THE SEARCH FOR THE
ISLANDS OF SOLOMON
1567–1838

ÁLVARO DE MENDAÑA

THE SEARCH FOR THE ISLANDS

OF

SOLOMON

1567-1838

BY

COLIN JACK-HINTON

CLARENDON PRESS · OXFORD
1969

Oxford University Press, Ely House, London W. 1

GLASGOW NEW YORK TORONTO MELBOURNE WELLINGTON
CAPE TOWN SALISBURY IBADAN NAIROBI LUSAKA ADDIS ABABA
BOMBAY CALCUTTA MADRAS KARACHI LAHORE DACCA
KUALA LUMPUR SINGAPORE HONG KONG TOKYO

PRINTED IN GREAT BRITAIN AT
THE UNIVERSITY PRESS
ABERDEEN

TO MY PARENTS

TEXTUAL FOREWORD

Footnotes:

References to archival sources relate to the *Bibliography of Archival Material*. They consist of an abbreviated reference to the site of the archive, followed by the archive reference and the page or folio number,

> e.g. MNM: MS. 921, f. 8.
>
> i.e. Museo Naval, Madrid: Manuscript 921, page 8.

The abbreviations used are:

AGI	Archivo General de Indias, Seville.
AGS	Archivo General de Simancas.
ANL	Australian National Library, Canberra.
ATL	Alexander Turnbull Library, Wellington.
AUS	Archivo de Universidad, Salamanca.
BCB	Biblioteca Central, Barcelona.
BM	British Museum, London.
BNM	Biblioteca Nacional, Madrid.
BNP	Bibliothèque Nationale, Paris.
BPM	Biblioteca de Palacio, Madrid.
CRO	Commonwealth Relations Office, London.
HL	Huntingdon Library, San Merino, California.
JCB	John Carter Brown Library, Providence, Rhode Island.
KB	Koninklijke Bibliotheek, The Hague.
LC	Library of Congress, Washington.
LRIHS	Library of the Rhode Island Historical Society.
MLS	Mitchell Library, Sydney.
MM	National Maritime Museum, Greenwich.
MNM	Museo Naval, Madrid.
NAH	National Archives, The Hague.
NAW	National Archives, Washington.
RAH	Real Academia de la Historia, Madrid.
Santa Casa	Archivo de Santa Casa de Loyola, Guipúzcoa.
VAGOFM	Vatican, Archivum Generale Ordinis Fratrum Minorum.
VAPF	Vatican, Archives of the Propaganda of the Faith.
VSdS	Vatican, Segreteria di Stato.

References to published sources relate directly to the *Bibliography of Published and Recent MS. Sources* which follows the *Bibliography of Archival Material*. They consist of the author's name, the year of publication (or, where a work consists of several volumes published over a number of years, the year of publication of the first volume), the volume number (in Roman numerals) where relevant, and the page/s referred to,

e.g. Zaragoza 1876: I: 75–81.

Where an author has published more than one work in any one year, a letter is added after the year in both the bibliography and the footnote,

e.g. Taylor 1930(a): 27.

Taylor 1930(b): 36.

References to newspapers and magazines are given in full.

Maps: References to maps and charts in the text and footnotes relate to the chronological *Bibliography of Maps Cited and Consulted* which follows the *Bibliography of Published Sources*.

Place-names

It will be appreciated that the considerable diversity in the spelling of place-names which is met with in a study of this kind represents a considerable problem and hindrance to uniformity. An attempt has been made in the text to explain the origin of particular spellings and to state those which are original, correct or in common usage. On grounds of historical accuracy it has often been necessary to depart from the Royal Geographical Society II system employed by the Admiralty, one of the lesser objects of this study being to determine the original names of particular islands and places. In those cases where the spelling given is neither that in common use, nor that which is earlier stated to be the original and correct one, it should be assumed that it is the spelling used in the text or MS. to which reference is being made.

Italics have been used for first references to place-names granted to localities; for archaic, mythical, misidentified, misrendered or confused place-names, for particular indigenous place-names, and in direct reference to the rendering of place-names on maps and charts.

Diacritical marks have been added according to modern usage except within direct quotations, titles and direct reference to names on maps and charts, where the original form is reproduced.

ACKNOWLEDGEMENTS

My grateful thanks are due to the following persons who have assisted me in the preparation of this study:

Professor J. W. Davidson, Mr. H. E. Maude and Dr. F. J. West of the Australian National University for their encouragement and interest, and for their learned and charitable comments on my drafts.

The late Mr. J. Forsyth of Avalon Beach, Sydney, for access to his valuable collection of notes and for the benefit which I derived from his considerable knowledge of Pacific discovery, both of which he made available with the absolute generosity of the true scholar.

Mr. P. Hurst, owner-master of the yacht *Staghound*, and Mr. R. Wraight for invaluable assistance and encouragement whilst at sea off the Solomons and New Hebrides on the *Staghound* recreating the routes and landfalls of the discoverers and early explorers.

Mr. A. A. Houghton Jnr. of New York for the generous gift of microfilms of the *derroteros* of Baena and Espinoza.

Professor R. W. Kenny of Brown University (Rhode Island) for information relating to the voyages of Captain Benjamin Page.

Father Celsus Kelly O.F.M. for the collection of MS. material relating to the Spanish exploration of the Pacific which is to be found on microfilm in the Australian National Library and of which I have made extensive use.

Dr. Helen Wallis of the British Museum Map Room, Mr. J. Louden, sometime of the Australian National Library, and Miss Joan Lancaster of the Commonwealth Relations Office for assistance in the search for material.

My wife, who gallantly bore the burden of typing the original complete manuscript, and numerous young ladies in the Australian National University who typed sections of the draft and revisions.

CONTENTS

LIST OF MAPS

INTRODUCTION

THIS study, which was completed in 1962, and is published on the fourth centenary of the discovery, is an attempt to trace the history of the European discovery, rediscovery and exploration of the islands lying immediately to the east of New Guinea which became known after their discovery by the attractive if historically inaccurate name Islands of Solomon. It attempts to narrate the story of the successive voyages to the archipelago in some detail, reconstructing the routes followed and identifying the landfalls made, and further attempts to relate those voyages to the background of pre-discovery knowledge and conjecture, the cartography of the Pacific, and the consideration given over the years to the position, composition and very existence of the archipelago by cartographers, chroniclers, hydrographers, geographers and historians.

The study represents the result of research conducted specifically between July 1960 and December 1961, supported by a previous knowledge of part of the Solomons and a voyage in 1961 in a 39 foot ketch to reconstruct the routes of the discoverers, rediscoverers and explorers, and to identify their landfalls.

The story of the discovery and rediscovery of the Solomons is perhaps well, if rather generally and incompletely, known. It has not, however, been previously studied both as a whole and in detail, or in relation to the all-important question of Pacific cartography which is in fact a mirror set up to its successive stages.

In 1567-8 Álvaro de Mendaña sailed westwards across the Pacific to discover, explore and name a substantial part of the eastern half of the islands which were shortly afterwards to become popularly known as the *Islands of Solomon*. He did so in a spirit of colonialism, commercialism, Catholic proselytism and romantic curiosity, against a background of supposition and belief that the South Pacific, from the area to the south of New Guinea and the Moluccas to a point in low latitudes as little as six hundred Iberian leagues west of Lima, contained a vast austral continent, the *Ophir* of King Solomon, the lands reported by Marco Polo and golden islands reputed to have been known to the Incas. He navigated in the belief that the Pacific was considerably less wide than is in fact the case, and in the further belief that the whole of this area lay within the hemisphere to which Spain laid absolute claim to explore, colonize, exploit and convert.

The techniques of navigation in the sixteenth century were such that the influence of the westerly-setting South Equatorial Current was insufficiently appreciated or allowed for, and in consequence the expedition considerably underestimated the distance sailed from Perú. By virtue of the current under-estimate of the width of the Pacific, however, an underestimate which remained undetected for much of the period in which navigators only crossed that ocean with the westerly-setting currents, the expedition was able to assume the proximity of its discovery to New Guinea, even though only the western half of the north coast of that land was known to them.

Within twenty years of the return of the expedition to Perú charts and maps had appeared in Europe on which the archipelago was laid down, exag-gerated in size, in close proximity to and to the east of New Guinea, with coastlines and nomenclature which generally conformed with the discoveries, exploration and conjectures made by the expedition in 1568. It was laid down at distances from Perú which varied according to the distance at which the cartographer plotted New Guinea, but which were generally less than that estimated by the discoverers. Chroniclers described the archipelago with varying degrees of accuracy, and as lying either 1,500 leagues from Perú or, quite inaccurately, as lying 800 leagues from Perú. The former distance was in fact reconcilable with the 1,600 plus leagues recorded by the discoverers from Perú to the mid-meridian of the archipelago where the first landfall was made, and with the exaggerated impression gained of the distance from that landfall to the eastern perimeter of the archipelago.

In 1595 Mendaña returned to colonize the archipelago, but discovered instead the island of Santa Cruz where he established an abortive and short-lived colony. Abandoning the colony after the death of Mendaña, the remnants of the expedition sailed for the Philippines and must have passed within a remarkably short distance of the main archipelago of the Solomons without sighting them. The outward trans-Pacific voyage had been meda in slightly higher latitudes where the South Equatorial Current is less pronounced, albeit in the trade wind season when that current tends to be strongest, and an appreciation of the existence of that current and improvements in the tech-niques of navigation had combined with this factor to produce a more correct, but still inadequate, estimate of the distance sailed. Nevertheless, Quirós, the Chief Pilot, was able to deduce that the Solomons lay to the west of Santa Cruz and that the expedition of 1567-9 had underestimated the distance of their discovery from Perú.

Quirós himself returned in 1606, burning with a desire to discover the austral continent and a Catholic zeal to save its inhabitants from perdition, and discovered the islands of Taumako and Tikopia and heard of Sikaiana. On this occasion an even more correct estimate was made of the distance sailed from Perú, and the fact established that Santa Cruz lay at a short distance to the westwards of the new discoveries. In the New Hebrides, which he took to be part of the supposed continent, the expedition became divided, Quirós returning to México and Spain, Torres, his second-in-command, heading westwards to discover the Torres Straits and demonstrate the insularity of New Guinea.

In 1616 Schouten and le Maire rounded Cape Horn and so defeated the letter of the Dutch East India Company's monopoly to the trade of the Spice Islands, and came westwards in search of the austral continent and a cargo of spices. Assuming the Hoorn Islands to be offlyers of Quirós' reputedly continental discoveries, unaware of Torres' voyage to the south of New Guinea and justifiably timorous of a possible lee shore extending southwards from New Guinea, they headed northwards to lower latitudes and discovered Ontong Java, Tau'u, the Green Islands, St. John's Island and the north-east coast of New Ireland, assuming the latter to be the extremity of New Guinea.

In 1643 Tasman, having sailed south of New Holland from the East Indies, and having entered the Pacific by way of Van Diemen's Land and New Zealand, sailed north from the Tonga Group to join what he thought to be the route of le Maire when he was in fact to the west of it. Misled by his chart to fear that Fiji might be Quirós' supposed continent he, like his countrymen before him, headed northwards to safety, to join their track and made the same landfalls amongst the outlyers of the Northern Solomons.

The seventeenth century saw the continued production of charts and maps of the Pacific which delineated the Solomons in a form similar to those of the late sixteenth century, often with improved dimensions, and the emergence of others of Iberian origin which delineated the discoveries of 1595 and 1606 but excluded those of 1568. It saw charts of the first category altered by the merging of the islands of the southern part of the Solomons to form a continental coastline extended southwards to accommodate the reputedly continental discovery of Quirós. It saw the Dutch discoveries added to all three types and their derivatives, the production of greatly improved Dutch charts from which the Spanish discoveries were excluded entirely, and the emergence of an erroneous type of map or chart on which the Spanish discoveries were identified with the chain of islands extending from New Guinea to Tierra del Fuego which cartographers had long postulated as a fringe of eroded fragments of the austral continent.

By the end of the century and the first quarter of the eighteenth century, however, some of the problems of reconciling the delineation of the Solomons in close proximity to New Guinea and also at the distance at which they were reputed to have been discovered, on charts which laid down a Pacific of considerably improved dimensions, had come to be appreciated. They were consequently and variously plotted 800 leagues, 1,500 leagues, or at such distances from Perú as the individual cartographers or their authorities understood them to have been discovered at. In the majority of cases all that was left of the Solomons for this repositioning was the one large island of *Santa Ysabel* and a few diminutive neighbours, the remainder having been lost in the period

2

of their cartographical absorption into the austral continent or Quirós' reputedly continental discovery. Of cartographers who seem to have run the whole gamut of possible locations for the Solomons de l'Isle is perhaps the most marked, beginning as he did by plotting them alongside the Marquesas, then moving them gradually westwards, and ending by plotting them in their earliest position in close proximity to New Guinea.

Dampier's circumnavigation of New Ireland and New Britain provided further information relating to the general area; whilst the voyages of Byron and Wallis, through the easterly position in which French charts in particular tended to delineate the Solomons, cast serious doubts on the accuracy of that location if not on the very existence of the Solomons. In 1767 Carteret, after becoming separated from Wallis, sailed westwards across the Pacific in as high latitudes as the winds would permit in an attempt to discover the austral continent. Driven into lower latitudes by contrary winds and shortage of provisions, he rediscovered and was subsequently to identify the Santa Cruz Group, probably discovered rather than rediscovered Vanikoro, discovered Ndai Island to the north of Malaíta, rediscovered but did not identify Malaíta, and discovered Kilinailau, Buka and the passage between New Ireland and New Britain.

The following year saw Bougainville rediscovering the New Hebrides, generally recognizing them as Quirós' Espíritu Santo, and, after sailing eastwards along the south side of the Louisiade Archipelago, discovering but not identifying the western perimeter of the Solomons. He discovered Ranongga, Vella Lavella, the south coast of the western extremity of Choiseul, Bougainville and its southern progeny, and the Bougainville Strait. In what was a veritable spate of maritime activity the Solomons were visited again the following year by Surville who, sailing south-eastwards from the Bashees in an attempt to reach the Eastern Pacific, coasted the northern and eastern perimeters of the archipelago, but failed to identify it or even to determine with certainty whether it was a mainland or an archipelago.

In 1769 Alexander Dalrymple, cantankerous, opinionated and ill-used by history, postulated the identification of the Solomons with Dampier's New Britain on the primary evidence of the location of the Solomons in close proximity to New Guinea on late sixteenth-century charts. His contemporary Cook evinced an interest in the area of the Solomons, without specifically implying that they might be found there, but failed to explore it when he was in the New Hebrides during his second Pacific voyage of 1772–5. It was not indeed until 1781 that Buâche made the major step in the identification of the Solomons by suggesting to the French Royal Academy of Sciences that they were in fact the lands 'discovered' by Carteret, Bougainville and Surville. Nevertheless, although he examined the correct evidence and arrived at a correct conclusion, his suggestion depended on a perhaps inadequate comprehension of the ramifications and complexities of their sixteenth-century cartographical delineation in close proximity to New Guinea, and on the apparently mistaken beliefs that Richard Hawkins had learned from the Spaniards that they lay 2,500 English leagues from Perú and that the discoveries of Carteret, Bougainville and Surville lay in that position.

The abortive attempt of the Spaniard Mourelle to make an easterly crossing of the Pacific south of the equator led him to sight the North-Western Solomons and unwittingly to rediscover what was probably the first landfall of his fellow-countrymen in 1568—Roncador Reef, although like most of his contemporaries who relied on contemporary French charts he supposed the Solomons to lie further to the east. For a time Dalrymple seems to have abandoned his identification of the Solomons with New Britain and New Ireland, and to have applied the name *Guadalcanal* to the coastline explored by Surville, probably in the face of Buâche's evidence, but in 1790 he returned with vigour to his assertions, denying the slightest resemblance between the discoveries to the east of New Guinea and those of 1568.

In 1787 an American merchantman under the command of Captain Read sailed northwards through the Western Pacific, having travelled by way of the South Atlantic, the South Indian Ocean and south of New Holland, *en route* to China. He coasted the south-western perimeter of the Solomons, and headed northwards along the western side of Bougainville and between Buka and New Ireland without identifying his landfalls. Moreover, despite the importance of his discovery of a passage to the west of Bougainville, his voyage seems to have been unknown in Europe and to have contributed nothing to contemporary cartography.

It was in the Santa Cruz Group that the expedition of la Pérouse, on its way towards the main archipelago of the Solomons and to what might well have been the last phase of this story of rediscovery, met its end on the cruel reef which embraces the island of Vanikoro like a circlet of thorns. There, at the hands of the natives or in an attempt to reach help in a vessel constructed on the island, the members of the expedition died. In the same year the rather more prosaic figure of Shortland, returning to England after the establishment of Port Jackson, coasted the southern perimeter of the Solomons and passed through the Bougainville Strait. He, like his predecessors, did not identify his landfalls, and seems indeed to have imagined them to be a quite new discovery.

The phase of rediscovery can be said to end with the publication in 1790 of Fleurieu's detailed defence of Buâche's hypothesis, and his production of convincing proof that the discoveries of Carteret, Bougainville, Surville and Shortland were the Islands of Solomon discovered in 1568. In the same year what can be described as the phase of exploration began, with Ball sailing north from Port Jackson to confirm Surville's rediscoveries in the south-eastern corner of the archipelago, with Hunter discovering Sikaiana and rediscovering Ontong Java, and with Edwards sailing west from Rotumah to discover Cherry, Mitre and Willis's Shoal or Indispensable Reef.

In 1792 Dentrecasteaux made the first of two visits to the Solomons, followed by Manning with his exploration of the passage between Guadalcanal and New Georgia, Santa Ysabel and Choiseul, and in the following year by Boyd with his discovery of Rennell and Bellona. Dentrecasteaux returned in 1793 to explore the south-eastern quarter of the Solomons and to make further advances in the identification of the islands discovered and named in 1568. In 1794 Wilkinson explored the passage between Malaíta to the east and Guadalcanal and Ysabel to the west, and added to contemporary knowledge as he was to do yet again by following the same general route two years later.

Taumako was rediscovered, though not recognized, by Wilson in the year 1797, and in the following year Cameron rediscovered but did not identify Tikopia. It was not, however, until 1824, with the discovery by Wellings of Nukumanu, that the whole of the Solomons can be said to have been discovered, if parts of it were still barely known; and it was not until 1838, when d'Urville explored the interior of the main archipelago from San Cristóval to the Manning Strait, and albeit to the neglect of Northern Guadalcanal and the area between Choiseul and New Georgia, that the next and last major piece of exploration was completed. By the time that the results of this voyage had been published the Solomons had been generally charted, though limited areas were still little known, and much progress still had to be made in the identification of the discoveries of 1568. The detailed completion of the chart, which was the work of naval surveys and Europeans residing in the Solomons, falls by its nature into the final and still uncompleted historical phase of survey, as opposed to exploration, and lies without the scope of this book.

In a study of this kind, where much emphasis must inevitably be placed on bare factual and technical details, the very humanity of the principal actors in the drama, the navigators and their crews, tends to be lost. It must, however, be remembered throughout that it was these men, of five nations and four centuries, bound together by the common bond of their often unwitting association with the Islands of Solomon and the pursuit of their occupations or aspirations upon the unquiet waters of the South Sea, who made the story what it is. They were not simply the shadowy authors of navigational records now fading in the archives of Seville, London or Paris, but men of flesh and blood who actually sailed the courses which they recorded, to whom the wind was not simply a group of letters on the page of a log-book but something to be felt on a living cheek, heard whining through the rigging or rattling a loose halyard. They were men who experienced hunger, thirst and fear, and who in a remarkably large number of cases ended their lives on the coral strands or in the blue waters of the Islands of Solomon.

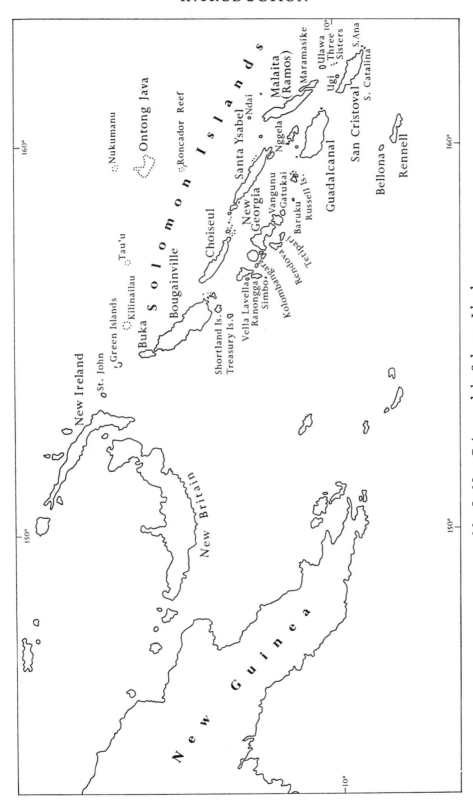

Map I New Guinea and the Solomon Islands

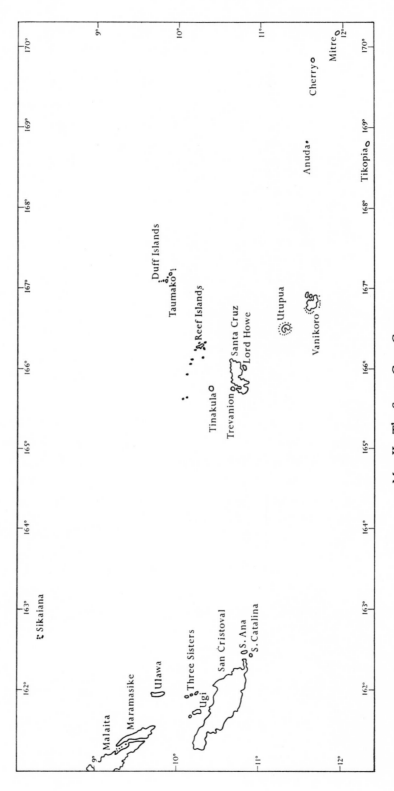

Map II The Santa Cruz Group

I

The Ophirian Conjecture

An age shall come, ere ages ende
　　Blessedly strange and strangely blest,
When our Sea farre and neere or'prest,
　　His shoare shall farther yet extend.

Descryed then shall a large land be,
　　By this profound sea navigation,
An other World, an other nation,
　　All men shall then discovered see.

Thule accounted heretofore
　　The worlde's extreme, the Northerne bound,
Shall be when Southwest parts be found,
　　A neerer Isle, a neighbour shoare.

Seneca. Tragedy of Medea.
Translation by Edward Grimston, 1604.

WHEN Ferdinand Magellan crossed the Pacific in 1520–21 and ushered in the period of European discovery in the South Sea, he brought to a head two problems which had dominated the relations of Spain and Portugal as those nations expanded westwards and eastwards from Europe. These were their rivalry for the Spice Islands and the trade of East Asia, and the allied question of the position of the antipode to the Atlantic line of demarcation agreed upon at the Treaty of Tordesillas in 1494, situated 370 leagues W of the Cape Verde Islands and dividing the spheres of influence and expansion of these two nations. These two problems were a result of the vagueness of the terms of Tordesillas, the several current concepts of the circumference of the earth,[1] and the existence in Europe of several different values for the league.[2] The Pacific, uncrossed,

---

[1] e.g. the concept derived from Ptolemy of a circumference of 180,000 *stadia*, which in fact gave the equatorial degree a length of $62\frac{1}{2}$ Roman miles (50 nautical miles); and the concept derived from Eratosthenes of a circumference of 252,000 *stadia*, which gave the equatorial degree a length of $87\frac{1}{2}$ Roman miles (70 nautical miles).

[2] e.g. the league of 3 Roman miles, the league of 4 Roman miles and the league of $3\frac{1}{2}$ Roman miles. It was also variously argued either that the equatorial degree consisted of $16\frac{2}{3}$ leagues (each of 3 Roman miles) or 50 Roman miles (40 nautical miles), or that it consisted of $17\frac{1}{2}$ leagues (each of 4 Roman miles) or 70 Roman miles (56 nautical miles), beliefs which seem to have derived from the acceptance of the Ptolemaic and Eratosthenesian concepts of the size of the earth, on the assumption that the *stadium* was equal to $\frac{1}{10}$th of a Roman mile. The league used by both Spanish and Portuguese pilots at sea during the last forty years of the sixteenth century at least was the 'sea league' of 4 Roman miles

unexplored and apparently the key to the problem of terrestrial circumference, had been variously underestimated in size by cosmographers, according to the circumferential figure which they postulated or espoused, but Magellan's voyage was to do little to clarify the question. With limited navigational techniques, and subject to the indeterminable currents setting from E to W across the Pacific, by the time Magellan had reached the Philippines he had logged an underestimate of the distance run which accorded reasonably with the underestimated distance which he expected to have to travel, and it was to be some quite considerable time before the width of the Pacific was determined with any accuracy.

In 1524 the representatives of Spain and Portugal met at Badajoz in an attempt to solve the threefold question of the antipodal *demarcación*, of their respective spheres of influence and expansion, and of their respective rights to the Spice Islands, but the junta, ending in dissension and confusion, served no other purpose than to reveal and amplify the nature and insolubility of the problem. It was not until 1529, when Charles of Spain, in urgent need of money and probably discouraged by the failure of his expeditions to discover the return sailing route across the Pacific, pledged his claim to the Moluccas and agreed at the Treaty of Saragossa to a provisional antipodal *demarcación* 17° E of the Moluccas, that any real agreement was reached, but even this was largely a fiction, for Spain continued her occupation of the Philippines in open defiance of it.

An interesting contemporary comment on the question, by an Englishman, is to be found in the *Booke* written in 1527 by Robert Thorne, a merchant at Seville, which he addressed to Doctor Ley (Lee), Henry VIII's ambassador at the Court of the Emperor, and accompanied with a map.[1] The *Booke* and the map are confused and confusing, though Thorne's intention can be understood, and are followed by a brief synopsis of the background to the rival Spanish and Portuguese claims to the Spice Islands, in which Thorne remarks that:

these Islands of Spicery fall neere the terme and limites betweene these princes . . . and it seemeth all that falleth from 160 to 180 degrees [i.e. E of Cape Verde 'an headland . . . which is over against a little cross made in the part Occidental'] should be of Portingal, and all the rest of Spaine.

He adds that both parties claim the Spice Islands without being able to determine their longitude, but that whilst the Portuguese, having discovered the Atlantic islands of Cape Verde and Brasil, were anxious to have them in

(equivalent to 3·2 nautical miles). For a detailed examination of the political and cosmographical background to the Spanish incursion into the Pacific see Jack-Hinton 1964(b) where the question of the league and its significance in the question of the *demarcación* is considered.

[1] Hakluyt 1903: II: 164–81. For the map see Nordenskiöld 1889: Plate XLI, and Parks 1928: Figure 14.

their hemisphere and accordingly agreed to the demarcation 370 leagues beyond Cape Verde, if they wish to maintain that limit then the limit 180° eastwards will exclude the Spice Islands. Even if they count the 180° from the meridian of Cape Verde, the Spice Islands are still within the Spanish hemisphere, and Thorne concludes that 'without doubt the sayd islands fall all without the limitations of Portingall, and pertane to Spaine, as it appeareth by the most part of all the cardes[1] made by the Portingalls, save those which they have falsified of late purposely.' His errors are apparent if understandable, and his reference to Portuguese charts may well be evidence that the Portuguese were extremely uncertain of their case, for if they had made anything like a correct estimate of the position of the Moluccas eastabout from Europe, their use of the degree of 70 Roman miles (56 nautical miles) would have probably led them to conclude that the Moluccas were beyond the antipodal *demarcación*,[2] even though they were in fact to the W of it and within the Portuguese hemisphere.

The possession of the Spice Islands was not, however, the only issue at stake in the dispute over the position of the *demarcación*. The view implied by Thorne in his map of 1527 was that a major consideration at Badajoz was the discovery and possession of *Ophir* and *Tharshish*, the lands from which King Solomon derived his wealth, and which Thorne concluded lay to the SE of the East Indies. At Badajoz itself the Spanish emissaries referred to the three year voyage of Solomon's ships to *Ofir* and *Zetin* as proof of the considerable distance of the Moluccas eastwards from Europe and the Middle East, and implied a general acceptance of the belief that these lands were to the SE of the Moluccas.[3] Outlining the relative geographical concepts of the two contestants Thorne concludes:

Et sic, licet insulae Tharsis+Ophir videntur attingere Portugalenses, tamen insule Capoverde dictae, quae intra supra dicta signa cadunt, videtur omittere. Et sic dum insulas Capoverde retinere volunt Portugalenses, illas Tharsis+Offir non possunt attingere.[4]

It was a view already put forward by Pirés and Encisco, and the latter's *Suma* of 1519 refers specifically to *Opir* or *Ofir*: '*de donde el rey Salomon truxo el ora para el templo . . . Y tarsis tengo que es el puerto de ciapangu que caen enel aurea. . .*'[5]

---

[1] 'Carde' = chart, probably derived from the Iberian *carta*.

[2] One of Thorne's purposes was to advocate an English approach to the Spice Islands via Newfoundland. Since England lay 39° S of the N Pole, and the Spice Islands lay on the Equator, Thorne concluded that, given a northern passage, English ships would only have to sail 129°, 2489 leagues or 7,440 miles (i.e. 3 miles to the league, and 19 leagues or 57·6 miles to the degree), as opposed to the 4,300 leagues which the Spanish and Portuguese were required to sail around the foot of America or the Cape of Good Hope.   [3] Blair 1903: I: 194.

[4] See the reproduction of his chart, on which this inscription occurs.

[5] Barlow 1932: 10–11. See Taylor 1932: xiv–xvi, where the possible relationship between Thorne's map and a *Mappa-mundi* prepared by Encisco for his *Suma* is discussed. *Ciapangu* was Japan.

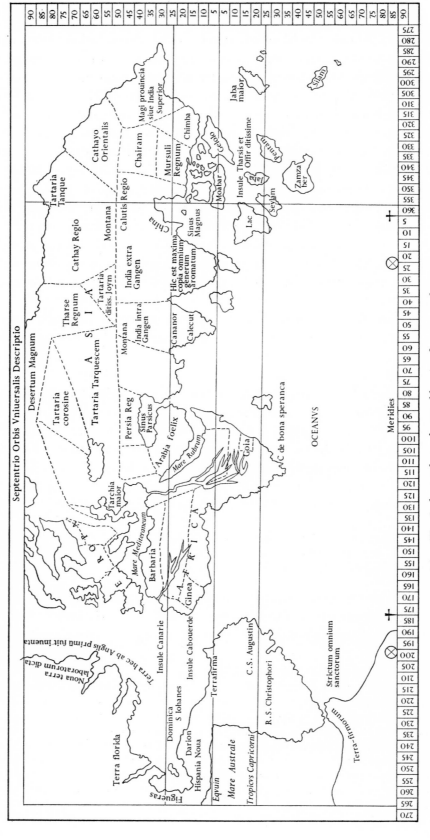

Map III Robert Thorne's *World-map* of 1527, redrawn.

The question of the existence and whereabouts of *Ophir* and *Tharshish* was one of the more dominant in the minds of Spanish and Portuguese cosmographers and pilots in the sixteenth and early seventeenth centuries, and was interwoven with the idea of a vast antipodean continent. The view that such a continent existed had been propounded since the days of Pythagoras, whose followers had advanced the theory of terrestrial sphericity on the grounds that the sphere was a perfect form, a view supported by Aristotle[1] and Pliny.[2] The corollary, dictated by the supposed natural laws of physics, was that the equilibrium of the sphere was maintained by equally balanced land masses in the north and east, the *Oikoumene* or known world, and in the south and west, the undiscovered and unknown *Antichthon* or *Southern Antipodes* described and mapped by Ptolemy.[3]

The idea of a southern continent persisted, with varying intensity, until as late as the eighteenth century, and was never without its advocates. Strabo[4] and Pomponius Mela[5] concerned themselves with its habitability and accessibility, whilst Cicero upheld, and Plutarch and Lucretius rejected, the whole spherical terrestrial concept. It was also opposed by Cosmas, 'who never tired of inveighing against those wrong headed pagans who believed in a round world and the Antipodes',[6] and by Lactantius. The Early Fathers as a whole were against the idea, not as a geographical concept but as a race of people, and St. Augustine and others of the Fathers held it heretical to believe in a race of people apparently cut off from the known world by impenetrable equatorial heat and a vast sea, contradicting a common descent from Noah and the divine assurance that the preaching of the Gospel and the offer of salvation had been for all mankind.

The concept found a champion in St. Isidore of Seville, who conceded the probable existence of the *Antipodes*, and upon whose view Beatus, an Iberian monk of the sixth century, based his material for a world-map in a commentary on the *Apocalypse*.[7] The earliest extant Beatus-type map, rectangular in shape and probably of the late ninth or early tenth century, represents the earth surrounded by water, with the Indian Ocean extending across the map to south of Africa and Asia and connecting the surrounding stream.

[1] Aristotle 1947: 292 *et seq.*   [2] Pliny 1938: 296–303.

[3] For Ptolemy's *World-map* see Wroth: 1944 Plate I. See also Nordenskiöld 1889 for a discussion on the several medieval editions of Ptolemy's *Geography*, and Stevenson 1922: Plate I which reproduces the *World-map* from the Ebner MS. of the *Geography* of *c.* 1460 illustrating the concept of a southern continent forming the southern boundary of a landlocked Indian Ocean.

[4] Rainaud 1893: 37–51.

[5] Bunbury 1959: II; 353 and Map 4. Mela (*c.* A.D. 50) considered it probable that Ceylon formed the tip of the unknown continent (Maggs 1927: I).

[6] Winstedt 1909: 8–9. 'But should one wish to examine more elaborately the question of the Antipodes, he would easily find them to be old wives' fables. For if two men on opposite sides placed the soles of their feet each against each . . . how could they be standing upright' (McCrindle 1897: 17).

[7] Wroth 1944: 164.

Beneath the Indian Ocean is a strip of land, the northern extremity of a southern continent, bearing the inscription '*Deserta Terra vicina solida ardore incognita nobis*', which seems to be derived from a statement by St. Isidore in his *Etymologiarum*, and which appears in full on a Beatus-type map of the thirteenth century as: '*Extra tres autem partes orbis, quarta pars trans Oceanum interior est in Meridie, quae solis ardore nobis incognita est, in cujus finibus Antipodes fabulose*

Map IV   The world according to Macrobius' *In Somnium Scipionis Exposito* of 1483

inhabitare produntur.'[1] As St. Isidore's idea found exposition in Beatus, so Cicero's concept of the *Antichthon* was perpetuated in the sixteenth-century work of Macrobius, his *In Somnium Scipionis Expositio*, where it was affirmed that, whilst reason permitted the assumption of its habitability, the intervening intense heat would prevent its exploration.

The two contributions to a unified concept of an antipodean continent, a *Terra Incognita*, were carried into the sixteenth century in a succession of maps. Of particular significance were those maps contained in the 1477 and later editions of Ptolemy's *Cosmographia*[2] and the Ptolemaic derived maps of Henricus Martellus. Of less significance, but no mean importance, were the

[1] Wroth 1944: 165-7 and Plate II.   [2] Wroth 1944: Plate I; and Skelton 1952: Plate 2.

maps in the 1483 Brescia edition of Macrobius' *In Somnium Scipionis*[1]; Johannes Eschvidus' *Summa . . . Anglicana*[2] of 1489; the *Margarita Philosophica* of Gregorius Reisch of 1503,[3] and the several late fifteenth-century editions of Pomponius Mela's *Cosmographia*.[4] In the early sixteenth century we find the continent represented on the globes by Schöner of 1515[5] to 1524[6] as a large *Brasilie Regio* centred upon the South Pole, on la Salle's *Mappemonde* of 1521[7] as a continental *Patalie Regio*, and on the maps of Leonardo da Vinci.[8]

In 1501 Amerigo Vespucci had been brought from retirement at the behest of King Manoel of Portugal, and despatched with three caravels to attempt the discovery of new lands by sailing as close to the Antarctic Pole as possible. He coasted Brazil and had reached 52° S by 3 April 1502. 'On the first day of April I discovered a Terra Australis which I coasted for 20 leagues.'[9] His discovery of Tierra del Fuego or the southern extremity of Argentina was probably more concrete than that of Paulmier de Gonneville who, despatched by the French in 1503 to follow up the advances of da Gama, was blown off course off the Cape of Good Hope, sailed 'southwards', and fetched up on the coast of a land which he named *South India* but to which the adjective austral appears to have been subsequently applied.[10]

Magellan's voyage through the *Estrecho de Magallanes* seemed, with its firm discovery of Tierra del Fuego, to provide physical proof of an antarctic and antipodean continent, and the identification of that land as the northern tip of a continental land-mass exercised a considerable influence over the cartography of the sixteenth century, and added yet another title, *Magellanica*, to the several already existing in relation to the supposed continent. The map of Franciscus Monachus in his *De Orbe Situ* of 1529,[11] which depicts a vast continent stretching from the Magellanic Straits to the South Pole, with the inscription '*Is*

[1] Wroth 1944: Plate III. See also Nordenskiöld 1889: Plate XXXI; and Rainaud 1893: 29.

[2] Nordenskiöld 1889: Plate XXXI.

[3] Nordenskiöld 1889: Plate XXXI. See also Bagrow 1951: 83.

[4] See Maggs 1927: 1–2, and Plate I, where the *World-map* in Mela's *Cosmographia* of 1482 (Venice) is reproduced, and Plate II where what is probably the first Spanish *World-map* in the Salamanca edition of the *Cosmographia* of 1498 is reproduced. In both cases the Indian Ocean is landlocked and bounded to the S by the antipodean continent. See also Bagrow 1951: Plate 56.

[5] Nordenskiöld 1889: Figure 47.

[6] On the Schöner (Schoener) globes see Nordenskiöld 1819: 77-79 and Figures 46-47; Stevens 1888: Figure 3; Wieder 1925: I: 1–4 and Plates I–III; Rainaud 1893: 248–255 and Figures 18 and 19; Marcell 1889; Jomard 1862: Plate XVII; Wieser 1882: 28, 64–66, 85, 109, Map 2; Gallois 1890: 82, 90, Plates III and V; Kretschmer 1891: Plate XI; Stevenson 1921: 84; and Bagrow 1951: 112.

[7] Nordenskiöld 1889: Figure 18.

[8] Morgan 1891: 91. See also Hemrig 1948: 36; Nordenskiöld 1889: Figure 45; Rainaud 1893: 248; and Major 1866: 1–4.   [9] Callander 1766: I: 60.

[10] Collingridge 1895: 93 and 210; Major 1859: xxiii; and Burney 1803: I: 379. The natural conclusion to be drawn is that he fetched up at Madagascar.

[11] Wroth 1944: Plate IX. See also Lewel 1850: Plate LXXII which reproduces a similar *Mappa-mundi* of 1526.

nobis detecta existit' near the Straits and the further inscription *'Haec pars ore nondum cognita'* to the south of India, reflects the effect of Magellan's voyage.

With Oronce Finé's map of 1531, *Nova et Integra Universi Orbis Descriptio*, we see the continent taking more definite shape and the title *Terra Australis*, in the inscription *'Terra Australis recenser inversa, sed nondū plene cognita'*, appearing, probably for the first time on a sixteenth-century map, together with the older titles *Brasilie Regio* and *Regio Patalis*.[1] Similarly, Mercator's double cordiform map of the world of 1538 depicts a large unnamed southern continent bearing the inscription *'Terras hu essᵉ certum est sed quātus quibus— limitibus finitas incertum'*.[2] The continued representation of an austral continent in the latter half of the sixteenth century is manifested on the *Universalis Exactissima atque Non Recens Modo. Rerum et Recentioribus* of Gastaldi (*c.* 1555),[3] on Mercator's *Nova et Aucta Orbis Terrae Descriptio ad usum navigantum emendat accomodata* of 1569,[4] and reached an extreme form, with the austral continent stretching from south of South America across to south of New Guinea, on the *Typus Orbis Terrarum* of Ortelius (1570)[5] and the *Orbis Terrae Compendiosa Descriptio of* Rumold Mercator (1587).[6] Further examples are to be found in the sixteenth-century maps of Plancius, de Jode, Rughesi and Wytfliet, for throughout the late sixteenth century the austral continent was a common cartographical feature.

The question of whether or not New Guinea, following the discovery of its western and part of its northern coasts, formed part of *Terra Australis*, or whether it was an adjacent island, was one which clearly perplexed carto-graphers; a perplexity reflected in Ortelius' map of 1570,[7] where New Guinea is given an insular character, and where an inscription admits that *'Nova Guinea nuper inventa que an sit insula an pars continentis Australis incertū est'*, and in Plancius' world-map of 1594,[8] where New Guinea appears as an extension of *Terra Australis* or *Magellanica*. Not all cartographers, however, accepted the evidence for a continent as sufficient to justify its inclusion on their charts. Ribeiro's *Carta Universal* of 1529, Ramusio's map of 1534 and Cabot's map of 1544,[9] are cases in point, and Sebastian Münster in his *Cosmographiae Universal* of 1559 also rejected the belief.[10] Drake's voyage in 1577 had provided reason-able evidence for the deduction that Tierra del Fuego was not part of an anti-podean continent and must have done something to weaken the belief in one, although the reply to the assertion that his voyage necessarily discredited

---

[1] In the *Novus Orbis* of Grijnaeus, Paris, 1532. Nordenskiöld 1889: Plate XLI. The Greeks had referred to the *'Antichthone: Altera australis'* (Rainaud 1893: 28).

[2] Nordenskiöld 1889: Plate XLIII. The map was copied, with modifications, by Mercator from Oronce Finé.

[3] In the Bibliothèque Nationale, Paris.   [4] Jomard 1862: Plate XXI.

[5] Nordenskiöld 1889: Plate XLVI.   [6] Nordenskiöld 1889: Plate XLVII.

[7] *Typus Orbis Terrarum.* Nordenskiöld 1889: Figure XLVI.   [8] Hakluyt 1903: IX: 474.

[9] Wroth 1944: 170–171.   [10] Maggs 1927: 7.

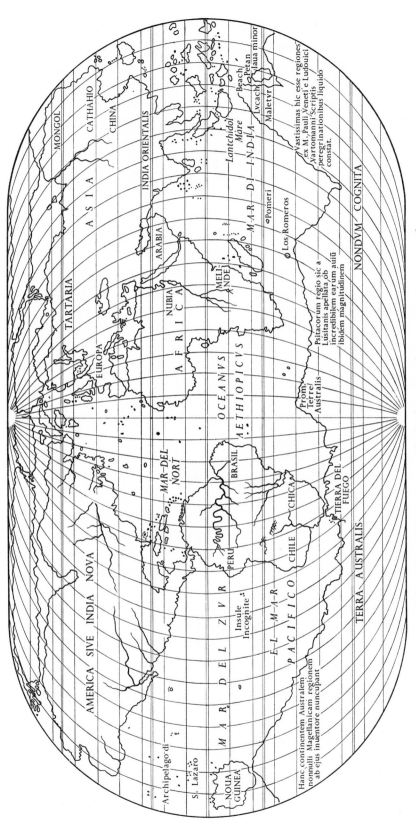

Map V The *Typus Orbis Terrarum* of Abraham Ortelius, Antwerp, 1570, redrawn

belief in the continent could well have been that it did not disprove the existence of a continent in higher latitudes S of Tierra del Fuego. In the *Hakluyt* or *Wright-Molyneux* map of 1598–1600[1] and in Tatton's map of the late sixteenth century,[2] disbelief consequent on Drake's voyage may be illustrated, for in both those maps the continent is omitted. As Bishop Hall remarked in his satirical *Mundus Alter:* 'If they know it for a Continent and for a Southern Continent why then doe they call it unknowne?'[3]

A matter of interest and concern to scholars and travellers of the sixteenth century was the existence and whereabouts of three reported places, the *Locac* of Marco Polo, the *Khryse Khersoneso* (*Aurea Chersonesus*) or *Golden Peninsula* of Ptolemy, and the *Ophir* of King Solomon, individually as separate places or collectively as different names for the one place.

According to the narrative of Marco Polo,[4] rich and unknown lands lay to the SE of Asia; the Kingdom of *Locac* (*Locach*) in which gold was to be found; the island of *Pentan* abounding in aromatic drugs, and 'a wild place with odoriferous trees'; *Malaiur*, with 'great trade in spices'; *Java Major* and *Java Minor*. In fact Polo was speaking of Malaya and the East Indian Archipelago, but, partly through the confusion of his narrative, particularly the interpolation of the name *Java* for what should have been *Champa* (East Indo-China), Renaissance scholars and cosmographers accepted the passage as information relating to the unknown parts to the SE of Asia. According to Mills the printer of the Basle edition of 1532 blundered, altered the *L* and first *c* of the *Locach* of his proof (or the *L* and first *a* of the *Laach* of his proof) and rendered the name as *Boeach* (or *Beach*).[5] It appears as *Beach*, or in hispanicized form as *Veach*, often together with the original *Lucach* or *Locach*, in a succession of maps and books of the sixteenth century. On the former it appears as a northern extension of the southern continent, and particularly clear examples may be seen on Mercator's world-map of 1569[6] and Ortelius' *Typus Orbis Terrarum* of 1570. The extent to which this particular extension may be indicative of an early knowledge of Australia will be referred to later, but it is most unlikely that it indicated an actual physical knowledge, and the location of Polo's reported lands in that area would seem to have been primarily the result of a failure to identify them with any of the lands so far discovered from Polo's description of them, with the result that they were located beyond the limits of immediate knowledge.

---

[1] Nordenskiöld 1889: Plate L; Markham 1880: Folio; Hakluyt 1903: I: 3, 56.

[2] Caraci 1926: I: Plates XV–XVII.

[3] Wroth 1944: 173. Bishop Joseph Hall's *Mundus Alter et idem, sive Terra Australis ante hac semper incognita longis interibus peregrini academici nuperime lustrata* (Frankfort 1605, Hanau 1607), published in England in 1609 as *The Discovery of the New World*, was probably the basis for Swift's *Gulliver's Travels* (Maggs 1927: 11).

[4] For a study of Marco Polo in South-East Asia see Jack-Hinton 1964(a).   [5] Mills 1930: 185.

[6] Jomard 1862: Plate xxi. See also Skelton 1958: Figure 8. An inscription below *Lucach* attributes the information on the promontory to Ludovicus Vartomannus (Varthema).

Against the background of the Indian campaign of Alexander the Great (334–323 B.C.), and its cultural and trade consequences of increasing indirect trade contact between the East and the Mediterranean, and of the extension of Imperial Roman trade influence at least as far as India and Ceylon, it is natural to expect the Classical geographers of Greece and Rome to offer some references to the East, and it is equally natural to expect these references to be at first vague and imprecise. The references of Eratosthenes (*c.* 234–196 B.C.), Pomponius Mela (*c.* A.D. 43), Pliny (*c.* A.D. 70) and Dionysius Periegetes (*c.* A.D. 120–30)[1] to the golden and silver islands *Khryse* and *Argyre* are indeed vague, and are almost certainly indebted through trade contact in India to Indian references to the Malay Peninsula and Archipelago under such mineral associated names as *Suvarnadvipa* and *Suvarnabhumi*.

Improved, but still vague, knowledge of South-East Asia is reflected in Classical references to *Khryse* as a peninsula: references which almost certainly permit the identification of *Khryse* with the Malay Peninsula, if not with Burma and the Archipelago as well, and which have their origin in the furthest extension of Graeco-Roman trade which occurred during the period from the Flavian Dynasty (A.D. 70–96) until the first half of the second century A.D. Mela had already referred to a peninsula named *Tamus*, in addition to and in close proximity to *Argyre* and *Khryse;* Pliny had referred to *Khryse* as both an island and a *promunturium;* and Josephus, writing in the first century, granted *Khryse* a peninsular character. The *Periplus of the Erythrean Sea*, which was probably compiled in the second half of the first century, still referred to *Khryse* as an island to which Indian vessels sailed: 'the last part of the inhabited world towards the east, under the rising sun itself', with 'the best tortoise shell of all the places on the Erythraean Sea'; but the voyage of the Greek skipper Alexander, reputedly beyond Malaya and to which Marinos of Tyre and the Ptolemaic *Geography*[2] were indebted, was possibly one of several which Mediterranean shipmasters made beyond India and which, with the indirect information obtained by the greater number of skippers who ventured no further east than Western India and Ceylon, provided the information not only for the improved geographical concept which is implied in the abandonment of the idea of the *Golden Island* in favour of the *Golden Peninsula* but also for the detailed but perplexing description of the *Khryse Khersoneso* in the Ptolemaic *Geography*.

On the ground that much of the *Geography* as we know it is believed to date from the tenth to eleventh centuries, it has been suggested that the detailed references to the *Golden Peninsula* which are contained in it, and which sparked

---

[1] Bunbury 1959: II: 475, 487, 364.

[2] On the Ptolemaic *Geography* see Bagrow 1945; Bagrow 1947; Stevenson 1932. There is some geological evidence to suggest that in quite recent times the Kra Isthmus of South Thailand emerged from the sea to make a peninsula out of what had previously been a Malayan island, although this is a doubtful point.

sixteenth-century enthusiasms, do not date from a period earlier than the fifth century when Martianus of Heraclea also wrote of the *Golden Khersonese* and the *Great Gulf* between it and China. This attitude to the Ptolemaic references to South-East Asia seems, however, to be an untenable one when we realize that Josephus had already written of the *Khryse Khersoneso* in the first century, and that after the second century A.D. eastern exploration by the Roman Empire came to an end. Admittedly trade did revive under the late Roman Emperors of Constantinople, but Graeco-Roman traders were no longer active in the Indian Ocean and their place had been taken by Arabians, Axumites and Persians. Indirect trade with the East continued, but it was in other than Roman hands, and increased geographical knowledge for the Roman and Byzantine worlds was not a likely by-product of it. Indeed, for the Roman world the period after the second century was one of regression in learning and scientific interest, to which the Church Fathers added their own particular form of encouragement. Geographical knowledge was forgotten rather than acquired, and the Arab conquests of the seventh century largely sealed off further information of South-East Asia for Europe until the Iberian navigators of the fifteenth century were able to obtain and utilize Arab knowledge, and until their successors were able to force their own way to South-East Asia. Such knowledge of South-East Asia as is to be found in classical writings, and which reached its peak in the Ptolemaic *Geography*, must inevitably be attributed to a period no later than the second century A.D.

References to *Khryse* and *Argyre* persisted into the Middle Ages in the works of such chroniclers as St. Isidore of Seville, and the numerous fifteenth-century editions of the Ptolemaic *Geography* perpetuated the information of the *Golden Khersonese*. With the exception of the more recent information which they were able to obtain from Arab sources, interested Europeans of the late fifteenth century were largely dependent upon Classical sources for their geographical information concerning the Near and Further East, and even the best of these sources were only available to them because Arab scholars had preserved them throughout the barbarian rape of Europe and from the depredations of some of the clergy of the Early Christian Church. It is hardly surprising therefore, particularly when it is realized that even Ptolemy had been vague about the produce of the *Golden Khersonese*, that when sixteenth-century European scholars looked to South-East Asia they entertained very golden expectations of it.

The arrival of the Portuguese in the Malay Peninsula brought the *Golden Khersonese* within their dominions, but, with a few exceptions, they do not seem, so extreme were the concepts held of this gold-bearing region, to have recognized it as such, or to have wished to recognize it as such, and the *Golden Khersonese* of their aspirations was, like Marco Polo's lands, identified with the yet undiscovered lands believed to lie to the south-east. Camões, however, reflecting one sixteenth-century theory which sought to reconcile the Ptolemaic description of the *Golden Khersonese* with a Malayan identification and the existence of Sumatra, remarks in his *Os Lusiadas*:

This noble island of Sumatra was said in ancient times to be joined to the mainland, until ocean breakers eating into the coast drove a wedge between. The Chersonese, the region was called, to which was added the adjective 'Golden' from its valuable seams of the metal. Some have imagined it to be the site of Solomon's Ophir.

From earliest times scholars had pondered the whereabouts of *Ophir*, from whence King Solomon had obtained gold with which to build the temple at Jerusalem. They had indeed little information on which to base their conjecture, other than the statement in the Biblical *Third Book of Kings*:

And King Solomon made a navy of ships in Eziongeber, which is beside Eloth, on the shore of the Red Sea, in the land of Edom. And Hiram sent in the navy his servants, shipmen that had knowledge of the sea, with the servants of Solomon. And they came to Ophir, and fetched thence gold, four hundred and twenty talents, and brought it to King Solomon.[1]
For the King had at sea a navy of Tharshish with the navy of Hiram, once in three years came the navy of Tharshish, bringing gold, and silver, ivory and apes, and peacocks.[2]

It was perhaps almost inevitable that *Ophir*, an unknown and uncertain place, should have become identified in men's minds with *Khryse*, *Argyre* and the *Golden Khersonese* of Ptolemy,[3] the lands described by Marco Polo and the antipodean continent, for so extreme does their concept of the wealth of *Odhir* seem to have been, that, as geographical knowledge extended eastwards and westwards without *Ophir* being recognized, its supposed position moved with that knowledge, always a little ahead of the latest discovery.

Josephus, in his *Jewish Antiquities* of the first century, writes quite categorically of 'the land anciently called *Sopheir* but now the *Golden Khersonese*; it belongs to *India*', by which, presumably, he meant *India beyond the Ganges*.[4] An *Indian* location was also ascribed to *Ophir* by Eusebius, St. Jerome, St. Basil, Procopius and Heyschius.[5] Roger Bacon (*c.* 1267) believed that Solomon's

[1] The passage occurs in chapter ix, of the *Third Book of Kings* in the Vulgate and Septuagint Versions. In the English Version of King James, where the *Third Book of Kings* becomes the *First Book of Kings*, as a result of the title *Book of Samuel* being applied to the first two books of *Kings*, the passage occurs in the *First Book of Kings*, chapter ix, verse 28. A similar passage occurs in chapter viii of the *Second Book of Paralipomemon* in the Septuagint Version, or the *Second Book of Chronicles*, chapter viii, verse 18, in the King James Version.

[2] Chapter ix of the *Third Book of Kings* (Vulgate Version) or chapter x, verse 22, of the *First Book of Kings* (King James Version). See also chapter viii of the *Second Book of Paralipomemon* (Septuagint Version) or chapter ix, verse 21, of the *Second Book of Chronicles* (King James Version).

[3] See Lelewel 1852: 158 where a possible connection between the name *Argyre*, or *Agyre*, on medieval maps and the *Ophir* of King Solomon is discussed.

[4] Josephus 1905: 660–1. Thackeray and Marcus translate Χρυσῆν ... Κολουμένην as 'Land of Gold' but it is clearly the same as the Χρυσῆς Χερσονήσου, *Golden Khersonese* or *Peninsula* of Ptolemy, and the fact that Josephus referred to it thus in the first century is very significant.

[5] Rainaud 1893: 61.

fleet sailed to *India*, which he placed at the furthest extremity of the Indian Ocean,[1] and d'Ailly, writing in 1410–14 in his *Imago Mundi*, respected Bacon's view. Columbus, who was much indebted to d'Ailly,[2] believed that he had discovered *Ophir* in Española,[3] but since he never renounced the view that Española was an eastern extremity of Asia this did not contradict d'Ailly. Rodrigo Fernández de Santaella y Córdoba, in the introduction to his Castilian translation of Marco Polo's *Travels* of 1503, according to the English translation of Frampton (1579), refuted Columbus' claim and wrote:

And whereas the vulgar people, and men for the most part, doe thinke that Antilla . . . be in the Indias, they be deceived therein. . . . And for bycause that in Spaniola, or new Spayne, they do find gold, some doe not let to say it is Tharsis and Ophir, and Sethin, from whence in the time of Salomon, they brought gold to Hierusalem. . . .

What is hee that in bringing gold from Antilla will prove it is from Ophir, or Sethin, or Tharsis from whence it was brought to Salomon . . . If for the golde that is founde in Antilla, wee should beleeve that it is Tharsis, and Orphyn, and Sethyn, by ye other things that be founde in Ophyn and not in Antilla, we must beleeve that it is not those, nor those it. And moreover, it appeareth that Asia and Tharsis, Ophyn and Sethyn, be in the East, and Antilla the Spanyola in the west, in place and condition much different.[4]

Whether or not Marco Polo himself expected to reach *Ophir* in the course of his Asiatic travels is uncertain, but the Portuguese, as they extended their activities across the Indian Ocean, certainly did.[5] Magellan believed that the *Lequios* were the *Islands of Ophir*,[6] and their East Indian location was implied by the Spanish emissaries at Badajoz.[7]

Pereira, like many Portuguese to follow him,[8] identified *Ophir* with the Portuguese discoveries in East Africa, and in his *Esmeraldo de Situ Orbis* of 1518 wrote:

in the second year of your reign 1497 A.D. . . . your Highness ordered the discovery to be continued from Ilheo da Cruz. . . . Your captains discovered anew the great mine which some hold to be that of Ophir and is now called Çofala whence the most wise King Solomon . . . drew 420 talents of gold with which he built the holy temple of Jerusalem.[9]

[1] Bacon 1928: 327–8. See also Kamal 1926: 1024 *et seq.*

[2] The edition of d'Ailly's *Imago Mundi* of 1410–14 by Buron (see D'Ailly 1930) is from a copy owned by Columbus and contains his notes.

[3] Jane 1930: I: cxviii–cxxi, 6; and Jane 1930: II: lxxxvi, 104. See also McNutt 1912: I: 61,86–87. Jane suggests that the true objective of Columbus lay to the south, the *Terra Incognita*.

[4] Penzer 1929: 6–9.

[5] See the Introductory Letter in Fernández' *O Livro de Marco Polo*, 1502. Fernández 1922.

[6] Denucé 1907: 435–61; Denucé 1911: 165.

[7] Blair 1903: I: 194–5; Navarette 1945: IV: Doc. XXXVII.

[8] See Theal 1898–1903: I: 22; Theal 1898–1903: VII: 275; and Theal 1898–1903: III: 354, where the views of Manuel de Faria e Sousa (1666), Friar João dos Santos (1609) and António Bocarro (1631) on the African location of *Ophir* are reproduced.

[9] Pereira 1937: 4–5. Kimble examines the claims of Sofala, Zimbabwe and the Omani coast of Arabia to the Ophirian identification, and refers to the archaeological evidence for the identification of the latter (Pereira 1937: 4 (footnote)). See Shattum 1908 for a study of the East African identification of *Ophir* and the case for its location between the Limpopo and Zambesi.

Enciso in his *Suma* of 1519 referred to the location of *Ophir*, arguing that since the Portuguese had already explored for 180° eastwards of the Atlantic *demarcación Ophir* must lie within the Spanish hemisphere. He also implied that *Ophir* must lie to the S or SE of the Moluccas, and identified *Ophir* with *Iocat (Locac)* and *Tharshish* with *Ciapangu* (Japan).[1] Barlow, treading more circumspectly in his version of the *Suma*, his *Briefe Summe of Geographie* of 1540–1, wrote:

And beiond Java 80 leges southest is another land called iocat, [locac] wherein is very moche golde and many elephants and apes and caracolitas. . . . And as they write of Ophir from whens Salomon had his golde for the temple, it is to be thought that this is the same that is Ophir. . . . Beiond the ilond iocat 30 leges is the ilond iava the lesse wch is by catigara, and w^tin this land is bredde the unicornes.[2]

In 1526 Sebastian Cabot was despatched by the Spanish authorities to traverse the Magellanic Straits and to 'discover Ophir and Tarsis and Eastern Cathay, as well as new spice regions believed to exist in the equatorial or southern Pacific and undoubtedly within the Spanish hemisphere'.[3] He was accompanied by Roger Barlow and Henry Latimer, both introduced to the expedition by Robert Thorne,[4] who had an investment of 1,400 ducats in the enterprise and whose interest in *Ophir* and the Moluccas has already been mentioned.

One of the most significant contributions to our understanding of the sixteenth-century idea of an antipodean continent, and its relationship in the minds of the time with *Ophir* and the lands reported by Marco Polo, is made by a group of cartographers who flourished in Dieppe in the mid-sixteenth century, through their *portolano* charts and written works. The particular feature of their charts which is of interest here is their representation of *Terra Australis* to the S and SE of the Malay Archipelago in a form which, allowing for what may be projectional distortion, unfamiliarity with a projection or hurried copying, and for a westerly transposition and proximity to Java, is, perhaps generally but not particularly, reminiscent of the configuration of North-Western Australia, although the idea of continental land is perhaps more significant than any familiarity in the actual configuration. This northern promontory bears the Poloesque name *Java la Grande*, but it is perhaps unlikely that this is a purely hypothetical delineation induced by the references of Polo and Varthema, and the fact that some of the Dieppe charts exclude all but this part of the supposed austral continent may indicate that the evidence for this part seemed to be reliable. Considerable interest has attached to these charts, primarily in an endeavour to prove or disprove a Portuguese knowledge

[1] Barlow 1932: 10–11 (footnote 3).   [2] Barlow 1932: 137.

[3] Williamson 1929: 262; Forsyth 1955: 37. See also the *cédula* of Carlos I, Toledo, 1525, in Torres y Lanzas 1925: No. 311.   [4] Forsyth 1955: 37.

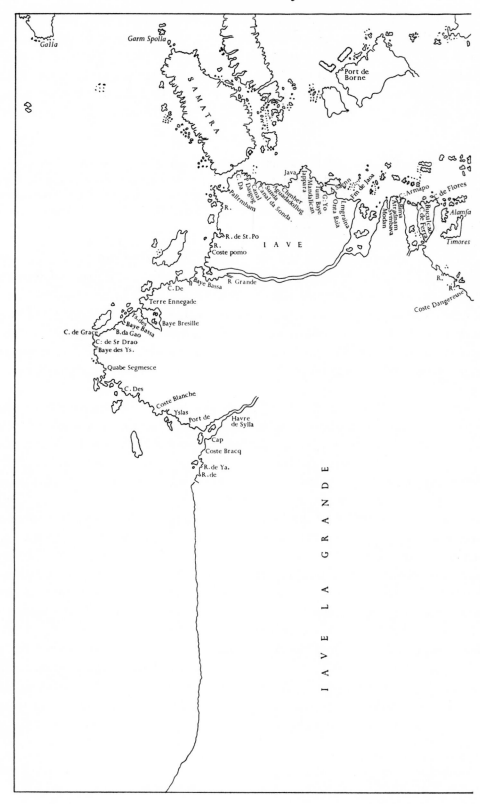

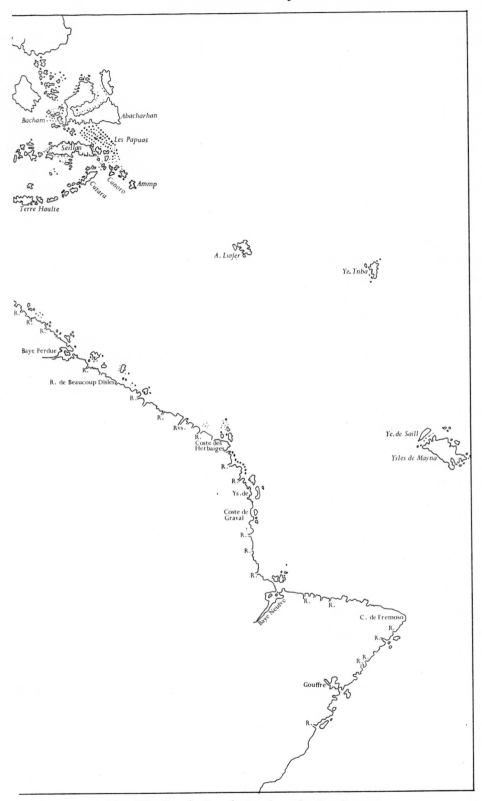

Map VI *Iave la Grande*, based on the *Dauphin* map.

of Australia prior to the Dutch exploration of it. Despite the attention and theorizing which this subject has received, including the unconvincing assertion that the prototypes were deliberately distorted to prevent knowledge of Australia by aliens, and to create an impression of unnavigability in the surrounding waters,[1] it is doubtful if anything more can be said than that the charts probably derived from a Portuguese origin and that they do indicate a knowledge of North-Western Australia. It is extremely doubtful, however, if the Portuguese prepared the original prototype on the basis of any physical knowledge of the area concerned. There is no other reliable documentary evidence to justify belief in a French or Portuguese discovery of Australia at that time, but it would be surprising if some Asiatic knowledge of Australia had not been obtained prior to the Portuguese settlement of the East Indies. Quite apart from the regular drift voyages still made by Indonesians and Timorese to North-Western Australia, which must have been going on for a considerable time and would have provided a native oral tradition of Australia, supposing that some of them managed to return, Macassan Bugis trade with this area is reliably reported for the late eighteenth century and some of the pottery types to be found on their trading sites appear to be similar to those excavated by the author and others in South Malaya in fifteenth- to seventeenth-century horizons. Moreover, it would be strange if Arab or Chinese seamen, who were well established in the trade of the East Indies long before the arrival of the Portuguese,[2] had not ventured, or drifted in the grip of local north-west winds, so far to the SE, and there is some evidence to support this assumption. Ludovico di Varthema, in his *Novum Itinerarium* (Milan, 1511), recorded how in the East Indies, in the first decade of the sixteenth century, he had been informed by a sea captain of lands to the S of Java whose inhabitants navigated at sea by the Southern Cross. He reported this information to the Portuguese, and it may well have encouraged them to press further to the E in 1512.[3]

What does seem probable, if we accept the relative accuracy of the charts as evidence of actual knowledge, is that when the Portuguese arrived in the East Indies they obtained information, oral and probably cartographical, of the north-western coast of Australia, and recorded that information without themselves ever proceeding to its exploration. That the Dieppe cartographers used a Portuguese model seems, from the contents of the maps alone, fairly certain, though how that model came to them, and whether it was the lost 'Javanese' chart copied by Francisco Rodrigues (the pilot of the Moluccan expedition of 1512) which Albuquerque sent to Portugal, is by no means certain. Of the Dieppe cartographers themselves little is known, other than can be pieced together from the slight information which we have about them individually. That they or their Portuguese cartographical predecessors should have

[1] Collingridge 1891–2: 100.   [2] On Arab seafaring see Hourani 1951: 61–79.
[3] Maggs 1927: 4.

identified these lands with those of Marco Polo is understandable, and it is al-most certainly from this origin that the whole series of maps and charts of the sixteenth century which depict *Terra Australis* with the familiar configuration of the coastline to the SE of Java and in the vicinity of North-Western Aus-tralia, and on which a Poloesque nomenclature (in original or adulterated form) is laid down, derive.[1]

That European knowledge was not obtained by discovery is supported by Guillaume le Testu, himself of the Dieppe School, who wrote concerning 'This part of the same land of the south called Australie which has not yet been discovered because there is no record that anyone has searched it out and be-cause it is only drawn from imagination',[2] though if it was 'imagination' it was inspired. The Jean Maillard *Mappe-monde* of 1536–42,[3] perhaps a prototype of the later charts produced by the Dieppe School, and certainly the earliest known chart of 'Australia' which bears any resemblance to reality, was prepared to illustrate a poetic geographical treatise addressed to Henry VIII of England,[4] and on it the antipodean continent bears the two titles *Terre Australle* and *La Catigare*.[5] Amongst the other productions of the School are the anonymous *Dauphin* map of 1542,[6] the atlas of Guillaume le Testu of 1555–6, on which the east coast of *Grande Jave* is named *Terre de offir*,[7] the *Hydrographie*[8] of Jean Alphonse Saintongeois of 1545,[9] the *Mappe-monde* of Nicolas Desliens of 1566[10] and the works of Jean Rotz.[11]

It is quite clear from the nomenclature of the *Dauphin* and Rotz maps in particular that an attempt has been made on them to reconcile an actual Portuguese knowledge of the north coasts of Java[12] and the Lesser Sunda Islands

---

[1] See for instance Ortelius' *Typus Orbis Terrarum* of 1570 and Rumold Mercator's *Orbis Terrae Compendiosa Descriptio* 1587 (Nordenskiöld 1889: Plate XLVII). Some argument can be advanced for a connection between the voyage from Honfleur of Paulmier de Gonneville in 1503 and the Dieppe *portolanos*, but a Portuguese-Asian source seems more probable.

[2] On le Testu's planisphere of 1566 (BNP: Res Ce AA625), in his illuminated atlas, the *Grande Jave* is only shown in faint outline, '*pour mémoire*', and in a legend on the planisphere he refers to certain Portuguese having been carried far S of the Cape of Good Hope and having seen it, but since no one else had discovered it he refrains from adding credence to it (Forsyth 1955: 29).

[3] In the British Museum. See Taylor 1930(d): 72.

[4] *Le Premier Livre de la Cosmographie en rhétorique françoyse.*

[5] *Cattigara*, the most easterly seaport of Ptolemy's known world.

[6] BM: MS. 5413. See Chicoteau 1959: 77; Major 1859: XXVII.

[7] MS. Atlas No. 607 in the Bibliothèque du Ministre de la Guerre, Paris (Maps 30–32). See Chicoteau 1959: 78; and Rainaud 1893: 291. Le Testu was with Drake in 1573 and may have influenced him in his designs on the antipodean continent (Williamson 1946: 127).

[8] BNP: MS. *fonds français* 676.   [9] BM: Add. MS. 24065. See Chicoteau 1959: 80.

[10] BNP: Res Ge D7895. See Chicoteau 1959: 80. Facsimile in the National Library, Canberra, and in Marcel 1886: Plate I.

[11] See for instance his chart (BM: Royal MS. 20 EIX, ff 29v–30) in Beaglehole 1955: xxviii; Parks 1928: 13.

[12] Sebastian del Caño's voyage in the *Victoria* with the remnants of Magellan's expedition past Timor and well to the south of Java early in 1522 seems to have been unknown to them, as does the

with the idea of an antipodean continent, and the division of *Iave* (Java) from *Iave la Grande* (the continent) by a hypothetical channel is clearly a rather ingenious attempt to reconcile the whole with Polo's distinction between *Java the Great* and *Java the Less*. Nevertheless, notwithstanding a due recognition that this reconciliation is the result of ignorance of the south coast of Java, there is no good reason for dismissing the suspicion if not assumption that the very idea of a promontory of the antipodean continent in this form and context was based on information of Australia: information which was so indeterminate that it was natural for cartographers of the Dieppe School to reconcile their total information as they did. What seems possible is that they had on the one hand a Portuguese cartographical record of the north coasts of Java and the Lesser Sunda Islands, and on the other hand they had the traditional hypothesis of an antipodean continent, Varthema's report, and indirect and deviously acquired Asian information of presumably continental land to the south-east of the archipelago. The combination of these bodies of information in the form in which it appears on the *Dauphin* and Rotz maps, where what may be Australia is placed in close proximity to the south of Java (and in the case of some of the Dieppe charts conjoined to it) was justified by one interpretation of what Polo had seemed to have to say about *Java the Great* and *Java the Less*.

Jean Alphonse or Fonteneau, the pilot of Saintonge, described the *Terre Australe* as being conjoined to *La grande Jayve* and stretching to Magellan's Straits, and referred to the *Terre de Offir* of le Testu.[1] In his *La Cosmographie avec l'Espère et Régime du Soleil et du Nord* he wrote:

And it is not yet known at present what land it is if not that Orfye is an island in the Pacific Ocean. And Tersye is mainland and is also on the shore of the Pacific Ocean. . . . So the memory of Tersye and Orfye was lost, and until now nothing more is known of it, but that it is searched for every year and is in the east of the Pacific Ocean. The Pacific Ocean aforesaid is all full of islands and other great lands of which it is not known whether they are islands. And for this reason one cannot know which they are. . . . There is not one, however, where gold and precious stones are not found. To the east of Java Minor . . . are the islands of Jacatte and Dorfy and the land of Tersye, and the island of White Men. . . . And in this land there is much gold and silver and elephants, and there are monkeys as in Barbary, and the aforesaid land lies in 21 degrees of south latitude and the islands in 8 degrees to 10 degrees. And I doubt that it is mainland and that it extends to join the 'Terra Australia'. And as it is written that Dorfy is the place whence Solomon had gold brought to build the temple, I conceive it to be one of these because in it there is a great quantity of gold and all

deduction of Francisco Rodrigues that Java had a south coast only slightly further to the south than is in fact the case (see his chart in Cortesão 1944). Rodrigues' deduction may have been speculative, and most early and mid-sixteenth century Portuguese charts only laid down the known northern coastline of Java. Post-Dieppe charts delineate the promontory as well separated from Java, even before the charting of Java's south coast, and reflect a recognition of the significance of del Cano's voyage in respect of the older delineation.

[1] Rainaud 1893:290. Fonteneau claimed to have navigated in this area. Rainaud 1893:290 (footnote 7).

things which were brought to Solomon. And from here to Peru eastwards there are approximately nine hundred or a thousand leagues at the most.[1]

Fonteneau's account, similar as it is to Encisco's, provides a very clear picture of the combined Ophirian-Poloesque-Antipodean concept, and of the distance at which *Ophir* was expected to lie from Perú. Where Fonteneau derived his information on latitudes and distance is uncertain, although the estimated distance was a reasonable deduction on the basis of an underestimated Pacific, and it is significant that it was in these latitudes that Mendaña, in 1567–8, sought for and was later reputed to have found the *Ophir* of King Solomon.

In 1518 Diogo Pacheco reported an island of gold over 100 leagues to the SE of *Baros* (Barus) in Sumatra,[2] and Pigafetta had reported New Guinea as gold producing. The Jesuit Father Joseph de Acosta, in his *Historia Natural y Moral de las Indias* (1570–87), published in 1587, discussed at some length the question of the *Antichthon* and the whereabouts of *Ophir* and *Tharshish*. He rejected the arguments of the Fathers against the existence of the *Antipodes* and the location of *Ophir* in Perú or Hispaniola, concluding that *Ophir* lay in the East Indies[3] and, of the southern continent, that: 'it sufficeth for our subject, to know that there is firme land on this Southerne part, as bigge as all Europe, Asia and Affricke.'[4] Mendoza, recounting the voyage of a Franciscan to China in 1576, follows a description of Malacca with the remark that: 'Over against this famous citie, of which so many thinges may be spoken of, is that mightie kingdome and land of Sumatra, called by the ancient cosmographers Trapouana, which is (as some say) the land of Ophir.'[5]

Of the English commentaries on this question, John Dee's *Great Volume of Famous and Rich Discoveries* of 1577 is perhaps the most significant for, as Taylor has pointed out, its purpose was to show how the English might bring back, not only the wealth of the East Indies and Cathay, but the riches of *Ophir*.[6] In it he states:

Upon the Premisses about the Ophirian voyage I have bestowed some days to make evident how, every three years once that most noble Ophirian provision might be got to Jerusalem,

and continues:

In sundry places afore hath mention been made of Iles in the Scythian Ocean, but ever with this respect, as to note the records thereof to some evidence of proving the Asian Periplus

[1] Forsyth 1955: 27; Fonteneau 1904: 278, 400. See also Fonteneau 1904: 388, 399–400. For comments on the Dieppe *portolanos* see Spate 1957(b); Collingridge 1891–2; Morgan 1891–2; Chicoteau 1959; Anthiaume 1916: I: 59–180, 494 *et seq*; Rainaud 1983: 286–92; Major 1859: xxvii *et seq*; and Forsyth 1955: 23–38.   [2] Baião 1939: II: 159.

[3] Markham 1880: I: 15–47. See also Markham 1880: I: xi–xvi.

[4] Markham 1880: I: 19 (from the English translation of Edward Grimston, 1604).

[5] Mendoza 1854: II: 319. *Trapouana* or *Taprobane* appears on early world maps, e.g. Beatus', as the north-eastern extremity of the *Antichthon*. *Taprobane* was in fact Ceylon, but came to be confused with Sumatra. See references in Jack-Hinton 1964(a).   [6] Taylor 1929: 127–8.

and the Navigation for Cape Comfort, or this most comfortable Brytish Kingdom to the lands of BEACH etc., to be open and commodiously enough possible to be made.[1]

Purchas rejected the idea that *Ophir* had been found in Perú or in the Americas and himself concluded that: 'This Golden Country is like Gold, hard to find and much quarrelled, and needs a wise Myner to bring it out of the Labrynth of darknesse', and that it should be identified with the area embraced by Bengal, Sumatra and the Coast of Coromandel.[2]

One of the most complete studies in the late sixteenth and early seventeenth centuries of this whole subject was made by the Malaccan Malayo-Portuguese Manuel Godinho de Erédia, whilst actually in the East Indies and with the prospect of making a voyage of exploration to the lands about which he wrote.[3] In a report, *Informação da Áurea Chersoneso, ou Península, e das Ilhas Áuríferas* . . . of 1597–1600, he identified the Malay Peninsula and Archipelago as the *Golden Khersonese*, suggested that *Tanasorir*, a West Malayan port, might have been 'the ancient port of Sophir', and added that Marco Polo and Lodovico Varto- mano (Varthema) both asserted the existence of 'the Lesser Java situated in the unknown Ocean . . . properly called the South Sea'. In his *Tratado Ophirico* of 1616 he identified *Ophir* with Siam, *Tharshish* with Canton, and described *Meridional India*[4] as consisting of 'the continental land of Lucach which reaches Southwards . . . as far as the Pole' and including 'the Java maior wherein Beach is situated or Luca Antara, and the Java minor . . . as is noted by Marco Polo'. He described Polo as having passed into the Southern Sea and as having reached 'Java major containing Beach or Veach, land of gold', and added that after 'leaving to Westward the shoal of Maletur . . . he passed to the South to the Island of Pentam, whence he crossed to Java minor'.[5] These were regions which Erédia himself wished to explore and for which venture he was licensed by the Viceroy of India on 5 April 1601. There is no evidence however to indicate that the voyage was ever embarked upon.

In his major work, his *Declaracam de Malaca e India Meridional com O Cathay* of 1613,[6] Erédia reiterated many of his earlier deductions and conclu- sions and located *Java Minor* on the latitude of Capricorn on the grounds that Polo had observed the constellation of Ursa Minor from the point of *Samara*. He adduced the evidence of the *Lontares* and *Annals of Java Major* as supporting his beliefs relating to *Meridional India*, 'as appears in the poems, vulgar songs, and histories of the Empire of Mattaron', and it is in these and other references to indigenous traditions of trade with *Java Minor*, and of voyages made by

---

[1] Taylor 1929: 127–8. See BM: Vitellius C VII Cotton MS. f 266.

[2] Purchas 1903: I: 92–94. Purchas devotes considerable space to the whole question of *Ophir*, reflecting contemporary interest in it. See Purchas 1903: I: 1–135.

[3] The Erédia sources referred to are all contained in Mills 1930. For a study of Erédia see Spate 1957(a).   [4] The southern land of Ptolemy's *Table 12 of Asia*.

[5] Mills 1930: 259–64.   [6] Mills 1930: 60 *et seq*.

the natives of the East Indies, that he provides perhaps the strongest documentary evidence for the belief that his own concepts, and those reflected in the Dieppe *portolanos*, derived from an early Asiatic knowledge of Australia.[1]

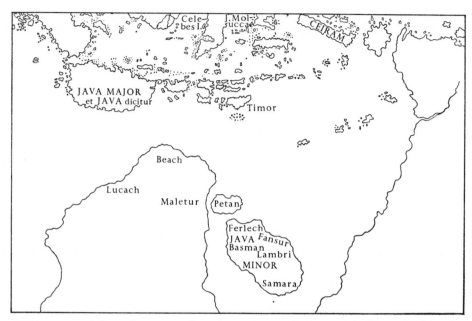

Map VII   Part of the only extant sheet from a second edition of Plancius' *Planisphere* of
c. 1595, redrawn.

On Mercator's world-map of 1569 there appears a group of three islands, some 10° W of Perú and in the latitude of Cuzco, bearing the inscription: '*Hic uspiam longius intra mare in paralello portus Hacari dicunt nonnulli Indi et Christiani esse insulas grandes et publica fama divites auro.*[2] These islands, which for want of a better name may be referred to as the *Uspiam Islands*, appear on several later charts and maps, on Ortelius' *Typus Orbis Terrarum* of 1570[3] and Poppelinier's world-map of 1582 with the name *Insulae incognitae*, on Postell's *Pola Captata Nova Charta Universii* of 1581 with the name *Ispiam*, and also on Mazza's *Americae . . . Descriptio* of 1583–9[4] and Rumold Mercator's *Orbis Terrae Compendiosa Descriptio* of 1587. In Ruscelli's translation of Ptolemy's *Geography* of 1599 they are described as '*Hic Uspia insulas esse auro divites nonulli volunt*', and in Lorenzo d'Anania's *L'Universale Fabrica del Mondo* (Venice 1597) as '*Hic Uspia Insules . . . auro divites*'.

What precisely induced cartographers to place these islands on their maps is a matter for some conjecture, but it would be wrong to dismiss them as

---

[1] Mills 1930: 60–64. Mills describes Erédia's *Map of Meridional India* (Mills 1930: 223) as a 'cartographic nightmare'.   [2] Jomard 1862: Plate XXI.
[3] Nordenskiöld 1889: Plate XLVI.   [4] Müller: 1894: I: Plate 12.

cartographical inspirations, even though sixteenth-century maps did have rather more than their fair share of decorative and monotony-relieving insular inventions. One is immediately struck in the several titles and inscriptions for the *Uspiam Islands* by their uncertainty, their suggestion of gold, and the possibility of the word *Uspiam* being a corrupt transcription of an adjectivally rendered *Ophir*. In fact there are no islands in or near the position ascribed to them on the several maps on which they appear, and they are certainly not the Galapagos. For their origin we must look to the sort of rumours and reports current in Perú and the Americas on the supposed contents of the Pacific, remembering at the same time the prevailing underestimate of the width of the Pacific and the conjecture that *Ophir* lay in the Pacific in close proximity to, if not part of, the austral continent, and at no great distance from Perú.

One such rumour current in Perú in the mid-sixteenth century was reported by Pedro Sarmiento de Gamboa in his *History of the Incas* of 1572,[1] where he described how Tupac Inca Yupanqui defeated the Huancavelicas by land and sea and overran Quito, dominating the country as far as the Ecuadorian coast in the area of Manta. In the course of his forrays, Tupac met merchants on the coast who had sailed into the Pacific on balsa rafts with sails, and had visited islands called *Avachumbi and Niñachumbi* 'where there were many people and much gold'. Dissatisfied with his own conquests, Tupac departed for these islands accompanied by 20,000 men on a vast fleet of balsa rafts.

Tupac Inca navigated and sailed on until he discovered the islands of Avachumbi and Ninachumbi, and returned, bringing back with him black people, gold, a chair of brass, and a skin and jaw bone of a horse. These trophies were preserved in the fortress of Cuzco until the Spaniards came. . . . The duration of this expedition by Tupac Inca was nine months, others say a year.[2]

That the story was based on some historical reality is perhaps indicated by the fact that the legend was not of any great antiquity in Sarmiento's time, Tupac's grandsons having met Pizarro[3]; that Sarmiento had made use of native chroniclers whose personal memories dated from pre-European days; that he tended if anything to understate rather than exaggerate Inca achievements; and that Inca oral traditions seem to have been strong and reliable. The story was repeated by Father Balboa in his *History of Peru* of 1586 and his *Miscelanea Antartica* of 1576,[4] and he was particularly interested in it and in attempting to reconcile it with the known geography of his day. Allowing for the possibility that the account of the relics brought back from the islands was

---

[1] Markham 1907. On Sarmiento see Madariaga 1947: 166, and Clissold 1954.

[2] Markham 1907: 136. Sarmiento was later to claim that he had sighted these islands during Mendaña's voyage of 1567–8.

[3] The actual dates of Tupac Inca's life are uncertain, Latcham suggests 1448–82 (Latcham 1928: 234), Rowe 1471–93 (Rowe 1944: 57, and Rowe 1946: 203). Sarmiento gave 1388 as the date of his birth and Balboa 1493 as the date of his death (Heyerdahl 1952: 557). Von Hagen gives 1471 as the year of his accession (Von Hagen 1957: 128).   [4] Heyerdahl 1952: 560–1.

distorted or, as Clissold points out, that they may have been obtained during the voyage but at Panama,[1] there seems no good reason to dismiss this story. The identity of the islands visited has been disputed, and although Markham identified them as the Galapagos,[2] Buck, Rivet and Christian have presented considerably stronger evidence for the identification of Mangareva, particularly by reference to Mangarevan traditions of the arrival of a chief named Tupa through an eastern passage known as the *Great Passage of Tupa*,[3] an identification which was within the range of balsa raft expeditions as Thor Heyerdahl and Eric de Bisschop have courageously demonstrated.

Whether or not the expedition of Tupac Inca Yupanqui occurred, or whether or not he visited the Galapagos or Mangareva, is unimportant in this context. What is important is that Sarmiento considered it so probable as to be worth recording, and that his feelings were echoed by Father Balboa. It is reasonable to conclude that the story was fairly generally known to the Spaniards in Perú, perhaps as one of several stories of this kind which, if accepted by Sarmiento and Balboa, were likely to have been generally accepted, even by those in authority. As Clissold remarks:

More than one old Spanish chronicler had spoken with assurance of the existence of islands in the Pacific. Cieza de Leon believed the Indians' tales of 'very great islands, inhabited by a prosperous people and having great store of gold and silver . . . and it is even said that they came to the mainland in great canoes to trade their wares, and some Spaniards of our nation say that in Acari, which is one of the valleys of which I have written, there may be seen a great piece of one of those canoes, which proves the truth of these reports.'[4]

Father Joseph de Acosta in his *Historia Natural y Moral de las Indias*, based on a sojourn in Perú from 1569 to 1585, contemplated a possible connection between the Old and New Worlds by land connections either north of California or south of Magellan's Straits, discussed the legends of Manta and Puerto Viejo about the arrival and departure of giants by sea, and remarked:

In like sort, the Indians of Yca and Arica report that in old time they were wont to saile farre to the Ilands of the West,[5] and made their voiages in Seales skinnes blowne up. So as there wants no witnesses to prove that they sailed in the South Sea before Spaniards came hither.[6]

That the reputed *Islands of the West* were closely associated with the Ophirian conjecture may be illustrated by an old, but unfortunately undated, manuscript record of an account given to Captain Francisco de Cáceres

---

[1] Clissold 1959: 238.   [2] Markham 1907: 136.
[3] Buck 1938: 22; Christian 1924: 525; Rivet 1928: 583, 603; Rivet 1943; 124. For further detailed comments on this question see Heyerdahl 1952; 556–67; Hornell 1946: 52–53; Lothrop 1932: 237; Means 1942: 17; Emery 1939.   [4] Clissold 1954: 25.
[5] '*que solian antiguamente navegar a unas Islas al Poniente muy laxos.*'
[6] The English translation of 1604, Acosta 1880.

(Cádres) by an Indian of the *Solomon Islands*.[1] Since the date is unknown there seems to be no good reason for associating the account with the actual voyage of discovery to the islands later to be named the Solomon Islands which forms the main subject of this study, and it is just as probable that the account was of an earlier vintage. Here again the truth of the report and the actual nature and position of the islands referred to are unimportant; what is significant is that de Cádres should have been sufficiently interested to record the story, and that the name Solomon should have been related to the islands. The same MS. contains an account of how Juan Montañés was blown off the coast of Chile for 50 days and discovered an exceedingly large island in 18½° latitude. The island was inhabited by amiable natives who, on Montañés' departure, produced the inevitable gold-plate as a farewell offering. The account is highly suspect, but once again this is irrelevant to its evidence of interest.

Antonio Galvano in his *Tratado* of 1563 states that:

In the yeere 1538 and 1539, after that Diego de Almagro was beheaded, . . . Pisarro was not idle. For he sent straight one Peter de Baldivia with a good companie of men to discover and conquere the country of Chili. . . . While he was in these discoveries he heard newes of a King called Leucengolma . . . and that this Leucengolma had an island, and a temple therein with two thousand prieste; and that beyond them were the Amazones, whose queene was called Guanomilla, that is to say, the golden heaven [whence the Spaniards concluded that there were great riches to be found there, and also at an Island called Solomon].[2] But as yet there are none of these things discovered.[3]

In a similar vein was *Don* Alonso de Montemayor's report of how, when fleeing from Perú 'for fear of Gonzalle Pizzaro', he visited an island in 15° S, about 600–700 leagues from Perú, called San Pablo,[4] and Arias,[5] in a memorial of about 1615, addressed to the King of Spain and designed to provoke the exploration and conversion of austral lands, recorded how:

A pilot named Juan Fernandez, who discovered the track from Lima to Chili by going to the westward [which till then had been made with much difficulty, as they kept along shore, where the southerly winds almost constantly prevail]: he sailing from the coast of Chili, in about the latitude of 40°, a little more or less, in a small ship . . . in courses between W. and S.W. was brought in a month's time to what was, to the best of their judgment, a very fertile continent.[6]

[1] BM: Egerton Add. MS. 1816, f 223; Zaragoza 1876: II: 126 (footnote). See Amherst 1901: II: 463–9, for an English translation. See also Heyerdahl 1952: 567–9, where the possibility of the islands being identified with Sala-y-Gómez and Easter Island is examined.

[2] '+ *assi de hua ylha que se chama de Salamam*'.

[3] Hakluyt's translation of 1601. Galvano 1862: 213–14.

[4] Espada 1891. See also Rozpides 1891.

[5] BM: *Papeles tocantes a la Iglesia Española* 4745, f 11; Markham 1904: II: 517–36; Major 1859: 1–30.

[6] Markham 1904: II: 526–7. Little is known of Juan Fernández. In 1563 he discovered the Lima-Chile route and the islands of San Félix and San Ambrosio. Arias suggested that the continental Pacific discovery was made during that voyage and cites a certain *Maestre de Campo* named Cortés as having reported so to the King. Mackenna and Markham rejected the account (Markham 1904: II:

In the preceding pages an attempt has been made to reconstruct the several prevailing concepts of the contents of the Pacific in the early part of the second half of the sixteenth century which might have been accepted, partly or as a whole, by enquiring Spaniards. In several cases the availability of material has necessitated the citing of sources of the late sixteenth century, but this has been done on the reasonable assumption that they illustrate the general tendency of ideas which prevailed in the mid-sixteenth century and persisted. It would be a mistake to look to particular concepts as providing incentive for particular exploratory projects, or to attempt for instance to relate the *Uspiam Islands* of cartography to any particular reputed island, for it is unlikely that Spaniards in Perú as a whole differentiated between particular concepts or viewed them other than *in toto*, as evidence of valuable and extensive lands within the unknown reaches of the Pacific.

To those who examined the available evidence there were strong grounds for believing that within the Spanish hemisphere and between the limits of Perú and the Moluccas, limits whose distance apart was underestimated, lay not only New Guinea but a vast antarctic continent stretching from Magellan's Straits towards New Guinea, of which the latter might itself be a promontory. In low latitudes it could not be far from Perú, and appeared to have another promontory to the S and SE of the Malay Archipelago identifiable with the southern lands of Marco Polo and Ptolemy. Prominent in all conjecture was *Ophir*; perhaps part of the antipodean continent, perhaps an island or islands in the Pacific close both to the continent and to Perú, and perhaps identifiable with those islands which some Spaniards had reported sighting and of which the *conquistadores* had heard from Inca historians.

It was against this background of geographical belief, this loose amalgam of biblical and classical tradition, scholarly and cartographical deduction and conjecture, report and rumour, fact and fiction, that the Spaniards embarked upon the exploration of the South Pacific.

528), Burney treated it seriously but doubted it (Burney 1803: I: 300–2), and Dalrymple accepted it as evidence for his belief in an antipodean continent. It seems probable that the story was a distortion of Fernández' discovery of San Félix and San Ambrosio.

Note: The possibility of a Portuguese contact with Australia during the sixteenth or seventeenth centuries cannot, of course, be entirely dismissed at this stage. Supposedly Portuguese cannon found in Napier-Broome Bay may well have come from an Indonesian trader, perhaps at a later date, and although there is some Aboriginal linguistic evidence of Portuguese influence, this may also have derived from contact with Indonesians. The Dieppe *portolanos* cannot themselves be accounted sufficient evidence of Portuguese contact on their own, since, as has been suggested, they can be adequately explained without postulating a direct contact, and if a two-way Portuguese contact had ever been established it would be surprising if some documentary reference to it had not survived. However, further archival research and field investigation may well throw new light on the question.

4

II

The Discovery of the Solomon Islands

The Voyage of Álvaro de Mendaña y Neyra to the South-West Pacific, 1567-9

Et cum anchoras sustulissent committebant se mari . . .
et levato artemone secundum aural flatum . . .

Acts xxxvii: 40

ON 24 July 1525, the King of Spain made a decisive move in the dispute over the Moluccas by despatching *Fray* García Jofre de Loyasa to occupy the archipelago, and by following this expedition with two abortive ones in 1526 under Diego García and Sebastian Cabot. In May 1522, Hernán Cortés had informed the King that he was constructing several vessels on the banks of the Zacatula in which he proposed to explore the western coast of México and the South Sea. His intention, once he had heard the results of Magellan's voyage, seems to have been to employ his vessels in securing control of the spice trade of Asia and the Moluccas, sending them northwards to discover the coastal North Pacific route to Asia, and to search at the same time for a strait through North America. His plans, however, were changed by the arrival of a royal *cédula*, dated 20 June 1526, in which the King, impatient to know the fate of his expeditions, ordered him to despatch his vessels direct to the Moluccas.[1]

Cortés entrusted the expedition to his kinsman Álvaro de Saavedra, instructing him to establish a fortification in the Moluccas and make trading agreements with the natives, with the object of dominating the islands as an outpost of New Spain. The expedition set sail on 31 October 1527, the flagship alone reaching the Philippines in February 1528. Here Saavedra discovered that Loyasa's flagship had proceeded to the Moluccas and, following it, found Hernando de la Torre entrenched on the island of Tidore, Loyasa having died *en route*. Two attempts were made by Saavedra to return to New Spain, but the unfavourable winds of the Central West Pacific prevented this, and after the second attempt, during which Saavedra died, the survivors returned to the Moluccas, where they remained for several years until they capitulated to the Portuguese.[2]

[1] Wright 1945: 62–63. For Loyasa's (Loaysa or Loiasa) expedition see Markham 1911: 1–89, Burney 1803: I: 127–47 and Navarrete 1825: V: 241–313.

[2] For Saavedra's voyage see Navarrete 1825: V: 465–75; Wright 1945: 64–67; Markham 1911: 111–32; and Burney 1803: I: 147–61.

The terms of the Treaty of Saragossa of 1529 put an end to Cortés' ambitions in the Spice Islands, and he devoted his attention to the exploration of the Pacific and the intended discovery of the rich islands believed to lie within it. In fact, although Cortés established ship-building yards and harbours, his main maritime and exploratory activities were along the Pacific coastline. In 1537 he despatched Hernán Grijalva in two vessels to the relief of Pizarro, threatened by Mango Ynca at Cuzco, with the further instruction that on completion of the relief he was to proceed on a voyage of discovery in the Eastern Pacific; to search for islands to the westward which were believed to abound in gold,[1] and to make further discoveries towards the Moluccas. He reached 29° S, but, failing to return to California against the contrary winds, his crew mutinied, murdered him, and then headed towards New Guinea where the survivors were captured by indigenes and finally sold to the Portuguese.[2]

Between 1535 and 1537 a series of agreements were made between the Spanish authorities and Juan Pacheco relating to a proposed voyage for the discovery of Pacific Islands, but nothing seems to have materialized from them.[3] Pedro de Alvarado, one of Cortés' captains who had become Governor of Guatemala, showed an interest in the question of Pacific exploration when he obtained a licence in 1527 to make discoveries in the South Sea. In 1534 he did in fact lead a fleet in search of golden islands believed to lie to the west of Guatemala, but en route arrived in Ecuador where Pizarro and Almagro purchased his vessels at a handsome price for use in a local campaign. He was in Spain in 1536 when the survivors of the expeditions of Loyasa and Saavedra returned there and, although forbidden by the King from further ventures to the Moluccas, he did secure, on 16 April 1538, a contract for discovery and trade in spices.

Returning to America, Alvarado constructed a fleet of eleven vessels at Acajutla, from which port he set sail in the autumn of 1540. At Santiago he began negotiations with Antonio de Mendoza, the Viceroy of México, who, with Cortés, was proposing a trans-Pacific expedition, and in 1541 came to an agreement with him to embark on a joint enterprise towards the *Western Isles*, by which they meant the Philippines.[4] Alvarado's death in the Mixton War left Mendoza as sole director of the enterprise and, in November 1542, he despatched Ruy López de Villalobos on the proposed expedition. Villalobos reached the Philippines in January 1543,[5] but shortage of food and the hostility of the indigenes drove him southwards to Tidore. In August 1543, he despatched one vessel under Bernardo de la Torre to return to New Spain with a report

[1] Couto 1612: 131.
[2] Galvano 1862: 201–5; Couto 1612: 131–2; Dalrymple 1767: I: 35–39; Wright 1945: 67–68.
[3] Torres y Lanzas 1925: I: 1069–80; Pacheco 1885: XVII: 24; Pacheco 1885: XX: 325.
[4] On this period see Wagner 1929.
[5] It was this expedition which named them *Las Felipinas*.

for Mendoza but in the summer of 1544 de la Torre rejoined Villalobos at Tidore, having been unable to sail eastwards against stormy winds.[1] In March 1545, the vessel was again despatched under Íñigo Ortiz de Retes,[2] but he was no more successful than de la Torre had been. Striking eastwards, he followed the northern coastline of the land, probably discovered by the Portuguese Jorge de Meneses in 1526[3] and known as *Os Papuas*, which Saavedra had also coasted to the north of in 1528 and 1529.[4] He now named it *Nueva Guinea*[5] (New Guinea) and, reaching a point in 5° S, was forced northwards by contrary winds and ultimately had to abandon the attempt and return to the Moluccas. At this stage Villalobos surrendered to the Portuguese, and the survivors of the expedition were repatriated to Spain.

The fact that Villalobos' expedition had visited the Moluccas despite a royal prohibition seems to have induced Charles to forbid all his Viceroys from sending expeditions to the Far East[6]; a prohibition based on a desire to appease Portugal, a potential ally against French incursion into the New World, and the belief that the mines of Perú and México could provide all the wealth which Spain needed. To the extent that this limited prohibition successfully diverted attention from the Moluccas, hitherto regarded as the immediate objective of maritime expansion, it may have focused attention on the Pacific itself as a potential source of wealth. Even if this is so, it was not until the change of policy which came with the accession of Philip II in 1556, and which culminated in Legazpi and Urdaneta's expedition to the Philippines in 1564–5, their settlement and the discovery of the return Pacific route, that Spain established a firm foothold in the Far East, satisfying a dominant longing and permitting the direction of attention towards the Central and South Pacific.

On 16 August 1550, Gómez de Solis urged Charles to discover '*ciertas islas de que se tiene noticia existan ay en esta mar del sur*',[7] and his petition seems to mark the first stages of the negotiations and proposals which led to the exploration of the South-West Pacific. Cieza de León records that when he left Perú in 1550 the Judges of the Royal Tribunal had entrusted the discovery of the 'various large rich islands from which it is told that they brought much gold to traffic with the natives of this coast' to Gómez de Solis,[8] but although this expedition never appears to have materialized there was no shortage of aspirants for the venture. About 1565 the *Licenciado* de Castro, the Governor of Perú, was approached by a merchant, Pedro de Ahedo, with an offer to despatch an expedition at his own expense. For a time the idea seems to have been well received, but although an agreement was made, it was cancelled after the alleged discovery that a gang of desperadoes intended to enlist in the expedition,

[1] Pacheco 1864: V: 117–209; Pacheco 1864: XIV: 151–65.
[2] Pacheco 1885: II: 206; Pacheco 1885: V: 153–61.   [3] Barros 1615: 53–54.
[4] Saavedra described New Guinea as '*del Oro*' (Markham 1911: 126).   [5] Galvano 1862: 238.
[6] Wright 1945: 72.   [7] Navarrete 1851: 591.   [8] Von Hagen 1959: 351.

mutiny, and divert the vessels to the 'lucrative business of piracy'.[1] In a letter to the King dated 23 September 1565, de Castro referred to the arrangements made with Ahedo for the discovery of 'some islands, called Solomon, which lie over opposite Chile, towards the Spice Islands',[2] a reference which is significant as evidence of the association of the proposed expedition with the Ophirian quest and as an indication of the immediate origin of the name which was subsequently to be given to islands actually discovered by the expedition.

The Spaniards were not alone in turning an enquiring eye in the direction of the South Pacific and, in view of the cartography and conjecture of the age, it would have been surprising if they had been. Early in 1566 Charles IX of France received a letter from Francisque d'Allaigne, a merchant residing in Lisbon, who claimed knowledge of the means to discover 3,000 miles of coastline, rich in precious metals, the extensive commerce of which might be enjoyed without infringing Spanish or Portuguese rights. He hoped to persuade a Portuguese pilot who knew of these lands to defect to France, and sought permission to offer a substantial bride and assurance of a reward for himself. The pilot was probably Bartholomeu Velho, a cosmographer indebted to the Dieppe *portolanos*, who defected from Portugal to France in 1566, followed or preceded by d'Allaigne. On 4 January 1567, the French Ambassador in Spain, Fourquevaux, wrote to the Queen Mother describing a meeting with d'Allaigne and pleading that the expedition be better led and organized than the recent ones to Canada, Florida and Brazil, by men able to govern colonies as well as to fight and to navigate. During 1567 Velho prepared for the expedition, but his death at Nantes in 1568 put an end to its immediate prosecution.[3]

Despite the failure of Ahedo's project, plans for a Spanish expedition were not abandoned, and on 2 April 1567, the *Licenciado* de Castro informed the King that he had decided to appoint his nephew, Álvaro de Mendaña y Neyra, as leader of the proposed expedition to 'certain islands and lands which lie in this part of the equinoctial between New Guinea and this coast and . . . are held to be very rich'.[4] The actual objects of this expedition, beyond the primary object of discovery, are open to debate. The view expressed by Gallego, the Chief Pilot of the expedition, in the *proemio* to his *relación*,[5] was that it was the conversion of the heathen, and it is certain that this object was constantly in the forefront of the minds of the leaders of Spanish expeditions into the South Pacific. The desire to discover new lands, to seek for wealth and trade, and to expand the Spanish Empire, were very real and very powerful incentives, which tend to obscure to twentieth-century scholars the realities

---

[1] Clissold 1954: 25. [2] Levillier 1921: III: 178–9; Kelly 1959; 14.

[3] Hamy 1894(a); Hamy 1894(b); Hamy 1899; Hamy 1903.

[4] Levillier 1921: III: 244; Kelly 1959: 14.

[5] MNM: MS. 921, f 1. For a description of the sources relating to this first voyage of Mendaña, particularly the extant versions of Gallego's *relación*, see the Bibiliography. MNM: MS. 921 has no pagination. I have numbered each page of the MS. and its reverse consecutively. Eg. f2v is referred to as f4.

and true position of religion as a motive behind the Spanish voyages of the sixteenth and early seventeenth centuries. As Madariaga remarks:

How can we . . . understand that age in which faith was like air and light, one of the very conditions of existence, the very breath with which people spoke? . . . All men . . . were either Christians, infidels, or liable to being enlightened and brought into Christianity. The Service of God was . . . to bring into the fold the unconverted. . . . This service to God was also service to the King—Emperor . . . State and religion, faith and civilization were one in those days. So that the service of God and the service of the King were but one in yet this other sense that conversion was, in the eyes of the century, less a religious-individual than a political collective act. *Cujus rex eius religio* was the principle of the era.[1]

The importance of the religious element in the Spanish colonial system was probably best summarized in the words of a Spanish Viceroy: 'in each friar the King had in the Philippines a captain-general and an entire army.'[2] The repeated religious references in the narratives of exploration, the presence of priests, the recourse of the *expedicionarios* to prayer and the sacraments, and the granting of saints' names to their discoveries, are all evidential of something more than pious hypocrisy. To suggest, as Amherst did,[3] that conversion was the official excuse for the expedition, conquest and spoliation the real motive, is, even though the materialist motives were very real, to express a view unsupported by the records of the expeditions, and to fail to understand the Spaniards of the sixteenth century against the background of their age and religio-political convictions, for though religion was by no means the major motive it was, like the oft-ignored motivations of exoticism and innate adventurousness, certainly a very real and important one.

The final preparations for the expedition included a general meeting of scholars, mathematicians and pilots, convened to determine the nature and position of the lands to be sought. The exact form and conclusions of the meeting do not emerge from the several narratives, and Gallego's *relación* speaks only of many men well versed in mathematics having deduced that certain islands existed in these positions.[4] Sarmiento de Gamboa, a member of the expedition who was later to distinguish himself as a historian, cartographer, sailor, soldier and ruthless extirpator of the surviving members of the royal Inca line, was to claim that the expedition derived from a proposal put by him to de Castro. He claimed that he knew the position of the islands from Inca information,[5] and it is natural to identify this assertion with his account of the reputed voyage of Tupac Inca Yupanqui to *Avachumbi* and *Niñachumbi*. He maintained that de Castro had agreed to his proposal and had offered him command of the expedition, an offer which he declined in favour of Mendaña on condition that he should retain control of the policy and navigation of the expedition.[6]

[1] Madariaga 1942: 106.   [2] Blair 1903: I: 2.
[3] Amherst 1901: I: vi.   [4] MNM: MS. 921, f2; Amherst 1901: I: 5.
[5] See his letter to the King of 4 March 1572, Espada 1879: xix; Markham 1895: xiii–xiv and his *History of the Incas*, Markham 1907: 11, 136.   [6] Rosenblat 1950: II: 172.

There is only Sarmiento's word for this, other than the dubious statements of several members of the expedition at a biased enquiry held by Dr. Barros in 1573 and in answer to leading questions framed in Sarmiento's interest.[1] The general impression to be gained from the report of the enquiry is that at moments of crisis and indecision during the expedition it was Sarmiento who saved the day but, although his information on Inca voyaging may have influenced de Castro, his claim that he was solely responsible is negated by our knowledge of the preceding negotiations. It is also negated by the reply of one of the *expedicionarios* at the Barros examination, who agreed that he knew that the expedition sprang from information supplied by Sarmiento, but added, 'and by many other means'. None of the several narratives record Sarmiento's position other than as captain of the flagship, and had he been responsible for the navigation his appointment would, in accordance with Spanish maritime custom, have been that of Chief Pilot.

According to Gallego the object of the expedition was 'the discovery of certain islands and a continent',[2] by which, one may reasonably adduce, were meant the *Western Isles* and the antipodean continent. Quirós, Mendaña's successor in the South-West Pacific, was later to remark that, whilst he did not know the object of the expedition, references in Gallego's *relación* to the reports of Ortiz de Retes and Bernardo de la Torre seemed to indicate that these were used by the expedition as navigational aids and that the objective was New Guinea.[3] However, with the little information about the Pacific available, such information as did exist would have been utilized, irrespective of the precise object of the expedition. Gallego also records that when they left Perú their course was determined by the fact that the *Presidente* had said that in 15° (S) there were many rich islands 600 leagues from Perú, and according to the priests on the expedition this was the distance at which the Cabo de la Cruz, supposedly sighted by Bernardo de la Torre in 1543 (and presumably part of the coast of New Guinea), was believed to lie from Perú.[4] Even within an underestimated Pacific this was no great relative distance, and in the course of the expedition, when the vessels were in 14° S, 280 leagues from Perú, and when a sailor thought that he had sighted land where no land exists, Sarmiento

---

[1] Conway 1946: 139–51; RAH: *Colección Muñoz, Vol.* X, ff197–212. See also Amherst 1901: I: 83–94; and Pacheco 1864: V: 210–21, for the 'Sarmiento narrative', which Forsyth has suggested is the concluding part of the *Barros Report* (Forsyth 1955: 37). In fact it seems certain that the 'Sarmiento narrative' (RAH: *Colección Muñoz*, Vol. XXXVII, ff3–7) is the work of Sarmiento, and is a brief version of an incomplete extant *relación* by Sarmiento (RAH: *Colección Muñoz*, Vol. XXXVII, ff266–283). However, since the brief version was made at La Plata, an association with the *Barros Report* seems very likely.

[2] 'el descubrimiento de Siertas Yslas Y tierra firme' (MNM: MS. 921, f2; Amherst 1901: I: 5).

[3] Zaragoza 1876: I: 188.

[4] 'por que avia dicho el Señor presidente que en quince grados de altura avia muchas yslas Ricas seis cientas leguas de el Piru' (MNM: MS. 921, f. 6). i.e. 1920 nautical miles from Perú. See also Amherst 1901: II: 207 for the belief that the Cabo de la Cruz was 600 leagues from Perú.

argued that it was the land of which he knew.[1] He was later to claim in his *History of the Incas*, when recounting the voyage of Tupac Inca Yupanqui to *Avachumbi* and *Niñachumbi* that: 'These are the islands which I discovered in the South Sea on the 30th November, 1567, 200 and more leagues to the westward, being the great discovery of which I gave notice . . . But Alvaro Mendaña . . . did not wish to occupy them.'[2]

Sarmiento's intention seems to have been that they should sail WSW as far as 23° S,[3] presumably on the deduction that the islands which he believed existed lay on that latitude, although this is contradicted by his complaint that they had been sighted when the expedition was in 14° S, 280 leagues from Lima.[4] Unfortunately Mendaña's instructions do not seem to have survived, but we can reasonably deduce that whilst the initial objective was the *Western Isles*,[5] in 15° S and at no great distance from Perú, as the navigation of the expedition indicates, the secondary objective was the antipodean continent, the *Terra Australis*, together with New Guinea. If contemporary charts had any basis in reality, this continent could have been expected to be found at no great distance from Perú, on that latitude. If the continent did, as cartographers suggested, extend to and perhaps adjoin New Guinea, then it could be discovered by running down a relatively low, warm, and not entirely unknown latitude, as an alternative to heading SW to higher, colder latitudes where the winds might be contrary or excessive.

Two vessels, the *Los Reyes* and *Todos Santos* of 200 and 140 tons respectively, were hastily prepared for the expedition, renamed the *Capitana* and *Almiranta* according to Iberian maritime custom, and despatched from Callao on 19 November 1567.[6] In the *Capitana* travelled the principal *expedicionarios*, Mendaña, Gallego, Sarmiento and Catoira[7]; in the *Almiranta*, Pedro de Ortega, as *Maestre de Campo*. The two vessels headed WSW until they were in 15° 45′ S, when they altered course to the W in search of their objective. No land had been sighted by 8 December, and Gallego determined to follow the latitude no further. On 16 December, whilst still in the latitude of 15° S, having sailed in that latitude for 620 leagues by Gallego's reckoning[8] and being then 800 leagues from Callao,[9] Gallego decided to alter course and they

---

[1] Conway 1946: 140; Amherst 1901: I: 85.   [2] Markham 1907: 136.

[3] Conway 1946: 140 (the fourth question in the Barros examination).

[4] Amherst 1901: I: 85. He may alternatively have deduced that the austral continent could be discovered in that position.

[5] Once the Philippines had been named *Las Felipinas* the title *Yslas del Poniente* seems to have been used to refer to any undiscovered islands believed to lie in the Pacific, and to have been used in a very general sense.

[6] There is some confusion on the date of departure between the several narratives, but Catoira's narrative, with its more detailed reference to the dates of movable feasts, gives a precise account of the years and dates referred to.   [7] Catoira was Chief Purser or Supercargo.

[8] MNM: MS. 921, f6.   [9] Amherst 1901: I: 162.

commenced steering '*a el hueste quarta del norhueste*' (to the W a 'quarter' NW).[1] Contrary to Sarmiento's opinion that they should have sailed S to 23° S, Gallego held his course for four days to 13° 45' S and then headed NW to decrease his latitude still further. On 30 December, in 6° 15' S, he headed due W, and on 15 January estimated his position to be 1,450 leagues from Perú and in 6° S. He altered course to the '*sudueste quarta del hueste*' (SW 11¼° W or SW by W), made 15 leagues on that course and sighted an island in 6¼° S at a distance of 6 leagues.[2] Several identifications have been made of this island, to which the Spaniards gave the name *Ysla de Jesús*, but the most convincing is that advanced by Maude, who identifies it with Nui in the Ellice Islands[3] (7° 16' S, 177° 10' E). Gallego's estimate of 1,471 leagues as the distance of Nui from Perú represents a considerable underestimate of distance sailed,[4] and this problem has been examined in more detail later.

[1] MNM: MS. 921, f6. In the Spanish system of boxing the compass, the 360° were divided into quadrants (*cuadrante*) of 90° reckoned from N, eastabout, and wind directions were often described as from the *cuadrante*, e.g. the *primero cuadrante* or N to E. To describe sailing directions the compass was further divided into octants (an *octavo*) of 45° and each *octavo* was further divided into four points, each of 11° 15'. This point, the *cuarta*, quarta or 'quarter', corresponded with the modern 'point', and should not be confused with the modern 'quarter' of 2¾° (Stanley 1874: 9; Santa Cruz 1918: 46–49). Gallego uses the words '*de*' or '*del*' throughout his *relación*, e.g. '*hueste quarta del norhueste*' (W 'a quarter' of the NW), but an alternative form seems to have existed in the use of the word '*al*', e.g. '*hueste quarta al norhueste*' (W a quarter to the NW). (See Vigneras 1960: 165; where the '*demonstración de los vientos*' or wind rose from Cortés' *Breve compendio . . .* of 1551 illustrates this usage.) It could be argued that these two alternative renderings in fact describe different bearings, e.g. '*hueste quarta del norhueste*', (W 'a quarter' of (or from) the NW) (NW 11¼° W), and '*hueste quarta al norhueste*', (W a quarter to the NW) (W 11¼° NW). That this was not the case, and that '*al*', and '*del*' were used alternatively, the latter as 'of the' as opposed to 'from the', and meaning the same, is indicated by the courses and bearings which Gallego gives, which can be checked against his recorded latitudes, distances run, and identifiable landfalls. When he speaks of a bearing or course being for instance '*hueste quarta del norhueste*', he means W 'a quarter' NW (W 11¼° NW), or as we would describe it W by N or 281¼°. This conclusion seems to be supported by the translations of Guppy and Amherst; in Morison's studies of Columbus; and, for example, by Gallego's statement that between 1 and 5 February 1568, he made a difference in latitude of 53' (between 6° 15' S and 7° 8' S), and drifted 15 leagues '*a el sur quarta del hueste*'. 15 leagues drifted N to S over 53' of latitude could only be on a course S 11¼° W, and not on a course W 11¼° S. The explanation for the alternative usage may be that on the wind rose from which the compass developed (the compass is still referred to as a *rosa dos ventos* in Portugal), the bearing was given as e.g. 'N a quarter of the W wind', which became reduced to 'N a quarter of W', and then amended to the more correct 'N a quarter to the W'.

[2] MNM: MS. 921, f10; Amherst 1901: I: 13. Mendaña records the date of the discovery as 15 January, as did Catoira, but Gallego says that it was 'on the morrow', i.e. the 16th. Mendaña, however, states that the island was named Ysla de Jesús since it was discovered on the day after the Feast of the Holy Name. As this feast was originally celebrated in Spain on 15 January, Gallego's date is apparently correct (Amherst 1901: I: 102).

[3] Maude 1959: 299–304; Amherst 1901: I: xx, 14; Woodford 1890: 402; Guppy 1887: 273; Sharp 1960: 43–44.

[4] Difference of Longitude (D./Long.) Callao-Nui = 105° 40', which, in the Middle Latitude of 9° 38', represents a distance of approximately 6,250 nautical miles, 7,812 Roman miles or 1,953 leagues E-W. The use of this reference, the Departure or linear distance of the Difference of Longitude in the

Strong currents and contrary winds prevented a landing, though some contact was had with the indigenes, and the expedition sailed WNW until on 21 January they were in 6° S. At this stage they encountered strong north-westerly winds typical of the season in these waters, and between 17 January and 1 February logged only 165 leagues by Gallego's reckoning. On the 1st they sighted a low line of shoals with several small islands in their midst, lying NE to SW, bearing W at a distance of 2 leagues, in 6° 15′ S.[1] From the latitude and the course alone it is immediately apparent that these shoals, to which were given the name *Los Bajos (Baxos) de la Candelaria* by virtue of their discovery on the Eve of Candlemas, were either the atoll of Ontong Java or Roncador Reef, an identification which is confirmed by the subsequent land-falls of the expedition. Ontong Java lies between 4° 56′ S and 5° 37′ S, Ron-cador Reef between 6° 10′ S and 6° 15′ S, N and S of each other between 159° E and 160° E; and whilst Gallego gives the latitude of the shoals as 6¼° '*con el medio de ellos*' [2] Catoira gives it as 6° 'full'.[3]

In several studies of the Spanish and Dutch voyages of the sixteenth and seventeenth centuries it has been suggested that an apparent consistency in errors of latitude determined by the navigator in question can be used as evidence in the identification of island discoveries, and can be regarded as confirming the identification of one or the rejection of another possibility. I am extremely doubtful about the validity of using such apparent consistency of error, even as secondary evidence combined with other indications, and have no doubts about its invalidity as primary evidence.

Sharp, for instance, when considering the identification of Los Bajos de la Candelaria, remarks that whilst both Ontong Java and Roncador Reef are possible identifications, 'The steady southerly error in Gallego's latitudes . . . points to Ontong Java'.[4] Furthermore, whilst it may be true, as Wallis remarks, that in most of the accounts of the Spanish Pacific voyages of this period an

---

Middle Latitude between Callao and the landfalls made in the Western Pacific, as the distance apart, has much to commend it. Although not as exact as the Great Circle distance, its error is slight in the low and between the limited latitudes in which it has been applied, and over the relatively considerable distances involved. It is conveniently simple to determine, and provides an adequate comparison with the estimates of the Spaniards. Its limitations of accuracy are compensated by the fact that it meets the Spaniards on their own navigational terms. Conditioned as they were to concepts of Parallel and rudimentary Plane Sailing, and practising what was primarily the former, they seem, although they recorded distances which were severally and variously total distances on various courses or rhumbs, or the distance on one course, to have generally thought of the distances of their Western Pacific discover-ies from Perú as the distances apart of meridians on a plane chart (though probably bearing in mind the convergence of meridians away from the equator). To compare their invariably unspecified 'distances' with the actual distances apart of the meridians of the two points referred to on a Middle Latitude, provided the Difference of Latitude is slight, seems to provide a comparison with the figure which the Spaniards were attempting to determine.

[1] MNM: MS. 921, f13.   [2] MNM: MS. 921, f13.
[3] Amherst 1901: II: 225.   [4] Sharp 1960: 44.

error of between +10′ and +1° is to be found,[1] this does not justify the kind of assertion made by Guppy to the effect that:

On making fourteen comparisons of the latitudes obtained by Gallego with the latitudes of the same places in the most recent Admiralty charts . . . I find that all but two are in excess of the true latitude. The excess varied between 11′ and 1° 7′ [about]; and since seven of the twelve latitudes vary between 38′ and 46′ excess, we may take 40′ plus as about the probable and average prevailing error.[2]

Quite apart from the admitted variability of the degree of error, the existence of any exceptions to the pattern of general consistency is sufficient in itself to impose a severe restriction on 'consistency' as a means of identification. Indeed, it seems somewhat dubious to postulate a consistent error on the evidence available, and to utilize that error, without attempting to offer any explanation for it; and in none of the studies which have been made of early Pacific discovery in which this factor is mentioned has any such attempt been made. If it could be shown, for instance, that the navigator in question was navigating by dead reckoning (DR), or that a series of latitudes were determined by DR in relation to an original latitude determined by observation, then it would be true to say that an error of latitude on one occasion would thereafter be continued consistently in subsequent plottings until obviated, reduced or increased by another error or a subsequent observation.

In the voyages of the sixteenth and seventeenth centuries with which this study is concerned we do know that latitudes were determined by observation of the sun's meridian altitude, and were reconciled with the DR position. When the latitude was determined by a solar observation, and that latitude was in error, the error could have been carried forward consistently over the few days which might elapse until another solar observation was taken, but this would only be a short-lived consistency. On the other hand, in a succession of solar observations, some degree of consistency might result from an error in the tables of declination, or from a failure to allow in the declination tables for the difference in longitude between the meridian of the vessel and the meridian of the place where and for which the tables of declination were compiled.[3] It might also result from a failure to allow for the refraction of the sun's rays, or from a particular error in the instrument used. It is not, however,

---

[1] Wallis 1954: 13.   [2] Guppy 1887: 274.

[3] John Davis, in his *Seamen's Secrets* of 1594, comments on the neglect of this necessary interpolation, and as late as 1771, Alexander Dalrymple, in his *Memoir on a Chart of the South Sea*, remarked of the latitudes of a Spanish chart of 1753, that he understood on the authority of one of the best Manila pilots that the Spaniards commonly took the wrong day's declination, Manila's date being taken from the westward. If allowance had been made for the difference in longitude between Manila and the place for which the tables were set, this factor would have been irrelevant. When it is appreciated that the sun's declination can alter by as much as 30′ in the space of 24 hours, particularly at the Equinoxes, failure to allow for even an approximate difference of longitude could cause a substantial error.

sufficient to show a possible cause of consistent error, particularly when such a cause might or might not have produced it; and if such error is to be relied on at all its cause or causes must be clearly explained and demonstrated. Gallego, for example, gives the latitude of Callao as 12½° S. It is in fact in 11° 56′ S, and, although this would only have affected DR navigation, it is possible that instruments and declination tables were set to this faulty latitude.

We do know that such instruments as the astrolabe and quadrant, although not dependent on the visibility of the horizon, suffered much greater disadvantages than the modern reflecting sextant, and that the circumstances of taking an observation on the deck of a low-freeboard vessel heaving on the breast of the Pacific would have tended to cause an error in the observation.[1] Furthermore, not only would these factors, even without being coupled to human errors, have tended to make an observation difficult, but they would have rendered an accurate observation virtually impossible, except by sheer chance or luck. They would not, however, have caused a consistent error, and even though a consistent error might have resulted from one or other of the factors which have been suggested in the preceding paragraph, that consistency would have been destroyed by the inconsistencies caused by the instruments or techniques of observation.

The extent of any error can only be gauged in relation to an identified landfall, and whilst some writers write blithely about consistency of error, they seem to fail to appreciate that in a trans-Pacific voyage on which few landfalls were made, the instances in which a recorded latitude can be checked represent but a small percentage of the total number of latitudes logged. To suggest, for instance, that a particular navigator showed a tendency to a southerly error in his latitudes on the strength of a few checks against identifiable landfalls (identifications which may in any case be disputed), when those latitudes may represent a very small proportion of the latitudes recorded, seems to be rather a rash assumption and statistically unsound.

In the light of these conclusions it would be wrong to invoke the apparent southerly error of Gallego's latitudes as evidence for the identification of Ontong Java; the relative positions of Ontong Java and Roncador Reef preclude the use as evidence of Gallego's estimate of the distance run from Nui, which was in any case considerably underestimated; and the later discoveries made by the expedition are of no great assistance in identifying the shoals by reference to courses sailed to them or estimated relative positions.

Fleurieu, Krusenstern and Burney[2] all identified the Bajos de la Candelaria with Roncador Reef, whilst Guppy and Amherst identified them with Ontong

---

[1] Quirós was to write in 1610: 'If four pilots, even though they be ashore, observe the latitude of the sun or stars with the same instruments, they will find more or less difference, seldom agreeing and when they repeat their observations they will find a new difference' (Zaragoza 1876: II: 363–4).

[2] Fleurieu 1791: 181; Krusenstern 1824: I: 182; Burney 1803: I: 288.

Java.[1] Woodford, in his several papers on the subject, reflected the difficulties of identification on the limited evidence available by alternating between the two possible identifications, but seems finally to have decided to be non-committal.[2] Guppy based his identification of Ontong Java on Gallego's estimate of the extent of the shoals of 15 leagues,[3] an estimate which is certainly excessive for Roncador Reef; but, as Woodford pointed out, the estimates of observed distance throughout the voyage seem to have been generally excessive.[4] Catoira records in his narrative that 'there did not appear to be anything but some reefs which might be six leagues in extent. . . . The sea appeared to be breaking over them in all parts'[5]; whilst Gallego states that he could not see the end of them (although he may have been referring to the far side, not to the extremities N and S), and that there were small islands in the middle of them. Mendaña and Catoira make no mention of the islands, and it may be significant that the word *bajos* (shoals) was used in the name rather than *arrecifes* (reefs), though Gallego does use both words in reference to them.[6] On the other hand the expedition made a determined effort to beat up to the shoals, an attempt which would seem to indicate the sight or expectation of some land, and Mendaña and Catoira record that their objective was wood and water. Whilst it can be argued that if there had been no indication of islands they would not have persevered, it is also possible that they simply hoped to see land beyond, and Catoira in fact states that they thought there might be low land.

Had they been approaching Ontong Java it would have been possible for them to approach on such a course as to see the reef in a position where none of the larger islands of the atoll, as opposed to smaller outcrops and sand keys, were visible. They were, however, in the vicinity for some time, at a distance by Catoira's estimate of one league, beating to and fro, and if their landfall had been Ontong Java they would have been likely to see at least one or two of the larger islands. Furthermore, the least islanded part of the atoll is towards the N, and further to the NW than the relatively large and more numerous islands on the south-eastern side. As the vessels later fell off to the SE they would, had their landfall been Ontong Java, have been likely to sight those larger islands, though not certain to do so. If the experiences of later navigators in the early stages of European contact are any indication, the *expedicionarios* would, had their landfall been Ontong Java, have been visited by the indigenes in their canoes, and that this did not occur seems to indicate that the 'islands' seen were not inhabited and were no more than the outcrops of Roncador Reef.

[1] Guppy 1887: 199, 273; Amherst 1901: I: xxi.
[2] Woodford 1890: 402; Woodford 1909: 545; Woodford 1916: 31.
[3] MNM: MS. 921, f13; Amherst 1901: I: 16.
[4] Woodford 1890: 403.   [5] Amherst 1901: II: 225.   [6] MNM: MS. 921, f18.

The only evidence which can really be adduced for the identification of Ontong Java is Gallego's reference to its size, a rather broken reed on which to lean, and if the islands to which he refers had existed as anything more than outcrops, and had they borne trees, it would have been surprising if Catoira, a chronicler reliable for his observation and detailed comment, had not described them as such. Gallego also describes the shoals as lying NE to SW,[1] a description which is certainly applicable to Roncador Reef when approached from the E, but which is only applicable to one part of the eastern side of Ontong Java, the south-western extremity, where several quite sizable islands would be visible. Even if it is argued that the description 'NE to SW' could be an error for 'NW to SE', and in the several extant versions of Gallego's *relación* east (*este*) and west (*hueste*) are often confused, the only part of the eastern side of Ontong Java to fit this description is at the southern extremity of the great bight in 5° 20′ S, from which position the expedition, as it fell off to the SE before the contrary winds, would have fetched up on the reef to the southwards. Although this question will be returned to briefly later, it seems fairly certain, on the evidence available and from the deductions possible, that Roncador Reef is the more likely identification.

Having coasted the reefs throughout the 1st of February in an unsuccessful attempt to approach them against the contrary winds, the vessels were forced to reef because of a squall at sunset, and, after a night of cross seas, they were headed N to lie, throughout the 2nd, under head sails with the wind veering to the NW. During the night of the 2nd to 3rd they lay under bare poles and fell off before the north-west wind. These conditions seem to have prevailed until Wednesday, 4 February, when a course was made '*al norueste quarta del nordeste*'[2] in the direction in which the shoals, now out of sight, were estimated to lie. On Thursday, 5 February, a course was shaped '*al sudueste quarta del lueste*' (SW by W) in order not to fall off to the SE or E; and on the 6th, after taking his first solar observation in four days, Gallego calculated his latitude to be 7° 8′ S and estimated that they had drifted 15 leagues '*a el sud quarta del hueste*' from the shoals. As the later landfalls show, this was probably a reasonable estimate of their position, for with the contrary north and north-westerly winds which they experienced, with the seasonal surface currents setting to the SSE,[3] and by attempting to sail towards the W, the vessels would have fallen off towards the S, but would probably have made a slight westing.

During the afternoon of the 6th they made sail and headed northwards, and on the following day, Saturday, 7 February, when, according to Catoira, they were headed NNW under a foresail with winds from the W, Gallego ordered a sailor to climb to the main-top and look to the southward for land,

---

[1] MNM: MS. 921, f13.   [2] MNM: MS. 921, f14 (NW 11¼° N, 326¼°).
[3] See Wyrtki 1960: 6–7; Woodford 1890: 403; United States 1944.

since he thought he saw something high in that direction.[1] The sailor reported that he could see land, and Gallego adds in his *relación* that it presently became visible to the others, and that he then ordered that the vessels be put on the other, the south-west, board or tack ('*el otro bordo en demanda de ella del sudueste*'). The land lay 15 leagues distant, and as the expedition approached 4 or 5 leagues closer its greater extent became more apparent. The *expedicionarios* had in fact made their first landfall in the group of islands which were to become known as the Solomon Islands, on the north-east coast of the island which they were themselves to name *Santa Ysabel*.[2]

It is possible to make a reasonable reconstruction of the route followed from Roncador Reef from the information in the narratives, but such a reconstruction is necessarily imprecise and hypothetical. The important thing to realize is that, with the rather severe and unfavourable weather conditions prevailing, the two vessels lay for much of the time between 1 and 6 February under bare poles, and between the 1st and 4th would have drifted SSE before the north-west winds and with the southerly setting current. When Gallego estimated on the 4th that the shoals lay NW by N he was probably correct, but the short runs made to the NW and SW by W on the 4th and 5th would have resulted in some westing. During the 6th they headed northwards in order to reduce the latitude, but it is doubtful if they would have made much progress, and probable that during the night they drifted southwards under reduced sail and at first light on the 7th were in approximately 7° 20' S, 159° E. The problem which seems to be presented by Gallego's statement that the land was sighted as they headed N, and which induced Guppy to conclude that this must be an error in the narrative,[3] is in fact no problem at all. If we accept that before dawn on the morning of the 7th the vessels were within daylight visibility of Santa Ysabel, and that they then recommenced tacking to the westwards, their first tack being a port-tack to the N, then the land could have become visible to the southwards as the dawn broke. That the land was sighted at dawn is indicated by Gallego's reference to its visibility to the look-out at the main-top, and subsequent visibility to the others on deck. He describes it as becoming visible to the others before he gave the order to alter course to the starboard or south-west tack, that is when they were still headed N and away from the land, a circumstance hardly possible except at dawn when the visibility and light would be increasing. That the land had not been sighted on the day previous can be attributed to a considerable southerly drift during the night of the 6th to 7th, which brought the vessels to the most southerly position yet reached on the morning of the 7th, or to bad visibility on the 6th.

[1] '*por que me avia parecido una cosa alta*' (MNM: MS. 921, f15).
[2] Alternatively referred to in the *relación* of Gallego as *Sancta Ysabel*.
[3] Guppy 1887: 200.

The land was not in fact reached until the evening of the 8th, when a boat was despatched in an unsuccessful attempt to find a harbour. During the following night the vessels passed over shoals without mishap, and on the following morning Gallego piloted them through the fringing reef and entered a bay, the latitude of which he estimated or observed to be 7° 50′ S[1] and at the entrance to which was a rock or islet, larger in size than the vessels. Gallego describes the bay as lying almost in the middle of the north coast of the island, 26 leagues '*sur quarta de norueste sudueste*' of the Shoals of Candelaria,[2] and Mendaña named it the port of *Santa Ysabel de la Estrella* and the island *Santa Ysabel*.[3]

The port of Santa Ysabel de la Estrella seems to have been correctly identified by Woodford, as it is now marked on the Admiralty charts,[4] and it seems highly probable that the expedition anchored in Kesuo Cove in 7° 55′ S.

[1] '*ocho grados menos dies minutos*' (MNM: MS. 921, f18). There may well be further support for my distrust of the use of so-called 'consistent errors of latitude' as evidence in the latitude which Gallego observed at Estrella Bay, Santa Ysabel, which, if the suggested identification of the bay is correct, was only in error by − 5′. This contrasts with the claim that Gallego's latitudes were subject to a consistently southerly or plus error, for if any of the observations which Gallego records were made on land and with great care, then this one certainly would have been. This being so, its relative accuracy would seem to indicate that no cause existed for a consistent error, and that the errors of other observations were the result of a variety of factors all tending to inconsistency.

[2] MNM: MS. 921, f18. The bearings in the extant long versions of Gallego's *relación* frequently suffer from two complications, the erroneous transcription of the Spanish words for east and west, the two having been confused by an amanuensis, and Gallego's often complicated rendering of them. That an amanuensis was the actual writer of the Museo Naval MS. is perhaps indicated by an alteration at page 5 of '*leste*' (E) to '*lueste*' (W), and the Seville MS. is described in its heading as oral. In consequence bearings must be read with considerable caution, reference to other versions, and with an eye to their conformity with each other and the other navigational information recorded. It is quite obvious that the bearing '*sur quarta de norueste sudueste*' (S ¼ NW, SW), is an erroneous rendering of either '*sur quarta de norueste su[d]este*' (S ¼ NW, SE) or '*sur quarta de nordeste sudueste*' (S ¼ NE, SW), the last two bearings being in each case the forward and back bearings towards the nearest of which the 'quarter' is to be measured. By comparison with the bearing given in the Santa Casa MS., '*sur quarta de Noroeste sueste*' (S ¼ NW, SE) (see also BPM: MS. 1686), it appears that the former was the one intended. On the other hand the information which Gallego gives of his route from the Shoals of Candelaria, and his estimated positions, would lead one to suppose that he meant the bearing to be S ¼ NE, SW. Guppy translated the BM MS. of Gallego's *relación* as meaning NE-SW (Guppy 1887: 202; BM: Add. 17 623, f21), and Amherst the MS. which he used as SW (Amherst 1901: I: 20; ATL: Gallego, f19), though both these MSS. agree with the Museo Naval MS. and the Seville MS. (AGI: Patronato, legajo 18, (1-1-1/18) No. 10, Ramo 4) in rendering the bearing as '*sur quarta de norueste sudueste*'. On the evidence of Gallego's previous information I prefer to accept the bearing as S ¼ NE, SW, i.e. S 'a quarter' SW or S by W (191¼°). With some provocation, Amherst was constrained to remark of Gallego that he is so careful about compass bearings 'that he defeats his object, for he generally gives the double bearings, but in so complicated a fashion that some of them are quite unintelligible' (Amherst 1901: I: ix); but, provided care is exercised, all his bearings can be translated with some measure of assurance, even where they are complicated by back-bearings and his use of *sueste* for SE instead of *sudeste*.

[3] The MNM MS. gives the name as *Sancta Ysabel*, the Santa Casa and other MSS. as *Santa Ysabel*. I have adopted *Santa* as the more convenient spelling.

[4] Woodford 1890: 403. See Admiralty Chart No. 3403 *Malaita Island and Santa Isabel Island*.

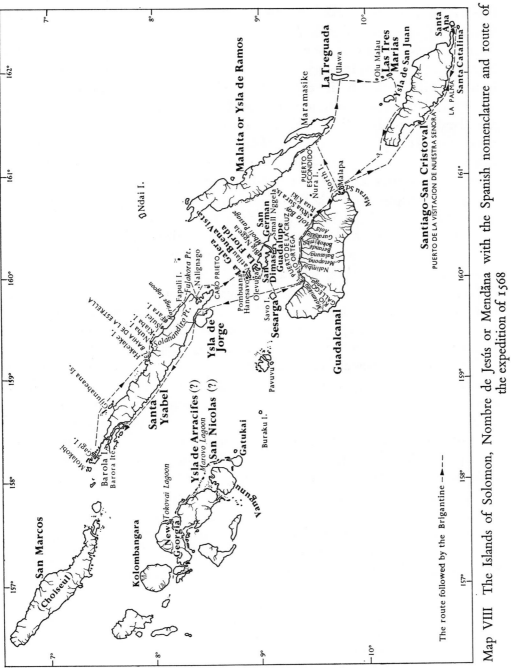

Map VIII   The Islands of Solomon, Nombre de Jesús or Mendāna with the Spanish nomenclature and route of the expedition of 1568

The route followed by the Brigantine — —

5

Gallego's description of the bay as lying halfway along the north coast of the island was supported by a subsequent circumnavigation of it, his bearing of the bay from the Shoals of Candelaria is close to the actual bearing of Kesuo Cove from Roncador Reef,[1] and his estimate of the distance of the bay from the Shoals of Candelaria of 26 leagues is only some 14 miles short of the actual distance between Estrella Bay and Roncador Reef. Three to four miles off Estrella Bay there are reefs such as Gallego describes, and on the reef immediately to the NE of the bay lies the small island of Hakelake, immediately to the W of which is the safest entrance to Estrella Bay through the reef. If this is not the island to which Gallego refers, there is yet another just off the headland which forms the north-eastern side of Estrella Bay, and in either case, whether Gallego is referring to the island as marking the entrance to the bay itself or the passage through the reef, they both have a unique appearance apposite to Gallego's description. Estrella Bay is one of the very few safe anchorages on the north-east coast of Santa Ysabel likely to be recognized by the Spaniards from a distance as suitable for use in the season of north-west winds, likely to be entered without mishap and deserving the title *puerto*. Woodford, who visited Estrella Bay in 1888 armed with a translation of the Catoira narrative, wrote that: 'It was not until I arrived within 20 miles of Estrella Bay that I found the natives speaking a language in which I was able to identify words recorded in the . . . diary of Catoira',[2] a statement which, in view of the linguistic diversity and fragmentation of the area, is particularly significant.

The Spaniards landed, took formal possession of the land in the King's name, and immediately commenced the construction of a brigantine for local exploration. Contact was made at a very early stage with the Melanesian inhabitants; a contact dominated initially by mutual suspicion. The nature of this first experience of Europeans by the indigenes, as it is reflected in the perhaps one-sided but interesting record of the Spanish narratives, is worthy of detailed examination; but the breadth of this study does not permit the inclusion of a detailed analysis of the nature of Iberian-Melanesian contact, or a recapitulation of the Spaniards' descriptions of the inhabitants, whom a late President of the Royal Geographical Society unkindly and incorrectly referred to, in the days when European contact had as yet not seriously affected their mode of life and customs, as 'interesting if unattractive specimens'.[3]

---

[1] This point is complicated by whether or not Gallego estimated the bay to lie S 'a quarter' SE, or S 'a quarter' SW of the shoals. He estimated the variation to be 'a quarter' E ($11\frac{1}{4}°$) (MNM: MS. 921, f21), so that he could be stating that the bearing was $191\frac{1}{4}°$, that is the true bearing of 180° magnetic or the magnetic bearing of $202\frac{1}{2}°$ true, or that it was $168\frac{3}{4}°$, that is the true bearing of $157\frac{1}{2}°$ magnetic or the magnetic bearing of 180° true. The chances are that this bearing was magnetic, in which case $168\frac{3}{4}°$ (magnetic), 180° (true), would be closer to the actual true bearing of Kesuo Cove from Roncador Reef, and the more likely if Estrella Bay is identified correctly. As Gallego's estimate must have been imprecise no reliance can be placed on either one or the other bearing.

[2] Woodford 1890: 404.   [3] Woodford 1916: 54.

Whilst the brigantine was under construction, two expeditions were despatched into the interior, and although the second expedition was much harrassed by the natives the Spaniards seem generally to have behaved with restraint. The advice of the Vicar, *Fray* Francisco de Gálvez, and Mendaña to the *expedicionarios*, on their conduct, are both classics of their kind, particularly when it is appreciated that the Spaniards were entirely dependent on the food which they could obtain locally for their very survival. The achievement of the second expedition in reaching the central ridge of Ysabel was remarkable, and an enterprise not lightly undertaken even in the early days of British administration at the beginning of this century. Another expedition went S along the coast to visit the territory of Meta, the local chief, *cacique* or *taurique*,[1] spending one night on an offshore island which may be identified from the narrative as Nuha Island. In all, seven expeditions seem to have been sent into the interior and along the coast from Estrella Bay.

By 7 April the brigantine had been completed, and was despatched on that day under the command of Pedro de Ortega, with Gallego and a number of the *expedicionarios* as crew. They followed the coast eastwards,[2] and on the second day arrived at two islands in 8° S, identifiable as Kiaba and the unnamed island to the W of it. Woodford identified these two islands as Kiaba (*Keaba*) and Nuha (*Ninuha*)[3]; but Gallego writes of them as being 6 leagues from Estrella Bay and on the same parallel, and at least implies a greater proximity than exists between Nuha and Kiaba. In the report of the voyage of the brigantine, probably written by Ortega and included in Mendaña's letter to de Castro,[4] the writer refers to the expedition anchoring on 9 April 'at the islet where we slept when we went to explore the territory of Meta'. It can only be concluded that he is not referring here to the two islets which Gallego describes as having been discovered, identified as Kiaba and the island to its W, but to Nuha, which Gallego, perhaps since this was the second visit made and was not a discovery, does not mention.

Continuing along the coast, and noting that it lay W by N–E by S[5] and that there was an easterly variation of the needle of $11\frac{1}{4}°$, they sighted many small islets in the same latitude, identifiable as the islets of the Maringe Lagoon,

---

[1] *Cacique* seems to have been the word used by the Spaniards for a chief, *taurique* the word which the natives of Ysabel used. The latter word may reflect an earlier Polynesian contact and be derived from the Polynesian word *Te-Ariki*.

[2] There is some divergence in the versions, the Museo Naval MS. giving the course as '*a el hueste*' (W) (MNM: MS. 921, f. 21), the Santa Casa MS. as '*alesueste*' (ESE) (Santa Casa: MS. *De Marina*, f105). It is quite clear from the subsequent narrative that the course was ESE.

[3] Woodford 1890: 405.

[4] AGI: *Patronato, legajo* 18, *No.* 10, *Ramo* 5; Pacheco 1864: V: 221–85; Amherst 1901: II: 97–158.

[5] This is the bearing as translated with reference to the several versions of the *relación* of Gallego. Having pointed out the pitfalls of the several versions in relation to the bearings given, I do not propose, except in particular instances, to cite discrepancies, but simply to state the bearings as I have translated them.

and anchored at a small island which was probably Fapuli. After an encounter with hostile natives, the brigantine tacked round 'the turn' of the land in order to obtain shelter from strong winds, and this would seem to mean that they rounded Fulakora Point. Here Gallego intersperses a paragraph in his *relación* which can only relate to the period immediately prior to rounding the point, and which was probably added as an afterthought, for he remarks that he observed the latitude after anchoring as $8\frac{1}{6}°$, and that the coast ran '*leste a hueste quarta de norhueste (a) hueste*'[1] (W by N–E by S) with the island of Meta, from which it was 7 leagues distant. The latitude of $8\frac{1}{6}°$, if it relates to Fapuli, is in error by $-10'$ as compared with the error of $-5'$ at Estrella Bay,[2] and the specific reference to the island of Meta (Nuha) is perhaps further evidence that it was not one of the two islands visited on the second day as Woodford suggested. The chronological confusion of Gallego's *relación* is clarified in Catoira's narrative and in Mendaña's letter to de Castro, which indicate that after leaving the anchorage (Fapuli) on Sunday, 11 April, the expedition had a brief sea-engagement with the natives and then encountered strong winds which compelled it to return to the coast. As the weather increased rather than abated, and as they were on what became a lee-shore as the winds veered to the NNW, Gallego stood out to sea. In the night which followed they were in some peril, but successfully rounded Fulakora Point and anchored in the lee of the land.

Gallego describes their anchorage as a large bay with seven or eight populous islands,[3] a description, brief as it is, which can only be related to an anchorage off Tanabuli.[4] From this bay a very large island could be seen to the eastward, known to the natives as *Malaíta*,[5] which is immediately identifiable with the island still known to the indigenes as *Mala* or, after European practice, as *Malaita*, the northern extremity of which is approximately due E of Tanabuli and Fulakora Point.[6] Since it was sighted on Palm Sunday, *el Domingo de*

---

[1] MNM: MS. 921, f22; BM: Add. 17 623, f25; ATL: Gallego, f23. The final *hueste* seems to be an error for *sueste* (SE).

[2] I am doubtful if any useful purpose is served by a comparative analysis of the latitudes estimated and observed by Gallego within the archipelago as was attempted by Guppy (Guppy 1887: 274) and Woodford (Woodford 1890: 415–16). Whilst several were certainly the result of observations made on land, other would have been the result of observations at sea, others simply estimated by dead-reckoning, and others, of islands not visited, by visual estimation. Those which were the result of an observation would have been subject to the limitations of the instruments, the normal hazards of taking a sight, the possibility of human or tabular errors, and if taken at sea these hazards would have been amplified and added to by the extreme difficulty of taking a sight in such an unstable vessel with instruments which depended on motionless suspension (the astrolabe) or relative immobility (the quadrant). [3] MNM: MS. 921, f22.

[4] See *Admiralty Chart 6039* which includes a sketch of part of this bay.

[5] MNM: MS. 921, f23. Gallego gives the name alternatively as *Malaita*, *Maylaita* and *Malayta*, Catoira gives it as *Mala* (Amherst 1901: II: 344).

[6] As Catoira rightly recorded, the native name was, and still is, Mala, and Woodford seems to have been the first to realize that what Gallego heard the natives say was '*Mala-ite*' or '*Mala-ita*', that is:

Ramos, it was named *Ysla de Ramos*.[1] According to Catoira's narrative Malaíta was sighted before they weathered Fulakora Point, and though Amherst was wrong in dismissing this as impossible, particularly when it is remembered that they stood out to sea before reaching Fulakora Point, Sunday seems to have been the day on which it was sighted. The report in Mendaña's letter to de Castro and Catoira's narrative both describe the Ysla de Ramos as being sighted on Palm Sunday, but also describe the rounding of Fulakora Point as occurring during the night of Sunday-Monday.[2] Gallego describes events which occurred on the day on which they anchored off Tanabuli as having occurred on 12 April, from which we may conclude that Malaíta was sighted on 11 April, Palm Sunday, before the expedition rounded Fulakora Point, and Gallego's reference to the island having been seen from the anchorage off Tanabuli should be taken as a reference not to the first sighting but to the fact that it was in view.

Gallego describes the point of Malaíta as lying E–W with the '*punta de meta*' and with the '*baxos de la Candelaria norueste sueste quarta de leste hueste cinquenta y dos leguas*'[3] (52 leagues NW by W–SE by E). If this bearing is laid off from the north-western extremity of Malaíta, together with the bearing and distance which Gallego estimated for Estrella Bay from the Bajos de la Candelaria, both bearings being laid down as if magnetic and also as if true, they bisect each other in positions slightly to the S of Roncador Reef. Although the difficulties of Gallego's navigation from the shoals to Santa Ysabel render this fact inconclusive as evidence for the identification of Roncador Reef with the Bajos de la Candelaria, it is certainly supplementary evidence.

His reference to the '*punta de meta*' is confusing, and would seem to refer to either Fulakora Point or Solanandiro Point, although the only cape or point which could properly be described as bearing E–W with the north-western extremity of Malaíta is the former. However, Gallego may have had difficulty in estimating the relative position of North Malaíta, for he records his own latitude off Tanabuli as 8° 10′ S, the latitude of the northern extremity of Malaíta as 8° S, and the latitude of Kiaba and its neighbouring island as 8° S. As the latitude of Kiaba is correct to within 1′, it seems likely that the other two latitudes were determined by dead-reckoning and visual estimation respectively, and that he obtained a distorted impression by failing to allow for the easterly magnetic variation, even though he had estimated it at $11\frac{1}{4}$°. His estimate of the distance of Malaíta from Santa Ysabel of 14 leagues (56 Roman miles or 44 nautical miles) is surprisingly accurate. Gallego records that mid-way between the

'Mala over there'. I refer to it by its now most common name, Malaita, but follow the precedent of Velasco in his *Demarcacion* of 1575–80 in using the hispanic accent on the *i* to preserve the indigenous pronunciation.

[1] The application of the name *Ramos Island* to the small island between Santa Ysabel and Malaíta is entirely erroneous.   [2] Amherst 1901: I: 138–9.

[3] MNM: MS. 921, f23; ATL: Gallego, ff24-24v; BM: Add. 17 623, f26v.

two islands were two small islands,[1] identifiable as the island so located on the modern chart with the erroneous name *Ramos*, and which from a distance has the appearance of two islands.[2] The five or six islands 'at the point' of Malaíta, which Gallego also mentions, are difficult to identify except as the north-western extremity of Malaíta seen from a distance, at sea level, and under conditions of visibility which gave it the appearance of five or six small islands.

Catoira and Mendaña record how on the following day, Tuesday, 13 April, the brigantine entered a large bay which appeared to be the mouth of a great river,[3] and some idea of the expectations of the *expedicionarios* is given in the statement that 'it was no small joy to us to think that, if we should find a great river, this was probably a continent'. It seems certain that they had entered the deep bay to the W of Tanabuli and, as they explored it further, the hopes raised by its estuary-like appearance were dashed, and they continued their voyage S along the coast. On 15 April they reached the southern extremity of the island, which Gallego placed in 9° S,[4] and in close proximity to which were several small islands, Mahige and the small islands between it and the coast. To the southern cape was given the name *Cabo Pueto* or *Cabo Prieto* [5] and that this was Vikenara Point is indicated by the expedition noting that the land thereafter terminated and trended towards the W. From this they concluded that Santa Ysabel was an island.

Continuing S from Cabo Prieto, the brigantine was headed towards 'some islands to the SE which are 9 leagues from the point', some of which lay '*Norte sur quarta del norueste sueste*' (S by E), others '*de norueste sueste*' (SE),[6] and 'to these last named we came this day, sailing SE with a fair wind'. It is clear that Gallego is referring to the group of islands lying SE of Vikenara Point, in 9° 5′ S, 160° 10′ E, which have the native name Nggela, and that the bearings which he gives are those of the apparent limits of the group. When it is appreciated that from Vikenara Point he would only be able to see the higher parts

[1] MNM: MS. 921, f23.   [2] Admiralty 1946: 338. Its position is 8° 21′ S, 159° 51′ E.

[3] Amherst 1901: I: 140; Amherst 1901: II: 283. The description of the voyage of the brigantine in Mendaña's letter to de Castro (a transcript of the report given to Mendaña, probably by Ortega) and in Catoira's narrative are generally similar. The latter seems also to have been derived from the report given to Mendaña.   [4] It is in fact 8° 33′ S.

[5] MNM: MS. 921, f24. In the BM MS. it appears as *Pueto*, *Puerto* and *Prieto*, in the ATL MS. generally as *Prieto*, and in the AGI MS as *Pueto*. *Prieto* would seem the most likely original title, *Cabo Prieto* meaning Dark Cape, a name which aptly describes the cape on occasions on which I have myself seen it, dark and forbidding, with the mountains rising steeply out of the sea. Gallego gives 16 April as the date on which they passed Cape Prieto, but Gallego also refers to Good Friday as the day following the one on which the Cape was passed. Since 16 April 1568, was Good Friday, Gallego seems to be in error, and Catoira, and Mendaña's letter to Castro, correct, in asserting that they passed the Cape on Maundy Thursday, 15 April. Gallego may, however, have been keeping sea time.

[6] MNM: MS. 921, f24; BM: Add. 17, 623, f28; ATL: Gallego, f25v. The bearing of the islands from Cabo Prieto given in the Santa Casa MS. is SSE (Santa Casa: MS. *De Marina*, f105v). In the Quirós-Bermúdez *relación* it is given as SW but this is contradicted by the bearings given of the limits of the group, S by E and SSE (Zaragoza 1876: I: 4).

of the group, and if allowance is made for easterly variation of approximately one point, his bearings are by no means unacceptable. His remark that it was to the last named, that is those bearing SE of the cape, to which they went, requires examination, since the names given to the Nggela Group by the Spaniards depend for their identification on the sequence in which they were given. The estimate of the distance of the group from Cabo Prieto of 9 leagues (28 nautical miles) is not unreasonable.

Arriving at the group on a south-easterly course from Cabo Prieto, the brigantine anchored at 10 at night off an island about 1½ leagues in circumference, low, reef-girt and covered with palms, which the *expedicionarios* named *La Galera* because of its similarity to a galley.[1] This would certainly seem to have been Pombuana, the most northerly of the islands in the Nggela group in 8° 51′ S, 160° 2′ E. Subsequent relative identifications support this, and, with the exception of Anuha Island (9° S, 160° 13′ E), it is the only island which fits the description of La Galera. It was 'the first island',[2] and Pombuana would have been the first island sighted and approached as the brigantine sailed towards the group. Gallego gives the time of arrival as 10 p.m. and the report in Mendaña's letter to de Castro gives the time of arrival as two hours after darkness, stressing the difficulties of anchoring, the reefs, and the anxiety of the night.

It is unthinkable that Gallego would have navigated in these waters at night, except through sheer necessity, and the only credible necessity in these circumstances would be that they had not reached a safe anchorage by dusk, and that La Galera was the first island which they reached; that is, Pombuana. Had the brigantine been heading along the northern coast of Nggela towards the eastern extremity of the group, Gallego could certainly have begun to look for an anchorage well before dark, and would have found one. The fact that they did anchor off a reef-strewn island is further evidence of their desire to anchor at the first possible opportunity, a bad anchorage being preferable to further navigation, and that La Galera was the first island reached in the group coming from Cabo Prieto. It is also most unlikely that Gallego would have passed the north-western islands in the Nggela Group during daylight without exploring them, this being after all the object of the expedition.

On the following day, 16 April, the brigantine was approached by many natives in canoes, who invited the Spaniards to a large island which Gallego describes as being about 1 league[3] distant from La Galera, 12 leagues in circumference, and with many small islands around it. The name *Buena Vista* was given to it 'because it appeared very fertile'; Gallego observed its latitude to be 9½° S and that it ran E to W,[4] and the report in Mendaña's letter to de

---

[1] MNM: MS. 921, f25; Amherst 1901: I: 141.
[2] Santa Casa: MS. *De Marina*, f105v; Zaragoza 1876: I: 4.
[3] Mendaña's letter to de Castro gives the distance as 1½ leagues (Amherst 1901: I: 142).
[4] MNM: MS. 921, ff25–26.

Castro adds that it was a land of 'bare mountains and *sabana* with many clearings sown with *panaes*'.[1] Apart from Gallego's estimate of its size, which in view of his generally unreliable estimates of size can hardly be said to detract from the identification, the description is recognizable as relating to the island of Vatilau at the north-western extremity of the group, immediately to the S of which is a veritable archipelago of small islands.

Although relations with the natives began reasonably, hostilities, perhaps due to misunderstanding or the realization that the Spaniards were after food, soon developed, and the expedition withdrew to a small island a quarter of a league distant. It seems highly probable that the canoes would have led the brigantine into the passage between Hanesavo and Vatilau, the only reasonable anchorage once the south-east trade winds had begun, the north coast of Vatilau being heavily reef-strewn. It is likely that the native village was in this passage, which is so narrow as to be unrecognizable as a through passage until its reef-blocked northern entrance is actually reached, and from such an anchorage the brigantine could have withdrawn to Nagotana (Ngangotanga) Island where there is another good anchorage. The *sabana* or grass covered hilltops of Vatilau are particularly extensive around the passage, and from the southern entrance to the channel the several smaller islands to the southwards are very obvious.[2]

Gallego gives the native name of Buena Vista as *Pela*,[3] and in the 'Sarmiento narrative' it is recorded as *Gella*,[4] both obviously derived from the surviving native name for the whole group, *Nggela*. Gallego adds that 'it is in a chain of five islands which lie east and west one with the other, and it is the first on the east side, because we discovered it coming from east to west.'[5] This statement seems to negate the suggested identifications of La Galera and Buena Vista and the W–E sequence of discovery in the group, though the conformity of these identifications with the descriptions recorded, and the unreliability of the tests of the *relación*, would be an effective counter to it. In fact the several

---

[1] Amherst 1901: I: 142. Dudley Stamp, in his *A Glossary of Geographical Terms*, quotes the Oxford *English Dictionary* to the effect that the words savannah, savanna and savana derive from the Carib zavana via Spanish, and mean a treeless plain. He adds that 'The derivation is not from Spanish, sabana (a sheet) which would place emphasis on the level terrain but from the Carib which is primarily in antithesis to woodland', and that 'the term has come to indicate essentially grassland with scattered trees or bushes'. Gallego is referring, in fact, to hilly grassland, interspersed with scattered trees and shrubs, and his usage of the word *sabana* to describe this terrain is clearly of some interest. *Panaes* are a root group, so named by the inhabitants of the Solomons.

[2] Whilst attempting to recreate parts of the route of the expedition in 1961, and whilst anchored in Hanesavo Harbour, I was particularly struck by the appositeness of the description in the *relación* and the report in Mendaña's letter to de Castro, and am convinced that this is certainly where the brigantine anchored.

[3] MNM: MS. 921, f28.   [4] Amherst, 1901: I: 89.

[5] '*i es la que esta en Cordillera de Cinco Yslas que estan leste hueste unas con otras esta es la primera que esta de la parte de leste por que las descubrimos de leste para hueste*' (MNM: MS. 921, ff25–26). The islands do lie E–W (magnetic) with each other.

texts of the *relación* are contradictory in their rendering of this passage, the MNM, ATL, BM and AGI MSS. all agreeing that the route was from E to W[1]; but the Santa Casa MS., which may well be either the earliest version or a corrected abbreviation of the long *relación*,[2] although describing the chain as '*deleste oeste*', adds that '*buena vista . . . es la primerapře deloeste*'[3] and that the later island of *San Dimas* was '*mas aleste*'.[4] The versions of the long *relación* subsequently agree, despite their reference to Buena Vista being 'the first on the east side', that the expedition went to other islands 'further to the east',[5] whilst still referring to the islands within the Nggela group. Mendaña, in his letter to the King of 11 September 1569,[6] names the several islands discovered in the Nggela Group commencing with La Galera and Buena Vista, and adds that 'The first of these is about 8 or 9 leagues from Santa Ysabel'. Figueroa, although very much a secondary source, described La Galera as 'that which they first saw'.[8] The greater preponderance of the evidence favours the belief that the exploration of the Nggela group proceeded from W to E, and that Pombuana was the first island visited, and this conclusion is the only one which can possibly be reconciled with the descriptions recorded.

On Easter Sunday, 18 April, the brigantine sailed along the south coast of Buena Vista and crossed to an island opposite, about a league distant.[9] To this island they gave the name *La Florida*,[10] and Gallego estimated it to lie in $9\frac{1}{2}°$ S, E and W with Buena Vista, and to be 25 leagues in circumference. This must have been the island of Olevuga, for although Gallego's estimate of its circumference is excessive, its appearance from the SW is deceptive, and more reliance should be placed on the relativity of Gallego's estimates of size than on the actual figures which he gives. On the same day the expedition continued towards other islands lying more to the E, to the first of which, of 25 leagues circumference, the name *San Dimas* was given. Although the further islands were not visited, one was named *San German*, the other *Ysla de Guadalupe*.[11]

According to Mendaña's letter to de Castro, the brigantine left Buena Vista to proceed to San Dimas, 'an island opposite', and on the way discovered 'many other islands on every side, some large, some small, some merely peaks rising from the water', to the largest of which they gave the name *Pascua*

[1] BM: Add. MS. 17 623, ff29–29v; ATL: Gallego, f27; AGI: *Patronato*, *legajo* 18 (1-1-1/18) *No.* 10, *Ramo* 4.   [2] Santa Casa: MS. De Marina, f106. See also Zaragoza 1876: I: 4.

[3] 'It is the first on the W.' '*buena vista . . . es la primera* [que esta de la] *pře* [parte] *de loeste*.'

[4] 'more to the east.'

[5] '*otras Yslas que estan mas adelante a el leste en la misma altura*.' See MNM: MS. 921, f28; BM: Add. MS. 17, 623, f32; Guppy 1887: 209; ATL: Gallego, f29v; Amherst 1901: I: 29; AGI: *Patronato*, *legajo* 18, (1-1-11/8) *No.* 10, *Ramo* 4.

[6] RAH: *Colección de Velázquez, Vol.* XXXVI, *No.* 8, ff185–194v; Zaragoza 1876: II: 15 *et seq*; Amherst 1901: I: 161.   [7] Amherst 1901: I: 173.

[8] Fleurieu 1791: 8, quoting from Figueroa's '*Hechos de Don García Hurtado de Mendoza . . .*' of 1613.

[9] Mendaña gives the distance as half a league (Amherst 1901: I: 146).

[10] Mendaña called it *Isla de Flores* (Amherst 1901: I: 173).   [11] MNM: MS. 921, f28.

Florida.[1] Gallego describes the group as a whole as consisting of five islands, and it is clear from the *relación* that after landing at San Dimas the expedition headed off to the S without exploring further. Gallego remarks that they did not visit San German and Guadalupe, to avoid delay, and it is likely that once the south-east winds had set in their progress, had they attempted to do so, would have been slow. San Dimas seems certainly to have been the island of Big Nggela, and although Gallego could not have been aware of the division of Big and Small Nggela by Mboli (Utuha) Passage, his impression that this part of the group consisted of three islands is understandable. Amherst and Woodford went to considerable pains to point out that the Nggela Group, when viewed from Savo Island to the SW, appears as five islands.[2] Unfortunately this approach to the identification collapses when it is realized that the appearance of Nggela from the S varies with the visibility and haze, that we do not know the visibility conditions when Gallego observed it, and that, in any case, the impression of five main islands appears to have been gained when the brigantine was actually in the Nggela Group.

The important point to realize is that from a position immediately to the S of Sandfly Passage, although Big and Small Nggela seem to constitute a complete land mass, the contours of the two islands give the impression that they may be three islands. The south-western extremity of Big Nggela, dominated by Mounts Barnett and Harold, appears as one island (San Dimas), with the indentation of Gavutu Harbour and the contours and ridges giving the impression of a separate island beyond it (San German). The southern extremity of Small Nggela, terminating to the westward in Tinete Point, also has the impression of probable separation from Small Nggela and was probably what the expedition called Guadalupe. Had Gallego been exploring the Nggela group from E to W he would certainly have realized that Big and Small Nggela formed a large land mass, and had he discovered Mboli Passage he would certainly have described it. In any case his description of the group would have been entirely different from the description which he does give, and which can only be reconciled with a partial exploration of the group from W to E along the south coast.

Leaving San Dimas at a point just S of Sandfly Passage, the expedition headed towards a large island which could be seen 'on the south side of these five islands', and 'in the middle of the way' discovered another one to which they gave the name of *Sesarga*.[3] Gallego describes this other island as volcanic, producing smoke, about 8 leagues in circumference, in the latitude of $9\frac{1}{4}°$ S

---

[1] Amherst 1901: I: 146–7.   [2] Amherst 1901: I: 29–30.

[3] Catoira gives the name as *Sesarga*, Mendaña as *Cesarga*, after the island of Sesarga W of La Coruña in Galicia (Amherst 1901: I: 149; Amherst 1901: II: 291). In the MNM MS. the name is given as *Sesagar* and *Sesarga*, and on one occasion the amanuensis seems to have begun to insert an *r* in *Sesagar*, but has crossed it out (MNM: MS. 921, ff. 28–30). In the Santa Casa MS. the name is given as *Ysla desarga* (Santa Casa: MS. *De Marina*, ff106).

and 5 leagues *'norueste sueste'*[1] of Buena Vista. Its description, even allowing for the faulty bearing and overestimated circumference, identifies it as the volcanic island of Savo, lying approximately midway between the Nggela group and the north-western extremity of the large island of *Guadalcanal*, so named by the Spaniards.[2] On the morrow they approached the coastline of the latter island at a point where a large river, which they named the *Río Ortega*, entered the sea. From this position, which Gallego estimated to be in 10½° S, the highest point of Buena Vista bore N, 9 leagues distant, and the highest point of Sesarga (*Sesagar*) bore NW. It is doubtful if the exact point at which they approached the coastline of Guadalcanal can be determined with any certainty, for if the bearings given are true they bisect at the mouth of the Lunga (Betikama) River, and if magnetic at the mouth of the Matanikau River. As the latter hardly deserves to be described as large, the former seems the more likely identification and is supported by later references. The differences between Gallego's estimated latitudes for Sesarga and Guadalcanal of 45', and between Guadalcanal and Buena Vista of 1°, hardly conform with his near-correct estimate of the linear distance between Buena Vista and Guadalcanal of 9 leagues (28 nautical miles). One can but conclude that the latitude of the north coast of Guadalcanal was determined by an observation which, not surprisingly, was incorrect by an excess of slightly more than 1°, and that Gallego included his estimated distance in qualification of the obvious discrepancy between his latitudes and estimated distances.

From Guadalcanal Ortega seems to have planned to pursue the exploration as far as 12° S, but Gallego's contrary advice, dictated by the limitations of the brigantine, prevailed, and they determined to return to Estrella Bay. Passing Sesarga[3] again, the brigantine headed towards Cabo Prieto, and on 21 April arrived at an island 7 leagues from the cape, 1 league from Santa Ysabel[4] and 15 leagues *'leste oeste quarta de noroeste sueste'* (W by N) from Sesarga,[5] ruled by a chief named Bene Bonesa and called by the natives *Veru*. The channel which separated this island from Santa Ysabel, and which ran *'les sueste oesnoroeste'*[6]

---

[1] MNM: MS. 921: f29. The Santa Casa MS. also gives *'noroeste sueste'* (Santa Casa: MS. *De Marina*, f106). This is clearly in error for *nordeste sudoeste* (NE-SW).

[2] The present use of the name *Guadalcanar* may derive from Figueroa's transcription of the name Guadalcanal in his *Hechos* of 1613 and its adoption by eighteenth- and nineteenth-century cartographers. Guadalcanal in Valencia was the birthplace of Pedro de Ortega. *Guadalcanar* is, however, the spelling given in the Santa Casa MS. (Santa Casa: MS. *De Marina*, f106v) and the Quirós-Bermúdez *relación* (BPM: MS. 1686, f5).

[3] Gallego gives the native name as *Guali* (MNM: MS. 921, f30) or *Cuali* (Santa Casa: MS. *De Marina*, f106v). When Woodford visited the island there was a village on the south-west side known as *Koila* (Amherst 1901: I: 32), and this could have been the name which Gallego heard.

[4] MNM: MS. 921, f30.

[5] Santa Casa: MS. *De Marina*, f106v. The MNM MS. gives the bearing, rather confusedly, as *'les norueste quarta del norueste'* (MNM: MS. 921, f30). The Santa Casa MS. bearing of E-W ¼ NW-SE (W by N-E by S) seems more reliable.

[6] Santa Casa: MS. *De Marina*, f106v. The MNM MS. is again confused (MNM: MS. 921, f30).

(WNW) for 6 leagues, offered a good anchorage for as many as 'a thousand' vessels, and could be entered either from the SE or through a narrow channel at its north-western extremity. The island itself, to which the *expedicionarios* gave the name of *Ysla de Jorge*[1] lay in 9⅓° S, and its circumference was estimated to be 25 leagues.[2] From the description it is clear that the expedition had discovered the island now named San Jorge, lying to the W of the south-eastern extremity of Santa Ysabel, that Gallego's erroneous latitude had been carried forward by dead-reckoning to give him an error of over 1° in excess, and that his description is of the large bay, now known as Thousand Ships Bay, which runs NW to narrow into a channel dividing San Jorge from Santa Ysabel. From the description given in the *relación* it may be concluded that the brigantine sailed up the continuous length of the bay to emerge on the south coast of Santa Ysabel through the channel. Here it seems to have been decided that the island of Santa Ysabel should be circumnavigated, in order to determine its size, and to discover whether or not any other islands lay to the southwards.

As the expedition followed the coastline north-westwards, and when they had progressed about a third of the way along it, two large reef-girt islands were sighted in 9⅓° S, lying 10 leagues W of San Jorge. They lay E and W with each other and were named respectively *San Nicolás*[3] and *Ysla de Arracifes*.[4] In the MNM MS. the latter is described as being to the SE, which could be interpreted as meaning to the SE of San Nicolás, but the Santa Casa MS. describes it as '*la otra de loeste*'.[5] Gallego adds that there was much land ahead running E by S to W by N, that his own latitude was 9° S, and that they were off a river mouth. His estimates of latitude and distance were certainly in error, but the lands to which he was referring can only be identified with Gatukai, Vangunu and New Georgia, though in what order is by no means clear. It is probable, as Woodford suggested,[6] that San Nicolás was Gatukai, that the Ysla de Arracifes was Vangunu, with the extensive reefs bounding the Marovo Lagoon, and that the 'much land' to which Gallego refers was the bulk of the island now known as New Georgia. It is also possible, however, that Gatukai was not named, and that San Nicolás was New Georgia. The expedition did not attempt to approach these new discoveries for, as Gallego remarks, there were many reefs and shoals on this coast, indicating perhaps that they were then sailing between the coast and the offshore reefs which extend from Tanabafe Island to Furona Island, and that the reefs seemed to offer an impediment to south-westerly exploration.

[1] In the Santa Casa MS.; '*su nombre san Gorge*' (Santa Casa: MS. *De Marina*, f107).

[2] Amherst 1901: II: 295 (the *Report of the Barros Enquiry*).

[3] Santa Casa: MS. *De Marina*, f107. The MNM MS. gives the name as *Sant Nicolas* (MNM: MS. 921, f32).

[4] Island of Reefs, as Gallego adds—'because there were many' (MNM: MS. 921, f32).

[5] 'the other to the W'. (Santa Casa: MS. *De Marina*, f107).   [6] Amherst 1901: I: 34.

At this point in his narrative Gallego interposes the comment that Santa Ysabel was 20 leagues wide: a conclusion based on his observation of the latitude at Estrella Bay, 7° 52′ S,[1] and his estimate of the latitude of a point on the south coast SSW of Estrella Bay, 9° S. At its widest point Santa Ysabel is only 15 miles across, but Gallego's errors of latitude had led him to overestimate the width by some 50 miles; a considerable overestimate, but of a kind to which one becomes accustomed as one reads the *relación*, and to which Quirós was presumably referring when he later wrote that:

pilots are accustomed, in the case, for example of a river of ten or twenty paces at the mouth, to give two or more leagues, and it is the same with a headland or cape, and in the case of a coast running E–W they increase it many leagues [and] . . . all the charts are defective.[2]

Following the coast north-westwards, Gallego noted many small inhabited and uninhabited islands and, further northwards, observed that the coast seemed to extend NE for another 6 leagues and the island to narrow. Here the expedition entered a channel which appeared to divide the island from the many other small islands round it, and emerged on the north side of Santa Ysabel in the latitude of 7½° S. As they emerged and headed E by S they sighted a large island in 7¾° S, lying '*leste hueste quarta de norueste sudueste*'[3] (W by S), to which they gave the name *San Márcos*,[4] and which was certainly the Choiseul Island of the modern charts.

Guppy, relying on Figueroa's secondary chronicle, in which it is stated that the expedition rounded the western end of the island, identified the passage through which the brigantine passed as Manning Strait,[5] whilst Amherst identified it as Austria Sound.[6] It is doubtful, in view of the several possible channels and the limited information, if an exact identification can be made. In favour of Austria Sound it may be said that Gallego's observed latitude is correct, that it does separate Santa Ysabel from the islands to the N, and that there are approximately 6 leagues of broken land lying to the NW of it. Against this identification may be cited the fact that the sound is not immediately

[1] He gives the latitude of Estrella Bay as 7° 50′ and 7° 52′ S (cf. MNM: MS. 921, f18; and MNM: MS. 921, f32).

[2] Zaragoza 1876: II: 363. Even allowing for understandable errors of judgement, much of this comment seems true of Gallego, who seems to have been inclined to exaggerate alarmingly in his estimates of the size of lands seen.

[3] MNM: MS. 921, f33. The Santa Casa MS. gives the bearing as '*de loeste 4ᵃ del sudueste*' (Santa Casa: MS. *De Marina*, f107v).

[4] *Sant Marcos* in the MNM MS. and the ATL MS., *S Marcos* in the BM MS.

[5] Guppy 1887: 212–13.

[6] Amherst 1901: I: 35. Amherst described Austria Sound as leading into Port Praslin, but this is not so. Woodford, on whose personal knowledge of the area Amherst based his identifications, identified the channel with the one leading into Port Praslin, by which presumably he meant Popu Channel (Woodford 1890: 407).

obvious as a continuous passage through to the north coast at any of its three southern entrances, that the high ground of Santa Ysabel and Barola Island add to this impression, and the probability that the *expedicionarios*, who had had one earlier and risky experience of following a blind channel, would have been unlikely to repeat the attempt with its incumbent risks to life and vessel. If the expedition did enter the sea on the north coast of Santa Ysabel through Austria Sound, then they would have had to go well out to sea towards the N after they had emerged from the channel to be able to sight San Márcos (Choiseul). Although Catoira states that they put out to sea to the northwards,[1] there would have been no necessity for them to head to the N for such a distance to be able to sight San Márcos.[2]

The evidence of latitude and the remaining extent of land are doubtful, and whilst Austria Sound does separate Santa Ysabel from the islands to the N, this remark could equally well have been made of Popu Channel or Kologilo Passage, since the fragmentation of Barora Ite, Barola and Gagi Islands is not certainly discernible from offshore. Catoira, and the report in Mendaña's letter to de Castro, state that the channel was amongst many islands, and refer to the current running through it with great force.[3] The abundance of islands mentioned seems to indicate that the passage which was followed was one towards the northern extremity of the archipelago, and that an impression of their considerable number had been gained by sighting them as it would not have been gained had they gone through Austria Sound. All the passages have strong currents and tidal streams; Austria Sound of 5 to 7 knots, Kologilo Passage of 2 to 4 knots, and Dart Sound and Popu Channel generally similar. Catoira states that Gallego entered the passage in the expectation of being able to get through to the other side, implying that the far end of the channel was not visible, although he could be referring to such possible obstacles to navigation as reefs, bars and tides, and adds that they were all day in the channel. Tidal currents and necessary caution could well have involved the expedition in a day's sailing through any of the passages, particularly if they had to row as well, but the 18 miles of Austria Sound, judging from their earlier rate of progress, seems perhaps an excessive distance to have sailed in one day.

---

[1] Amherst 1901: II: 297.

[2] Since they presumably headed northwards in order to clear the fringing reefs, and to beat against the south-easterly and easterly winds which prevented a direct course for Estrella Bay, little purpose would have been served by heading due N and running with the wind over the starboard stern quarter or beam, and their course was more likely to have been north-easterly. Unless they went through Austria Sound, it would have been necessary, other than by heading N from the northern exit of Austria Sound as far N as 7° 20′ S, to go out to sea eastwards for at least 35 miles before the most easterly peak of Choiseul was at the same angle above the horizontal as the high ground of Barola, and at the distance at which that peak might be visible and recognizable as land beyond Barola it would be too distant to be visible.

[3] Amherst 1901: II: 297; Amherst 1901: I: 155. The report in Mendaña's letter to de Castro states that the islands must have numbered more than eighty, large and small.

It seems likely that the blind channel which the expedition entered earlier was the southern entrance to Austria Sound, on either side of Bero Island, and that they were daunted by the narrowing of the channel and the background hills of Santa Ysabel. In the face of this proliferation of considerations, the only conclusion which can be drawn is that the channel followed was either Kologilo Passage or Popu Channel. That Choiseul was not sighted until they had emerged on the north side, and not as they entered the channel, can be attributed to bad visibility or preoccupation with the navigation of the vessel. It is a common phenomenon of these waters that whilst throughout the day high land to the W may not be visible across 60 miles of water, in the early evening, as the sun sets behind it, that land becomes quite clear and distinct. This may well explain the failure of the expedition to sight Choiseul until the latter part of the day.

Gallego concluded that Santa Ysabel was 95 leagues (304 nautical miles) long and 200 leagues (640 nautical miles) in circumference.[1] In fact it is only 128 miles long, including the adjacent islands at the northern extremity, or approximately 40 Iberian leagues. Gallego had determined the extremities of the island to lie in 9° S and 7° 30' S, a difference of 1° 30', only 16' in excess of the actual latitude difference. In assuming that the island could extend for 95 leagues within these narrow limits, Gallego must have pictured Santa Ysabel as lying lengthways E to W rather than NW to SE, an impression which could be attributed in part to the errors of his latitudes, his own mistrust of his latitudes and, most of all, to a failure to appreciate thoroughly the effects of easterly magnetic variation.[2] Leaving the islands off North-Western Ysabel on 28 April, the expedition put out to sea to beat against the south-easterly winds and to avoid the reefs and shoals off the coast,[3] and arrived at Estrella Bay on 5 May.

Leaving Estrella Bay on 8 May, the total complement of the expedition proceeded towards Guadalcanal, which they reached on 12 May, anchoring initially in an insecure position 2 leagues to the W of the Río de Ortega. A better anchorage was found in the lee of what Gallego describes as a small island, Catoira as a point, a league to the W of their first anchorage, to which they gave the name *El Puerto de la Cruz*, naming a river in the vicinity the *Río Gallego*.[4] The only point on this coastline which can be related to the probable situation of the Río de Ortega, and which conforms with the description of the Puerto de la Cruz, is the site of the present township of Honiara. The small island or point still exists as a small coral island joined to the coast by a spit of sand and shingle, which may, in 1568, have been lower than it now is

[1] MNM: MS. 921, f33.

[2] The consequences of this fault seem to be reflected in sixteenth-century charts.

[3] Catoira aptly describes the reefs and shoals as 'a thing to frighten one coming with ships among these islands' (Amherst 1901: II: 297).   [4] MNM: MS. 921, f37.

and covered at high tide.[1] The expedition must have anchored on the west side of the spit, an anchorage which is still used by vessels of a similar size during the season of south-east winds. The Río Gallego would seem to have been the Matanikau River, an identification which in its turn seems to confirm the identification of the Río de Ortega with the Lunga (Betikama) River, although Gallego's estimate of 3 leagues as the distance apart of these two rivers is exaggerated.[2] Catoira's account, with its detailed narration of the several Spanish incursions into the hinterland of Guadalcanal, its description of the coastal terrain and its record of native names, provides added evidence for these identifications.

On 19 May[3] the brigantine was despatched under the *Alférez-General* [4] Don Hernando Henríquez, with Gallego as pilot. They sailed eastwards along the coast,[5] noting the large number of well-populated villages in an area which is now almost denuded of inhabitants, and passed the Río de Ortega and the heavily populated mouth of a river to which they gave the name *Río de San Bernardino*.[6] The Nalimbiu (Nalimbu) is a likely identification for this latter river, dominated as this part of the coast is from seawards by the conspicuous mountains of Tatuve (Lions Head) and Yellow Scar, one of which may be what Gallego describes as a very high rounded hill behind the Río de San Bernardino. Further along they came to another large river mouth, to which they gave the name *Río de Santa Elena*[7] and which is probably identifiable with the Bokokimbo River,[8] and Gallego describes the coastal plain with its palm groves and background *cordillera* of mountains.

Sailing on down the north coast, the expedition came to a large well-populated village, 'near to the beach', half a league to seaward of which were two small islands and, 'further on', a small sand cay to their NW. Two leagues to the SE they passed yet another pair of islands, also with a sand cay to the N.[9]

The well-populated village seems likely to have been in the vicinity of Aola Bay, and the first pair of islands to have been Neal and Bara Islands within that bay. To the N of the former lies the small sand and coral outcrop, Weldon Reef. The second pair of islands would seem certainly to have been the offshore islands of Rua Sura and Rua Kiki, to the NW of which lies a reef and sand

---

[1] Recent port development has altered the shape of the spit, now known as Point Cruz, but its essential character still remained intact in June 1961.   [2] They are barely five miles apart.

[3] May 9 in the Santa Casa MS.   [4] *Alférez Real* in the Santa Casa MS.

[5] The MNM MS. gives the course as '*de les sueste a les norueste*' (MNM: MS. 921, f39), the Santa Casa MS. as '*alesueste*' (Santa Casa: MS. *De Marina*, f108v).

[6] The MNM MS. gives *Sant Bernardino*, the Catoira narrative *San Bernaldino* (MNM: MS. 921, f39; Amherst 1909: II: 330).   [7] Catoira gives *Santa Helena* (Amherst 1901: II: 337).

[8] The identification of the rivers E of the Lunga is by no means certain, so limited is the descriptive evidence and so exaggerated are Gallego's estimates of distances sailed between them.

[9] MNM: MS. 921, f43.

outcrop named on modern charts North West Reef.[1] Still following the coast-line south-eastwards, and searching for a port which the expedition might use in an emergency, the expedition arrived at the south-eastern end of Guadal-canal. Here, in 10° 45′ S by Gallego's observation, they found a collection of islets, shoals, and one particularly large island with a harbour. This was the Marau Sound; the particularly large island being Malapa, to the W of which there is excellent anchorage in all seasons.[2]

As they left Marau Sound an island was sighted bearing SE by E and 7 leagues distant,[3] but the brigantine was headed towards Ramos (Malaíta),[4] which it reached on 26 May. It anchored in a good harbour, surrounded by reefs and entered by a narrow passage which concealed its inner width, to which was given the name *Puerto Escondido*.[5] From the description of the nar-ratives it seems likely that they anchored in what is now known as Uhu Harbour (9° 29′ 30″ S, 161° 15′ 30″ E), although it could have been one of several anchorages fitting the description between Uhu and Waisisi (9° 18′ 30″ S, 161° 4′ 45″ E).[6] From Puerto Escondido they sailed for '4 leagues' down the coast to the mouth of what seemed to be a large river, as Gallego remarks: 'dividing the country in two', and which Catoira tells us was found to be not a river at all.[7] This was the Maramasike Passage, a stretch of navigable water which has, with its many bends and jungle-clad banks, the appearance of a large river, and which divides Malaíta from Small Malaíta or Maramasike. The expedition did not enter the passage, but continued on down the coast for four leagues to another anchorage, at the entrance to which was a small island to starboard of the channel, and to which they gave the name

[1] Catoira only mentions two islands and a small sand island lying between Guadalcanal and Ramos (Malaíta), by which he is certainly referring to Rua Sura and Rua Kiki (Amherst 1901: II: 339).

[2] 9° 50′ S, 160° 51′ E. Catoira provides a slightly fuller description of the area. Gallego's recorded latitudes along the north coast of Guadalcanal seem to be based on a DR estimate and perpetuate the 1° error made by observation at the Rio de Ortega. Only when he got to Marau Sound does he actually state that he determined his latitude by observation. As he was still in error by almost +1° at this point one is inclined to wonder whether or not his latitude was entirely the result of an observation, or if it was not influenced by his earlier latitudes.

[3] The island now known as San Cristóval (*San Cristóbal* on the Admiralty Charts). The bearing given, if taken as magnetic, is correct.

[4] In his letter to the King, Mendaña, reporting this voyage, becomes confused and writes: 'From there he discovered an island known to the natives as Malay, near Ramos, the same that the natives called Malayta' (RAH: *Colección de Velázquez, Vol. XXXVI, No. 8*, ff185–194v; Zaragoza 1876: II: 32–33). As Amherst suggested, Mendaña may have been confused by the native expression '*Mala-ite*' (or '*Mala-ita*'), 'Mala over there' (accepted by Gallego as the name *Malayta*), when the Spaniards first enquired as to the name of the islands, and their later use of the name *Mala*, as Catoira recorded it (Amherst 1901: I: 177).   [5] MNM: MS. 921, f45.

[6] Gallego remarks that this island had already been named Ramos, but Catoira states that Gallego named it *San German*. As the latter name had been applied to the Nggela Group, and as we have Gallego's *relación* as evidence of his nomenclature, it seems certain that Catoira was misinformed or confused.   [7] Amherst 1901: II: 348.

6

Puerto de la Asunción in honour of their arrival there on the Feast of the Assumption.[1]

Having remarked that the southern extremity of Ramos was found to be in 10° 15′ S, a statement in contradiction to his observed latitude of 10° 20′ S for Puerto Escondido to the northwards, Gallego interjects some comments on the general topography of the group which are important, not only for the light they throw on his impression of the lands seen but as a written record on which subsequent cartographers might have based their charts. Gallego remarks that the southern cape of Malaíta is:

NE to SE [SW?] with the Island of Jesus which is the first which we saw and which is in 7° S and 85½ leagues from the cape of the Island of Malayta which is to the NE W with the point of the same island which is E and W with Meta in 8° the width of the cape which is at the other point in 7° which is the one point with the other NE to SE [SW?] 'quarta' N to S [NE by N–SW by S] E and W with the Island of Jesus 135 leagues.[2]

The difficulties of comprehension in this confused and unpunctuated passage are considerable, and are conducive of a bewilderment shared by both Guppy and Amherst. The Santa Casa MS., though slightly better, is still confusing, for it reads:

and it is with the Island of Jesus NE to SE [SW] which was the first discovered at a distance 85½ leagues, and with the cape of the Island of Malaita which is to the NW NE–SW with the point of the same island, E and W 8° and the width of the cape which is at the other point in 7° and the points lie one with the other NE to SE [SW?] ¼N to S [NE by N–SW by S] E and W with the Island of Jesus 135 Leagues.[3]

As far as the sense of the passage in its two forms can be determined, Gallego is stating that the southern point of Malaíta lies SW of the Ysla de Jesús, the first island discovered, which is in 7° S and 85½ leagues from the northern cape of Malaíta. The northern cape lies to the NW of the southern cape, E and W with Meta in 8° S, and the Ysla de Jesús bears NE to SW from it. The width of the southern cape is the same as the width of the point in 7° (i.e. the northern extremity of Santa Ysabel), and it bears NE by N to SW by S with the Island of Jesus, distant 135 leagues.

---

[1] This would seem to have been Teriari or Ariel Harbour (9° 39′ 15″ S, 161° 26′ E).

[2] MNM: MS. 921, ff46–47; BM: Add. 17, 623 ff49v–50; ATL: Gallego, ff47–47v. '*Esta a nordeste sueste con la Ysla de Jesus que es la primera que vimos la qual esta en siete grados de la parte del sur que son ochenta y cinco leguas y media con el Cabo de esta Ysla de malayta que esta al Nordeste hueste con la punta de la misma Ysla que es esta con meta leste hueste ocho grados el gordon de el Cabo que hace otra punta en siete grados que esta una punta con otra nordeste sueste quarta de Norte sur leste hueste con la Ysla de Jesus ciento y treinta y cinco leguas.*'

[3] Santa Casa: MS. *De Marina*, ff110v–111. (See also Zaragoza 1876: I: 11–12; and BPM: MS. 1686, f11.) '*i esta con la Isla de Jesus Nordeste sueste que la primera que se descubrio distançia ochentos i çinco leguas i medio, i con el cabo desta Isla de Malaita que esta al Noroeste Nordeste sudueste con la punta de la misma Isla, Leste oeste ocho grados i el gordon del cabo que haze otra punta en siete grados i esta una punta con otra Nordeste Sueste quarta del Norte sur Leste oeste con la Isla de Jesus çiento i treinta i çinco leguas.*'

What is important about the passage, and what emerges even from its complexities, is the information it conveys of Gallego's concept of the relative positions of the Ysla de Jesús and Malaíta. Recalling his considerable under-estimate of the distance sailed from the Ysla de Jesús to Los Bajos de la Candelaria, and his overestimates of the size of the lands which he sighted or visited whilst voyaging eastwards from Estrella Bay to the southern cape of Malaíta, it is not surprising that he should have visualized the Ysla de Jesús as lying relatively close to Malaíta and, indeed, as part of the archipelago. Gallego continues his topographic summary by remarking that:

The Island of Malayta is 114 leagues long,[1] but I did not visit the north coast and therefore do not know how wide it is. The island of Guadalcanal is very large. I do not estimate its size, because it is a great land, and its circumnavigation would take half a year; but I am able to say that it is very great, having gone along its northern part for 130 leagues,[2] without coming to the end of it, and at the eastern headland the coastline trended westwards and I saw a very great number of large villages.[3]

From the southern cape of Small Malaíta another island was sighted bearing '*leste quarta al sueste*' (E by S),[4] 8 leagues distant, towards which the brigantine sailed. They anchored off a small river and a village, but their sojourn was brief and terminated when the natives, hitherto friendly, suddenly turned on the Spaniards and attacked them. They departed, naming the island *La Treguada* or 'truce island, because they attacked us after a broken truce'.[5] The native name for the island was understood to be *Uraba*, and it can be identified with the island of Ulawa bearing E 8° S and 23 miles from the southern cape of Small Malaíta.[6] Three leagues to the S by W were sighted three low, shoal-girt islands, to which were given the collective name *Las Tres Marías* and which are identifiable with the three low islands of Olu Malau. Three leagues beyond was another low island in 10⅔° S, 6 leagues in circumference and with a good harbour, which must have been the island of Ugi (10° 15′ S, 161° 43′ E), and to this was given the name *San Juan*.[7]

From San Juan the expedition continued, inevitably as the modern chart reveals, to explore the large island to the S. Gallego describes it as 40 leagues in extent, narrow, mountainous, populous and lying in 10¾° S, and states that it

[1] 114 leagues = 456 Roman miles = 364·8 nautical miles, i.e. an estimate 3·5 times the actual length of 103 nautical miles.

[2] 130 leagues = 520 Roman miles = 416 nautical miles, as compared with the 60 or so nautical miles which Gallego had actually sailed along the north coast of Guadalcanal, and the remaining 30 miles which he might have seen from a distance.   [3] MNM: MS. 921, f47.

[4] BPM: MS. 1686, f13. The long *relación* of Gallego gives the bearing as '*leste quarta a el hueste*' (MNM: MS. 921, f47; BM: Add. 17, 623, f50; ATL: Gallego, f48), the Santa Casa MS. as '*aleste 4ᵃ*' (Santa Casa: MS. *De Marina*, f111).   [5] MNM: MS. 921, f48.

[6] Gallego gives the latitude as 10½° S, describes it as 25 leagues in extent, and adds that he took an observation of 10° S on the highest point of the island, and the other half (i.e. of the degree, 30′) being the southern end. The southern end of Ulawa is in 9° 50′ S.

[7] Gallego also gives the name as *Sant Joan*.

was given the name of *Ysla de Santiago*.[1] He makes no reference to its identification with the land sighted to the SE of the Marau Sound, but, unless some island has disappeared in the intervening four hundred years, it is almost certainly the same, that is the island which now bears the name San Cristóval. A gale from the NE, which suddenly appears to have sprung up, now drove the brigantine to the western end of the island of Santiago. From this point a large island was seen to the SW, 18 leagues distant and in 12½° S,[2] to which they gave the name *San(t) Urban*. It seems certain that the wind was from the NE, and that the vessel was driven to the western end of the island, for Gallego adds that San Urban lay 4 leagues from Guadalcanal. The identification of this island is perplexing, for a glance at the chart shows that there is indeed nothing between the western extremity of San Cristóval and Guadalcanal. Gallego was ill at the time, and Catoira, who mentions an island sighted 12 leagues to the E of south-eastern Guadalcanal, remarks that Gallego was suffering from a tertiary fever. It seems very likely that Gallego's observation, or later memory of this part of the voyage, was confused, and that if land was seen at all it was probably Guadalcanal. Mendaña does not mention San Urban in his letter to the King, and though the fact that the island was given a name seems to indicate that it was in fact seen and thought to be a new discovery by the members of the brigantine's complement, they may subsequently have realized it to be Guadalcanal. Perhaps it was only Gallego, sick as he was, who retained the memory of San Urban as a separate discovery. Guppy's assumption that San Urban was the south-eastern extremity of Santiago, which does from a distance and under certain conditions of visibility seem to be a separate island, accords neither with the wind direction recorded, the bearing given in all the versions of the *relación*, the implied relative position of San Urban with Guadalcanal, nor with the succeeding account of the voyage of the brigantine which leads one to suppose that the expedition proceeded directly from the cape to Guadalcanal.

It is by no means impossible that the brigantine was driven beyond the western extremity of Santiago, and that the island sighted was Rennell Island in 11° 40′ S. Rennell is only 500 feet high, so that, if the brigantine did sail just far enough S for it to be sighted, the *expedicionarios* might well have imagined that it was larger, higher and more distant than it in fact was, hence a southerly error of some 50′ in the latitude of 12½° S as compared with the error in

---

[1] MNM: MS. 921, f50.

[2] Santa Casa: MS. *De Marina*, f111v. The long version gives the latitude as 10½° S (ATL: Gallego, f51; MNM: MS. 921, f50; BM: Add. 17, 623, f53v), but if it bore SW from Santiago, the north coast of which was in 10¾° S, it could hardly be less than 10¾° S, although 12½° S seems rather distant. Gallego gives the latitude of South-Eastern Guadalcanal as 10° 45′ S, so that if San Urban was in 12½° S it was considerably more than 4 leagues from Guadalcanal, unless Gallego assumed that Guadalcanal extended further to the S than he had seen it to extend. In fact he did assume a considerable extent for Guadalcanal, but this would not explain his precise estimate of 4 leagues. On the other hand, if San Urban was in 10½° S it must have been NE of the south-eastern extremity of Guadalcanal.

the latitude of the north coast of Santiago of approximately 20′. The estimate of 4 leagues as the distance from Guadalcanal of San Urban could be a guess by Gallego, influenced by his impression of Guadalcanal's considerable size.

The brigantine was now put to leeward, and since, according to Catoira, Gallego's intention of exploring Ramos was frustrated by the sickness of the crew, was headed back towards the Puerto de la Cruz which they reached on 6 June. On 13 June the whole expedition set sail for 'the place which we had discovered with the brigantine', and proceeded eastwards along the north coast of Guadalcanal. Leaving the area of the Marau Sound on 18 June, they attempted to beat against the easterly winds towards Santiago and San Juan, their intention being to careen at the latter. Unable to beat against the wind, the vessels fell off to the S and Gallego attempted to make an anchorage in the lee of the western cape of Santiago. Unable to do even this, the vessels fell off to the S of the western cape and began to follow the southern coast. Here Gallego again became confused, for he remarks that they went 'coasting along an island which had not been seen by the brigantine'[1] to which they gave the name *San Cristóval*. Catoira is a little more explicit, and records that they 'discovered another large island near that of Santiago, although it was barely visible and seemed to be either all one island or divided by a small arm of the sea'.[2] In fact, having passed to the S of the western extremity of Santiago, the expedition had mistaken the southern coast of the one island for a separate island, and Gallego adds later, of the anchorage which he found, that it was 'very close' to the Island of Santiago.[3]

Worn out by their endeavours the expedition attempted to find an anchorage, and one was found by Gallego in the brigantine. Contrary winds and heavy seas drove the vessels to leeward of it, and Gallego then had to find another. From the second anchorage, which cannot be identified with certainty, the brigantine was again despatched eastwards on a voyage of reconnaissance along the coast of San Cristóval, the native name of which was learned to be *Paubro (Pauvro)*.[4] Gallego describes the south coast of San Cristóval, reasonably,

---

[1] MNM: MS. 921, ff57–58.   [2] Amherst 1901: II: 386–7.

[3] This error is to be seen reflected on sixteenth-century post-discovery charts of the archipelago in the delineation of two separate islands, Santiago and San Cristóval, separated by a strait. It was probably the result of the adverse weather conditions, imprecise navigation, and the fact that the north-western end of San Cristóval-Santiago is low-lying in comparison with the remainder of the island, which is divided by two distinct ranges of peaks running NW to SE. The name *San Cristóbal* of the modern charts is an alternative spelling of San Cristóval resulting from the Spanish *v* having the same sound as the Spanish *b*, softer than the English *b* at the beginning of words and soft like the English *v* when used elsewhere. San Cristóval is, however, the only reasonably phonetic spelling on an English chart or in an English speaking or written context. Gallego uses both spellings (and *San Christoval*) in the long version of his *relación*, *Cristoval* in the short Santa Casa version. In his letter to the King, Mendaña gives the name as *San Chrisptoual* (Zaragoza 1876: II: 40). As Santiago was the first name given to the island it is the more correct one to apply.

[4] Probably a corrupt rendering of the surviving native name *Bauro*.

as trending SE by E for about 20 leagues as far as the middle of the island and then E by S.

At the eastern end of the island Gallego discovered two small islands, estimated his latitude to be 11° 30′ S, and calculated that the island of San Cristóval was about 100 leagues in circumference and 7 leagues broad. Heading first for the smallest of the two small islands, the brigantine was met by a canoe containing twelve natives who, on enquiry, informed the Spaniards that there was no land ahead (?), but that there was land to the SE. Gallego adds that 'we saw it' but, as this would have been quite impossible, it seems likely that he means that they understood the natives. He also adds that when they landed on the island a sailor who climbed a palm tree was unable to see any land. In all probability the natives were indicating land in the direction of the Santa Cruz Group or New Hebrides, of both of which areas they probably had some knowledge. To the island was given the name *Santa Catalina*, and Gallego describes it as low and flat, 40 (presumably an error for 4) leagues in circumference, with many palm trees, reefs and inhabitants, and lying 2 leagues from the point of San Cristóval in 11⅔° S. Heading NNW, they visited the second island, which lay a 'short league'[1] from Santa Catalina and 3 leagues E by S of the point of San Cristóval in 11° 36′ S. It was 7 leagues in circumference and larger than Santa Catalina, and was given the name *Santa (Sancta) Ana*.[2] The brigantine then returned to the main body of the expedition, anchoring *en route* in a sheltered but unidentifiable anchorage to which was given the name *La Palma*.[3]

Mendaña still seems to have been anxious to pursue the original plan of the expedition, to sail S as far as 20°–22° S in search of the *tierra firme*, of which it was felt the archipelago might be an off-lier, or of which the lands discovered to the W might even be promontories. At a meeting of the captains and pilots the further prosecution of the search was agreed upon, but on 7 August, immediately prior to their departure, Gallego protested that they should be satisfied with the discoveries made and that the ships were worm-eaten and in a state of disrepair. He argued that they could no longer hope or expect to obtain food from the natives, either by friendly agreement or by seizure, and that, short of food and water as they were, it would be foolish to head further S when their return to Perú could only be effected by passing N of the equator beyond the south-east winds and the westerly equatorial current. The remainder of the expedition seem to have been persuaded by Gallego's arguments.

The deliberations which occurred at this time, as they are recorded in the several narratives, reveal something more of the background concepts behind

[1] i.e. a 'land' league of 3 Roman miles or 2·4 nautical miles.
[2] Santa Ana and Santa Catalina can only be the islands so named on the Admiralty chart, in 10° 50′ S, 162° 28′ E, and 10° 54′ S, 162° 27′ E.   [3] MNM: MS. 921, f65.

the expedition. Catoira, describing Mendaña's opinion on the plan to be followed after leaving San Cristóval, remarks that:

he thought that we should go forward to 20 and 22 degrees in quest of the land which, as your Lordship has been informed, lay within from 700 to 1,000 leagues or more from the kingdom of Peru, in the latitude of 15 degrees. . . . For as to Cabo de la Cruz, which Pedro Sarmiento informed your Lordship was 1200 leagues from the Kingdom in 8 degrees south latitude, with a long stretch of coast extending for 500 leagues and more in the latitude of 1 to 8 degrees, though we had navigated 1500 leagues, and 1000 from east to west in a lower latitude than 8 degrees, we had not seen it, nor found it to be so.[1]

The estimate of 700 to 1,000 leagues is greater than the 600 leagues at which Gallego states that they originally expected to find land, but the fact that the expedition sailed eastwards for over 1,600 leagues by their estimate is perhaps an indication that they did not expect to find land at much under 1,000 leagues. Mendaña seems at this stage to have been influenced by Sarmiento, who argued that the lands sought should be found in 23° S.[2]

From Catoira's remarks it appears that Sarmiento, earlier at least, had subscribed to the view that Cabo de la Cruz,[3] a supposed promontory of Nueva Guinea, lay 1,200 leagues from Perú. In the anonymous narrative the narrator refers to the opinion of Ortega and the clergy, who voted against settlements in the islands, that the *Licenciado* de Castro:

had been informed in Peru that this land [presumably meaning the lands discovered, identical with or adjacent to the lands sought] was very near to Lima, and it was 600 leagues at most to Cabo de Cruz and the coast of New Guinea, which was discovered by Inigo Ortiz de Retes . . . and therefore it was resolved to go forward in quest of that land.[4]

Presumably the meaning of this is that 600 leagues was the distance at which the clergy understood the Cabo de Cruz to have been discovered from Perú, and that, as they had not passed it, it must lie in close proximity to them, and there is clearly a close relationship between the belief that the Cabo de la Cruz (New Guinea) was 600 leagues from Perú and the *Presidente's* belief that the objective of the expedition lay at the same distance. Catoira provides a more detailed picture of the considerations given by the whole expedition to their future plans, and it appears from his comments that Mendaña's instructions were to settle in such good lands as were discovered. The objections to this, apart from the state of the ships and the navigational problems of returning to Perú,

---

[1] Amherst 1901: II: 420.   [2] Conway: 1946: 140.

[3] *Cabo de la Cruz* appears to have been the name applied by Bernardo de la Torre, who attempted in 1543 to sail from Tidore to New Spain, and who, according to Gallego, claimed to have discovered Nueva Guinea (New Guinea). Gallego adds of New Guinea that it 'is in no greater latitude than 4° S . . . and Inigo Ortez de Retes discovered it, and no one else, for Bernardo de la Torre did not see it, nor is there a Cabo de Cruz as he says' (ATL: Gallego, ff70v–71). See also Galvano 1862: 238.

[4] Amherst 1901: II: 207.

were the hostility of the natives, shortage of provisions, the insufficiency of their armaments and the absence of certain evidence of gold and silver. The Fathers argued that the Viceroy had assumed that the lands sought lay much closer to Perú than these which had been discovered, that had he anticipated such a distant discovery he would not have ordered colonization, and that the proximity of New Guinea to the islands discovered seemed to suggest either settlement or refreshment there. Some of the soldiery, who were convinced of the existence of gold, and Sarmiento, if the *Barros Report* reflects his true feelings,[1] advocated settlement, further discovery to the SE or a return to Perú by way of the South Pacific in the hope of discovering mainland or the lands which he believed to lie there.

It seems more than likely that the expedition owed its survival to Gallego, for neither settlement nor a course to the SE could have ended other than in ultimate tragedy, in the foundering of the steadily deteriorating vessels, in the starvation of the *expedicionarios*, their decimation by indigenes, or their abandonment on another island. Leaving *El Puerto de la Visitación*, as their last anchorage at San Cristóval was named, on 11 August, and having taken six hostages, the expedition was at sea for seven days before they had doubled Santa Ana and Santa Catalina. Despite Gallego's arguments, Mendaña, still clinging to the hope of discovering more lands to the SE and to the belief that the winds would change with the equinox and permit a direct course for Chile,[2] persistently ordered the ships to be headed to the SE whenever the wind veered to the northward. On 4 September the pilots made a formal protest at this waste of time, food and water,[3] and Mendaña acceded to their request, permitting the vessels to pass N of the equator.

On 20 December 1568, after a voyage of over three months, of acute suffering, extreme hardship and severe privation, during which the brigantine was abandoned and the *Almiranta* and *Capitana* were separated, those in the *Capitana* sighted the coast of California. Following the American coastline southwards, the two vessels were reunited at Santiago de Colima, where they remained for forty days, and eventually anchored off Callao on 11 September 1569. On the American coast Sarmiento, whose mutinous behaviour, preoccupation with his own ideas of where lands might be discovered, and not entirely unjustified belief in his own navigational prowess, made him a difficult if not a dangerous *expedicionario*, was arrested.

Unfortunately the contents of Gallego's *relación* do not permit a reconstruction of the actual distances logged by the expedition between San Cristóval and California. It is certain, however, from the narratives that they realized that the distance traversed on the return journey was greater than the 1700 leagues '*del golfo*' which Gallego estimated to lie between San Cristóval and

[1] RAH: *Colección Muñoz, Vol.* X, ff197–212. See also Amherst 1901: I: 93.
[2] Amherst 1901: I: 183–4.   [3] Amherst 1901: II: 430–5.

México[1] and, in view of the circumstances of the return voyage and weather experienced, the failure of Gallego to record any detailed navigational inform-ation is hardly surprising. On 4 September 1568, when by his estimate they were in 4° S, and were in fact probably in the region of the Gilbert Islands, Gallego interpreted floating debris as signs of the proximity of New Guinea. When it is realized that from Santa Ana to 4° S the course was predominantly to the NE, and that the time was 19 days, it appears that Gallego imagined the archipelago discovered as lying to the SE of New Guinea, if not to the S of its most easterly, unknown and unexplored, promontory. Gallego was able to deduce, correctly as it turned out but for the wrong reasons, that New Guinea was in close proximity to the archipelago and to the course which was followed to the equator. He was able to deduce this because of the current underestimate of the width of the Pacific and the distance of New Guinea from Central America, and because, since the eastern extremity of New Guinea was unknown, even the underestimated distance logged between Perú and the Solomons did not negate the possibility.

[1] MNM: MS. 921, f66.

III

Navigation, Cartography,
Chronicle, and Rivalry

WHILST there are many differences between the several narratives of the expedition of 1567–9, they do as a whole provide a comprehensive account of the expedition and create a fairly complete picture of the islands discovered. It is one thing, however, for the historian to identify known lands from the narratives, but it was quite a different matter for contemporary and later chroniclers and cartographers to create a picture, impression or actual chart from these narratives, particularly from Gallego's *relación*, the most important but also the most complex and confused of them.

Several factors which emerge from the records of the expedition are worthy of emphasis, as bearing upon the subsequent history of attempts to relocate the archipelago of the Solomons, and its delineation on subsequent charts. Principal among these are the underestimated distance of the archipelago from Perú and from the Ysla de Jesús; the idea that the Ysla de Jesús was relatively close to the Ysla de Ramos[1]; the generally correct latitudes ascribed to the archipelago[2]; the over-estimate of the sizes of the islands in the archipelago; the failure of the expedition to circumnavigate the coasts of Guadalcanal, San Nicolás, Ysla de Arracifes and San Márcos, which resulted in uncertainty as to their insular or continental character; the belief that what was in fact one island was two islands—named Santiago and San Cristóval; the existence of some confusion over magnetic variation, and the deduced proximity of the archipelago to New Guinea.

The Navigation of the Expedition

It is particularly necessary to examine in some detail the estimate made by the *expedicionarios* of the distance of the Islands of Solomon from Perú; for it was upon that estimate that the whole question of the subsequent rediscovery and recognition of the islands developed.

From the outset it must be appreciated that in the late sixteenth century longitude in a navigational fix could only be determined by dead reckoning

---

[1] This is well illustrated in the *relación* of Gallego when, five days and 78 leagues out from Santa Ana on a north-easterly course, he notes that he was in 7° S and 36 leagues E by S of the Ysla de Jesús.

[2] Correct enough, that is, to permit their rediscovery.

(DR), or by the reconciliation of a DR position with the observed latitude. The inadequacies of both techniques are well known, but will be illustrated, for it was a necessary reliance upon them which was to bedevil navigation and cartography until the late eighteenth century; a bedevilment only relieved by the invention and introduction of reliable chronometers, despite the considerable time and energy devoted to such theoretically correct but then practically impossible techniques as lunar distances and lunar eclipses. The best that the Spaniards could manage by way of a time piece was an hour glass on the poop turned by a ship's boy, a mechanism far removed from the precise standards necessary to determine longitude.

In determining a position by DR, four ingredients are required: a knowledge of the course steered, derived from a magnetic compass with allowance for variation and deviation; an estimate of the ship's leeway caused by wind; an estimate of the influence of surface currents, their set (direction) and drift (strength or speed); and a knowledge or estimate of the distances made good.

That Iberian pilots of the sixteenth century were able to determine magnetic variation is amply illustrated in the narratives of the expeditions with which this study is concerned, and that Gallego did determine variation is illustrated by such entries in his *relación* as: '*torne à mirar a el aguxa por ver si se avia apartado del derecho del polo por el medio dia y norhueste ay un tercio de quarta*'[1]; or again that: '*la mesma aguja estava fixa al Polo y que no bajava ni alçaba al Sueste y nor Sueste y estaba buena.*'[2]

The first remark would seem to indicate either that Gallego was using a shadow compass or that he was simply taking the angle between ship, sun and compass-needle at noon. The latter method could have been tolerably accurate, but in the low latitudes in which Gallego was navigating the height of the sun would have precluded anything other than a rough estimate. It is doubtful if any allowance for deviation caused by the magnetic fields of the ship's metal fittings was made, and although the vessels were largely wooden the amount of ironmongery on board could well have exercised a not inconsiderable effect upon the needles.

[1] MNM: MS. 921, f8; ATL: Gallego, f7v. 'at mid-day I examined the needle to see if it deviated from the direction of the pole, and it deviated NW a third of a quarter', i.e. the variation was 3° 45' W.

[2] MNM: MS. 921, f5; ATL: Gallego, f4v. 'the needle was steady on the Pole, and varied neither to the south-east nor south-west (?) which was good'. Gallego also remarks that 'we carried the compasses pointing due N, for those which they make in the Kingdom of Spain, particularly in the town of Seville, are, in these waters, NW a quarter, and we had no need to make any alterations, nor did anything as compensation, nor pay any attention to this quarter' (MNM: MS. 921, f3), from which we can conclude that the Spanish compasses were invariably offset to allow for a standard variation in Iberian waters, but that the expedition carried unadjusted compasses, the variation of which was determined from time to time as the voyage proceeded. Sarmiento de Gamboa remarks in the account of his voyage of 1579 to the Straits of Magellan that 'the compasses (made in Spain) have the needles changed nearly a point from the fleur-de-lys' (Markham 1895: 29–30).

It would be surprising if, in determining leeway, any technique other than a regular observation of the angle between the ship's wake and bow-stern line was employed, and if it was not, more probably, determined by a rough guess based on past experience of the ship's leeway under different wind strengths and under different spreads of canvas. A considerable amount has been written on the subject of Spanish vessels of the sixteenth century which would lead one to suppose that they were cumbersome, difficult to handle, and incapable of sailing other than before the wind without making considerable leeway. This is very far from the truth of the matter. With the limited exception of the Manila galleon, designed primarily with an eye to cargo capacity and seasonal trade-wind sailing, the vessels constructed on the Pacific coast were as good as, and ultimately became better than, the best in Europe. The weatherliness of Spanish vessels constructed on the Pacific coast is well illustrated in the comment of Hawkins in his *Observations* that such vessels were 'ever moulded sharp under water and long', a design necessitated by the constant tacking and beating to be done along the Pacific coast against the prevailing winds, and that they were superior in speed and manoeuvrability to his own *Dainty*, one of the most modern vessels designed and built in England at that time.[1] Diego García de Palacio includes in his *Instrucion Nauthica* of 1587 the outline of the body sections and sheer plan of a ship of 150 tons which well illustrates this point[2]; and whilst Maldonado claimed in 1610 that some Spanish vessels could sail up to 5 points[3] off the wind,[4] the contemporary English opinion seems to have been that the most that could be expected was 6 points.[5] That these comments can be applied to the vessels of the expedition of 1567-9 is illustrated by the fact that when the ex-flagship, the *Los Reyes* or *Capitana*, was later captured by the English at Valparaiso, she had just sailed 1,200 miles to windward from Callao on a normal commercial voyage.[6]

No reliable technique was available for determining drift due to currents in unknown waters, and navigators were forced to rely solely on observations of the surface of the sea, the possible influence of prevailing winds on the sea, and the apparent movement of the ship. In consequence DR positions were liable to considerable error when the ship's course was subjected to strong surface currents from any direction. For the determination of distance run they were hardly better equipped, their normal techniques being to estimate the ship's speed either by throwing a billet of wood into the sea astern and timing the pay-out of a measured line attached to it[7] or, alternatively, by pacing a piece of jetsam thrown over the bow down the known length of the ship, timing its passage with a sand glass or the rate of the human pulse. As often as not pilots seem to have relied on their knowledge of the ship and the

[1] Purchas 1905: XV: 150, 152, 197-8.   [2] Tate 1941: 191-5.   [3] $56\frac{1}{4}°$.
[4] Pacheco 1864: V: 440.   [5] $67\frac{1}{2}°$.   [6] Medina 1956: 384, 402.
[7] The embryo log-line.

speed it had previously made good in close proximity to known land, where speed could be determined more accurately, under different wind strengths and different spreads of canvas. Indeed, some contemporary and later manuals provided tables related to the amount and tautness of the canvas carried to determine the speed, though this would necessarily have varied with the design of the ship concerned.

The limitations of DR, particularly in respect of surface currents, though still contested, are too obvious to require detailed reference in this context; but it is surprising how many navigators still persist in arguing the consistent accuracy of the technique. Sölver and Marcus,[1] attacking this argument in Morison's work on Columbus,[2] enumerate the fallacies in it and reiterate the several factors likely to contribute to navigational error. They cite the experience of Albo on Magellan's voyage, and his considerable underestimate of the distance sailed from the Straits of Magellan to the Philippines, as 'perhaps the classic example of the extreme difficulty—not to say impossibility—of keeping a good dead reckoning through an ocean passage of a good many hundreds of miles'.[3] Whilst it is certainly true that DR is the foundation of navigation, and that most systems of celestial navigation begin with an assumed DR position, subsequently corrected by celestial observations, this does not obviate its very real limitations even today; particularly if, as in the sixteenth century, the only celestial observation is one to determine latitude, when the course is along the latitude.[4]

It was a similar underestimate to that of Albo, though to a lesser extent, which was made by the expedition of 1567–8; an underestimate which can be attributed to the shortcomings of DR navigation over a long ocean crossing, and in particular to the inability of the DR technique to make anything like even an approximate allowance for the drift and set of E–W surface currents.

The difference of longitude between Roncador Reef and Callao is 123° 20', which, in the middle or mean latitude of 9° S, is an actual distance of 7,309 nautical miles (approximate), 9,136 Roman miles or 2,284 Iberian leagues,[5] a figure considerably in excess of those recorded in the several narratives.

Gallego recorded the distance from Callao as 1,450 leagues in a direct line to a point 15 leagues NE by E of the position from which the Ysla de Jesús was sighted 6 leagues to the westwards. From the Ysla de Jesús he estimated that the expedition sailed 165 leagues to a point from which the Candelaria Shoals (Los Bajos de la Candelaria) lay 2 leagues to the W, giving a total

---

[1] Sölver 1958: 18–34.   [2] Morison 1942(b): I: xxxv, 248.

[3] Sölver argues that Albo's error was so extreme as to indicate deliberate falsification of his log, but this idea is untenable.   [4] Freidsleben 1960.

[5] Latitude of Callao, 12° S. Latitude of Ontong Java-Roncador Reef, 6° S. Middle Latitude 9° S. D./Long. Callao-Roncador Reef, 123° 20' or 7,400'. Distance in nautical miles Callao-Roncador Reef (approximate), 7,400' × cosine 9° S (·98769) = 7308·9 nautical miles.

approximate distance of the Candelaria Shoals from Callao of 1,638 leagues.[1] In the short version of his *relación* Gallego gives the distance from Callao to the Ysla de Jesús as 1,450 leages, and from the Ysla de Jesús to the Candelaria Shoals as 165 leagues,[2] but this is a condensed version and it is clear that only some of the figures of the long version have been included. The total of the actual daily distances run on different courses recorded in his long *relación* is only 1,610 leagues, but it must be assumed that several have been omitted in the compilation, transcription or dictation of the *relación*. At San Cristóval, in August 1568, Gallego informed Mendaña that on the return journey they would have to cross 1,700 leagues of *golfo*,[3] but since this was probably the total distance which Gallego estimated they would have to sail to México, it cannot be accepted as an estimate of the direct distance of the Solomons from Perú. Mendaña, in his letter to the *Licenciado* de Castro estimated the distance of the Ysla de Jesús from Perú as 1,400 leagues, and mentions the daily runs between 19 January and 1 February 1568, from the Ysla de Jesús to the Candelaria Shoals, as totalling 170 leagues.[4] In his letter to the King he gives no composite total, but mentions that the Candelaria Shoals lay about 180 leagues from the Ysla de Jesús.[5] The anonymous narrative gives the distance of Santa Ysabel from Truxillo as 1,700 leagues,[6] in the 'Sarmiento narrative' the total distance is given as 4,130 leagues,[7] an obviously worthless figure, and Catoira gives it as 1,575 leagues.[8]

Of the several figures, Gallego's in his long *relación* must be accounted the most reliable, that is 1,638 leagues, 6,552 Roman miles or 5,241·6 nautical miles, an underestimate of 646 leagues or 2,068 nautical miles.[9] It must be assumed that Gallego was employing the league value of 4 Roman miles,[10] on the evidence of contemporary usage, and the fact that Quirós, when he later examined Gallego's *relación*, made no suggestion that Gallego used any other kind of league, as he assuredly would have done as a Portuguese and as one concerned with the accuracy of the distances which Gallego recorded.

Noting that the voyage of 1567–8 to the Solomons was performed within narrowly circumscribed latitudes and in an E–W direction, it is immediately obvious that the underestimate of distance run can be attributed to the limitations of DR navigation, and to Gallego's failure to allow sufficiently for the

---

[1] MNM: MS. 921, ff10–13.   [2] Santa Casa: MS. *De Marina*, f104v.
[3] MNM: MS. 921, f66.   [4] Amherst 1901: I: 99–107.
[5] Amherst 1901: I: 163.   [6] Amherst 1901: II: 198.
[7] Amherst 1901: I: 86.   [8] Amherst 1901: II: 217–27.

[9] Expressed another way, 1,638 leagues represent 5,241·6 nautical miles, or a Difference of Longitude of 88° 45′ (D./Long. = Distance in nautical miles × secant of the middle latitude, 9°) as compared with an actual D./Long. of 123° 20′. Gallego would have expressed 1,638 leagues as 93° 36′ if he applied the degree value of 17½ leagues and if he made no correction for the decreased length of a degree of longitude in 9° S.

[10] He certainly employed the degree value of 17½ leagues, as is evidenced by such entries in his *relación* as: 'we went 1 degree north and south which is 17½ leagues' (Amherst 1901: I: 65).

generally consistent E–W current of the waters in which they sailed when making his daily estimate of the distance run. On such a course, errors of leeway and errors caused by a current setting to or from the N or S would have been indicated by solar observations of the latitude; but with a current setting E–W, and with the ships on an E–W course, there were absolutely no adequate means by which the extent of the westerly setting current could be determined, additional as it was to the actual speed of the vessel on the surface of the ocean.

For purposes of simplicity it is reasonable to divide the South Pacific into three zones of hydrographic differentiation; the South-East Trade Wind Zone from 5° N to 25° S, the Variables of Capricorn from 25° S to 30° S, and the Westerly Wind Zone from 30° S to 40° S. Between April and October the Trade Wind Zone, with which we are concerned, is characterized by fresh winds and occasional squalls, and between November and March, the period with which we are concerned, it recedes to 20° S and is characterized by prolonged calms in Central Pacific waters, with occasional cyclones, and hurricanes S of 10° S. Generally the disturbances travel in a southerly or south-westerly direction and, whilst cyclonic storms are rarely experienced N of 10° S, the area around and to the E of the Solomons is subjected to severe gales from the NW and W. Throughout the year the predominant ocean swell is from the SE, but between March and November it subsides at times and becomes confused.

The Pacific Ocean Current sets westwards along the equator, and in close proximity to it achieves a drift of as much as 80 miles daily, weakening rapidly S of 6° S. Strongest during the trade wind season, it weakens and becomes variable during the cyclonic period. From the available pilot charts of the South Pacific a reasonably clear picture of the winds and currents normally experienced throughout the months of the voyage can be obtained. From Lima to 95° W, during the month of November, the expedition would have experienced a current setting from the SE and veering gradually towards the E, drifting at 10–20 miles per day, with winds predominantly (40–75 per cent) from the SE, Force 4, or from the E (30–60 per cent), Force 4. West of 95° W the current would have continued setting from the SE, from the NE in the area of the Marquesas, from the E and NE as far as the Ellice Islands, and from the SW as the Solomons were approached. The minimum-maximum drift would have been 10–15 miles daily, increasing to 10–20 miles daily between 110° W and 160° W, 15–25 miles daily E of the Ellice Islands, dropping to 10–25 miles daily near the Gilberts, and 10–15 miles daily near the Solomons.

West of 95° W the winds would have been predominantly from the E, average Force 3–4, but increasing beyond 110° W and veering to the NE and SE. W of 150° W and as far as 180° W they would have been predominantly from the NE, veering to the N and NW with increasing velocity beyond 180° W and towards the Solomons. The present pilot charts of the Central Pacific are still based on inadequate observations and, although currents setting at as much as 80 miles per day are experienced, the average drift indicated on the charts, based on perhaps two or three observations, rarely exceeds 25 miles per day. As the *Pacific Islands Pilot* comments:

A considerable proportion of currents experienced in the region of the South Equatorial current exceed the rate of one knot [24 n. miles per day], and rates of up to 2 knots are frequent [48 n. miles per day]. Rates exceeding 2 knots are rare in most longitudes and seasons; very occasional currents have been recorded with a rate of about 4 knots [96 n. miles per day].[1]

This synopsis of the present prevailing hydrographic conditions conforms well with the conditions recorded by Gallego in his *relación*, but it is also immediately apparent that if the underestimate of the distance run is to be attributed to the prevailing current, and to the inability of the navigational technique to adequately note or compensate for this underestimate, then the current must have been persistently strong. Over the total period of the voyage from Callao to Los Bajos de la Candelaria, from 19 November 1567, to 1 February 1568, a period of some 72 days actual sailing time, Gallego estimated that he had made 1,638 leagues more or less E–W, an underestimate of the actual distance made good E–W of 646 leagues (2,068 nautical miles), or an average of slightly less than 9 leagues or 28·7 nautical miles underestimated daily. However, if the underestimates made between Callao and Nui (Jesús), and between Nui and Roncador Reef (Los Baxos de la Candelaria), are compared, it can be seen that the average over the Callao–Nui run was not so great as over the Nui–Roncador Reef run, for which the estimate of distance run was probably little more than guessed at.

	Gallego's Estimate	*Actual*
Callao–Roncador	1,638 leagues 5,242 n. miles	2,284 leagues 7,309 n. miles
Callao–Nui	1,471 leagues 4,708 n. miles	1,953 leagues 6,250 n. miles
Nui–Roncador	167 leagues 534 n. miles	331 leagues 1,059 n. miles[2]
Callao–Nui	19 November 1567–16 January 1568 [58 days]. Underestimate 482 leagues or 1542 n. miles, an average of 26½ n. miles or 8⅓ leagues daily.	
Nui–Roncador	18 January–1 February 1568 [14 days]. Underestimate 164 leagues or 526 n. miles, an average of 37½ n. miles or 11·7 leagues daily.	

[1] *Pacific Islands Pilot* 1946: I: 7.
[2] Longitudes: Callao 77° 10′ W, Nui 177° 10′ E, Roncador Reef 159° 30′ E.

Even if we take the slightly reduced daily average of 26½ nautical miles underestimated daily, it is still quite a high figure for an average. Two factors should, however, be taken into account; firstly, the prevailing favourable winds, which may have been insufficiently allowed for in determining the ship's speed; and, secondly, the possibility of drifts in excess of those normally or averagely expected, such as are occasionally experienced.

The *expedicionarios* were by no means totally ignorant of the existence of the E–W current, or of its effect on their navigation. Gallego himself remarks that it was very strong,[1] and Catoira states that:

the leagues which we travelled are stated above, and the account of how we went up and down. The distance travelled from east to west was more than was put down in the day's run, for we always had a calm sea and a fresh wind astern. And upon our return voyage also we found the way longer than we expected.[2]

Writing considerably later, Dampier was to comment on westerly Pacific navigation that:

we should rather increase than shorten our Estimate of the length of it [the distance run], considering that the easterly Wind and Current being so strong, and bearing therefore our log after us, as is usual in such cases,[3]

and Herrera, in his *Historia*, remarks that:

between the Tropics a current flows so strongly and persistently from the east that for many days the sailors do not need to touch the helm or sails, because they sail in that great ocean as if it were a canal or a peaceful river.[4]

Of the shortcomings of navigation by DR, *Don* Hernando Colón stated at the Junta of Badajoz that:

a much greater difference will result when the said leagues are measured by sea, for there are . . . obstacles that alter or impede the correct calculation of them, such as . . . currents, tides, the ship's . . . speed, because [of] . . . winds, or because of heavy seas . . . athwart the bows, or from other directions. In addition . . . one may be deceived by the ship's burden or bulk; or by reason of the ship's bottom being cleaner or dirtier . . . or whether it carries old or new sails, and whether they are of good or ill pattern, and wet or dry. Whether the day's run is estimated from the poop, prow or amidships; and other special consideration which I pass by.[5]

Even though the underestimate of distance made good across the Pacific can be adequately explained, one is bound, so considerable was that underestimate, to look for a further additional cause or causes. Inevitably one must examine the navigational techniques employed by Gallego, for although he employed a simple DR technique he reconciled his DR position with his latitude by celestial observation. An examination of the ramifications of the technique,

[1] MNM: MS. 921, ff8–9; Amherst 1901: I: 10–11.   [2] Amherst 1901: II: 461.
[3] Dampier 1729: I: 290.   [4] Herrera 1601(b): *dec.* 1, *lib.* IX, *cap.* XII, ff318–19.
[5] Blair 1903: I: 201–2.

particularly the likely technique of reconciliation, reveals the insufficiency of the evidence available; but such evidence as does exist would seem to suggest that the technique of reconciliation did not influence the estimate of longitudinal distance made good. That the latitude was determined by celestial observation emerges clearly in all the narratives of the expedition, and that the observation was a noon solar observation is evidenced by such statements as 'on this day we took the sun, and found $5\frac{1}{4}$ degrees of latitude',[1] and 'on the said Monday, January the 19th, Hernan Gallego took the sun',[2] by Mendaña; and Gallego's own repeated 'I took my altitude', although Gallego is rarely explicit as to whether his observation was of the sun or of the Southern Cross.

When Gallego's DR position did not agree with his observed latitude, which, when his course was other than E–W and in view of the tendency of his observations to error, must have been quite often, established techniques were available by which he could reconcile the two to arrive at a mean position. If the DR position did agree with the observed latitude, then the course and distance run would have been accepted as correct, and would not have revealed an underestimate of distance run.

Cortés, the leading navigational exponent of his day, in his *Arte de Navegar* of 1545, laid down rules for the reconciliation of a DR position with an observed latitude when the two did not agree. He concluded that the true position should be plotted at the intersection of the estimated course line with the observed latitude, relying on the course rather than on the estimated distance, except when the course was actually along a parallel of latitude.

In recommending reliance on course rather than on the estimated distance run, Cortés was in fact making an understandable suggestion, for the course was determined by an instrument, even though other factors influenced it, whilst the distance run was largely the result of guess-work or the use of a very primitive 'instrument'. Theoretically, the observed latitude, if correct, would compensate for an underestimate or overestimate of the distance sailed, provided the course was correct; but where the drift was lateral and the course steered was no longer the course run, the observed latitude would not reveal or compensate for the error in the estimate of distance.

The method suggested by Cortés was not, however, the only method employed, and later navigators came to realize that course and distance in any DR plot might be equally subject to error; so that, depending on the relationship of the observed latitude to the DR position, the one, course or distance, most likely to be in error needed to be determined. Two rules seem to have been formulated during the sixteenth century, the first—that where the course was nearer a parallel than a meridian reliance was to be placed on the estimated

[1] Amherst 1901: I: 105.

[2] Amherst 1901: I: 105. In the log of his later voyage of 1579, to the Straits of Magellan, Sarmiento de Gamboa is quite explicit in describing the taking of noon sights (Markham 1895: 29–30).

distance run rather than upon the course, the other—that where the course was nearer a meridian than a parallel reliance should be placed on the course rather than on the estimated distance. The application of these two rules produced results which were often far from accurate, but they were an improvement on the technique of Cortés, and were probably used by the more sophisticated pilots of the late sixteenth century, including, perhaps, Gallego.

A third technique of reconciliation would have been to plot a position midway between the position plotted if the course was assumed to be correct, and that plotted if the estimated distance was assumed to be correct, in the rare circumstances when the course was midway between a parallel and a meridian. It is possible that some pilots used this technique as a standard one for every situation, but nevertheless it is unlikely that its effects, plus or minus, on the longitudinal difference would have been significant.

It is quite clear that any attempt to arrive at a conclusion relating to the influence of the actual technique of reconciliation on the calculated longitudinal position must depend on knowledge of the particular daily DR positions and the observed latitudes. On the evidence available the most that can be said is that whilst the technique of reconciliation employed could have led to an increase or a decrease in the longitudinal error, so manifold are the ramifications and so limited is the evidence available that it is impossible to determine whether or not, and to what extent, it did occur. Even if the technique employed did contribute to an increase in the longitudinal error made, and this seems unlikely, it could hardly have been very significant.

Within the narratives of the three Spanish expeditions with which this study deals, there appears to be only one reference to the technique of reconciling the observed latitude and the DR position. This occurs in the Quirós-Bermúdez *relación* in relation to Quirós' later expedition of 1606. He writes, of an occasion during the voyage when the question of the distance sailed had been raised, and when a meeting of the pilots was called to hear their several opinions, that:

The pilots showed their charts and notes. As they were solely by dead-reckoning there were considerable differences, especially in the calculations of the Chief Pilot... Presently the Chief Pilot showed on his chart the track he had drawn upon it from Callao to 26°S, which the ships reached, the course being nearly WSW. It appeared to be here that he made his principal mistake, for he multiplied degrees on the WSW course, the direction in which we had to navigate... and he laid down the route by the course... and by the latitude, when it should have been, for greater accuracy, by the estimated leagues and the known latitude,

and Quirós concludes that

He did not calculate for errors in determining distances in a route from east to west, and the two quarters, caused by the variation of the needle, more or less leeway, winds, sails and other necessary considerations and calculations to enable him to mark on the chart the most correct position; and was only accustomed to navigating off the Peruvian coast.[1]

[1] Zaragoza 1876: I: 276–7.

The remarks are significant, not only in revealing that Quirós applied the rule of relying on the estimated distance rather than on the course when navigating on a course close to a parallel, but also in revealing that the Chief Pilot, the senior navigating officer, was employing a faulty system which, in effect, seems to have been little better than no system at all. If the Chief Pilot of the expedition of 1606 was at fault in this way, is it not also possible that Gallego, in 1567–8, employed a faulty system which tended to increase the error in his estimate of longitudinal distance made good caused by the current?

Despite Gallego's assumption that the Solomons must lie close to New Guinea, this realization in no way served to indicate the underestimate of distance which he had made. On 4 September 1568, 16 days after leaving Santa Ana and in the vicinity of the Gilbert Islands, Gallego saw driftwood and flotsam which he took as an indication of the proximity of New Guinea.[1] Quirós' comments on this deduction will be examined shortly, but that Gallego was able to deduce the proximity of New Guinea to a point bearing NE from the Solomons, and at a distance consequently less than that of the Eastern Solomons from Perú, is perplexing, particularly since the impression to be gained from Gallego's *relación* is that at that time he imagined his position to be to the E of the Ysla de Jesús.[2] One would have expected him to have concluded that at the Candelaria Shoals he had been even closer to New Guinea, since they were further to the W. As Quirós was later to point out, there was probably an error in Gallego's reckoning, although he does not state how close was the proximity of New Guinea indicated by the floating debris.

If we ignore this particular allusion, even though Gallego may have conceived of New Guinea as having a peninsular projection N of the Solomons, and concern ourselves solely with Gallego's undoubted conviction that the Solomons were close to New Guinea, his belief is understandable. At Badajoz the Spaniards had claimed that the Moluccas lay 210° E and 150° W of the *demarcación*, and if 30° are allowed as the approximate distance of the Peruvian coast from the Brazilian or Atlantic *demarcación*,[3] only 120° (2,100 leagues) would have been accounted left between the Peruvian coast (Callao) and the Moluccas. Miguel Rojo de Brito had reported that New Guinea and the Moluccas were close together, and on the evidence of de Brito and of de Retes (Rates), who had sailed eastwards along the north coast of New Guinea as far as 5° S and had then headed N, Quirós was himself to conclude that New Guinea, by which presumably he meant known New Guinea as far as the most easterly

[1] 'hallamos grandisimas señates de la tierra por que hallamos muchas palmas atadar y leños quemador y otra palos y Rossuras que saca la mar de la tierra . . . aunque no la descubrimos nos parecio que era la nueba guinea' (MNM: MS. 921, f71).

[2] MNM: MS. 921, ff68–69; Santa Casa: MS. De Marina, f115.

[3] See for instance Herrera's chart 'Descripcion de las Yndias Ocidentalis' of 1601. Herrera 1622: before f2.

point reached by de Retes, was 2,000 leagues from Perú.[1] Since de Retes had not sailed to the eastern extremity of New Guinea, there was nothing to hinder Gallego from believing that it extended for a considerable distance. The approximate distance between the point reached by de Retes and Eastern New Ireland is 13° or 244 Iberian leagues, so that, ignoring the underestimated width of the Pacific, there were in fact 244 leagues of land extending eastwards of the position reached by de Retes to the end of what may properly be called New Guinea. If de Retes' position was accepted as 2,000 leagues from Perú, then it would have been no myth of illusion to believe that the eastern extremity of New Guinea might lie 1,756 leagues from Perú and Gallego could well in the absence of any negative evidence, have believed that it extended much further E.

The view suggested by Guppy, that the distance of the Solomons from Perú was deliberately underestimated in order to ensure a general belief that they were within the Spanish hemisphere and to conceal them from the English,[2] deserves less respect than the opinion that the Albo log of Magellan's voyage was falsified. Quite apart from the fact that the underestimate can be adequately explained in terms of navigation and hydrology, the suggestion relating to the *demarcación* founders on the facts that by 1568 the Spaniards were in effective control of the Philippines despite the *demarcación*, and that even the *demarcación* or *raya* plotted by the Portuguese was well to the W of both the actual and supposed position of the Solomons. The concealment theory collapses on the tactical limitations of the Solomons for the English, whose interests, despite some proposals, were elsewhere, and the obvious desire of the Spaniards to distract them from the American Pacific coasts rather than attract them to islands supposed to be in close proximity to those coasts.

The Origin and Application of the Name Islands of Solomon

Despite the Ophirian aspirations of Mendaña's expedition and the use of the title Island of Solomon in relation to the object of the search prior to its departure, in none of the narratives does the name Island or Islands of Solomon occur, either in relation to the object of the voyage or to the discoveries made. It would indeed have been strange if it had been applied to the discoveries made, for none of the principal *expedicionarios* could have imagined that they had discovered the *Ophir* of King Solomon, although Mendaña, when he

---

[1] Zaragoza 1876: I: 187. Galvano in his *Tratado*, describing the voyage of Grijalva, reported the island of *O Acea* as lying over 1,000 leagues from Perú, and 500 leagues from the Isle of Cloves (Moluccas), giving a total distance Perú—Isle of Cloves of somewhat over 1,500 leagues. Encisco and Pirés had estimated the distance from Figuera, the then most westerly known point in South America, to *Cattigar* as 1,650 leagues.   [2] Guppy 1887: 255.

wrote in his letter to the *Licenciado* de Castro of 'the discovery of the islands', did perhaps imply that the islands which had been sought were the same as those which had been discovered.

The earliest use of the name Islands of Solomon after Mendaña's return from the Western Pacific seems to have been in a despatch of the *Licenciado* Juan de Orosco (Orozco), dated Guadalajara, 20 March 1569, in which he reported the arrival of Mendaña's vessels off the Mexican coast.

On the 8th of February there put into the port of Santiago ... two battered ships without masts or victuals which had set out from the Port of Lima in Peru, in quest of the Western Isles, the Solomon Islands, and New Guinea, in accordance with information which they had of them ... on the other side of the Line towards the South, they discovered many thickly populated islands in the latitude of 10 degrees to 12 degrees.... In my opinion, according to the report that I have received, they were of little importance, although they say they heard of better lands, for in the course of these discoveries they found no specimens of spices, nor of gold and silver, nor of merchandise, nor of any other source of profit, and all the people were naked savages.[1]

Orosco writes only of the discovery of the Islands of Solomon as the object of the expedition, not as its result, and seems to imply that none of the *expedicion-arios* had claimed such a discovery when reporting to his informant, the *Alguacil-Mayor* of México City. Whilst his words may reflect a mercenary outlook and some jealousy, Orosco's reaction to the accounts of the expedition was natural, and was to be echoed in Spain and Perú.

One early document in which the discoveries are named the Islands of Solomon is the *Report of Dr Barros' Enquiry* of 4 June 1573, to which reference has already been made. The *Report* is headed: 'Report which the illustrious Doctor Barros, Judge of this Royal Audience, ordered prepared by instructions of His Excellency, with regard to the discovery of the Solomon Islands'[2]; the preamble states that 'His Excellency, wishes especially to be informed regarding the discovery of the Solomon Islands, which *Licenciado* Castro entrusted to Álvaro de Mendaña'[3]; and folio 199 begins, 'The following questions shall serve to examine the witnesses who testify regarding the information on the discovery of the Western Islands in the South Seas, commonly called the Solomon Islands'. The last phrase seems to indicate that neither Barros nor *Don* Francisco de Toledo, the Governor of Perú, believed that the islands discovered were in fact the Islands of Solomon and, in a document so obviously biased in favour of the dissident Pedro Sarmiento de Gamboa, this is hardly surprising.

Sarmiento himself, thwarted as he thought in his quest for the real *Ophir* or Inca-known islands of gold, seems to have been the most vehement in his

[1] Zaragoza 1876: III: 115; RAH: *Colección Muñoz, Vol.* XXXVII, ff9–10; Amherst 1901: I: lviii; AGI: *Guadalajara*, 51, doc. 145.   [2] RAH: *Colección Muñoz, Vol.* X, f197; Conway 1946: 139.
[3] RAH: *Colección Muñoz, Vol.* X, f198; Conway 1946: 139.

denial of the Ophirian identity of the islands discovered, and in a MS. document dated Seville, 18 January 1571, signed by him and headed '*Probanza de los servicios de Mase Agustín Felipe Carpintero de Ribera en el descubrimiento de las islas del Nombre de Jesus, o de Salomon, y en el extrecho de Magallanes*', he writes of '*las yslas del nombre de Jesus bulgarmente llamados de Salamon*'.[1] In the dedicatory preface to his *History of the Incas* he also writes:

By this same title [i.e. the King's title to all the Indies] Your Majesty may also, without scruple, order the conquest of those islands of the archipelago of 'Nombre de Jesus', vulgarly but incorrectly called the Solomon Isles, of which I gave notice and personally discovered in the year 1567; although it was for the General Alvaro de Mendaña; and many others which are in the same South Sea. I offer myself to your Majesty to discover and settle these islands, which will make known and facilitate all the commerical navigation, with the favour of God, by shorter routes.[2]

He seems to have been the only member of the expedition who, ultimately at least, gave a name to the archipelago, and it may be significant that on the *Molyneux Globe* of 1592[3] the *Insulae Salomonis* are depicted with the title, '*Islas estas descubrio Pedro Sarmiento de Gamboa por la Corona de Castilla y Leon des de el anno 1568 llamolas islas de Jesus ennq bulgarmente las llama ISLAS de SALOMON*'.

As we have already seen the name Ysla de Jesús was applied by Mendaña to the island of Nui by virtue of its discovery on the Feast of the Holy Name (Nombre de Jesús). When it is recalled that the 'Island of Jesus was the first we had discovered before we saw the archipelago',[4] that the distance between the Ysla de Jesús and the Bajos de la Candelaria was considerably underestimated, and that a reconstruction of Gallego's impression of the topography and relative position of the islands discovered puts the Ysla de Jesús in close proximity to the archipelago, Sarmiento's use of the name *Islas de Jesús* for the whole group was neither unreasonable nor inappropriate.[5]

Elsewhere Sarmiento refers to the Islands of Solomon by name, but always with reservation. In an account of the depredations caused by Drake on the Peruvian and Chilean coasts in 1578,[6] he refers to a vessel captured by the English at

---

[1] AGI: *Patronato, legajo* 18, *No.* 10, *Ramo* 6; 'the islands of Nombre de Jesus vulgarly called of Solomon'. The name Salomón is variously rendered as *Salomon* or *Salamon*.

[2] Markham 1907: 11.

[3] An example of the 1592 edition is at Petworth. There is also one of 1603 in the Middle Temple. See Wallis 1951; Wallis 1952; Wallis 1953; Wallis 1955; and Stevenson 1921: I: 193.

[4] MNM: MS. 921, f69.

[5] In a seventeenth-century *derrotero*, almost certainly derived from official sources, the list of the islands discovered by Mendaña in the archipelago, and their positions, commences with '*La Primera Ysla que llaman El nombre de Jesus esta En altura de Nuebe Grados—9*: gra—. . .', and in the absence of any longitudinal information the reader would have been justified in assuming that this was the most easterly island, but part of the archipelago (A. A. Houghton Jnr. Collection: Espinoza—*Descripcion y Derotero*).

[6] Navarrete 1842: XCIV: 432; '*Relación de lo que el corsario Drake hizo y robo en la costa de Chile y Perú y las diligencias que el Virey Don Francisco de Toledo, hizo contra el, 1578*'.

Valparaiso as 'named *La Capitana* because she had served as such in the voyage of discovery to the Solomon Islands'[1]; but he does not write of the discovery of, only the discovery to, the Solomon Islands, adding, in reference to the Peruvian coastal winds, 'as I learnt from experience when I discovered the islands commonly called of Solomon, in the year 1568'.[2]

It may well have been that Mendaña refrained from naming his discoveries in the hope that they would subsequently be named after him personally, and Juan de Iturbe, a later participant in Spanish exploration in the Western Pacific, in a summary of the voyages made to that area which he wrote after his return from Quirós' expedition of 1606, referred to the islands as '*Islas que llamaron de Salomon u de Mendaña*'.[3]

At some stage between 1569 and the end of 1570 the name Islands of Solomon came to be applied, in common parlance at least, to the discoveries of Mendaña. Though the leaders of the expedition might protest that these were not the Islands of Solomon, Mendaña would have been foolish to do so too vehemently, and the bulk of the *expedicionarios* must have returned to tell their stories in the taverns and *bordellos* of the Central American waterfront; stories of land actually discovered. Theirs had been a romantic enterprise deserving of a romantic name and, so they might have argued to themselves, even if the *Ophir* of King Solomon had not actually been discovered, it could hardly have been far distant and might well have been any of the lands or islands which they had seen in the distance. One of the informants at the Barros Enquiry stated that, according to the natives, Guadalcanal was an island small in comparison to a very large land in the vicinity. More important perhaps were the reports of gold found in the islands for, although no indubitable evidence of gold in any quantities had been found, Gallego reported the existence of some evidence of it, and Mendaña claimed that the natives recognized it and called it *aburu* and *tereque*. At the Barros Enquiry the witnesses asserted that there was evidence of gold in the islands, and that the natives also reported it, and in fact there was truth in these beliefs and assertions.

The name Islands of Solomon was slow to be accepted officially. In the *Letters Patent* of 27 April 1574, granting the islands to Mendaña, they are referred to as *Yslas del Poniente* and *Islas del Mar del Sur*, and in[4] an *Instrucción* from the King to Mendaña, dated 25 May 1575, on the question of the longitudinal position of the islands and observations to be made there, he is addressed as '*Nuestra Governador de las Yslas ocidentales*'. Common usage may however have been instrumental in ending official reluctance to use the name, for in June 1580 the King addressed a longer *Instrucción* to Mendaña from Badajoz in which he referred to him as '*Nuestra Governador de las Yslas de Salamon*'

---

[1] Nuttall 1914: I: 66.   [2] Nuttall 1914: I: 85.
[3] AGS: *Estado, legajo* 219; BNM: MS. 3099, f109v, '*Sumario brebe . . .*'.
[4] Pacheco 1864: XXII: 189; Zaragoza 1876: III: 116.

(later spelt *Salomon*).[1] It is with this royal use of the name in relation to the archipelago, which, by Mendaña's acts of possession, the Treaties of Tordesillas and Saragossa, and by contemporary European concepts of sovereignty, were within and part of the King's provinces, that the islands became in name, if not in historical fact, the Islands of Solomon. It is indeed from this royal assent, or from previous royal assents in hitherto unknown documents, that the name legally and properly derives.

Between 1570 and 1587 the Jesuit Father, Joseph de Acosta, wrote in his *Historia Natural y Moral de las Indias*:

In this South Sea, although they have not yet discovered the ende towards the West, yet of late they have found out the Ilands which they call Salomon, and which are many and great, distant from Peru about eyght hundred leagues. And for that we find by observation, that wereas there bee many and great Ilandes, so there is some firme lande neere unto the Ilands of Salomon, the which doth answere unto our America on the West part, and possibly might runne by the heigth of the South, to the Straightes of Magellan. Some hold that Nova Guinea is firme Land, and some learned men describe it neere to the ilands of Salamon.[2]

His erroneous figure of 800 leagues, derived from none of the primary narratives of Mendaña's expedition, is perplexing. That it is not a deliberately false figure created to mislead aliens seems to be indicated by the reference to the proximity of New Guinea, and it is possible that one origin of the error is to be found in another statement of Acosta's in the same context to the effect that:

I have observed, as well by my own navigation, as by the relation of others, that the Sea is never divided from the lande above a thousand leagues. And although the great Ocean stretcheth farre, yet does it never passe this measure. . . . I say and affirme, that of that which is this day discovered, there is no land distant from any other land, by direct line, or from some Islands neere unto it above a thousand leagues.[3]

and in the conclusion to be drawn that Acosta could not have accepted the distance of the Solomons as being greater than 1,000 leagues from Perú. It seems unlikely that the Spaniards would have disseminated a false estimate of the distance of the Islands of Solomon from Perú, for by spreading an under-estimated figure they ran the risk of attracting aliens near to Perú and México.

---

[1] MNM: MS. 328, ff123–133v.

[2] Markham 1880: I: 18 (Edward Grimston's translation of 1604).

[3] Markham 1880: I: 17. The figure 800 leagues was repeated by other chroniclers and historians besides Acosta. Acosta also states: 'Wee see even now that they cut through the Ocean to discover new lands, as not long since Alvaro Mendaña and his companions did . . . and at the end of three months they discovered the Ilands which they call the Ilands of Salomon, which are many and very great, and by all likelihood they lie adioyning new Guinnie, or else are very neere to some other firme lande.' Markham 1880: I: 46–47. Grimston's translation ensured that information on the position of the Islands of Solomon was available in England by 1604, but the Spanish (1590, 1591), Italian (1596), French (1597, 1600), Dutch (1598) and Latin (1602, 1603) editions of Acosta's *Historia* would have been available earlier.

Moreover, in view of the large extent of hypothetical lands on contemporary charts of the Pacific, which could attract aliens in any case, any attempt at concealment of the position of the Solomons would have seemed quite futile and unlikely to succeed.

The Islands of Solomon on Sixteenth-Century Charts

In the narratives of the expedition of 1567–69 there is only one reference to a chart having been prepared of the discoveries made, by Gallego, in his remark in the opening lines of his *relación* in which he mentions an accompanying *carta de marear*.[1] As yet no certain example of this chart has been found, either in or separated from the extant versions of the *relación*, and its absence presents a considerable drawback in any attempt to analyse the existing sixteenth-century charts of the Pacific on which the Islands of Solomon are laid down.

It is reasonable to conclude that Gallego's chart reached the Spanish authorities and that a copy was lodged in the *Casa de Contratación*,[2] its details being added to the official master-chart. It is also reasonable to suppose that at least one other chart was prepared and so lodged, perhaps by Sarmiento de Gamboa; for, although Gallego was the Chief Pilot and bore the responsibility for preparing the chart of the discoveries made, Sarmiento was an accomplished cartographer whose later charts of Magellan's Straits are still deserving of admiration, and he laid claim to a place of prominence and responsibility in the conduct and navigation of the expedition.

Assuming that lodgement of a chart or charts in the *Casa de Contratación* did occur, then one might expect to find derivatives of it or them amongst later charts which had a certain origin in the *Casa* and were based on the prototypes held there. Amongst the charts for which such a certain origin can be claimed, and then albeit with qualification, are those contained in the *derroteros*, rutters or pilot-books, issued under the strict control of the *Casa* to pilots in the Indies fleets, and guarded zealously by them. In one of these, the seventeenth-century *Derrotero General* of Pedro Baena,[3] occurs a chart of the Solomons.

[1] MNM: MS. 921, f1; Amherst 1901: I: 3.

[2] Founded in 1503, the *Casa de Contratación* combined the functions of a Board of Trade, Emigration Office, Trade Clearing House, Mercantile Tribunal and Nautical College. In its early days it also acted as a Colonial Office, a function later assumed by the *Consejo de Indias*. The *Casa* played a significant role in the development of nautical science, acted as a repository and co-ordinating agency for cartographical, nautical and astronomical information, and to its activities are due the survival of many charts of the sixteenth and seventeenth centuries.

[3] In the private collection of Arthur A. Houghton, Jnr., New York (f149) to whom I am most grateful for the gift of microfilms of this and another *derrotero*. My attention was drawn to the existence of this chart by Mr. J. Forsyth and later by a reference by Father Celsus Kelly (Kelly 1960: footnote 29). The other version of the *derrotero* to which Fr. Kelly refers is in the Biblioteca Nacional, Madrid (MS. 2957, f150).

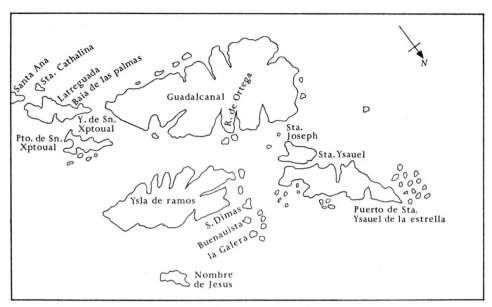

Map IX The chart of the Yslas de Salomón in Pedro Baena's *Derrotero General*, redrawn

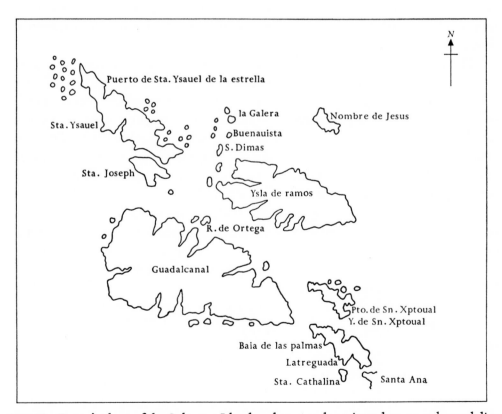

Map X Baena's chart of the Solomon Islands redrawn and reoriented on a north-south line

When the Baena chart is oriented on a N–S line, its similarity to the known configuration of the archipelago is striking, and by no means unacceptable. It would, however, from the appearance of relative accuracy, and general conformity to the contents of Gallego's *relación* alone, be rash to suggest any more of this chart than of any of several which will also be examined: that it could possibly be derived from the *carta de marear* of Gallego. Cartographical accuracy in the sixteenth century was by no means as fervently sought after as one might expect, and a considerable distortion or inaccuracy of delineation and topography is no real evidence that a chart is not the original prototype. On this particular chart can be noted a nomenclature generally though not entirely similar to the nomenclature of Gallego's *relación*, the delineation of the Ysla de Jesús (*Nombre de Jesus*) in close proximity to the *Ysla de ramos* (Malaíta), and the division of the one large island to the SE of Guadalcanal (San Cristóval) into two islands. However, whilst Gallego identified the north coast of San Cristóval as one island and named it Santiago, the south coast of San Cristóval as another island and named it San Cristóval, on the Baena chart San Cristóval[1] is placed N of *Latreguada*, the island which has already been certainly identified with Ulawa. Allowing for Gallego's erroneous impression that Santiago and San Cristóval were two separate islands, the island on the Baena chart named *Latreguada* should be named San Cristóval, the island named *S* *Xptoual* (San Cristóval) should be named Santiago, and *Latreguada* should be the name applied to an island to the SE of Ramos.

The distorted position of the chain of islands, *S Dimas, Buenauista*, and *la Galera*, between Ramos and Santa Ysabel (*Ysauel*), may reflect the difficulties which Gallego had in determining the relative positions of the islands, but his *relación* clearly describes that group as occupying a position between Guadalcanal, Santa Ysabel and Ramos, the position of the Nggela Group. The chart as a whole does not reflect the considerable longitudinal distortion of a reconstruction of Gallego's description of the archipelago, resulting from his overestimate of the size of the islands, but, as has already been suggested, Gallego may have stated overestimated figures without actually plotting them. The coastlines of Southern Guadalcanal and Eastern Malaíta are laid down with a convincing display of creeks and islands, although neither coastline was visited by the expedition or even sighted from a distance. Several islands, for example San Nicolás and Ysla de Arracifes, are not laid down on the Baena chart, though it is possible that the extant chart is only part of a larger chart which included those islands, together with San Márcos and Los Bajos de la Candelaria.

The inscription at the foot of the chart is perplexing, for it reads '*Estas yslas todas estan de la parte de la Linea Equinozial desde siete hasta catorze Grados*

---

[1] *Y. de S* *Xptoual.*

de Altura—y estan um mil y ciento y setenta leguas del puerto del Callao.[1] The estimated distance of 1,170 leagues from Perú conforms with none of the narratives, although it is possible that the inscription bears no relation to the chart in its original form, and was added by Baena from such information as he had of the position of the Solomons, and that his information was incorrect.

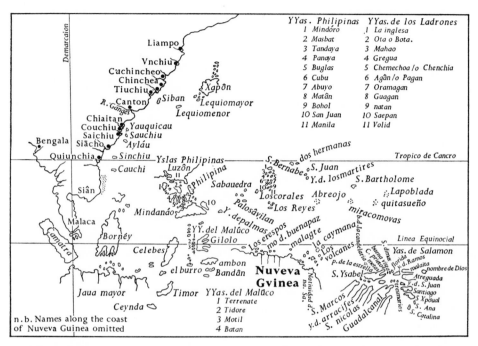

Map XI López de Velasco's *Descripcion de las Yndias del Poniente* of *c.* 1575, redrawn

Whilst the Spanish official archives must have had a prototype chart of the Solomons by 1570 at the latest, it was not until López de Velasco published his *Demarcacion y Diuision de las Indias* between 1575 and 1580,[2] a summary of his earlier but apparently chartless *Geografía y Descripción Universal de las Indias* of 1571–4,[3] that a chart of the archipelago came into even limited circulation. As the leading cosmographer of his day, whose cartography is almost certainly derived from official sources, his work is of considerable importance, all the more since the period of his writing immediately followed the return of Mendaña's expedition, when it is possible that he obtained information, directly or indirectly, from the *expedicionarios* themselves.

---

[1] All these islands are to the south of the equator between 7° and 14° of latitude—and are one (or 'west one') thousand one hundred and seventy leagues from the port of Callao.

[2] I have used the MS. copy in the John Carter Brown Library, Providence, Rhode Island. There are at least four other MS. copies, three of these being in the Biblioteca Nacional, Madrid; the Archivo General de Indias, Seville; and the Provincial Library, Toledo, respectively.

[3] Zaragoza 1894.

In the MS. *Demarcacion . . .* occur two charts, a chart of the Pacific, Americas and Far East, entitled *Demarcacion y Nauegaciones de Yndias*, and a more detailed chart of the Far East and Western Pacific entitled *Descripcion de las Yndias del Poniente*. Taking the latter chart first and examining Velasco's delineation of the Y*as*. *d. Salamon*, it is immediately obvious that, despite some distortions which give a superficial impression of inaccuracy, in many respects the chart is a more faithful illustration of the details of Gallego's *relación* than the Baena chart, and is also hardly less faithful to reality. The extension of *Guadalcanal, S. nicolas* (San Nicolás), *y. d. arracifes* (Ysla de Arracifes) and *S. Marcos* (San Márcos) southwards illustrates what the expedition suspected: that these islands might be promontories of continental land; and although the southerly elongation is unjustified by what the expedition saw, the non-completion of coastlines not actually seen or explored is no less honest than the completed coastlines of the Baena chart.[1] San Cristóval (*S. Xpoual*) and *Santiago* appear as separate islands, but they appear in their correct position relative to Gallego's description, and although *Atreguada* (La Treguada, Ulawa) is exaggerated in size relative to *y. d. Ramos, Ramos* and *malaita* are mistakenly separated. The *tres marias* are located to the W instead of the E of the *Ya. d. S. Juan* (San Juan) (Ugi); *Sesarga* (Savo) is reasonably correct, and *florida, buena vista* and *S. dimas* (the Nggela Group) are better located than on the Baena chart. *nombre de Dios* (Nombre de Jesús, Ysla de Jesús)[2] is laid down close to *malaita; Los Bajos de la Candelaria* are depicted; and if the archipelago as a whole is moved on its axis through some 10° to compensate for easterly magnetic variation not allowed for by the cartographer, a greater conformity to reality and an honest attempt to chart the group as it appeared are evident.

In the text of his *Demarcacion . . .* , under the heading 'Poniente: Yslas de Salomón', Velasco describes the archipelago as being 1,500 leagues from Callao, the City of the Kings, and lying between 7° and 12° S, adding that its proximity to New Guinea is to be deduced from the racial characteristics of the indigenes. He refers to eighteen principal islands, some of 300 leagues in circuit, two of 200 leagues, one of 100 leagues, one of 50, and others smaller, in addition to which 'are several, the coasts of which have been only imperfectly traced'.[3] *Sancta Ysabel* he describes as lying between 8° and 9° S, 150 leagues in extent, 18 leagues wide, and having the good harbour of *la estrella*.

To the S of Sta. Ysabel lie S. Jorge or Borbi, 30 leagues in circumference, and the Ysla de arracífes, the latter of the same extent as S. Marcos or S. Nícolas, lying SE[4] of Sancta Ysabel, and 100 leagues in circumference. To the west of Sancta Ysabel is S. Geronimo, of 100

---

[1] The unnamed promontory to the SE of Guadalcanal may be intended to represent the doubtful discovery of San Urban.

[2] The interpolation from Nombre de Jesús to Nombre de Dios is understandable.

[3] JCB: Velasco, f73.   [4] *Sueste* is presumably an error for *sudueste*.

leagues circumference,[1] and to the SW, the largest of the islands, Guadalcanâl. To the E
lie San dinas, la ysla Florída, the ysla de buena vista, each of 20 leagues circumference, and
also La ysla de Ramos of 200 leagues, in close proximity to Malayta, La Atreguada of 25
or 30 leagues, and Las tres Marías. S. Juan, between Sanctíago and la Atreguada and to the
S of Malayta, is 12 leagues, whilst to the SE of Malayta is the island of San Xpobal [Cristóval],
as large as Malayta, in close proximity to which are the small islands of Sancta Ana and
Sancta Cathalina. The island of nombre de Díos is 50 leagues from Sancta Ana and in 7° S
and lastly, to the N of Sancta Ysabel are Los báxos . . . de la candelaría.[2]

This gazetteer does not entirely agree with Velasco's chart and, apart from
the confusion over San Márcos, San Jerónimo and Ysla de Arracifes, which can
be related to an attempt to reconcile the contents of Mendaña's letter to the
King with Gallego's description of the islands, the laying down of Ramos and
Malayta as two separate islands, and the use of only four of the names given to
the islands in the Nggela group, La Galera, Buena Vista, San Dimas and Florida,
all point to the fact that Velasco had access to Mendaña's letter to the King and
used it as a source.

The general chart, *Demarcacion y Nauegaciones de Yndias*, is worthy of particular attention, illustrating as it does the established trade route between
Acapulco and the Philippines, the return route discovered by Arellano,[3] and,
optimistically perhaps when compared with the other 'trade' routes, the route
to the Solomons from Perú. Ignoring the grid squaring of the chart, which is
quite irrelevant, it can be assumed that the distance between the two lines of
demarcación represents 180° of longitude. The distance from Callao to the eastern
extremity of the Y^{as}. *de Salamon* represents only one-fifth of that total distance
or 36°, but by no calculation can this be reconciled with Velasco's stated distance
of 1,500 leagues. Velasco accepted the equatorial degree of longitude as being
20 leagues or 70 Italian (Roman) miles, so that 36° would represent 720 leagues
or 2,520 Roman miles. The attribution of Velasco's underestimate to deliberate
falsification, a popular kind of explanation, is negated by the existence of a
figure close to the actual reported distance of the Solomons from Perú in his
narrative. Similarly, its attribution to a desire to show that the Solomons were
within the Spanish hemisphere can in turn be negated by plotting 1,500
leagues westwards from Perú on his chart, according to his scale of 20 leagues
to the equatorial degree, when it will be seen that a point 1,500 leagues distant
from Perú would still be well within the Spanish hemisphere. The only reasonable explanation is that Velasco did not accept the figure of 1,500 leagues as
definite when he prepared the chart.

[1] In his letter to the King (Zaragoza 1876: II: 15 *et seq*), Mendaña mistakenly reported that three
islands were sighted to the SW of Santa Ysabel, named *San Marcos, San Jerónimo* and *Ysla de Recifes*.
In fact the islands sighted were San Nicolás (Vangunu?) and Ysla de Arracifes (New Georgia?). *San
Jerónimo* may have been the name given to the background hills of New Georgia. San Márcos was of
course Choiseul.   [2] JCB: Velasco, f73v.
[3] After his separation from Legazpi's expedition of 1564–5. Urdaneta made the return voyage two
months later.

It is clear from the configuration of the Yslas de Salomón (*Yas. d. Salamon*) that their detail was added after Velasco had obtained information of them, for they are laid down in a form roughly reduced from that of the chart *Descripcion de las Yndias del Poniente*. However, if we recall that the *Western Isles* were expected to be found 600 leagues from Perú, 'because the *Señor Presidente* had said that',[1] and if we also convert Velasco's distance of 36° into leagues at the alternative, and then still acceptable, value of $16\frac{2}{3}$ leagues to the degree,[2] it can be seen that Velasco's chart, on that scale, lays down the Yslas de Salomón 600 leagues from Perú. This can be suggested as evidence that Velasco, or a cartographer on whose prototype he based his chart, had prepared a chart on which the *Western Isles* were laid down at the distance from Perú at which they were expected to be found, and that, perhaps because he had already distributed or published charts on which they were so laid down and was reluctant to recant, even after he had learned that the Yslas de Salomón were 1,500 leagues from Perú, he still laid them down in the position in which he had previously laid down the *Western Isles*.

This suggestion may be reinforced by a comparison of his chart of the *Yndias del Poniente* with the chart *Demarcacion y Nauegaciones de Yndias*. On the former it can be seen that the coastline of *Nu(v)eva Guinea* has been longitudinally shortened, and that the Yslas de Salomón are relatively much closer to the Moluccas and South-East Asia than on the smaller scale chart, perhaps indicating that Velasco had corrected his earlier error and had necessarily reduced the longitudinal extension of Nueva Guinea to enable the Yslas de Salomón to be located 1,500 leagues from Perú.

A map which has a tentative claim to being perhaps second to Velasco's two charts in depicting the Solomons at an early date, is Chart No. 15 in a MS. atlas of 18 folios in the Huntingdon Library.[3] Cortesão states of this map that it was described in the catalogue of its sale as being 'on native paper, probably executed at . . . Macao, about 1580',[4] and he agrees with the dating. The style is a little behind that of contemporary Portuguese cartography, although a colonial origin would explain this, but if a colonial origin is to be postulated it can hardly be dated with such certainty from the style alone, and Cortesão admits the possibility of a later date. If it is of 1580, then it is perhaps the first Portuguese, and certainly one of the earliest extra-Hispanic maps, to show the Solomons. Although the Solomons are not named, either individually or collectively, the islands laid down close to the eastern extremity of the similarly unnamed New Guinea are recognizable as the Solomons, and by comparison with Velasco's chart, the islands of Ysabel, Malaíta, Santiago, San Cristóval, and probably Las Tres Marías, Guadalcanal, Sesarga, Arracifes, San Nicolás and San Márcos, can be identified. It is, however, extremely doubtful

---

[1] Amherst 1901: I: 8.   [2] $36° \times 16\frac{2}{3} = 600$ leagues.
[3] HL: HM 39, f15.   [4] Cortesão 1935: I: 168.

if its date of origin is as early as 1580, although it is certainly an early map on which the Solomons appear.

The first definite example of cartographical knowledge of the archipelago outside Spain is to be found in two maps by Abraham Ortelius dated 1587, the world-map *Typus Orbis Terrarum* in his *Theatrum Orbis Terrarum* of 1590,[1] and his *Americae sive Novi Orbis Nova Descriptio*.[2] Whilst these maps are significant, they are less important in this context than Ortelius' *Maris Pacifici* (*quod vulgo Mar del Zur cum regionibus circumiacentibus, insulis que in eodem passim sparsis novissima descriptio*)[3] of 1589, from which they differ slightly. The map *Maris Pacifici* lays the *Insulae Salomonis* down in close proximity to *Nova Guinea*, as do the two former maps, extending over some 18° of longitude, with their eastern extremities 72° W of Callao,[4] and between the latitudes of 1° and 10° S. *Nova Guinea* is itself exaggerated in size, and the easterly error of its position, relative to Perú, is but one aspect of the typically underestimated width of the Pacific. The configuration of the *Insulae Salomonis* is similar on all three maps, and generally similar to that of the charts of Baena and Velasco, although San Márcos is omitted. There is some distortion of the position of the *Isola Atreguada* in relation to *Nombre de Iesus*, and, unlike the Velasco chart, the coastlines are all filled in to give a complete representation of an archipelago. On the map *Maris Pacifici* the position of the group of five islands between *Maialata* (Malaíta), *Guadalcanal* and *Isabella* (Ysabel), with the name *Buena Vista*, is a considerably more accurate representation of the Nggela Group, as reported by Gallego and as they in fact exist, than that of either the Baena or Velasco charts. *Nombre de Iesus* is, as is to be expected, located close to Malaíta; San Cristóval and Santiago are recognizable, though unnamed, as a divided San Cristóval; and, unlike Velasco, Ortelius lays down Malaíta (*Maialata*) as one island. Whilst generally similar to the charts of Baena and Velasco, the Solomons configuration on the Ortelius maps, particularly in their clearest form on his *Maris Pacifici*, have certain features indicative of derivation from another source, or of a more correct derivation from the same or a similar prototype. Whilst such differences can be attributed to an attempt to reconcile a

[1] Wroth 1944: Plate XIV; Amherst 1901: I: lxxiii; Wagner 1937: II: No. 148. Although it did not appear in the *Theatrum* until 1590, the map is dated 1587, and was presumably published individually. I have only examined it in the *Theatrum* of 1601.

[2] In the *Theatrum* of 1601, later, and possibly earlier editions. See also Wagner 1937: II: No. 147. This map is strikingly different from the *Typus Orbis Terrarum* in that it shows New Guinea attached to *Terra Australis*. In the *Theatrum* of 1590 this map does not depict the Solomons.

[3] It first appeared in the *Additamentum* to the *Theatrum* of 1590, a copy of which is in Trinity College Library, Cambridge, and later as Map 6 in the *Theatrum* of 1592. It appears, however, to have been published separately in 1589, the date which it bears (Skelton 1958: Fig 128; Amherst 1901: I: 1).

[4] In this latter respect the map *Maris Pacifici* differs from the *Typus Orbis Terrarum* and the *Americae sive Novi Orbis . . .*, the two latter maps laying the islands down over 23° of longitude, with their eastern extremities 57° and 61°, respectively, W of Callao.

8

prototype with the actual narratives of discovery, these few charts and maps already examined offer some suggestion that more than one prototype did exist.

In his *The First Discovery of Australia and New Guinea*, Collingridge reproduces a map which he reputes to be by Mazza and describes as the earliest known map of the Solomons.[1] Coote, in the Introduction to Müller's *Reproduction of Remarkable Maps . . .*, refers to a map reproduced in that work,[2]

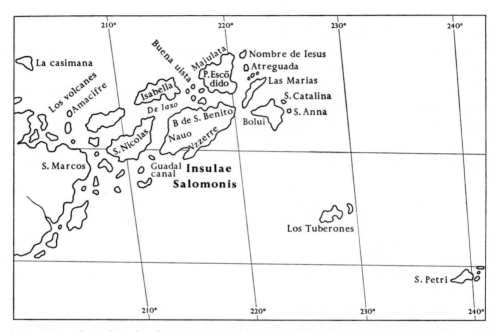

Map XII   Enlarged and redrawn section from Mazza's *Americae et Proximar* of *c.* 1589, after Ortelius

entitled *Americae et Proximar Regionvm Orae Descriptio* and of about 1583, as 'a clever adaptation by Gio. Babtista Mazza the engraver of the "Maris Pacifici" map dated 1589'.[3] This appears to be the map to which Collingridge refers and which he reproduces. Neither Collingridge, Coote nor Müller adduce any evidence for the date 1583, and whilst it is possible that Ortelius' map may have been in the engraver's hands some time prior to 1589, there seems no reason to deduce that it was as early as 1583 or that Mazza published his plagiarized version immediately, even though Mazza's position as an engraver rather than a cartographer, and his access to the *Maris Pacifici* map, do support the allegation of plagiarism. One thing is certain: that Mazza's map was not the earliest published map of the Solomons.

[1] Collingridge 1906: 72.
[2] Müller 1843: I: Plate 12. The map is from the Bodel Nyenhus Collection.
[3] Müller 1843: I: 12.

The Solomons appear again on a map by Bartolomeo Lasso, in his *Este Libro de Cosmographia denevegar fey Bertholomeu Laso Ano de 1590*,[1] which is discussed by Cortesão.[2] This map is important in relation to a map by Petrus Plancius, *Nova et Exacta Terrarum Orbis Tabula Geographica ac Hydrographica*, published concurrently in Amsterdam and Antwerp by Claesz and Vrient in 1592. Discussing this latter map, Wieder indicates Plancius' indebtedness to a Portuguese world-map which he had obtained, to Mercator's world-map of 1569, and his use of the former when he found the latter less well informed, as it was in all that pertained to navigation.[3] He adds that Plancius had purchased a planisphere by Lasso in Lisbon[4] and, although this has not survived, concludes that the series of special maps by Lasso dated 1590 probably agree with the planisphere, and uses them to judge the extent of Plancius' indebtedness to Mercator and the Portuguese map. One of these special maps by Lasso is his *Map of New Guinea and the Solomon Islands*, and Wieder remarks of it, and of Plancius' planisphere, that

on the eastern part of his planisphere Plancius shows New Guinea as part of the great southern continent, but on the western part he follows Laso's picture, and adds his Islas de Salamon. . . . The Solomon Islands of Laso are entirely devoid of names, which may be due to incompleteness. On Plancius the names are given.[5]

The publication of Lasso's[6] maps, and their use by Plancius, affords another instance of probable derivation from copies of prototypes held by the Spanish authorities, for Lasso's appointment as Cosmographer Royal would have provided him with ready access to the chart or charts prepared during Mendaña's expedition.

Another earlier map by Plancius, dated 1590, is his *Orbis Terrarum Typus de Integro Multis in Locis Emendatus*.[7] On this the Solomons extend over some 20° of longitude, are laid down 2° E of New Guinea, with their eastern extremities 62° W of Callao, and reflect considerable indebtedness to Ortelius. On the planisphere of 1592, however, the Solomons extend over 15° of longitude, and are laid down between 8° S and 17° S, with their eastern extremities 82° W of Perú, their western extremities $2\frac{1}{2}°$ E of New Guinea. The Pacific distance of 82°[8] is a considerable improvement on that of the maps already examined, and much closer to the estimated distance recorded by the *expedicionarios*. On

[1] Reproduced in Mollema 1925: Plate LXVI, Map XII. See also Mollema 1925: 408 *et seq.*

[2] Cortesão 1935; II: 286–9. See also Cortesão 1915: 269–74.

[3] Wieder 1925: II: 33–34, Plates 26 and 31.

[4] According to the resolutions of the States General, in 1592 'the printer, Cornelius Claesz . . . had obtained, with the help of Plancius, from Bartolomeo de Lasso, 'Cosmographer of the King of Spain', a collection of sea charts of the whole world, with descriptions of the sailing routes' (Linschoten 1885: xxxii). 　　　　　　　　[5] Wieder 1925: II: 35.

[6] The name is either Lasso or Laso. 　　　[7] BM: PS 0/8955, 920(279).

[8] On the equator 82° would be 1,435 leagues (at $17\frac{1}{2}$ leagues to the equatorial degree), and in 10° S would be 1,413 leagues. Alternatively, at 20 leagues to the degree, it would be 1,615 leagues in 10° S.

both of the maps of Plancius the configuration of the Solomons is generally similar to that of Velasco, but with the enclosure of the southern and north-eastern coastlines, and in the maps of Velasco, Lasso and Plancius can be seen the emergence of a distinct configurative pattern, thereafter continually reproduced with only minor variations. In 1594 Blundeville published a description of Plancius' planisphere in which he wrote:

Magellanica. This is the sixt part of the worlde, which as yet is but little knowne, in such sort as we cannot write anything touching the provinces of the same, notwithstanding it is thought the arovince of Beach is verie rich, and hath abundance of Golde, the chief iles of Magellanica pre these Iava maior, and Iava minor, Timor, Banda, the Molucques, Romeros, the Iles of Salomon.[1]

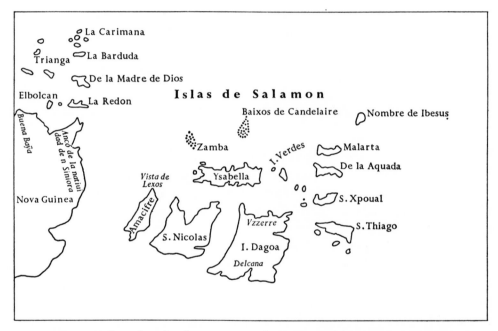

Map XIII   Enlarged and redrawn section from de Jode's *Novae Guineae* of 1593

A map almost identical to Plancius' world-map of 1592 is Cornelius de Jode's *Novae Guineae, Forma et Situs* in his *Speculum Orbis Terrae* of 1593. It is accompanied by a commentary referring to the *Golden Khersonese, Oriental India*, and *Tharsim Auriferam regionem*. New Guinea appears on the map as an island, though de Jode follows Plancius who, in an inscription, admits his ignorance as to whether or not New Guinea is insular or continental, declaring: '*Continens nē ad terrā Australē, an Insula sit, incognitā est*'. In the *Speculum* . . . appears another map, an antarctic polar-projected hemisphere, entitled *Hemispheriv̄ ab Aeqvinoctiali Linea, ad Circulv̄ Poli Ātarctici*, which certainly

[1] In the footnote to Plancius' planisphere in the British Museum.

pre-dates the map of 1593 and is significant primarily for its projection and the vast *Ter Australis incognita* which it portrays.

In 1594 Plancius produced another world-map, his *Orbis Terrarum Typus de Integro Multis in Locis Emendatus*.[1] Here the configuration of the Solomons is generally similar to that of his world-map of 1592, but the hypothetical southern coastlines of Guadalcanal, San Nicolás and *Arracifre*[2] have been obliterated, and open coastlines similar to those of Velasco's charts replace them, suggesting continental promontories. The archipelago itself extends over 15°, and its eastern extremities are approximately 84° W of Callao.

There is evidence to suggest that a further edition of Plancius' planisphere was published in London in 1595, although no definitely identifiable copy has yet been discovered. In the Nederlandsch Historisch Scheepvaart Museum, Amsterdam, is a single sheet of a second edition planisphere, which may or may not be part of the London edition. Wieder notes that the watermark may date it around 1605–6, indicating perhaps that the planisphere was re-printed in Amsterdam at that time by Henricus Hondius, and concludes:

This single unique sheet, identical neither with the ... 1592 map nor the ... map of Van Langren, shows ... how many original maps may have been entirely lost and how cautious we must be when building theories, remembering that existing documents form only a part of the total number actually produced.[3]

It consists of an antarctic polar hemisphere, significant in that it depicts the Solomons in the form of Plancius' map of 1592, but at a distance of 85° from Perú, and of a map of the East Indies which is of interest in this context only because it depicts *Beach, Maletur* and *Lucach*.

The *Hemisphere* of Theodore de Bry, of 1596,[4] shows the Solomons with a configuration which seems to be a further adaptation of the earliest maps. On the Plancius map of 1594 we saw the insular character of Guadalcanal, San Nicolás and Arracifes abandoned in favour of the alternative Velasco-type open coastlines suggestive of continental promontories. On de Bry's *Hemisphere* these coastlines are rejoined as a whole, with the result that one large island is formed out of what was earlier depicted as the separate islands of Guadalcanal (*Dagoa*), San Nicolás and Arracifes, bearing the name *Dagoa*. This in itself may reflect an attempt to illustrate the supposed continental character of Guadalcanal, but the firm separation from the austral continent may reflect Gallego's belief that Guadalcanal was a large island.

[1] In the BM copy of Linschoten's *Itinerario* of 1604–5. See also the reproduction in Hakluyt 1903: IX.

[2] Only *Dagoa* (Guadalcanal) and *Arracifre* (Arracifes) are named, and the *S. Nicolas* of the planisphere of 1592 appears unnamed as two promontories.

[3] Wieder 1925: II: 56, and Plate 40 ter.

[4] Forrest 1779: Plate XIV; Fleurieu 1790: Chart X; Dalrymple 1770: I: 16.

Two maps by Fausto Rughesi, dated Rome, 1597, his *Carta dell Americana* and *Mappiamondo*,[1] illustrate a total divergence from the configurations of the Solomons so far noted; so extreme in fact, and so different even between themselves, that one is tempted to conclude that Rughesi laid down a collection of islands, collectively in close proximity to *Nova Guinea*, but individually at random, and applied to them the nomenclature of the *Isole de Salomone*. On the *Carta dell Americana* the archipelago is laid down between 3° S and 23° S, 65° W of Callao, and on the *Mappiamondo* 60° W of Callao; but a significant feature of both maps, particularly the latter, is that the longitudinal extent of the Solomons has been reduced to some 10°–12°.

In 1597 Cornille Wytfliet produced his *Descriptionis Ptolemaicae Augmentum* [2] which contained a map, *Chica sive Patagonia et Australis Terra*,[3] delineating the *Insulae Salomonis* in close proximity to *Nova Guinea*, extending over 20° of longitude, and with a configuration generally similar to that of Ortelius' *Maris Pacifici*. In the text Wytfliet wrote:

Du costé droit sont ioinctes à la Guinee les Isles Salomoniennes, qui sont de large estendue & de grande nombre, & qui furét dernierement decouuertes par Aluarez Médanie, car luy desireux de la pousser la fortune & de chercher des regions non encore cognues, desancra d'vn port du Peru dit Linano, apres auoir nauigé trois mois continuels, ayant touiours le vent Oriental en poupe, vint aborder en ces Isles lesquelles il nōma Salomoniennes, plustot à la volée que pour quelque certaine raison: car de la flotte que Salomon envoya és regions d'Ophir & de Tarsis de laquelle fait mention le 3 livre des Roys au Chap. 9. & 12. nous avons beaucoup de raisons & d'arguments qui nous sont croire qu'elle ayt tiré deuers l'Orient.[4]

One of the major Dutch cartographers of the late sixteenth century was the celebrated Jan Huychen (Huighen) van Linschoten who, returning to Holland in 1592 after six years residence in Goa, gave considerable impetus to the development of a Dutch Far Eastern trade by the publication of three works, his *Reys-gheschrift Vande Navigatien der Portugaloysers in Orienten* of 1595, and his *Voyage ofte Schipvaert . . .* and *Beschryvinghe van de gantsche Custe van Guinea* of 1596, published together in 1596 as his *Itinerario*. Apart from containing the Plancius world-map of 1594, the *Itinerario* also contains a chart of the East Indies, destined to play an important part in the Dutch expansion to the East.[5] This chart does not show the Solomons, but in the British Museum copy of *John Huighen van Linschoten his discours of Voyages unto ye Easte and West Indies*, printed in London in 1598 by John Wolfe and the earliest English translation of the *Itinerario*, occurs a chart entitled *Insulae Moluccae*. [6] This

[1] Amalgià 1948: IV: Plates 23 and 25.

[2] Wytfliet 1597; Wytfliet 1605. The latter is the French version, published at Douay in 1605, under the title *Histoire Universelle des Indes Orientales et Occidentales*.

[3] Wytfliet 1605: 70–71.   [4] Wytfliet 1605: 71–72; Wytfliet 1597: 101.

[5] Wroth 1944: 192–3, Plate XV; Nordenskiöld 1897: Plate LX (dated incorrectly 1599).

[6] See Hakluyt 1903: XI: Endpiece. For a discussion of the English edition of the *Itinerario* see Burnell's comments in Linschoten 1885: xxiii–lii.

chart is identical with a later chart by Visscher, known to have been derived from Linschoten, and whilst it is generally assumed that Linschoten derived much of his cartography from Portuguese sources and prototypes, many of his charts bear a striking resemblance to those of Lasso's *Atlas* of 1590, and the chart *Insulae Moluccae* may derive as much from Lasso, through Claesz, who acquired a collection of sea-charts by Lasso in 1592 and was associated with Plancius, as from a Portuguese source. In view of Linschoten's knowledge of

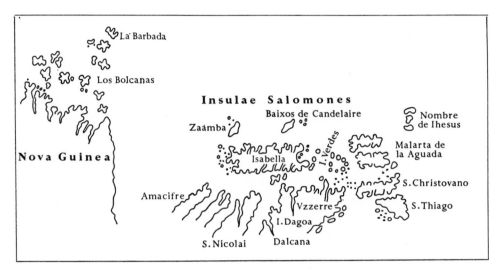

Map XIV   Enlarged and redrawn reproduction of relevant detail on Wolfe's *Map of the Moluccas* of 1598, after Linschoten

the Portuguese possessions in the Far East, and his association with Claesz[1] and Plancius, this chart is clearly of major importance.[2] In the Linschoten-Plancius-Claesz association, linked with Lasso, we have considerable evidence of the direct derivation of Dutch charts from official Spanish sources, evidence which is confirmed, not only by Lasso's position as Cosmographer Royal, but also by the similarity between the configuration of the Solomons on charts by Visscher and Linschoten and their configuration on the charts of Velasco.

The publication of Linschoten's *Itinerario* in England in 1598 almost certainly exerted a major influence on the English cartography of the Pacific. This is reflected on a world-map of 1598–1600, known variously as the *Shakespeare New Map*, the *Molyneux-Hakluyt* or *Wright-Molyneux* map, now generally accepted to be the work of Edward Wright and 'sometimes, but rarely found in copies of the Second Edition of the Principall Navigations' of

---

[1] Claesz also printed the *Itinerario*.

[2] The chart *Insulae Moluccae* of Visscher, 1617, and a section of the Wolfe chart of 1598 have been reproduced.

Hakluyt,[1] on which an inscription in the top right hand corner refers to the voyage of 'Francis Gaulle a Spaniard in the yeare 1584', and is almost certainly derived from Linschoten's account in his *Reys-gheschrift* . . . of the voyage of Francisco Galli from Macao to Acapulco, the first printed account of a return voyage across the Pacific.[2] However, whilst the configuration of the Solomons on the *Wright-Molyneux* map is similar to that on the map by Wolfe, *Insulae*

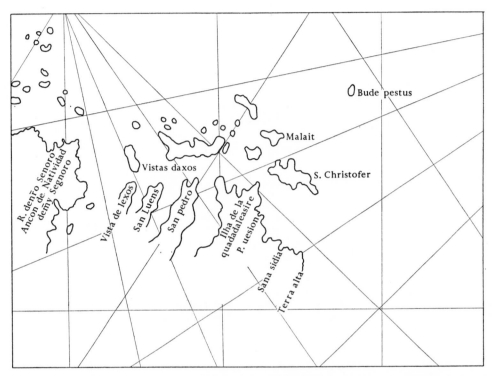

Map XV   Enlarged and redrawn section from the *Shakespeare New* or *Wright-Molyneux* map of 1598-1600

Moluccae, derived from Linschoten, it is considerably more akin to that of the *Molyneux Globe* of 1603. The authorship of the *Wright-Molyneux* map is, as its several names suggest, rather an open question; some scholars arguing that it is the work of Edward Wright,[3] though Linton, a contemporary of Wright's who wrote in praise of his work, only admitted that the map was based on his projection. A relationship with Molyneux seems impossible to

[1] Hakluyt 1903: I: xii. 'it is now believed to be the Map alluded to by Shakespeare in "Twelfth Night", Act III, Scene 2, in the passage "He does not smile his face into more lines than is in the new map with the augmentation of the Indies" ' (Hakluyt 1903: I: xii).

[2] See Hakluyt 1903: IX: 326–37, where the account of the voyage is given.

[3] See for instance Markham 1880: lxxxv–xcv, where C. H. Coote argues this authorship of a version of the *New Map*, slightly different from the one in Hakluyt 1903: I: Endpiece, published as an annexure to Markham 1880. See also Nordenskiöld 1889: Plate L.

avoid or dismiss, and from this relationship an interesting conjecture emerges. The *Molyneux Globes* of 1592 at Petworth, and of 1603 in the Middle Temple, London, show the Solomons as *Insulae Salomonis* with a configuration similar in a general way to that of the maps of Wolfe, Linschoten and Velasco, particularly in their open southern coastlines and continental suggestion, and similar to the maps of Wytfliet, Mazza and Ortelius in showing only three large islands on the eastern perimeter of the archipelago. Most important of all, however, is the inscription naming the islands Islands of Jesus 'or commonly Islands of Solomon', and attributing their discovery to Sarmiento in Spanish phraseology strikingly reminiscent of the actual phrases used by Sarmiento in reference to the archipelago. Not only may this indicate the influence of Sarmiento on English cartography, a direct result of his sojourn in England as a prisoner and later as a welcome and informative guest, but it may also indicate that of the charts and maps which have been examined a considerable number may derive from a prototype prepared by him.

Obviously, with the limited extant charts available, and allowing for the errors and idiosyncrasies of successive cartographers, any firm judgement would be futile and audacious. It may, however, be suggested that in attempting to analyse and classify historical maps configuration is more important than nomenclature, itself all too susceptible to errors of transcription as the nomenclature of the Solomons on the *Molyneux Globe* illustrates.[1] In the possible influence of Sarmiento on Solomons cartography, as the creator of a prototype and later as the creator of a new or adaptor of existing English maps, may perhaps be evidenced the validity of this opinion. In other words, if Sarmiento's association with English cartography is to be deduced from his residence in England and from Molyneux's reference to him, then it seems reasonable to conclude that earlier maps, Spanish or of probable Spanish derivation, which are similar in configuration to these English maps with which he would seem to have been associated, may illustrate the form of his original prototype.

A final comment on the *Wright-Molyneux* map is necessary, since it is particularly important in laying down the Solomons 90° W of Callao. The map is itself based on the English degree value of 20 leagues, so that in the latitude of 10° S 90° of longitude would represent 1,773 leagues, but it is possible that in plotting a reported distance in Spanish leagues English cartographers used the Spanish value for the degree of $17\frac{1}{2}$ leagues, so that 90° would represent 1,550 leagues.[2] In either case the distance is much closer to that

---

[1] For instance Molyneux renders Nombre de Jesús as *Tumbu de prosus*, Malay as *Naloj* and Baxos de la Candelaria as *Baixos de la cancalana*. The suggestion that the *Molyneux Globe* owes much to Sarmiento has also been made by Wallis. My own recognition of this rather obvious possible derivation was, however, reached before I had read Wallis' work on this subject, and the suggestion is perhaps strengthened by this independently dual recognition.

[2] At 20 leagues to the degree 90° represents 1,800 leagues on the equator, or 1,773 leagues in 10° S. At $17\frac{1}{2}$ leagues to the degree 90° represents 1,575 leagues on the equator, or 1,550 leagues in 10° S.

reported by the *expedicionarios* than are the distances laid down on the earlier charts and maps so far examined. This may in itself only be due to the fact that the *Wright-Molyneux* map reflects the improved concept of the width of the Pacific which began to prevail after Linschoten's publication of the account of the voyage of Francisco Galli, and that the more correct positioning of the Solomons relative to the distance from Perú estimated by the discoverers themselves was an accidental result of applying this improved Pacific width, for the inscription on the map reads:

It appeareth by discoverie of Francis Gaulle a Spaniard, in the year 1584, that the sea betweene the west part of America and the east of Asia [which hath bene ordinarily set out as a straight and named in most maps the streight of Anian] is above 1,200 leagues wide at the latitude of 38 degr.

An English map of the late sixteenth century on which the Islands of Solomon are laid down in a way similar to the Linschoten chart is the *Map of the Pacific* of Gabriel Tatton in the National Library, Florence.[1] In a note on this map Caraci suggests that:

the cartographer wanted to design above all what was known of the Pacific Ocean in his time, and particularly the islands which lie between the eastern coast of Asia, the Japanese Archipelago and the Solomon Islands. . . . The periplus of Java, New Guinea and the Solomon Islands is left indeterminate southwards, so that we cannot see which is the real conception our cartographer had of Terra Australis. The outline and nomenclature of New Guinea do not show fortuitous coincidences with the printed Dutch and Italian maps of the second half of the 16th and early years of the 17th century.[2] However, there are no sufficient reasons to exclude that such coincidences instead of deriving from the printed maps, came from the Iberian models, which served as prototypes for the same charts.[3]

He describes the outline of New Guinea and the Solomons as 'like that in the Herrera map (1601)',[4] but adds that 'there are some data showing that Tatton cannot descend from Herrera (see for instance the spelling Ballona instead of Vallena, Susana instead of S. Ana, the position of Rio S. Augustin)'. It is doubtful, however, if any of the details mentioned by Caraci do disprove descent from one source or another, for nomenclature in particular is subject to linguistic variation, illegibility in the prototype, and the human error of the cartographer; and the use of other prototypes for comparative purposes could well result in the intrusion of differences. Caraci is perhaps misled in relating Tatton's work to Herrera, for Herrera's maps were derived from Velasco, with differences which are not relative to either the configuration of New Guinea or the Solomons; and to the extent to which any comparison can be

---

[1] Caraci 1926: I: Plates XV, XVII. National Library, Florence, Port No. 33.

[2] See Hamy 1896: 187.

[3] Caraci 1926: I: 12–15. Caraci's negative 'do not show fortuitous' seems to be incorrect in this context and should presumably read 'do show fortuitous'.

[4] The Herrera map of 1601 is examined later, it was derived from Velasco.

made, it should be with Velasco, Linschoten and contemporary English maps, charts and globes.

Antonio de Herrera's *Descripcion de las Yndias Occidentales*, published in Madrid in 1601, was an expansion of Velasco's *Demarcacion ... of* 1575–80.[1] Describing the discovery of the *Insulae Salomonis* which, unlike Velasco, he attributes to 'Alvarus de Mendoza', he writes: '*Insulae Salomonis 800 à Peru leucis nomen illud fortitate sunt, propter conceptam de ijs magnarum opum+divitarum opinionem*', but he continues several lines later: '*Sitae sunt inter gradus altit, polaris* 7+12 *ad latus Aequatoris meridionale* 1500 *penè ab urbe de los Reyes leucis*'.[2]

The inclusion of both the 1,500 leagues recorded by Velasco and the conflicting and contradictory 800 leagues of other chroniclers in his text, as the distance of the Solomons from Perú, is confusing. It is likely that Herrera was confused by the discrepancy between Velasco's textual figure of 1,500 leagues, and the much shorter distance at which the Solomons were laid down on his general chart *Demarcacion y Nauegaciones*, but he departs from Velasco in his own version of this chart, his *Descripcion de las Yndias Ocidentalis*, by laying down the *Yas de Salamon* some 75° W of Callao.

In the introduction to his *Descripcion* he discusses the several current concepts of the linear length of an equatorial degree, and though he seems to prefer the value of 17½ leagues or 70 Roman miles,[3] he also refers to the value of 60 Roman miles or 20 leagues. If the position of the Solomons on his chart is to be reconciled with the stated distance of 1,500 leagues, then it seems likely that he has laid off 75° as 1,500 leagues (i.e. 20 leagues to the equatorial degree)[4] or 4,500 Roman miles (at 3 Roman miles to the league). Alternatively, if the 75° are laid down as equatorial degrees of 17½ leagues or 70 Roman miles, then they would represent 1,312½ leagues or 5,250 Roman miles; a shorter distance in 'leagues' but a longer distance in Roman miles. To the extent to which, by one value of the degree, his chart does conform with the textual distance of 1,500 leagues, Herrera improves on Velasco; and he improves even further in conforming the position of the Solomons on his detailed East-Indian chart *Descripcion de las Indias del Poniente* with their position on the former. Since his detailed local chart is similar to Velasco's, it appears that all he has done is to correct the small-scale chart and remove Velasco's inconsistency, although he has added a longitudinal scale to both charts.

The inclusion of the 800 leagues recorded by other chroniclers such as Acosta can only be explained as an attempt to obtain the best of both worlds

---

[1] See Herrera 1622, the Latin edition of his *Descripcion* under the title *Novus Orbis sive Descriptio Indiae Occidentalis*.   [2] Herrera 1622: Chapter XXVII.

[3] Herrera concludes his comments on the degree by preferring the degree of 17 leagues, but this appears to be a misprint for 17½.

[4] No allowance being made for the decreased length of a degree at 10° S.

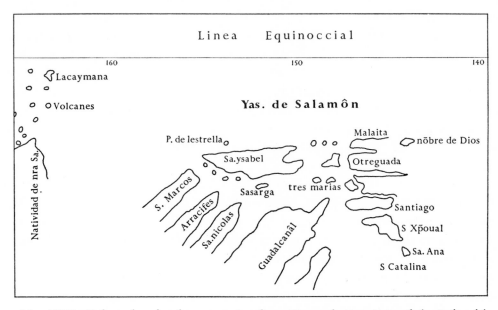

Map XVI   Enlarged and redrawn section from Herrera's *Descripcion de las Indias del Poniente* of 1601

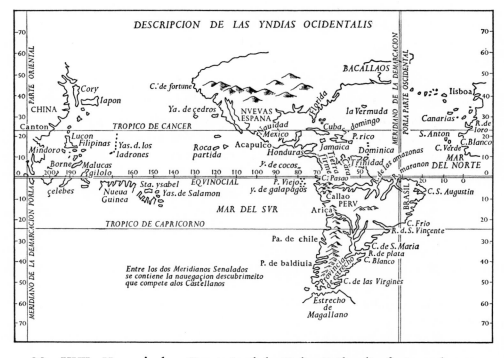

Map XVII   Herrera's chart *Descripcion de las Yndias Ocidentalis* of 1601, redrawn

and to guard against the possibility of error by reporting both of the figures then current or available to him. He follows Velasco in his description of the islands in the archipelago and their relative positions and sizes, omits the supposed southern continent from his charts, and remarks of New Guinea:

The coast of new Guinea begins 100 leagues to the east of the island of Gilolo in approximately 1° S and stretches from there to the east 300 leagues until it goes up to 5° or 6° S. It has been doubtful up to now whether it is an island or mainland, extending as it does for such a distance as to be possibly conjoined with the land of the Solomon Islands or to the Provinces on the S side of the Magellan Straits. But this doubt has been resolved by the affirmation of those who have travelled S of the Magellan Straits, namely, that there is no continent there, but only islands, and that the Straits are succeeded immediately by a vast sea.

In the preceding pages an attempt has been made to provide some indication of the types of maps and charts which laid down the Islands of Solomon within a period of thirty years following their discovery. No reference has been made to the large body of extant maps of that period which do not show the Solomons, the aim of the study being to indicate the extent to which the islands were mapped, the extent to which some knowledge of them was consequently available in Europe, and the several dominant forms which the configuration of the archipelago took on those maps. Wieder's comment on the extant charts of the period derived from Iberian sources is still valid, for:

The study of early Portuguese and Spanish cartography is not yet so far advanced that we can describe with any certainty the development of the official Spanish world-map, the *padrón-real*, or decide from what sources the maps privately printed were derived, and whether their authors had access to the *padrón-real* or not. Owing to our scanty knowledge of the relatively poor remains which survive from the total output of maps of the first 'colonial' century, there is naturally much confusion of relationship . . . and it is hardly possible to establish a direct affinity between any two of them.[1]

Nevertheless it is possible and necessary to indicate such evidence of affinity and derivation as does exist; and although much of the once extant material is no longer available, one can only hope that it is reasonable, particularly when dealing with one limited feature of the maps available, to assume that those which are still extant do represent a cross-section of the original material. In this particular case, this assumption seems to be supported by the limited variation in the configuration of the Solomons.

It is doubtful, however, if any certain conclusions are to be derived from a comparison of the different forms which the Solomons take on the maps examined, and it is certain that no definite direct derivation can be so adduced. It does seem likely that the extant material derives from more than one prototype prepared during or as a result of the expedition of 1567–9, but it is quite impossible to decide what form these took. It is of course quite possible that all the material derives from one prototype, the differences which subsequently

[1] Weider 1932: I: 36.

developed between its many derivatives being the result of erroneous copying, brief access to a prototype, or the adaptation of the maps to conform with some particular information which the cartographer possessed. It is possible, for instance, that the open southern coastlines found on several of the maps examined were an adaptation, perhaps by Velasco, of a prototype which showed the islands with complete coastlines; an adaptation made in the knowledge that the southern coastlines had not been seen or explored, and in the belief that a southern continent did exist.

If anything should be emphasized about the several maps and charts examined, it is their generally correct delineation of the archipelago as it seemed to appear to its discoverers, with the addition to that delineation of such coastlines as could reasonably be deduced. Five general features are worthy of note: the cartographical knowledge of the Solomons in Europe at the end of the sixteenth century which they reflect; their delineation of the Solomons in close proximity to New Guinea; their exaggeration of the size and extent of the Solomons; the varied underestimated width of the Pacific which they demonstrate; and their laying down of the Solomons at a distance equal to or even less than that which the *expedicionarios* had underestimated from Perú.

If we accept the width of the Pacific as the distance between Panama and the Philippines and as 150°, it can be seen that the maps examined display considerable diversity in their degree of accuracy. Leaving aside the charts of Diego Ribeiro, which, with the Pacific laid down 134° in width from the Moluccas to Central America, are a possible indication of a more correct knowledge of the width of the Pacific by the Spanish authorities than might generally be supposed, Velasco's Pacific, 97° wide, is typical of the period. The publication of Linschoten's *Reys-gheschrift* in 1595, with its reference to the voyage of Francisco Galli from Macao to Acapulco, and its report that in 38° N the Pacific was 1,200 leagues wide, certainly contributed considerably to an improved concept of the width of the Pacific, although as early as 1563 Galvano had stated in his *Tratado* that in 32° N the Pacific extended from 1,000 to 1,200 leagues.[1]

One immediate consequence of the underestimated Pacific was that, since the position of New Guinea was plotted in relation to its known distance from the East Indies, the position in which the Solomons were laid down was itself dictated by the position of New Guinea, even if the eastern extremity of the latter was laid down closer to Perú than the position in which the *expedicionarios* had reported the Solomons to lie. Recalling that all that was known of New Guinea was its western extremity and its northern coast as far E as the position in 5° S reached by Íñigo Ortiz de Retes in 1545, or something like half of its actual longitudinal extent, it might be expected that this would have compensated for the underestimated width of the Pacific by permitting a

[1] Galvano 1862: 210.

more westerly delineation of the Solomons than if the total extent of New Guinea had been known. In fact the reverse occurred, for on almost all the charts examined New Guinea's northern coastline is itself exaggerated in extent, due perhaps to the supposition of its continental character and the tendency of sixteenth-century pilots and cartographers to exaggerate little known coastlines.

This is perhaps the principal reason why on several of the maps examined we have to contend not only with the underestimated distance of the Solomons from Perú reported by the expedition of 1567–9 but also with a further under-estimate by the cartographer himself.

Except where a scale is given on the map in question, we cannot be certain what a degree represents in leagues, although it seems likely that even on non-Iberian charts and maps the cartographer generally laid down 'Spanish' leagues at the value of $17\frac{1}{2}$ to the equatorial degree. Examining the several maps which have been reproduced and discussed, a gradual improvement in the positioning of the Solomons relative to Perú is to be observed, until on those, for example, of Herrera and the *Wright-Molyneux*, they are laid down at least at distances closer to if not exactly that recorded by the *expedicionarios*. This improvement was the direct result of an improving concept of the width of the Pacific, and for the moment at least it did not reveal the underestimate of the distance of the Solomons from Perú. It was not in fact until the next century, as the Pacific became increasingly more correctly delineated and as the limits of New Guinea became known, that New Guinea was moved further to the west and more correctly charted and that the problem of whether or not the Solomons should be laid down in close proximity to New Guinea, as on the charts of the late sixteenth century, or should be laid down at the distance at which they were reported by their discoverers to lie from Perú, emerged.

At the end of the sixteenth century there were therefore in existence in Europe a not inconsiderable body of charts and maps which laid down the Solomons with a recognizable configuration, within relatively correct lati-tudinal bounds, and reasonably correctly positioned in relation to New Guinea. Using such charts navigators could, had they been prepared and equipped, have left the American coastline and sailed westwards down the latitudes of 8°–10° S with a reasonable expectation of reaching the Solomons. That they and later navigators did not do so for a considerable time thereafter was itself due to the current underestimated width of the Pacific, and to uncertainty as to the accu-racy of the charts available. In consequence they feared that, once the supposed longitude of the Solomons had been passed, they might find themselves upon a coastline formed by the eastern extremity of New Guinea and the perhaps adjacent and conjoined antipodean continent. South-easterly winds would make this a lee shore and create the danger of embayment, whilst seasonal north-westerly winds might prevent a northerly passage around New Guinea.

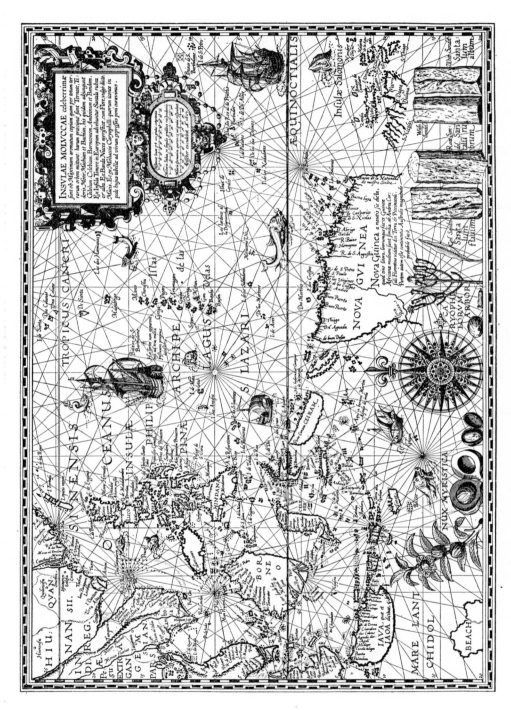

Map XVIII   Visscher's chart *Insulae Moluccae* of 1617, after Linschoten

English and French Interest in the Pacific in the Late Sixteenth Century

In the mid-sixteenth century England was lagging behind Spain and Portugal in trade, overseas expansion and navigational knowledge. The absence of national subsidies and of an institution comparable with the *Casa de Contratación*, and the dependence placed on private capital and enterprise for overseas ventures, retarded development. Even though Henry VII had patronized John Cabot in 1497, it was not until relative internal stability came with the reign of Henry VIII that preparations for expansion could be begun. National policy in the early sixteenth century had precluded the incitement of Spain and Portugal, but the religious breach with Rome and Catholic Europe, the spread of education and the growth of national feeling, provided a climate favourable to expansion, induced by the need to secure foreign markets.[1]

The Spanish and Portuguese monopolies seemed to preclude access to the markets of the East, and initially the English concerned themselves with the search for routes other than those via the Cape of Good Hope and the Magellanic Straits to the Spice Islands and the markets of Cathay. Thorne's suggestion of a Polar Passage was pursued by his associate Roger Barlow in 1541, without success,[2] and in 1548 Sebastian Cabot, for thirty years Pilot-Major in Spain, was induced to settle in England and suggested a North-East Passage. Willoughby's successful if expensive voyage to Russia in 1553, which resulted in the formation of the Muscovy Company by a charter of Queen Mary, did not divert attention from the search for a passage to Cathay and the Pacific, but when in 1566 Humphrey Gilbert sought a royal grant to search for a North-West Passage, he was thwarted by the Muscovy Company's monopoly.

On 19 April 1570, Guerau de Spes wrote to Philip of Spain from London:

I have reported the arrival here of Bartolomé Bayon, a Portuguese. . . . They invite him to return with a good number of ships to Guinea, and some of the Council have communicated with him about a project that was discussed here before, to occupy and colonize one or two ports in the Kingdom of Magellanes, in order to have in their hands the commerce of the Southern Sea . . . as well as getting as near as they wish to Peru,[3]

and in a pamphlet of 1579–80 Richard Hakluyt was to develop the same plan.[4] De Spes' report seems to be the first reference to a series of English projects for occupying various regions in the southern hemisphere which were considered between 1570 and 1588, and in 1572 it was rumoured that the French intended to seize Madagascar (St. Laurence Island) as a base for exploring New Guinea as a supposed part of *Terra Australis*.[5]

[1] See the *Dedication* in the Second Edition of Hakluyt's *Principal Navigations* where English motivations for overseas expansion are outlined.　　　[2] Hakluyt 1903: II: 176–7.
[3] Taylor 1935(b): I: 87.　　　[4] Taylor 1935(b): I: 139.　　　[5] Taylor 1935(b): I: 87 (footnote 3).

At the time of Mendaña's arrival off the coasts of México and California in 1568 there were several English merchants resident in México, trading under licence and sending cargoes in the Spanish fleets. One of these, Henry Hawkes (Hawke or Hawks), returned to England in 1572 and passed on the news of Mendaña's expedition to Richard Hakluyt and other interested persons.[1]

Foure yeeres past, to wit 1568, there was a ship made out of Peru, to seeke Salamon's Islands, and they came somewhat to the South of the Equinoctiall, and founde an Island with many blacke people. . . . And because they had bene long upon the voyage, their people were very weake, and so went not on land, to know what commoditie was upon it. And for want of victuals, they arrived in Nova Hispania . . . and thence returned backe againe unto Peru, whereas they were evill entreated, because they had not knowen more of the same islands.[2]

Such news of Mendaña's voyage may have been instrumental in inducing William Hawkins, Richard Grenville and several 'gentlemen of Devon and Cornwall', to seek the Queen's approval in 1573-4 for an expedition, the objects of which were set out in a document endorsed by Burleigh and entitled *A Discovery of lands beyond the Equinoctial*,[3] which was concerned with the

discoverie, traffique and enjoyenge for the Queen Majestie and her subiectes of all or anie landes, islandes and countries southwards beyonde the aequinoctial, or when the Polie Antartick hathe anie elevation above the Horizon. . . .

Williamson suggests that:

Their further particulars show without doubt that the region in view was the Terra Australis or Magellanic Continent of Mercator and Ortelius, embodying the Lochac and Ophir about which Dee was writing secret memoranda and talking confidentially to the Queen. . . . The enterprise would yield results to England comparable with the benefits derived by Portugal and Spain from the East and West—increase of shipping, sale of manufactures, work for the unemployed, discovery of gold, silver and pearls, and the propagation of the gospel. In sum the projectors were putting forth the complete programme of a colonial empire.[4]

At first the proposal was approved, but Elizabeth later rescinded the licence, presumably to avoid conflict with Spain. No projects for Pacific expansion being forthcoming from the Muscovy Company, Frobisher, supported by Locke, John Dee, Gilbert and Stephen Borough, presented a letter from the Queen to the Company in 1574, exhorting them either to take steps themselves or to grant a licence to someone else. In the absence of a satisfactory reply the Queen granted a licence to Frobisher in 1575, and in 1576 Gilbert published his *Discourse for a Discovery of a New Passage to Cathaia*. However, Frobisher's voyage of 1576 to Baffin Land, and the voyages of 1577 and 1578 under the auspices of the new Cathay Company, were equally unsuccessful in their main objective.

[1] Taylor 1935(b): I: 10. Hawkes was a confidante of Gutierrez who had made the return voyage to the Philippines with Urdaneta.   [2] Taylor 1935(b): I: 108; Hakluyt 1903: IX: 392.
[3] BM: Landsdowne MS. C, ff142-6.   [4] Williamson: 1946: 150-1.

Despite a deterioration in Anglo-Spanish relations in the years immediately prior to 1577, Elizabeth strove, albeit with scant success, to refrain from antagonizing Spain. The activities of Drake and Hawkins in the West Indies and the plying of the English slave trade contrary to the edicts of Spain, with the consequent and understandable retaliations of Spain which the English regarded as an unnecessary and illegal attempt to prohibit commerce, seem, however, to have forced the issue.

Drake's Pacific voyage of 1577–8, the South Sea Project, emanated from a syndicate composed of Leicester, Walsingham, Hatton, Lincoln, Minto, Hawkins and Drake himself. Whilst its main avowed objects[1] were the discovery of *Terra Australis*, trade with the Spice Islands and a search for the *Straits of Anian*,[2] there seems little doubt that Drake envisaged a profitable excursion up the Peruvian coast at the expense of Spain, and that in this second intention he had the connivance of the Queen. In fact, the secondary and secret motive seems to have absorbed all his attention, and when he did depart on his voyage he made no attempt to search for *Terra Australis*. He did, however, succeed in indicating that Tierra del Fuego was probably not the northerly extension of a continent and, after a series of successful raids, in crossing the Pacific in low latitudes N of the equator.[3]

Perhaps the most significant feature of Drake's voyage in this context, other than its indication of English interest in the South Pacific, was its influence on Spanish policy; a policy which was not so much dictated by the need to keep the English out of the Pacific and away from the potentially wealthy lands reputed to exist there, for its own sake, as by the need to concentrate vessels, resources and manpower on the defence of the West American coastline and the Manila trade-route. Drake's activities emphasized the already realized inherent dangers of a vast empire and extended lines of communication; and the authorities, particularly those on the Pacific coastline to whom he had demonstrated all too clearly the weakness of their defences, were not particularly well-disposed to expend men, money and materials on further voyages of exploration which, even if successful, could only render their problems more acute. Even if *Terra Australis* and *Ophir* were discovered, their colonization and exploitation might only be achieved at the expense of the existing Empire, to the detriment of Spanish enjoyment of these new discoveries, and certainly to the benefit of other European nations.

---

[1] The draft plan of the enterprise is in the British Museum (BM: Cotton MSS. Otho E VIII).

[2] Taylor 1929(a): 128–9.

[3] Williamson 1946; Taylor 1930(b): 46–47; Taylor 1929(a); Taylor 1930(c); Nuttall 1914: 57–88. It is of interest to note, in relation to the formation of Drake's plan, if not its execution, his association with the Dieppe cartographer Le Testu (Tetu). The latter was a Huguenot corsair who had allied with Drake in the capture of the Panama baggage train in 1573, and was killed whilst in command of the rearguard. His maps refer specifically to *Ophir* in *Java le Grand*.

One of Spain's first attempts to curb the English incursion was to despatch Sarmiento de Gamboa to the Straits of Magellan to site and erect a series of blockade forts.[1] Sarmiento was captured by the English, 'carried to England, and being afterwards set at liberty . . . conferred often with Drake, and even with the Queen on the subject of his design of settling a colony in this part of the world'.[2] That Sarmiento, one of the leading members of Mendaña's expedition, should have been in England within little more than ten years after his return, and apparently in a talkative mood, is, as has already been suggested, almost certainly reflected in several English charts of the Pacific of the late sixteenth century. That the English did not pursue their interest in the South Pacific is understandable in view of the rich harvests to be gleaned by piracy elsewhere, and Cavendish's voyage of 1586, in emulation of Drake, abandoned even the self-deluding pretensions of discovery and concentrated on the acquisition of loot. Nevertheless, proposals for the exploration of the South Sea were made from time to time, and in 1586, for example, the voyages of Solomon's fleet were cited as evidence for the existence of a North-West Passage in a proposal which named the contents of the Pacific.[3]

Hakluyt reproduces the *Historie* of a Portuguese, López Vaz, who was captured by Captain Withrington on the River Plate in 1586; a work which provides a fascinating contemporary comment on the Spanish American colonies, and the depredations caused by the English corsairs. Of the Spanish voyages of exploration from Perú and New Spain, López Vaz reports that 'the most notable discovery that hath been made from these parts now of late, was that of the Isles of Salomon'.[4] He attributes the discovery to 'Alvares de Mendanio', and locates the Solomons 800 leagues from Perú in 11° S, a figure which he may have derived from Acosta, or from the same source as Acosta. He describes the discovery of the archipelago, of *Santa Izabella* and:

eleven great islands, being one with another of eightie leagues in compasse. The greatest Island that they discovered was according unto the first finder, called Guadalcanal, on the coast whereof they sailed 150 leagues, before they could know whether it was an island or part of the maine land: and yet they know not perfectly what to make of it, but thinke that it may be part of that continent which stretcheth to the Streights of Magellan; for they coasted it to eighteene degrees, and could not find the ende thereof.

He continues with an exaggerated picture of bounteous islands abounding in food and spices, and probably reflects the sort of exaggerated belief then current in the Americas. He is, however, cautious on the subject of gold and, though recording that grains were seen, adds that the difficulties of communicating with the natives, and their hostility, prevented the Spaniards from discovering where the gold had been obtained. In conclusion he remarks:

---

[1] Markham 1895; Callander 1766: I: 376.   [2] Callander 1766: I: 378; Markham 1895: 341–3.
[3] Sainsbury 1862: 94. He cites his source as BM: Harl 167, ff100–108.
[4] Purchas 1905: XVII: 289.

The discoverer of these Islands named them the Isles of Salomon, to the end that the Spaniards supposing them to be those from whence Salomon fetched Gold to adorne the Temple
at Jerusalem, might be the more desirous to goe and inhabit the same[1]; now the same time
when they thought to have sent Colonies unto these Islands, Captaine Drake entered the
South Sea; whereupon Commandement was given, that they should not be inhabited, to
the end that such Englishmen . . . might have no succour there. . . .[2]

In 1578 a Portuguese pilot had been compelled to accompany Drake, and
on 23 May 1579, he appeared before the Holy Inquisition of México, called
to explain his collaboration. In his deposition he stated:

Between Lima and Panama lies the Cape of San Francisco where he [Drake] seized the
Nao Rica. From this Cape to Chile he could take the same route as the Lima ships, that take
to the open sea as far as the Islands of Solomon and from thence return to the coast of Chile,
whence he could go on through the Straits of Magellan.[3]

It is almost certain that the pilot, named da Silva, was not referring to the
islands discovered by Mendaña, but to the islands of San Félix and San Ambrosio, sighted by Juan Fernández when he discovered the sea-route from Lima
to Chile. That the name Islands of Solomon had become associated with these
islands, as part of the rumour that Fernández had discovered a great southern
continent, and also possibly as a result of the association of any Pacific islands
close to Perú with Inca legends and the Ophirian conjecture, is hardly surprising. Also typical of the misconceptions which seem to have developed concerning the Islands of Solomon is the report of an English vessel, carried to
64° S in 1599, the captain of which, on sighting mountainous snow-clad land,
concluded that it must extend towards the Islands of Solomon, a conclusion
apparently based on the belief that the Solomons were part of or adjoining
the Antipodean continent.[4]

The proposals of the d'Allaigne brothers were not the only French schemes
for exploration and colonization in the South Pacific in the sixteenth century.
During the religious war preceding the Peace of St. Germaine, the French
Ambassador in Spain was approached by an Iberian seaman who proposed
the discovery and conquest of extensive lands in the south. The Ambassador,
an enthusiast for such schemes although somewhat easily impressed, endeavoured to secure the support of the Queen Mother and the Duc d'Anjou, but
the natural reaction to the vagueness of the proposals and the extravagance of
the seaman's remunerative expectations was unfavourable. Following the

---

[1] The error of such an assertion has already been illustrated.

[2] Purchas 1905: XVII: 292. If a 'commandement' was ever given, it was revoked in 1595 when the
second expedition of colonization was despatched to the Solomons. Vaz' appreciation of the effect
of Drake's voyage is basically correct, although it is doubtful if anyone, other than Mendaña, thought
of colonization with any enthusiasm. The reluctance of the Spanish authorities to support new colonizing ventures, particularly to such unpromising lands, was dictated by considerations which were
appreciated before Drake's voyage, but which were emphasized by it.

[3] Nuttall 1914: 318.   [4] Guppy 1887: 248.

death of Velho, Francisque d'Allaigne attempted to pursue his project, but seems to have perished in the massacre of the Huguenots which followed the murder of their leader, an advocate of French maritime expansion, Admiral Coligny. His brother, André d'Allaigne, presented a *remonstrance* to King Henry III in which he offered to perform the voyage and claimed to possess the necessary information, maps and instruments. Despite his exhortations to the Crown to save the souls of the heathen of the austral lands, the advantages to be derived from the transportation of unquiet spirits to their shores, and the rather cruel reminder that Columbus had unsuccessfully offered his project and his services to France, he met with no consideration.[1]

In 1577 the *Marquis* de la Roche was granted a commission to carry colonists to new lands and to settle there,[2] and though the English were reassured that their suspicions that the expedition was directed against overseas English interests were unfounded, the precise object was kept a close secret.[3] In 1578 Sir Humphrey Gilbert was granted a patent to explore, and it seems probable that one of his objectives was *Magellanica*. He approached the French Ambassador, Castlenau, with the suggestion that if the French and English should meet on the high seas they would avoid hostilities. Castlenau, in reporting to the King, referred to the proposals of d'Allaigne, and explained that his plan had been to settle rich lands outside the spheres of Spain and Portugal, reached by heading E or W in the South Atlantic, behind America, and convenient to the Portuguese and Spanish Indies. Pilots who had been there had described them as rich in gold and inhabited by naked, unarmed and vulnerable natives. Castlenau added that he had heard of them when he was in Portugal[4], a reference which could relate either to the voyage of Mendaña or to the speculative stories current at the time.

[1] Hamy 1903; Hamy 1894(b); Hamy 1899.   [2] Anthiaume 1916: II: 45.
[3] Murdin 1759: 305.   [4] Jameson 1926: 288.

IV

Mendaña's Expedition of 1595

'la tragedia de las islas donde faltó Salomon'
['the tragedy of the islands where Solomon was wanting']

Zaragoza 1876: II: 119

ON his return from his expedition of 1567–9 Mendaña determined to return
to his discoveries and establish a colony. His report to the King of 11 September 1569[1] provides a description of the archipelago and an inventory of its
products, varying from gold to a specific for gout, which, though not exactly
dishonest, is considerably more attractive than the realities of the discovery
justified. This is understandable, as is the emphasis in the letter on the number
of souls awaiting salvation and the signs of potential wealth.[2] It is all the more
understandable in terms of the assumption that the Solomons might be outliers
to a more attractive continent and perhaps *Ophir* itself, of Mendaña's desire to
establish a colony in the area as a base for rurthei exploration, and his realization that a bald statement of the achievements of the expedition of 1567–9
would be unlikely to win royal support for a further venture.

It seems likely, however, that the Spanish authorities were more impressed
by the distance of the group from Perú, and the imperial, strategic and commercial problems of Spain, as arguments against its colonization, than by
Mendaña's picture of its potentialities. They could well have argued that since
Mendaña had originally been despatched with the intention of founding a
colony, the arguments which had necessitated his return in 1568 were the
strongest arguments against the further prosecution of a colonizing venture.[3]
Nevertheless, Mendaña did succeed in making some progress in the pursuit of
his object, largely it would seem through the intervention and favour of his
uncle, the *Licenciado* de Castro, who had returned to Spain from Perú in 1569.
In April 1574, he received *Letters Patent* appointing him Governor of the islands[4]
and permitting him to colonize at his own expense, which were subsequently

---

[1] RAH: *Colección de Velázquez, Vol. XXXVI, No. 8*, ff185–194v; Zaragoza 1876: II: 15 *et seq*;
Amherst 1901: 159 *et seq*.

[2] Zaragoza 1876: II: 36–39; Amherst 1901: I: 180–3.

[3] See Mendaña's *memoriales* of 1573 (AGI: *Indiferente General* 1383B).

[4] AGI: *Patronato, legajo 18, No. 10, Ramo 8, Expedientes* of Doña Ysabel and de Castro (1597) ff3–4,
Expediente of de Castro (1598) ff16–37; Pacheco 1864: XXIII: 189; Zaragoza 1876: III: 116.

amplified in three *cédulas* dated 12 May, 14 July and 20 August of the same year.[1]

The royal *Instrucción* of 25 May 1575,[2] ordering him to make observations of lunar eclipses expected to occur on 26 September 1575, and 15 September 1578, to determine the longitude of the archipelago and to chart it correctly, would seem to indicate that the King at least expected Mendaña to depart immediately. The *Instrucción* relating to the first eclipse was certainly over-optimistic, for it was not until mid-1576 that Mendaña embarked at Seville, arriving in Panama in January 1577.[3] Here he was imprisoned on a trivial charge by the President, Loarte, and kept under close arrest until he left for Perú. In a letter of 3 February 1577, he protested to the King at the treatment which he had received,[4] imploring him to send orders to Toledo, the Viceroy of Perú, not to interfere with the expedition. His fears seem to have been justified, for in a letter of 24 March 1580, addressed to the Council of the Indies (*Consejo de Indias*) from Lima (Los Reyes), he complained that Toledo had twice prevented the expedition from sailing and had imprisoned him.[5]

That the King still expected him to depart soon is reflected in the second *Instrucción*, addressed to him as '*Governador de las Yslas de Salamon*', instructing him to determine the correct latitudes and longitudes of the Solomons, their distance from the Spanish kingdoms, and to observe the time of a lunar eclipse in July 1581.[6] It was not, however, until 1590, with the commencement of the vice-reign of *Don* García Hurtado de Mendoza, 4th *Marquis* of Cañete,[7] that the obstacles to his enterprise began to diminish and that preparations for the voyage were recommenced. That Mendaña remained in Perú throughout this interminable delay seems likely,[8] but it was not until 1595 that the expedition was finally in a state of readiness.

The expedition consisted of four vessels carrying settlers, soldiers and wives, and Mendaña was himself accompanied by his wife, *Doña* Ysabel de Barreto, and her brothers. The Chief Pilot was a Portuguese, Pedro Fernández de Quirós, probably one of the most competent Iberian pilots of his day, who, in

---

[1] Zaragoza 1876: III: 118; Zaragoza 1876: II: 62; AGI: *Patronato, legajo* 18, *No.* 10, *Ramo* 8, *Expedientes* of *Doña* Ysabel and de Castro (1597), ff4v–23, *Expediente* of de Castro (1598) ff28–41; AGI: *Patronato, legajo* 51, *No.* 3, *Ramo* 8, ff94–6v. See also AGI: *Indiferente General* 1384, and *Indiferente General* 1085, containing five *memoriales* from Mendaña to the King and five to the *Consejo de Indias*, 1574–5.

[2] MNM: MS. 328, f123. This document is further evidence of the real uncertainty of the Spaniards as to the exact position of the Solomons, and the absence of duplicity or falsification in the records of the previous expedition. Sarmiento elsewhere refers to orders being sent to the Indies respecting the eclipses of 1577 and 1578, and he himself made observations at Lima (Markham 1895: 215).

[3] Zaragoza 1876: III: 117.　　　　　　　　[4] Zaragoza 1876: III: 118. MLS: MS. c404, ff 1–18.

[5] MLS: MS. c402, ff1–7; AGI: *Lima* 125; Zaragoza 1876: III: 119; AGI: *Patronato, legajo* 18, *No.* 10, *Ramo* 8; Amherst 1901: I: lxviii. See also his letter to the King of 30 March 1580 (AGI: *Lima* 125, *carrete* 21).　　　　　　　　[6] MNM: MS. 328, ff123–123v.

[7] Zaragoza 1876: III: 65; Zaragoza 1876: I: 23.　　　　　[8] Amherst 1901: I: lxviii.

the course of the voyage, was to become imbued with a desire, ultimately developing into something little short of fanaticism, to discover the supposed austral continent and to convert its inhabitants to the Catholic Faith. On Friday, 9 April 1595, the fleet weighed anchor in the port of Callao and, sailing off the valleys of Santa, Truxillo and Saña, collected men and provisions, often, it would seem in the case of the latter, by the simple expedient of robbing.[1] In the bibliography the several sources which describe the conduct of the expedition have been discussed, and it is in the major account, the Quirós-Bermúdez *relación*, that the clearest picture of this phase of the expedition is drawn.

Immediately prior to their departure from the South American coast, Mendaña instructed Quirós to prepare five charts, one for himself and one for each of the pilots. On these he was to lay down nothing more than the Peruvian coastline and two points in 7° S and 12° S, 1,500 leagues from Lima, 'which he said was the extreme distance of the islands which he sought, the longitude of which was 1,450 leagues, the other 50 leagues being added to afford some margin, and no other land was to be charted in case some ship should steer to or desert to it'.[2] The instruction is interesting, not only as reflecting the scant knowledge of the Pacific of the pilots employed and the danger or fear or mutiny and desertion, but for the light it throws on Mendaña's knowledge of the distance of the Solomons from Perú. In his *relación* Gallego had recorded a distance from Perú to Los Bajos de la Candelaria of 1,638 leagues,[3] and Mendaña himself, in his two letters to the King and de Castro, had implied that the distance was at least 1,580 leagues.[4] It is probable, as a result of the impression gained that the Island of Jesus (Ysla or Nombre de Jesús) was in close proximity to the eastern coast of Ramos (Malaíta), that Mendaña regarded the Ysla de Jesús as the most easterly of the Islands of Solomon, and accordingly instructed Quirós to lay down his objective marks at the distance from Perú which Gallego had recorded on the day prior to their sighting the Ysla de Jesús, 1,450 leagues, but that he added 50 leagues for safety. In a *discurso* on the position of the Solomons included in his *relación* Quirós refers to Gallego's *relación* as giving the distance of the Solomons from Perú as 1450 leagues,[5] and in the Santa Casa MS. of Gallego's short *relación* the distance of the Ysla de Jesús from Perú is given as 1,450 leagues.[6]

Having watered at Paýta, the expedition finally set sail on 16 June 1595, with a complement of 378 persons,[7] in a fleet consisting of two galleons, a

---

[1] The preparations for the expedition, chaotic, disorderly and ill-commanded as they seem to have been, set the note for the further conduct of the enterprise.   [2] Zaragoza 1876: I: 29–30.

[3] MNM: MS. 921, ff10, 13, 66. Although Gallego spoke of their return course from San Cristóval to México being over 1,700 leagues of gulf, it is probable that he meant the total distance to be sailed.

[4] Amherst 1901: I: 91, 163.   [5] Zaragoza 1876: I: 183; Santa Casa: MS. *De Marina*, f46.

[6] Santa Casa: MS. *De Marina*, f104v.

[7] AGI: *Patronato*, *legajo* 18, No. 10, *Ramo* 5,[3] '*Lista de la gente* . . .' lists 354 persons.

galeot and a frigate, named respectively the *Capitana*, *Almiranta*, *San Felipe* and *Santa Catalina*.[1] Heading WSW as far as 14° S, the course was then changed to W 11¼° N, and on Friday, 21 July, in 10° 50' S, an island was sighted to which was given the name *Magdalena*.[2] This was the first of several island discoveries within the Marquesas Group, which, for no apparently good reason, Mendaña immediately concluded to be the islands which he sought, although Quirós had only logged 1,000 leagues from Callao.[3] Certainly these islands were nearer to the position which, during the voyage of 1567-9, Mendaña had hoped to find land, but to have concluded that they were the archipelago discovered by that expedition was rash, and Mendaña soon realized his error. At no great distance from Magdalena three other islands were sighted and named *San Pedro*, *Dominica* and *Santa Cristina*, and to all four were given the collective name which they bear today, *Las Marquesas de Mendoza*.

Continuing on a course which varied from W by S to NW and W, the expedition sailed for a further 400 leagues and, on 10 August sighted four islands in 10° 20' S, to which they gave the name *Islas de San Bernardo*,[4] and which would seem to be identifiable with Puka Puka (10° 53' S, 165° 49' W) in the Cook Islands.[5] Leaving these astern and maintaining a course between 12° S and 8° S, though generally between 10° S and 11° S, the expedition logged another 135 leagues and sighted a low round island in 10° 40' S, which they named *Isla Solitaria*,[6] and which is identifiable with Niulakita in the Ellice Islands (10° 45' S, 179° 30' E).[7]

Even at this stage in the voyage the disaffection which was ultimately to contribute to the collapse of the enterprise became pronounced, and from Quirós' *relación* emerges a depressing picture of unchecked mutinous assemblies and undisciplined *expedicionarios*. By this time they had sailed by their reckoning 1,535 leagues, and were beyond the point at which Mendaña had expected to sight the Yslas de Salomón. The disaffected soldiery began to voice their doubts as to the existence of the islands which they sought, to suggest that the pilots were incompetent, and to complain that they would be in Tartary before they had discovered the islands. The Quirós-Bermúdez *relación* also adds that according to some of the pilots they were sailing on rocks and over land, and had been doing so for many days, 'because the place where they had been painted had been erased' from the charts[8]; a reference perhaps to the fact that the blank charts which Quirós had issued had previously laid down either the

[1] Zaragoza 1876: I: 34.

[2] Zaragoza 1876: I: 35. In his letter to de Morga, Quirós gives the latitude as 'fully 10°'.

[3] Zaragoza 1876: I: 39.

[4] Zaragoza 1876: I: 52-53. In his letter to de Morga Quirós gives the latitude as 10° 45' S (Markham 1904: I: 152).

[5] Maude 1959: 306-7. The distance of 1,400 leagues from Perú represents an underestimate of some 230 leagues.   [6] Zaragoza 1876: I: 54.

[7] Maude 1959: 306, 308-9.   [8] Zaragoza 1876: I: 57.

Solomons or *Terra Australis* in the area in which the vessels were now thought to be sailing.

On 7 September, as they continued their westerly course, a mass of dark smoke was sighted dead ahead, and as a precautionary measure the galeot and frigate were sent ahead to investigate. During the following night the rain clouds which had previously limited their vision cleared, and land could be seen. The dawn revealed a single pointed volcanic mountain, rising out of the sea and erupting violently, and, to the SE, the land which had been sighted during the night. The dawn also revealed the absence of the *Almiranta*, and indeed nothing more was ever heard of either her or her crew and passengers. Quirós estimated the position of the expedition to be in 10° 20′ S, 1,850 leagues from Perú[1]; and there is no doubt that they were off the island of *Santa Cruz* (10° 40′ S, 166° E), so named by Mendaña, and the now quiescent volcano of Tinakula. Quirós' estimate of 1,850 leagues as the distance of Santa Cruz from Perú is an underestimate of 295 leagues, its actual distance being approximately 2,145 Iberian leagues (of 4 Roman miles).

It is perhaps reasonable to expect to find more correct navigational information in the narratives of the expedition of 1595 than in those of the expedition of 1567–8, and to expect from Quirós, the Chief Pilot, a more accurate estimate of the distance sailed E–W across the Pacific. In the period of over twenty-five years which elapsed between the return of the first and the departure of the second expedition it is doubtful, however, if any radical improvements had occurred in the navigational science of the Iberian peninsula. Spain, largely through the stultifying and limiting effects of the *Casa de Contratación*, once the envy of Europe and the genesis of many navigational innovations, but later dominated by conservatism and a reluctance to innovate, had become a country of navigational stagnation. This is not to suggest that some improvements did not occur, and in the main the problems of development were problems related to the determination of longitude, were common to Europe, and were to remain so until the eighteenth century. The limitations of the existing navigational techniques could not be obviated, but they could be reduced by a greater awareness of their existence and a consequently increased care, caution and allowance for them, and it would seem to have been this kind of improvement which did occur. From Quirós himself one might expect a good record of navigation, not only by virtue of his known reputation and reflected competence, but also by virtue of his ability to view the navigation of the 1567–9 expedition in retrospect and at leisure, and perhaps to notice the likelihood of and reasons for such errors as might have occurred.

That Quirós was a competent navigator can hardly be doubted. His knowledge is reflected in two treatises on navigation which he prepared in

[1] Zaragoza 1876: I: 60, 76. In his letter to de Morga Quirós gives the distance as 1,800 leagues (Zaragoza 1876: II: 56).

1602[1] and 1610,[2] in which he reveals his appreciation of the imperfections of the navigational techniques of his day, and in the comments on his proficiency by the Duke of Sesa in letters to the King and to *Don* Pedro Franqueza from Rome dated 2 February 1602.[3] In his treatise of 1610 he remarks, significantly, that:

the navigational charts which are in use today, are compiled solely from the information of the pilots ... The observations which they make are with uncertain instruments, and with declination tables of the sun much the same. They are unable to give true reports regarding longitude, latitude and size, and ... all the charts are defective.[4]

In expecting to find improved navigation reflected in the narratives of the voyage of 1595 the reader is not disappointed, but it is doubtful if all the credit for the improvement is due to Quirós, and much of it may well be due to the absence of the extreme conditions of E–W drift experienced by Gallego in the slightly higher latitudes in which Quirós sailed for much of the time, and at the time of the year in which he made his passage.[5]

Between Callao and San Bernardo (Puka Puka) Quirós recorded a direct distance of 1,400 leagues for an actual distance of 1,630 leagues, an underestimate of 230 leagues.[6] Between San Bernardo and La Solitaria (Niulakita) he logged 135 leagues, an underestimate of half the actual distance between the two islands, giving a total underestimate Callao–La Solitaria of 365 leagues.[7] Overall between Callao and Santa Cruz, however, the underestimate made was only 295 leagues, since he estimated the distance of Santa Cruz from Callao as

---

[1] AGS: *Estado, legajo* K, 1631, *doc.*245. This treatise follows AGS: *Estado, legajo* K, 1631, *doc.*244, which is a *memorial* to the King, and may originally have accompanied it. Santa Casa: MS. *De Marina,* ff100–104.

[2] Zaragoza 1876: II: 356–67. See also the documents in the Santa Casa MS. *De Marina, 'Platica entre un Cap^{an} y un Piloto mayor de una Armada para el buen açertamiento dela nabegaçion'* (ff1–15), *'Fabrica de la aguxa'* (ff15–31), *'Como sesabra La Variaçion, i de que parte el Aguxa tiene por la estrella del Norte esto no puede sur sino es estando de su parte'* (ff31–32) ... *'por el cruzero'* (ff32–44v).

[3] AGS: *Estado, legajo* K, 1631, *docs.*33–34. The letter to Franqueza refers to two instruments designed by Quirós, one a 'compass of variation' (shadow compass?), the other 'an instrument to take better altitudes' (an improved Jacob's staff or quadrant?).

[4] Zaragoza 1876: II: 363.

[5] S of 6° S the drift of the South Equatorial Current drops appreciably and suddenly.

[6] Puka Puka is in 10° 53′S, 165° 49′ W, Callao in 12° S, 77° 10′ W.
D/Long. Callao—Puka Puka = 88° 39′, 5320′
Middle Latitude = 11° 26′ S.
Distance (approximate) Callao—Puka Puka = $5{,}320 \times$ Cosine 11° 26′ = 5,215·7 n. miles = 6,519·6 Roman miles = 1,629·9 Iberian leagues.

[7] Niulakita is in 10° 45′ S, 179° 30′ E.
D/Long. Puka Puka—Niulakita = 14° 41′, 881′.
Middle Latitude = 10° 49′ S.
Distance (approximate) Puka Puka—Niulakita = $881 \times$ Cosine 10° 49′ = 865 n. miles = 1081 Roman miles = 270 Iberian leagues.

1,850 leagues, as compared with an actual distance of 2,145 leagues.[1] If the identification of Niulakita with La Solitaria is correct, then Quirós' estimate of 315 leagues as its distance to the E of Santa Cruz represents an over-estimate of 69 leagues (276 Roman miles or 221 n. miles),[2] and has the effect of reducing the total underestimate made by the time the expedition had reached Niulakita within the total distance estimated between Callao and Santa Cruz.

Between Callao and Niulakita Quirós had estimated 1,535 leagues for an actual distance of 1,900 leagues, a considerable underestimate, but not of the same extent as Gallego's estimate of 1,471 leagues over the roughly similar distance between Callao and Nui[3] (1,953 leagues). Nevertheless, it must be appreciated that from the Marquesas to Niulakita Quirós was sailing slightly to the S of the route followed by Gallego, in higher latitudes beyond the maximum influence of the South Equatorial Current, where his navigation was less susceptible to errors due to oceanic influences than Gallego's navigation had been. It is reasonable to conclude then that over this period of the voyage his navigation was little better than Gallego's.

Quirós' overestimate of distance between Niulakita and Santa Cruz is difficult to understand, and there appears to be no convincing or adequate explanation for it on the evidence available. From the information contained in the modern pilot charts it does not appear likely that the surface currents would have been appreciably greater or less than those experienced between the Marquesas and Niulakita, but the winds would have been more confused, the percentage of favourable winds decreasing and the percentage of unfavourable winds increasing. It is possible that with the confused winds the navigation became more difficult, and that Quirós succumbed to a tendency to log the sort of daily runs which he had logged previously, partly in appreciation of the probable E–W current, when in fact he was not making anything like the same daily runs he had been making previously. It may also be that he belatedly realized, in view of the time already spent at sea and the realization that Gallego had probably underestimated the distance sailed, that he himself was falling into the same error as Gallego, and that he attempted to compensate by deliberately overestimating the distance sailed thereafter, although this seems most unlikely.

---

[1] Santa Cruz is in 10° 40′ S, 166° 10′ E.
D/Long, Callao—Santa Cruz = 116° 40′, 7000′.
Middle Latitude = 11° 20′ S.
Distance (approximate) Callao—Santa Cruz = $7,000 \times$ Cosine 11° 20′ = 6,863·5 n. miles = 8,579 Roman miles = 2,145 Iberian leagues.
[2] D/Long. Niulakita—Santa Cruz = 13° 20′, 800′.
$800' \times$ Cosine 10° 42′ (Middle Latitude) = 786 n. miles = $982\frac{1}{2}$ Roman miles = 246 Iberian leagues.
[3] Nui is in 177° 10′ E, Niulakita in 179° 30′ E.

The thirty-ninth chapter of the Quirós-Bermúdez *relación* consists of a *discurso* or analysis by Quirós of the reasons for the expedition of 1595 failing to find the Islands of Solomon discovered by Mendaña and Gallego in 1568.[1] This document is also to be found independently, perhaps as a copy of the original if not as the original itself, initially written by Quirós and subsequently included in the *relación*.[2] The two forms of the *discurso*, in the *relación* and in the Santa Casa MS., differ only in respect of occasional words and phrases, but it seems likely that the latter is the older form; perhaps written by Quirós for submission to the Viceroy of Perú, *Don* Luis de Velasco, in 1597. In the Santa Casa MS. it is immediately followed by a *discurso* addressed to Don P° de Velasco, and the index page refers to the addressee of this second document as Viceroy of Perú.

Quirós opens by stating quite categorically that the Islas de Salomón of which Hernán Gallego, who discovered them, writes in his *relación*, and of which Álvaro de Mendaña went in search, were neither the Islas de Marquesas nor those of Santa Cruz. He suggests three possible impediments to their rediscovery in 1595: first, the possibility that they were at a greater distance than was believed; secondly, that for some motive of private interest their true latitudes were concealed and erroneous ones given; or thirdly, that inadequate instruments, ignorance, errors of judgement in navigation or an error in recording, had prevented the correct determination or recording of their position. Whilst admitting the second possibility, Quirós considers it to be out of character with Gallego, an honourable man who, although he had a subsequent disagreement with Mendaña, was in a state of amity with him at the time when Mendaña requested a record of the navigation from him. Gallego himself had never sought to negotiate at court on his own behalf for the settlement of these islands and, although Mendaña could have been easily deceived, Gallego's observations were known to the other four pilots of the expedition of 1568, and he could hardly have hoped to keep them secret.

The third alternative Quirós suggests as probable, adding that in navigating E to W along the same latitude, longitude could only be determined 'by such estimation as each one may make',[3] and that such estimates might be considerably in error as a result of either the pilot's calculation or the difficulty of determining the distance run by the ship. Quirós expresses his own conviction that the first possibility is probably the correct one, that the true longitude of the Islands of Solomon had not been given to the expedition of 1595, and that in fact they lay to the W of Santa Cruz. He cites Mendaña, Mendaña's instructions and the *relación* of Gallego, as giving the position of the Solomons as between the latitudes of 7° and 12° S, 1,450 leagues from Lima. In fact in the long versions of Gallego's *relación* 1,450 leagues is the distance logged on the

[1] Zaragoza 1876: I: 182–92; BPM: MS. 1686, ff96 *et seq.*
[2] Santa Casa: MS. *De Marina*, ff45–51v.   [3] Zaragoza 1876: I: 184.

day before the Ysla de Jesús was sighted, but in the Santa Casa short version, which appears from Quirós' quotations from it, and from its discovery together with his *discurso* in the same volume in the Santa Casa Archives, to be the one to which he is referring, the distance of the Ysla de Jesús from Perú is recorded as 1,450 leagues. Accepting the natural deduction, to which I have already referred, that the Ysla de Jesús was in close proximity to the archipelago, perhaps part of it, Quirós' reading of the *relación* is understandable, even though the short version of the *relación*, like the long version, also states that 165 leagues lay between the Ysla de Jesús and Los Bajos de la Candelaria.

Quirós supports his conclusion that the Solomons lay to the W of their reported position by citing Gallego in his *relación*, and Mendaña in conversation, as stating that during the return voyage of the expedition of 1567–9 the vessels were in 8° 40′ N, amongst '*las islas de San Bartolomé*. . .', in the position of the Barbudos. Gallego was at that time amongst the Marshall Islands, and seems to have concluded that the islands which he visited were the same as those discovered and named *San Bartolomeo* by Toribo Alonzo de Salazar in 1526, and estimated by him to lie 328 leagues from the Marianas.[1] Whilst Gallego makes no reference to their identity with the *Barbudos*, Quirós, perhaps from Mendaña, does so, and adds that the Barbudos were known to lie at least 2,000 leagues from Perú.[2] He concludes, rationally and logically, that Gallego could hardly have sailed from the Islands of Solomon on a NE to northerly course, and then be 2,000 leagues from Perú, if the Islands of Solomon were only 1,450 leagues from Perú.[3] He adds, and his remark reflects his belief that islands were indications of continents, the eroded fragments of a larger land mass, that inhabited islands indicated the proximity of New Guinea. He cites Gallego's statement that on 4 September 1568, between 2° and 4° S, he had seen driftwood and flotsam which indicated the proximity of New Guinea, and deduces that since he himself had travelled 1,850 plus 40 leagues from Perú, and had then followed a NW course from Santa Cruz towards Manila without actually sighting New Guinea (as he was to do during this second expedition), how could Gallego have been near New Guinea if he had only gone 1,450 leagues and then headed N to NE?

[1] Krustenstern 1824: Part II: 49. *San Bartolomeo* was an island discovered and so named by Salazar, the successor to del Cano and Loyasa in their voyage from Spain to the Philippines in the *Santa María de la Victoria* in 1525–6. Sighted on 21 August 1526, in 14° 2′ N, twelve days short of the Ladrones, it can be identified with Taongi, the most northerly of the Marshall Islands in 14° 30′ N, 169° 20′ E (Navarette 1837: V: 241–313; Navarette 1866: V: 5–67). The island which Gallego and Mendaña visited and identified with *San Bartolomeo*, and which they named *San Mateo* (Amherst 1901: I: 67, 185; Amherst 1901: II: 209), would seem to have been Namu Atoll in the Marshalls (8° N, 168° E.)

[2] In his own voyage, from Santa Cruz to Manila in 1595–6, Quirós sighted islands in 6° N, probably some of the Carolines, which he identified with the *Barbudos*. (Zaragoza 1876: I: 155.)

[3] The *Barbudos* were *Los Barbudos* of Legazpi, who had discovered them during his voyage of 1565 from México to the Philippines, in 10¼° N, and can be identified with Mejit in the Eastern Marshalls in 10° 20′ N, 171° E (Pacheco 1885: II: 373–95, 217–52).

He refers to Gallego's allusion to the claims of Bernardo de la Torre and Íñigo Ortiz de Rates (Retes)[1] to have discovered New Guinea, and his acceptance of the latter's claim.[2] In fact de Retes had been no further E along the north coast of New Guinea than about 143° E (Greenwich), and the eastern extremities, from 143° E to the east coast of New Ireland (156° E), were quite unknown. When Gallego and Quirós, on separate occasions, expressed the opinion that they were close to New Guinea, their opinions reflected the current underestimate of the width of the Pacific if they thought that New Guinea terminated at a point close to that which de Retes had reached; approximately 13° W of New Ireland. When Quirós, in 5° S and probably to the E of Ontong Java, was to think he saw signs that New Guinea was close at hand, he was at least 1,000 miles from the easternmost part of New Guinea which de Retes had visited and which had been charted.

He goes on to quote 'the *relación* of Gallego to the *Licenciado* de Castro',[3] in which Gallego stated that when 30 leagues from the Ysla de Jesús and in 7° S, he believed that if they had gone on they would have discovered another land in close proximity. Quirós interprets this as an implied reference to New Guinea, and sees the references to de Retes and de la Torre as evidence that the object of the expedition of 1567–9 was New Guinea. He adds that Gallego could not have believed himself to be close to New Guinea without also believing, on the evidence of Miguel Rojo de Brito, who had stated that *Nueva Guinea* and *Maluco* (the Moluccas) were close together, that New Guinea was at least 2,000 leagues from Perú.[4]

He again cites Gallego as having told Mendaña that the voyage from San Cristóval to Perú would be over 1,700 leagues of ocean, but adds that Gallego, having sailed from San Cristóval on a course N–NE for 78 leagues to 7° S, recorded that in that latitude his position was '30 leagues from the Island of Jesus to the E of it'.[5] He argues that if the Ysla de Jesús was in 6° 45′ S and 1,450 leagues from Perú, and if the course from San Cristóval to a point 30 leagues

---

[1] Zaragoza 1876: I: 186.

[2] New Guinea was probably discovered by the Portuguese Jorge de Meneses in 1526 (Barros 1615: Decada 4: 53–54), but de Retes, in 1545, sailed further to the E along the north coast of New Guinea than anyone previously, and the point in 5° S at which he left New Guinea and headed northwards was still the most easterly known point in Quirós' time.

[3] He means the short version (Santa Casa: MS. *De Marina*, f115). In this same quotation Gallego speaks of the Ysla de Jesús as 'the first we discovered as we saw the archipelago of islands', indicating why Quirós accepted the distance of the Ysla de Jesús recorded in the short version of Gallego's *relación* as the distance of the Solomons from Perú.

[4] Quirós states that he appended a chapter of the narrative of de Brito to his *discurso*, but this does not appear in the papers in the Santa Casa MS. or in the Quirós-Bermúdez *relación*. It does however appear, perhaps in an abbreviated form, in a later *memorial* by Quirós to the King dated 1610 (Zaragoza 1876: II: 294–6).

[5] Santa Casa: MS. *De Marina*, f49v; BPM: MS. 1686, f99v, '*apartado de la Isla de Jesus de la parte de leste della*', i.e. his position was to the E of the Ysla de Jesús. See also Zaragoza 1876: I: 189.

to the E of the Ysla de Jesús was N to NE, then the Ysla de Jesús must be
N of San Cristóval and at the same distance from Perú. This he sees as indicative
of carelessness or an error in calculation. If the error over this short distance
was 250 leagues, how much greater could it have been over the long distance
from Perú to the Solomons? Quirós is probably mistaken in relating Gallego's
reference to the Ysla de Jesús to his estimate of 1,700 leagues, for this was
almost certainly his estimate of the total distance to be sailed to México, a
greater distance than that logged between Perú and the Candelaria Shoals.

In the long version of the *relación* Gallego states that, after leaving San
Cristóval, he sailed for 78 leagues[1] on courses between N and NE, and that
on 23 August, in 7° S, his position was 'east and west a quarter north-west to
south-east thirty-six leagues from the Island of Jesus *de la parte de el leste*'.[2] He
does not say that his own position was to the E of the Ysla de Jesús, '*de la
parte de el leste dela*' but only '*apartado de la Ysla de Jesus de la parte de el leste*',
a phrase which could as equally well refer to the Ysla de Jesús being to the E
of his position as to his position being to the E of the Ysla de Jesús. In the
short version of the *relación*, however, the source which Quirós appears to have
used, Gallego records his courses between N and NE, the distance travelled as
78 leagues,[3] and then states that he was 'in 7° S east and west a quarter north-
west to south-east and thirty leagues from the Ysla de Jesús which was the
first which we discovered'.[4] In the short version he makes no mention of
whether or not he was to the E or W of the Ysla de Jesús, but since in both
versions he does record the latitude of the Ysla de Jesús as $6\frac{1}{4}$° S, Quirós was
naturally correct in assuming that in 7° S, on a bearing of E by S to W by N
from it, Gallego must have believed himself to have been to the E of it, since
the Ysla de Jesús was in a more northerly latitude, and therefore bearing W by
N. In view of his false impression of the relative positions of San Cristóval and
the Ysla de Jesús, Gallego's belief is, of course, understandable.

Quirós refers to other inconsistencies in Gallego's *relación* indicative of
error, including his estimate of the size of Guadalcanal, and supports his
conclusion on the proximity of Santa Cruz to the Solomons by reference to the
similarity of the natives, adding the interesting conclusion that both peoples
originally came from the Philippines by way of New Guinea, driven out 'by
Moors and other Indians and kinsmen to the aborigines of Luzon'. He reports
Mendaña and other pilots in the expedition of 1567–9 as stating that Gallego
had underestimated the distance to be sailed on the return journey by 700

---

[1] He lists the daily courses and distances between 18 and 23 August.

[2] MNM: MS. 921, ff68–69; ATL: Gallego, ff68v–69, '*leste ueste quarta del norueste sueste treinta
y seis leguas apartado de la parte de el leste*'.

[3] He lists the daily courses and distances.

[4] Santa Casa: MS. *De Marina*, f115, '*en siete grados largos parte del sur leste oeste quarta de noroeste
sueste treinta leguas apartado de la Isla de Jesus que fue la primera que descubrimos*'.

leagues,[1] and, accepting the probability of such an explanation, remarks that it confirms his suspicions, that the distance 2,150 leagues would be beyond the 2,000 leagues which he himself believed to lie between Lima and New Guinea, and that at that distance Gallego could have sailed N to NE from San Cristóval, and have passed close to New Guinea and through the Barbudos.[2]

Whilst this explanation of the underestimated distance of the Solomon from Perú is not entirely impossible, it seems strange that Mendaña, who was one of Quirós' informants of this supposed error by Gallego, should have clung to the idea in 1595 that the Solomons lay 1,450 leagues from Perú. Admittedly Mendaña, as Quirós suggests when he points to the facility with which Gallego could have deceived him had he so wished, was no navigator, but at the same time he was no fool, and a known error of 700 leagues would have been a considerable one to ignore.

What seems extremely probable is that Quirós missed the real point of the report of Mendaña and the pilots, that the distance from the Solomons to México was 700 leagues further than anticipated. On the outward journey Gallego, for reasons of current, wind and the limitations of navigational techniques employed, underestimated the distance sailed, logging rather more than 1,450 leagues to the Island of Jesus, and 167 leagues to the Candelaria Shoals. On the return journey, however, when he no longer had to contend with a favourable current, and when the winds were more variable, he was able to log a more correct distance, 700 leagues greater than the distance which he expected to have to navigate to México. This is entirely understandable, and is supported by Catoira's remark that 'the distance travelled from east to west was more than was put down . . . and upon our return voyage we found the way longer than we expected'.[3] Quirós suggests that Gallego had made an error of calculation rather than that the distances recorded for the outward voyage were the distances actually logged, and to the extent that he interprets the report of Mendaña and the pilots as evidence of the wrong sort of error, an error of calculation rather than an error of DR navigation, he misses the point of that report.

As we have already seen, Gallego deduced a distance of 1,638 leagues from Perú to the Candelaria Shoals from the distances which he logged. If we add the 700 leagues discrepancy on the return journey to this figure (1,638+700 = 2,338 leagues) the result is rather in excess of the actual distance between Callao and Roncador Reef (7,310 nautical miles or 2,284 Iberian leagues). This

---

[1] 'Hernan Gallego yendo navegando a la costa de Mexico se hizo çierto dia en tierra i que despues se navego para llegar della seteçientas leguas' (Santa Casa: MS. De Marina, f51), i.e. in sailing to México (on the return journey), Gallego expected to reach the land on one day, the day on which they would have sailed the distance across the Pacific which he expected to have to sail from the Solomons to México, but in fact he had to sail a further 700 leagues before sighting México.

[2] This part of the discurso is confusing, but I hope that I have rendered the meaning correctly.

[3] Amherst 1901: II: 461.

excess was probably due to the fact that the return voyage, which involved varied courses and crossing the line, was probably subjected to counter currents which tended to result in an overestimate of the distance sailed. A comparison of the three figures does illustrate and support the deduction that the outward underestimate of 646 leagues was the result of a failure to allow sufficiently for the E–W current, and that on the return journey, when the currents were varied or contrary, no such error was made; the error then, if Gallego estimated the distance of México from the Solomons relative to the distance logged from Perú correctly,[1] being one of overestimation of approximately 54 leagues.

The frigate was now despatched to circumnavigate the volcano and search for the *Almiranta*, and as the fleet waited off the island they were visited by natives in canoes. Quirós' description of the natives, their canoes and accoutrements, is a readily recognizable one of the natives of this island as they appeared to visiting Europeans in the eighteenth and nineteenth centuries and, to some extent, as they appear today. The first occasion of contact between the Spaniards and the indigenes was brief and bloody, and the latter quickly learnt the futility of discharging their arrows at these strange 'canoes' from another world. Mendaña, misled by the similarity of the natives to those of the islands which he had discovered in 1568, declared that their goal had been reached, and indeed seems to have identified the island, though which island he identified it with is not recorded.[2]

When the frigate returned, without news of the *Almiranta*, an anchorage was found in the mouth of a bay, in the lee of some rocks, on a bad bottom. As the tide rose the position of the ships became perilous, and during the night it became necessary to weigh anchor and put out to sea.[3] On the following morning a better anchorage was found in 12 fathoms, SE of the volcano, and sheltered to the SE; but this appears to have been unsatisfactory, for Quirós records that at night the ships were at sea, and that another anchorage was discovered on the following day, sheltered from all winds, in 15 fathoms. The actual location of each of these three anchorages can hardly be ascertained with any certainty, though they were certainly three of the four bays situated between Cape Byron and North Point on the north-east coast of the island,

---

[1] He presumably estimated the total distance to be sailed from San Cristóval on different courses as 1,700 leagues. This could well have been in error relative to the distance which he estimated from Perú to the Candelaria Shoals, for since the latter was 1,638 leagues, the total distance from San Cristóval to México should have been anticipated at more than 1,700 leagues. However, since Gallego thought the eastern end of San Cristóval to be more to the E of the meridian of the Candelaria Shoals that it in fact is, this is not surprising.

[2] '*el adelantado . . . los tuvo por la gente que buscaba, y decia: este es tal isla, ó tal tierra*' (Zaragoza 1876: I: 63).

[3] Swallow Bay, which is a likely identification for this anchorage, offers poor holding ground for anchors, and has rocks at the extremities of both of its arms.

but the last anchorage seems to be identifiable with either Carlisle Bay (10°
40′ 20″, 166° 3′ 40″ E) or Byron Bay (10° 40′ 20″ S, 166° 2′ 30″ E).[1]

From this anchorage the frigate was again despatched, under the command
of *Don* Lorenzo de Barreto, to explore the coastline and continue the search
for the *Almiranta*. It returned after several days with the report from Barreto
that, in the course of circumnavigating the island, a more populous bay had
been discovered which afforded as good an anchorage as that which they already had. During his circumnavigation Barreto had passed two well-populated and fair-sized islands close to the mainland, and to the SE at a distance
of 8 leagues (25⅗ nautical miles) he had sighted another island. To the *lesnoroeste*
(WNW) of the position from which the expedition had first sighted Santa
Cruz,[2] at a distance of 9 or 10 leagues, he had discovered three palm covered
islands, one seven leagues in circumference, the other two very small, bearing
NE from the volcano,[3] girt with reefs which extended to the WNW, and
inhabited by 'light brown people of a clear colour'.[4]

It seems clear from the narrative that during the circumnavigation the
expedition had noticed the insular character of the Trevanion[5] and Lord
Howe[6] Islands of the modern chart, and had sighted the island of Utupua
lying 37 miles to the SE of Santa Cruz in 11° 20′ S, 166° 33′ E. Utupua is
normally visible from off the east coast of Santa Cruz, and there seems to be no
good reason for concluding that they also saw the island of Vanikoro. *Don*
Lorenzo only reported seeing one island, and although it is possible that under
conditions of exceptional visibility Vanikoro is visible behind Utupua, and
that he did in fact see part of it without realizing that it was a separate island,
it is most uncertain. In his letter to de Morga, Quirós remarks of Utupua,
without naming it, that it must be linked with others[7]; a statement, not only
correct by virtue of Utupua's proximity to Vanikoro and the Northern New
Hebrides, but particularly important in relation to the subsequent ambitions of
Quirós and his belief that these islands were but outliers to the southern continent. The one large and two small islands to the NE of the volcano are identifiable as the Polynesian inhabited islands of Nibanga,[8] Banepi,[9] Lom Lom
and Namomblo-U, part of the Swallow or Reef Islands of the modern

---

[1] Quirós later remarks that they moved to a better anchorage in the same bay, distant half a league
(1⅗ nautical miles). With the exception of Swallow Bay, there is no bay on the north coast of Santa
Cruz of a greater width than half a mile, and it seems likely that we are here faced with the usual
exaggeration of distances.   [2] Zaragoza 1876: I: 70.

[3] Zaragoza 1876: II: 56 (his letter to de Morga).

[4] 'gente Mulata, color clara' (Zaragoza 1876: I: 70).

[5] *Te Motu Neo* in local Polynesian, *Matemotu* in Santa Cruzian.

[6] *Temotunoi* in Santa Cruzian and local Polynesian.   [7] Zaragoza 1876: II: 57.

[8] *Banga Ndene* (*Ndeni*), *Nimbanga Nendi* or *Nibanga Nede* in Reef Island language; *Pangani* in Polynesian. The native name for the island of Santa Cruz is *Ndeni*.

[9] *Banga Netepa* or *Nibanga Tema* in Reef Island language. *Pokoli* in Polynesian.

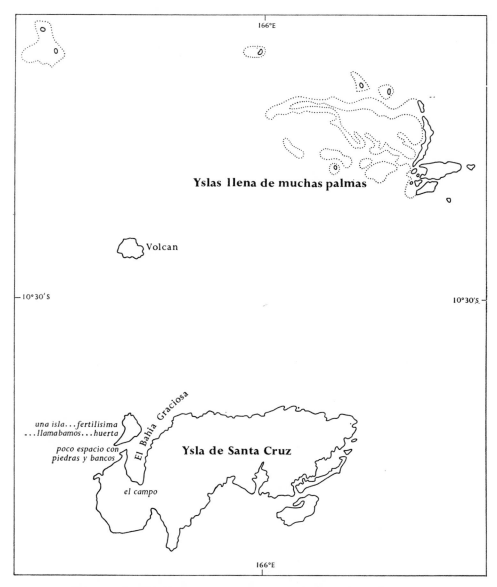

166°E

Yslas llena de muchas palmas

Volcan

10°30'S

10°30'S

una isla...fertilisima
...llamabamos...huerta

poco espacio con
piedras y bancos

El Bahia Graciosa

Ysla de Santa Cruz

el campo

166°E

Map XIX   The Ysla de Santa Cruz etc. as named by the expedition of 1595

charts.[1] The two latter islands in 10° 18′ S, 166° 15′ E would probably have appeared as one island, the large island of Quirós' narrative, and from Don Lorenzo's description it seems clear that the expedition did not proceed further N than Namomblo-U, and that Banepi was seen from a distance. Had they visited Banepi they would have realized that Lom Lom and Namomblo-U are two separate islands.[2] The reefs extending to the WNW would have been the

[1] I am grateful to Dr. William Davenport, an expert on the languages, social organization and cultures of Santa Cruz and the Reef Islands, for information relating to nomenclature.

[2] Known collectively to the indigenes as Ngailo.

Great Reef, known to the natives as *Tekauloa*, *Teakauloa* or *Ngamolo*, and extending WNW for a quite considerable distance.

As a result of *Don* Lorenzo's report the expedition now moved to the large bay which he had discovered; identifiable with the large bay at the north-western extremity of the island which is bounded to the NW by the island of Te Motu and was named by Mendaña *Graciosa*[1] *Bay*. Here at the foot of the bay, in a position which is identifiable today from Quirós' description of it,[2] an attempt was made to found a colony. It would be irrelevant in this context to

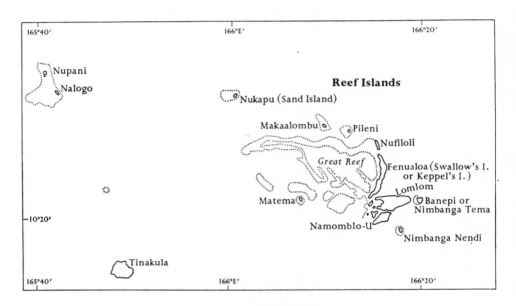

Map XX   The Reef Islands

attempt to describe in any detail the story of human frailty and disaster which emerges from the narrative of the settlement. Established with high hopes but little organization, the colony foundered as a result of bad leadership and the factional squabbles which divided its builders. Mendaña was certainly over-sanguine in granting the word *graciosa* to the bay in which the colony was established, for although it does not lack scenic attractions, anyone who knows the bay is bound to conclude that the *expedicionarios* were either easily pleased or were thoroughly sick of being at sea. It was in fact a most unsuitable island on which to attempt to establish a colony, and as the innate difficulties of the environment became apparent, as sickness spread and the vessels slowly rotted at anchor, it is not surprising that the soldiery became more mutinous and uncontrollable. Relations with the natives of the neighbourhood, which had begun on a mixed but generally amicable footing, deteriorated as Spanish

[1] *graciosa*—beautiful, pleasing.   [2] Zaragoza 1876: I: 75–81.

hunger, foraging and ill-discipline increased, and after the unprovoked murder of the local chief, Malopé, the hostility of the natives rendered permanent settlement impossible. Quirós himself ascribed all the blame to the Spaniards, and states quite categorically that the discontented soldiery deliberately provoked the natives to excite their hostility and render settlement impossible. Mendaña, sick in body, and apparently more concerned with the future of his immortal soul than with the future of the enterprise and his responsibilities, seems to have sunk into a state of penitential misery and to have failed completely in his duties and responsibilities as *Adelantado*. He took decisive action on only one occasion; action which even then he instigated as little more than the vassal of *Doña* Ysabel and her brothers, and which ended in Spaniard turning on Spaniard, bloodshed and butchery. The deaths of Mendaña,[1] and later of *Don* Lorenzo, rang the funeral bell of the whole enterprise, and in the face of an increasing death toll, opposition from the natives, and the unsuitability of the site, the settlers pleaded for their removal before the vessels became more unseaworthy.[2]

On 7 November 1595, little over two months after they had discovered the island, the colony was abandoned and the survivors moved out to the ships. As Quirós remarks: 'had only ten determined natives come, they could have killed us all ... The settlement remained a spectacle for sentiment and reflection on the disastrous and short-lived events which took place in it.'[3]

Only one more voyage was made within the group, when the frigate was despatched for a third time to search for the *Almiranta*, and when it seems to have revisited the Reef Islands, for Quirós records that whilst visiting 'the three islets already mentioned, surrounded by reefs', eight youths were captured.[4] The proposal of *Doña* Ysabel, Mendaña's widow and now *Gobernadora* or Governess, was that they should attempt to find the island of San Cristóval, in the hope that the *Almiranta* might have proceeded there, and to fulfil the real object of the voyage. In the event of their failing to find San Cristóval, her further proposal was that they should then sail for Manila, engage priests and settlers, and return to the discovery and settlement originally planned. The view of all was that after leaving Santa Cruz a course should be followed

---

[1] Zaragoza 1876: III: 126 (footnote 1).

[2] See Zaragoza 1876: II: 62–63; MNM: MS. 142, *Doc. No.* 5; AGI: *Patronato, legajo* 18, *No.* 10, *Ramo* 8, ('*Expediente formado en Mexico* ... 3°, *Testamento de* ... Mendaña ... 5°, *Una informacion* ...').   [3] Zaragoza 1876: I: 134.

[4] Zaragoza 1876: I: 129. Four subsidiary voyages seem to have been made in all:
  A. When the smoke of Tinakula was sighted and the frigate and galeot were despatched to investigate.
  B. When Santa Cruz had been sighted and the *Almiranta* had been missed, the frigate was despatched to circumnavigate Tinakula.
  C. The voyage of the frigate around Santa Cruz and to the Reef Islands.
  D. This last voyage in search of the *Almiranta*, to the Reef Islands and probably elsewhere.

to the WSW as far as 11° S, from which latitude, if neither the *Almiranta* nor the island of San Cristóval had been sighted, they should head for the Philippines.

The most significant feature of the proposal was the realization implicit in it that the Solomons in fact lay to the W of Santa Cruz and at no great distance, an idea which seems to have come from Quirós and on which he was later to enlarge. Quirós had determined the latitude of Graciosa Bay as 10° 20′ S, so that he could have estimated that a west-south-westerly course towards 11° S, if a true course, would have taken them approximately 96 miles to the W of Santa Cruz before they reached 11° S, but would have taken them approximately 200 miles if it was magnetic. Whilst Quirós estimated or observed the latitude of Graciosa Bay to be 10° 20′ S, Te Motu or Trevanion is in 10° 40′ S, and from that latitude 11° S would be reached 48 miles westwards on a true west-south-westerly course, or 100 miles westwards on a magnetic west-south-westerly course. Santa Ana and Santa Catalina lie 185 miles W of Santa Cruz, so that if Quirós determined 11° S correctly when he reached it, he would have been at the most only 100 miles W of Santa Cruz and still out of sight of San Cristóval. On the other hand, if he made an error of observation similar to that at Graciosa Bay, i.e. of −20′, he would not have thought himself to be in 11° S until he was in fact in 11° 20′ S, when he could have been as much as 200 miles W of Santa Cruz. There is, however, no reason to suppose that he would have made the same mistake; on the contrary he could have made a converse error, putting himself in 11° S, believed or actual, at between 48 and 100 miles W of Santa Cruz. Quirós would have expected to log a difference in latitude of 40′, presumably anticipated a westing of 96 or 200 miles, depending on whether the course was true or magnetic,[1] and would have been as likely to rely on the DR position of 11° S as on the solar observation of 11° S. It must also be appreciated that leeway and drift, beyond or below Quirós' estimate of it, could have increased or decreased the distance sailed from Santa Cruz before Quirós reckoned his latitude to be 11° S.

There is no suggestion in the narrative that when the expedition reached 11° S they would follow the latitude, and in view of the reasonable conclusion that San Cristóval lay quite close, in view of the westing to be made and Gallego's report that San Cristóval lay in 10° 40′ S, the distance and course planned were reasonable. From the advantageous position which we occupy, of being able to visualize Quirós' proposed route on an accurate chart, it is possible to conclude that although the expedition had a sporting chance of reaching San Cristóval, the odds were against them, and that they were likely to head for the Philippines at a point just short of that from which they could have sighted San Cristóval.

[1] 96 miles (30 Iberian leagues) if true, 200 miles (62½ Iberian leagues) if magnetic. The latter seems the more probable.

On 18 November the three surviving vessels weighed anchor in Graciosa Bay, contrary to the advice of Quirós who had advised the use of one vessel only, and set sail. The parlous condition of the vessels seems to have rendered their chances of reaching Manila rather slight, and Quirós records that he had to give the pilot of the frigate a chart, and explain its use, since he neither possessed nor knew how to use one. Between the 18th and noon on the 19th the expedition held a course to the WSW, when Quirós observed the sun and pronounced their latitude to be 11° S. As no land had been sighted *Doña* Ysabel gave the order to alter course to the NW and to sail for Manila, estimated by Quirós to lie 900 leagues distant.[1] It is not possible to determine the exact location of the vessels when they altered course, but it is certain that they did so at no great distance from the island of San Cristóval. Heading NW they must initially have run parallel to the archipelago, but if their course was magnetic they would have subsequently increased their distance from it as they ran to lower latitudes. The moment at which the decision to head NW was made is perhaps one of the most disappointing in the history of Pacific discovery and exploration, for the expedition must have been so very close to rediscovering the Islands of Solomon. Considering the state of the vessels and their occupants, however, it is probably just as well for them that they did not sight San Cristóval, for any delay, and any further attempt to establish a colony, might have ended in total disaster.

The expedition must have crossed Mendaña's route to the Solomons of 1568, and in all probability passed between Malaíta and Sikaiana. It is unlikely, however, that they passed S of Ontong Java, for on a magnetic course they would have crossed the latitude of 5° S more to the E. In his letter to de Morga Quirós remarks that he steered NW 'to avoid meeting islands on the way, for we were ill-prepared to go amongst them',[2] and in the Quirós-Bermúdez *relación* states that he headed NW before the south-east winds in order to avoid New Guinea, which was very close, and in order not to get amongst islands or other lands. He also adds that if it had not been for the unseaworthiness of the ship he would have given orders to coast along 'that land' to discover what it was.[3] It seems certain that Quirós is referring to New Guinea, the Solomons and such islands as might be off the eastern and north-eastern extremities of New Guinea. His desire to avoid them was sound, for the vessels were obviously in no condition for the hard pounding which their tackle might be subjected to in beating or tacking in the vicinity of unknown islands. At the same time Quirós' repressed desire to explore New Guinea was natural to the man himself, for the determination of its easterly extent was, with the discovery of the supposed antipodean continent and the rediscovery of the Islands of Solomon, one of the major tasks with which Spanish navigators were faced. By 17 November the expedition was in 5° S and Quirós, seeing a

---

[1] Zaragoza 1876: I: 142-3.   [2] Markham 1904: I: 146.   [3] Zaragoza 1876: I: 143.

tree trunk, reeds, straw and snakes in the water, concluded that New Guinea was close to, although in all probability the nearest lands were the atolls of Nukumanu and Ontong Java.

The account of the voyage to Manila which is recorded in the Quirós-Bermúdez *relación* is probably one of the classic horror stories of maritime travel. *Doña* Ysabel, with food and water in her larder, allowed the *expedicionarios*, their women and children, to sicken and die for want of it. The *Capitana*, early separated from the galeot and frigate, made slow progress with her rotting, leaking hull and exhausted half-starved crew, and reached Cavite, Manila, on 11 February 1596. The frigate eventually made Mindanao, but of the galeot Quirós reports a rumour to the effect that she was found on the coast of the Philippines with her sails set and her crew and passengers dead and decomposed. In the Philippines *Doña* Ysabel married a young nobleman, *Don* Fernando de Castro, who took possession of the assets of the expedition and arranged for the revictualling of the expedition for the voyage to New Spain.[1] Of the voyage to México Quirós tells us little more than that it was beset by hardships and trouble, but at last, on 11 December 1596, they arrived at Acapulco, where Quirós left the vessel and made his own way to Perú.[2]

---

[1] For documents relating to Quirós' sojourn in Manila, see AGI: *Patronato* 51, *No.* 3, *Ramo* 8, *Papeles de* . . . *Quirós*, ff114 (14 May 1596)—185v (28 June 1596). In folio 186v, a *petición* by Quirós, the object of the expedition of 1595 is referred to as the colonization and pacification of '*las Islas Occidentales del Mar del Sur que se dicen de Salomon*', indicating that officially at least the name Islas de Salomón was still used with reserve.

[2] The part of the Quirós-Bermúdez *relación* dealing with the expedition of 1595 concludes with the discourse by Quirós on the reasons for their failure to rediscover the Islands of Solomon.

V

The Expedition of Pedro Fernández de Quirós, 1605-1606

IT was during his voyage to Santa Cruz as Mendaña's Chief Pilot that Quirós became obsessed with the idea which was to dominate the remainder of his life; the discovery of the antipodean continent, or *Nuevo Mundo* as he was later to call it,[1] which he believed must occupy a quarter of the globe,[2] and to the supposed inhabitants of which he wished to offer the means for the salvation of their immortal souls. Of Quirós it surely can be said, with little reservation or qualification, that his motives were religious, his interests those of a curious, enquiring, Renaissance cosmographer and explorer. The several concepts of an antipodean continent which were prevalent during the sixteenth century have already been examined, together with some of the considerable body of scientific, cosmographical and cartographical evidence which seemed to justify belief in it. Quirós was not only a competent pilot[3] and cosmographer,[4] but he was also highly literate, as the contents of the Quirós-Bermúdez *relación* reveal, and it is certain that he would have been acquainted with earlier and contemporary writing on the subject of that continent. We have already seen evidence of his belief that all islands were indications of a neighbouring continent, the daughters of a great land-mother and the result of erosion, and it is certain that to him the existence of the islands discovered in 1568 and 1595, the Solomons and Marquesas in particular, indicated a continent to the S, since 'not one of the inhabited islands in all the discoveries made has been found far from some mainland'.[5] In a *discurso* which appears to have been delivered to the Viceroy of Perú in 1598(?),[6] he outlines in considerable detail his belief that the austral continent extended from New Guinea towards the Straits of Magellan, that the Marquesas, Santa Cruz, the Islas de Salomón and the Philippines

---

[1] See his *memorial* to the King of 1607, Zaragoza 1876: II: 191; RAH: *Papeles Varios de Indias* D90.

[2] Quirós' *memorial* to the King (BPM: MS. 2227, ff254-257), '*La parte incognita Austral es justamente quarta del Globo*'.

[3] In a *cédula* to the *Casa de Contratación* of 31 March 1603, the King referred to Quirós as a '*gran Piloto y muy platico de las navegaciones delas Indias orientales y occidentales*' (BNM: MS. 3099, f17).

[4] He produced more than 200 maps and globes, etc. (Zaragoza 1876: II: 281).

[5] Quirós' *memorial* to the King (1602) commencing '*Con liçensia de VM el Adelantado . . .*' (AGS: *Estado, legajo* K, 1631, *doc.* 244). The theory of erosion had been well expounded by Bourne in 1578 (Bourne 1578: V: 9), and persisted in the cartography of the seventeenth century, in relation to the antipodean continent, as a string of off-shore islands fringing that hypothetical continent.

[6] Santa Casa: MS. *De Marina*, ff51v-80.

formed a penetrable barrier to it, and that the continent itself equalled Europe and Asia in size.[1]

If his zeal to discover and to proselytize can be traced to any one moment during the voyage of 1595, it must surely have been that moment, so poignantly described in the Quirós-Bermúdez *relación*, when, off the Marquesas, a ten-year-old boy approached the ship in a canoe.

His eyes were fixed on the ship, his countenance angelic, with an aspect and vigour that promised much, of a good colour, not fair but white, his locks like those of a lady who prized them greatly. He was everything that I am able to say with reason about him, so that I never in all my life felt such anguish as when I thought that so beautiful a creature should be left to go to perdition.[2]

That Quirós had a particular interest in the Marquesas and in the inhabitants of that part of the continent which he believed to be immediately to the S of them is apparent from his early correspondence after the expedition of 1595.[3] His interest is understandable, for the Polynesian inhabitants of those islands must have seemed not only attractive in themselves, but doubly attractive when compared in retrospect with their painted and bellicose Melanesian counterparts on Santa Cruz. That he considered the Marquesas to be particularly important is indicated in the concluding words of his report on the voyage of 1595 to de Morga in which he wrote:

I beg you to keep it secret, for man does not know what time brings: for looking at it rightly, it is fit that the first islands [i.e. the Marquesas] should remain concealed until His Majesty be informed, and order whatever may be most for his service, for as they are placed, taking a middle position between Peru, New Spain, and this country [the Philippines], the English, on knowing it, might settle in them, and do much mischief in this sea.[4]

Quirós arrived in Paýta from Acapulco on 3 May 1598(7),[5] and here he wrote to *Don* Luis de Velasco, Viceroy of Perú, by whom he was received after an overland journey to his residence at Lima. Having reported on the voyage and the discoveries of 1595, Quirós requested a vessel of 60 tons and 40 sailors to enable him to return to discover 'those lands that I should find in those seas'.[6] Velasco, perhaps to avoid committing himself financially, perhaps

---

[1] See also his letter to the Viceroy of Perú (Santa Casa: MS. *De Marina*, ff81–92v) and his *memorial* to the Viceroy (AUS: MS. CCCXXXVII, f122) in which he writes of '*Muchas yslas o tierra firme antipodas*'.   [2] Zaragoza 1876: I: 36–37.

[3] '*Por todas las razones dichas digo que piadosamente se puede creer que aquestas quatro Islas trinen dela parte del sueste por el sur hasta quasi a el oeste otras Islas o tierra firme*' (Santa Casa: MS. *De Marina*, f85). See also AUS: MS. CCCXXXVII, ff121–125v.   [4] Markham 1904: I: 157.

[5] Zaragoza 1876: I: 195. Quirós gives the year as 1598, but 1597 appears to be the correct year.

[6] Zaragoza 1876: I: 196. Quirós states in his *relación* that he wrote three letters or petitions to *Don* Luis de Velasco, one from Paýta (1598), and two from Cartagena (1598 and 1599). See AUS: MS. CCCXXXVII, ff121–125v, where three *memoriales* of 1597, apparently written at Los Reyes (Lima), are contained; ff121–123v '*Copia del Memorial de los motivos y de otros dos que di en la ciudad de los Reyes a Vissorey don Luys de Velasco el año de 1597 . . .*' '*Porque es parte de çirculo la sombra . . .*', ff123v–124 '*Copia del segundo Memorial*', '*Mucho qui siera . . . criaturas*'; ff124–125v '*Copia del 3° Memorial . . .*', '*Dos sin esta . . . memoriales*'. The Santa Casa MS., *De Marina*, contains two *memoriales* written by

for the reasons which Quirós gives, replied that he was unable to accede without Royal approval. He suggested, in view of the importance of the proposal, that Quirós was the person best fitted to plead his case and that he should proceed to the Court of Spain. From Cartagena Quirós wrote to Velasco giving a more detailed account of his proposals, so that, should he die *en route*, his proposals would not die with him.[1] Proceeding to Havana and thence for Spain, the treasure fleet in which he was travelling was hit by a storm and forced to run for Cartagena, and it was not until February 1600, that he reached Spain.

There he discovered that the year 1600 had been proclaimed a Holy Year, and accordingly determined to make a pilgrimage to Rome. Here he had the good fortune to be received by the Duke of Sesa, the Spanish Ambassador to the Holy See, to whom he described his recent voyage, his plans for another, and his purpose to convey the means of salvation to the benighted indigenes of the austral lands. He prepared a treatise on navigation for the Duke, in which he pointed to the limitations of the practices of his day, and the value which might be derived from a voyage to the austral lands followed by a circumnavigation of the globe. During this voyage he could test instruments which he had devised, study the important question of magnetic variation, and generally pursue such research as might lead to the improvement and simplification of the art of navigation.[2] Impressed by Quirós' competence as a navigator and cosmographer,[3] de Sesa arranged for him to be examined by reputable

Quirós to the Viceroy, the first indexed as '*Carta y discurso del Capitan Pero fernàndez Quiros al Virey del Peru . . . el descubrimiento de las partes inconitas del nueuo Austral*' (ff51v–80), the second as '*Otra carta del . . . Capitan Quiros*' (ff81–92v). The second is followed by '*la respuesta que hizo del Virrey della*' (ff92v–93) ('*La respuesta del Virrei a estos dos memoriales*'). These appear to be the Cartagena *memoriales*.

[1] Zaragoza 1876: I: 196–7.

[2] This treatise is to be found in the Santa Casa MS. *De Marina*, ff100–104v, and attached to a letter of de Sesa to the King of 1602 (AGS: *Estado, legajo* K 1631, *doc.* 245, ff1–4, '*Punto en la navegacion . . . noticia de la navegacion*'). Ff100–101v of the Santa Casa MS. and ff1–2 of AGS: *Estado, legajo* K 1631, *doc.* 245 are similar to the opening pages of what appears to be a revised form of the treatise included in a *memorial* by Quirós to the King of 1610 (Zaragoza 1876: II: 357–9, '*Punto en la navegacion . . . sí daña su parte*'). The Santa Casa MS. and AGS versions are similar, only varying in respect of occasional words and phrases, but whilst in the AGS version (AGS: *Estado, legajo* K 1631, *doc.* 245, f4) he writes of his proposed circumnavigation as a remedy for the problem of variation, in the Santa Casa version (Santa Casa: MS. *De Marina*, f102) he describes it as a remedy 'for all the impediments of navigation'.

[3] See AGS: *Estado, legajo* K, 1631, *doc.* 33 and *doc.* 34. Quirós illustrated his negotiations with maps which he had prepared (Zaragoza 1876: I: 198), but of the total output of his maps only one appears to have survived. This, dated 1598 and in the possession of *Signor Avv.* Franco Novacco of Venice, has been referred to in one of two papers (Kelly 1961(a): Map 1) by Kelly which appeared after the completion of this book. These papers (Kelly 1961(a) and (b)), of which Kelly 1961(a) offers some comments on the question of cartography and apparently owes much to Forsyth, have been cited in the Bibliography. The Quirós map adds little to our knowledge, for it does not lay down the discoveries of 1595, but lays down the Solomons and New Guinea in the rather standard form of late sixteenth-century Pacific charts and with hypothetical coastlines extending southwards to create a promontory bearing the name *Terra Australis Incognita*. To the extent that Quirós saw and used Gallego's *carta de marear* it is possible that this outline of the Solomons, albeit roughly copied, is the outline laid down by Gallego. See Plate XXI.

pilots and cosmographers in Rome and, on the strength of their approval, secured an audience for him with the Holy Father. Again he was well received, and obtained encouragement for his enterprise in the form of letters of recommendation to Philip III and other dignitaries of the Spanish Court, and six papal briefs.[1]

It was not, however, until the spring of 1602, due to bureaucratic delays in the Vatican, that Quirós was able to leave for Spain, but he now had the support and approval of the Pope, a support which no Catholic monarch could

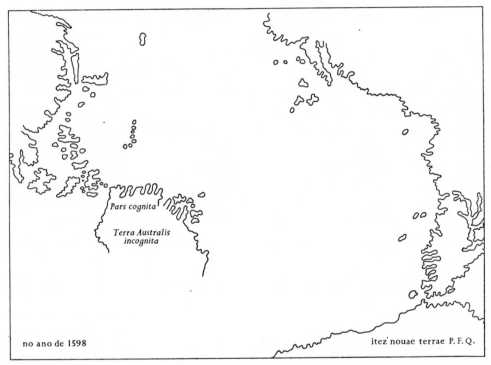

Pars cognita

Terra Australis
incognita

no ano de 1598   itez nouae terrae P. F. Q.

Map XXI   A chart by Quirós of 1598 in the collection of *Signor* Avv. Franco Novacco of Venice, redrawn.

ignore, and the added support of the Duke of Sesa. The support of the Duke was hardly less important than that of the Pope for, with the recommendation of the pilots and cosmographers of Rome behind it, it offered some assurance of success and a tangible return for the Spanish authorities. In a letter to Philip III dated Rome, 3 February 1602, the Duke referred to the opinion of those cosmographers, and to their agreement with Quirós' proofs and reasoning that a great continental tract or number of islands stretched from the Straits of Magellan to New Guinea and *Java Major*. They had agreed that much of this

[1] See Quirós' *memoriales* to the Pope, Rome, 1602 (VSdS: Vol. CCCXIX, ff73–77v), the Papal Brief to the ecclesiastics of the Indies dated March 1602, and Brief to the Franciscan prelates of Perú in the same collection of documents. See also Zaragoza 1876: II: 251.

continent or tract must lie in the vicinity of 15° S,[1] and that its discovery should be effected without loss of time. He also commented on the report which he had received of Quirós as 'a great pilot' from Diego de Soria, Dominican Prior at Manila, and expressed his own belief in Quirós' diligence, experience, decency, zeal, disinterestedness and desire to serve God and King.

Arriving at Valladolid in the early summer of 1602, Quirós presented two *memoriales* to the King,[2] received an assurance of consideration,[3] and then addressed himself to the various members of the *Consejo de Estado* likely to be able to assist him.[4] Although his reception was mixed, some arguing that Spain had quite sufficient territory already, that the real problem was settlement not discovery, and that distant colonies were difficult and costly to maintain,[5] on 5 April 1603 he received the King's consent and orders for the proposed expedition. Three royal *cédulas* dated 31 March 1603 are included in the Quirós-Bermúdez *relación*, the first of which, addressed to Velasco as Viceroy of Perú, or his successor the Count of Monterey, ordered that Quirós be provided with two good ships, fitted out. manned, victualled, armed and equipped at the royal expense, reiterated the good reports which he had received of the project from Rome, and implied a partial agreement to the proposed circumnavigation. The Viceroy was further instructed to report immediately to the King by the first ship for Spain after Quirós' arrival in Perú on the arrangements which he had made, and the King added that whilst the plan had been effected through the *Consejo de Estado*, instead of through the more normal channels of the *Consejo de Indias*, this was not to be used as an excuse for the creation of delays and difficulties.[6]

The second *cédula*, also addressed to the Viceroy of Perú, repeated the strict injunctions of the King for the immediate execution of his orders, stressed his personal interest in the venture, and gave the object of the voyage as 'the discovery of the Austral islands and lands as far as Nueva Guinea and Java Major'.[7] The third *cédula*, addressed to all his administrators, of whatever title, quality, nation or condition, instructed them to receive, protect, and succour the *expedicionarios*, to provide them with the necessities of their travel, and stated the object of the voyage as the discovery of 'Nueva Guinea and

---

[1] AGS: *Estado, legajo* K 1631, *doc.* 33. The King repeated this report in a *cédula* to the Viceroy of Perú dated 31 March 1603 (Zaragoza 1876: I: 203).

[2] AGS: *Estado, legajo* K 1631, *doc.* 243, 'Pedro F. de Quiros, digo questa por descubir . . .', doc. 244, 'con liçensia . . .'.

[3] For Quirós' movements between 1600 and 1602 see Zaragoza 1876: I: 198–202.

[4] Of these *Don* Pedro Franqueza seems to have been particularly sympathetic, probably in consequence of a letter which he received personally from the Duke of Sesa. (See *Duque* de Sesa to *Don* Pedro Franqueza, Rome, 2 February 1602, AGS: *Estado, legajo* K 1631, *doc.* 34.)

[5] Zaragoza 1876: I: 201.

[6] Zaragoza 1876: I: 202–7; AGS: *Estado, legajo* 196; see also AGI: *Patronato* 51, f228v; and BNM: MS. 3099, ff9–12v.

[7] Zaragoza 1876: I: 208–9; AGS: *Estado, legajo* 196; BNM: MS. 3099, ff13–13v.

Java Major, and other austral islands and lands'.[1] On 9 May 1603, the King issued yet another *cédula*, at the instigation of Quirós, in which he ordered that, in the event of Quirós' death,[2] the expedition be prosecuted under another commander.

The circumstances of Quirós' departure are summarized in Torquemada's *Monarchia Indiana*, probably on information derived from Quirós himself, in which the author gives the itinerary of the expedition as being:

> to circumnavigate the world, returning to Spain by the East Indies, first discovering—since that was their prime object, the unknown lands of the south; thence proceeding via New Guinea to arrive at China, Maluco, and the two Javas, the Great and the Less, and all the other famous islands abounding in silver, gold, gems and spices.[3]

Proceeding to Seville, where he obtained a passage through the *Casa de Contratación*,[4] Quirós sailed for New Spain and arrived in Guadalupe on 2 August 1603. After considerable delay and misfortune he reached Callao on 6 March 1605, but, even after he had been received by the Viceroy, it required a succession of *memoriales* and a determined struggle against opposition before arrangements for the expedition were finally concluded in December 1605.[5] Among his opponents Quirós mentions *Don* Fernando de Castro, husband of *Doña* Ysabel de Barreto, who regarded his proposals as entrenching upon his own rights to the Solomons, inherited through his wife from Mendaña, and of which he was titular *Adelantado*[6]; but Quirós appears to have assured him of his intentions and to have secured his goodwill.

The fleet consisted of three vessels, the *Capitana* (*San Pedro*), the *Almiranta*, and a *zabra* or inshore sloop; had a complement of 300 sailors, soldiers, and six Franciscan friars; and was supplied with victuals for twelve months and seed and animals for those who intended to settle. The Chief Pilot, reluctantly it appears, was one Juan Ochoa de Bilboa who, according to Quirós, did much harm, and the second-in-command or *Almirante* was Luis Váez de Torres. According to Quirós' sailing orders and instructions,[7] the fleet was to head WSW as far as 30° S,[8] when, if no land had been sighted, the course should be

---

[1] Zaragoza 1876: I: 209. The different wording and change of emphasis in describing the object of the voyage in this more public *cédula* was probably designed to conceal the immediate object of the expedition.   [2] See also the *cédula* in BNM: MS. 3099, ff15–15v.

[3] Torquemada 1723: Tome 1, Book V, Cap. LXIV: 738.

[4] See also AGS: *Estado, legajo* 196, 'Al Presidente de la Casa de Contratacion de Sevilla. De Valladolid a 31 de Marco 1603. Embarcacion y dos instrumentos del Capitan P. F. de Quiros.'

[5] Zaragoza 1876: I: 212–24.

[6] For de Castro's assumption of the title of *Adelantado* see AGI: *Patronato, legajo* 18, No. 10 *Ramo* 8; Zaragoza 1876: II: 62; MNM: MS. 142, *doc.* No. 5; and AGI: *México* 116. Fernando de Castro was in fact the fourth Governor of the Islands of Solomon.   [7] Zaragoza 1876: I: 225–41.

[8] According to Juan de Iturbe, the Purser to the expedition, the southern limit was 40° S (BNM: MS. 3099, f136, *memorial* to the King, México, 25 March 1607), and Arias, in a *memorial* written 1615–21, records that the route conformed with that followed by Juan Fernández when he made his supposed continental discovery in 40° S (Markham 1904: II: 526, 528).

altered to NW as far as 10° 15′ S, after which a westerly course should be followed in search of Santa Cruz, 1,850 leagues from Perú. If any vessel arrived
there alone it was to remain in Graciosa Bay for three months to await the
others. Once the fleet was reunited the further route of the expedition would
be decided upon, but in the event of only one vessel reaching Santa Cruz it was
thereafter to head SW to 20° S, then NW to 4° S and westwards in search of
New Guinea.[1] After coasting Northern New Guinea the vessel was to proceed
to Manila, thence via the East Indies to Spain.

By making a scale sketch-map of the Pacific as Quirós probably viewed it,
by laying down the principal land areas in their relative positions as Quirós
reported or believed them,[2] and by plotting his proposed route, some indication can be obtained of the approximate limits of the *tierra firme austral* as
Quirós deduced and expected to discover them. In heading WSW from Callao
to 30° S it seems clear that he hoped to encounter the eastern low latitude limits
of the continent at their shortest distance from Perú. If he failed to make such a
discovery, he intended to head for better-known latitudes in which the navigation to Santa Cruz was known to be possible, perhaps with the hope of sighting
some north-eastern promontory of the continent *en route*, but prudently
avoiding further navigation southwards or westwards in higher latitudes and
unknown waters where the prevailing winds and currents could only be
guessed at. In heading SW from Santa Cruz he would have expected to strike
the continental coast in fairly low latitudes, particularly if New Guinea was a
promontory of it, and it is clear that he would by then have been in the supposed longitude of the most easterly known part of New Guinea.

In proposing, in the event of continued failure, a course NW to 4° S and
thence westwards, which would have brought him well to the westward of
the eastern extremity of known New Guinea, it seems likely that Quirós had
two ideas in mind; one, in the event of the distance of New Guinea having
been underestimated, of determining the exact position of its eastern extremity; and a second one, probably the more likely, that New Guinea might be an
island, in which case he could follow its southern coast westwards and sail
thereafter for Java or the Moluccas. In risking putting himself under the southern or a south-eastern coast of New Guinea, a risk which Torres was subsequently to take, Quirós was prepared to brave what his successors were for
many years to fight shy of, namely the danger of finding themselves within a
deep bay, held on a lee shore by the south-easterlies, or prevented from rounding the eastern extremity of New Guinea by the Asiatic monsoon. In view of
his firm belief in the austral continent it is doubtful if Quirós really expected
that this phase of the plan would have to be attempted, and probably anticipated

---

[1] When it is recalled that the most easterly known limit of New Guinea lay in 5° S, the plan to
proceed to 4° S before heading W is understandable.

[2] See Zaragoza 1876: I: 39, 76, 180-92.

that the continent would be discovered much earlier in the voyage. It is particularly interesting, in view of Quirós' deductions on the position of the Solomons[1] and his conclusion that they lay between New Guinea and Santa Cruz, that his proposed course seems, if anything, to have been designed to avoid them. This is understandable, for the Solomons were a group to which he had no claim, and to enter which would have infringed the rights of de Castro. It is probable that de Castro's earlier opposition to Quirós' voyage was in fact removed by Quirós' assurances, illustrated by reference to his proposed route, that he had no designs on the Solomons and only intended to use Santa Cruz as a rendezvous.

The sailing orders also set out the duties of the *Almirante*, Torres. They required him to take solar observations and observations of *Crucero*[2]; to plot the daily courses and positions with due allowance for current, leeway and magnetic variation; to take due account of natural phenomena indicative of land; and to chart such lands as were discovered or visited in their observed or deduced latitudes and longitudes, and in a manner representative of their size and configuration. They further required him to make a detailed record of the social organization, religion, appearance and customs of the native peoples encountered, and provided rigid rules for the conduct of the *expedicionarios* with native peoples, enjoining charity and restraint, but ordering the seizure of hostages as a safety-precaution. In addition, they laid down rules on religious observances, the discipline of the crew, the daily rationing of the expedition, and communication between the vessels of the fleet.

On 21 December 1605, the fleet weighed anchor off Callao and headed WSW. By January they were in 26° S, but the variable winds, a strong swell from the S and the natural uneasiness of navigating in unknown waters, induced them to head WNW to 25° S.[3] On 26 January they discovered an island in 25° S, 800 leagues from Lima, to which Quirós gave the name *Lunapuesta*[4] or *Encarnación*,[5] and which can be identified with Ducie (24° 40' S, 124° 48' W).[6] In that latitude the expedition continued westwards and, at a distance of 870 leagues from Perú, in 24° 45' S, discovered another island which Quirós named *San Juan Bautista*[7] and which may be identified with Henderson Island (24° 22' S, 128° 18' W).[8] Heading WNW, land was sighted on 3

---

[1] Zaragoza 1876: I: 180–92.   [2] The Southern Cross.

[3] According to Arias, in his *memorial* to the King after 1614, Torres urged that the voyage be prosecuted to 40° S (Markham 1904: II: 528), but in his letter to the King of 12 July 1607 (Markham 1904: II: 456) Torres only states that he considered it proper that they should have continued to 30° S.

[4] Zaragoza 1876: I: 243.

[5] *Memorial* of 1609 (Zaragoza 1876: II: 229). In de Leza's journal it is named *Anegada* and its distance from Perú is given as 1,000 leagues. De Leza named the sea between Perú and *Anegada* the *Golfo de Nuestra Señora de Loreto* (Zaragoza 1876: II: 87).   [6] Maude 1959: 310–11.

[7] Zaragoza 1876: I: 244. De Leza names it *Sin Puerto* (Zaragoza 1876: II: 86) and gives its distance from Perú as 1,075 leagues.   [8] Maude 1959: 310–11.

February which eventually revealed itself as another island, lying in 20° 30′ S, 1,030 leagues from Lima, to which was given the name *San Telmo*[1] and which must have been South Marutea.[2] Further to the WNW four islands were sighted on the 4th, in 20° S and 1,050 leagues from Perú,[3] to which were given the name *Las Cuatro Coronadas* and which are identifiable with the Actaeon Group.[4] On 9 February they passed an island 75 leagues further to the W, in 18° 30′ S, which they named *San Miguel*[5] (Vairaatea),[6] and on the following day yet another, in 18° S and 1,180 leagues from Lima, which they named *La Conversión de San Pablo*[7] (Hao Island).[8] In the following few days they sighted and named *Deçena* (Tauere), *Sagitaria* (Rekareka) and *Fugitiva* (Raroia).[9]

Their apparently never-ending voyage was by now becoming irksome to the crew and, encouraged by the Chief Pilot, Ochoa de Bilboa, whom Quirós accused of sabotage and of altering the course,[10] mutinous murmurings began. Quirós was himself disturbed by the fact that they had already reached low latitudes without sighting 'the mother of those islands ... which had been passed',[11] and perhaps also by the suggestion of the crew that the course followed must have been parallel to the continental coastline, and that they would shortly find themselves engulfed by contrary winds. He now determined to head NW to 10° 40′ S in order to reach San Bernardo, discovered during the voyage of 1595 (Puka Puka),[12] and on 18 February in 10° 45′ S, the expedition altered course to the W to search for it and for Santa Cruz.[13] Three days later an island was sighted in 10° 40′ S, 1,400 leagues by Quirós' estimate from Perú, which he identified as *San Bernardo*, although Torres appears to have realized that it was not. In fact this island was probably Caroline Island (10° S, 150° 14′ W),[14] which, assuming that San Bernardo was Puka Puka, was considerably to the W of San Bernardo. On 1 March, whilst they were still on a westerly course, another island was discovered in 10° 20′ S, 1,600 leagues

---

[1] Zaragoza 1876: I: 247. Torres made the distance 1,110 leagues, his pilot (Fuenti Duenas) 1,140 leagues, Bernal 1,240 leagues, and all were agreed that they were SSW of the Marquesas (Zaragoza 1876: II: 89). Their position must in fact have been almost SSE of the Marquesas.

[2] Maude 1959: 310-11. [3] Zaragoza 1876: I: 247.

[4] Maude 1951: 310-11. De Leza gives their name as *las Anegadas* (Zaragoza 1876: II: 91), and their position as 350 leagues W of '*destas islas de Mendosa*'.

[5] Zaragoza 1876: I: 248. [6] Maude 1959: 311-15.

[7] Zaragoza 1876: I: 256. [8] Maude 1959: 311-15.

[9] Zaragoza 1876: I: 257; Maude 1959: 311-15. Sharp 1960 identifies *Deçena* as Amanu, *Sagitaría* as Raroia, and *Fugitiva* as Takume. The identifications are an open question.

[10] Zaragoza 1876: I: 257-8. [11] Zaragoza 1876: I: 259.

[12] The complainants had some grounds for discontent, for whilst Quirós' reluctance to linger in higher latitudes is understandable, whilst shortage of water necessitated his making a known island soon, the austral continent, as cartographers conceived and mapped it, would have been more certainly reached by heading SW. Quirós clearly hoped to find the continent in more equable climes in the vicinity of islands which he had previously visited.

[13] Zaragoza 1876: I: 259. The Quirós-Bermúdez *relación* gives the date as the 19th, de Leza's log as the 18th. [14] Maude 1959: 311-15.

from Lima, to which Quirós gave the name *Peregrina*[1] and which is identifiable with Rakahanga (10° 02′ S, 161° 05′ W).

Continued failure to make the expected landfall, shortage of water and the plottings of malcontents, had reduced the crew to a state of mutiny, and doubts were expressed as to the reality of Quirós' continent. On 25 March the Chief Pilot claimed that they had now sailed 2,220 leagues from Perú, a distance well in excess of the 1,850 leagues at which Quirós had said the island of Santa Cruz lay, and Quirós called a meeting of the pilots in order to determine the general consensus of opinion on their position. Considerable disparity in their several reckonings was immediately apparent, their estimates varying from 2,300 leagues to 2,000 leagues, and Torres, who estimated the latter distance, confessed to doubts at the accuracy of his estimate. According to Quirós[2] an examination of the Chief Pilot's chart revealed an error of 600 leagues, apparently the result of his having calculated longitude along the west-south-westerly course of the first phase of the voyage instead of calculating the difference in longitude, of failing to correctly reconcile the estimated distances run and the DR positions with the observed latitudes, and of failing to allow sufficiently for variation, leeway and current. This particular passage throws considerable light on the navigational techniques employed, in particular on the method of reconciling the DR position with the observed latitude, but it seems very likely, in view of the estimate of Torres, that Quirós overstated the error made by the Pilot in order to support his earlier estimate of the distance of Santa Cruz from Perú.[3]

[1] Zaragoza 1876: I: 272. In a *memorial* of 1609 (Zaragoza 1876: II: 229) Quirós gives the name as *la del Peregrino*, Torres calls it *Matanza* (Markham 1904: II: 457), and Torquemada calls it *Gente Hermosa* (Torquemada 1723: Tome 1, Book V, Cap. LXVI).   [2] Zaragoza 1876: I: 275–7.

[3] The Chief Pilot's error seems to have been the considerable one of regarding the distance run WSW from Callao to 26° S, converted from leagues to degrees, as the Difference of Longitude between Callao and the meridian reached in 26° S. It is doubtful, however, if Quirós would have calculated the Difference of Longitude with any exactitude, for he almost certainly treated the 'nautical triangle' (composed of the Distance, Difference of Latitude, Difference of Longitude and Course Angle) as a Pythagorean triangle, used a plane chart, and only allowed for the sphericity of the earth by applying tables of the length of a degree of longitude in different latitudes to distances sailed along a parallel which he might wish to express in degrees. As early as 1513 Johann Stoeffler had stated the principle of Plane or Mid-Latitude sailing: that the Difference of Longitude should be taken as if in the Middle or Mean Latitude, but the correct demonstration of the 'nautical triangle' of Plane Sailing (i.e. calculating the Departure as the Distance Run × the Sine of the Course Angle, or as the Difference of Longitude × the Cosine of the Mean or Middle Latitude, and calculating the Difference of Longitude as the Departure × the Secant of the Mean or Middle Latitude) was an English achievement occurring at this time. The correct demonstration of the Mercator projection (which permitted the 'nautical triangle' to be drawn) and of the principles of Mercator Sailing was another contemporary English achievement, and as late as the end of the seventeenth century Spanish and Portuguese pilots were still taught to use plane charts. Although Quirós probably knew of the contemporary advances, and certainly appreciated the shortcomings of the techniques commonly employed, it is doubtful if he employed anything other than the established techniques, and in the low latitudes and parallel sailing of much of the voyage the effect would not have been too serious.

The westerly course was maintained, 'with much anxiety, on account of the confusion which existed in determining the distance of the ships from the port of Lima, and more, on account of the allowance [of food and water] being so short'.[1] On 3 April, de Leza noted in his log-book that they must have gone by guess or dead-reckoning at least 2,120 leagues, and that since Santa Cruz was reported to lie 1,850 leagues from Perú, then either they themselves had overestimated the distance run, due to occasional calms, or the expedition of 1595 had underestimated the distance to Santa Cruz.[2] On 7 April, at 3 p.m., the lookout of the flagship sighted high land to the NW, and the ships' bows were brought round on to a course for it. Hove-to during the night, the expedition found itself at dawn on the following day above a 12 fathom bank which was crossed in safety, and it was not until the 9th that they made and anchored off the land, the *zabra* and a ship's boat being sent forward to reconnoitre.

The land revealed itself as one of a small chain of islands, of which it was the largest, and although the *expedicionarios* were met by hostile natives, one arquebus shot was sufficient to disperse them. Peaceful relations were established at the intervention of the local chief, whose name the Spaniards understood to be Tumai (*Tamay* or *Tomai*). Collectively, the several narratives of the expedition provide a very complete picture of the island, the native name for which was *Taumaco*,[3] its inhabitants and their relations with the Spaniards, and permit its undoubted identification with Taumako, the largest of the Polynesian inhabited Duff Islands in 9° 57′ S, 167° 12′ E. Estimated to lie in 10° 20′ S and 1,650 leagues from Perú,[4] it is described in the narratives as being ten leagues in circumference, well-wooded and moderately high. Two leagues to the W was another inhabited island of much the same size, known to the natives as *Temelflua*, and to the NE were two other small rocky islets. De Leza records that three islets lay to the W of the main island, which from a distance appeared as two humps. The village of the chief lay on the south side of the island, situated on a small island and fortified by a wall, and earned from the Spaniards the appropriate name of *Venecia*.[5] The natives were tall, '*mulatto*', and armed with bows and arrows, and Torres remarks of them that 'they are great seafarers; they have much beard, are great archers and hurlers of darts; the vessels in which they sail are large and can go a great way'.[6] Their

---

[1] Zaragoza 1876: I: 280.

[2] Zaragoza 1876: II: 117. He estimated that Santa Cruz must be 2,000 leagues from Perú, an estimate later supported by Torres (Markham 1904: II: 459).

[3] The spelling of the Quirós-Bermúdez *relación*.

[4] Zaragoza 1876: I: 287. Torres gives the distance from Perú as 1,940 leagues (Markham 1904: II: 459), its circumference as 6 leagues, and the native name as *Taomaco*. De Leza gives the position as 10° 10′ S, 1,950 leagues from Perú (Zaragoza 1876: II: 118–20).

[5] The main village is still on this site and still has its fortification wall.

[6] Markham 1904: II: 460

clothing was of a woven substance, and they had large well-found canoes, with planked decks and outriggers, which were capable of carrying 30 or 40 persons. On being asked about the Volcano discovered by Mendaña in 1595, Tumai, who implied that he had heard of Europeans and their weapons,[1] informed Quirós that it lay at a distance of five days' sailing to the W, that its native name was *Mami*, and that it was close to the island of *Indeni*. The latter the Spaniards recognized as the native name for Santa Cruz.[2] To their new discovery were given the several names of *Nuestra Señora del Socorro*,[3] *Nuestra Señora de Loreto*[4] and *Monterrey*.[5]

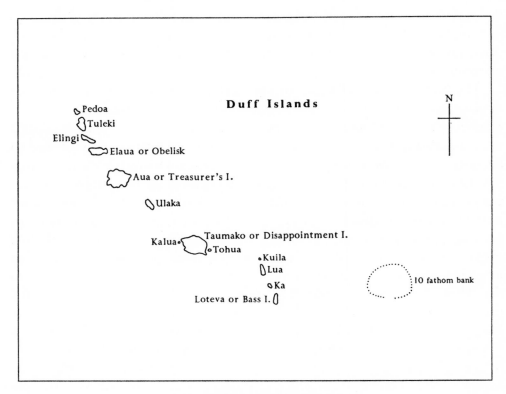

Map XXII   The Duff Islands

When Quirós departed from Perú on his second voyage to the Western Pacific in 1605, he had behind him his experience as a navigator, the particular experience of a previous voyage to these regions, and a background of considerable thought applied over several years to the whole question of Pacific

---

[1] According to de Prado, he gave them to understand that he was at Santa Cruz when the Spaniards killed Małope (Stevens 1929: 108–9).

[2] The local Polynesian name for Santa Cruz is *Deni*, and the volcano of Tinakula is known to the Santa Cruzians as *Temami* and to the local Polynesians as *Tenakula*.

[3] Zaragoza 1876: I: 287 (Quirós).   [4] Zaragoza 1876: II: 120 (de Leza).

[5] Quirós, in a *memorial* of 1609; Zaragoza 1876: II: 229.

topography and navigation, particularly to the question of his own and Gallego's previous navigation. Whilst the basic techniques of navigation were essentially the same in 1606 as they had been in 1595, some improvements had resulted from a realization that two major sources of error in celestial observations of latitude were the dip of the horizon and the sun's parallax, and attempts to counteract them were being made throughout maritime Europe.[1]

Quirós' instructions to the *Almirante* and pilots of the expedition reflect a rigorous approach to the problems of navigation, even though his pilots were by no means all fitted or able to implement them. He ordered daily sun sights and the nightly observation of the Southern Cross[2] to determine the latitude; the daily plotting of the ship's position with allowance for leeway of divergence from the intended course due to wind, current and the variation of the compass needle; the correction of the needle against the sun or against a known star when on its meridian; and the careful recording of the number of leagues logged, wind changes, showers, currents, flights of birds, shoals of fish and all signs of land.[3] The several accounts of the voyage itself provide a more complete picture of the navigation than do the narratives of the two earlier expeditions, this being particularly true of the Quirós-Bermúdez *relación* and the log-book of the Chief Pilot, de Leza. In addition, considerable evidence of the shortcomings of DR navigation is to be found in a comparison of the recorded estimates of the several pilots of the distances run across the Pacific.

Taking several of the landfalls as examples, some idea of the accuracy of the navigation can be obtained. Between Perú and La Encarnación (Ducie), a distance of 800 leagues was determined, an underestimate of the actual distance,

[1] In 1599 Edward Wright had published tables of dip and parallax, and had examined the question of determining magnetic variation correctly with the aid of tables of amplitude (of which the earliest known printed ones appeared in 1608 in the *Hydrografía* of the Portuguese Figueiredo).

[2] It is doubtful if the Southern Cross was used to any real extent, and this was probably just as well, for there is some doubt as to the accuracy with which *Crucero* was used. Apparently mentioned for the first time by John de Lisboa in his *Tratado de agulha de marear*, on the basis of his observations of it in the East in 1505, *Regimentos* of the Southern Cross appeared in navigating manuals during the sixteenth century (e.g. the sixteenth-century Italian manual in the Library of the Royal Geographical Society, see Taylor 1931). John Winter, the English voyager, describing his voyage of 1577-8, refers to the 'Crosiers' as 30° in latitude from the South Pole, and advises that 'the lowest star of the said Crosiers is to be taken: when it is directly under the uppermost: and being so taken, as many degrees as it wanteth of thirty, so many you are to the northward of the Equinoctial, and as many degrees more than thirty so many degrees you are to the southwards of the Equinoctial'. Argenzola, in his *History of the Conquest of the Moluccas* (Madrid 1609) describes *La Cruzera* as 30° from the Antarctic Pole and refers to Sarmiento's view of it on his voyage to Magellan's Straits, and the *Regimento* in Vaz Dourado's Portuguese *Atlas* of 1571 also gives 30° as the altitude of the *Cruzeira*. If the height of the foot of the Cross was taken as 30°, then an error would result, for when vertically positioned the lower star has an altitude of 28°, the upper an altitude of 33°. Nightly observations are now rarely taken, the modern sextant being dependent upon the visibility of a good horizon. However, with an astrolabe or quadrant, positioned on the horizontal by suspension or an incorporated plumb-line, no horizon was necessary, and night sights were possible, though subject to inaccuracy.

[3] Zaragoza 1876: I: 229-30.

but between Callao and *San Bernardo* (Caroline Island) they estimated a total distance of 1,400 leagues for an actual distance of approximately 1,363 leagues; an overestimate of 37 leagues or 118 n. miles. Between Callao and Gente Hermosa (Rakahanga) they estimated 1,600 leagues for an actual distance of 1,564 leagues; still an overestimate, of 38 leagues, but barely increased upon since Caroline Island.[1]

It is at once apparent from an examination of these figures that the navigation of the expedition showed a considerable improvement on that of previous expeditions, at least as far as Rakahanga. With an early underestimate and a subsequently fairly constant over-estimate, the results are commensurate with the limitations of the navigational techniques employed, but seem to indicate an intelligent and careful use of those techniques and a realization of the hydrographic factors likely to influence the reckoning. However, between Rakahanga and Taumako the navigation was subject to much more considerable error, and for an actual total distance of some 6,810 nautical miles or 2,128 leagues between Callao and Taumako[2] the narratives of the expedition record an estimate of 1,950 leagues by de Leza, 1,940 leagues by Torres and 1,650 leagues by Quirós. If we take de Leza's estimate, in all charity since it is the most accurate, it is significant that his underestimate of 178 leagues or 570 n. miles, whilst less than the underestimate made by Quirós in 1595 at Santa Cruz, conflicts with the overestimate which prevailed in the reckoning at Rakahanga. Bearing in mind that the expedition had sailed in predominantly higher latitudes W of the Marquesas than had Gallego in 1567–8, S of the latitudes in which the maximum effect of the South Equatorial Current is experienced, and that over the first part of the voyage it had been in higher latitudes than had Quirós in 1595, an improvement in the navigation was to be expected, the oceanic influences contrary to accurate DR navigation being somewhat reduced. The inconsistency in the error between Rakahanga and Taumako, as compared with the error between Callao and Rakahanga, cannot be attributed with any evidence to hydrological influences, and in view of the improved use of the existing navigational techniques it is perplexing.

There is evidence to suggest that in the last phase of the voyage, before Taumako was sighted, the pilots allowed Quirós' estimate of the position of Santa Cruz, and their own uncertainty and conjecture or *fantasia*, to influence them in their estimates and to sway them from a rigid adherence to the reckonings which they had made. On 25 March Torres had estimated their position to be 2,000 leagues from Perú, but had expressed doubts as to his findings. On 3

---

[1] D/Long. Callao-Caroline I. = 73° 4'.
   D/Long. Callao-Rakahanga = 83° 55'.
[2] D/Long. Callao-Taumako = 115° 38', 6,938'.
   Middle Latitude = 11°.
   Approximate distance Callao-Taumako = 6,938 × Cosine 11° = 6,810 n. miles.

April de Leza had estimated their position to be 2,120 leagues from Perú, and yet on 9 April, the day on which they anchored off Taumako, these same two navigators estimated their position to be 1,940 and 1,950 leagues, respectively, from Perú. In giving their earlier estimates both had expressed uncertainty as to their findings by reference to the supposed distance of Santa Cruz from Perú of 1,850 leagues, and it is understandable, in view of the known limitations of DR navigation and Quirós' reputation and presence in the expedition, that they should have had doubts on that score, particularly when, at Taumako, they were informed by the natives that Santa Cruz did lie to the W.

It must be assumed that they were not prepared to admit the possibility of Quirós having been in error at Santa Cruz to the extent to which he in fact was in error, and that, in recognition of the limitations and uncertainty of DR and of Quirós' reputation, they altered their estimates and reduced them to figures reasonably balanced between their estimates and Quirós' earlier estimates. De Leza's estimate of 2,120 leagues on 3 April, four days before Taumako was sighted, must have been a reasonably accurate estimate. Between 3 and 7 April de Leza recorded a distance sailed of 36 leagues, and on the 7th Taumako was sighted bearing WNW '10 leagues' distant.[1] Taking the total distance of (2,120 + 36 + 10 =) 2,166 leagues as the distance which de Leza really estimated from Perú to Taumako, it represents an overestimate of approximately 121 n. miles or 38 leagues, and it may be presumed that Torres' estimate would have been some 10 leagues less of an overestimate. In his entry for 3 April de Leza suggests that those who discovered Santa Cruz put down its position to the E of its true position, thinking that they had not gone as far as the true distance to Santa Cruz. He makes this remark in relation to his estimate of 2,120 leagues, and the fact that Santa Cruz was supposed to lie 1,850 leagues from Perú, but he uses the two figures in such a way as to imply that they refer to the same sort of distance, that is, the direct distance of Santa Cruz from Perú, and the direct distance of the vessels from Perú. However, in his entry for the 19th he remarks that he had gone 2,250 leagues from Perú 'on different courses', but that Taumako lay 1,950 leagues in a direct line from Goumey on the Peruvian coast.

In view of the nature of his comment on the 3rd, it is reasonable to suspect that de Leza used the varied courses to conceal his true estimate, giving the distance which he had calculated as the direct distance from Perú as the total distance sailed, and giving the compromise and adjusted figure of 1,950 leagues as the direct distance. That the daily distances which de Leza records from Perú were normally the distances calculated on a direct E–W line or the daily Departures, and not the total distances sailed, is evidenced by an addition of his daily runs. On 14 February, for instance, he declared that he calculated that they had gone 1,475 leagues from Perú, or 1,398 leagues in a direct line.[2]

[1] Zaragoza 1876: II: 116–18.   [2] Zaragoza 1876: II: 102.

On the 26th he recorded the distance from Callao, by which he presumably meant the total on different courses, as 1,740 leagues, although he had logged 274 leagues in the interim period; and when on 3 April he estimated the distance from Callao as 2,120 leagues, he had in fact logged a total of 499 leagues since the 26th. If his estimate of 1,740 leagues on 26 February was the total distance run on varied courses, then on 3 April that total should have been increased to 2,239 leagues, indicating that the estimate of 2,120 leagues was of the direct distance from Callao. It is more than probable that there is some confusion in the narratives, not least because, as de Leza himself admits: 'toda la diferençia del rumbo para el sol viene á deçir cartear por escuadria ó fantasía.'[1] This notwithstanding, it seems reasonable to assume that the expedition did deduce a greater direct distance from Callao to Taumako than was recorded.

In the analysis of the longitudinal estimates of the three Spanish voyages between 1567 and 1606, and of the factors and techniques which influenced or enabled these estimates to be made, a steady improvement in navigation and in the estimates made is apparent. By 1606, with the estimate of Taumako's position 570 n. miles E of its true position, an estimate which could perhaps have been 90 n. miles W of the true position if the pilots had abided by their real estimates, the maximum accuracy of the three expeditions had been achieved. Against the knowledge gained at Taumako that Santa Cruz lay to the westwards, and against Quirós' conclusion that the Islas de Salomón lay to the W of Santa Cruz, the general positioning of the islands in this area could have been approximately deduced, some 10° E of their true position.

The Spaniards noted with interest the sea-going abilities of the natives, and were particularly interested in their knowledge of adjacent islands, with the inhabitants of which they waged war and from which they obtained slaves. Tumai himself claimed to rule over fourteen islands, and whilst these may have been no more than the fourteen islands and rocks which comprise the Duff Group, it is possible that he exercised suzerainty over the Reef Islands to the NE of Santa Cruz. Torres records that on their arrival a canoe was despatched to Santa Cruz to pass on the news, and Quirós was naturally particularly anxious to ascertain the position, size and distance of the known adjacent islands.

According to the Quirós-Bermúdez relación Tumai named seventy islands of which he had knowledge, one of these being a large land which he called Manicolo.[2] In none of the existing documents which have been examined is the 'gazetteer' of Tumai reproduced, but in a memorial of 1609 Quirós refers briefly to the information provided by him,[3] and then goes on to list and describe a number of islands reported to him by Pedro, a native taken hostage at

---

[1] Zaragoza 1876: II: 103, that is, that all the variations of course for the sun (i.e. to maintain the correct latitude, determined by solar observation), result in the position being charted by guesswork.

[2] Zaragoza 1876: II: 284.

[3] In this memorial he refers to Tumai as having described sixty islands.

Taumako who eventually accompanied Quirós to Perú.[1] Pedro described himself as a native of *Chicayana*, a low-lying island four days distant from and slightly larger than Taumako, inhabited by people with 'a good colour' and long loose hair, who were tattooed slightly on the face, shoulders and breast. In addition he described other natives of a paler complexion with long red hair, and implied that the social organization of *Chicayana* was essentially rigid, hierarchial and adapted to a state of continuous warfare, within which his own position and occupation as a weaver and soldier-archer was firmly determined. He described their fear of the devil Tetua and their use as spoons and fish-hooks of five species of shell in which the surrounding waters abounded, and from his description it is easy to identify *Chicayana* with the Polynesian islands of Sikaiana[2] in 8° 22' S, 162° 45' E.

Three days' sailing from Taumako and two from *Chicayana* was another island, larger than both and named *Guaytopo*. Its inhabitants were friendly and as white as the Spaniards, had black or red hair, spoke one language and greeted by kissing on the cheek. Pedro had not visited this island, but he reported how fifty of its people had previously set out in a canoe for another inhabited island named *Mecayrayla* to obtain turtle or tortoise shell for ornaments. Prevented by contrary winds from reaching their destination, they had eventually landed at Taumako. Pedro described the men as very white, with the exception of one who was brown, and the three women in the party as white, beautiful, having long red hair and wearing blue-black veil-like garments which covered them from head to foot and which they called *foa foa*. A survivor of this party, named Olan, was seen by Quirós and confirmed Pedro's description of his home island, and Pedro added that on another occasion a vessel with two hulls (a double canoe) had gone from *Guaytopo* to *Chicayana* bearing 110 people, white and beautiful, amongst whom were some very handsome girls. It is extremely doubtful if Guaytopo can be identified with any certainty. Its inhabitants seem certainly to have been Polynesian, but the only island in close proximity to Taumako with a name even slightly similar is Utupua. The inhabitants of Utupua are now Melanesian, although it is quite possible that they have displaced earlier Polynesian inhabitants. The estimates of distance which Pedro gave may have been incorrect or misunderstood, for the garment worn by the women of *Guaytopo* seems to be recognizable as the traditional neck to ankle *tapa* cloth of Polynesian women, its veil-like appearance being the result of only one or two layers of *tapa* being used, and the colours black or dark blue are traditionally associated with *haute couture* in Tonga and Fiji.

In attempting to identify the islands named by Pedro the reader is perhaps

---

[1] Zaragoza 1876: II: 229-36; Purchas 1906: XVII: 232-46; Markham 1904: II: 487-503; Burney 1803: II: 179-82; Guppy 1887: 276-7; Woodford 1916: 40.

[2] *Hikaiana* in local Polynesian. Teatua is the Sikaiana ancestor spirit, who is worshipped as an image. See Woodford 1916: 39.

tempted unduly to identify them with islands in close proximity to Taumako, on the grounds that nearer islands would have been known, and to forget that some islands were probably only known of indirectly as a result of drift voyages or war parties from them. Moreover, whilst Tumai may have named all the local islands in his list, Pedro may have tended to describe islands which were of particular interest to him by virtue of their distance and the difference and strangeness of their inhabitants. That Pedro, a Polynesian himself, who had lived in Sikaiana and Taumako, should have commented on the dress of the women of *Guaytopo* seems to indicate they were in this respect different from his own neighbouring women, and seems to indicate their more distant origin. Remembering the association which seems to have existed between Taumako and Santa Cruz, it is almost impossible to avoid the conclusion that Utupua must have been much better known than *Guaytopo*, to which none of the inhabitants of Taumako seem to have gone.

It is important to note that Tongan traditions refer to activities in Fiji, Tikopia and Ontong Java,[1] and Peter Dillon learned in 1826 of a canoe of Tongatabuans (Tongatapuans) being killed at Vanikoro[2] in about 1788. He learned that the inhabitants of Tikopia, who deliberately prevented coconuts from growing on Mitre Island (Fataka) lest they offer sustenance to raiders from the E,[3] had knowledge of Tonga and Rotuma,[4] and he also heard of Tongan excursions to Tikopia.[5] In 1906 Woodford was informed at Sikaiana of two traditional invasions by Tongans, both apparently in the early seventeenth century, which ended in massacres, and from the last of which the Tongans carried on towards Taumako.[6] He was also informed of a renowned navigator named Kaidakita who, a few years after the Tongan invasion, had sailed to Malaíta, Ysabel, Ontong Java, Taumako, Tikopia, Nupani, Tinakula and *Fenuahala* (Fenualoa), and learnt that the Sikaiana natives knew of Anuta (Cherry Island) and *Fatutaka* (Fataka or Mitre Island).[7] It is certainly reasonable to assume that the drift voyages which frequently occur from the outlying islands of the Solomons were at least as prevalent before 1606 as they are now, and that within limited areas deliberate voyages, one-way and return, were made. It is interesting however to note, despite Tongan traditional knowledge of Tikopia, that Dillon was informed by Tubou (*Tupou*), the Tongan chief, that he had never heard of 'the Mannicolos', by which Dillon meant Vanikoro, or of Tikopia,[8] though this could have been his own personal ignorance or an indication that Tongan visits to the Eastern Solomons were generally one-way voyages. Given the assumption that *Guaytopo* and *Mecayrayla* were reasonably distant, Vaitupu (Tracy Island) and Nukulaelae in the Ellice Islands seem

---

[1] Gifford 1929: 14–15.
[2] Dillon 1829: II: 269.
[3] Dillon 1829: II: 111.
[4] Dillon 1829: II: 103, 135.
[5] Dillon 1829: II: 112.
[6] Woodford 1916: 42–43.
[7] Woodford 1916: 42–43.
[8] Dillon 1829: I: 294.

phonetically acceptable, although a Tongan or Fijian identity cannot be excluded.

Pedro informed Quirós that five days' sailing distance from the island of *Tucopia*, an island which Quirós later visited and which was unquestionably Tikopia, was that '*gran tierra*' of *Manicolo* inhabited by a non-cannibal, foreign-tongued, dun-coloured or *mulatto* people, a land of large villages, high mountains and large rivers. In navigating towards it from Tikopia the point at which the sun rose on the horizon was kept on the left side, and from this Quirós concluded that it lay between S and SE of Tikopia.[1] The island of Vanikoro (11° 40′ S, 166° 55′ E) has often been cited as a probable or certain identification of *Manicolo*. When Dillon heard of the island at Tikopia, in 1826, he understood its name to be *Malicolo*, but subsequently learnt that its more correct spelling and pronunciation was *Mannicolo* or *Vannicolo*[2] and today the local Polynesian name for Vanikoro is *Vanikolo*. On the other hand the south-south-easterly course which Pedro described from Tikopia to *Manicolo* is not the course for Vanikoro, which lies W by N $\frac{3}{4}$ N, but is the course for Fiji and Tonga; and the sailing time estimated from Tikopia to *Manicolo* would not, assuming *Manicolo* to have been in the Fiji area, have been beyond the capabilities of a seagoing double-canoe during the season of north-west winds. Pedro certainly conveyed the impression of a large land, even if Quirós did exaggerate it to justify his belief in a neighbouring continent, but although Vanikoro is larger than Taumako it is not as large as Santa Cruz. Accordingly an identification in the Fiji area is perhaps more likely than one in the immediate area of the Eastern Solomons.

Three days' sail from Taumako, or two days with a fair breeze, Pedro described another land named *Fonofono*, an archipelago of many small low-lying islands, inhabited by tall dun-coloured and *mulatto* natives, who spoke a different language but with whom his people were at peace. Near to these islands were two others, *Pilen* and *Nupan*, from which names it is possible to identify *Fonofono* with the three main islands of the Reef or Swallow Group (10° 15′ S, 166° 15′ E). They are charted on modern charts as Lom Lom but are known collectively to the indigenes as *Ngailo*, and the most northerly

---

[1] According to Andia y Varela (Corney 1915: II: 284) the Polynesians 'have no mariners compass, but divide the horizon into sixteen parts, taking as the cardinal points those at which the sun rises and sets ... when setting out from port the helmsman reckons with the horizon thus partitioned, counting from the East, or the point where the sun rises: he knows the direction in which his destination bears'. Despite the not inconsiderable attention which has been paid to the question of Polynesian navigation, our knowledge of it is scant, and such attention as has been paid to it has been in support of preconceived theories of Polynesian dispersal and voyaging, on little indigenous information, less practical knowledge and even less experimentation. Gatty hardly went far enough in his research (Gatty 1943) and de Bischop, who had probably amassed the greatest amount of indigenous material, and had gained the most practical experience, was regrettably killed before he had completed his writing.

[2] Dillon 1829: I: 33.

island is known as *Fenualoa*.[1] *Pilen* may be identified with the small island of Pileni off the northern reef, and *Nupan* with Nupani, the neighbouring reef island in 164° 50' E.

Pedro also informed Quirós of the exploits of a native pilot who 'knew the names of many countries wherein he had been many times', and who had visited a large country called *Pouro*, inhabited by dun-coloured natives living in a state of continued internal warfare, from which he had brought back a red-breasted parrot and white-tipped arrows. Guppy identified this country with San Cristóval in the Eastern Solomons,[2] on the evidence of Gallego's discovery that the native name of that island was *Paubro*,[3] and the survival of the name *Bauro*, now related to a district but originally applied to the whole island.[4] Hale, somewhat imaginatively perhaps, interpreted *Pouro* as a joint reference to *Bouro*, the traditional home of the Fijians, Samoans and Tongans, and the Bouro of the Malay Archipelago.[5]

Whether or not *Pouro* was a reference to San Cristóval or not, if the indigenes of Taumako did regard a place named *Bouro* or *Pouro* as their ancestral home, then it is more than likely that either Tumai or Pedro would have mentioned it, indicating the direction in which it was traditionally reported to lie. Although the successive Polynesian voyages, dispersals or drifts, which culminated, as far as the Taumakoans were concerned, in the settlement of Taumako, would not necessarily have distorted the originally supposed directions of the ancestral home, they might well have distorted the concept of its distance. To the extent that the homeland of *Bouro* may have been mythically adapted or even adopted, its identification can be no more than conjectured upon until we have amassed a greater knowledge of the fabric of Polynesian dispersal and corpus of Pacific pre-history than we at present possess. The fact that Pedro described a native pilot, whose chronological period can be determined, as having an actual knowledge of *Pouro*, seems to indicate that *Pouro* was a land in fairly close proximity to Taumako, distinct from any traditional homeland. A final island mentioned by Pedro was *Taucolo*, which he described as close to Taumako, and although Guppy's suggestion that this was a reference to Tinakula[6] cannot be dismissed, the fact that Tumai had already referred to Tinakula by its Santa Cruzian name of *Mami* (Temami) seems to indicate

---

[1] In 1906 Woodford was informed by Kwaisulia, a locally well-known chief of North-Eastern Malaíta, that he knew of two islands to the E and SE of Malaíta, Sikaiana and *Fonofono* (Woodford 1916: 41). This provides additional evidence for the identification of the Reef Islands.

[2] Guppy 1887: 277.   [3] MNM: MS. 921, f60.

[4] Guppy remarks that: 'Had Quiros been in possession of Gallego's journal . . . he would have at once recognized in this Pouro . . . the Paubro of Mendaña's expedition' (Guppy 1887: 252). In fact Quirós did have Gallego's journal, at least during the voyage of 1595, although it is hardly surprising that he did not remember or recognize the name. Guppy also suggests that the white-tipped arrows were silver-tipped relics of the 1568 expedition, but it seems more likely that they were the lime-tipped arrows still seen today in the islands of the Western Pacific.

[5] Guppy 1887: 277.   [6] Guppy 1887: 277.

that *Taucolo* was Tekauloa or Teakauloa, the Great Reef of the Reef or Swallow Islands.

Having replenished their supplies, the expedition put to sea on 18 April and headed SE in the direction in which Pedro claimed the great land of *Manicolo* lay.[1] Three days out from Taumako, running before the north-west wind,[2] an island was sighted in the distance, with a high rounded peak on its eastern side, which they eventually reached on the 24th. As they coasted it, numerous natives were seen on a wide beach, and Torres, embarking in the tender, was received with a demonstration of welcome, was presented with a 'cape of fine palm leaves' and informed of the proximity of other lands.[3] The name of the island was ascertained to be *Tucopia*,[4] *Chucupia*,[5] or *Chiquipia*,[6] and Torres estimated its latitude as 12½° S, de Leza as 12° S. It can be certainly identified with the island of Tikopia[7] (12° 18′ S, 168° 49′ E), bearing 135° (magnetic) from Taumako. From Tikopia the south-easterly course was maintained for another day, when, having drifted to 14° S as a result of a strong northerly wind during the preceding night, Quirós ordered the helmsman to give the ship her helm. The result, apparently, was a south-westerly course, although Torres appears to have protested that they should continue into higher latitudes[8] more directly.

The details of the voyage immediately following the expedition's departure from Tikopia are not particularly relevant in this context and may be dismissed briefly. On a south-westerly course the expedition entered the northern islands of the group now known as the New Hebrides, discovering and naming *San Márcos* (Star Peak or Mera Lava), *Verjel* (Merig), *Vírgen María* (*Santa María*[9] or Gaua), *Margaritana* (Aurora), *Las Lágrimas de San Pedro* (South-Eastern Vanua Lava) and *Los Portales de Belén* (Vanua Lava).[10] This abundance of islands seemed to confirm Quirós' theories and to indicate that

---

[1] It is significant that in the Quirós-Bermúdez *relación* Manicolo is referred to as '*una muy grande tierra*' (Zaragoza 1876: I: 284–5), not as '*una muy grande isla*', and both there and in a *memorial* of 1609 Quirós remarks how Tumai, when he spoke of the '*grande tierra*', opened both his arms and hands 'without making them meet' (Zaragoza 1876: I: 284), 'showing that it continued' (Zaragoza 1876: II: 231). This part of the *memorial* of 1609 is almost a transcript of the Quirós-Bermúdez *relación*. Cf. Zaragoza 1876: II: 230–1, '*las fui escribiendo á todas . . . Mostró deseo de bolver á su casa*', and Zaragoza 1876: I: 284–5, '*fué escribiendo los nombres . . . Mostró deseo de volverse á su casa*'.

[2] They were at the tail-end of the north-west season, or *kumburu* as it is called by the indigenes of the Solomons.

[3] Zaragoza 1876: I: 292. The cape, which from Torres' description seems to have been a sheet of *tapa* cloth (Markham 1904: II: 461), was presented by two natives who came off in a canoe. Torres did not land.   [4] Zaragoza 1876: II: 229 (Quirós' *memorial*).

[5] Markham 1904: II: 460 (Torres' letter to the king).

[6] Stevens 1929: 118 (De Prado's *relación*).

[7] Polynesian: *Tikopia* or *Sikopia*. Santa Cruzian: *Tukopia*.

[8] Zaragoza 1876: I: 293; Markham 1904: II: 461.

[9] *Santa María* was the name recorded by Torres (Markham 1904: II: 461).

[10] Zaragoza 1876: I: 293–300.

he was approaching a large land mass. More misled perhaps by enthusiasm, and adherence to his theories, than by any lack of observation, he concluded, as he approached a large land area in 15° S, that he was approaching the *tierra firme* of his dreams and aspirations. In fact he was approaching the largest of the islands in the group, to which, as he anchored in the great bay on its northern coast, he gave the name which it bears in part today: *la Austrialia del Espíritu Santo*.[1] To the great bay itself he gave the name of *San Felipe y Santiago* (St. Philip and St. James), and to their anchorage in the south-eastern corner the name *Vera Cruz*. As they approached the bay from the E the expedition had sighted what appeared to be a chain of mountains stretching to the SE, and Quirós, taking them to be confirmation of his discovery of a new continent, named them *La Clementina*, and an island in the foreground *Cardona*. The chain of mountains was in fact the island of Pentecost, and Cardona was Leper's Island or Oba.

To dwell on the circumstances of the Spanish settlement at Vera Cruz is inevitably to detract from the very real achievements of the expedition. Knowing as we do that this was no continent, the grandiose proceedings which followed, the acts of possession, plans for a great city, creation of a government and initiation of an order of knights, all smack of tragi-comedy. Seen however, as they must surely be seen, against the background of Quirós' conviction that this was the *New World*, against the natural demonstrativeness of seventeenth-century Iberia and, more importantly, against the achievements of seamanship which culminated in this discovery, contempt, pity or amusement are emotions to which the twentieth-century reader is hardly entitled. After only 35 days at Vera Cruz, in the face of increasing hostility from the natives and in an attempt to revitalize the *expedicionarios*, Quirós decided to pursue the voyage towards the chain of mountains sighted to the SE.

There is some disagreement between the several narratives in their accounts of what happened during the next phase of the voyage. According to the Quirós-Bermúdez *relación* the fleet left the bay on 8 June but met a wind veering to the SE and increasing in force which made progress impossible. Quirós, realizing presumably that this was now the season of south-easterly winds, decided to return to Vera Cruz, to build a fort, sow crops, build a

---

[1] Quirós claimed that he had changed the traditional spelling *austral* to *austrial* in cognizance of the King of Spain's imperial Austrian title (see his *memorial* to the King of 1607, Zaragoza 1876: II: 201), but de Prado gives the name as *la grande australia del spíritu santo* (Stevens 1929: 124), and de Leza as *la parte Austral del Espíritu Santo* (Zaragoza 1876: II: 156). Torres simply calls it *Espíritu Santo* (Markham 1904: II: 462), the name it bears today, and in two later memoriales Quirós writes of *las tierras Australes* (BNM: MS. 3099, f192), and *la Australia* (BNM: MS. 3099, f192). Whilst *Austrialia* is the spelling in the BPM MS. of the Quirós-Bermúdez *relación*, in the MNM MS. the spelling is *Australia*. It seems likely that the *i* was a later gesture by Quirós to please the King, but that at Espíritu Santo he used the older *austral* and actually named the island *la Australia del Espíritu Santo*.

brigantine for local exploration and attempt to determine the seasonal winds and their duration. Only the *Almiranta* and the *zabra* were able to make the anchorage, for they were carrying more sail and were consequently able to make longer tacks than the *Capitana*. As the wind increased during the night, the *Capitana*, carrying only a fore-course, fell off to leeward. Quirós was ill and in no condition to command the vessel, and by dawn they had fallen off beyond the north-west cape of Espíritu Santo. Ordered to sail to windward the Pilot argued that such a course would be dangerous for the vessel's timbers and, after beating off the bay for three days in the hope that the other vessels would join them, the *Capitana* fell off past Vírgen María, Belén and Ureparapara (*Pilar de Zaragoza*), until eventually, on 19 June, they lost sight of land and estimated their latitude to be 12° S.[1]

This account of the events is supported by de Leza's log, inevitably perhaps since he was responsible for sailing the ship and may also have been a party to the incident which Torres and de Prado offer as an explanation for the separation. According to Torres the *Capitana* left the bay during the night of 11 June without informing the other vessels,[2] for her crew 'were mutinous, designing to go directly to Manila . . . from whence succeeded what Your Majesty knows, since they made him turn out of his course'.[3] De Prado records that the fleet left the bay, were compelled by the weather to return, and that in the night the *Capitana* disappeared. He adds that: 'I told them that they need not search, for the crew had mutinied',[4] and stated in a letter to the King that 'Quirós, the imposter, discovered some reefs and small islands, for the people mutinied'.[5] Irrespective of the actual circumstances of the separation (and de Prado's story of a mutiny seems only to be based on his expectation of one), a mutiny would hardly have been surprising, for by this stage in the expedition we see revealed in the narratives a Quirós whose enthusiasm had assumed almost fanatical proportions, and who was by no means the well-balanced Chief Pilot of Mendaña's expedition of 1595.

Torres,[6] attempting to comply with the spirit and the letter of his instructions, remained at Vera Cruz for 15 days, and then sailed down the east coast

[1] Zaragoza 1876: I: 347–50. In reference to the failure of the *Capitana* to beat into the bay, Markham remarks that 'ships built in Peru would not work to windward' (Markham 1904: I: XXVI), presumably basing this conclusion on his translation of the phrase in de Leza's log-book 'todos estos nauíos del Pirú ser malos de arriuar con poca vela, y ansí podiamos embestir primero que el nauío hiziese buelta' (Zaragoza 1876: II: 174), as 'all the ships built in Peru are bad under little sail, and so we had time to look out before she went round' (Markham 1904: II: 394). In fact ships built in Perú were designed for beating to windward, and slowness in going about is a feature of a weatherly not an unweatherly vessel.   [2] Markham 1904: II: 462 (Torres' letter to the King, Manila, 27 July 1607).

[3] Markham 1904: II: 457–8.   [4] Stevens 1929: 128–9.

[5] Zaragoza 1876: II: 188 (letter from Goa, 24 December 1613). See also Zaragoza 1876: II: 190 (letter from Goa, 25 December 1613).

[6] Torres was really the leader of this section of the expedition, although de Prado may have been the Viceroy's nominee as Quirós' successor. See Stevens 1929: 202–3.

12

of Espíritu Santo, realized that it was in fact an island, and ran SW to 20½° S. From there he stood to the NW, and eventually sighted the south-east coast of New Guinea which he identified. Crowding on sail he attempted to sail eastwards and round its eastern extremity, but contrary winds made this impossible. He now took the only reasonable course open and headed west-wards, in the hope that New Guinea was an island which he might safely pass to the S of. In doing this he took a considerable risk, although the only alterna-tive to it would have been to lie up until the season of north-west winds came round, a risk which later navigators, ignorant of his successful voyage through the straits which now bear his name, were reluctant to take. On a variable course he passed between Northern Australia and New Guinea, and eventually reached the Moluccas, Ternate and Manila.[1]

When the *Capitana* was out of sight and in 12° S, she must have been approximately NW–NNW of Ureparapara but out of sight of Hiw and Tegua, the Torres Islands. According to the Quirós-Bermúdez *relación* argu-ments were then put to Quirós, which he seems to have been glad to accept, to the effect that the delays endured in Perú had robbed the expedition of two and a half months of the supposed 'summer season' during which it was feasible to navigate in the South-West Pacific.[2] It was argued that the favour-able season for westward trans-Pacific voyaging extended over eight months from early October to the end of May. Since the voyage from Perú to Manila took three months at the most, five months remained in the summer season for exploration. If the expedition had completed its exploration and had reached Manila by the end of the summer season, it would have had to remain there for some time until the seasonal south-west winds ended and the advent of northerly winds permitted a southerly passage through the East Indies and past the 'two Javas',[3] in search of new lands in the Southern Indian Ocean. This would have enabled the expedition to round the Cape of Good Hope between the months of January and March, the best months for that passage, and to arrive in Spain in the summer between July and September.

Quirós now determined to proceed to Santa Cruz[4] where they could collect supplies and await Torres.[5] In expecting that Torres would proceed to Santa Cruz he seems, however, to have interpreted the instructions which he issued at the commencement of the voyage rather strangely, for the planned rendez-vous at Santa Cruz had presumably been abandoned when they headed S from Taumako, and they were by now in the next phase of the plan. The

[1] See Torres' letter to the King, Manila, 12 July 1607 (Stevens 1929: 214–37); Torres' letter to Quirós, Manila, 15 June 1607, which is included in part in a *memorial* of Quirós of 1610 (Zaragoza 1876: II: 296–8); and the *relación* of de Prado (Stevens 1929: 130–203).

[2] Zaragoza 1876: I: 351–3.

[3] *Java the Less* and *Java the Great*, the north-western promontory of the austral continent on sixteenth-century charts and maps which delineated such a continent; Java and the Sunda Islands on others.   [4] Zaragoza 1876: I: 353.   [5] Zaragoza 1876: II: 175.

latitude of 10° 30′ S was reached on 21 June when, according to de Leza, since the direction of Santa Cruz, E or W, was unknown, and since a westerly passage might have caused the expedition to be embayed upon an eastern or southern shore of New Guinea in the season of *bendeuales*, it was decided to head for the latitude of Guam and the Philippines. Sailing northwards, an island was sighted in 3° 15′ N, and on 24 July, when they were in 15° 10′ N, Quirós ordered 'the customary navigation from the Philippines to Acapulco'.[1] According to the Quirós-Bermúdez *relación*, however, the decision to proceed to Acapulco was made before they reached the latitude of Santa Cruz. Quirós, considering the problems presented by the prevailing south-east winds, the dangers of sailing too far to the W in search of Santa Cruz, the furious westerlies of the Philippines which lasted until late October and rendered navigation there impossible, the shortage of water and food, the unknown winds of the equatorial region which they would have to cross, the sick and the mutinous, the uncertainty of the fate of the other two vessels and the need to report on the discoveries made, convened a council of the pilots at which a passage to Acapulco was agreed upon.[2] He consoled himself with the thought that Torres could be expected to prosecute the discoveries as his instructions ordered.

It is fairly certain that, in heading NE to N from their position in 12° S, the expedition must have passed through the Eastern Solomons, probably between Vanikoro and Tikopia, and to the E of Taumako, without sighting land. The island sighted in 3° 15′ N, named *Buen Viaje* by the expedition, would seem to have been Butaritari in the Northern Gilbert Islands.[3] Between 24 June and 19 August they headed slowly north-eastwards to 38° N,[4] headed E, and arrived at Navidad on 20 October after a voyage of considerable hardship, privation and danger. From Navidad they sailed to Acapulco, which they reached on 23 November 1606, and here Quirós handed his ship over to the authorities and proceeded independently to México City where he was received by the Viceroy and *Don* Luis de Velasco. Although the Viceroy, then Viceroy-designate of Perú, gave Quirós little assistance for his return to Spain, he assured him of his favour and assistance should Quirós return to Perú to prosecute his discoveries further.[5] In a state of penury Quirós obtained a passage to Cádiz, and from there made his way to Seville and Madrid, which he reached on 9 October 1607.[6]

---

[1] Zaragoza 1876: II: 175–9.   [2] Zaragoza 1876: I: 353–7.   [3] Maude 1959: 318–20, 326.

[4] De Leza estimated that their position when they reached 28° N bore N by E from Espíritu Santo, and was 400 leagues E of Japan and 700 leagues W from 38° N in Nueva España (New Spain). This is a total distance of 1,100 leagues between Japan and New Spain, 4,400 Roman miles or 3,520 nautical miles. The Great Circle distance of Yokohama from San Francisco is in fact 4,732 nautical miles, representing a considerable underestimate by de Leza presumably based on the supposed distance of Japan from America.   [5] Zaragoza 1876: I: 387–8.

[6] Zaragoza 1876: I: 388–9. He was aided in Seville by Francisco Duarte (see Duarte's letter to the King, Seville, 18 September 1607, AGS: *Estado, legajo* 206).

After eleven days in Madrid Quirós was received by the Count of Lemos, President of the *Consejo de Indias*, to whom he presented his *relación*, by the Duke of Lerma, then First Minister to the King and a member of the *Consejo de Estado*, and by the King. He now began to write the succession of *memoriales* with which he was to deluge the councils over the next seven frustrating years, in an attempt to prosecute the further discovery, colonization and conversion of the austral lands which he believed he had discovered. Whilst his objective was the austral continent and Espíritu Santo as a supposed part of it, and not the Solomon Islands, his proposals and attempts to implement them are relevant to this study to the extent that a further voyage to the South-West Pacific might have led to their rediscovery, and as illustrating the reasons why, and the way in which, the Spanish authorities refused to permit further voyages of discovery and colonization. In a *memorial* of 1607[1] Quirós described his recent voyage, justified his decision to alter course in 26° S and his later separation from Torres, and propounded his conviction that the austral lands extended at least from Espíritu Santo to the Straits of Magellan. In this, as in the total collection of extant *memoriales* submitted between 1607 and 1614, can be observed the dominant theme of praise of the lands which he had discovered, their beauty, potential wealth and abundance of souls awaiting salvation. It may be uncharitable to suggest that Quirós deliberately attempted to mislead the King, but to anyone who knows the island of Espíritu Santo the excesses of his description are at once apparent, and at least indicative of an enthusiasm and optimism which led him to see the island in a much rosier hue than the other *expedicionarios* must have done. As Charles Clerke, a member of Cook's expedition of 1774, remarked of Quirós' description of Espíritu Santo:

He has given a most pompous description of this Country in his Memorials to the King of Spain, wherein he solicits the settlement of these Isles, however I firmly believe Mr Quiros' Zeal and warmth for his own favourite projects has carried him too far in the qualities he has ascribed to this Country.[2]

His *memoriales* aroused a mixed response, but when, on 6 March 1608, the King passed the handling of Quirós' affairs over to the *Consejo de Indias*, their attitude was generally unfavourable. Quirós' attribution of their reaction to jealousy that his first expedition had been arranged through the *Consejo de Estado*[3] is weakened by the record of their deliberations and by the very cogent reasons which existed for not prosecuting further voyages of discovery. Their instructions to Quirós, conveyed by Francisco de Trejada, were to proceed to Perú and there await the Viceroy's pleasure; but he, having seen and experienced the frustrations of attendance on the pleasure of Spanish colonial

---

[1] Zaragoza 1876: II: 191–212; RAH: *Papeles Varios de Indias*, D90 B, '*Que gobernando el Pirú . . . y gloria de Dios*'.   [2] Beaglehole 1961: 516–17.   [3] Zaragoza 1876: I: 390.

administrators, found such instructions unattractive. In reply he subjected Spanish officialdom to another spate of *memoriales*, of which one in particular, written in December 1608, and his eighth,[1] was subsequently published and distributed widely throughout Europe.[2] In it he reiterated his plea for the settlement of *Austrialia Incognita*, and stressed his own penury, exertions, privations and pious motivations. He extolled the beauties of the land, its advantages over even Spain, and suggested that the lands seen in the distance from the Bay of St. Philip and St. James might well be an earthly paradise.

On 22 June 1608 a letter was received at Court from Torres,[3] accompanied by five charts prepared by de Prado and sketches of the indigenes of the lands visited.[4] In it Torres reported his dissatisfaction with Quirós' failure to sail S to 30° S, implied his poor opinion of him as a commander able to cope with mutiny, and reported his discovery of the fact that Espíritu Santo was an island.[5] At about the same time a letter arrived from Juan de Esquibel, Camp Master at Ternate, reporting Torres' arrival there and his discoveries,[6] and at much the same time Quirós must himself have received a letter from Torres.[7] Despite the latter's discovery that Espíritu Santo was an island, Quirós continued to assert his belief that he had discovered part of the austral continent; and in his longest extant *memorial*, in which he quotes from Torres' letter to him, he excludes any reference to the insular character of Espíritu Santo. It is possible of course that there was no such reference in his own letter from Torres, and that he did not see Torres' letter to the King for some time after its receipt, if at all, is indicated by the fact that he had

---

[1] '*digo: que con este son ocho los memoriales . . . el defensor della*', Zaragoza 1876: II: 216–28; Markham 1904: II: 477–86; Pacheco 1866: V: 497–506; RAH: *Colección Muñoz, Vol.* XXXVIII, ff42–48; MNM: MS. 196, ff1–6 (prologue absent); MNM: MS. 142, *doc. No.* 8 (truncated): MNM: MS. 328, ff145–54; BM: Add. MS. 13,974.

[2] For instance by Hessel Gerritsz in his *Detectio Freti Hudsoni* of 1612, and by Purchas (Purchas 1906: XVII: 218–31).

[3] *Carta de Luis Báez de Torres*, Manila, 12 July 1607, BNM: MS. 3099, ff29–42; AGS: *Estado, legajo* 209.

[4] AGS: *Mapas', Planos y Dibujos*. These are the four charts referred to by Stevens (Stevens 1929: 36–40). The fifth is generally supposed to have become separated from the four extant charts, and is suspected to have been a general Pacific chart. However, unless the microfilm copy of the maps in the General Archives at Simancas which I have examined has led me astray, the four maps of de Prado consist of five sheets, the chart *Pvertos . i . Bayas . de-San-Buenaventura* being in two sections. It seems likely that this may account for the reference to five and the existence of only four complete maps. See Stevens 1929: *Facsimilies of the Four Prado Maps;* and Markham 1904: Map 1. De Prado also appears to have prepared a general map to accompany his *relación*. See *Parecer: Consejo de Estado*, 21 August 1610, referring to a letter of de Prado dated 20 July 1608 from Manila. AGS: *Estado, legajo* 228.

[5] Stevens 1929: 226–9.

[6] See *Minuta de Consejo de Estado* to the King, 2 August 1608, AGS: *Estado, legajo* 2638. See also Zaragoza 1876: I: 390. Esquibel's letter is to be found in AGS: *Estado, legajo* 209 and AGI: Filipinas 19 and 20, dated 31 March 1607.

[7] An extract from the letter dated Manila, 15 June 1607, was included by Quirós in a *memorial* of 1610, '*V.M. Ordena y Manda á su Consejo de Indias . . .*' (Zaragoza 1876: II: 296–8).

to petition for access to it.[1] Indeed, it would have been politic for the authorities to conceal Torres' letter from him, lest he be forewarned of any of its contents detrimental to his proposals, and to give him the opportunity to overstate and destroy his arguments and claims. Whilst the insular character of Espíritu Santo did not negate Quirós' belief that the land seen to the further S might be continental, he does later refer to having seen Torres' letter in the possession of the *Condestable* of Castille,[2] and in his long *memorial* of 1610 refers to 'the greatness of the lands discovered, judged by what I saw and by that which Luis Váez de Torres . . . had written to Your Majesty and myself'.[3] It seems likely that Quirós had advanced to the state of enthusiasm where self-deception led him to regard the unfavourable as favourable.

A *consulta* of the *Consejo de Indias* of 12 July 1608[4] recommended against the prosecution of his proposals; a recommendation echoed in a further *consulta* and in a report of the Duke of Lerma of 29 July,[5] in which the resultant loss of manpower, the exhaustion of the treasury, the dangers of foreign aggression and the ethical and moral dubiety of conquering unprovocative heathens were stated as reasons for such an attitude. It was suggested that Quirós be employed as a cosmographer and cartographer, a view adopted by the *Consejo de Estado* in a *consulta* of 25 September 1608,[6] who added that since the *Consejo de Indias* were unsympathetic to him he would have to be employed by the *Consejo de Guerra* (Council of War).

General suspicion of Quirós' abilities must have increased with the receipt on 26 November of a letter from Luis de Castro which emphasized his failings and unsuitability for further command.[7] Quirós, however, still continued to submit *memoriales* describing his plans, comparing himself with Columbus and requesting one thousand settlers, twelve Franciscans, surgeons, armaments, sheet iron, ships and a provisional budget of 500,000 *ducados*.[8] In a *memorial* of

---

[1] *Memorial*, 'Digo y tengo en mi poder . . . al servicio de Dios y de V. Mgd.', AGS: *Estado, legajo* 2640. The King's *endorso* to the *memorial* states that Quirós should be told verbally that the Torres letter is lost. In a *minuta* of September, 1608, the *Consejo de Estado* express their curiosity as to how Quirós has come to hear of Torres' letter (AGS: *Estado, legajo* 2640). According to Quirós himself, in the Quirós-Bermúdez *relación*, he saw the letter when it was in the possession of the *Condestable* of Castille (Zaragoza 1876: I: 390.).   [2] Zaragoza 1876: I: 390. He may not have read it though.

[3] Zaragoza 1876: II: 282.   [4] AGS: *Estado, legajo* 219; BNM: MS. 3099, ff79–84.

[5] AGS: *Estado, legajo* 209; BNM: MS. 3099, ff27–28.

[6] AGS: *Estado, legajo* 209; AGS: *Estado, legajo* 219; BNM: MS. 3099, ff25–26 (duplicated at ff75–76v); Stevens 1929: 210–13.

[7] Luis de Castro to the King, Lima, 2 March 1608, AGS: *Estado, legajo* 209; BNM: MS. 3099, ff21–23v.

[8] See his sixteenth *memorial*, 'En razon del caso . . . doña Isabel con Colon. . . .', AGS: *Estado, legajo* 219; BNM: MS. 3099, ff51–58v; Zaragoza 1876: II: 242–58. See also his *memorial* 'digo que para la poblaçcion de las tierras . . . mucho menos de lo que yo deseo servir a V. Mgd.', AGS: *Estado, legajo* 219; BNM: MS. 3099, ff95–96; his *memorial* 'Buelbo á mi tema y digo . . . que es lo mismo que en Hispaña 62. v. 500', AGS: *Estado, legajo* 719; BNM: MS. 3099, ff68–69; and his *memorial* 'Las razones que doy para que esta jornada . . . gran priesa V. Mgd. me mando que las fuese á descubrir', AGS: *Estado, legajo* 219: BNM: MS. 3909, ff89–94.

March 1609 he refers to the depopulation of the Indies and the consequent loss of tribute, arguing that the inhabitants of his new world would render more in ten years 'for heaven and earth' than the American Empire had rendered in 117 years.[1] It can certainly be said of Quirós that he was most concerned that the welfare of the indigenes of newly colonized lands should be the major concern of the colonists, and in this *memorial* he refers to those mistakes of his predecessors in the Americas which had led to the demoralization and depopulation of the indigenes.[2]

On 7 February 1609, Quirós received a *decreto* granting him aid and money,[3] but a second *decreto*, which passed the responsibility for implementation and further consideration to the *Consejo de Indias*, dashed his new-found hopes.[4] The views of the individual members of the *Consejo de Estado* are contained in a *consulta* of 18 February 1609.[5] Reiterating the objections voiced earlier to Quirós' proposals, though admitting his competence and honest purpose, they recorded that the English Ambassador had reported to his monarch on Quirós' voyage, and emphasized their particular concern with the ethical dubiety of conquering inoffensive heathens. This last consideration was raised again in a *consulta* prepared by the King's Confessor, *Padre Fray* Luis de Aliaga, in consideration of the opinions expressed by the *Consejo*, in which it was stressed '*que sola la infidelidad no basta y es cosa llana en toda theologia y entiendo que procede de derecho civil pero esto quedará a determinacion de juristas*', although Quirós' pious intentions and the existence of a Catholic duty to convert the heathen by peaceful means were admitted.[6]

The question of the ethical and moral right to conquer and thereafter to convert was one which had long exercised the minds of Spanish lawyers and theologians, and from the first the Empire had endeavoured to justify itself on a basis of principle. When the Count of Lemos asked Quirós, 'What right have we to these regions?', meaning the austral lands, he was asking a pertinent and relevant question, to which Quirós' reply: 'The same right that we had to possess ourselves of the others' was, in the light of contemporary concern with the question, neither diplomatic nor particularly intelligent.[7] Much earlier in Spanish history, when las Casas, who opposed the despatch of Columbus,

---

[1] His *memorial*, '*Buelbo á mi tema y digo . . . pues ha de ser por una vez*', AGS: *Estado, legajo* 219; RAH: *Colección Muñoz*, Vol. XXXVIII, within ff49–54; BNM: MS. 3099, ff61–64 (duplicated at ff65–67); Zaragoza 1876: II: 237–41; Pacheco 1866: V: 507–10; Markham 1904: II: 504–7; see also his *memorial* '*No puedo desar de mostrar por punto . . . servir á V. Mgd. toda mi vida*', AGS: *Estado, legajo* 219; BNM: MS. 3099, ff71–71v, and his *memorial* '*ya he dicho á V.M. que de la parte del Sur . . .*', Zaragoza 1876: II: 229–36; Markham 1904: II: 487–503; Purchas 1906: XVII: 232–46; Dalrymple 1770: I: 145, and the summary of papers concerning the proposals of Quirós at AGS: *Estado, legajo* 219, and BNM: MS. 3099, ff73–74v.   [2] See also his will, Zaragoza 1876: I: 362–5.

[3] Zaragoza 1876: I: 391.   [4] Zaragoza 1876: I: 391.

[5] BNM: MS. 3099, ff85–88; AGS: *Estado, legajo* 219.

[6] 22 March 1609. AGS: *Estado, legajo* 219; BNM: MS. 3099, ff97–99.

[7] Zaragoza 1876: I: 389.

had argued against the doctrine of Dr. Juan de Sepulveda that it was right to wage war to spread the faith, Charles V had felt the matter to be of sufficient importance to lay it before a congregation of jurists and theologians at Vallado-lid. They accepted the view of las Casas, many of the members being influenced by Francisco de Vitoria, perhaps the genius of his age, and had denied the Spaniards any right to be in the Indias at all, other than the right of all men to trade peacefully anywhere, and the right of every Christian to convert the heathen by peaceful means. The congregation had in fact established a princi-ple, not always applied but invariably considered, that it was unjust to 'wage wars known as conquests' against Indians who had committed no guilty act other than that of their infidelity.[1]

The reaction of the two *Consejos* to Quirós' demands were eminently reasonable, their reasons for advocating the non-prosecution of his project entirely logical, and it would be a mistake to allow ourselves to be misled by the existence of departmental rivalries, bureaucratic inertia and a natural mistrust of Quirós. To appreciate the policy of the Spanish authorities towards Pacific discoveries and future discovery it is necessary to understand something of the condition of Spain and its Empire at the close of the sixteenth and commence-ment of the seventeenth centuries. By the time of his death in 1598 Philip II had brought Spain to the brink of ruin. As early as 1583, although he had completed the formidable task of unifying Spain within the one Faith, he was an old and broken man faced with increasing dissension at home and in Europe. In 1587 the Spanish Netherlands had declared their independence; an indepen-dence, once achieved, which opened the way for the maritime expansion of Holland and the emergence of a threat to Spanish sea-power. In 1587 Drake had attacked the Spanish fleet in Lisbon and Cádiz, wreaking considerable havoc, and in 1588 the Invincible Armada pitted itself against the inclement weather of the Channel and England's casual defences and, hampered by orders to avoid a direct action, met disaster. The importance of the Armada has perhaps been overstated, for it did not decide the Anglo-Spanish War, which dragged on for fourteen years, nor did Spain decline immediately thereafter. By 1603 Spain had not lost a single colony to England, whilst England, due largely to the hostilities with Spain, had been compelled to delay the coloniza-tion of Virginia. For some time prior to the Armada the English fleet had been generally superior in strength to the amalgamated fleets of Spain and Portugal, but after 1588 the margin of superiority, if anything, diminished. For the Spanish mercantile marine the years immediately after the Armada were perhaps amongst its most successful, and between 1588 and 1603 more American treasure reached Spain than in any other fifteen years in Spanish history. Other factors were of course important, but it is a measure of the strength of the Spanish marine that even after Essex's raid on Cádiz in 1596 it was not ruined.

[1] Madariaga 1947: 12.

The accession of Philip III in 1598 brought no change in Spanish fortunes. Philip II had attempted to leave a legacy of peace but had failed, and a second Armada in 1601 and an attempt to support an Irish rising were both abortive. The advent of James I to the throne of England brought peace in 1604, and it was hoped in Spain that merchant fleets would thereafter be able to cross the Atlantic without being subject to attacks. A period of pacification with France was cemented by an alliance, but although Philip did succeed to a limited extent between 1604 and 1610 in curbing the dissident factions within Spain, his incapacity as a monarch soon became all too apparent. After 1611 silver imports dropped to one-tenth of those in the peak years, and corruption, industrial depression, excessive taxation, social indiscipline and sinecurism were the symptoms of a nation in decay. After 1615 Spain strove to avoid participation in the renewed conflicts of the preceding century, but finally participated in a series of long and ruinous conflicts with France, Holland and England. The seventeenth century was a period of decline which contrasts sharply with the success, spirit of enthusiasm and expansion which characterized the sixteenth century.

By the late sixteenth century there seems little doubt that the Councils of Madrid were all too well aware of the increasing problems with which they had to contend, problems in the Empire of over-extended and largely in-defensible lines of communication, and extensive and virtually indefensible territories. The problem of man-power and shipping was a very real one to an Empire whose boundaries were so vast, lines of communication so extended and subject peoples relatively numerous, and when they were combined with other considerations, including a dwindling treasury and the threat of foreign aggression, they rendered further colonization an impracticable proposition.

The recorded deliberations of the *Consejo de Estado* on Quirós' proposals continually refer to the dangers of English, Dutch and French aggression, and to the fear of Quirós' defection to an alien power.[1] He in his turn seems to

[1] *Parecer de Consejo de Estado*, 2 May 1609, AGS: *Estado, legajo* 219; BNM: MS. 3099, ff101-101v.

Consulta de Consejo de Estado, July 1609, Zaragoza 1876: II. 259-65; AGS: *Estado, legajo* 219; BNM: MS. 3099, ff43-47v.

Duque de Lerma to the *Conde* de Lemos, 5 October 1609, AGS: *Estado, legajo* 219, covering a *consulta* of the *Consejo de Indias* of 15 September 1609, AGS: *Estado, legajo* 219.

Consulta de Consejo de Indias to the King, 2 November 1609, AGS: *Estado, legajo* 219.

Consejo de Estado to the King, 5 November 1609, AGS: *Estado, legajo* 219; BNM: MS. 3099, ff157-157v.

Consejo de Estado to the King, 10 April 1610, AGS: *Estado, legajo* 2640.

Consulta de Consejo de Estado, 19 June 1610, AGS: *Estado, legajo* 228; BNM: MS. 3099, ff181-4.

Minuta de Consejo de Estado, 3 October 1613, AGS: *Estado, legajo* 2644.

See also the *Minuta de Consejo de Estado*, 17 March 1612, AGS: *Estado, legajo* 2642, which refers to the report of *Don* Francisco de Uarte of the new voyage of the English into the South Sea. *Relación* of two letters from *Don* Jorge de Castelblanco, *capitán de la fortaleza de Ormuz*, 17 December 1612, and 28 January 1613, AGS: *Estado, legajo* 252.

have attempted to turn this fear to his advantage, for in one *memorial* he refers pointedly to the proximity of the Dutch-held Moluccas to the austral continent,[1] and in another to his conversations with an English geographer in 1594.[2] If anything he probably only engendered more suspicion and fear of his defection, and the reaction of the Councils is reflected in their attitude to his publication of some of his *memoriales*. In a *minuta* of 13 November 1609[3] the *Consejo de Estado* drew the King's attention to the danger of such publications being distributed. Again on 31 October 1610, they drew his attention to Quirós' continued publication and distribution of *memoriales*, including 'a long one',[4] stressing not only the inherent dangers but also the fact that much of the information in his *memoriales* was misrepresented. At their suggestion the King ordered the *Consejo de Indias* to receive the *memoriales* which Quirós was to recover, and to limit their circulation.

That the dangers of foreign aggression were real and considerable is evidenced by the English forays on the American Pacific coastlines, and by later Dutch proposals to occupy Tonga as a base from which to harry the Peruvian coastlines, and it would have been in Spanish interests, had it been possible, to deny to foreigners knowledge of the Marquesas at least. The Solomons and Espíritu Santo were not of the same strategic importance, but the supposed austral continent, for the exploration of which these discoveries might have been considered as bases, was already attracting Dutch interest. If the austral continent did exist, its colonization by an alien power would be to the serious detriment of Spain's imperial defence and trade, but the Spanish authorities must have realized the impossibility of concealing the facts of their recent voyages into the South Pacific. Indeed, the quite considerable amount of information circulating in Europe, which is reflected in contemporary charts and publications, should be seen, not as evidence of the failure of Spanish attempts to suppress information, but rather as evidence of a policy of denying to aliens any more information than they might reasonably be expected to obtain, information of the kind contained in Quirós' *memoriales*. It is perhaps significant that Quirós was not forbidden to publish and distribute his *memoriales* until he had in fact done so.

Shortly before 15 May 1609 three letters were received at Court from Juan

---

[1] '*Obligando estoy en conçiençia . . . al menos no lo desdore*', AGS: *Estado, legajo* 2644.

[2] '*Por lo que devo a Dios . . . mas me justifico*', AGS: *Estado, legajo* 228; BNM: MS. 3099, ff177–180v.

[3] AGS: *Estado, legajo* 219; BNM: MS. 3199, f165.

[4] RAH: *Colección Muñoz, Vol.* XXXVIII, ff49–54; Zaragoza 1876: II: 388–9; Markham 1904: II: 516; BNM: MS. 3099, f286. The 'long one' was perhaps the longest extant one, which included a restatement of the eighth and sixteenth memorials, a report of the voyage of de Brito, an extract from Torres' letter to Quirós, Quirós' treatise on navigation, and a report by Sequeira, Governor of the Moluccas, Zaragoza 1876: II: 280–388; RAH: *Salazar*, F23 ff59v–139v, '*V.M. ordena y manda á su Consejo*'.

de Iturbe, the Accountant or Purser of Quirós' expedition,[1] together with an account by him of the voyage of 1606.[2] Although he stressed the glories and importance of the newly discovered land of Espíritu Santo: '*tan grandes...*, *como es la de Guadalcanal, que habiendola prolongado mas de 140 leguas, no le hallaron Cabo*', Iturbe threw considerable doubt on Quirós' competence, reliability and suitability for further employment. It is doubtful if Iturbe's letters did anything more than reassure the Councils in their decision to recommend the refusal of Quirós' requests, for by that time their minds were obviously made up. They are referred to in a *minuta* of the Duke of Lerma of 15 May 1609, and again in a *consulta* of the *Consejo de Estado* of July 1609,[3] with reference to the earlier documents recommending the non-prosecution of Quirós' proposals, and in relation to a *consulta* of the *Consejo de Estado* of 18 January 1609. This July *consulta* recommended that Quirós be pacified by being sent to Perú, but that copies of Iturbe's correspondence be sent to the Viceroy under a *contra-despacho*, leaving the matter to his discretion and ordering him to entertain but not to assist Quirós. On 30 August 1609, the Duke of Lerma informed the Count of Lemos of the King's decision to despatch Quirós as recommended.[4]

It is possible that Quirós was entertaining thoughts of the rediscovery or settlement of the Solomons, or at least that his negotiations had conveyed this impression, for on 28 September 1609, a letter was received at Court from *Don* Fernando de Castro, *Adelantado* of the Islands of Solomon, dated Lima, 29 December 1608,[5] in which the writer expressed his belief that Quirós was asking for the duty of settling and pacifying 'the islands called of Solomon'. He reported the friars who had accompanied Quirós in 1605-7 as testifying that he had not obeyed his instructions, had been deaf to all advice, had deliberately avoided possible discoveries, and that the land which he had discovered

[1] Letter to the King, México, 25 March 1607, AGS: *Estado, legajo* 219; BNM: MS. 3099, ff129-139v.

Letter to the King, Panama, 10 May 1608, AGS: *Estado, legajo* 219; BNM: MS. 3099, ff141-143v.

Letter to the *Condestable* of Castille, Panama, 10 May 1608, AGS: *Estado, legajo* 219; BNM: MS. 3099, ff145-147v. See also the digest of their contents, '*Sumario de lo que contienen las Cartas de Juan de Iturbe*', AGS: *Estado, legajo* 219; BNM: MS. 3099, ff149-152v.

[2] '*Sumario brebe de la Relacion y Derrotero del Viaje que hizo el Capitan ... de Quiros ... en el descubrimiento de las tierras incognitas de la parte Austral de la Mar del Sur ... año de 1605.*' '*Porque mejor se entienda esta Relacion ... y en lo demas vá cierto y verdadero*', AGS: *Estado, legajo* 219; BNM: MS. 3099, ff109-128v; RAH: *Colección de Jesuitas*,CXVIII, 87; MNM: MS. 196, ff16-27v.

[3] AGS: *Estado, legajo* 219; BNM: MS. 3099, ff43-47v; Zaragoza 1876: II: 259-65.

[4] AGS: *Estado, legajo* 219. See also '*Despachos: Consejo de Estado*', 7 September 1609, BNM: MS. 3099, f262; and *Consulta: Consejo de Estado*, 11 September 1609, BNM: MS. 3099, ff257-258.

[5] AGS: *Estado, legajo* 213 (*copia*); AGI: *Indiferente General, legajo* 750; RAH: *Colección Muñoz, Vol.* XXXVIII, f51; Zaragoza 1876: II: 213-15; Pacheco 1864: V: 513-15; Markham 1904: II: 508-10. It was sent under a letter from Gabriel de Hoa to the Secretary Andrés de Prada, AGS: *Estado, legajo* 213 (*original*).

was part of New Guinea[1]: 'seen many times by those navigating to the Philippines, and on the discovery of the Solomon Islands which are very near it, and the inhabitants and lands are truly the same as those in New Guinea.' He promised to write again by the next fleet, restated his claims to the Islands of Solomon, and added that he was about to depart for 'these kingdoms' (Spain?), with the intention of making his plea for the good settlement of the islands (the Solomons), and besought the King to prevent Quirós from obtaining a concession injurious to himself.

After several conciliar exchanges between 5 October and early December 1609,[2] a royal *cédula* was issued on 15 December, signed by de Hoa and witnessed by the *Consejo de Estado*, ordering Montes Claros, the Viceroy of Perú, to receive and prepare Quirós for his proposed voyage.[3] This was accompanied by a letter from de Hoa to the Viceroy urging the quick despatch of Quirós in the King's name.[4] Quirós saw both these documents, but he did not see the *contra-despacho* which accompanied them and which effectively prevented the prosecution of his project.[5] Nevertheless he was dissatisfied with the terms of the *cédula* and began once again to memorialize the King and Councils, estimating his expenses and listing his requirements.[6] In a *minuta* of 16 June 1610,[7]

---

[1] When it is recalled that Quirós had only seen the north coast of Espíritu Santo, and Torres had only seen the north, east and south coasts, the supposition that Espíritu Santo was an eastern extremity of New Guinea was neither unreasonable nor disproven.

[2] *Duque de Lerma, 5 October 1609, AGS: Estado, legajo 219.*

Parecer: Consejo de Indias, 30 October 1609, BNM: MS. 3099, ff253–254.

Duque de Lerma, 2 November 1609, AGS: Estado, legajo 219.

Parecer: Consejo de Estado, 5 November 1609, BNM: MS. 3099, ff157–157v; AGS: Estado, legato 219.   [3] Zaragoza 1876: I: 391–4; Markham 1904: I: 314–15.

[4] Zaragoza 1876: I: 394–5; Markham 1904: I: 315.   [5] BNM: MS. 3099, ff280–280v.

[6] *Memorial, '... demostrará á V.M. ... y razon que ofrezco', Zaragoza 1876: II: 268–79.*

Memorial, 'V. Md. mando al Consejo ... y á mi con ella', BNM: MS. 3099, f188; AGS: Estado, legajo 228.

Memorial, 'V. M. ordeno al Consejo ... me tiene concedido', BNM: MS. 3099, ff189–189v; AGS: Estado, legajo 228.

Memorial, 'Mucho qui siera ... Dios para estas su obra', BNM: MS. 3099, ff192–193v; AGS: Estado, lagajo 228.

Memorial, 'Lo que à V. Mgd. ofrezco son Reynos ... su Monarquia', BNM: MS. 3099, ff173–174; AGS: Estado, legajo 228.

Memorial, 'Supplico a V.M. con todo encarecimiento ... en esta grande servicio de Dios, y de V.M.', BNM: MS. 3099, ff267–270v.

Memorial, '... digo que ha dos meses ... pedido y justicia Vᵃ.', BNM: MS. 3099, f272.

Memorial, 'Digo que el S.ʳⁱᵒ Pedro de Ledesma ... estare cóntento', BNM: MS. 3099, ff275–276.

See also the *minuta, Duque de Lerma to the Presidente de Indias, 24 July 1610, AGS: Estado, legajo* 2640; BNM: MS. 3099, ff265–265v, which lists Quirós' requirements in Spain and Perú.

As the *memoriales* of Quirós are invariably undated in their extant MS. form it is necessary to date them according to their contents and/or position amongst other dated documents, but errors of chronology may well result, particularly since most of the material has been examined on microfilm.

[7] AGS: *Estado, legajo* 223; RAH: *Colección Muñoz, Vol.* XXXVIII, ff49–54; BNM: MS. 3099, ff163–163v; Zaragoza 1876: II: 266–8; Markham 1904: II: 514–15.

the *Consejo de Indias* referred to a *memorial* in which Quirós had stated that many people would accompany him,[1] and suggested, in view of the inconveniences likely to result if Quirós and a large body of colonists became destitute in Perú, that the plan be changed. They suggested that Quirós be informed that, although his proposals were considered to be valuable, the moment was inopportune, but that he might expect approval in two or three years' time, and further suggested that he be given a well-paid appointment at Court.

However, on 1 November 1610 he was provided with another *cédula*, different from the first one only in that it granted him 6,000 *ducados* for expenses and specified sheet iron with which he was to be supplied, indicating presumably that the chances of Quirós' defection were considered greater than the inconvenience of his followers being stranded in Perú.[2] A *minuta* of 21 August 1610,[3] refers to the receipt of a letter from *Don* Diego de Prado y Tovar, dated Manila, 20 July 1609, in which de Prado reported detrimentally on Quirós and his conduct on the expedition of 1605–6. This letter was a precursor to two others received on 12 October 1614,[4] less than a month before Quirós received the assurances of the Viceroy-designate of Perú, Francisco de Borja, Prince of Esquilache, with whom he was to travel to Perú, that he would be despatched to settle the '*tierra Austrial*'.[5]

Despite his assurances to Quirós there is little doubt that de Borja had been well advised of the negative part which he was to play in the abortive enterprise, and in a *minuta* of 2 September 1614, the *Consejo de Estado* reported that the President of the Indies had advised him of what he was to do.[6] Quirós' departure with de Borja was the pathetic outcome of all his endeavours, and his death *en route* to Perú saved him from further frustration and humiliation and the Spanish authorities from further inconvenience.

Further Proposals for the Exploration of the South Pacific

Quirós' failure to conduct a further expedition to the South-West Pacific did not, despite the attitude of the Spanish authorities, mark the end of Spanish aspirations towards that region, though such proposals for further exploration

---

[1] Perhaps the *memorial* '*Mucho qui siera . . . Dios para estas su obra*', BNM: MS. 3099, ff192–193v.

[2] Zaragoza 1876: I: 396–9; BNM: MS. 3099, ff278–279V.

See also *Minuta: Consejo de Estado*, 19 June 1610, BNM: MS. 3099, ff181–184; AGS: *Estado, legajo* 228.   [3] *Consejo de Estado*, AGS: *Estado, legajo* 228; AGS: *Estado, legajo* 2026.

[4] De Prado to the King, *per* Antonio de Arostegui, dated Goa, 24 December 1613, AGS: *Estado, legajo* 252; BNM: MS. 3099, ff207–210; Stevens 1929; 239–40; Zaragoza 1876: II: 187–9; Markham 1904: II: 511–12. De Prado to the King, dated Goa, 25 December 1613, AGS: *Estado, Legajo* 252; BNM: MS. 3099, ff210v–211; RAH: *Colección Muñoz, Vol.* XXXVIII; Pacheco 1864: V: 517–18; Stevens 1929: 240; Zaragoza 1876: II: 189–90; Markham 1904: II: 512–13.

[5] '*Certificacion de Don Francisco de Borja*', Zaragoza 1876: I: 402.   [6] AGS: *Estado, legajo* 2644.

as were made seem to have come from individuals, in particular from members
of Missionary Orders. It is indeed in this latter period, fertile with plans but
damned to sterility by the uncontrollable vicissitudes of Spanish fortunes, that
the religious motivations of the Spaniards stand out most clearly, and their
sense of obligation and duty to convert the inhabitants of the South-West Pacific is most marked. Economic, military, strategic and political necessity might
compel statesmen to abandon the souls of the *Indios* to perdition, but the Missionary Orders could admit of no such necessity.

Oral traditions, written accounts and the cartography of the era all served to
keep memories of the three voyages fresh in men's minds, and to stir their
interest and imagination. The Pacific still offered all the attractions which it had
offered before Mendaña's departure in 1567, for the three voyages between
1567 and 1607 had been but preliminary forays in low latitudes. The austral
continent was still an unknown and elusive entity, and the great expanses of
the South Pacific might well conceal lands whose contents were beyond the
imaginations of men. Quirós himself had never failed to emphasize the potential wealth of his discoveries and the perhaps greater wealth of their neighbours,
and in a *memorial* of 1609 had quoted Sequeira, Portuguese Captain-Major of
Tidore, to the effect that New Guinea was a '*tierra de mucho oro*',[1] and the
Licenciado Hernando de los Ríos, *Procurador* of the Philippines, as declaring on
the authority of de Brito that the natives of New Guinea '*tienen oro que traen en
las orejas, y al cuello, que son mercaderes*'.[2]

In 1609 Dr. Antonio de Morga produced in México his *Sucesos de las
Islas Philipinas*,[3] in which he included a brief account of Mendaña's second
voyage and a transcript of Quirós' letter to himself.[4] He describes Mendaña's
purpose in 1595 as being 'to people the islands of Solomon which he had
discovered many years before in the South Sea', referred to Santa Cruz as
'an island of negroes, close to New Guinea', and provided, in effect, brief but
accurate accounts of the last two voyages for interested readers of the early
seventeenth century.[5] In 1613 Dr. Christóval Suárez de Figueroa produced in
Madrid his *Hechos de Don García Hurtado de Mendoza, Cuarto Marqués de
Cañete*, a work which was to provide French and English historians and cartographers of the eighteenth century with sufficient information of Mendaña's
first voyage to enable them to identify the Islands of Solomon with recent
discoveries. Guppy had 'no doubt that Figueroa derived almost all his information from the journal of Gallego',[6] which seems likely, but his account seems
to have been predominantly based on the brief account at the beginning of

[1] Zaragoza 1876: II: 299.   [2] Zaragoza 1876: II: 295.
 [3] Stanley 1868. This is a translation of the BM. copy (Grenville Library). On de Morga see Stanley
1868: ii; Maggs 1927: 12.   [4] Stanley 1868: 65–74; Markham 1904: 149–57.
 [5] The distribution of this work was probably very limited, and even by 1736 it was very rare.
See Stanley 1868: i–ii.   [6] Guppy 1887: 272.

the Quirós-Bermúdez *relación*, although the contents may indicate that Figueroa also had access to the accounts of Mendaña and Catoira.[1] He describes the Ysla de Jesús as 1,450 leagues from Perú, Los Baxos de la Candelaria as being a further 160 leagues to the W in $6\frac{1}{2}°$ S.[2] For his description of Mendaña's second voyage of 1595 he used Quirós' own account in the Quirós-Bermúdez *relación*,[3] and his was the only account of that voyage available to the later historians of Pacific discovery, Dalrymple and Burney.[4]

The year 1613 saw the Franciscans urging the need to discover and convert within the Pacific and austral lands in two *memoriales* submitted by *Fray* Juan de Silva in Madrid and approved by *Fray* Juan de Torquemada, the Provincial of the Order in México.[5] In 1621 de Silva again raised the Ophirian quest as a motive for discovery, remarking that 'it is certain that the fleets that went to Solomon laden with gold and silver . . . were from the Austral Provinces . . . and the island called Ophir whence the very pure and refined gold came together with other riches was also of these Provinces,'[6] and in 1615 Torquemada published in Seville his *Primera Parte de los veynte y un libros rituales y Monarchia Yndiana con el origen y guerras de los Indias Occidentales de sus poblaçones descubrimento conquista conversion y otras cosas maravillosas de la mesma tierra*, which included an account of Quirós' voyage of 1605–6, probably obtained from Quirós himself,[7] and a map of the Americas and Pacific which seems to be a crude version of the similar map to be found in Herrera.

Between the years 1615 and 1621[8] an advocate of Santiago in Chile, Dr. Juan Luis Arias, presented a *memorial* to Philip III[9] urging the evangelical obligations of the state, reiterating the traditional arguments for the existence of the *Antipodes* and advocating the further exploration of the lands already discovered. Referring to the lead taken by de Silva and the Franciscans, he warned against the activities of the English and Dutch, the 'most poisonous venom of their apostasy' and their incursions into Florida, California and Virginia. He stated that:

[1] If he had access to Gallego's *relación* then it is likely that he would have had access to other relevant documents in the same place. His description of the return voyage is confined to the voyage of the *Capitana*, indicating that his sources were only those written by *expedicionarios* on that vessel, and his reference to 18 soldiers accompanying the first voyage of the brigantine is only to be found in Catoira's narrative.

[2] See Fleurieu 1791: 5–16. The work is to be found as a whole in the *Colección de Historiadores*, introduced by D. Barros Amaña, Santiago, 1861.   [3] Markham 1904: I: xiii.

[4] It was also used by de Brosses (see De Brosses 1756) (Pingré 1767: 30).

[5] BNM: $\dfrac{2}{51255}$ (two printed *memoriales* with succeeding papers).

[6] Silva 1621: 60.

[7] Torquemada 1723: I: 738–56 (The Madrid edition), Markham 1904: II: 407 *et seq.*

[8] The death of Quirós, which occurred in 1614, is mentioned, and Philip III died in 1621.

[9] Markham 1904: II: 517–36. A copy of the original is in the BM (*Papeles Tocantes a la Iglesia Española*, 4745, f11) and is translated in Dalrymple 1770; and Major 1859.

that which we now propose to have explored, discovered and evangelically subdued is part of the said hemisphere [the austral hemisphere] which lies in the Pacific Ocean, between . . . the coast of Peru, as far as the Baia de San Felipe y Santiago and the longitude which remains up to Bachan and Ternate,

and agreed that this land 'is greatly stored with metals and rich in precious stones and metals'. Describing the discoveries already made he wrote:

The Adelantado, Alvaro Mendaña de Neyra, first discovered New Guadalcanal, which is a very large island very near New Guinea, and some have imagined that what Mendaña called New Guadalcanal was part of New Guinea, but this is of no consequence whatever. New Guinea belongs to the southern hemisphere. . . . It is a country encompassed with water . . . The Adelantado . . . afterwards discovered the archipelago of islands which he called the Islands of Solomon, whereof, great and small, he saw thirty-three of very fine appearance, the middle of which, according to his account, is in 11° S. After this he discovered, in the year 1565, the island of San Christobal, not far from the said archipelago the middle of which was in from 7° to 8° of South latitude. . . .

Subsequently, in the year 1595, the said Adelantado sailed for the last time from Peru . . . with the purpose of colonising the island of San Christobal, and from thence attempting the discovery of the southern *tierra firma*. He shortly after discovered, to the east of the said island of San Christobal, the island of Santa Cruz in 10° S latitude.[1]

He went on to describe Quirós' voyage of 1605–6, the information of 'lands very fertile and populous and running down to a great depth towards the south' which he obtained from the native chief at Taumako, the discovery of Espíritu Santo, and Torres' voyage south of New Guinea, during which 'he sighted a very extensive coast, which he took for that of New Guadalcanal'.[2] The Arias *memorial* is important in this context as expressing the belief that the Solomons were close to New Guinea, and in its near-correct statement of the relative positions of Taumako, Santa Cruz and the Solomons.

Joannes de Soloranzo Pereira, in his *Disputationem de Indiarum Jure* of 1629 refers to the Islands of Solomon, the discoveries of Quirós, the works available on these subjects, enumerating the Quirós papers then in Perú and citing the writings of Herrera, de Morga, Torquemada and Acosta.[3] In 1646 Father Alonso de Ovalle SJ, a native of Santiago in Chile and Procurator of his Order in Rome, produced *An Historical Relation of the Kingdom of Chile* which was published in Rome in 1649 and in England in 1703. Of Tierra del Fuego he writes that:

Formerly before the . . . Streights of Le Maire, were discovered, this land was thought to be joined to some other great continent of the Terra Australis which was supposed to join to New Guinea or the Islands of Solomon; and Ortelius in his geography is of this Opinion,

---

[1] Markham 1904: II: 523–4.

[2] Though this deduction was not mentioned by Torres, who identified the coastline along which he sailed as that of New Guinea, he may initially have thought that the southern coast of New Guinea was Guadalcanal, or have concluded as others did that Guadalcanal was the eastern extremity of New Guinea. [3] Pereira 1629: 74.

but upon the discovery of the other Streights of St. Vincent that doubt has been cleared. . . . Having also mentioned the Islands of Solomon and New Guinea to which antiently it was thought that the land of Tierra del Fuego was joined, it will be well to say something of them. The Author who writes the best of them is Antonio de Herrera, and from him is taken what John and Theodore de Brye say of them; which is this. The Islands of New Guinea run from something more than One Degree South of the Pole Antartick. Three hundred Leagues East to the Fifth or Sixth degree; according to which reckoning, they fall upon the West of Paita. The islands of Solomon fall to the West of Peru about Eight Hundred Leagues from its Coast, and extend themselves between the Seventh and Twelth Degree: They are distant from Lima about Fifteen hundred leagues; they are many, of a good size.[1]

During the seventeenth century several petitions seem to have been presented to the Pope seeking his support for the further exploration of the South-West Pacific, but even if the Pope himself approved of these projects they received no support in Spain. In 1622, for instance, two *memoriales* were submitted to Pope Gregory XV by Dr. Sebastián Clemente, outlining proposals for the conversion of the natives of the austral lands.[2]

In 1647-61 a Peruvian astronomer and cosmographer, Andrés de Medina-Dávila, presented a petition to the King in which he pointed out the advantages to be derived from the colonization of the Islands of Solomon, and sought permission to conquer them.[3] His proposal seems to have been received with some favour, primarily perhaps because he was prepared to bear the expense of the expedition himself, in return for the generalship of the Manila galleon for three years. This lucrative post was normally awarded annually and alternately by the Governor of the Philippines and the Bishop of Manila, but the King acceded to the proposal and ordered the Viceroy of New Spain to hand the galleon over to Dávila on his arrival there in 1663, and to place vessels at his disposal for the conquest and exploration of the Solomons. Having few vessels at his disposal the Viceroy decided to pass the latter responsibility to the Governor of the Philippines, and ordered the commander, García, to vacate his command of the galleon. On 25 March 1663, the galleon put to sea, but once out of sight of land Dávila was deposed by *Don* Diego de Salcedo, the Governor-designate of the Philippines and a passenger on the vessel.[4]

Dávila sought the assistance of *Fray* José de Paternìna, an Augustinian previously condemned to the galleys for disreputable conduct, who had been

[1] Churchill 1704: III: 53. This is the English translation of 1703. Ovalle perpetuated, as did the de Brye (Bry) brothers, Herrera's double statement of the distance of the Solomons from Perú of 1500 leagues and 800 leagues. According to Buâche (Fleurieu 1791: 317, 221), Ovalle gave the distance of the Solomons from Perú as 7,500 miles.

[2] VAPF: *Scritture originali riferite nelle Congregazioni Generali, Memoriali del an 1622*, CCCLXXXII, ff156-157v and 164-167v.

[3] See BM: *Gayangos FU/65 Medina*; BNM: MS. 3048, ff53-58v; Dalrymple 1770: 56; Blair 1906: XXXVII: 227. There is some doubt as to whether the petition was presented in 1647 or 1661.

[4] Blair 1906: XXXVI: 261; XXXVII: 227-30.

13

subsequently reprieved and appointed Father Commissary to the Holy Office of the Inquisition in Manila. He had already quarrelled with Salcedo in México City, over a lady relative with whom Salcedo had apparently had an *affaire*, and he now quarrelled with him over Dávila's deposal, and over Salcedo's refusal to appoint his nephew to an office in the Philippines.[1] On arrival in the Philippines Paternìna seized the opportunity presented by a quarrel between the Governor and Archbishop Poblete of Manila to denounce the former to the Inquisition for communicating with the Dutch[2] and, when this accusation failed, for failing to fulfil his religious obligations. In 1667 the Archbishop died, and in October 1668 the Commissioners of the Inquisition despatched armed Franciscans led by Paternìna to arrest the Governor and throw him into prison.[3]

It is hardly surprising, against this background, that Medina-Dávila's plans for the exploration and settlement of the Solomons were frustrated. He did eventually obtain a ship and, with support from the Augustinians, sailed for Cochin-China, presumably to obtain more supplies. He was never heard of again, though some of his instruments were later offered for sale to Portuguese traders on that coast.[4]

By this time the incentive to pursue the exploration and settlement of the South Pacific seems to have passed from the Franciscans to the Jesuits. In 1662 the Jesuit Father Diego Luis de San Vitores left New Spain for the Philippines and Japan. The galleon in which he was travelling called at the Ladrones, and it was here, he decided, that his mission really lay. Having failed to win the support of the Governor of the Philippines for his proposed mission, he returned to Spain, where his father, *Don* Gerónimo San Vitores, was influential at the court of Philip IV, and secured the support of the King and of Queen María Anna.[5]

In June 1665, orders were despatched to the Governor of the Philippines to assist him in his project, and he himself arrived in Guam in 1668. In 1669 a *memorial* was published in México under his name, the object of which had apparently been to persuade the Society of Jesus to found a mission in the Ladrones, renamed the *Marianas* in honour of Queen María Anna by San Vitores, with a view to exploring and christianizing the *Tierra Austrialia* and the 'Southern or austral islands'.[6] The first part of his *memorial* describes the advantages to be derived from using the Marianas as a stepping stone to the austral continent, and refers to an appended *memorial* of 1610 by Quirós,

---

[1] Blair 1906: XXXVII: 26–7, 49, 56–8, 122, 226; XXVIII: 112–3, 196.

[2] Lea 1908: 311–12. Salcedo was himself a Fleming in origin.

[3] Blair 1906: XXXVII: 23–32, 262–8.   [4] Blair 1906: XXXVII: 234

[5] Burney 1803: III: 274–8. On the mission settlement of the Ladrones see Burney 1803: III: 271–315. Burney cites as his source Gobien's *Histoire des Isles Marianes nouvellement converties à la Religion Chrètienne, et de la mort glorieuse des premieres Missionaires qui ont prêché la Foy*. See Vidal 1674, and Blair 1906: XXXVII: 266–7.

[6] San Vitores 1669. There is a copy in the Dixson Collection, Sydney (66/4).

whose beliefs he cites in support of his proposals. The *memorial* contains an account of Mendaña's voyage of 1595, a copy of Quirós' eighth *memorial*, and concludes with a discourse on the reasons for not delaying 'the conversion of the innumerable souls throughout . . . the unknown Austral land'.

In 1670–1 a further *noticia* was published in México reporting on the progress of the mission of San Vitores between 15 May 1669, and 28 April 1670.[1] Included in it are extracts from the reports of San Vitores in which he expresses the opinion that, given the men and ships, a long string of islands might be discovered in the Pacific connecting 'the Marianas with the great austral land to the south and the islands of Japan to the north'. It concludes with a plea for support to explore the many ports and islands 'from the Island of Guam to very near Perú, as related in the relation of Captain Pedro Fernández de Quirós which was presented with the other papers a year ago'.

The idea of a chain of islands fringing the austral continent was one to which Quirós had subscribed, and is to be seen illustrated on several charts and maps of the period, sometimes with the discovery of the islands attributed to Gallego, sometimes to Quirós.[2] San Vitores, from his study of the discoveries of Mendaña and Quirós, seems to have concluded that the chain of islands stretched from Japan through the Marianas to the Island of Solomon, the discoveries of Quirós, and thence towards South America. Although the concept of such islands forming a continuous indication of an austral continent extending from New Guinea to the S of Tierra del Fuego had been largely belied by the voyage of Tasman, the island discoveries of Mendaña, Quirós, le Maire and Tasman did offer considerable evidence for the idea of a continuous chain of islands running eastwards across the Pacific in increasingly high latitudes south of the equator, which might in their turn indicate a southern continent extending eastwards from Tasman's Nova Zeelandia or Staten Landt. A map which was apparently prepared by San Vitores and *Fray* Marcelo de Ansaldo to accompany the first report,[3] a rather crude map centred on the antarctic pole, depicts a large *Tierra Austral No Conocida* of which Nueva Guinea is a narrow promontory, with a chain of islands fringing the coast of Nueva Guinea and several more extending eastwards into the Pacific.

San Vitores' settlement of the Marianas was not effected without difficulty or physical opposition, and in 1672 he was himself killed.[4] A period of strife and turmoil followed, with the natives in revolt, but the Jesuits still continued to press for a vessel in which to expand their activities towards the south, and in 1681 the Governor of the Philippines had in hand the construction of a

---

[1] San Vitores 1670. Copy in the Dixson Collection, Sydney (67/5). Both documents are described in Maggs 1927: 24–27.

[2] See for instance the *Leconsfield-Edwards* map of 1618–25, Gerard's *Carte Universelle Hydrographique* of 1634, and Janssonius' *Mar del Zur Hispanis, Mare Pacificum* of 1650.

[3] *Ministerio de Fomento* 1877: *Mapa* I, *Mapa de la Australia*.   [4] Maggs 1927: 31.

vessel of 120 tons.[1] In view of the strained relations which had developed between the Jesuit Mission and the Governor of the Philippines it was decided in 1680 that a separate administration be established in the Marianas, and in 1681 *Don* Antonio de Sarabia (Saravia) departed from Acapulco as Governor-designate with a commission to conquer, explore and govern all the adjacent islands and austral lands.[2] Arriving in Guam in June 1681, in poor health, Sarabia found himself faced with a task of local pacification and administration of sufficient magnitude to preclude any immediate hopes of southerly expansion. The promised vessel from the Philippines did not arrive until August 1683,[3] and just before the death of Sarabia she parted her cables in a storm and was driven on a reef, destroying 'our hope of exploring the southern islands which lead to the unknown Austral lands and are the goal of our endeavour'.[4] On Sarabia's death the administration of the Marianas was assumed by a creole, Esplana, who had brought the vessel from the Philippines in August, 1683, but insurrections and disorders seem to have put an end to any further attempts to explore towards the south which might have been envisaged.

The Franciscans and Jesuits were now joined by the Dominicans in their proposals for the settlement and conversion of the Solomons and other austral islands, and in 1674–5 *Fray* Ignacio Muñoz put forward proposals which constitute valuable historical documents in themselves.[5] In a proposal dated 15 April 1674, he reiterated the idea of a chain of Pacific islands extending over 2,240 leagues from the coast of Perú to New Guinea, within 25° S of the equator, but it is quite clear that when Muñoz wrote of the Islas de Salomón, 'the name . . . which has been given to the Islas Australes', he meant all the islands of the South Pacific within the vicinity of the eastern point of New Guinea, which he believed to lie 2,240 leagues from Perú. He gave the relative positions of Lima and Manila as separated by 157° 12' or '*2790 leguas Españolas y 40 minutas*', and described Magellan's island discoveries as the first of the *Solomon or Austral Islands*, and Mendaña's discoveries in 1568, 1 700+ *leguas* from Perú and 540 *leguas* E of easternmost New Guinea, as the second. He goes on

---

[1] See Maggs 1927: 40–41, where the relevant *Relacion de los Sucessos mas Notables de las Islas Marianas desde Junio 1681 hasta junio 1682* of Padre Manuel de Solorzano, dated Agadña (Guam), 3 May 1682, is described and translated. See also Maggs 1927: 35–38.

[2] Maggs 1927: 40. Dahlgren 1916 notes that in 1681 Sarabia sailed from Acapulco, and sites the Jesuit chronicle of Stocklerin, *Der Neue Welt-Bott*: 1, i, page 3 of 1726, to the effect that Sarabia intended to conquer some islands to the S of the Marianas and explore the Southland.

[3] *Padre* Gerardo Bonwens to the Duchess of Aveiro, Guam, 30 May 1685, Maggs 1927: 47–49.

[4] *Fray* Manuel de Solorzano to the Duchess of Aveiro, Agadhña, 25 April 1684, Maggs 1927: 46.

[5] AGI: *Filipinas*, 82 ('*Fray Ignacio Muñoz O.P. al Consejo de las Indias: Propone su parecer . . . Sobre la Manutencion, y Extension de la Fë en la Cordillera de las Islas Marianas y sus confinantes, y sobre el Descubrimiento, y Conquista de las Islas Australes de Salomon, 15. IV. 1674*').

See also RAH: *Don Beníto de la Mata y Linares, a. tom. 3, ff115–128, 'Propone en su parecear sobre las Islas Marianas y las Islas de Salomon por Fr. Ignacio Muñoz, O.P., 1675*'; and BM: Egerton No. 1816, item 24, ff225–228.

to refer to the several foreign incursions into the Pacific of Drake, Cavendish, de Cordes, Oliver del Norte and Spilbergio (Speilbergen), and returns to the Spanish discoveries with an account of Mendaña's voyage of 1595. In the concluding phases of this expedition he confuses it with Quirós' voyage of 1606, which he does not describe, referring to Santa Cruz as the *Isla Sancti Spiritus*, to *Vera Cruz* and the *Puerto de San Felipe y Santiago* as part of it, and mentioning a great island sighted to the SE which was named *San Christoval*.

It is almost certain that more proposals for the discovery and settlement of the *Solomon or Austral Islands* were submitted during this period, but they were not implemented. Whilst their references to the Solomons were often vague, their aims directed not only towards the discoveries of Mendaña but to all the islands discovered in the South Pacific, it is very likely that if they had been supported and implemented they would have led to the rediscovery of the Solomons, and to an increased knowledge and rapidly improved cartography of the South-West Pacific. Heading south-eastwards towards the discoveries of Quirós, the positions of which in relation to the Marianas were tolerably accurately charted, and using New Guinea as a stepping-stone, any expansion southwards from the Marianas and Carolines could hardly have failed to involve the rediscovery of the Solomons.

The Islands of Solomon, Santa Cruz and Espíritu Santo in the Pacific Cartography of the Early Seventeenth Century

The Pacific cartography of the early part of the seventeenth century provides an interesting commentary on contemporary concepts of the Islands of Solomon, all the more so since these concepts can be related to the further discoveries of Mendaña in 1595 and Quirós in 1606 whether it be by their delineation on or absence from those charts.

As is to be expected, the majority of the Pacific charts of the early part of the century which depict the Islands of Solomon derive directly from proto-types of the late sixteenth century. On the great majority of these we see the archipelago laid down in what, by the end of the sixteenth century, had almost become the standard configuration of the group: situated close to New Guinea and with open southern and western coastlines, reflecting the limits of the exploration actually made in 1568 and the possibility of connection with New Guinea and/or *Terra Australis*. Whilst variations of delineation and nomenclature within this general form can be observed, they are largely irrelevant, can be attributed to errors of transcription or copying, and do not detract from the existence of this general form. The *Molyneux Globe* of 1603 falls within this category, as does Jodocus Hondius' map of the world of 1608,[1]

---

[1] Published in 1927 by the Royal Geographical Society, London, with a memoir by Eastwood.

and, on a smaller scale, his *Typus Orbis Terrarum* of 1608–9.[1] The same general form is to be observed on Petrus Kaerius' *Nova Guinea et In. Salomonis* of 1609,[2] itself identical to Linschoten's *Insulae Moluccae* of 1596 in its representation of the Solomons, and to Visscher's reproduction of the latter in 1617.[3] The map in Torquemada's *Monarchia Yndiana*,[4] with its probable derivation from Herrera,[5] is in the same category, as are Guiljelmo Blaeu's *Nova Totius Terrarum Orbis Geographica* of 1635, the *Globis Terrestris Planisphericus* of Ottavio Pisani (1637),[6] and a Pacific chart by António Sanches of 1641.[7] The same form is continued on the map *Nova Totius Terrarum Orbis geographica ac hydrographica tabula* by Kaerius and Janssonius of 1645, which seems to be a copy of Blaeu's *Nova Totius Terrarum Orbis* of 1635.

Santa Cruz, discovered in 1595, is rather conspicuous by its frequent absence from the charts of the century as a whole, and whilst this absence during the early years of the century can be attributed to the slow dissemination of reliable reports of the discovery,[8] and to the continued reproduction of sixteenth-century prototypes without corrections or additions, the same cannot be said of charts produced during the later years of the century. It is possible that the Spanish authorities were quite successful in suppressing information concerning this voyage, for such information was certainly limited, and the strategic importance of the Marquesas imposed a very decided need for secrecy. Furthermore, knowledge of the failure of the Santa Cruz settlement, the insignificant size of the island, and its dissociation from the Ophirian conjecture, may have rendered it of little interest, and of even less interest once the rumours of Quirós' discoveries of 1606 began to circulate.

A chart which does depict Santa Cruz and the discoveries of Quirós is to be found in Pedro Baena's *Derrotero*[9] in Hack's translation of the Spanish *derrotero* captured by Captain Sharp in 1681,[10] in another Spanish *derrotero* of 1669 in the Huntingdon Library,[11] and reproduced by Zaragoza from an original in a private collection in Spain.[12] These charts are all basically identical, although there are some differences in the nomenclature. As can be seen from any of

[1] Langenes 1609: 1.   [2] Langenes 1609: 755.
[3] Müller 1894: II: No. 3.   [4] Torquemada 1723: 1.
[5] His *Descripcion de las Yndias Ocidentalis*.   [6] Bagrow 1951: 359. This map is in reverse.
[7] This is one of five illuminated charts on vellum, all dated Lisbon, 1641, to be found in a MS. *Atlas* of 16 charts in the Koninklijke Bibliotheek, The Hague (Press Mark, 129A.25). Sanches' Pacific chart is No. 10 in the *Atlas*, which also contains 11 charts by Gio. Battista Cavellini, dated Leghorn, 1642. See Cortesão 1935: II: 293.
[8] The publication of de Morga's *Sucesos de las Islas Philipinas* in 1609 with Quirós' report of the voyage was, judging from the surviving copies, for limited circulation.
[9] Collection of Arthur A. Houghton, Jnr, New York.
[10] BM: MS. Harl 4034 (the last in the *derrotero*).   [11] HL: HM 918.
[12] Zaragoza 1876: III: End Map. The BM and Huntingdon versions bear the date, Panama, 1669. I understand that there is a further version of this *derrotero* chart in the Biblioteca Nacional, Madrid, (MS. 2957, ff150v–151) which I have not seen. See Kelly 1961(a): 240.

these examples, particularly the British Museum version, it is an attempt at a pictorial or panoramic representation of the discoveries in the South-West Pacific, as well as a chart, and should be adjudged as such.

The Spanish *derroteros* of the seventeenth century were essentially pilot-books, and accordingly provided sketches of coastlines and ports on what was often an attempt at a combined vertical (showing the delineation of the

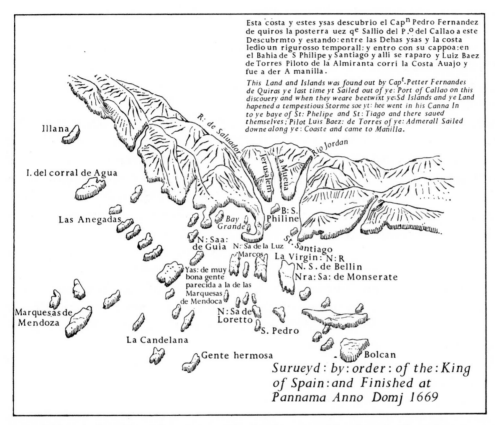

Esta costa y estes ysas descubrio el Cap^n Pedro Fernandez de quiros la posterra uez q^e Sallio del P.^o del Callao a este Descubrmto y estando: entre las Dehas ysas y la costa ledio un rigurosso temporall: y entro con su cappoa: en el Bahia de S Philipe y Santiago y alli se raparo y Luiz Baez de Torres Piloto de la Almiranta corri la Costa Auajo y fue a der A manilla.

This Land and Islands was found out by Capt. Petter Fernandes de Quiras ye last time yt Sailed out of ye: Port of Callao on this discouery and when they weare beetwixt ye: Sd Islands and ye Land hapened a tempestious Storme soe yt: hee went in his Canna In to ye baye of St: Phelipe and St: Tiago and there saued themselves: Pilot Luis Baez: de Torres of ye: Admerall Sailed downe along ye: Coaste and came to Manilla.

Map XXIII   A chart from the *rutter* or pilot-book captured by Captain Sharp in 1681 and translated by Hack, redrawn

coast) and horizontal (showing the coast as it appeared from the sea) plane. In an age when navigation was imprecise such panoramic charts, if they can be properly called charts at all, were probably of more value than inaccurate charts on a vertical plane when it came to identifying a landmark or finding a port. Indeed, the continued value of accurate panoramic views of coastlines, islands and harbour or channel entrances is to be seen today in the sketches which adorn some Admiralty charts.

Whilst such panoramic views, even when combined with an attempt to show the coastline on a vertical plane, were of value in showing a limited coastline, they were relatively useless when it came to depicting collections of islands, particularly if they were separated by any distance. In the case of this representation of some of the discoveries made in the Western Pacific in the *derroteros*, the draughtsman has, perhaps from limited information, perhaps because he only intended to convey an impression, or perhaps because he knew no better, attempted to do just this. The result, as can be seen, is a gross distortion of relative distances and positions, meaningless island silhouettes, and the conveyance of little more than a confused impression.

Against the southern background of an exaggerated representation of Quirós' *La Nueba Jerusalem* (La Austrialia del Espíritu Santo) and *Bahia de San Phelipe y Santiago*,[1] Santa Cruz[2] is laid down in the north-western corner, with the volcano (*Bolcan*) of Tinakula to its NW, and with several unnamed islands around it which may be presumed to represent the Reef Islands, the islands off Santa Cruz, and Utupua. Taumako (*Taumaco*) is delineated under the name *Nuestra Senora de Loreto* (*Loretto* in the BM version), and it is probable that the island and shoal bearing the name *La Candelana* (in the Huntingdon and BM version) or *La Candelario* (in the Zaragoza version) represents Los Baxos de la Candelaria (Roncador Reef) of 1568. These are the only islands of immediate interest in this context, but it may be noted that the contents of the chart are so compressed as to permit the proximate inclusion of even the Marquesas, that the name of one island, *Nuestra Senora de Gracia* (on the Zaragoza version, *de Guia* on the BM, Huntingdon and Houghton versions), does not derive from any of the extant narratives of the three expeditions examined, and that the island of *San Pedro* may be either the erroneously dissociated San Pedro of the Marquesas, so named by Mendaña in 1595, or the San Pedro of Magellan. One is perhaps forced to the conclusion that the draughtsman of this work relied on secondary narratives for his delineation of these islands, and not on a prototype chart.

Map No. 16 in the so-called *Duchess of Berry Atlas*[3] lays down an insular *Nova Guinea* with a southern coastline probably derived from a knowledge of Torres' discoveries. Santa Cruz (*S: braz*) is delineated, and to its NE are laid down what can only reasonably be identified as the Reef Islands and, to the NW, a group of islands which presumably represent the single volcanic island of Tinakula. The name *Palmos*, which almost certainly derives from *Don* Lorenzo's reference to the Reef Islands as '*llena de muchas palmas*'[4] has

---

[1] *feliphe* on the Zaragoza version; *Philine* on the Huntingdon version.

[2] Bearing the name *Sta Cruz* on the Zaragoza version, but on the other versions named only with a Maltese cross, or a Maltese cross preceded by *Sta*.

[3] BNP: Ge FF 14409. Cortesão dates this atlas between 1615 and 1623 and attributes it to a Portuguese cartographer.

[4] Zaragoza 1876: I: 70. As the Reef Islands were not named by the expedition of 1595, *Don* Lorenzo's description would be the only reasonable source for a name, either *Yslas de muchas palmas* or *Las palmas*, corrupted to *Palmas* or *Palmos*.

here been incorrectly applied to what should have been delineated as the single island of Tinakula instead of to the Reef Islands. To the E of Santa Cruz are five unnamed islands which must surely be intended to represent Taumako (*Taumaco*) and the other Duff Islands. To the SE of Santa Cruz we see delineated Quirós' actual discovery of Tikopia (*Chuquipia*); the reported island of Sikaiana (?) (*Chuquiseria*); and Espíritu Santo (*Noua gerusalē, Terra do Spō Panto*) with its bay of San Felipe y Santiago (*S:tiago e S:felipe*) and Rio de Vera Cruz

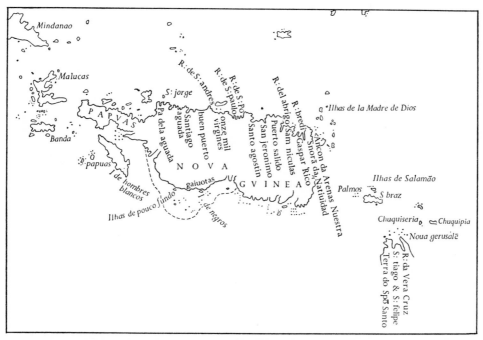

Map XXIV   Map No. 16 in the *Duchess of Berry Atlas, redrawn*

(*R:da Vera Cruz*). None of Mendaña's discoveries of 1568 are delineated, but the name *Ilhas de Salamão* appears in large print as if to apply to Santa Cruz and its immediate neighbours.

The first map in the *Duchess of Berry Atlas* is a world-map *Typus Orbis Terrarum* which roughly reproduces the relevant contents of Map No. 16, with the one name *Ilhas de Salamaō*. Apart from Espíritu Santo (unnamed), the only two relevant islands actually laid down are *Santa Cruz* and *Palmos*, which are laid down 95° and 90° W of Perú and, although unnamed, are identifiable when compared with similar world maps by Manuel Godinho de Erédia. Erédia's *Typus Orbis Terrarum* in his *Declaracam de Malaca* of 1613[1] is similar, although without nomenclature, but two world-maps in a MS *Miscellaneous-Atlas* of Erédia's in the private collection of Señor Machado

[1] In the Bibliothèque Royale, Brussels (MS. 7264).

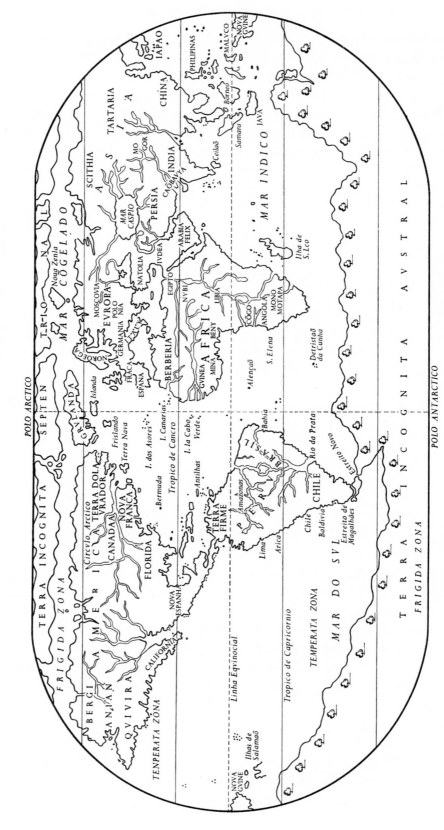

Map XXV   Map No. 1 in the *Duchess of Berry Atlas*, redrawn

Figueira of Lisbon[1] are even more revealing. These two world-maps, each entitled *Typus Orbis Terrarum*, are similar in their relevant detail to the world-maps of the *Declaracam* and the *Duchess of Berry Atlas* (Chart 1), and in both cases the names *S Bras* and *Palmos* are applied to the two islands to the N and NW of *Nova Gerusalem* (Espíritu Santo). On the one[2] Espíritu Santo is delineated with an open southern coastline, but on the other[3] the southern coastline is completed, a feature which may indicate that it post-dates Erédia's contact with de Prado and that the former map pre-dates it, for de Prado would almost certainly have told him of the insular character of that discovery.

In the same MS. *Miscellaneous-Atlas* are to be found a Pacific chart[4] and a detailed chart of *Nova Gervsalem*.[5] Within the limits of relevance to this study it is true to say that their detail is similar and also similar to that of Chart No. 16 in the *Duchess of Berry Atlas*. Santa Cruz bears the mis-copied name *S Bras*, and whilst on the Pacific chart the name *Palmos* is applied to the group of islets occupying the position of Tinakula, on the chart of *Nova Gervsalem* the name is correctly applied to the islands to the NE of Santa Cruz, the Reef Islands. As on Map No. 16 in the *Duchess of Berry Atlas*, *Chuquipia* (Tikopia) and *Chuquecema* (*Chuquiseria* on the Berry Chart, *Chusesena* on the Pacific chart—Sikaiana?) are laid down, together with unnamed features which may be identified as Taumako and the remainder of the Duff Islands.

Two of the charts examined within the category of those depicting the discoveries of 1568, in close proximity to New Guinea and with open southern coastlines, lay down some of the discoveries of Quirós. On Sanches' chart of 1641 Quirós' discoveries of *Gente Ermosa* (Gente Hermosa), *De ermanas* (La Decena, La Sagitaria, La Fugitiva), *Y: de muin buena gente* (Ysla de muy buena gente), *Las anegadas*, *Coral de Aqua*, *Y: de muin buen vista* and *Luna Puesta* in 1606; the *Marquesas de Mendoza*, *San Bernardo* and *Solitaria* of the expedition of 1595; and the *Nombre de Jesus* of the expedition of 1568, are all delineated to the E of the *Y^{as}. de Salamão*, as well as the *Da tubarones* (Las Tiburones) and *Ysla de San Pedro* of Magellan. However, no attempt has been made to lay down either Santa Cruz, Espíritu Santo, Taumako or Tikopia, perhaps because their delineation would have conflicted with that of the *Yas de Salamão*, or perhaps because the cartographer concluded that these were part of the Solomons.

<hr>

[1] On Erédia see Mills 1930; Spate 1957(a); Hamy 1878; Faro 1955. Faro refers to a notebook owned by Erédia containing maps relevant to the Spanish discoveries of 1595 and 1606, which may explain his delineation of these discoveries alone. The maps of this notebook, the *Miscellaneous-Atlas*, are reproduced in Cortesão 1960: IV: Plates 414A, 414B, 419D, 419E. It is certain that Erédia was in contact with *Don* Diego de Prado y Tovar in 1613.

[2] Cortesão 1960: IV: 414B.   [3] Cortesão 1960: IV: 414A.   [4] Cortesão 1960: IV: 419E.

[5] Cortesão 1960: IV: 419D. The Pacific chart shows Espíritu Santo's southern coastline open, the detailed chart of *Nova Gervsalem* (Espíritu Santo) shows it enclosed, again perhaps dating their composition pre and post Erédia's contact with de Prado respectively. The chart of *Nova Gervsalem* depicts an island at its eastern extremity bearing the names *Nuestra Senora de Loreto* (the name given in 1606 to Taumako) and *Matacas* (the Matanza of Torres?). This is clearly an erroneous addition.

An earlier chart by Sanches, his world-map of 1623,[1] shows a concept similar to that of the sixteenth chart in the *Duchess of Berry Atlas*. Sanches has here abandoned or deliberately neglected the late sixteenth-century delineation of the Solomons to which he returned, or which he adopted, on his chart of 1641. Although the name *Yas de Salamão* appears, as on the Berry chart it applies to Santa Cruz and its immediate neighbours, the Reef Islands, Taumako, Tikopia and perhaps Sikaiana. These, like Espíritu Santo, are unnamed, although their identity is ascertainable by comparison with the Berry chart, or with Erédia's Pacific chart or chart of *Nova Gervsalem*.

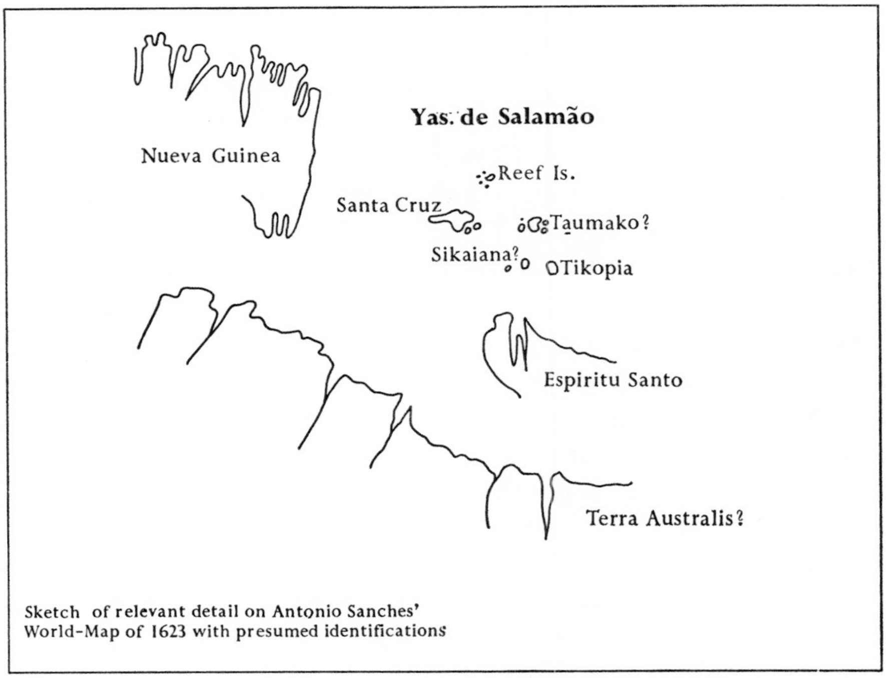

Yas. de Salamão

Nueva Guinea

Reef Is.

Santa Cruz   Taumako?

Sikaiana?   Tikopia

Espiritu Santo

Terra Australis?

Sketch of relevant detail on Antonio Sanches'
World-Map of 1623 with presumed identifications

Map XXVI   Sketch of relevant detail on Antonio Sanches' *World-map* of 1623 with presumed identifications

In summary it may be suggested that the Pacific charts and maps of the early seventeenth century which delineated the Solomons generally followed their late sixteenth-century prototypes in laying them down in close proximity to New Guinea, invariably with the islands of the 'Southern' Solomons laid down with open southern coastlines suggestive of a continental character. As we will shortly see, the supposed continental discovery of Quirós seems to have induced some cartographers to take this suggestive delineation a stage further, and on a body of charts of the period following the dissemination of reports of Quirós' discovery of La Tierra Austrialia del Espirítu Santo (e.g.

[1] BM: Add. 1 MS. 22874.

the *Van Langren Globe* of *c.* 1625) we see the promontory-like representations of the 'Southern' Solomons (Guadalcanal, Arracifes, San Nicolás and San Márcos) merged or blurred to form a continuous coastline, the eastern limit of which is extended southwards to include Quirós' Bahía de San Felipe y Santiago. The Tierra Austrialia del Espíritu Santo, or *Terre de Quiros* as the

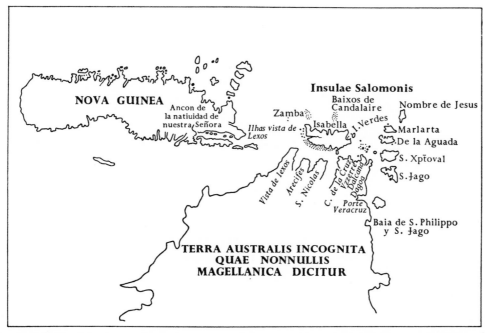

Map **XXVII**   A section of the *Van Langren Globe* of *c.* 1625, redrawn and with some detail deleted

French charts of the period name it, and the 'Southern' Solomons appear as different parts of the greater austral continent. Yet another body of charts, of Iberian origin and such as have just been examined, laid down the South-West Pacific discoveries of 1595 and 1606 alone, omitting the discoveries of 1568 entirely, and to both bodies of charts were subsequently added the discoveries of the Dutch of 1616 and 1643.

VI

The Dutch in the South-West Pacific, 1616-1643

Holland, that scarce deserves the name of land,
As but the off-scouring of the British sand;
And so much earth as was contributed
By English pilots, when they heaved the lead.

Andrew Marvell

Dutch and English Interest in the Pacific and East Indies
(1590-1616)

THE English voyages to the East of Lancaster in 1591 and Wood in 1596, though unsuccessful, seemed to indicate that the Portuguese were unable to prevent interlopers on their East Indian preserves. The produce of the Indies and Americas had previously been carried from Seville and Lisbon by Dutch vessels for distribution through Antwerp, and later, after the fall of Antwerp in 1585, through Amsterdam. The closure of Spanish and Portuguese ports to Dutch shipping during the Dutch-Spanish wars led the Dutch merchants to consider the question of direct trade with the East as a matter of some urgency, and in 1592 a company was formed in Holland with this objective. Initially the idea of a North-East Passage was entertained, largely at the insistence of the carto-grapher Peter Plancius, who espoused the idea of an open polar sea, and such a passage was in fact attempted by Willem Barentszoon (Berents) between 1594 and 1596.[1] Perhaps the most immediately effective impulse to Eastern trade came from Linschoten who, after six years' residence in Goa, published his *Reys-gheschrift* of East Indian sailing directions (1595) and *Itinerario* (1596), and exhorted his countrymen to trade in the East.

The voyage of Cornelius de Houtman to Bantam between 1595 and 1597, with the aid of Portuguese charts, gave further incentive; and the return of van Neck's fleet in July 1599, with a realized profit of 400 per cent on spices procured in Bantam and Java, after establishing trading posts in Banda and a refreshment port at Mauritius, provided the final encouragement needed. Almost immediately companies were established throughout the United Provinces, to be amalgamated in 1602 in a joint stock corporation, the United East-India Company (*Vereenigde Oost-Indische Compagnie*). Contrary to their

---

[1] Beynen 1876.

expectations, the Company's first voyages met with considerable Portuguese opposition; hostilities developed, and in 1603 van der Hagen was despatched with twelve ships to take up a position at Mozambique, to attack Spanish and Portuguese shipping, to clear the Moluccas and to show the flag off Goa. By 1607 the Dutch had established factories in Sumatra, Palembang and Bantam, and had effective access to the Moluccas and control over the Portuguese factories in the Banda Islands. Following a reversal in 1611, when the Spaniards drove them out of Tidore and Bantam, the Dutch had by 1612 established themselves in Timor, and by 1619 were in effective control of the European trade with the East Indies.[1]

The merchants of London were somewhat slow to follow the lead of their Dutch contemporaries in seeking an Eastern trade via the Cape of Good Hope. A series of bad harvests led to a trade depression in 1596 and 1597, most of the available capital and energy had been absorbed in the Levantine trade, and it seems likely that the English merchants waited to see how the Dutch would fare before committing themselves to new spheres of commercial activity. The successful return of van Neck removed any doubts in their minds and, since the death of Philip II of Spain seemed a likely prelude to an Anglo-Spanish peace, it was urged that a physical claim be established in the East in anticipation of the question of incursion into the Portuguese sphere being raised in any peace talks.

On 25 September 1599 a meeting of English traders was convened, the object of which, and for which £30,133 6s. 8d. had been subscribed, was to 'set forthe a vyage this present year to the Est Indies and other islandes and cuntries thereabouts'.[2] What precisely these founders of the East India Company meant by their reference to 'other islandes and cuntries' emerges later, but the meeting agreed to the submission of a petition to the Privy Council requesting incorporation as a 'joint and unyted stock'.[3] The impending peace negotiations with Spain compelled the Lords of the Council to defer making a definite reply to the submission, it being held 'more beneficiall for the generall state of merchandize to enterteyne a peace, then that the same shuld be hindered by the standing with the Spanishe commissioners for the mainteyning of this trade to forgoe the opportunety of the concluding of the peace'. Nevertheless, although the Council had kept its hands free, there is little doubt that it was fully aware of the benefits of an Eastern trade and the need to establish an English claim.

After some delay peace negotiations began at Boulogne in the summer of 1600, at which the English commissioners were provided with a memorandum prepared on behalf of the interested merchants, together with a report thereon by Fulke Greville, Treasurer to the Navy. These documents listed the regions

---

[1] Mutch 1942: 303–52.   [2] Sainsbury 1862: 102.
[3] As distinct from the Levant Company which was 'regulated'.

in the East not considered to be under the jurisdiction of either Spain or Portugal, and to which the English demanded the right to trade if they so desired. Included in these regions were 'the rich and goulden land of Sumatra . . . Java Major . . . Java Minor . . . Os Papua and the Long Tracte of Nova Guinea and the Isles of Solomon'.[1] In June 1600 the Commissioners were ordered to yield nothing in this connection but, if possible, to allow it to be passed over in silence. In July the negotiations collapsed, ostensibly over a question of precedence, the way now seemed clear, and the merchants were assured that a licence would be granted to them.[2] A licence was granted on 31 December 1600,[3] and in the following spring the first East India Company fleet under James Lancaster and John Davis sailed for the East.

Whilst significant within the background picture of English enterprise, the aspirations of the London merchants are important in this context as reflecting not only knowledge of the existence of, but interest in, the Islands of Solomon as a sphere of possible commercial activity to which the Spaniards, presumably by their failure to settle or exploit, had no greater claim. In fact no English attempt was made at this time to either explore or trade to the S and SE of the East Indies, or in the South-West Pacific. During the first half of the seventeenth century English attempts to establish effective trade in the East Indies were hindered by the Dutch, and after continued conflict the English virtually withdrew to India.

English interest in the Pacific was certainly indebted to the publication in 1589, and in a more extensive form in 1598–1600, of Richard Hakluyt's *Principall Navigations* [4] with the references to the Spanish expeditions which that work contained. It was sustained by the publication of Purchas' *Hakluytus Posthumus or Purchas His Pilgrimes* in 1622 and 1625, with its additional references to the voyage of 'Pedro Fernandez Giroz Portugez', a note on that voyage and his projected second voyage by Walsingham Gresley, and two of Quirós' *memoriales*.[5] The *Observations* of Sir Richard Hawkins, published in 1622, but written in 1602–3, described his capture by the Spaniards in 1594–1603 and stated how:

In the height of this Port of Santa, some seaven hundred and fiftie leagues to the westwards, lie the Ilands of Salomon, of late years discovered. At my being in Lyma, a fleete of foure sayle was sent from thence to people them; which through the emulation, and discord that arose amongst them, being landed and setled in the Countrey was utterly over throwne,

---

[1] Bruce 1810: 112–26; Sainsbury 1862: 103–5.

[2] For the negotiations with Spain see Winwood 1725: 186, 209, 211.

[3] See Purchas 1905: II: 366, for the *Privilige* or *Patent* of the Company.

[4] Hakluyt had attended meetings of the organizers of the East India Company in 1599, had delivered papers to them, and had provided three maps for the voyage of 1601. See Markham 1878: iii–iv; Parks 1928: 261; Jones 1850: 151–71; Rundall 1849: 151–71; Bruce 1815: I: 115–21.

[5] Purchas 1905: XVII: 217 *et seq*.

onely one shippe, with some few of the people, after much misery, got to the Philippines.[1] This I came to the knowledge of, by a large relation written from a person of credit, and sent from the Philippines to Panama. I saw it at my being there, in my voyage towards Spaine.[2]

In 1604 Hakluyt received a report from one Simon Fernández 'a pilot of Lisbone' to the effect that:

He having beene in the Citie of Lima in Peru, did perfectly understand that foure ships and barkes departed from the said Citie of Lima, about the yeere 1600 in the month of February towards the Philippines. Their Generall was a Mestizo, that is to say, the Sonne of a Spaniard, and an Indian woman. And that seeking to make way towards the Philippinas, they were driven with strong Northerne winds to the South of the Equinoctiall Line, and fell in with divers rich Countreyes and Ilands, as it seemeth, not farre from the Iles of Salomon. One chiefe place they called Monte de Plata, for the great abundance of silver that is like to be there.

The reference may be a garbled one to Mendaña's second voyage, for Hakluyt continues:

Concerning this Voyage also; the Licentiate Luis de Tribaldo ... told me ... that two yeeres past he saw at Madrid, a Captaine of quality suing for license to conquer this place, & that he obtained the same. And that divers religious men and Fathers were to goe to convert them to Christianitie. They arrived at their returne from this Voyage at Peru, in the moneth of August.[3]

This is almost certainly a reference to the proposals of Quirós, though the reference to the return of the expedition is perplexing since Tribaldo's letter to Hakluyt was dated Valladolid, July 1605.[4] It is possible of course that Hakluyt may have added the final sentence in 1607 when news of Quirós' return had reached England, for in July 1605, he received a letter from Ludovicus Tribaldus Toletus in Vallodolid in which he was informed that no news of the 'voyage to the Iland lately found out towards Nova Guinea' had as yet arrived.[5] Purchas concludes his discourse on the true position of *Ophir* with the remark:

Let us leave the Spaniards magnifying the present riches of their Mines, as that of Guadalcanal, one of the best in the world by the King's Treasurer reported in a letter to our Author, dated 1607, and another of Francisco Tesada his sonne, so farre extolling the Spanish beyond those of Potossi.[6]

---

[1] Mendaña's expedition of 1595.

[2] Williamson 1933: 120. According to Buâche (Fleurieu 1791: 318) Hawkins reported the Solomons to lie 2,500 leagues from Perú, but 750 leagues is the distance given in the original 1622 edition of the *Observations* as well as in the Purchas reproduction of it. See Purchas 1905: XVII: 152; Markham 1878: 260–1. Purchas had a MS. of the *Observations* in 1614, six years before its publication. It is possible that Hawkins was deliberately misled by the Spaniards in respect of the longitude of the Solomons, but his figure is close to the erroneous 800 leagues recorded by Acosta, etc.

[3] Purchas 1905: XVII: 247.   [4] Purchas 1905: XVIII: 76.

[5] Taylor 1935(b): II: 490   [6] Purchas 1905: I: 134.

14

By the end of the sixteenth century 'the English people in full force had accepted the doctrine that their future lay upon the oceans',[1] and with this acceptance came a sustained but very limited interest in the Pacific, reflected in periodic proposals for further exploration and trade presented during the seventeenth century, but which seem to have received only limited support or attention. On 26 July 1612, however, a grant was issued which referred to the despatch in April 1610, by certain private backers and the Muscovy and East India Companies, of a voyage of discovery under Henry Hudson 'to search and find out a passage by the north-west of America to the Sea of Suz, commonly called the South Sea'. It continued to the effect that they:

have in that voyage found a strait or narrow sea by which they hope and purpose to advance a trade to the great kingdoms of Tartary, China, Japan, Solomon's Islands, Chili, the Philippines . . . for the better accomplishment . . . of which they have sued for licence to join with others and be incorporated into a company,

and authorized the formation of the 'Governor and Company of the Merchants of London, discoverers of the North-west passage'.[2]

In the *Court Minutes* of the East India Company for 31 March 1614, reference is made to the frequent proposals of Sir James Lancaster 'to have a ship appointed to go through the Straits of Magellan to the Isles of Solomon',[3] but James I does not seem to have been attracted by the proposal, and when the Company failed to take any action Lancaster abandoned the proposal.

The Voyage of le Maire and Schouten

Apart from the Spaniards the only two European nations in a position to rediscover the Solomons in the early seventeenth century were Holland and England, but for neither nation was it a likely eventuality. England was unsuccessfully attempting to establish a foothold in the East Indies, was otherwise occupied in the profitable pastime of looting the Spanish treasure fleets and ill-defended American coastal towns, and was unlikely to waste time and money on voyages into the Pacific for any purpose other than plunder. The Dutch were more concerned with trade than discovery, regarding the latter as a necessary prelude to or accidental consequence of the former, and had neither the ships nor the capital to waste on possibly fruitless expeditions into the Pacific when both were needed for the development of the East Indies. Nor were the Dutch normally likely to rediscover the Solomons in the process of proceeding to and from the East Indies, for the route via the Cape of Good Hope was a known and infinitely preferable one to the riskier and less-known route via the Straits of Magellan and the Pacific.

---

[1] Williamson 1946: 393.   [2] Sainsbury 1862: 238–41.   [3] Sainsbury 1862: 288.

Despite these considerations, it was Dutchmen who explored far south of the East Indies in search of new trade on the austral continent, and it was Dutchmen who, on two separate occasions, came within a very short distance of the main archipelago of the Solomon Islands. On the first of these two occasions the near-discovery was the result of an attempt by a rebel faction to beat the trade-monopoly of the Dutch East India Company, by discovering a route to the East Indies other than the known ones, and by discovering new markets on the austral continent or in the islands reputed to lie in the South Pacific. As Harris remarks:

The States General of the United Provinces having granted to the East India Company an exclusive Charter, prohibiting thereby all their subjects, except the said Company, from carrying on any Trade to the Eastward beyond the Cape of Good Hope, or Westward through the Streights of Magellan, in any Countries either known or unknown, under very high Penalties, this Prohibition gave very great Distaste to many rich merchants, who were desirous of fitting out Ships, and making Discoveries at their own Costs, and could not help thinking it a little hard, that the Government should thus, against the Laws of Nature, bar those passages which God had left free.[1]

One of these Dutchmen:

Isaac Le Maire, a wealthy Amsterdam merchant, approached Cornelius Schouten, an experienced navigator and Indies trader and sought his opinion as to whether there was likely to be another passage to the South Seas, and whether the great continent to the South of these seas might not offer possibilities for trade and exploitation equal to those of the East and West Indies. Schouten thought that there was every reason to believe so, and the two entered into partnership, Schouten being backed by several dignitaries and merchants of Horn.[2]

The company which they formed was named the *Zuid Compagnie of Australische*.[3]

The antipodean or austral continent had been as much a feature of Dutch cosmographical interest as of the other maritime nations of Europe, as the Dutch cartography of the period reflects, and this must have been considerably stimulated by such information of the Spanish expeditions into the Pacific as had reached Holland. The exact objects of the *Zuid Compagnie* are contained in the surviving *Secret Instructions* addressed to Jaque le Maire, the son of Isaac, as 'princepaele persoon', and these *Instructions* recapitulate the background to the voyage. Le Maire was to find a route into the Pacific other than by the Straits of Magellan, and to attempt the discovery of *Terra Australis*[4] with a view to

[1] Harris 1744: I: 51.
[2] Harris 1744: I: 51. The possibility of a route existing to the S of Tierra del Fuego was supported not only by the evidence of Drake's voyage but also by several cartographers, perhaps influenced in part by the results of Drake's voyage, who abandoned the idea that Tierra del Fuego was a northern promontory of *Terra Australis* and depicted either an archipelago of islands in that area or an open sea.
[3] Bakhuizen 1865: 43. Bakhuizen examines the question of Le Maire's opposition to the monopoly in some detail.   [4] Bakhuizen 1865: 48.

trading there. Whether successful or not in his search for the austral continent, he was to proceed N of New Guinea towards the Moluccas and, if possible, to sail S of Java into latitudes 25° or 30° S with a view to discovering *de landen van Reach Maletur*.[1] If no cargo had been obtained by this time the expedition was to proceed to the Dutch East India Company trading factory at Jacatra, in the hope of obtaining a cargo for the return voyage. It was not expected that the Governor, an old acquaintance of Isaac le Maire, would prove difficult once their route to the East Indies had been explained to him, and if he did then they were to attempt to blackmail him by threatening to carry a competitive English cargo.[2]

The expedition, which departed from Hoorn via the Texel in June 1615, consisted of two vessels, the *Eendracht* or *Unity* of 360 tons, with Willem Schouten as Master, and the *Hoorn* of 110 tons, with John Schouten, Willem's son, as Master. On the former sailed Jaque Le Maire in his capacity as Merchant or Principal, and on the latter the Factor or Supercargo, Aris Claessen.

A considerable number of accounts of the voyage have been published, at least forty-two appearing in Dutch, French, English, Latin, German and Spanish between 1618 and 1690.[3] The earliest account, entitled *Journal Ofte Beschryvinghe van de wonderlicke reyse, ghedaen door Willem Cornelisz Schouten van Hoorn*, appeared in 1618, and the earliest account under the other distinct Dutch title *Australische Navigatien, ontdeckt door Jacob le Maire, inde jaeren Anno 1615, 1616, 1617 . . .* appeared in 1619 as the eighth published account. The authorship of the narratives is by no means certain, and Villiers' comment, that the question is so involved as to render the true authorship unknown, still appears to be entirely valid.[4] Whilst the two distinct titles[5] under which the published narratives appear might seem at first to offer some indication of their authorship, in attributing as they do the command of the expedition to either le Maire or Schouten, there are not in fact two separate accounts. All the accounts are generally similar, but there are considerable discrepancies over dates, omissions and additions, differences and similarities within the publications and outwith the limits of the two titles. For instance, the *Australische Navigatien* of 1619 begins in the same way as the *Journal* of 1618, but differently from the *Spieghel der Australische Navigatien* of 1622, and subsequently there are differences between all three publications.

Whilst Schouten and le Maire are the principal contenders for the authorship of an original, de Brosses, who reproduced a version of the voyage, attributes the authorship of the narrative to Claessen *'et sur le récit de plusieurs*

[1] Bakhuizen 1865: 22. The *Beach* (*Locac*) and *Maletur* of Marco Polo, identified by cartographers with a promontory of *Terra Australis* S of the East Indies.   [2] Bakhuizen 1865: 51.
    [3] See the chronological list in Villiers 1906: 239–44.   [4] Villiers 1906: xlvii.
    [5] All the other titles of the several publications seem to be the same as, translations of, or derivations of, one of these two titles.

personnes de l'équipage.[1] Bakhuizen suggests that Schouten did prepare an account at the instigation of the United East India Company, with the intention that it should be detrimental to le Maire,[2] and Harris informs us that:

the Proprietors . . . determined . . . to follow the dying Advice of Jaques Le Maire, and to publish an Account of the Discovery. . . . In order to do this, they caused the Journals of Le Maire and Clawson to be transcribed, examined, and compared, and then drawing out of them such Points as seemed in any Degree obscure . . . recommended them to the View of the Masters, and other officers . . . for Explanation: And, having thus procured an authentic Relation . . . they published it the very next Year in Dutch.[3]

It seems likely that the extant narratives are derived from several original accounts, with varying degrees of reliance on one or the other of them, bound together by a common subject, if not by one particular master-journal, and Villiers has suggested that 'the history of the publication of the earlier accounts is nothing more than the record of an unseemly squabble between Willem Cornelisz Schouten and the friends of Jacob Le Maire'.[4]

In reconstructing the voyage in this study three of the narratives have been used: the earliest 1618 edition of the *Journal ofte Beschryvinghe van de wonderlicke reyse* . . . , published by Willem Jansz (Blaeu) in Amsterdam[5] and referred to hereafter as the 1618 *Journal*; the 1619 edition of the *Australische Navigatien, ontdeckt door Jacob Le Maire* . . . ,[6] published in Leyden by Geelkercken, appended to Joris van Spielbergen's *Niewe Oost ende West-Indische Navigatien* and referred to hereafter as the 1619 *Australische Navigatien;* and the 1622 edition by Michiel Colign of Amsterdam of the *Spieghel der Australische Navigatien door den Wijt vermaerdeb ende cloeckmoedighen Zee-Heldt, Iacob Le Maire* . . . ,[7] which is referred to hereafter as the 1622 *Spieghel*. The Latin edition of the latter, publiched by Colijn in 1622 as *Ephemerides sive Descriptio Navigationis, institutae Anno MDCXV, ductu et moderamine fortissimi . . . Jacobi Le Maire*, which is referred to hereafter as the 1622 *Ephemerides*[8] and which is similar to the 1622 *Spieghel*, has also been utilized.

Leaving the English Channel at the end of June 1615, the two vessels sailed S via the Canaries and Sierra Leone to Patagonia and Tierra del Fuego. Reduced to one vessel when the *Hoorn* burnt out at Patagonia, the expedition rounded Tierra del Fuego by passing between it and *Staten Eylandt*, naming the strait *de Strate Le Maire* and the southern tip of Tierra del Fuego *Caap Hoorn*, and entered the Pacific on 31 January 1616, having successfully achieved

[1] De Brosses 1756: I: 349; Callander 1766: II: 217.   [2] Bakhuizen 1865: 55.
[3] Harris 1705: I: 62. At least three Dutch versions appeared in 1618.   [4] Villiers 1906: xlvii.
[5] Reproduced in Engelbrecht 1945: 149–218.   [6] Translated in Villiers 1906: 165 *et seq.*
[7] Reproduced in Engelbrecht 1945: 1–101.
[8] The 1622 *Spieghel* and 1622 *Ephemerides* were appended by Colijn to his Dutch and Latin translations respectively of Herrera's *Descripcion de las Yndias Occidentales*. See also Harris 1705: I: 62, which contains English translations based on Philipp's translations of 1619.

their first object.[1] They now headed NW as far as 15° S, altered course in that latitude to the westward and, as they crossed the Pacific, visited Puka Puka (*Honden Eylandt*) and discovered Takaroa and Takapoto (*t'Eylandt sonder grondt*), Manihi (*Waterlandt*), Rangiroa (*Vliegen Eylandt*), Tafahi (*Cocos Eylandt*), Niuatobutabu (*Verraders Eylandt*) and Niuafou (*Eylandt van goede Hope*).[2]

As early as 24 March the 1622 *Spieghel* records that at a distance of 460 *mijlen* from Perú they were longing to see land, that they feared that no *Terra Australis* existed, and that the *Skipper* (Schouten) had expressed the opinion that if he had known that there were no Dutch Indies or an *Australis Terra* on this side of the *Salomons Eylanden* he would never have set foot on the ship.[3] The same narrative records that on 15 April it was concluded that the contrary nature of the current indicated the proximity of land, 'of the Islands of Solomon, from "Terrae Australis" '.[4] On 18 May they were in 16° 5' S, with uncertain winds, and a consultation was held as to the further prosecution of the voyage. Schouten estimated their position to be 1,600 *mijlen* from Perú, and was of the opinion that as they had not as yet discovered any part of *Terra Australis* they were unlikely to do so now. He added that they had already sailed much further W in their present latitude than originally intended, and that if they pursued their course they would certainly fall to the S of *Nova Guinea* (New Guinea—as conceived at the time). There, if no strait or passage was found, they would inevitably be lost, for it would be impossible to beat back eastwards against the easterly winds. He proposed that they should sail northwards in order to clear *Nova Guinea*, and the company agreed to his proposal.[5]

Allowing for the current underestimate of the width of the Pacific, and the uncertainty as to whether or not *Nova Guinea* was conjoined to *Terra Australis*, this was a reasonable deduction and precaution. The results of Torres' voyage of 1606 were apparently known to a limited group within both the Portuguese and Spanish worlds, as is evidenced by charts of the period, but they appear to have been little known elsewhere. Moreover, the *Duyfken's* voyage of 1605–6 to the S of New Guinea, in the Arafura Sea and along part of the north coast of what is now Australia, had not clarified this question. In the several accounts of this voyage repeated reference is made to the use of a chart, and from these references we can deduce that it laid down the discoveries of Quirós. Quirós had believed that the Bahía de San Felipe y Santiago lay 1,700 leagues from

[1] Engelbrecht 1945: 39, 167; Villiers 1906: 189.   [2] Engelbrecht 1945: deel XLIX.
[3] Engelbrecht 1945: 45.   [4] Engelbrecht 1945: 49.
[5] Engelbrecht 1945: 197. (1618 *Journal*). This account gives the month, incorrectly, as April. See also the 1622 *Spieghel* which describes how, on 18 May, at a distance of 1550 leagues from Perú, the proposal to head N was mooted on the grounds that the present winds would not hold out much longer. In view of the opinion that land might be near, it was decided to continue for 500 *mijlen* before heading N (Engelbrecht 1945: 60). The 1619 *Australische Navigatien* dismisses the deliberations on the change of course in one sentence and gives the date as prior to 28 April (Villiers 1906: 205).

Lima,[1] Santa Cruz 1,850 leagues, Taumako 1,650 leagues, and had expressed the current belief that New Guinea was 2,000 leagues from Perú. If the Dutch were using a chart based on Quirós' estimates, then when they were 1,600 *mijlen* from Perú they would have regarded that as equal to 2,000 Spanish leagues,[2] a distance in excess of that at which Quirós had made his discoveries. Following their new northerly course, two more islands were discovered on 19 May to which were given the name *De Hoornsche Eylanden* [3] and which are identifiable with Futuna and Alofi, the Hoorn Islands of the modern chart.

Le Maire was of the opinion that the Hoornsche Eylanden and the Eylant van goede Hope were the same as those named Islands of Solomon, since they conformed with the account of Quirós,[4] and expressed his belief that the *Australia Terra* would be discovered in their vicinity.[5] Le Maire was much influenced by the beliefs and reports of Quirós, possessed a copy of one of his *memoriales*, and chose the latitude in which he crossed the Western Central Pacific from Quirós' report that in that latitude he had discovered La Austrialia del Espíritu Santo. Quirós' estimate of the distance of that discovery from Perú must have given le Maire very reasonable grounds for concluding that the Hoornsche Eylanden and Eylandt van goede Hope were part of the Islands of Solomon or the islands which Quirós had discovered. It seems strange, however, in view of his conclusions that they had reached the outposts of the islands and possible continent discovered by the Spaniards, that le Maire was unable to insist on the further prosecution of the voyage westwards. Two answers seem likely. Schouten's fears of becoming embayed on a lee-shore of *Nova Guinea* were still valid enough in the light of contemporary cartography, and at the distance which they had come it was quite possible that they had passed the longitudes of most of Quirós' discoveries and were almost below *Nova Guinea* and perhaps on to a continental coast. Secondly, it seems likely that Schouten, a merchant-navigator with a considerable financial stake in the venture, was primarily concerned with reaching the East Indies and obtaining a cargo, as he expected to be able to do by virtue of having beaten the Company's monopoly. There is evidence in the narratives to suggest that a real cleavage of purpose existed between Schouten and le Maire, and this, in view of the several objectives planned, was perhaps inevitable.

---

[1] De Leza had estimated it at 1,900 leagues (Zaragoza 1876: II: 185).

[2] 1,600 *mijlen* = 6,400 nautical miles (1 Dutch *mijle* = 4 nautical miles) = 8,000 Roman miles = 2,000 *leguas*.

[3] Engelbrecht 1945: 61 (1622 *Spieghel*). The 1619 *Journal* gives the month, incorrectly, as April (Engelbrecht 1945: 188); the 1619 *Australische Navigatien*, also incorrectly gives the date as 28 April (Villiers 1906: 205). The Dutch name for these two islands appears variously in the narratives and on later charts as *Hoornsche*, *Hoornse*, *Hoorn*, *Horensche* and *Horn*.

[4] It seems likely that the name Islands of Solomon was here being used loosely to include Quirós' discoveries of 1606.

[5] Engelbrecht 1945: 75 (1622 *Spieghel*).

On 1 June 1616 the expedition left the Hoornsche Eylanden, and Engelbrecht cites the 1646 Amsterdam edition of the *Australische Navigatien*[1] as
listing the opinions of the *skippers* and *stiersmen* as to their distance from Perú
on 6 June,[2] opinions which varied from 1,610 to 1,730 *mijlen*. By 15 June they
had reached 4½° S and were now following a westerly course. The 1622 *Spieghel*
notes that they were experiencing a disturbing south-easterly swell, perplexing
in view of their expectation that by now they would be to the N and W of the
eastern promontory of *Nova Guinea* and in the lee of the land. In fact they
were still well to the E of New Guinea, and their perplexity reflects not only
the current underestimate of the width of the Pacific and the easterly error in
the charting of New Guinea, even though the eastern bulk of New Guinea was
unknown, but, more importantly, the fact that the Dutch had navigated much
more correctly than their Spanish predecessors. Applying their more correct
estimate of the distance run to the faulty charts, they imagined themselves to
be well to the W of their actual position. Perplexing though it was for them,
their improved navigation was to provide a more accurate indication of the
true width of the Pacific, and to provide the navigational information on which
the greatly improved seventeenth-century Dutch cartography of the Pacific
was to be based.

Towards evening on 20 (21?) June[3] a low island was sighted bearing SSW
to W in 4° 47′ S, with sandbanks stretching away to the NW and three or
four neighbouring islets covered with trees. Canoes came off manned by
tattooed natives armed with bows and arrows, similar to but rather darker than
the natives with whom the Dutch had previously had contact. They made
signs to indicate that more land and refreshment lay to the westward where
their chief lived, and the Dutch accordingly maintained a westerly course.[4]
On 21 (22) June, whilst following a course to the W by N in order to maintain
a low latitude, and when in 4° 45′ S, twelve or thirteen islands were sighted
to the WSW. They lay close together and extended NW to SE, were reckoned
to be 32 *mijlen* from the previous landfall, and were given the name *Marcken*.[5]

Leaving these islands to 'larboard' (port: i.e. to the S), the course was
maintained until 24 June when three low, green and tree-clad islands, two of
which were apparently about 2 leagues in length, the other small, were sighted
to the SW. The shore was rugged and cliff-girt, making anchoring difficult,

[1] In Isaac Commelin's *Begin ende Voortgangh vande . . . Oost Indische Compagnie*, 1646.

[2] In the original the date is given as 6 May, but Engelbrecht has corrected it to 6 June (Engelbrecht
1945: 221).   [3] The dates here are uncertain.

[4] Engelbrecht 1945: 199; (1618 *Journal*). The 1622 *Spieghel* is much less detailed (Engelbrecht 1945:
75–76), the 1619 *Australische Navigatien* is even more brief, the date which it gives, 1 July, being
erroneous (Villiers 1906: 214). How the natives succeeded in conveying this information by signs is
not stated.

[5] Engelbrecht 1945: 77, 99. The alternative spellings of *Marcken* are *Marquen* and *Marqueen*. I have
adopted *Marquen* hereafter.

so that the expedition passed to the northwards of them, naming them *De Groene Eylanden*. On the same day a high island was sighted to the NW on which were seven or eight 'hovels' (rude huts, or perhaps hillocks = *heuvels* in modern Dutch) and to which was given the name *St. Jans Eylandt*, and on 25 June a large expanse of land was sighted to the W which was presumed to be *Nova Guinea*.

From the descriptions given it is quite certain that the Groene Eylanden, St. Jan's Eylandt and *Nova Guinea* of the narratives were the Green Islands, St. John's Island and New Ireland of the modern chart, and these identifications provide considerable assistance in the identification of the two more easterly landfalls. In view of the sailing times between the landfalls it seems certain that the first of the two easterly landfalls were either Ontong Java or Nukumanu. The latitude determined was 4° 47' S, a latitude approximately midway between these two atolls, and Sharp, in identifying the landfall as Nukumanu, suggests that 'the persistent southerly error in the latitude of Le Maire's voyage south of the line can be taken to rule out Ontong Java'.[1] Some reference has already been made to the dubiety of this kind of evidence, and to the greater reliance which should be placed on the differences in recorded latitudes between a proximate and known landfall and the landfall to be identified. Even allowing for errors of DR, likely to be slight over a short distance, the stated course and the difference in observed or deduced latitude between two landfalls are obviously of more value than a doubtful and unexplained consistency of latitude errors. Moreover, the historian must be prepared to assume some competence on the part of the navigators concerned, and their ability to determine whether or not the difference in latitude between any two landfalls conformed with the steered and sailed course between them.

Without anticipating the logical sequence of deduction, it is relevant to point out that the latitude ascribed to the second group, Marquen, of 4° 45' S, a group which must have been either Tau'u or Kilinailau, both of which are bisected by 4° 45' S, is clearly not subject to a consistent error, but is in fact correct. This being so, the suggestion that a 'consistent error' can be used to rule out the identification of Ontong Java seems even more dubious.[2]

Leaving aside the evidence of latitude as inconclusive, the evidence of description may now be examined. The narratives describe the first group as a low island, lying SSW and W from the ship when sighted, with several sandbanks stretching NW from the land and with three or four neighbouring

[1] Sharp 1960: 76.

[2] Sharp 1960: 76, accepts the obvious identification of Marquen with Tau'u, without comment on the near-accuracy and northerly error of le Maire's latitude. Le Maire admitted that the latitude of Marquen was estimated in relation to an earlier landfall, which may have been either Ontong Java or Nukumanu. This would seem to indicate, since the northern extremity of Ontong Java bears in relation to Tau'u as 4° 47' S (the estimated latitude of the first landfall) bears in relation to 4° 45' S over the same distance, that Ontong Java is the more likely identification.

tree-covered islets. Nukumanu is a relatively small atoll composed of some thirty-nine islets, one considerably larger than the others, and it is difficult to see how the description can be applied to it. On the other hand, if the expedition had sighted Ontong Java in approximately 5° S they would have seen the low island of Pelau, with the several smaller islands which lie to the N of it, and the sandbanks of the northern extremity of the reef running away to the NW. It is unlikely that any land would have been visible to the S, and the expedition could easily have passed to the N of the reef without gaining any sight whatsoever of the low-lying atoll of Nukumanu.

It seems reasonable, in view of the estimated distance, the sailing time and the recorded latitude ascribed by the expedition to the second group, Marquen, to identify it with Tau'u Atoll. Whilst the latitude would be equally valid for Kilinailau, the application of the recorded sailing times to the distances between Ontong Java, Kilinailau and the Green Islands is unconvincing. The description of a group of twelve or thirteen islands is much more applicable to Tau'u, a group of about twenty low islands lying on an atoll reef about 7 miles long, with most of the islands lying close together on the eastern side of the lagoon, than it is to Kilinailau, an atoll of six islands.

The course steered from the first to the second group was W and W by N, and the latitude of the second group was calculated or observed to be 2′ to the N of the latitude of the first group (i.e. 2′ less). If the first group sighted was Nukumanu, then with an ESE wind, as stated, on the course given, the vessels would have been unlikely to strike Tau'u. It is possible that the southerly set of the prevailing current would have been sufficient to bring Tau'u on course, but it would also have brought Kilinailau on course or within sight, and no island group is mentioned as having been sighted between Marquen and the Groene Eylanden. Furthermore, we are probably justified in assuming that the course recorded was the magnetic one, and although no estimate of the variation is given, the record of Tasman's voyage in these waters twenty-six years later reveals that then, as now, it was in the vicinity of 8′ E. If the course recorded was magnetic, then it was to the N of W and W by N, and the course between Nukumanu and Tau'u is even less likely to have been the one followed. It must be remembered that the main thought in the minds of the pilots at this stage was to clear the north coast of New Guinea, a consideration which would have impelled them to head at least due W, and to counter any apparent tendency to drift to the southwards due to leeway or current. With these factors in mind the identification of Nukumanu as the first landfall becomes increasingly doubtful, the identification of Ontong Java more probable. On a magnetic course of W to W by N, with an ESE wind and even with a strong southerly set, the vessel could have sailed from Ontong Java to Tau'u. It is extremely unlikely that they could have sailed from Nukumanu to Tau'u, and even less likely that the *Skipper* and pilots would have permitted such a falling off to the S, discernible to them when and if they took a noon sight on the 21st.

The scanty information given about the indigenes of the first landfall provides no evidence for the identification of it, and it is doubtful if the Dutch were able to communicate with them to the extent implied in the narratives. If the natives pointed to anything in the W it was probably to the entrance of the lagoon at the northern extremity of Ontong Java, so providing the information which these strange seafarers would be most likely to want. On the other hand they may, understandably, have been encouraging them to pass on quickly.

The information and evidence available would seem to indicate that the expedition sighted, in succession, Ontong Java, Tau'u (Marquen), the Green Islands (de Groene Eylanden), St. John's Island (St. Jan's Eylandt) and New Ireland (*Nova Guinea*). Of the remainder of the voyage little need be said other than that their sanguine expectations of a friendly reception in the East Indies were unjustified. In Jacatra the vessels and their contents were seized by the newly appointed Governor, Coen, and the survivors completed their circumnavigation as prisoners in the care of Speilbergen, Jaque le Maire dying *en route*.

The Claims of the United East India Company to the Islands of Solomon

In 1605 the yacht *Duyfken* has been despatched from Banda under Jan-lodewykssen Roossengin, with Willem Jansz as *Skipper*, with the object of exploring *Terra Australis*, and during 1606 had coasted S of New Guinea and along the western side of the Cape York Peninsula of Australia.[1] In 1616 Dirk Hartog, pursuing the recently discovered southerly route from the Cape of Good Hope to the Indies in the *Eendracht*, had discovered the western coast of Australia between 23° and 26° S. When, in 1618, Isaac le Maire was litigating against the United Company, litigation which eventually terminated in a decree of the *Hooge Raad* recognizing his rights and ordering the return of the confiscated property with interest,[2] certain *Instructions* were drawn up 'to serve as a basis for Answers on the part of the General United East India Company to the advice given by Lords States of Holland, touching the Charter

---

[1] Wieder 1925: VL 176-9. The discoveries of the *Duyfken* were laid down on a map by Jansonnius, *India Orientalis*, published in the Mercator-Hondius *Atlas* of 1633, and, more importantly, on a chart in the *Secret Atlas of the East India Company* in the *Atlas* of Prince Eugene of Savoy, Vienna, of 1670 (Wieder: V: Plate 125).   [2] Bakhuizen 1865: 54-55.

of the Australia Company', and were laid before the Council of the United Company on 2 August. Among other things these *Instructions* remarked:

So that the East India Company opines that in every case the Australia Company aforesaid ought to be excluded from the Southern parts, situated between the Meridian passing through the Eastern extremity of Ceylon and the Meridian lying a hundred miles eastwards of the Salomon Islands; seeing that the United East India Company has repeatedly given orders for discovering and exploring the land of Nova Guinea and the islands situated east of the same, since, equally by her orders, such discovery was once tried about the year 1606 with the yacht de Duyve by skipper Willem Jansz . . . who made sundry discoveries on the said coast of Nova Guinea, as is amply set forth in their journals.[1]

The territorial claim made here by the United Company was a considerable one, for a patent to all lands S of the equator between Ceylon and a point 100 *mijlen* E of the *Salomon Islands*, particularly if the latter title was used generically to embrace all the Spanish discoveries in the South-West Pacific, would have ensured for the Company exclusive access to the lands sighted by Jansz and Hartog, the extensive presumed reaches of *Terra Australis*, the *Javas* and *Locac* or *Beach*,[2] and the discoveries made in the South-West Pacific by the Spaniards. It was to be expected, moreover, if sixteenth-century cartographic representations of the austral continent bore any relation to reality, that it would be between the meridian of Ceylon and a point to the E of the Solomons that that continent would extend to low latitudes, be most accessible and likely to be of value.

The claim of the Company to have repeatedly ordered the exploration of the 'islands situated east' of New Guinea, by which they presumably meant the Spanish discoveries, seems to have little foundation in fact. Moreover, in view of the motives behind the statement and the necessity of proving an expansionist and exploratory intention and policy, it may be doubted if the implied claim that the voyage of the *Duyfken* had such an object in view had itself any basis in fact. However, the fact that the *Duyfken* did follow the south coast of New Guinea eastwards for some 880 miles, and then headed southwards at the entrance to the Torres Straits, together with the particular delineation of the New Guinea and Cape York coastlines on early charts depicting the route and discoveries of *Duyfken*, seem to support the claim. They do perhaps indicate that the aim was to attempt to sail S of New Guinea to the Pacific, towards the Spanish discoveries of 1568 and 1595, with the major object of determining whether or not New Guinea was insular or peninsular, but that the expedition failed to realize that a navigable strait did exist, although a break in the coastline is made on a MS. chart of the route of the *Duyfken* in the Dutch National Archives, The Hague.[3]

[1] Heeres 1899: 4-5.
[2] When Frederick de Houtman, *en route* to Batavia in 1619, sighted the West Australian coast in 32° 21′ S, he concluded that it was the *Southland of Beach*.   [3] Collection of Leupe 493.

English Interest in the Western Pacific (1616-1700)

On 15 February 1618 the voyage and discoveries of Le Maire were noted in the *Minutes of the English East India Company*,[1] and on 20 March 'the Governor made known that his Majesty had acquainted him by letter of a suit made for a patent for the south west by a strait (beyond that of Magellan) discovered by Isaac Lanneere[2] "a business that his Majesty hath a very great affection unto" '. A committee was formed to examine the suggestion, 'esteeming it a project fit for the Company to hearken unto',[3] and on 10 April the *Court Minutes* record that they had again raised the question of a South-West Passage, 'which it was intended to conceal', and had despatched Sir Thomas Ditchington to meet 'Isaac Lameers', 'who gave such encouragement that the King will not have it neglected'.[4]

Between 14 and 15 April the 'proposition to join in the discovery of a South-west passage' was considered by the East India Company, but by this time King James seems to have granted a patent to the original petitioners, though they were anxious to secure the support and partnership of the Company. The *Minutes* record that:

Sir Thomas Ditchington and other patentees inform the Company that it is a new passage towards Mare Zur, under the tropics towards the Isle of Solomon, where the navigators passed by 300 islands, and saw ginger, cloves, and other spices in the land of the inhabitants.

The Company then noted various reasons for rejecting the proposal, adding that the patent had already been rejected by the new Scottish East India Company, on the advice of Sir Richard Hawkins 'that nothing more was discovered [by le Maire] than had been formerly by himself'.[5] The Directors appointed a committee to draw up a politic reply to the King, and on 15 April this was considered. Their main point was that, whilst they were prepared to suit the King's wishes, they did so as the Company to whom the passage to be sought and used had already been granted in their patent of 1609, and that, whilst Sir Thomas Ditchington and his three associates might join the Company in the project, it would be a Company enterprise. The Committee met the King on 17 April and he, expressing some astonishment at their reluctance to incur expense without immediate profit, replied that:

the right of discoveries should be to such as made them; but aiming only at mines, of the discovery of which he has hopeful expectations, the King's desire is to have the business prosecuted as soon as possible; he cares not by whom, so long as it be effected, that he may not seem to neglect these proferred hopes as his grand-father did the West Indies.[6]

---

[1] Sainsbury 1870: 125. A *Minute* for 30 October 1617 records that the English Ambassador at The Hague had secured a copy of the 'journal of Le Maire' and a map which he promised to send to Secretary Winwood (Sainsbury 1870: 69).   [2] Le Maire.

[3] Sainsbury 1870: 141.   [4] Sainsbury 1870: 147.   [5] Williamson 1933: lxxxvi–lxxxvii.

[6] Sainsbury 1870: 150–1.

There the question rested, a final threat issuing from the King to the effect that Ditchington might raise the capital elsewhere and secure his authority to prevent an expedition by the Company. The *Court Minutes* recorded on 24 April that, whilst the King was still desirous to have the discovery effected, a month's respite had been granted to the patentees, who had refused to join the Company and whose patent the King was reluctant to overthrow.[1] At this stage the proposal appears to have foundered, perhaps because Ditchington was unable to raise the capital, perhaps also because the King and Company were diverted by the worsening situation and increasing hostility of the Dutch in the East Indies.

In 1625 William Courteen petitioned the King for a patent to discover and colonize at his own expense:

all the lands in ye South parts of ye world called Terra Australis incognita extending Eastwards and Westwards from ye Straights of Le Maire together with all ye adjacente Islands &c., ... yet undiscovered or being discovered are not yet traded unto by any of your Maties subjects,

for the conversion of infidels, the honour of King James and the extension of his Kingdom, the increase of customs and revenue, and the employment of His Majesty's subjects. Courteen, however, was fobbed off and pacified with a bad title to the Barbados,[2] and such English interest as was maintained throughout the century received little or no support or encouragement, for capital and energy were required elsewhere. That the Pacific and the *Antipodes* remained an object of limited interest throughout the century is, however, reflected in the occasional published references to them. Such references could be as humorous as Peter Heylyn's *Cosmographie in foure Bookes* ..., the *Appendix* to the second edition of 1657 of which was entitled 'An Appendix ... endeavouring a Discovery of the Unknown Parts of the World. Especially of Terra Australis Incognita, or the Southern Continent.' It was a combination of fact and fiction, reality and jest, dealing simultaneously with 'Terra del Fuego, Solomon Islands, New Guinea, Mundus Alter et idem (a witty and ingenious invention of a learned Prelate),[3] Utopia (a country first discovered by Sir Thomas More), New Atlantis (discovered by Sir Francis Bacon), Faerie Land, the Painter's Wives Island, Land of Chivalrie, and the New World of the Moon', and the voyages of Quirós and Le Maire.[4]

Dutch Charts of the Pacific in the Early Seventeenth Century

Of the several Dutch charts and maps produced after the return of the survivors of le Maire and Schouten's expedition to Holland, on which their route and discoveries were laid down, one or two are of particular interest in this context. Of these perhaps the most interesting is the chart of the South

---

[1] Sainsbury 1870: 154.   [2] Mackaness 1943: 6.   [3] Bishop Hall.   [4] Maggs 1927: 23.

Sea published in 1622 by Hessel Gerritsz, Cartographer to the Netherlands East India Company from 1617 to 1632.[1] Rediscovered in 1912 by Dr. Wieder of Leyden, who announced his find at the Seville Congress of 1914, the original chart is coloured and bears an inscription stating its authorship and the date of its preparation as 1634, but Wieder produces convincing reasons for believing that the latter is a later alteration of the original date, 1622.[2] Not only does

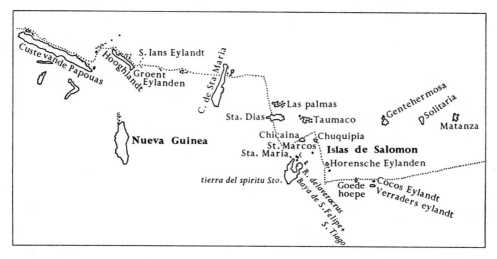

Map XXVIII   Relevant detail on Hessel Gerritsz' *Great Chart of the South Sea* of 1622, redrawn

the chart lay down the route of le Maire and Schouten, and the Australian discoveries of Janlodewykssen Roossengin and Willem Jansz (Janszoon) in the *Duyfken* (1606), but it also lays down Santa Cruz (*Sta Dias*), the Reef Islands (*Las palmas*),[3] and Quirós' discoveries of Taumako (*Taumaco*), Tikopia (*Chuquipia*), La Austrialia del Espíritu Santo (*Tierra del spiritu S^to*), San Márcos

---

[1] See Mutch 1942: 303–52; Henderson 1933: 64; Wieder 1914. The original is in the Dépôt de la Marine, Paris, and there is a hand-painted copy in the Mitchell Library, Sydney.

[2] Henderson 1933: 63.

[3] It is quite obvious that these two delineations on the chart are Santa Cruz and the Reef Islands when the chart is compared with Maps Nos. 1 and 16 in the *Duchess of Berry Atlas* (1615–23) (BNP: Ge FF 14409), where their configuration is similar and where they are named *S braz* and *Palmos*, and with Antonio Sanches' map of 1623 (BM: Add. MS. 22874). The corruption of Santa Cruz to *Sta Dias* is understandable, and the application of the name *las Palmas* to the Reef Islands (which were not named by the expedition of 1595) probably derives from *Don* Lorenzo's report that they were *llena de muchas palmas* (Zaragoza 1876: I: 70). Their position, configuration and the fact that only they are laid down negate any suggestion of identification with the San Dimas (an island in the Nggela Group) and La Palma (a bay on San Cristóval) of the expedition of 1567–9, both of which were very minor items in the nomenclature of the discoveries of that expedition. Furthermore, Gerritsz lays down others of the discoveries of 1595 in the Central Pacific, so that it is reasonable to expect to find Santa Cruz and the Reef Islands in some form on the chart.

(*St Marcos*) and Virgen María (*Sta Maria*, as it was called by Torres), and the reported island of Chicayana (*Chicaina*) (i.e. Sikaiana), all exaggerated in size.

The name *Islas de Salomon*, extends in large script over the chart to the E of Quirós' New Hebridean discoveries, and seems to have been applied generally by Gerritsz, perhaps following the conclusion of le Maire that the Hoorn and Good Hope Islands were part of it, to all the lands delineated in the South-West Pacific. Mutch's statement that 'the reference to the "Yacht of Quiros"[1] indicates that Hessel Gerritsz had come into possession of Spanish charts or manuscripts that revealed the voyage of Torres is plausible, although the information seems to have been very scanty judging from Gerritsz' failure to lay down anything on the chart indicative of Torres' voyage S of New Guinea other than to breach the coastline charted by Jansz, as Jansz himself had done.[2]

The chart seems to have at least two origins so far as its South-West Pacific configurations are concerned, a Spanish prototype similar to Maps Nos. 1 and 16 in the *Duchess of Berry Atlas* and Antonio Sanches' chart of 1623, and the chart prepared during and immediately subsequent to the voyage of le Maire and Schouten. It is possible, however, that Gerritsz' chart is derived solely from the chart prepared as a result of le Maire's voyage, seized by the East India Company and available to him as its Cartographer, and that it was this latter chart which was indebted to a Spanish prototype for its configuration, if not its longitudinal delineation, of the Spanish discoveries in the South-West Pacific of 1595 and 1606.

A comparison of the longitudinal delineation of the islands and mainlands laid down with the actual positions which they occupy reveals some interesting facts, and the chart as a whole reflects the greatly improved concept of the width of the Pacific to which le Maire's voyage made an important contribution. The Difference in Longitude (D/Long.) between Gilolo and the meridian of Callao is only 1° 9′ short of the actual D/Long., and part of this is offset by the fact that the eastern promontory of Gilolo is over-extended eastwards. Quirós' New Hebridean discoveries are laid down some 1,759 *mijlen* W of the meridian of Callao, 117° 16′ as the Dutch would correctly have regarded that linear distance on the equator, or 2,199 Iberian leagues, as compared with an actual D/Long. of 115° 50′, 1,738 *mijlen* or 2,172 Iberian leagues, and the Spanish estimate (in the latitude of Espíritu Santo) of 1,900 leagues.[3] In fact Gerritsz

---

[1] In an inscription on the chart.

[2] See for instance the chart of the discoveries of the *Duyfken* in the National Archives (Algemeen Rijksarchief), The Hague (Collection of Leupe 493). This chart of the *Duyfken's* discoveries shows a break in an otherwise continuous coastline in the position of the Torres Straits where Jansz, deterred by reefs and shoals from exploring eastwards, had obviously not felt justified in assuming that a continuous coastline lay.

[3] Torres estimated 1,900 leagues, although Quirós had estimated only 1,700 leagues. For Gerritsz' chart I have used his own scale, and have taken all the D/Long^s. and distances on the equator relative to the meridians, not to the distances apart of the land-marks in their respective latitudes.

has plotted Espíritu Santo, relative to Perú, not only to the W of its reported position but to the W of its actual position.

The Horensche Eylanden are plotted by Gerritsz, 1,706 *mijlen* (113° 44′) W of the meridian of Callao, but when it is recalled that the pilots of Le Maire's expedition varied in their estimates between 1,600 and 1,730 *mijlen*,[1] and when it is noted that the Hoorn Islands in fact lie 101° W of the meridian of Callao, or less than 1,515 *mijlen* if allowance is made for the length of a degree at that latitude, it is at once apparent, not only that the pilots had overestimated the distance run across the Pacific to the Horensche Eylanden,[2] but also that Gerritsz had plotted those islands almost at their maximum estimated distance and certainly well to the W of their actual position.

Two features of Gerritsz' chart stand out: the proximity of the Horensche Eylanden to Espíritu Santo, and the curious dog-leg course which seems to have been deliberately plotted to avoid the Spanish discoveries, but which does cut *Sta Dias* (Santa Cruz), passes *Chuquipia* (Tikopia) and *Chicaina* (Sikaiana), and crosses the supposed *C de Sta Maria*.[3] As one of the first Dutch cartographers to lay down the Spanish discoveries of 1595 and 1606 Gerritsz perhaps considered such inconsistencies as justified if unfortunate and inexplicable, and the delineation of the Spanish discoveries does give the chart a particular value.

Examining the Gerritsz chart alone one might be tempted to conclude that the dog-leg course between the Horensche Eylanden and the latitude of $4\frac{1}{2}°$ S was an attempt by Gerritsz, albeit only partially successful, to relate le Maire's route to the Spanish discoveries as he felt bound to lay them down, for the narratives do not mention the south-westerly course which he lays down, nor would such a course have been followed by the expedition for such a distance, concerned as they were with the avoidance of New Guinea's supposed lee shore, even had they experienced contrary winds from the NW. In fact the route as laid down by Gerritsz is also to be seen laid down on earlier charts of le Maire's voyage on which the Spanish discoveries are not delineated, and it

[1] Five days after leaving the Horensche Eylanden their estimates varied from 1610 to 1730 *mijlen*, by which time they must have been to the N but also somewhat to the W of the meridian of the islands.

[2] It should be noted that they were sailing in higher latitudes than the Spaniards had done and further from the main force of the South Equatorial Current, but even so their overestimate does reflect improved navigation, particularly when their trans-Pacific navigation is viewed as a whole.

[3] According to Tasman the *Cabo Santa María* was the name given to the supposed eastern extremity of New Guinea by the Spaniards (Burney 1803: III: 97). He identified it with the north-east coast of New Ireland, the *Hooch Landt* of post-le Maire Dutch cartography. It may be the same as the *Cabo de la Cruz* reported by Bernardo de la Torre (see Gallego's *relación*, MNM: MS. 921, 671). Alternatively, perhaps, the *Cabo Santa María* may have been the name given to the most easterly point along the northern coastline of New Guinea in 5° S reached by Íñigo Ortiz de Retes in 1545. On some contemporary charts the eastern extremity of the north coast of New Guinea, as laid down, terminates in a bay and a headland in 5° S with the name *Ancon de la Natividad de Nuestra Señora* (Bay of the Birth of Our Lady), and a relationship with *Cabo Santa Maria* (Cape of the Holy Mary) seems likely.

15

may be concluded that this was the route plotted by le Maire and Schouten on their chart. It is quite apparent from the narratives that they used a Spanish chart on which the width of the Pacific was underestimated and on which the discoveries of Quirós were laid down at their reported distance from Perú; that by the time le Maire and Schouten had reached the Hoorn (Horensche) Islands they were to the W of the discoveries of Quirós as they were laid down on that chart, and that when they headed W in $4\frac{1}{2}°$ S they shortly expected to be in the lee of New Guinea.

It is probable that this Spanish chart had the discoveries of 1595 and 1606 laid down in the general pattern in which they appear on the Gerritsz chart, on the *Duchess of Berry* map of 1616–23 and on Sanches' map of 1623. If this was so, then it is possible that when Schouten and le Maire came to correct their chart, in the light of their realization that the Pacific was wider than the Spaniards had estimated and their deduction that Espíritu Santo must lie to the W of the Horensche Eylanden, that they moved the delineation of the Spanish discoveries *in toto*. They were bound, in view of the Spanish estimates of the distance of Espíritu Santo from Perú, at least to lay it down close to the Horensche Eylanden (not appreciating that they had overestimated the westerly position of those islands relative to Perú), but they were also bound to lay down Santa Cruz and the other Spanish discoveries in the positions relative to Espíritu Santo in which they were laid down on the Spanish chart.

It is quite apparent from the Gerritsz chart that the problem which would then have faced them, of plotting a direct route bearing W of due N to $4\frac{1}{2}°$ S which did not cut through the Spanish discoveries, was insurmountable. With the Horensche Eylanden plotted at their maximum estimated distance from Perú, and well to the W of their true position, and with the Spanish discoveries plotted as far to the W of their reported positions as seemed reasonable, a confused course was inevitable. Short of moving the Spanish discoveries further to the W, or of plotting a course due N from the Horensche Eylanden to $4\frac{1}{2}°$ S (which would have almost doubled the distance actually sailed westwards in that latitude), their only answer was to plot a course through the Spanish discoveries which, though not true and though not entirely successful in its avoidance of those discoveries, did at least convey an impression of avoidance. Equally importantly, such a course would account for the total distance run, and presumably plotted, from the Horensche Eylanden to Ontong Java. That this was all worked out in retrospect seems likely in view of the probability that at least by the time they reached the Moluccas the Dutch must have become aware of an error of overestimation in their navigation.

As their value of 15 *mijlen* to the equatorial degree reveals, by 1616 the Dutch had arrived at an accurate estimate of the world's circumference and the linear length of a degree, and the position of the Moluccas was by then known with fair accuracy. Between the Horensche Eylanden and Ontong Java they traversed 22° 25′ of longitude, as compared with the 16° 40′ laid down on the Gerritsz chart, and between Ontong Java and Gilolo they traversed 30° 40′, as compared with the 22° 32′ of the Gerritsz chart. Whilst on this latter stage of the voyage an underestimate may have resulted from sailing conditions and the limitations of the navigational techniques employed, and whilst the same may have been true to a lesser extent during the former stage, it seems likely that simply in order to plot the distance actually sailed between the Horensche Eylanden and Ontong Java they would have plotted a dog-leg course such as is laid down. The problem as a whole was not one related to the underestimates made by the Spaniards, for their discoveries are plotted to the W of their actual positions, but derived entirely from the over estimate of the distance of the Horensche Eylanden from Perú made by the Dutch, and their conclusion that the Horensche Eylanden were close to Espíritu Santo.

In the 1619 *Australische Navigatien* are contained a map and chart of the route and discoveries of le Maire and Schouten.[1] The first of these, *Nova Totius Orbis Terrarum Descriptio*, is an undated and anonymous world-map on which the route of the Dutch is superimposed, and has an inset map demonstrating their route along the north coast of *Nova Guinea*. The former is clearly a late sixteenth-century map on which the width of the Pacific is underestimated, and on which *Terra Australia Incognita* is laid down with typically bold and vast proportions to which *Nova Guinea* is a rather reluctant extension; 'antiqa descriptio Portagisorum'. The Islands of Solomon are laid down with a configuration similar to that of Plancius' *Nova et Exacta Terrarum Orbis Tabula Geographica ac Hydrographica* of 1592, exaggerated in size, in close proximity to *Nova Guinea* and between 88° and 105° W of Perú. None of the discoveries of Schouten and le Maire have been added.

The inset map is quite different from the relevant section of the world-map and, since it is found in other editions of the narrative of their voyage, probably derives from the chart prepared by Schouten and le Maire. Gilolo, the north coast of Papua, Schouten Eylandt and the north coast of *Hooch Landt* (New Ireland) are laid down with tolerable accuracy, and, to the E of *De Grone* and *S. Ians* islands, the landfalls of Ontong Java and Tau'u (Marquen) are laid down without names, approximately 4° and 2½° E of *De Grone Eylandt*.

The second chart in the 1619 *Australische Navigatien*, which is also to be found in the 1618 *Journal*,[2] bears the title: 'Chart of the Itinerary of Jacob Le Maire. Showing Your Honours in what manner the aforesaid . . . passed (into) the South Sea by a new Strait and so to the Indies.' The chart in the 1619 *Australische Navigatien* also has an inset, generally similar to the inset map of the route of the expedition N of New Guinea on the map *Nova Totius Orbis Terrarum Descriptio*, which is absent from the map in the 1618 *Journal*. The

[1] Villiers 1906: 10, 186.   [2] Villiers 1906: 186–7; Engelbrecht 1945: 172–3.

main *Chart of the Itinerary* lays down a route similar to that already seen on the Gerritsz chart, does not delineate any of the Spanish discoveries, and confines its coastlines to those well known, and those discovered or explored by the Dutch. Meridians of longitude are marked on the equator, and a comparison of the relative delineations of the chart with reality reveals an interesting picture.

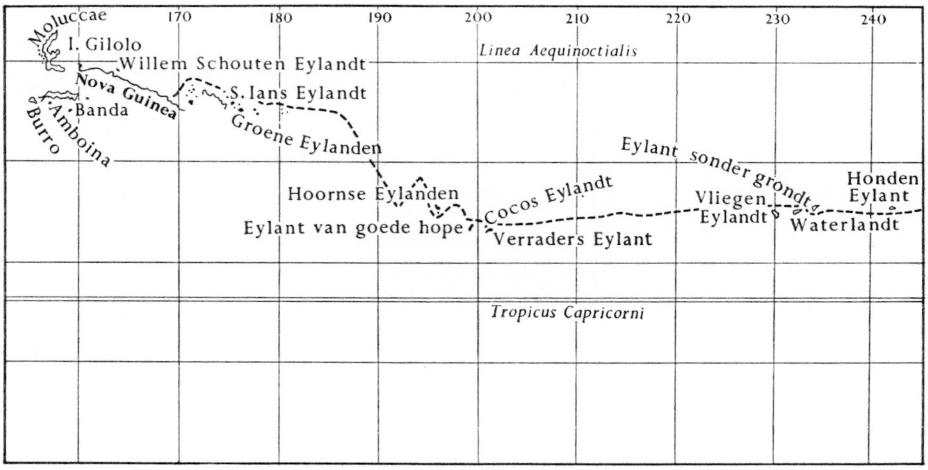

Map XXIX   Part of the *Carte van de zeylage van Iacob le Maire over de Zuydzee* . . . from the 1622 *Ephemerides* and *Spieghel, redrawn*

Recalling the minimum distance at which the pilots of the expedition reckoned the Hoorn Islands to bear from Perú, it is apparent that this chart, as compared with the Gerritsz chart, has them at their minimum estimate but still 5° to the W of their true position. As on the Gerritsz chart the D/Long. between the Hoorn Islands and Gilolo is underestimated, but whereas on the former this resulted in some compensation for the westerly error in their position, on this chart the total width of the Pacific is considerably underestimated.

In the 1622 *Ephemerides* and the 1622 *Spieghel* are to be found two similar charts, a *Carte vande Landen vande Papouas ofte Nova Guinea nae de besejlinge en ondecking van Iacob Le Maire gedaen in den Iare* 1616, depicting the route followed along the north coast of *Nova Guinea* from Ontong Java, and only differing from the inset maps already referred to in respect of its prime meridian; and a *Carte van de zeylage van Iacobe le Maire over de Zuydzee* . . . .[1] This latter chart is generally similar to the Pacific charts of the 1618 *Journal* and the 1619 *Australische Navigatien*, but differs in the longitudinal differences of its delineations which are more in accordance with the Gerritsz chart, the distance of the Hoorn Islands from Perú, 112° or 1,680 *mijlen*, being close to the maximum estimated by the expedition and considerably in excess of reality.

[1] Herrera 1622; Engelbrecht 1945: 100-1, 90–91.

The charts produced as a result of the voyage of le Maire and Schouten made a substantial contribution to Pacific cartography, confirming that an underestimate of relative distances in the southern half of that ocean had previously been made, and offering considerable, indeed excessive, evidence, when related to the narratives of the voyage, that the Spanish discoveries of 1606 were to the W of their reported positions. To the extent that it would have been reasonable to conclude that the discoveries of 1595, and to a lesser degree the discoveries of 1568, lay in positions relative to the discoveries of 1606 such as the Spaniards had deduced, the result could have been a much more accurate appreciation of the position of those discoveries as a whole. It was of course largely chance that the Dutch estimated the position of Quirós' discoveries approximately in or just beyond their correct positions, for had their navigation been more precise, and had they not over estimated the position of the Hoorn Islands westwards, they would presumably have located them in the approximate position of Fiji.

The charts as a whole provide some evidence for the identification of the landfalls made by le Maire to the E of De Groene Eylanden. The longitudinal differences of the four island or atoll landfalls made prior to sighting New Ireland, and the difference of latitude between the two easterly atolls, the most easterly one being slightly to the S of the other, do support the identification of Ontong Java rather than Nukumana, and of Tau'u.

The Voyage of Abel Janszoon Tasman (1642–1643)

By 1641 the United Netherlands East India Company was in virtual control of the trade of the East Indies and the sea-routes to them.[1] A succession of voyages between 1618 and 1636[2] had further discovered and charted the western coast of Australia, or *Nova Hollandia* (*Nieu Nederland*) as this western seaboard was to be named, and part of the south coast. In most instances these were the result not of deliberate discovery or exploration, but of plying a favourable route to Batavia from the Cape of Good Hope, but they had all contributed to the emergence of a clearer picture of that seaboard and of West New Guinea.[3]

In 1642 Fransz (Francoijs) Jacobsen Visscher published a *Memoir concerning the Discovery of the South-land*, in which he proposed the further exploration of the South-West Australian coastline and beyond. He suggested that a vessel be sent eastwards from the Cape of Good Hope in the latitudes of 52° or 54° S, pursuing that course until land was sighted, or until the longitude of easternmost New Guinea was reached, when it would head N by W. Alternatively,

---

[1] Hyma 1953: 83–127.   [2] Nordenskiöld 1897: 199.
[3] See for instance Gerritsz' *Chart of the East Indies and Southland* of 1628–43 (MLS: Huydecoper MS.) and Jacob Aertz Colom's chart *Oost-Indische PasCaart Nieulycks Beschreven*... (Maggs 1927: Plate XI).

it might sail eastwards as far as the supposed longitude of the Islands of Solomon, head N in an attempt to rediscover them, and then return to Batavia via the north coast of New Guinea. As Visscher remarked: 'we do not in the least doubt that divers strange things will be revealed to us in the Solomon Islands.'

Visscher's proposal was of immediate interest to the United Company, not only because it would reveal whether or not the western seaboard of Nova Hollandia was part of the supposed austral continent, but, more particularly, because it might reveal the feasibility of a Dutch fleet sailing southwards around it from the Indian Ocean to the Pacific to seize the island of Chiloe off Chile and plunder the Spanish mines and trade routes.[1] Callander suggested that their aim was 'to learn whether or not Australia was an island so that, as they did, it could be mapped however roughly, and held out as their sphere of undivided influence', and likened the Company to the Carthaginians who 'as Diodorus Siculus tells us, preserved a fruitful island in the African Ocean, suffering none to cultivate it, and reserving it as a home to fly to'.[2]

In 1642 an expedition was fitted out and placed under the command of Abel Janszoon Tasman, Visscher himself being appointed as *Opperstierman* or Chief Pilot, and two vessels, the *Heemskercq* and the *Zeehaen*, were commissioned in Batavia. Whilst Tasman was granted considerable discretionary powers, individually or with the Fleet Council, his instructions followed the proposals originally put forward by Visscher. Always, however, with an eye to ready profit, the Company also instructed him to make landings on all lands discovered, to treat the natives kindly, and to obtain information on the commodities available, particularly gold and silver, making the natives 'believe you are by no means eager for precious metals, so as to leave them ignorant of the value of the same; and if they should offer you gold ... you will pretend to hold the same in slight regard'.[3] With the possibility that he might rediscover the Islands of Solomon, Tasman was equipped with a Spanish description of them, and a vocabulary of native words.[4]

The details and itinerary of Tasman's expedition can be obtained from two narratives attributed to Tasman himself, and two general charts of the voyage. The two narratives are a MS. journal, signed by Tasman, in The Hague, commonly known as the *State Archives Journal*,[5] and an unsigned journal in the Mitchell Library, Sydney, commonly known as the *Huydecoper* MS.[6] The relative merits of the two MSS. have been discussed by Heeres[7] and

[1] Heeres 1898: 131–7, 141–2, Appendices D F K.   [2] Callander 1766: II: 369.
[3] Henderson 1933: 40–41; Major 1859: 43–58; Burney 1803: II: 304; Burney 1803: III: 178.
[4] Which natives and which words is not clear.
[5] Published in facsimile with an English translation: See Heeres 1898.
[6] An English translation by P. K. Roest is also in the Mitchell Library.
[7] Heeres 1898: 59 *et seq.*

Meyjes,[1] and their contrary opinions summarized by Henderson.[2] For the purposes of this study the two MSS. are perhaps of equal value, the former as Tasman's original journal, the latter as possibly a transcription of the journal presented by him to the Governor and Councillors of the United Company,[3] and differ little one from the other. The two most important general charts of the voyage are Tasman's own *Kaart* of 1644,[4] generally known as the *Bonaparte Map* by virtue of its original possession by Prince Roland Bonaparte, and a chart prepared after 1666, probably by Nicolaus Witsen, commonly known as the *Eugene Map* from its inclusion in the *Great Atlas* of Prince Eugene of Savoy in the National Library, Vienna. Wieder convincingly suggests that this latter chart is a copy of a general chart prepared by Visscher,[5] and, pointing to its accuracy and the features which differentiate it from the *Bonaparte Map*, argues that it may have been intended for inclusion in the *Huydecoper* MS., which contains Visscher's special or local charts and from which a general chart is absent. Of subsidiary interest, among others, are a chart after Visscher (*c.* 1687) in the British Museum,[6] and a map included in Thevenot's *Recueil des Voyages* of 1681.[7] Both the MS. journals contain special charts of particular localities or discoveries.

Tasman weighed anchor off Batavia on 14 August 1642, and, having fitted out at Mauritius, proceeded to carry out his instructions. His intention was to follow an easterly course in 44° S as far as 150° E (of the Peak of Teneriffe), to head N to 40° S and eastwards to 220° E, and then to head northwards, searching to the E and W for the Solomon Islands. On 24 November 1642, he discovered *Van Diemen's Landt* (Tasmania), and on 13 December sighted the western seaboard of New Zealand, or *Staeten Landt* as he named it, and began to follow it northwards. Leaving the North Cape of New Zealand on 6 January, without in fact discovering whether or not this land was an island or a western seaboard of the 'austral continent', he headed NE and discovered the southern islands of the Tonga Archipelago, *Hooge Pylestert* (Ata or Pylstaart), *Moddleburgh* (Eua or Moddleburch), *Amsterdam* (Tongatabu) and *Rotterdam* (Nomuka). Passing through the group in a generally north-easterly direction, he reached the latitude of 17° S on 4 February 1643, and then headed W. In following this new course he was acting in accordance with a resolution of the Ship's Council of 6 January that they should make and keep 'full in the course of Jacob Le

[1] Meyjes 1919.   [2] Henderson 1933: 72–90.

[3] Heeres 1998: 65. As additional secondary sources see Burney 1803: III: 59–112; Callander 1766: II: 371; Harris 1744: I: 325 *et seq.*

[4] The original is in the Mitchell Library, Sydney. See Wieder 1942.

[5] Wieder 1925: IV: 138–9, Plates 94–96.

[6] BM: Sloane MSS. No 5222 Art 12. See Heeres 1898: 73 (note 2).

[7] Thevenot 1681: 10–11. See Nordenskiöld 1897: 197, where the same map is reproduced from Thevenot's *Relation des . . . Voyages* of 1666, without Tasman's route. Thevenot's map first appeared in 1663, a further edition appeared in 1666, and Tasman's route was added to the edition of 1681.

Maire, and run straight in sight of the Coques and Hoorense Islands'.[1] He expected, from the estimated longitude in which he had made 17° S, and from the reports of Schouten and le Maire, that in heading W in that latitude he would encounter the Cocos and Verraders Eylanden (Tafahi or Boscawen and Niuatoputapu or Keppel). In fact these islands were already behind him to the NNE, as he headed westwards, and on 5 February he sighted Nuku Mbasanga in the Fiji Group.[2]

At Nomuka Tasman had estimated his longitude to be 206° 19′ E of Teneriffe, and prior to leaving the island on 1 February had entered in his journal under 31 January: 'These islands are in the average longitude 185 *mylen* more to the eastward than the Salomonis Islands, and according to my estimation are situated 230 *mylen* east of the easternmost Salomonis Islands'.[3] Henderson has examined this statement in some detail, and has shown how, with other remarks to follow, it can only be understood if read in conjunction with Hessel Gerritsz' *Chart of the South Sea* of 1622-3. Wieder and Henderson are both of the opinion that the *Great Chart of the South Sea* referred to by Tasman in his journal was in fact Gerritsz' *Chart of the South Sea*, and, in view of Gerritsz' appointment and the way in which the details of Tasman's journal do become understandable when related to it, this seems very likely. Henderson states categorically that Tasman is here referring to the *Islas de Salomon* as they appear on that chart, and to the *Horensche Eylanden* as being the easternmost of them.[4]

It will be recalled that le Maire had concluded that both the Horensche Eylanden and the Eylandt van goede Hope were parts of the Islands of Solomon, and it will be immediately noted that Tasman's statement that he was 185 *mylen* E of the *Salomonis Islands*, but that he was 230 *mylen* E of the most eastern of them, is confusing and contradictory. If he is referring to the Horensche Eylanden as lying 230 *mylen* to the W of his position, then from the Gerritsz' chart he would have deduced that the Eylandt van goede Hope lay 185 *mylen* to the W, that island being laid down on the Gerritsz' chart, according to the scale, 45 *mylen* to the E of the Horensche Eylanden, and he may be referring to this island.

Whilst Henderson's assertion seems to be correct, there are, however, other factors to be considered; firstly, Tasman's reference in his journal to the additional use of the chart of Jacob le Maire, and, secondly, the fact that the details of Tasman's journal cannot be entirely reconciled with Gerritsz' chart alone.

[1] Heeres 1898: 24.

[2] See Visscher's chart in the *Huydecoper* MS. (Henderson 1933: 46), a derivative of it by Vingbooms (*c.* 1665) (Wieder 1925: IV: Plate 100 and note at p. 143), and Tasman's sectional chart in the *State Archives Journal* (Henderson 1933: 50), (Heeres 1898).

[3] Heeres 1898: 32 (i.e. he estimated his position to be 920 nautical miles E of the 'easternmost' Solomons, as the name Solomon Islands was applied on his chart).

[4] Henderson 1933: 46–47, 65–66; Wieder 1925: IV: 143.

Thirty days out from Mauritius, Visscher had delivered his advice on the navigation to be followed, and had referred to the fact that on the terrestrial globe 'the easternmost islands of the Salomonis' were laid down 205° (E) of the longitude of Tanneriffe (Teneriffe), between 7° and 14° or 15° S. He then referred to the 'great chart of the South Sea' which, 'using the longitude beginning from the Peak of Tinnariffe', indicated that Batavia lay on 127° 5′ and the south-west point of Celebes on 138° 25′.

Now from the south-west point of Celebes to the easternmost islands of the Salomonis where the chart reads 'Hoorensche eylanden' we reckon 47° 20′ so that we get for the longitude of the Hoorentsch islands 185° 45′.... Now from the Hoorentse islands to the Cocos or Verraders island, discovered by Willem Schouten, we reckon still more to eastward 8° 15′, so that for the longitude of Coques and Verraders island we get 194°. Should one wish to consider the Hoorentse islands, situated in Longitude 185° 45′, to be the easternmost of the Salomonis, then the charts and the globe would show a difference of about 19°; but if one should look upon the Cocos and Verraders island, situated in 194° Longitude ... as the easternmost of the Salomonis islands then the difference between the charts and the globe would ammount to no more than 11 degrees, the globe placing the islands 11 degrees more to the eastwards than the charts; now to avoid all mistakes, we think it best to disregard the indications to eastwards, both of the globe and of the charts.[1]

Quite what Visscher meant by this last remark is not clear, but if it was that they would not rely on the chart being exact in its delineation of the lands in the eastern reaches of the expedition, then it was an intention by which they did not abide. Now whilst the fact that Visscher had to apply a scale of longitude to the *Great Chart* is further evidence that this was Gerritsz' chart, which itself lacks meridians, Visscher's deductions cannot be applied to the Gerritsz' chart precisely; though the differences are slight and probably no more than might reasonably have been allowed for the decreased length of the degree of longitude in the latitude of the Horensche and Cocos Islands by Visscher, if he allowed for it at all.

Tasman himself states that the expedition was also using le Maire's chart of his voyage across the Pacific, though whether this chart was similar to that in the 1618 *Journal*, the 1622 *Spieghel*, or was yet a third, is not determinable. Quite involved theories can be postulated to show a relationship between the extant charts of le Maire's voyage, the Gerritsz' chart and the remarks of Tasman and Visscher, but it is doubtful if they do anything more than emphasize the complexity of the problem, and the confusion which faced Tasman and Visscher and which is reflected in their recorded disagreement on the question of longitude.[2]

It seems certain, however, that Tasman regarded the *Horensche Eylanden* of the *Great Chart* as the easternmost of the *Islas de Salomon*, though whether his

[1] Heeres 1898: 9.
[2] Compare for instance the local charts in the *Huydecoper* and *State Archives* MSS.

additional reference to them being 185 *mylen* to the W from his position at Nomuka should be regarded as a reference to a mean of the different positions for Nomuka estimated by Tasman and the pilots (45 *mylen* to the W of the position which Tasman determined), as a reference to either the *Cocos* and *Verrader's Eylanden* or *Goede hoep Eylandt*, or can be attributed to the difficulties of reconciling the *Great Chart* with le Maire's chart, is not certain.

Wieder remarks of the Gerritsz map that the principal aim of it was 'to check the position of the Insulae Salomonis of the Spanish charts, and the aim of Tasman's voyage was to find them again',[1] and whilst it is certainly true that Tasman's secondary aim was the rediscovery of the Islands of Solomon, quite what Wieder meant by the principal aim of the map being to 'check' their position is not clear. It may be that the chart was prepared, with only the Spanish discoveries of 1595 and 1606 plotted in their supposed positions relative to the route and discoveries of le Maire, in order that the Islands of Solomon might be charted when rediscovered, and that Gerritsz wrote the name *Islas de Salomon* on the chart, not as a generic name for the Spanish discoveries of 1595 and 1606 and the Western Pacific discoveries of le Maire, but as a name intended for a later addition. However, the size of the name and the fact that Le Maire had identified his Western Pacific discoveries with the Islands of Solomon renders this unlikely.

On 4 February Tasman estimated his latitude to be N of 17° S, accordingly headed W 'full in the course of Jacob le Maire', as he thought, and at noon his position was 16° 40' S, 205° 25' E. Tasman and Visscher's local charts both show the change of course occurring in the longitude of Late Island (18° 48' S, 174° 36' W Greenwich) and on Tasman's chart the change of course is plotted in 17° S, 206° 20' E.[2] Tasman calculated his longitude E from Teneriffe, and reckoned the south-east point of Mauritius to be 78° 47' E of it. As Mauritius is in fact 74° 10' E of Teneriffe, Tasman's longitude should be estimated from Mauritius, subtracting the difference of 21° 7', between his estimated longitude of Mauritius from Teneriffe (78° 47' E) and the known longitude of Mauritius from Greenwich (57° 40' E), from the longitudes of his journal or charts, thereby adapting his longitudes to Greenwich and removing the error at Mauritius for which he was not responsible. His position when he altered course in 206° 20' E was therefore 185° 13' E of Greenwich (174° 47' W), an error of only 11' and a staggering achievement.

When related to any of the charts of le Maire's route and discoveries, Tasman's belief, as he headed westwards in 206° 20' E, that he was sailing towards the Cocos and Verraders islands is understandable. On 5 February having recorded a noon position of 16° 30' S, 203° 12' E, he passed the Ring-gold Islands and entered the Fiji archipelago. On the 6th he passed through the Nanuku Reef (*Heems Kercks Droochton*), sailed as far S as Taviuni, which, with

<hr/>

[1] Wieder 1925: IV: 143.   [2] Heeres 1898; Henderson 1933: 50; Burney 1803: III: 30-31.

its adjacent islands, he named *Prins Wyllem's Eylanden*, and between the 6th and 8th sailed between the Ringgold Islands and Vanua Levu.

On the 7th Tasman noted in his journal that Visscher had expressed the opinion that the islands sighted on the 6th had in fact been the 'islands which in the great chart are drawn south-west' of the Horensche Eylanden, that is Quirós' Espíritu Santo, and that the course ought to be shaped 'close to the wind somewhat to the north in order to keep clear of the coast of Nova Guinea since this is a lee shore and the season unfavourable so that it would be impossible to put off from the shore again.' On the 8th Tasman records that he again asked Visscher if he persisted in his opinion, that the latter replied in the affirmative, and that he accordingly called the Ship's Council together to consider the situation. His own opinion was that:

The islands . . . 18 or 20 . . . are situated full in the course of Jacob le Maire. But since in this latitude he ran for 430 *mylen* due west and did not find any such islands there we might conclude that these islands do not lie in the line of the said course. But in the Great Chart of the South Sea certain islands are marked which agree with these as regards latitude, but this would make a difference with our reckoning of more than 200 *mylen*, the said islands being marked in the chart so many miles more to the westward.

He records that the general opinion was that they should head due N to 4° S, then W as far as the coast of *Nova Guinea*, and that this was agreed to.

When Tasman reached the latitude of 17° S and headed W, he had in fact completed the principal object of his voyage, of determining whether or not it was possible to sail S of New Holland from the Indian Ocean into the Pacific, and this in itself may have been an added inducement to him to shy off the bogey of the unknown eastern coasts of *Nova Guinea* and, like le Maire and Schouten, head for lower latitudes to the N. Applying his own very accurate longitudinal estimate to the Gerritsz chart, he was of the opinion that he still had 200 *mylen* to travel westwards before reaching the longitude of Quirós' Espíritu Santo as it was laid down on that chart. Nevertheless, in the face of the opinions of Visscher and the pilots, and apparently without taking due account of the possibility that le Maire and Schouten might have over-estimated their distance run or that the charts might be in error, Tasman was sufficiently uncertain of the accuracy of his navigation to admit the possibility of an error therein of some 800 nautical miles. His position, in fact, was approxi-mately 600 miles to the E of Espíritu Santo, and well over 120 miles SW of the Hoorn Islands, but it is necessary before Tasman is criticized to appreciate the perplexity which the discovery of the Fiji group must have caused him. Irres-pective of le Maire's navigation, it was reasonable to assume that the Fiji Group was either part of the discoveries of Quirós or part of *Nueva Guinea*, if not both, and he was neither alone amongst seafarers in the days of sail, nor lacking in either seamanship or courage, when he fought shy of a lee-shore. As Visscher himself remarked:

it is now the bad season and the period of rain in the Molucques, and here we have every day rain and strong north-east winds, which cause the east side of Nova Guinea to be a lee shore. Also it is a rule all over the East Indies, the nearer a lee shore the worse the weather.

Relying on the *Great Chart* as he was, Visscher's conclusion that the Fiji group must be 'the islands which in the great chart are drawn south-west of the Hoornsche Eylanden' was natural, if not the only deduction which he could have made. Tasman's own comment that if this was so then there must have been a difference of reckoning of more than 200 *mylen*, 'the said islands being marked . . . so many miles more to the westward', can be related to Gerritsz' chart with some accuracy. From his estimated position on the 6th, in 201° 35′ E, a point 200 *mylen* to the W would have been in 188° 15′ E, that is 41 *mylen* to the W of the Horensche Eylanden (assuming Tasman to have been referring to the latter islands when at Nomuka and in 206° 19′ E he described the eastern-most of the *Salomonis Islands* as 230 *mylen* to the W) in 191°, the distance at which Quirós' Espíritu Santo is plotted on the Gerritsz' chart to the W of the *Horensche Eylanden*.

It was not until 15 February that the expedition did eventually head N, by which time their position was some 7° W of the eastern extremity of Vanua Levu, in approximately 173° E (Greenwich). Between 15 February and 21 March the expedition experienced mixed weather, which made their generally north-westerly course somewhat erratic. Between 13 and 15 March their position, as a reconstruction of the route as it is laid down on Tasman's *Kaart* of 1644 and the Visscher-Witsen *Eugene Map* reveals, must have been very close to Taumako (Duff Islands). At noon on 21 March Tasman estimated his position to be 4° 25′ S, 180° 20′ E, and he maintained a westerly course with light breezes from the E and NE. On the 22nd, with the same good weather, he estimated his noon position to be 5° 2′ S, 178° 32′ E and at once sighted land dead ahead, about 4 *mylen* distant.

. . . in order to run north of it we set our course first west by north, and then west-north-west; towards evening we sailed close along the land north-west. These islands are close upon thirty in number, but very small, the largest of them not being more than 2 (*mylen*) in length; the rest are all small fry, all of them being surrounded by a reef, to the north-west runs off from this another reef on which there are three cocoa-nut trees, by which it is easily recognisable. These are the islands, which Le Maire has laid down in the chart; they are about 90 (*mylen*) distance from the coast of Nova Guinea. In the evening we still saw land north-north-west of us, we therefore turned our course over to north-north-west close to the wind, in order to steer north of all shoals, brailed up our foresail, and in this way drifted until day break. To these islands we have given the name of Onthong Java because of the great resemblance they bear to the latter; they are also surrounded by reefs and appear as shown here,[1] when they are south-west of you at 2 (*mylen*) distance.[2]

---

[1] See Tasman's sketch of Ontong Java, reproduced in Dalrymple 1770: I: 83.
[2] Heeres 1898: 41.

Making sail at daybreak, Tasman headed WNW, the 'small islands we had passed the previous day' lying S at a distance of 3 *mylen*. His estimated noon position was 4° 31' S, 177° 18' E, and during the following night the vessels hove to lest they 'come upon the island to which Le Maire has given the name of Marcken'.

In the morning [of the 24th] we made sail again, shaping our course to westward. Towards noon we saw land right ahead of us, this land was very low lying and showed as two islands bearing south-east and north-west from each other; the northernmost bears some resemblance to the island of Marcken in the Zuyder Zee, as Jacob Le Maire says, for which reason he gave it the name.[1]

At noon the estimated position was 4° 55' S, 175° 30' E, and Tasman remarks that, whilst the course was held W as far as could be estimated, a strong current was experienced setting towards the S. In the evening the course was altered to the N, in order to clear the islands, and during the night the vessels drifted in a calm.

On the 25th, having drifted close inshore, contact was made with the islanders, and the course was again set to the N to clear the islands. Tasman describes the group as:

15 or 16 in number, the largest of them being about a mile in length, the others looking like houses, they all lie together surrounded by a reef. The said reef runs off from the islands to the North-west side; at about a swivel-gun shot's distance there is another small islet; the reef extends another half mile farther into the sea, so that the reef runs out to sea in a north-westerly direction fully 3 miles from the islands.[2]

At noon the estimated position was 4° 34' S, 175° 10' E, and the course seems to have been predominantly NW with some variation to the W.

On the 26th and 27th the noon positions recorded were 4° 33' S, 174° 33' E and 4° 1' S, 173° 36' E respectively, with the course generally NW but altered to W at noon on the 27th. Towards noon on the 27th an island was sighted ahead, and from a position in 4° 11' S, 172° 32' E at noon it lay 4 *mylen* distant. Tasman notes in his journal that:

This island is in 4° 30' S . . . 172° 16' longitude; it lies 46 (*mylen*) to the west and west by north of the islands which Jacob Le Maire has named Marcken. . . . To these islands Le Maire has given the name of Groene Eylanden because they looked green and beautiful.[3]

At the end of the dog-watch[4] on the 29th the Groene Eylanden were finally cleared. To the WNW a high island, with two or three small ones in close proximity, became visible; and beyond could be seen high land 'which looked like a mainland coast'. Tasman identified the high island as St. Jan's Eylandt,

---

[1] Heeres 1898: 41. Tasman also refers to it as *Maercken*.

[2] Heeres 1898: 42. In the *State Archives Journal* there is a sketch.

[3] Heeres 1898: 42. In the *State Archives Journal* there is a sketch.

[4] 2000 hours. The dog watches are between 1600 hours and 2000 hours and are each of two hours' duration.

and on the 30th recorded in his journal that it lay NW at a distance of 6 *mylen*. On 1 April 'we got the coast of Nova Guinea alongside in 4° 30' S Latitude', and at noon the observed and estimated position was 4° 30' S, 171° 2' E.[1]

From the details of the journal and the charts of Tasman and Visscher, it is quite certain that when Tasman sighted and identified the Groene Eylanden (Green Islands), St. Jan's Eylandt (St. John's Island) and *Nova Guinea* (New Ireland) his identifications were correct, and these identifiable landfalls enable us to determine the approximate extent, if any, of Tasman's longitudinal error. A brief comparison of his noon longitudes, corrected to Greenwich, with the modern chart, reveals the existence of such an error, for when *Nova Guinea* (New Ireland) was 'alongside' his position must have been in approximately 153° 10' E, an error in Tasman's estimate of −3° 15', and at the Groene Eylanden his position was in error by −3° 3'. That an error did exist is hardly surprising in view of the unfavourable conditions experienced between Prins Wyllem's Eylanden and Onthong Java and the varied course which was followed.

Tasman describes the Groene Eylanden as 46 *mylen* W by N of Marcken, that is 184 nautical miles or a slight overestimate of the actual distance between the Green Islands and Tau'u, the Marquen of le Maire. If allowance is made for Tasman's longitudinal error, then the noon position which he recorded for 25 March corrects to between 157° 3' and 157° 18' E (Greenwich), as compared with the longitude of Tau'u of 157° 2' E, and his description of Marcken accords well with the appearance of Tau'u.

Tasman's latitude when he sighted Tau'u 'right ahead' was in error by only +4' so that it is reasonable to assume that, even though his latitude two days previously would probably have been determined from an earlier solar observation, it would, if only by virtue of the reconciliation of the two observations with the dead-reckoning course and the short distance sailed from Onthong Java to Marquen, be fairly correct. At noon on the 22nd Tasman had sighted Onthong Java about 4 *mylen* to the W and on course, his own estimated position being 5° 2' S, 178° 32' E (157° 25' E Greenwich). Allowing for his later known longitudinal error at Tau'u of −2° 59', his position must have been in approximately 5° 2' S 160° 24' E, or 12 *mylen* to the E of the most easterly islands of the atoll which now bears the incorrectly spelt name Ontong Java. His description accords well with an approach to Ontong Java in the vicinity of Avaha Islet in 5° 7' S, 159° 36' E, with the many reef islets lying N and S of it, and Tasman's reference to the land still visible to the NNW as night approached could well apply to the islands extending along the reef NNW from Pelau in 5° S, 159° 36' E to the northern extremity of the atoll. That he should have followed the route of le Maire and Schouten in these latitudes with such

---

[1] His identification of New Ireland as a promontory of New Guinea is understandable, as was le Maire's.

exactitude is hardly surprising. With his use of le Maire's chart and his firm intention of avoiding the east coast of *Nova Guinea* in higher latitudes, the course followed was one which was determined by prudence and limited knowledge. It seems fairly clear that it was his intention to follow the charted and feasible route of le Maire and Schouten, and his ready identification of their landfalls with his own is evidence of this intention.

Tasman had come even closer to rediscovering the Yslas de Salomón than had Schouten and le Maire, but like them, and irrespective of the cartographical factors which determined the moment of his failure, he had failed to do so because the risks involved in sailing further to the W in latitudes S of 5° S, and of becoming embayed on a possible eastern coast of *Nova Guinea*, seemed to be unjustified. In fact he was probably right; for having discovered that Nova Hollandia was not part of an antarctic antipodean continent, and having demonstrated that it was possible to sail from the Indian Ocean S of Nova Hollandia into the Pacific, and thence to Perú or Tierra del Fuego, he had obtained information which it was necessary to report without undue delay or risk of loss.

Nevertheless, despite his considerable achievements the results of Tasman's voyage were limited. So far as the Dutch East India Company was concerned, no commercial potentialities had been revealed by the voyage, and, so far as geographical knowledge was concerned, he had not discovered exactly how far Nova Hollandia extended to the eastwards, whether or not *Nova Guinea* was an extension of it, where the Yslas de Salomón lay, or whether or not Staeten Landt was part of an antarctic continent, perhaps conjoined with le Maire's Staten Landt.

His discovery of the islands of the Tonga and Fiji archipelagos resulted in the United Company considering their settlement and use as bases from which to harry the Spanish treasure fleets. Le Maire had suspected that his Western Pacific discoveries were part of the 'Solomon Islands', Tasman had been prepared to admit that even the Tonga islands might be,[1] and Gilsemans had 'trusted' that the Fiji islands were.[2] To this extent, and despite their very generic use of the name,[3] the proposal of the Company to explore, survey and settle 'the southlands lately discovered in the East, like the Solomon Islands',[4] is relevant to this study, and had such exploration and settlement eventuated, it might well have led to the rediscovery of the Yslas de Salomón of Mendaña. That the Dutch intended to 'fortifie' their new discoveries was a view expressed by Ralph Cartwright, President of the English factory at Bantam, in a rather confused letter to his Directors dated 10 January 1644.[5] The original

---

[1] Heeres 1898: 32.   [2] Heeres 1898: 37.

[3] Generic to the extent that the position of the Spanish-discovered Yslas de Salomón was uncertain, and that there might well be a southerly part of them.

[4] Heeres 1898: 115, Appendices K and O.   [5] Foster 1911: 551; Wieder 1942: 77.

intention seems to have been to despatch an expedition in 1643, but the maintenance of the East Indies trade and renewed hostilities with the Portuguese
compelled the Company to postpone it until the following year.

In 1644 Tasman was again despatched, this time with the object of determining whether or not a passage existed between *Nova Guinea* and Nova Hollandia.
If he did find such a passage he was to follow it through to the eastwards, and
then coast the eastern limits of Nova Hollandia as far S as Van Diemen's
Landt. He was to attempt to circumnavigate the latter, determining thereby
whether or not it was part of Pieter Nuyt's Landt,[1] or Nova Hollandia, and
then to follow the south coast of Pieter Nuyt's Landt as far westwards as the
islands of SS. Peter and Francis, completing the circumnavigation of the
Southland. Like his predecessor, Jansz of the *Duyfken*, Tasman failed to discover
the strait between New Guinea and Australia, previously navigated by
Torres,[2] and instead followed the western coast of the Cape York Peninsula
southwards, coasted Arnhem Land, and eventually headed away from the
west coast of Nova Hollandia in 24° S and returned to the East Indies. Thereafter, although the Dutch maintained a waning interest in the *Southland*, with
one exception no voyages likely to lead to the rediscovery of the Yslas de
Salomón, even indirectly or accidently, were despatched, and Dutch interest
was concentrated upon the very real, certain, and tangible returns of the East
Indian factories.

Further Pacific Cartography of the Seventeenth Century

On the *Van Langren Globe* of 1625(?),[3] where the *Insulae Salomonis* are laid
down close to New Guinea and with open southern coastlines, the east coast of
Guadalcanal (*Dalcana, Dagoa* as it is named) is extended southwards to form
the Pacific coast of *Terra Avstralis Incognita Qvae Nonnvllis Magellanica Dicitvr*.
At the point where, on other maps or charts of similar delineation, the east
coast of Guadalcanal would end, an indentation in the coastline is named
Porte Veracruz, and an indentation slightly further to the S is named *Baia de S
Philippe y S Iago*. In effect, Quirós' New Hebridean discoveries are shown as
part of the Pacific coastline of *Terra Avstralis*, of which Guadalcanal, and probably the other islands in the 'Southern' Solomons, the *S Nicolas*, *Arecifes* and
Vista de lexos of the chart (the New Georgia Group and Choiseul), form a
northern promontory, and from which *Nova Guinea* is distinctly separated.[4]

---

[1] That is the southern coast of Australia (Nova Hollandia) discovered and coasted as far E as the
islands of SS. Peter and Francis by Thijssen in the *Gulden Zeepaert* in 1627.

[2] See Tasman's *Kaart* of 1644.   [3] BNP: Globe room.

[4] The delineation and nomenclature of the south coast of *Nova Guinea* reflects Torres' voyage.
The origin of this supposedly continental coastline southwards from Guadalcanal may perhaps have
been Quirós' own cartography. See, for instance his Pacific chart of 1598.

This identification of Quirós' Espíritu Santo as part of a continental coast-line, contiguous with Guadalcanal or the 'Southern' Solomons as a whole, is quite a common feature amongst the Pacific charts of the seventeenth century. Its origin may lie in the configuration anticipated and presented on Quirós' map of 1598, and its development may be noticed particularly clearly on two maps by Sanson (d'Abbeville), his *Mappe-monde* of 1670–8 and a *Mappe-monde* of about 1678.[1] On the former the *Isles de Salomon* follow a normal form, but the south-eastern coast of Guadalcanal bears the two titles *Porto de Vera Cruz* and *Porto de San Phillipo y S Iago*, and immediately to the E of the latter port the discoveries of le Maire and Schouten, *Horn I, Bonn Esperance* and *I de Cocos*, are delineated. The second *Mappe-monde* is basically the same, but in this case the 'southern' islands discovered in the Solomons are joined together to appear as promontories of a single land mass and, instead of bearing the individual names given to them by the discoverers, or the corrup-tions of them produced by subsequent cartographers, they bear the single name *Terre de Quir*. The Espíritu Santo of Quirós and the 'Southern' Solomons are thus identified as different parts of the one continental or large insular land mass.[2] This second *Mappe-monde* also lays down both the discoveries of Schou-ten and le Maire and the *Terre de Diemen* and *Nouvelle Zeelande* of Tasman.

The same identification of the New Hebridean discoveries of Quirós with the Islands of Solomon is to be seen on William Berry's *Map of the World in Two Hemispheres* of 1680, based on Sanson's work; on de Wit's *Novissima et Accuratissima* (c. 1685?), which appears to be derived from, or from the same source as, N. Visscher's *Novissima et Accuratissima Totius Americae Descriptio;* and J. Danckert's *Recentissima Novi Orbis sive Americae Septentrionalis et Meridion-alis Tabula* (1795?); Carol Allard's *Recentissima Nova Orbis* and *Planisphaerium Terrestre sive Terrarum Orbis* of 1696, Jaillot's *Mappemonde* of 1694; and on Gio. Lhuilier's *Mappa Mondo o Vero Carta Generale* of 1674.[3]

The merging of the coastlines of the 'Southern' Solomons to form a continental coastline can also be seen in process of development in a comparison of Edward Wright's *World-map* of 1610 with the *Wright-Molyneux* map of 1598–1600 or the *Molyneux Globe* of 1603. The Wright map belongs to the second edition of his *Certaine Errors of Navigation*, although it has never been

---

[1] *Mappe-monde pour Connoitre les Progrés et les Conquestes les plus Remarquable*, 1670–8. National Lib-rary, Canberra (uncatalogued). *Mappe-monde ou Carte Generale du Globe Terrestre representée en deux plan-hémisphères*, 1678. National Library, Canberra (uncatalogued).

[2] The idea that Quirós' discoveries were on the coast of *Terra Australis* is also expressed in Francisco de Aefferden's *El Atlas Abreviado* of 1697, in which, in a chapter on 'Unknown Lands', it is 'stated that Unknown Australia extends into different climates and zones ... and that one Fernandez Quir, a Spaniard, Juan de More and various Dutchmen have discovered many mouths of rivers. ... These lands comprise the Tierra Grande, Tierra del Fuego, Island of New Guinea, Islands of Horn, Cocos, Traydores, and others...' (Maggs 1947: 54).

[3] In G. G. Rossi's *Mercuris Geografico* (BM: Maps 39 f7).

16

found in a copy of it.[1] It is generally similar to the *Wright-Molyneux* map, a similarity which offers some further support for the general belief that the latter was the work of Wright. A comparison of the delineation of the Solomons on the two maps shows that, whilst the basic configuration is the same, on the Wright map the Solomons have uncertain coastlines, the 'Southern' Solomons are not as decisively insular as they are on the *Wright-Molyneux* map (though they bear the more correct names *dagoa*, *S Nicolas*, *Arrasifre*), and the name *Nova Guinea* extends across the map to the S of the Solomons implying a probable unified identity with New Guinea.[2] An English map which shows the adaptation of the 'Southern' Solomons to form a continuous coastline is the so-called *Leconsfield* or *Edwards* world-map of 1618–25. This anonymous map, which clearly owes much to Wright's map of 1610,[3] retains the nomenclature of the 'Southern' Solomons (*Arrasifre*, *S Nicholas*, etc.), but such is the configuration of these discoveries that the names relate to headlands or promontories separated by uncharted bays, rather than to separate islands.[4]

Both the Wright map of 1610 and the *Leconsfield-Edwards* map show a long chain of islands extending from a point immediately to the SE of the Solomons across the Pacific in a south-easterly direction. On the Wright map the inscription 'These islands lying both in the Torride and temperate zones were lately discovered by Pedro Fernande de Quiros and Luis Baez de Torres' would seem to apply to the chain of islands, but it could also be applied, as it may suppositiously have been intended to apply, to the Solomons. This chain of islands is a feature of several charts and maps of the period, with inscriptions attributing their discovery to either Gallego or Quirós, and is laid down either additionally, or as an alternative, to the more normal delineation of the Solomons discoveries of 1568 and the New Hebridean discoveries of 1606. Such a chain had been delineated by Hondius in 1589 and 1602, and its origin is probably to be found in the continental coastline plotted in a similar position on earlier maps; in the current belief, also espoused by Quirós, San Vitores and William Bourne, that a chain of islands did exist, the eroded offspring and an indication of the austral continent; and in confused reports of the discoveries of Gallego and, after 1608, of Quirós.

On Joannes Janssonius' *Mar del Zur Hispanis Mare Pacificum* of 1650,[5] which otherwise only lays down the discoveries of Schouten and le Maire, this chain of islands extends from a point to the SE of the *Cocos Eylanden* as far as a point S of *T del Fuego* (Tierra del Fuego), with the inscription: '*Insulas esse a*

---

[1] A copy was found bound in an Ortelius atlas in the Bodleian Library.

[2] A small world-map appears on the title page of the second edition of *Certaine errors . . .* which differs somewhat from this map. It shows some islands off the north-eastern coast of New Guinea named *Islands* which would seem to be identifiable with the Solomons.

[3] See Francis Edwards, Ltd., Catalogue No. 603.

[4] This can also be seen on a chart by J. Daniell (1639) as *Portolano* 23 in a collection of charts in the Bibliotheca Nazionale, Florence.   [5] Nordenskiöld 1897: Plate LVII.

Nova Guinea usque ad Fretum Magellanicum, affirmat Hernandus Galego, qui ad eas explorandas missus fuit a Rege Hispaniae Anno 1576.'

On J. Seller's *Chart of the South Sea* of 1675 the chain appears with the same inscription in English: 'These islands as affirmeth Hernan Gallego who was sent by the King of Spain to discover those parts in Anno 1576 to be in a continued tract reach from New Guinea to the Straits of Magellan,' and it also appears on a chart in William Hack's *Charts of the Pacific Coasts of America*[1] together with the discoveries of Tasman, le Maire and Magellan, and with a similar inscription.

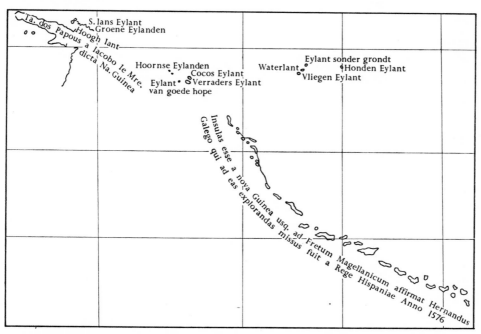

Map XXX   A section of Joannes Janssonius, *Mare Pacificum* of 1650, redrawn

Nordenskiöld, referring to the Janssonnius map of 1650, suggests that Gallego 'must have made at least one more voyage to the islands of the Pacific'.[2] Apart from the contents of the chart, and the date 1576 (which seems likely to be a misprint for 1567, the date of the departure of Gallego and Mendaña from Perú), there is no evidence to suggest that such a voyage did take place, and the fact that no such chain of islands exists seems to indicate that the explanation of its origin which I have suggested is the correct one. Uncertain as to the position of the discoveries made by the Spaniards in their three voyages to the South-West Pacific, and against the background of belief that such a chain of islands did exist and was probably what the Spaniards had in fact discovered, a cartographer would have felt reasonably justified in laying down the configuration of these particular charts.

[1] BM: Harl. 4034.   [2] Nordenskiöld 1897: 191.

A French chart of 1634(?), Guerard's *Carte Universelle Hydrographique*, lays down the chain of islands with the inscription '*isles que pedro Fernandes de quiros et louis baez de Torres ont descouuertes*', together with the mythical austral coastline and the discoveries of le Maire and Schouten. Another French map, Pierre du Val's *La Mer de Sud* of 1679, provides an example of perhaps the most fascinating extent to which a combination of the current cartographical concepts of the South Pacific, correct, mythical or distorted, could be combined. *Nouvelle Guinéa* is shown as a distinctly insular configuration, separate

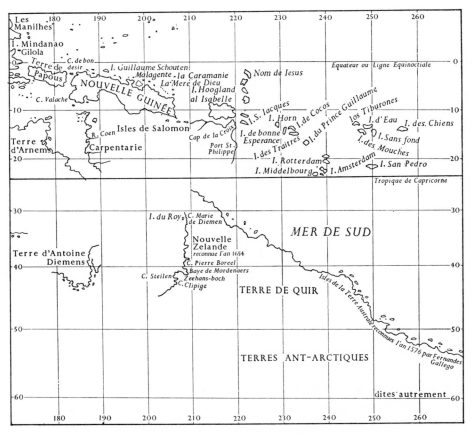

Map XXXI   Du Val's *La Mer de Sud* of 1679, *redrawn*

from the Dutch charted coastlines of *Carpentarie* and *Terre d'Arnems* to the S. To its E are the *Isles de Salomon*, with their southern members obliterated to form a continuous continental coastline of which Quirós' *Port St Philippe* (San Felipe y Santiago) is an east-coast indentation. *Isabelle* has become the largest and most dominant island of the archipelago, and the five islands of the Eastern Solomons of earlier charts have been extended to six, though they may still be identified from N to S with *Nombre* (Ysla) *de Jesús* (named); Malaíta and Ramos (unnamed and incorrectly differentiated, as they are on some other charts of the period); La Treguada (unnamed); and San Cristóval (unnamed) and *S Iacques* (Santiago), also incorrectly differentiated, as they had been by Gallego. The north-eastern cape of what was once Guadalcanal, but has now become part of the continental coastline composed of the 'Southern' Solomons and Quirós' Bahía de San Felipe y Santiago, bears the name *Cap de la Croix*. It seems very likely that this is an identification with the Cabo de la Cruz, reputedly discovered by Bernardo de la Torre and referred to by Gallego and Quirós, although it could also derive from the Point of the Cross on Guadalcanal where Mendaña raised the cross. To the E of the *Isles de Salomon* are situated the Western Pacific discoveries of Magellan (*I San Pedro* and *los Tiburones*), the discoveries of le Maire and Schouten,[1] and the discoveries of Tasman. The route of le Maire is plotted through the Solomons, and it will be noticed that *Isabelle* is given the alternative name of *Hoogland*, thus identifying it with the Hooch Landt of le Maire (New Ireland). The atoll discoveries of le Maire and Tasman in the Northern Solomons are not delineated. S of 25° S are delineated, to the W, Tasman's discoveries of the *Terre d'Antoine Diemens* and *Nouvelle Zelande*, and to the E, a combination of the traditional coastline of *Terra Australis* (*Terre Ant-Arctiques dites autrement*) and the off-shore chain of islands, respectively bearing the name *Terre de Quir*(os) and the inscription '*Isles de la Terre Australe reconnues l'an 1576 par Fernandes Gallego*'. Du Val had in fact taken all the information available from a variety of charts of different derivations and attempted, with remarkable success if not with consequent accuracy, to combine it into the one chart.

Some reference has been made to the incorporation of the discoveries of le Maire and Tasman on the maps and charts so far examined, but it is interesting to note that, generally, where the Solomons are laid down in one or other of the forms developed during the late sixteenth century, even though the discoveries of the Dutch as far W as the Hoorn (Horensche) Islands and Fiji (Prins Wyllem's Eylanden) are laid down, the discoveries between these groups and New Guinea (New Ireland), Onthong Java, Marcken, de Groene Eylanden and St. Jans Eylandt, are not. In several cases this omission can be attributed to and justified by their diminutive size, but in most of the examples noted their delineation would have conflicted with the traditional and oversized representation of the Solomons. On Jansonnius' map of 1650, from which the Solomons are omitted, except to the extent that they are identifiable with the concept of the chain of islands extending across the Pacific, the *Groene Eylanden* and *S Ians Eylant* are laid down, but le Maire's more easterly discoveries in the same latitudes are not.

On a considerable number of charts of the latter half of the seventeenth century, predominantly of Dutch origin, no attempt is made to delineate the Solomons at all, and only those discoveries made by the Dutch are laid down.

[1] To the W of their true relative positions.

It should not, however, be supposed that this is evidence of a denial of the existence of the archipelago by the cartographers concerned, though in some cases this may well have been the case. One explanation, the origins of which have already been noted in the comments of le Maire and Tasman, is indirectly suggested by Ioannes Blaeu on his map *Archipelagus Orientalis sive Asiaticus* of 1659,[1] where he remarks that:

The Solomon Islands are held by some to be the following: Honden-Eylandt, het Eylandt sonder gront, Waterlant, t'Vliegen Eylant, Cocos Eylant, Verraders Eylant, het Eylant van goede Hope, de Hoornsche Eylanden, de Groene Eylanden, S Ians Eylant, most of them visited by Willen Corneliusz Schouten in his voyage and named thus by him.[2]

The extreme difficulties which Dutch cartographers were faced with in attempting to reconcile the Solomons of earlier charts and maps with the recent discoveries of their own seamen, and the uncertainties surrounding the exact positions of the Spanish discoveries (uncertainties which were increased if credence was given to the possibility of the Western Pacific discoveries of the Dutch being the same as those of Mendaña, even though they were in higher latitudes), would have been quite sufficient justification for them to abandon anything other than the lands of which they had recent certain, and probably accurate, knowledge.

This was the classical age of Dutch cartography, an age when accuracy was sought in Pacific cartography as it had never been sought before, and which resulted in the creation of sound cartographical foundations upon which the subsequent exploration and charting of the contents of the Pacific could improve. This search for accuracy, and the fact that Dutch cartography dominated the century, seems to have had one important effect. In striving for accuracy the Dutch, understandably, omitted the vague and often conflicting delineation of their predecessors, but so extensive was the output of Dutch charts during this period, and so reliable and greatly improved were they quickly seen to be, that they in fact created a break in the continuous delineation of the Spanish discoveries. Even though earlier charts might have contained many errors, they did nevertheless record the fact that the Solomons existed as an archipelago, with particular island names, in close proximity to New Guinea and between particular latitudes. It seems very likely that this break in the chronological sequence of their delineation contributed considerably to the emergence of extreme doubts as to the very existence of the Solomons.

To the extent that a cartographer would naturally tend to rely for his prototypes on recent charts, to the extent that these were probably Dutch, and

---

[1] Originally in the Preussiche Staats Bibliothek, Berlin.

[2] Wieder 1925: III: 73. Recalling that Honden Eylandt was the first island in the Central Pacific discovered by le Maire and Schouten, this belief, that the Solomons extended over the 65° of longitude which le Maire charted between Honden Eylandt and St. Jans Eylandt, reflects an extreme generic use of the name Islands of Solomon.

to the extent that earlier charts would become rarer as time went on, the inevitable result would have been the continued exclusion of the Solomons from at least one line of maps. Even if a cartographer felt bound to lay the Solomons down on a chart, he might well have found considerable difficulty in obtaining a chart which showed that archipelago as it had been delineated by his earlier predecessors, and if he attempted to lay them down with limited information at his disposal, or with the corrupted information of charts which had attempted to show too many features, real and mythical, the result was likely to be erroneous. As Wieder has remarked in his monograph on Blaeu's world-map of 1648:

In the Pacific Ocean, the Solomon Islands and the eastern part of New Guinea have disappeared.... The answer to the question how it came about that this more accurate information [more accurate that is than the information leading to other delineations on the map] was abandoned, is one of the results that we may expect to obtain from a study of the history of geographical discoveries in its relation with the expression of those discoveries on contemporary maps.[1]

My suggestion here is that this information was abandoned in the Dutch search for accuracy because it was uncertain, and because it seemed to conflict with what was more recently known.[2] It was not abandoned because it was disbelieved, but its very abandonment did, through the process of time, encourage disbelief and create other errors on the charts of those who still attempted to delineate the unknown and uncertain as well as the known and certain. Indeed it seems likely that as a result of this abandonment or break many later cartographers were automatically denied the knowledge that on the earliest charts the Islands of Solomon were laid down in close proximity to New Guinea.[3]

Other examples of this category of Dutch Pacific cartography are F. de Wit's *Nova Totius Terrarum Orbis Tabula*,[4] which 'became and remained for many years, the standard map of the world',[5] Blaeu's *Nova et Accuratissima Totius Terrarum Orbis Tabula* of 1662(?),[6] and Visscher's *Nova Totius Terrarum*

[1] Wieder 1925: III: 64. In relation to the idea of a break in the continuous delineation of the Solomons, it may be relevant to note that the tendency for cartography to be a family affair, particularly in Holland, may have contributed much to its perpetuation.

[2] The exaggerated size of the Solomons and their longitudinal position in relation to Perú on late sixteenth-century charts seemed, by the mid-seventeenth century, to be contradictory and probably erroneous.

[3] At first the Dutch cartographers produced both maps which laid the Solomons down and others which did not. Cf. Blaeu's world-map of 1648, *Nova Totius Terrarum Orbis Tabula* (Wieder 1925: III: Plate 51), with the *Weltkarte* in his *Atlas* of 1648 (Bagrow 1951: Plate 99).

[4] Wieder 1925: III: Plates 74 and 75. See also de Witt's *Nova Totius Terrarum* of 168? (MLS Dixson Collection: Cb 68/8), and its derivative, Danckert's *Nova Totius Terrarum* of 169?

[5] Wieder 1925: III: 66.

[6] See also an Italian map, J. P. Coronelli's *Mar del Sud* ... , which lays down the route and discoveries of le Maire and excludes the Solomons.

... of 1652.[1] A particularly good example is Pieter Goos' *Pascaerte vande Zvyd-Zee* of 1665–6, which lays down and names the four discoveries of le Maire and Tasman to the E of New Ireland but excludes all the Spanish discoveries south of the equator except for Magellan's *I de S Pedro* and *I de los Tiburones*. North of the equator the Spanish discoveries are laid down and named.[2] As an example of the Dutch striving for accuracy, and their remarkable success therein, it is relevant to refer again to the Dutch derived chart of Thevenot (1666),[3] which illustrates well how the exclusion of uncertain and doubtful cartographic material produced a result comparably better, but perhaps less interesting to the historian, than the cluttered chaos of, say, du Val's *La Mer de Sud*.

[1] In Donckers: 1660.

[2] Another chart by Goos, his *Pascaerte beschreven door Arent Roggeveen* of 1676, lays down nothing whatever between *Nova Guinea* and *Hoorne Eylandt*, excluding even the atoll and small discoveries of le Maire.   [3] Thevenot 1696: 10–11.

VII

The Rediscovery of the Islands of Solomon

It was not till after the middle of the [eighteenth] century, under the influence of the Romantic Revival, as well as an increasing interest in scientific research, that commanders boarded their ships once again to make discoveries in the South Pacific.

Henderson 1933: 105

IF we examine the Pacific charts of the late seventeenth century we see a type emerging, and increasing in number with the turn of the century, on which the Solomons are laid down, often as one large island (Santa Ysabel) with several small ones in close proximity, situated either in a position immediately to the E of the Marquesas, or else between the Marquesas and New Guinea. This delineation of the Solomons as one large island, with several small ones in close proximity, seems to have been a direct result of the merging of the coastlines of the 'Southern' Solomons to form a continental coastline contiguous with the New Hebridean discoveries of Quirós.[1] The consequence of this merging, reinforced by the identification of the 'Southern' Solomons on some charts with the Hooch Landt (New Ireland) of Schouten and le Maire,[2] was a reduction of the total area and island content of the Solomons to the one large island of Ysabel and the chain of apparently smaller islands running from N to S in the east (Ramos, La Treguada, etc.). When the Solomons were moved from the position which they had previously held, in close proximity to and to the E of New Guinea, it was in some cases only Ysabel and its eastern neighbours which were moved, the islands originally laid down to the S having disappeared. Unless the cartographer referred to earlier charts which delineated the Solomons in their originally mapped totality (and some did), and relied only on those charts on which the 'Southern' Solomons had been obliterated, this reduced delineation of the archipelago was inevitable.

The movement of the Solomons to the position of the Marquesas, or to a position between the Marquesas and their true position, seems to have had its origins partly in the exclusion of the Solomons from Dutch charts, which threw considerable doubts on the accuracy of earlier charts and, in particular, on the reliability of their delineation of the Solomons in close proximity to New Guinea; partly in an attempt to place the Solomons on the chart in the position and at the distance from Perú which the Spaniards had earlier ascribed to them;

[1] See, additionally to those examples already examined, João Teixeira's map of 1649 in Thevenot's *Rélations de Divers Voyages Curieux*, Paris, 1664.

[2] See for instance du Val's *La Mer de Sud* (1679).

and partly in an attempt to locate them in a position which did not conflict with other islands whose locality and identity seemed more certain. The gradual improvement in the concept of the width of the Pacific which followed the establishment of the return trans-Pacific route to the Americas from Manila and to which the voyage of Schouten and le Maire had also made a significant contribution, and which reached its peak on the Dutch charts of the mid-seventeenth century, threw considerable doubts on the traditional delineation of the Solomons in close proximity to New Guinea. If cartographers utilized narratives of the voyage of 1568, they must have realized that the delineation of the Solomons in close proximity to New Guinea on more recent charts (on which the Pacific had been widened) contradicted the distance at which the discoverers had estimated the Solomons to lie from Perú. They must also have realized that the belief that the Solomons were in close proximity to New Guinea rested on nothing more than the assumption of the *expedicionarios*, an assumption which was probably influenced by sixteenth-century misconceptions as to the distance between Perú and New Guinea. In addition, if the cartographer relied on nothing more than the secondary accounts of the expedition of early chroniclers, he was likely to be faced with the conflicting estimates of 1,500 leagues and 800 leagues, or the latter alone. Whilst a considerable area immediately to the SE and S of the Hooch Landt (New Ireland's north coast) of le Maire remained unexplored, the exaggerated delineation of the Solomons on early charts did seem to conflict with the apparently islandless areas in which both le Maire and Tasman had sailed.

In Dudley's *Arcano del Mare* of 1661 appears a chart of Asia[1] on which the Solomons are combined with the Marquesas to form one group, and in a note Dudley remarks that:

The Islands of Solomon, discovered by Alvarez de Mendaña, in 1580, were found at 800 Spanish leagues west from Lima; nevertheless the ordinary charts place them at 1800 leagues, but very falsely.[2]

His acceptance of the distance of 800 leagues had the authority, confused though that might be, of the chroniclers Herrera, de Bry and Ovalle and, once it had been accepted, the similar location of the Solomons and the Marquesas was hardly surprising. In fact the Solomons are laid down by Dudley immediately to the E of New Guinea with individual island names and a delineation common to late sixteenth-century charts, but with the denial that these are the Islands of Solomon.[3]

[1] In his *Arcano* of 1646 Dudley had laid down the Solomons in a traditional manner in close proximity to New Guinea, with the southern members joined to form a promontory.

[2] Dudley 1661: (Book 6, Tome III, Part 2); Fleurieu 1791: 314.

[3] It is most unlikely that the positioning of the Solomons with the Marquesas had anything at all to do with Mendaña's initial erroneous conclusion in 1595 that the Marquesas were the Solomons, or with the distance at which the Islands of Solomon were reputed to lie from Perú before 1567. Dudley's chart is reproduced in Dalrymple 1790.

According to Buâche,[1] Dudley's precedent was followed by others, in particular by the cartographer de l'Isle (Delisle), who was induced to follow it: 'rather by the reputation of its author than by any profound reflection.'[2] De l'Isle's mid-Pacific positioning of the Solomons can be seen on his *Mappe-monde* of 1700,[3] on an undated *Mappa Totius Mundi* (*c.* 1700) and on his *L'Amerique Méridionale* of 1708, and Buâche refers to his first application of it as being on his charts and globe of 1700.[4] The same positioning of the Solomons is to be seen on an undated *Mappe-monde* by M. Sanson (*c.* 1700); on A. F. Zuerner's *America tam Septentrionalis;* on Seutter's *Diversi Globi Terr-Aquei* of 1730; and on two maps by H. Moll, his *New Correct Map of the World* of 1709, and his map in Nicholson's *Atlas Geographus* of 1717. On these charts as a whole the Marquesas are laid down some 57° W of Lima, with the Solomons immediately to their E and between 45° and 55° W of Lima.[5] It would be a mistake to assert, as has been asserted, that some eighteenth-century cartographers identified the Solomons with the Marquesas, for on these charts the two groups are shown separately though close together.

The delineation of the group on the de l'Isle *Mappe-monde* of 1700, the undated Sanson *Mappe-monde* and Zuerner's *America tam Septentrionalis* of 1709,[6] is similar, and although on the latter the 'Southern' Solomons as a whole have survived from earlier charts as a single large *Guadalcanal*, on the two former maps their existence is doubted in the dotted outline of *Guadalcanal*. On these maps the Marquesas are laid down, but on the maps by Moll and on de l'Isle's *L'Amerique Méridionale* they have been omitted, and the Solomons as a whole have been cut off across Guadalcanal and Ysabel.

Buâche informs us that de l'Isle renounced this positioning of the Solomons in 1714, 'and in that year in his Southern Hemisphere he placed the Solomons 1,635 Spanish leagues from Peru in 205° E of Ferro', and this stage in de l'Isle's recantation may be noted on his *Hémisphère Méridional pour voir plus distinctement les Terres Australes*, printed in 1740 with some additions and revisions but substantially the same as his *Hémisphère* of 1714.[7] On this the Solomons are laid down twice, once to the immediate E of and adjoining the Marquesas, but without any nomenclature other than the title '*Isles de Salomon selon Dudley*' (i.e. in 255° E of Ferro, 45° W of Lima), and again in 205° E of Ferro with a configuration similar to that of his *Mappe-monde* of 1700 and with the general

---

[1] In a memoir of 1781 to the French Royal Academy of Sciences. See Fleurieu 1791: 309–23.

[2] Fleurieu 1791: 314.   [3] BM: Maps 37: f13.   [4] Fleurieu 1791: 314.

[5] Lima-Marquesas, estimated in 1595 to be 1,000 leagues. $1,000 \div 17\frac{1}{2} = 57°$. Lima-Solomons, according to Herrera and Acosta, 800 leagues. If the league was taken at the value of $17\frac{1}{2}$ to the degree, then 800 leagues would be 45°.

[6] And also on Seutter's *Diversi Globi Terr-Aquei* of 1730. See also Zeurner's *Planisphaerium Terrestre* of 1709.

[7] For Buâche's statement see Fleurieu 1791: 314, and for the *Hémisphère* of 1740 Corney 1908: Map V.

title '*Isles de Salomon selon Fernand Gallego*'. In the two titles may be observed de l'Isle's reason for abandoning Dudley's lead, for he cites the authority for the positioning of the Solomons with the Marquesas as Dudley, but gives the authority for positioning them in 205° E of Ferro as Gallego himself. Clearly, in the period between 1700 and 1714, de l'Isle had given the question the 'profound reflection' which he had not given it before following Dudley's lead, and had concluded that the most reasonable thing to do was to plot the Solomons at the distance from Perú at which Gallego had estimated them to lie.[1] To plot them at this distance did not, as his *Hémisphère* shows, conflict with any post-Spanish voyages prior to his time, for those longitudes and latitudes had not been visited by any vessel since 1568, and the Solomons might well have lain there.

De l'Isle did not maintain that positioning for long, for, as Buâche remarks:

In 1720 when he published his Map of the World and Memoir on the Situation and Extent of different parts of the Earth [to the Academy of Sciences] he approached still nearer to the positions of the early charts. He placed the Solomons in 190° longitude.[2]

This positioning can be seen on his *Mappe-monde* of 1720, but Buâche apparently did not follow de l'Isle's recantation of Dudley's positioning through to its conclusion, for on his *Hémisphère Occidental* of 1720 the Solomons were moved yet again, this time to 180° E of Ferro, to a position due N of the *Terre Australe Du S Esprit* of Quirós (to which they are joined by a dotted line) and close to the *Nouvelle Bretagne* (*Nova Brittannia*) of Dampier.[3] De l'Isle, in fact, went full circle in his positioning of the Solomons, and the final result can also be seen on another state of his *Hémisphère Méridional pour voir . . . les Terres Australes*.[4] On both this last map and his *Hémisphère Occidental* of 1720 occur the inscriptions '*selon N. Struyck de Nouv. decouvert en 1705*' and '*selon N*

---

[1] It will be recalled that in his *relación* Gallego had recorded the distance between Perú and the Baxos de la Candelaria as being 1,638 leagues (1,450 + 15 + 6 to the Ysla de Jesús + 165 + 2 leagues). Presumably de l'Isle had used some source which gave him the accurate figure of 1,635 leagues which he applied on his *Hémisphère*, and on which he also plotted Santa Cruz immediately to the SW of the *Isles de Salomon* (in 199° E of Ferro and 11° S). Quite where de l'Isle obtained the figure 1,635 leagues is difficult to determine.   [2] Fleurieu 1791: 315.

[3] In 1700 Dampier had sailed eastwards from the Moluccas and above New Guinea, had followed the north-east coast of what is now New Ireland south-eastwards (passing the St. Jans Eylandt of le Maire) and, without realizing that New Ireland was separated from New Britain, had sailed southwestwards to discover the strait between New Britain and New Guinea, and thence westwards along the north coast of New Guinea back to the Moluccas. The two islands of New Ireland and New Britain he charted as one island, and named *Nova Brit(t)annia* (New Britain). (See Dampier 1906: II: 451–573, map between 372–3). The appearance of *Nova Britannia* is to be noted, following Dampier's voyage, on several of the maps (post 1700) which have been examined, with its north-eastern coast line (i.e. the north-eastern coast of New Ireland) correctly identified with the Hooch Landt (Hoogh Landt) of le Maire.

[4] Date uncertain but certainly post 1740; this may well be a later reproduction of de l'Isle's original. MLS (Dixson) Cb74/7.

Struyk' after the names *Isles de Salomon*, and on the *Hémisphère Méridional* may be observed a coastline to the immediate SE of *Nouvelle Bretagne* (Dampier's *Nova Britannia*) which seems to be an extension westwards of the old coastline formed by the merging of the 'Southern' Solomons bearing the name *Geelvinks Bay*.

In 1705 the Dutch *yacht Geelvink* (*Pinson Jaune*, *Yellow Pigeon*) was despatched to explore the south-eastern part of New Guinea.[1] The extent to which the *Geelvink* did explore eastwards along the north coast of New Guinea is not immediately relevant to this context, but what is relevant is that many cartographers who heard of the voyage plotted its reported discoveries in the form of a northern coastline immediately to the S and SE of Dampier's *Nova Britannia*. Nicolas Struyck, referred to in de l'Isle's two inscriptions, was the author of a Dutch work, referred to by de Brosses, which included details of the discoveries made by the *Geelvink*.[2] On the map *Hémisphère Méridional* Dampier's Strait between *Nouvelle Bretagne* and *Nouvelle Guinée* is inscribed '*Passage de Dampiere ou Guadalcanal*', thus associating it with the discoveries of the *Geelvink*, and they in turn with the coastline remnants of the 'Southern' Solomons (the coastline from which *Isabelle* alone remains separated), of which, on several of the maps already examined, *Guadalcanal* is the only surviving name. The delineation of *Nova Britannia*, and to a lesser extent the incorrect delineation of the coastline reputedly seen by the *Geelvink*,[3] were important additions to the cartography of the South-West Pacific, for they imposed limits on conjecture and, in particular, on the tendency of cartographers to indulge in continental conjecture.

Early eighteenth-century Pacific charts were the inheritors of a diversity of types of delineation and representation of the Solomons, and in a general examination of the charts and maps of that period as a whole on which they are laid down the bulk of them appear, with varying degrees of exactitude, to follow de l'Isle's second phase when he laid them down 205° E of Ferro, 95° W of Lima. Of the many extant examples within this category, I. Tirion's

---

[1] See De Brosses 1756: II: 437–50. See also Dalrymple 1770: I: 16 (*Plan of Part of Papua*). The *Geelvink* does not seem to have gone very far eastwards along the north coast of New Guinea at all.

[2] De Brosses 1756: II: 437. De Brosses refers to the work as published in 1753. Whilst it is possible that the two inscriptions on the maps referring to Struyck were added later, and were not on de l'Isle's original maps, it is more likely that Struyck had published or circulated some reference to the voyage of the *Geelvink* before 1753.

[3] It is invariably plotted running W-E and trending NE at its eastern extremity. Although some charts of Spanish origin or derivation did, as we have seen, delineate the south coast of New Guinea discovered by Torres, they were very limited, and even though Torres had determined the south-eastern extremity of New Guinea. (See de Prado's chart *Puertos . I . Bayas . Detiera . Desanbuen-aventura* (*Ports and Bays of the land of San Buena. Ventura*, i.e. the extremity of New Guinea) (Stevens 1930: 2 maps in pocket) this fact was little known outside Iberia. Nevertheless a continuous sequence of charts delineating the south coast of New Guinea can be traced from the time of Torres to the eighteenth century.

Wereld-Kaart of 1744; Emmanual Bowen's *A New and Accurate Map of the World* (1744),[1] *A New and Accurate Chart of the World* (1750–2),[2] *and A New and Accurate Map of all the Known World* (1752)[3]; R. de Vaugondy's *Orbis Vetus in Utraque Continente* (1752); F. Valentijn's *Kaart der Reyse van Abel*

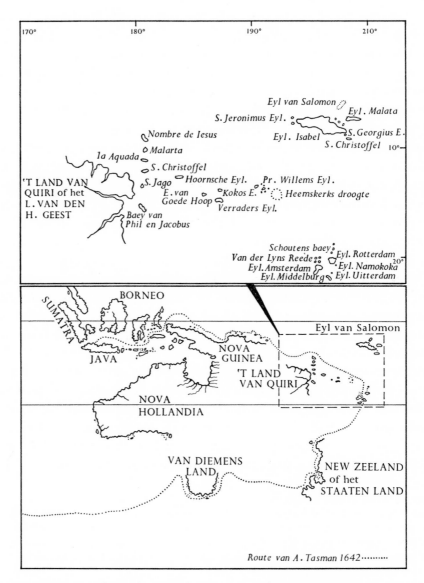

Map XXXII   Valentijn's *Kaart der Reyse van Abel Tasman* of 1726, redrawn

[1] Harris 1744: I: 6–7. The Solomons consist of *St. Elizabeth* (Ysabel—with a dotted and doubtful western coastline) with *St. Croix* (Santa Cruz) to the SW. Meridians E of Greenwich.

[2] Here the Solomons consist simply of one coastline named *St. Elizabeth, Jesus Island* to the NE and an unnamed Santa Cruz to the SW. Greenwich meridian.

[3] Similar to his map of 1744. Meridian of Ferro.

Tasman[1]; Ottens' *Magnum Mare del Zur* (173?)[2]; Tirion's *Nieuwe Kaart* of 1754[3]; and Juan de la Cruz' *Mapa Nautico* of 1756[4] may be cited. Buâche cites Bellin as having begun by plotting the Solomons 195° E of Ferro (105° W of Lima) by having subsequently, in 1756, moved them to a position 205° E of Ferro (95° W of Lima)[5]. The lead of Dudley and of de l'Isle's early charts was, however, perpetuated, and we see the Solomons plotted between 40° and 60° W of Lima on Lowitz' *Planiglobi Terrestris* of 1746, 60° W of Lima on R. W. Seale's *Chart showing the Track of the Centurion* (c. 1745).[6] The lead of de l'Isle's final maps was also followed in, for example, Philippe Buâche's *Carte Physique de la Grande Mer* (1744), where the Solomons are laid down in the form of de l'Isle's *Mappe-monde* of 1720 (i.e. 110° W of Lima). It would seem true to say that by the mid-eighteenth century the majority of charts of the Pacific tended to represent the Islands of Solomon with a much reduced content and delineation, to the E of their true position, and that they were the object of an increasing doubt and scepticism typified in the inscription on Lowitz' *Planiglobi Terrestris* of 1746: '*I Salomonis dubiae positionis*' and in the inscription on later charts: *Imaginary Isles of Solomon*.[7]

English and French Interest in the Pacific

The religious and political problems of Europe in the mid and late seventeenth century left little time for exploration, and between the voyage of Tasman and the end of the seventeenth century there was a hiatus, a hiatus reflected in the dearth of travel literature between the publication of *Purchas His Pilgrimes* in 1625 and the appearance of the 'Buccaneer' literature of Queen Anne's reign. The translation of Esquemeling's *History of the Buccaneers in America* in 1684, the publication of several buccaneer narratives, often of particular merit and sensitivity, and the much lauded writings of Dampier,

---

[1] Valentijn 1726: opp. 46. Here the 'Eastern' Solomons are left appended to the combination of the 'Southern' Solomons and Quirós supposed continental coastline '*T land van Quiri*. The chart is of particular interest for this additional inclusion of the remnants of the earlier delineation of the Solomons with the *Land van Quiri*, with Santa Ysabel removed. It clearly illustrates the division and denudation of that earlier delineation and the confusion which had developed.   [2] Publisher.

[3] On this map, as on several others, *Santa Cruz* is given the alternative name of *Guadalcanal*. This identification is similar to, if not derived from, J. N. Bellin's argument (in his *Observations sur la Construction de la Carte des Mers comprisés entre l'Asie et l'Amerique*, Paris, 1742) that Santa Cruz was Guadalcanal, which Mendaña had failed to recognize.

[4] The delineation of the Solomons is similar to that of Bellin's map of 1744. *Santa Cruz* is given the alternative name of *Guadalcanar*, the *Basas de la Candelarai* are named, as is a relatively minute *Malaita*, and a *Volcan* (Tinakula?) is laid down NE of *Santa Cruz*. Quirós' *Tierra del Espíritu Santo* is plotted to the S of *Nueva Bretaña*, on a dotted and suppositious eastern coastline of *Nueva Holand*, linking *Nueva Guinea* and the *Tierra de Diemen*, and *Taumago* (Taumako) is plotted mid-way between the Solomons and *Espíritu Santo*. These latter features are common to several maps and charts of the period.

[5] Fleurieu 1791: 315.   [6] A chart of Anson's voyage of 1741-4.

[7] See for instance Sayer and Bennet's *Chart of the Greater Part of the South Sea* of 1783.

stimulated an interest in maritime activity of which Defoe and Swift were to take advantage.[1]

Spain, as we have seen, was in no position to consider further exploration; and Portugal, effectively ousted from the East Indies, was primarily concerned with her fight for independence from Spanish rule and the maintenance of her Brazilian and African possessions. The Dutch, secure in the East Indies, occupied themselves with the task at which they were happiest, of attempting to wring every ounce of profit from their possessions, and the abortive proposals of Jean Pierre Purry in 1717 and 1718 to settle Pieter Nuyts Landt fell on deaf ears. The voyage of Jacob Roggeveen in 1721–2 in search of the southern continent, which led to the European discovery and naming of Easter Island and which latterly pursued the general track of le Maire in passing N of the Solomons, was the last of the Dutch voyages of exploration and ended as unsuccessfully as did that of le Maire. England and France were preoccupied throughout the seventeenth century with colonial expansion in America and the West Indies and in preparing the way for the establishment of their Indian Empires, and such activity as England did indulge in within the Pacific was confined to the Eastern Pacific, in 'reprisals' against the Spaniards and, indirectly or unofficially, in the activities of the buccaneers.

The death in 1700 of Charles II of Spain, the last of the Spanish Hapsburgs, offered a new threat to a not very peaceful world, for the prospect of a French candidate on the Spanish throne, and of Frenchmen in control of the Spanish Americas and Philippines, was not one to gladden the hearts of either Englishmen or Dutchmen. In 1702 began that decade of bloodshed known as the War of the Spanish Succession, a war which seemed likely to end the Spanish Pacific Empire and which consequently focused European attention in that direction. The Treaty of Utrecht, which ended the war and brought a partition which could as easily have been achieved before as after the conflict, dashed the hopes of those European powers which had hoped for a slice of the imperial cake, for it admitted Spanish claims to the Pacific.

Dampier's voyage of 1699–1701, which included the navigation of the northern, eastern and southern limits of New Britain and New Ireland and their cartographical delineation as the one island of *Nova Britannia*, and which really ended at Ascension Island in the Atlantic when the *Roebuck* 'founder'd thro' perfect Age', was the first of a series of expeditions despatched by Great Britain for the exploration of the Pacific. The publication in 1697 of his *New Voyage round the World*, an odyssey of twelve years occupied primarily as a buccaneer, during which he had visited New Holland and heard from Captain Davis of continental land in 27° C, 500 leagues from Chile, came at an opportune

---

[1] Swift's *Gulliver's Travels* and *Tale of a Tub* both contain considerable allusion to the Pacific, and his satirical *Project for the Universal Benefit of Mankind* (1704) was particularly aimed at belief in an austral continent.

moment when the question of the Spanish succession was to the forefront of European minds, the Pacific the object of their immediate interest, and when the English reading public were particularly receptive to the romantic escapism offered by the literature of travel.

Lionized with good reason in literary society, Dampier was consulted as an oracle of geography, natural sciences, hydrography and meteorology, and when he suggested, at the instigation of Orford, Halifax, Pepys and Pembroke, a voyage to 'the remoter part of the East India Islands and to the neighbouring coast of Terra Australis', he was suggesting a voyage which he hoped would afford him the opportunity to explore the east coast of New Holland. It engendered, and on his return was to engender still more, the interest of the English public in the Pacific; and was to bring him within a very short distance of the island now named Bougainville, the most north-westerly of the major islands of the archipelago of the Solomon Islands. Indeed, his original plan was to cross the Pacific westwards as far as the coast of New Holland, and then to follow that eastern coastline northwards towards New Guinea. Had he done this he might have preceded both Bougainville and Cook, and might well have rediscovered the Solomons.[1]

Dampier's description of *Nova Britannia* attracted English attention to it as a possible strategic base in the new concept of Pacific activity which an increasing expansionist inclination, the circumstances of the War of the Spanish Succession and the romantic pictures which the Pacific conjured in the minds of the inhabitants of the Britannic Isles, had combined to create. In 1713 Captain John Welbe, who had accompanied Dampier and was reputed to be an ingenious but financially distressed projector seeking primarily to relieve his distress, proposed to go round Cape Horn to Juan Fernández,

thence to the Solomon Islands, discovered 150 years ago by the Spaniards . . . to search and discover what the country abounds in, and to trepan some of the inhabitants on board and bring them back to England, who when they have learnt our language will be proper interpreters.

Suspicious of his motives, the Admiralty passed the matter to the directors of the South Sea Company, who found it to be without their bounds, and, although Welbe several times repeated his proposals, his last attempt was from a debtors' prison and as unsuccessful as his previous ones.[2]

In 1720 an English captain named Betagh was a prisoner of the Spaniards in Perú following a privateering foray. On his return to England he produced an account of Perú in which he referred to 'the discoveries that have been talked

---

[1] Woodford cites Dampier as having identified the Islands of Solomon with *Nova Britannia*, and as mentioning the map of de Bry (1596), which he correctly concluded to be a map of the discoveries made during Mendaña's first voyage, and the Ortelius' map of 1589 (Woodford 1890: 417). I have been unsuccessful in my attempts to find this extract in Dampier's writings.

[2] See BM: Sloane MS. 4044, ff214v–217; Mackaness 1942: 8–11.

of amongst the Spaniards', of which 'that which has made the most noise, is the island or islands of Solomon'.

These are supposed to be the same with those discovered by the famous Ferdinand de Quiros: he reported them to be excessively rich, as well as extremely populous, and desired, by repeated memorials, that he might be authorized . . . to proceed in and finish that discovery; but, as all his instances were neglected, in the space of a few years it became a question, whether there really were any such islands or not; and the treating of this matter as a romance, was, for some time, a political maxim with the Viceroys of Peru.[1]

Betagh follows this with a confused account of Mendaña's (Alvaro de Miranda as he calls him) voyage, which he dates 1695, and also refers to a Spanish ship which had arrived in Callao during his stay there, 'the master of which reported, that, being driven out of his course, he made the Islands of Solomon'. It had been followed by yet another ship with the same story, and in consequence an indigent French trader had been despatched in a ketch to look for the islands. He had apparently sailed westwards in 10° S without sighting them, and Betagh reasonably suggests that he probably did not sail far enough, adding that he was probably uncertain of his latitudes: 'for I have been informed in London, that the said island or islands lie more southerly in the Pacific Ocean, than where they are laid down in the Dutch maps'.[2]

The English and French buccaneers had been the major 'representatives' of their respective nations in the Eastern Pacific in the late seventeenth century, and although the former had been the first there, they were quickly followed by a host of Frenchmen who were particularly active from 1695 to 1726. During the Spanish Succession War they were employed by the Spaniards to fight the English, and the geographical knowledge which they accumulated was an important factor in inducing the French, like the English, to consider official Pacific voyages. During the war itself buccaneering donned a cloak of respectability, English privateers such as Woodes Rogers and Dampier harried the Spanish-American Pacific coast, and England carried into the peace which followed Utrecht the rivalries which had come to fruition during the war.

The formation of the South Sea Company in 1711 was the only English attempt, for the moment, at actual commercial activity, but it never launched an expedition and its association with the South Sea was a tenuous one of expectation and speculation. Created in anticipation of the commercial gains to be made at the end of the War of the Spanish Succession, the year 1720, the Year of the Bubble, saw English expectations of wealth from the South Seas dashed. As Dr. Johnson remarks of Pope:

[1] Pinkerton 1813: XIV: 12.

[2] The two ships which reported sighting the Solomons may have sighted islands, but it is most unlikely that they were anywhere near the Solomons.

In this disastrous year of national infatuation, when more riches than Peru can boast were expected from the South Sea, when the contagion of avarice tainted every mind, and even poets panted after wealth, Pope was seized with the universal passion, and ventured some of his money.

Nor was England alone, for in France the *Compagnie des Indes* met the same disastrous end, an end which must have been particularly gratifying to Spain, who saw both companies as threats to her Pacific monopoly.

The expansion which both England and France were attempting was hardly colonial expansion, but rather domination over sea-routes and the trade and wealth of foreign shores, and it was with such objectives that the Admiralty despatched Anson in 1740, during the Anglo-Spanish war of 1739–48. His mission was to incite the Spanish colonists of Chile and Perú to rise against Spain so that, once they had gained their independence, trading treaties might be made with them. Handicapped by poor equipment and losses *en route*, he found his initial task impossible, and compensated for it by a brilliant raid and the capture of the Manila galleon.[1] By the mid-eighteenth century the Spanish seem to have believed that the English and French were already established in settlements on the South American coast,[2] and the degree of rivalry between Spain and England is reflected in an article in the *London Chronicle* of March 1771, which reported how, in 1748, sloops had been fitted out to explore Pepys and Falkland Islands or the South Sea, but so vehemently did the Spanish Ambassador oppose the project and protest the right of Spain to the exclusive dominion of the Pacific that the Ministry revoked its original intention.[3] It is a measure of the tenacity of Imperial Spain that, despite her misfortunes, she maintained her dominion over the Americas and the Philippines; that in the face of English ambitions, Don Manuel de Amat, Viceroy of Perú, annexed Easter Island in 1772 and sent expeditions to Tahiti in 1773 and 1774; and that missionary activities were extended during the second half of the century.

The report of Anson's voyage revealed the necessity for Pacific bases, and, in addition, achieved considerable popularity as another addition to the much sought-after literature of travel and maritime activity. In 1744 Campbell produced his edition of Harris' *Navigantum atque Itinerarium Bibliotheca* [4] the first of the several 'Voyages' of which this was to be the age, in which he (Campbell) outlined a plan for the South Pacific involving the colonization and fortification of Juan Fernández as a way-station for vessels proceeding to a proposed colony in *Nova Britannia*.[5] Campbell argued that with the products

---

[1] The *derrotero* captured on the galleon, whilst of considerable value, revealed that the return route of the galleons from Manila to California was essentially fortuitous and hazily understood. From Macao or Guam they committed themselves to wind and current in the vicinity of 40–50° N.

[2] Corney 1913: I: xix–xx.

[3] *London Chronicle* No. 2225, 16–19 March, 1771, p. 26.   [4] Harris 1744.

[5] This was also an idea conceived by Roggeveen, who saw Juan Fernández as an ideal base for the exploration of the South Pacific.

of *Nova Britannia* itself, of New Guinea and the neighbouring Indies, the colony could hardly fail, and that it would offer a unique opportunity for the discovery of Eastern New Holland and of *Terra Australis* itself. Harris had provided a rather corrupt account of the discovery 'of the islands of Solomon by Alvarez de Mendoca, about the year 1527' and of 'Captain Pedro Fernandez Quiros (who) made Two Voyages . . . about the latter End of the Sixteenth Century; but the exact time does not appear', derived, as he himself states, from one of Quirós' *memoriales* of 1607. He refers to Quirós' eighth *memorial*, and to another larger *memorial* in which Quirós enumerated twenty islands which he had discovered.[1] Harris admits his uncertainty over the date of the first voyage of 'Mendoca', and in Campbell's edition were included a chart by Bowen, which laid the Solomons down in mid-Pacific, and Captain Betagh's report, neither of which could have been in the earlier edition of 1705.

Campbell's edition of Harris' *Navigantum* appeared in the middle of the period of renewed hostilities with Spain between 1739 and 1748, when several petitioners had urged particular activities against Spain in her Pacific colonies and of which Anson's voyage was the result. According to Campbell it was agreed that 'the best way to reduce her (Spain's) strength and to prevent the bad effects of her evil intentions would be to attack her in the South Seas'.[2] Campbell's proposals were ignored, primarily it would seem because the entry of France into the war on the side of Spain offered a threat to considerably more than England's potential Pacific trade and influence, and the Government was anxious to terminate the war as speedily as possible. Such peace as did come in 1748 was chimerical, and was followed by almost eight years of hostility and sparring which culminated in 1755 in the outbreak of the Seven Years War.

French interest in the Pacific had also continued unabated, much of it centred upon the existence of the austral continent. Against the background of the Sieur de Gonneville's reputed discovery of the *Terra Australis*,[3] which made the whole question one of immediate and national interest, the proposals put by Lozier-Bouvet to the French East India Company for the discovery of the austral continent were received with some enthusiasm. He sailed from France in July 1738, and concentrated his search for de Gonneville's continent in the South Atlantic. In 54° S, and to the SSW of the Cape of Good Hope, he imagined, in conditions of fog and bad visibility, that he had actually seen and coasted the austral continent[4] and, when he returned to France in 1739, he endeavoured to interest the Company in yet another voyage.[5] In his proposals and plans, submitted between 1740 and 1741, he anticipated most of what

---

[1] Identifiable with a *memorial* of 1609 (Zaragoza 1876: II: 229–36).   [2] Harris 1744: I: 327.
[3] Of de Gonneville's voyage Rainaud remarks that, although not properly a voyage of discovery, '*il a exercé une très heureuse influence sur la multiplication des voyages aux mers australes*' (Rainaud 1893: 269).   [4] Bouvet Island, to which Bouvet gave the name *Cap de la Circoncision*.
[5] On Lozier-Bouvet see Rainaud 1893: 394–406; Burney 1803: V: 30–37.

Cook was later to propose and implement in his search for the austral continent but the Company was unimpressed by his previous achievement and he was not permitted to implement them.

In 1756, as the Seven Years War was beginning, Charles de Brosses published his *Histoire des Navigations aux Terres Australes*,[1] a work begun at the instigation of Pierre Louis de Maupertius (1698–1759) who, in a *Lettre sur le Progrès des Sciences*, had stressed the urgent need for foreign discoveries, particularly of *Terra Australis*. De Brosses' publication consisted of a collection of narratives of all the known voyages of discovery, real and supposed, to the southern hemisphere, and an analysis of the evidence for the existence of an austral continent. It was an important publication, if only for the fact that it marked an advance from the idea of exploration justified by trade prospects to the idea of exploration justified by the consequent expansion of civilization and the increase of European knowledge. He visualized a French Empire which was at once the concept of a scholar, a liberal and a humanitarian, and saw the establishment of a French colony near to and resembling those of the Dutch in the East Indies as being of more immediate importance than the exploration of the South Pacific. He recommended *Nova Britannia* as a land lying

advantageously on the fifth parallel of South latitude; its length is four and a half degrees, by a breadth of three, neither too close to, nor too distant from the Moluccas and the Philippines, within reach of Quantong in China, and, what is perhaps no less important, of the Ladrones, and of the countless number of islands not yet visited which are found in the great Pacific Ocean, at the approach to which New Guinea is located. . . .

No better situation could be chosen . . . from which to explore the vast lands of Carpentaria and of the Southern Land of the Holy Spirit, situated a considerable distance away to the south.

De Brosses' *Histoire* contains two maps prepared by Robert Vaugondy on which the Solomons are laid down in the position and with the delineation common to most Pacific maps and charts of the period, 95° W of Lima. They are delineated as the one large island of *Isabelle*, the neighbouring *I Ste. Croix ou Guadalcanal*, and several small islands to the E, of which only *Malaita*, *Nombre de Dios* (Jesús) (which appears twice, once as *I. Jesus*), *Volcan* (Tinakula?) and the *Basses de la Chandeleur* are named. The *Terre du St. Esprit* is part of a hypothetical eastern coastline of *Nouvelle Hollande* (New Holland), *Taumaco* or *Taumago* (Taumako) is situated between *Ste. Croix* and *Nouvelle Hollande*: 'aux environs de laquelle il y a 3 isles savoir Pilen, Pupam et Fonfono',[2] *Chicayama*[3] is situated S of *Taumaco*, and *Tucopia* (Tikopia) is plotted close to the *Terre du St. Esprit*. The discoveries of the Dutch are also plotted, the *Horn*, *Esperance*,

---

[1] De Brosses 1756.

[2] The *Pilen*, *Nupan* and *Fonofono* described to Quirós by the Sikaiana native Pedro (i.e. the Reef Islands).   [3] *Chicayana* (Sikaiana), reported to Quirós but not visited.

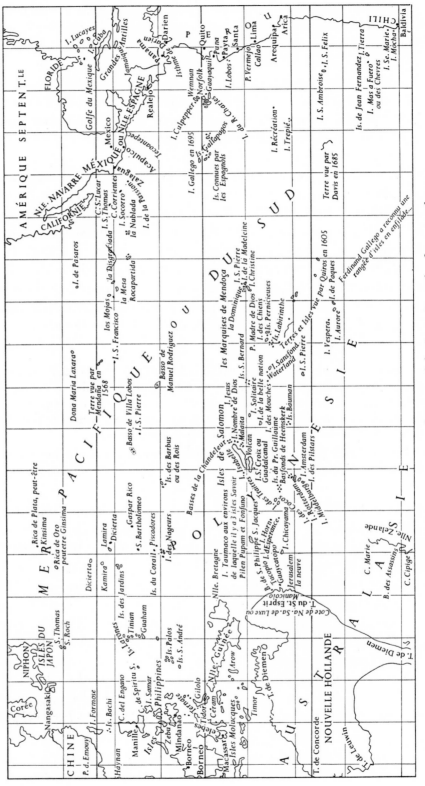

Map XXXIII　A section of Vaugondy's *Carte Generale* of 1756, redrawn

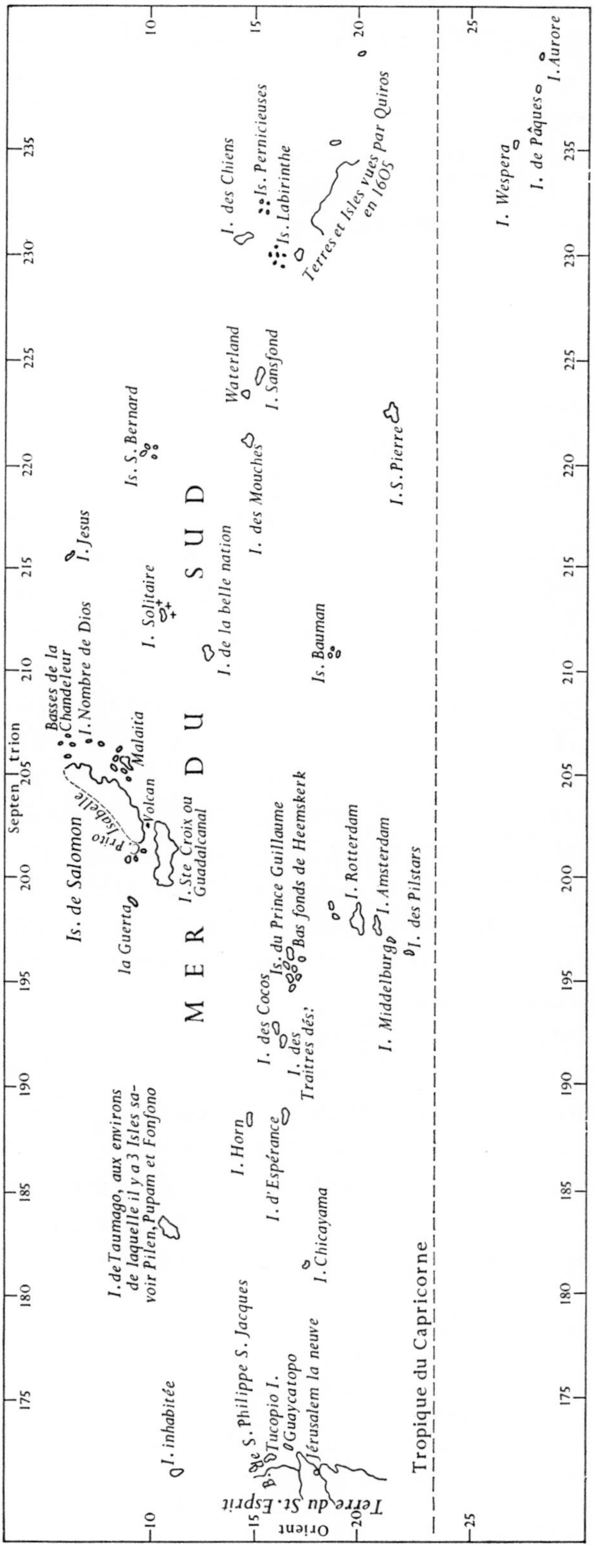

I. inhabitée

I. de Taumago, aux environs de laquelle il y a 3 Isles savoir Pilen, Pupam et Fonfono

I. Horn

I. d'Espérance

Septen | trion

Basses de la Chandeleur
I. Nombre de Dios
I. Jesus

I. de Salomon

la Guerta

Prin Isabelle
Volcan
Malaita

I. Ste Croix ou Guadalcanal

I. Solitaire

Is. S. Bernard

I. des Chiens
Is. Pernicieuses
Is. Labirinthe

Terres et Isles vues par Quiros en 1605

I. des Cocos
Is. du Prince Guillaume
I. des Traitres dés;
Bas fonds de Heemskerk

I. de la belle nation

I. des Mouches

Waterland
I. Sansfond

M E R   D U   S U D

Is. Bauman

I. S. Pierre

I. Rotterdam
I. Amsterdam
I. Middelburg
I. des Pilstars

I. Chicayama

Tropique du Capricorne

S. Philippe S. Jacques
Tucopio I.
Guaycatopo
Jérusalem la neuve

Orient
Terre du St. Esprit

I. Wespera
I. de Pâques
I. Aurore

Map XXXIV Vaugondy's *Carte Réduite de la Mer du Sud* of 1756, redrawn

Cocos and *Traitres* islands of le Maire being situated to the W instead of to the E of Tasman's *I^s du Prince Guillaume* (Fiji). As evidence of the austral continent are the supposed *Terre vue par Davis en 1685*[1]; an inscription referring to the island chain found on several contemporary charts extending NW-SE across the South Pacific; and, in 18° S, 235° E, *Terres et Isles vue par Quiros en 1605*, a confused representation of Quirós' Central Pacific discoveries, of which only the *I. de la belle nation* (Gente Hermosa) is otherwise delineated.[2]

Mad Jack Byron

The years of peace brought by the Peace of Paris in 1763 saw the French and English governments, thoroughly stimulated by the changes and emotions of the preceding years of the century, embarked upon a policy of exploration and territorial aggrandizement. The Falkland Islands replaced Juan Fernández in the minds of strategists, and in 1764 and 1765 were visited in turn by Louis Antoine de Bougainville, with a small party of French colonists, and by Commodore John (Mad Jack) Byron. The latter's visit was followed by the establishment of a British settlement in 1767, only discovered when the French withdrew after Spanish protests, but although the Spaniards captured the English colonists in 1770, the threat of war induced Spain to restore the Falklands to England. Byron's instructions[3] laid down a general objective of discovery, and specifically ordered him to possess the Falklands, to search for land in the South Atlantic between 33° and 53° S and to take 'possession of convenient situations'. He was to enter the Pacific and follow the western American coastline northwards in search of the long-sought strait leading to Hudson's Bay, for the discovery of which the British government had in 1745 offered a reward of £20,000.

After leaving the Falkland Islands he made for the Straits of Magellan and, after a rather lengthy and hazardous passage, entered the Pacific on 9 April 1765.[4] Clearing the South American coast, he headed northwards and visited the island of Masafuera, the most westerly of the two islands of Juan Fernández. Leaving this island on 30 April, he continued to head northwards, but on 2 May appears to have abandoned any intention of fulfilling his instructions to search for the North-West Passage, for on that day he headed westwards:

---

[1] Reported to Dampier.

[2] The *I^s. S Bernard* is almost certainly the San Bernardo of 1595. The maps lay down the Central Pacific discoveries of Mendaña in 1595 and the landfalls of Roggeveen in 1722.

[3] See Corney 1915: I: xix–xx; PRO: Ad 2/1332, pp. 99–100.

[4] Hawkesworth 1773: I: 3–139, contains an account of Byron's voyage. It is of interest to note that Byron was accompanied by Lieutenant Carteret (as First Lieutenant of the *Tamar*, and later of the *Dolphin*, the two vessels under Byron's command), an officer whose name will recur in the story of the rediscovery of the Solomons.

to make the land, which is called Davis's Land[1] in the charts, and is laid down in latitude 27° 30′ S and about five hundred leagues west of Copiapo in Chili; but on the 9th, finding little prospect of getting to the westward, in the latitude which I at first proposed, being then in latitude 26° 46′ S, longitude 94° 45′ W, and having a great run to make, I determined to steer a north west course till I got the true trade-wind, and then to stand to the westward till I should fall in with Solomon's Islands, if any such there were, or make some new discovery.[2]

Running generally to the WNW, Byron came on 7 June to two low inhabited islands which, since the hostility of the natives prevented him from landing, he named the *Islands of Disappointment*, and which may be identified with Napuka and Tepoto in the Northern Tuamotus. On the following day he came to two more islands which he named *King George's Islands*, and which may be identified with Takaroa and Takapoto; and on the 13th came to an island in 15° S, 151° 53′ W which he named the *Prince of Wales's Island*, and which is identifiable with Manihi. On 21 June he came to the three islets and rocks which comprise the Pukapuka of the Northern Cook Islands (10° 53′, 165° 49′ W), and which he named the *Islands of Danger*, a name which they still bear. After quitting these islands:

Nothing worthy of notice happened till Monday the 24th, when, about ten o'clock in the morning, we discovered another island, bearing SSW distant about seven or eight leagues ... low, but covered with wood, among which were cocoa-nut trees in great abundance. It had a pleasant appearance, and a large lake in the middle ... is near thirty miles in circumference, a dreadful sea breaks upon almost every part of the coast, and a great deal of foul ground lies about it. ... At first I was inclined to believe that this island was the same that in the 'Neptune Francois' is called 'Maluita', and laid down about a degree to the eastward of the great island of Saint Elizabeth, which is the principal of the Solomon's Islands; but being afterwards convinced of the contrary, I called it the Duke of York's Island. ... There is indeed great reason to believe that there is no good authority for laying down Solomon's Islands in the situation that is assigned to them by the French: the only person who has pretended to have seen them is Quiros, and I doubt whether he left behind him any account of them by which they might be found by future navigators.[3]

The Hawkesworth account does not record the estimated position of the *Duke of York's Island*, but from Byron's course and description it is possible to identify it with Atafu, the northernmost of the islands in the Tokelau Group, in 8° 32′ S, 172° 31′ W. On the Pacific chart at the front of the first volume of Hawkesworth's *Voyages*, the Duke of York's Island is plotted, though unnamed, in 8° 20′ S, 171° 15′ W, almost 95° W of Lima and almost 40° E of the centre of *Nova Britannia*, the position then currently occupied on French

[1] The land reported to Dampier. See, for instance, Vaugondy's world-map in De Brosses 1756.
[2] Hawkesworth 1773: I: 90.
[3] Hawkesworth 1773: I: 110-11. That Quirós should have displaced Mendaña as the discoverer of the Solomon Islands is, in view of the limited information available, hardly surprising, and Betagh had reported Quirós as the discoverer.

charts[1] by the *Isles de Salomon*. Byron was reasonably correct in his assumption that he was in the immediate vicinity of the Solomons as they were charted on the majority of contemporary charts, and his initial identification is entirely understandable.

Continuing his westerly course in the charted latitude of the Solomons, Byron records than on the 28th they were:

now giving up all hopes of seeing Solomon's Islands; which we had expected to visit; and should certainly have found had there been any such islands, in the latitude in which they are placed in our maps.[2]

On the 29th:

being then ten degrees to the westward of their situation in the chart, without having seen any thing of them, I hauled to the northward, in order to cross the equinocial, and afterwards shape my course for the Ladrone Islands.[3]

Byron thereafter proceeded via the Ladrones, Batavia, the Indian Ocean and Cape of Good Hope, and came to anchor in the Downs on 9 May 1766. As a Pacific voyage it had achieved little, but it did throw considerable doubt on the reputed position of the Islands of Solomon on contemporary charts, and by his discoveries Byron did direct further British attention towards the Central and Western Pacific.

The Voyage of Carteret

Byron's voyage emphasized the need to reinforce the strategic value of the Falkland Islands with a further base in the South Pacific, and seems to have led the British Government to take active steps in the search for the southern continent of *Terra Australis*. Within four months of Byron's return to England Captain Samuel Wallis had received his sailing orders and had weighed anchor in Plymouth South with a fleet of three ships, the *Dolphin*,[4] the *Swallow* and the *Prince Frederick* storeship. His secret orders clearly reflect the Admiralty's intention to discover and possess the austral continent and, though he ostensibly cleared for the Leeward Islands, he was instructed to search for land between longitudes 100° and 120° W in the seas to the W of Cape Horn. If he found nothing there he was to head NW to 20° S, and to attempt further exploration.[5] At Port Famine Bay, Patagonia, the *Prince Frederick* detached herself from the

---

[1] See, for instance, the world-map in De Brosses 1756. When Byron wrote that there was no good authority for positioning the Solomons some 93°–95° W of Lima he was wrong, for this was in fact the approximate distance at which the discoverers had estimated the islands to lie from Perú if the cartographer applied the Spanish estimate of $17\frac{1}{2}$ Iberian leagues to the degree ($94° \times 17\frac{1}{2}$—1,645 leagues).   [2] Callander 1766: III: 711.

[3] Hawkesworth 1773: I: 111.   [4] Byron's ship.

[5] On Wallis' voyage see Hawkesworth 1773: I: 141–302; and Carrington 1948. For his *Secret Instructions* see PRO: Ad. 2/1332, pp. 146–52.

fleet and departed for the Falkland Islands with relief stores for the British settlement there.

By this time the limitations of the *Swallow* as an expeditionary vessel had become all too apparent, for she sailed badly and,

notwithstanding an alteration which had been made in her rudder, she steered and worked so ill, that every time they got under way they were apprehensive that she could never safely be brought to an anchor again[1]. She was an old ship, having been in the service thirty years ... by no means fit for a long voyage, having only a slight thin sheathing upon her bottom;

and her Captain, Philip Carteret, previously Byron's First Lieutenant, was constrained to record that, though he had been given to understand that he was to accompany the *Dolphin*, 'the disparity of the two ships, and the difference in their equipment' made him think that they could not be intended for the same duty, and that

if the 'Dolphin' was to go round the world, it could never be intended that I should go farther than Falkland's Islands, where the 'Jason' a fine frigate ... sheathed with copper and amply equipped, would supply my place.[2]

On 11 April 1767, as the two vessels passed into the Pacific, after a hazardous voyage through the Straits of almost four months' duration, they became separated, and a rising sea, fog, unfavourable winds and currents, prevented Wallis from returning to search for the *Swallow*. Continuing the voyage independently, he headed WNW, and by early June was amongst the Tuamotu Islands where he made several minor discoveries. On 18 June he made the important discovery of Tahiti (*Otaheite*), or *King George the Third's Island* as he called it, and its immediate neighbours; a discovery which was to justify the romantic expectations of interested Englishmen, with its attractive, intelligent, amiable and obliging inhabitants, and was to provide a justification for the idea of the 'Noble Savage' which was to pervade European literary and political writing during the late eighteenth century. From the Society Islands Wallis headed W, visiting Niuatobutabu and Tafahi and discovering Uvea, and then headed north-westwards through the Ellice, Gilbert and Marshall Islands areas to the Ladrones, eventually reaching England on 19 May 1768, by way of Batavia, the Indian Ocean and the Cape of Good Hope.

His achievements had not been inconsiderable, but his search for the austral continent had been rather less than the Admiralty, in their instructions to him, would seem to have intended.[3] His route was very similar to that of his predecessor Byron and, like Byron, he had hoped to find *Davis's Land*. What both he and Byron had in fact shown, though not realized, was the near impossibility

---

[1] Hawkesworth 1773: I: 177.   [2] Hawkesworth 1773: I: 305–6.
[3] The journal of Robertson, Master of the *Dolphin*, reveals Wallis as rather deficient in enterprise and curiosity. See, for example, Carrington 1948: 233.

of a sailing ship making headway against the variable but generally westerly winds of the southern South Pacific, and of the necessity, if that area was to be searched for the austral continent, for the approach to be from the west. As Williamson has remarked of Wallis:

his crossing was tropical, and it was fairly well known by this time that the continent was not. The tropic zone drew these expeditions like a magnet. For there was the trade-wind, fair from the eastward, and fine weather, and islands yielding fresh water and vegetables for scurvy-stricken men.[1]

Meanwhile, Carteret in the *Swallow*, whom we left in the western approaches to the Straits of Magellan, had almost immediately reconciled himself to the prospect of making the voyage to England alone. Not only was his vessel 'so foul, that with all the sails she could set she could not make so much way as the "Dolphin", with only her top-sails and a reef in them'[2] but she had no trade goods with which to barter for supplies, and was much less well-equipped for the Pacific crossing than the *Dolphin*. Carteret did not in fact clear the Straits of Magellan until 15 April and, since the ship was short of water, he then decided to haul to the northwards to replenish his stocks at Juan Fernández or Masafuera.[3] On 10 May he made Juan Fernández but, discovering that it had been fortified by the Spaniards and prevented by contrary winds from approaching sufficiently close to anchor, proceeded to Masafuera and, with considerable difficulty on account of the unfavourable weather, succeeded in taking on water.

Leaving Masafuera on 24 May 1767, he stood to the N in order to catch the trade-winds, determining initially to visit San Ambrosio and San Félix,[4] to 'perform an acceptable service by examining if they were fit for shipping to refresh at, especially as the Spaniards have fortified Juan Fernandez'.[5] Misled by the information at his disposal, Carteret missed the islands, but concluded, probably correctly, that the *Davis's Land* for which Byron had searched was almost certainly nothing more than San Ambrosio and San Félix,[6] and that 'if there had been any such place as Davis's Land in the situation which has been allotted to it on our sea charts, I must have sailed over it, or at least have seen it'.[7] On 2 July, in 25° 2′ S, 133° 21′ W, he discovered and named *Pitcairn*

---

[1] Williamson 1946: 57.   [2] Hawkesworth 1773: I: 310.

[3] For the account of Carteret's voyage I have relied primarily on Carteret's log-book (MLS Dixson Collection Add. 371). The edited narrative in Hawkesworth 1773: I: 303–456, though eminently readable, is at times slightly confusing in respect of navigational details (see Jack-Hinton 1961(b); Jack-Hinton 1962).   [4] Discovered by Juan Fernández.   [5] Hawkesworth 1773: I: 337.

[6] Hawkesworth 1773: I: 338–9. The two islands accord well with the description of *Davis's Land* given at second-hand by Dampier (Dampier 1906: I: 357) and at first-hand by Davis' surgeon, Wafer (Wafer 1934: 125–6), and are on course from the Galapagos to Juan Fernández. *Davis's Land* was certainly not Easter Island, although Carteret remarks that when Roggeveen's discovery of that island was reported, it was accepted by some as evidence of the existence of *Davis's Land*.

[7] Hawkesworth 1773: I: 339.

Island, and on the 11th and 12th of the same month discovered Tematangi (or Mururoa?) (*Bishop of Osnaburgh's Island*) and two of the three islands of Nukutipipi, Anuanurunga and Anuanuraro in the Tuamotus, which he named the *Duke of Gloucester's Islands*.

By 22 July, his estimated position was 18° S, 161° W. As yet he had found no sign of a continent, although he had made a more determined attempt to search for it than had Byron or Wallis; his crew were rotten with scurvy; and bad weather, variable winds and the defects of the ship, frustrated all his attempts to keep in high latitudes and rendered his progress slow. Choosing the survival of his ship and crew as his first responsibility, he determined to head N for the trade-winds and the area where the charts showed islands to exist, his purpose being to obtain the refreshment of which his crew stood in need, to put the ship into proper condition, and then return southwards with the changed season in search of any continent which might lie there. If he found it, he intended to coast it eastwards or westwards, and then return to England.

It was not until he reached 16° S that he eventually found the trade-winds, and between 22 and 26 July he ran N to NW with thick weather and gales behind him. In 10° S, 167° W, by his calculations, he headed westwards 'in hopes to have fallen in with some of the islands called Solomon's Islands, this being the latitude in which the southernmost of them is laid down'.[1] By 3 August he was in 10° 18′ S, 177° 51′ E:

five degrees to the westward of the situation of those islands in the charts. It was not our good fortune however to fall in with any land; probably we might pass near some, which the thick weather prevented our seeing; for in this run great numbers of sea birds were often about the ship: however, as Commodore Byron in his last voyage sailed over the northern limits of that part of the ocean in which the Islands of Solomon are said to lie, and as I sailed over the southern limits without seeing them, there is great reason to conclude that, if there are any such islands, their situation in all our charts is erroneously laid down.[2]

On 11 August Carteret recorded a noon position in 10° 49′ S, 167° 00′ E[3] and, having noticed driftwood during the morning, concluded that he was not far from land. Scurvy was now raging amongst the crew; those not laid low by it were exhausted; the deficiencies in the vessel's equipment were becoming daily more noticeable, and at 4 p.m. on the 11th she sprang a leak in her bows, and three feet of water in the hold added to the already considerable distresses of the voyage.

[1] Hawkesworth 1773: I: 345. He was, as we have already seen on contemporary charts which laid down the Solomons, some 3° to 4° E of them. These comments in the Hawkesworth narrative on the search for the Solomons, and his position relative to their charted position, do not appear in the log-book. [2] Hawkesworth 1773: I: 345–6.

[3] Carteret calculated his DR position from Masafuera, the position of which he knew within 1′ of latitude. His longitudes were calculated from London.

At $\frac{1}{2}$ past 5 a.m. [on the 12th] we saw land ahead we hauld up for it, it appeared like a large Island, soon after as the daylight came on we saw two more Isl^ds to the Southward about SSE, these two I named Lord Edgcombe, and the other Ourrys Island, there were more Islands but could not see them plain enough to name them, at the same time we saw another island on our lee beam to the northward about NW seemed to been low and flat this I named Keppels Island, all this Islands could only be seen from the masts heads, we keep on for those ahead, which we found to be two Islands, the Southernmost I named Lord Howes, and the other or Northermost Lord of Egmonts Island, the passage between these two

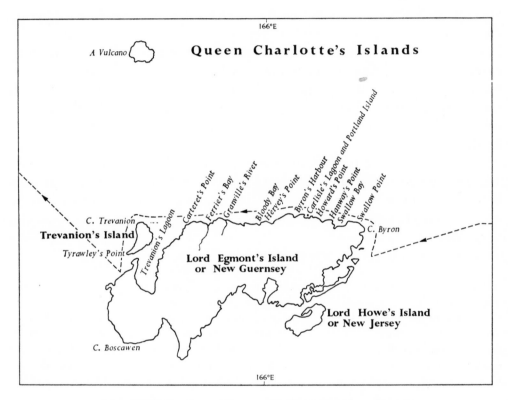

Map XXXV   Carteret's route in the Santa Cruz Group

Islands seemed to be about 4 or 5 miles broad, the Northermost is much the largest Island, both of them high land covered with trees at 8 we was within a couple of miles of this latter one, this was the East or weather side, the wind blew very strong on it, we bore up and runed along, we found this side of these two Islands to run about NbW and SbE 10 or 11 leage^e including the passage between them, when we Come off the NE end of Egmont Island, which is Called Cape Byron, we saw a high round Peeked Island, the top making like a funnel, out of which issued much smoke by which I imagine it is a vulcano, it bears from Cape Byron by compass WNW$\frac{1}{2}$N about 13 Leagues, here we brought too and hoisted the boat out and sent her in shore to find out anchorage . . . at noon the NE point or Cape Byron E by S$\frac{1}{2}$ S 7 or 8 miles so that it is very nearly in this L and Long^d.[1]

[1] Carteret's log-book, f134.

Carteret had come upon the eastern coast of the island of Santa Cruz, discovered by Mendaña in 1595; sighting *en route* the islands of Vanikoro (*Ourry's Island or New Alderney*)[1] and Utupua (*Lord Edgecombe's Island or New Sark*) to the southwards, and to the northwards the Reef Islands (*Keppel's or Swallow's Island*) which he took to be one low-lying island. Rounding the north-eastern promontory of Santa Cruz he had sighted the volcanic island of Tinakula to the NW, then, as at the time of Mendaña's visit, in a state of activity. In his log-book Carteret estimates the position of *Cape Byron* to be 10° 40′ S, 164° 49′ E (London), but on the chart of the islands in Hawkesworth's edited narrative[2] he lays it down in 10° 42′ S, 164° 32′ E. Its actual position is 10° 41′ 30″ S, 166° 9′ E. (Greenwich) and, since Carteret logged a noon position on the 12th of 10° 38′ S, 164° 43′ E, at which time Cape Byron bore 7 miles 'E by S½ S', his correct noon position must have been 10° 38′ 15″ S, 166° 2′ 40″ E (Greenwich) and his error of longitude one of −1° 19′ 40″.

During the afternoon of the 12th the *Swallow* anchored in the north-eastern bay of the island, which they named *Swallow's Bay*, but the unsuitability of this anchorage soon became apparent, and on the following morning the Master was ordered to take the cutter along the north shore of the island and search for a more favourable one. Contrary to his orders he was lax in his precautions, and suffered an assault from the indigenes[3] in which he, a midshipman and six of the crew were wounded. Attempts to establish friendly relations with natives who had appeared on the beach in the immediate vicinity of the *Swallow* had met with similar reactions and a flight of arrows.

With considerable difficulty the expedition managed to take on water at Swallow's Bay and to reduce the leak in the ship's bows. By this time the condition of the expedition was becoming parlous for, with the crew either sick or wounded, the Master dying of his wounds, and both the Lieutenant and Carteret apparently seriously ill, there seemed a strong possibility that before long there would be no-one left to navigate and insufficient crew left to work the vessel. Confined to his bed, unable to command the ship effectively, and in the expectation of death, Carteret conferred with the Lieutenant and Master on the plan to be followed. They agreed that, in view of the hostility of the natives and the unsuitability of the island, the only reasonable plan was to head northwards with all speed in order to reach Batavia before the season changed. Carteret's log-book seems to reflect a very genuine disappointment that he was not able to pursue the voyage to the southwards. As he wrote:

---

[1] Possibly, but improbably, seen in 1595 by *Don* Lorenzo de Barreto, the brother-in-law of Mendaña, and certainly not recognized by him as a separate island from Utupua.

[2] Hawkesworth 1773: I: 348–9.

[3] The fault would seem to have been the Master's for, whilst the cutter crew were initially well received, his thoughtless order to cut down a coconut tree seems, not surprisingly, to have incited the indigenes to violence.

My ill state of health, the Little reguard that had been paid to my Orders, the incensing and falling out with these people notwithstanding all my precautions with the ill consequences attending it, the lose of so many of my best men from duty with the master and midshipman the great number sick we already had the bad condition of the ship the little liklyhood there was of getting any refreshments wont of Cutlery ware and other things for to trade with the Indians and wont of officers to do the ships duty, were dispiriting incedents that at once blasted and dompd all my hopes from being again in a condition to persue the voyage any farther to the Southward and this at the time when I had flattered myself I was on the point of dowing someting to the porpose towards the desired intention we were now so much reduced in strength it was with much difficulty we could weigh our anchors or work the ship.[1]

At 6 in the morning of 17 August the *Swallow* weighed anchor and began to run westwards along the north coast of the island. Carteret had not yet realized that he had rediscovered the Santa Cruz of Mendaña, for although the account in Hawkesworth's *Voyages* contains the phrase: 'it certainly is the same to which the Spaniards have given the name of Santa Cruz, as appears by the accounts which their writers have given of it',[2] no such remark occurs in his log, and the realization of his rediscovery did not come until later. Coasting the island the expedition named the several bays and points visited by the boats or seen now for the first time, and in the afternoon passed the northern entrance to Graciosa Bay where Mendaña had attempted to found his ill-fated colony. Carteret named the island of Te Motu, which forms the northwestern side of the bay, *Trevanion's Island*, and coasted its western shore as far S as the western entrance to Graciosa Bay. However, the hostility and large numbers of the indigenes in this area, and the uncertainty of the entrance, induced him to make sail and head WNW[3] without seeking further refreshment.

At 10 a.m. on 20 August, whilst pursuing a course generally WNW from *Lord Egmont's Island*, as he named Santa Cruz, Carteret sighted a small island, the latitude of which he observed in 7° 53′ S. The day's work in his log-book is from Cape Byron, the longitude still being calculated from Masafuera, and even without plotting the successive days' work from Cape Byron to this new landfall, its latitude and difference of longitude (i.e. Carteret's longitude) from Cape Byron permit its identification with Ndai Island, the small island in 7° 53′ S, 160° 38′ E to the N of Malaíta. By the early afternoon Carteret had rounded the northern end of the island, and had launched the boat in order to determine whether or not an anchorage might be found. Unsuccessful in their objective, the boat's crew returned with several coconuts obtained from three unarmed natives, who had made signs to them to go round to the western side of the island. Continuing round the island, the expedition found a bay on the western side, but this also proved to be unsuitable as an anchorage and, after

---

[1] Carteret's log-book, f138.   [2] Hawkesworth 1773: I: 356.
[3] Carteret noted that his Lieutenant and Master estimated Egmont's Island (Santa Cruz) to extend 50 miles E-W, but that he himself doubted if it was so large. It is in fact only 24 nautical miles long.

making further contact with natives in canoes from whom they obtained more coconuts, the *Swallow* was stood off from the shore for the approaching night. Making sail, they stood on and off throughout the night with the intention of returning to the island on the following day to obtain more coconuts and such other refreshment as it might offer.

As daylight broke the expedition found that a strong current setting to the S had carried them during the night well to the S of the island, named by Carteret *Gower's Island*, and within sight of two more islands, one of which was small and to the eastwards of the other, 'a fine large Island'. The largest and most westerly of the two islands was given the name *Carteret's Island*, and to the other was given the name *Simpson's Island*.[1] As these islands were to windward Carteret was unable to explore them, as he wished, but from his description[2] it is at once apparent that the two islands were the north coast of Malaíta (Carteret's Island) and Manaoba Island (Simpson's Island). He had in fact rediscovered one of the main islands in the Islands of Solomon, the Ramos of Mendaña, but in approaching it from the N he was not made immediately aware of its more considerable size, and only saw an island of little more than 15 miles extent from E to W. The sketch-map of Gower's, Carteret's and Simpson's Islands, included as an inset in the chart of *Queen Charlotte's Islands* (the Santa Cruz Islands) in Hawkesworth's *Voyages*, is in error in its longitudes, for it lays down Gower's Island in 7° 56′ S, 156° 2′ E, whereas Carteret records the position of the north-eastern point of the island in his log-book as 7° 53′ S, 158° 56′ E (London).[3]

Running back to Gower's Island, the expedition found several canoes awaiting them, apparently with the intention of seizing the *Swallow's* boat as it came to collect refreshments. Turning the tables on the indigenes, the English seized 'a fine handsome Canoe' and 100 coconuts and then put to sea. At noon (21 August) the north-east point of Gower's Island lay 3 miles distant bearing N$\frac{1}{2}$W; at 12.30 the cutter was hoisted inboard, sail was made, and Carteret set a course for the NW. Like his predecessors he was concerned with the bogey of New Guinea's supposed or probable lee shore, for he notes in his log that:

we now hauld up NW finding so strong current I was afraid in case we should fall in with the main land of New Guinea too far to the south-ward we should not be able to get

---

[1] *Simpson* in the log-book and in Hawkesworth's narrative, but *Simson* on the chart in Hawkesworth.   [2] More detailed in the Hawkesworth narrative than in the log-book.

[3] He took this as his noon position for the 20th, calculating his day's work for the 24 hours preceding it, and his day's work for the voyage to noon on the 22nd from it (there being no day's work in the log-book for the period from noon on the 20th to noon on the 21st when the *Swallow* was in the vicinity of Gower's Island). The Hawkesworth narrative also gives the position of Gower's Island as 7° 56′ S, 158° 56′ E. Carteret estimated Carteret's Island to lie 10 or 11 leagues (30 or 33 miles) to the S of Gower's Island, a slight overestimate, understandably the result of attempting to judge the size of the former from a distance.

round to the North-ward of it, or had we fallen into any deep bay or gulf we should never been able to have got out of it with such a miserable tool of a ship as we have.

The crew was here depleted by one marine, Patrick Dwyer, who fell overboard and drowned, and the increasingly parlous condition of the crew is reflected in such entries in the log as:

at 8 James Cooper Armorour, died of the Scurvy, at 10 departed this life likewise Samuel Smith the [leading] seaman, he was one of these that had been wounded, he was a young-man, he was taken with pain in his belly then what they Call the locked Jaws, and soon after died.

By noon on the 22nd the *Swallow* had made 122 miles to the N 43° W of the north-eastern extremity of Gower's Island and was experiencing a strong current setting to the S. Carteret states that he allowed for this in estimating his position; in the course plotted, and by shortening the distance sailed. By noon on the 23rd they made 94 miles to the N 60°, W and by noon on the 24th a further 70 miles to a position which Carteret calculated to lie in 5° 07′ S, 155° 08′ E. At 11 p.m. on the 24th the expedition:

saw the land right ahead and very near us, we instantly, hauld off but with difficulty we got clear of it, it prouved several small Islands which I take to be those called O'hong Java discovered by Tasman ... at daylight[1] found these to be 9 small islands [except one which is tollerably large] some scarce better than rocks but all well Cloathed with ... trees.[2]

At noon on the 25th, when Carteret estimated his position to be 4° 32′ S, 154° 06′ E, the westernmost of the islands lay W by S distant about 5 leagues, and he concluded that the islands as a whole lay in 4° 36′ S, 154° 17′ E.

At about 5 p.m. on the 25th, as they continued westwards, an island was sighted to the S 'making in hummocks which we at first took to be so many Islands', and at 10.30 p.m., during a very dark night, the *Swallow* came within 2 or 3 miles of more land which was avoided with difficulty. With the dawn the latter landfall revealed itself as 'a fine low flat Island green and pleasant', which Carteret named *Sir Charles Hardy's Island*, and which he deduced to be in 4° 50′ S, 15 leagues W of the northernmost of the *Nine Islands*. The island sighted earlier, 'making in three hummocks', was named the *Earl of Winchel-sea's Island*,[3] and lay 10 leagues to the S by E of Sir Charles Hardy's Island. At about 10 a.m. high land was sighted to the northward which Carteret 'judged to be St. Johns Island as by Schouten the discoverer and mentioned by Dampier'. Shortly afterwards very high land was sighted to the W, 'what Dampier had named Nova Brittannia', and at noon, when their estimated position was 4° 46′ S, 153° 17′ E, *Nova Britannia* bore from W by S to WNW, and St. John's Island bore NNW ½ W about 10 or 12 leagues distant.

[1] i.e. daylight on the 25th.   [2] Carteret's log-book, f 142.
[3] *Lord Anson's Island* on the chart in Hawkesworth 1773: I: 374-5.

Carteret had now reached, as he correctly concluded, the eastern coast of Dampier's *Nova Britannia* (which Dampier's chart spells as *Nova Brittannia*), he was shortly to discover what Dampier had not discovered, that *Nova Britannia* consisted in fact of two separate islands separated by a wide and navigable strait. From the identification of this coastline, and in particular of the southern extremity of what Carteret was himself to name *New Ireland, Cape St. George*, it is possible to reconstruct his route from Gower's Island and identify his landfalls. If Carteret's several days' workings recorded in his log are plotted from the north-eastern point of Gower's Island, it becomes apparent from the noon positions for 26 to 28 August that Carteret underestimated the longitude made good during that part of the voyage and, recalling his own note to the effect that he had compensated for the effects of current upon his estimated position by shortening the distance sailed, his underestimate is understandable. If allowance is made for it, it becomes at once apparent that from Gower's Island the *Swallow* had passed to the S of and close to Roncador Reef (the probable identification of Mendaña's Baxos de la Candelaria), had passed to the S of and close to the atoll of Tau'u (the Marquen of le Maire and Tasman), without sighting either of them, and had come upon the atoll of Kilinailau. Beyond it had been sighted Buka (Winchelsea or Lord Anson's Island) to the S, le Maire's Groene Eylanden (Sir Charles Hardy's Island) to the N, and Carteret had also sighted and recognized the St. Jans Eylandt of Schouten and le Maire (St. John's Island) further to the NW. The description of the Nine Islands which Carteret gives is not one immediately reconcilable with the description of Kilinailau Atoll contained in the available hydrographic sources, but a reconstruction of Carteret's course on the modern chart indicates that he was well past Tau'u by the evening of the 24th, and his underestimate of longitude made good between Gower's Island and New Ireland indicates that his true position was to the W of his estimated position. There is therefore no doubt that the Nine Islands were Kilinailau, as opposed to Tau'u, and that from a particular position, and under certain conditions of visibility, Kilinailau must have the appearance of nine islands which Carteret describes.[1]

Set by the current into what Dampier had named *St. George's Bay*, Carteret was able to find a suitable anchorage where he heeled the *Swallow* and made further repairs to her deteriorating hull, and where he was also able to obtain refreshment. Prevented by strong winds and a contrary current from following Dampier's track to the S of *Nova Britannia* and through Dampier's Passage, he sailed northwards with the current, on the assumption that it must indicate a strait, and successfully passed between the islands which he now named *New Ireland* and *New Britain*. His passage homewards via Batavia and the Cape of Good Hope was to last until 20 March 1769, when the *Swallow* eventually came to anchor at Spithead. Carteret's achievement was a considerable

[1] See Jack-Hinton 1961(b) and Jack-Hinton 1962.

one, for, had he made no discoveries at all, his determination, fortitude and ability in bringing an old, awkward, ill-equipped and increasingly foul vessel around the world, in the face of almost every conceivable impediment, would have received just acclaim in the annals of nautical endeavour. He had, however, made several important contributions to geographical knowledge: determining the actual position and existence of the Santa Cruz of Mendaña; discovering the existence of a passage between New Ireland and New Britain; discovering and charting Ndai Island; rediscovering but not recognizing the northern extremity of Malaíta; and discovering Kilinailau Atoll[1] and the island of Buka (*Bouka*).

The successive voyages of Byron, Wallis and Carteret had made not insignificant contributions to contemporary knowledge of the contents of the Pacific and, perhaps more importantly, provided further incentives to European interest, particularly in their revelation that discoveries of fertile populated lands could be made there. In this they helped to create a climate of English opinion of which the three major voyages of Pacific exploration of Captain James Cook were to be an immediate result.

[1] Wrongly assuming it to be the Onthong Java of Tasman, an assumption which was to add to later confusion surrounding the charting and identification of the five atoll reefs off the Northern Solomons.

VIII

The Further Rediscovery and Recognition of the Islands of Solomon

Among the ancient discoveries, the loss of which deserved regret, Mendaña's archipelago of Solomon's Islands . . . held the foremost rank.

Fleurieu 1791: 210

The Voyage of Bougainville

IN the last stage of Carteret's voyage, when the *Swallow* was making her laborious way from Ascension Island to the Channel, she was overhauled by a vessel which struck French colours and exchanged greetings. This vessel, the *Boudeuse*, was commanded by Louis Antoine de Bougainville, a French soldier turned navigator, who had himself circumnavigated the globe and, like Carteret, was on his way home. Despatched from France in November 1766, to effect the French handover of the Falkland Islands to Spain, he was further instructed to make a voyage of exploration and to provide an opportunity for the French astronomer, de Commerçon, to make observations to determine longitude at sea. Having executed his business in the Falkland Islands, he sailed via Río de Janeiro and the Straits of Magellan and entered the Pacific in January 1768.[1]

Heading NW, he passed through the Tuamotu Archipelago, making several minor discoveries, and on 16 April, after heading southwards and then northwards, came to Tahiti, previously discovered by Wallis. Continuing westwards he rediscovered Manua and Tutuila in the Samoa Group, previously discovered by Roggeveen, and remarks in his account that:

La longitude de ces îles est à peu-près la même par laquelle s'estimoit être Abel Tasman, lorsqu'il découvrit les îles d'Amsterdam et de Rotterdam, des Pilstaars, du Prince Guillaume, et les bas fonds de Fleemskerk. C'est aussi celle qu'on assigne à peu de chose près, aux îles de Salomon.[2]

Further westwards he passed the islands of Futuna and Alofi, the Hoorn Islands or Horensche Eylanden of Le Maire and Schouten, which he named *l'Enfant perdu*, and on 22 May came in sight of more islands. As he approached,

---

[1] An account of Bougainville's voyage was published in 1771 (see Bougainville 1771), and an abbreviated version is to be found in Fleurieu 1790 and Fleurieu 1791. His log-book is preserved in the French National Archives, but for the purposes of this study the published account has been found reasonably adequate. [2] Bougainville 1771: 240.

two islands became particularly prominent, one lying to the S which Bougainville named *île de la Pentecôte*, the other lying ahead which he named *l'Aurore*.
The positions which he ascribes to these two islands on his chart,[1] although
subject to an easterly error of slightly over 1°, and their configuration, clearly
reveal them as the easternmost of the New Hebrides Archipelago discovered
by Quirós. Rounding l'Aurore, Bougainville sighted more land and, as he
headed SW, gained the impression that he was now completely surrounded
by land. His description bears a striking resemblance to that recorded by
Quirós, and Bougainville concluded that he was in fact approaching the
Austrialia del Espíritu Santo of that explorer. As he wrote of these islands:

> *Les apparences sembloient se conformer au récit de Quiros, et ce que nous découvrions chaque jour
> encourageoit nos recherches. Il est bien singulier que précisément par la même latitude et la même
> longitude où Quiros place sa grande baie de Saint-Jacques et Saint-Philippe, sur une côte qui parois-
> soit au premier coup d'oeil celle d'un continent, nous ayons trouvé un passage de largeur égale à celle
> qu'il donne à l'ouverture de sa baie.*[2]

Bougainville was not, as he thought, in the Great Bay of St. Philip and St.
James, but on the south-eastern side of the land which Torres had shown to
be an island, Espíritu Santo. Naming the whole archipelago *l'archipel des
grandes Cyclades*, he now determined to follow the passage which he thought
he had discovered on the western perimeter of the bay, but which was in fact
the passage between Espíritu Santo and Malekula navigated by Torres, with a
view to resolving the question of whether Espíritu Santo was or was not conjoined to New Guinea. Many contemporary charts showed Quirós' Espíritu
Santo as part of a continental coastline linking New Guinea and Van Diemen's
Land, and although de Brosses and others had produced charts on which New
Guinea was separated from New Holland and although the cartographical
record of Torres' New Guinea discoveries had survived, Torres' voyage was
relatively unknown.[3] The only answer, as Bougainville concluded, was to
head westwards for 350 leagues in the hope of sighting the east coast of New
Holland. This he did, only to be impeded by the Great Barrier Reef and,
although several of the crew claimed to have sighted land, this was not confirmed, and the ships were headed to the N. Nevertheless, Bougainville concluded that he was close to some extensive land and, in running westwards
from Espíritu Santo, he had dared to face the risk of the legendary lee-shore
of New Holland and New Guinea, even though prudence, shortage of food
and the condition of his vessels would have justified his heading northwards at
an earlier date.

---

[1] Bougainville 1771: 240–1.   [2] Bougainville 1771: 252.

[3] Dalrymple, to whom reference is made later, was an exception. Charts were in existence (e.g. in
the *Neptune François* of 1700) which recorded the New Guinea discoveries of Torres, but little credence
seems to have been given to this particular feature.

On 10 June, at daybreak, the navigators found themselves confronted by a large expanse of land extending from the E to NW. Bougainville does not appear to have realized that this was probably the south coast of New Guinea, but he hoped that if he headed westwards he would be able to find a passage between New Holland and New Guinea. As Forsyth has remarked:

Bougainville's decision to sail westwards from the Great Cyclades, was, considering the state of his ships and crews, and his belief that there was a passage between New Guinea and New Holland, enterprising to the verge of recklessness. It has frequently been stated that Bougainville believed that such a passage 'probably existed'. What he wrote[1] was '*Rien n'étoit à la vérité plus problématique que l'existence de ce passage*'.[2]

For the moment the favourable south-east winds had failed him, and his passage northwards to the coastline which he named the *Terres de la Louisiade* had been far from easy. In view of this, and of the fact that he seemed to be in a gulf,[3] he determined to sail to the ESE around the Terres de la Louisiade and then northwards around New Guinea. Almost immediately he found himself faced with the sort of situation which his predecessors had dreaded, for, short of food and with vessels which by now were in need of extensive overhaul, he had to contend with the resurgent south-east winds which threatened to drive him upon his most recent discovery. For two weeks he tacked to and fro in an attempt to make headway to the E:

and still, however much the ships worked to south, day after day there was land to the north-east, islets, reefs, shoals, the interminable archipelago which formed the eastern extremity of New Guinea; day after day discovered the endless line of breakers.[4]

Eventually, on 25 June, land was sighted which seemed to end in a cape, and on that day the expedition was able to head northwards undeterred by the prospect of further land or reefs to the eastwards, naming what was in fact the eastern extremity of Rossel Island the *cap de la Délivrance*. As Bougainville remarks:

Tous les navigateurs que sont venus dans ces parages, avoient toujours redouté ce tomber dans le Sud de la nouvelle Guinée, et d'y trouver un golfe correspondant à celui de la Carpenterie d'où il leur fût ensuite difficile de se relever. En conséquence ils ont tous gagné de bonne heure la latitude de la nouvelle Bretagne, sur laquelle ils alloient atterrir. Tous ont suivi les mêmes traces; nous en ouvrions de nouvelles, et il falloit payer l'honneur d'une première découverte.[5]

His claim was modestly put, for in the context of this study his successive decisions had put him in a position in which, accidental though it was, he was able to make a significant contribution to the further discovery, rediscovery and recognition of the Islands of Solomon. But for the change of weather and course his predecessor Torres might well have found himself, instead of discovering the strait between New Guinea and Australia, following the route

---

[1] Bougainville 1771: 249. [2] Forsyth 1959: 122.
[3] He was in fact at the edge of the Gulf of Papua.
[4] Beaglehole 1934: 268. [5] Bougainville 1771: 261.

which Bougainville himself was to follow. In foul weather he headed NE for
60 leagues to the latitude of 8° S, and on the morning of 28 June, sighted land
to the NW, 9 or 10 leagues distant, and more land to the ESE and ENE.
Bougainville's own chart of his route and landfalls[1] is adequate evidence in
itself for the recognition of his position as one in approximately 7° 40′ S,
156° 15′ E (Greenwich), to the SE of the Treasury and Shortland Islands and

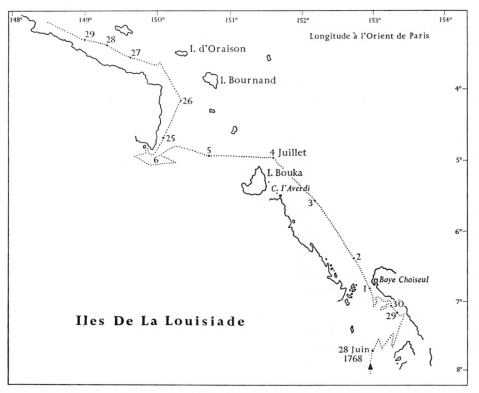

Map XXXVI   Chart of Bougainville's landfalls in the Choiseul, Bougainville and New
Ireland area, redrawn from Fleurieu's *Découvertes des François*

to the W of the island of Vella Lavella. As the vessels headed to the NE the
coastline to the eastwards could be seen to extend to the N and then to the
NW, interrupted for a time to the S by what 'could have been a channel or
a large bay'.[2] What Bougainville could in fact see was the coastline of the
island which he was himself to name *Choiseul*,[3] separated from Vella Lavella
by the expanse of water now known as the New Georgia Sound.

   As they coasted Choiseul during 29 and 30 July, boats were sent ahead to
attempt to find a suitable anchorage, but returned with the report that the

---

[1] Bougainville 1771: 264–5.   [2] Bougainville 1771: 264.
   [3] The San Márcos of Mendaña. In the text of his narrative Bougainville spells the name *Choiseul*,
but on the charts and illustration it is invariably spelt *Choiseuil*.

coastline was open. In the interim period the ships were visited by natives in well constructed canoes, of whom, although they did not attack, Bougainville was constrained to remark '*il parut que leurs dispositions n'étoient pas pacifiques*'.[1] a strong current from the N offered hopes that a passage might be found there, for the position of the vessels, apparently almost surrounded by land and off a rather inhospitable and forbidding coastline, was far from pleasant. The coastline was soon seen to trend to the northwards and apparently to terminate, and at the north-western extremity an attractive bay revealed itself and offered prospects of an anchorage and refreshment.[2] By now the two vessels were in a strait four or five leagues wide between the island of Choiseul to the E and more land to the W, and were experiencing the rather unpleasant combinations of tide and current for which this particular stretch of water is locally renowned. Boats were sent into the bay but were attacked by the indigenes in ten canoes,[3] with a skill and determination which only waned after two fusillades from the muskets of the *matelots*.

Discouraged by this display of antipathy for strangers, Bougainville continued to the NW, passing through the strait and coasting the land to the W which slowly revealed itself as long and high, with 'prodigious' mountains rising from the water until they were lost in the clouds. Slowly, the island of Choiseul receded to the S, and by the morning of 3 July was no longer visible. On the same day the land to the W terminated in what Bougainville describes as a remarkable cape, to which he gave the name the *cap l'Averdi*, and to the NW of which no more land could be seen. At daybreak on the 4th more land was sighted to the W which Bougainville deduced to be separate from the large island which he had just coasted, more to the W than, and separated from the Cap l'Averdi by '*un vaste espace formant ou un passage ou un golfe considérable*'. He was, of course, correct in identifying this new land as separate from the former, but he was insufficiently close inshore to see that the land trended W from Cap l'Averdi, then NW, and terminated in a narrow promontory, separated from the latest discovery (Bouka) by a narrow strait. To this new land which had already been discovered by Carteret and named by him Lord Anson's Island or Winchelsea, Bougainville gave the name *Bouka*,[4] a word much used by the indigenes who came off-shore in canoes and tempted the

---

[1] Bougainville 1771: 265.

[2] See the *Plan de la Baye Choiseuil* in Bougainville 1771: 266–7, which is clearly identifiable with the Choiseul Bay of the modern chart (Admiralty Chart No. 3268).

[3] Bougainville's description of the indigenes and their canoes (Bougainville 1771: 208–9) is both excellent and interesting, and accords well with later descriptions of them. His comment of them: '*Leur audace a nous attaquer, l'usage de porter des armes offensives et défensives, leur adresse a s'en servir, prouvent qu'ils sont presque toujours en état de guerre*' (Bougainville 1771: 269) was correct, for the inhabitants of this region seem, particularly after the introduction of steel axes by whalers during the early nineteenth century, to have ranged to the SE in head-hunting expeditions, and to have been notorious for their bloodthirstiness.

[4] The name which it bears today with the corrupt spelling *Buka*.

voyagers with coconuts. Contrary winds and currents prevented the vessels from approaching and anchoring, and Bougainville decided to head for *Nova Britannia* which he concluded could not be far distant.

As he headed westwards, two islands were sighted to the N and NNW, identifiable with the Green Islands, and almost immediately afterwards more land was sighted to the NW and W, of considerable height and extent and with several bays, which was identified as *Nova Britannia*. Here the expedition was able to anchor and effect necessary repairs, but little food was to be found and rations were reduced to a minimum. Whilst at anchor the expedition made a careful exploration of the neighbourhood, in the course of which the remnants of Carteret's camp were found, though Bougainville was not of course aware of his predecessor's identity. Unlike Carteret he did not attempt to follow Dampier's route to the SW, through the strait between New Britain and New Guinea, and in consequence failed to discover what Carteret had discovered, that Dampier's *Nova Britannia* was in fact two separate islands, and continued in the belief that Dampier's Bay of St. George was indeed a bay and not a strait.[1] From this anchorage he headed northwards, passing to the W of St. John's Island which he named the *Ile Bournand*, and proceeded via Boero and Batavia, where he discovered Carteret's identity, and Mauritius. He arrived at the Cape of Good Hope to find that Carteret was only three days ahead of him and, eventually overhauling him off the West African coast, recorded with sympathy '*Combien il a dû souffrir dans une aussi mauvaise embarcation!*'

Like Carteret he had no idea that he had passed through the Islands of Solomon, and this is hardly surprising in view of the considerable stretch of water which still remained unknown within this area. Even if he had had access to the detailed narratives of Mendaña's voyage of 1568, they would not really have permitted the identification of his discoveries, for he had passed through a part of the archipelago which Mendaña's expedition had not visited, and had in fact made the entirely new discovery of the islands now known as Bougainville, Vella Lavella, the Treasury Islands, and of the north-western coastline of Choiseul. With Carteret he had reduced the limits of the unknown areas of the South-West Pacific, and his rediscovery and recognition of Espíritu Santo, like Carteret's rediscovery and recognition of Santa Cruz, provided a concrete addition to the chart of the Pacific, in relation to which cartographers and historians were able to postulate the position of the Islands of Solomon. Of these islands he himself remarked, in the *Discours Préliminaire* to his *Voyage* of 1771:

Alvar de Mendoce et Mindana, partis du Péro en 1567, découvrirent les îles célèbres que leur richesse fit nommer îles de Salomon; mais, on supposant que les détails rapportés sur la richesse de

---

[1] On his own chart (Bougainville 1771: 264–5) the southern extremity of New Ireland is joined to the east coast of New Britain by a dotted line, and the whole is named *Partie de la Nouvelle Bretagne*. In his narrative Bougainville notes that there were signs that the Bay of St. George might be a strait.

ces îles ne soient pas fabuleux, on ignore où elles sont situées, et c'est vainement qu'on les a recherchées depuis. Il paroît seulement qu'elles sont dans la partie australe de la ligne entre le huitieme et le douzieme parallele. L'île Isabella et la terre de Guadalcanal, dont les mêmes voyageurs fait mention, ne sont pas mieux connues,[1]

and on the world-map in his *Voyage* they are laid down in mid-Pacific in the manner of contemporary French charts with the inscription '*Isles Salomon, dont l'existence et la position sont douteuses*'.

The Voyage of Surville

On 2 June 1769, Jean François Marie de Surville sailed from Pondicherry in the French armed merchantman the *St. Jean Baptiste* bound for the South Pacific. The precise object of his voyage is uncertain,[2] but it seems likely that it was to establish trading interests in Tahiti in forestallment of the English. The enterprise was a privately backed one, the *St. Jean* having been fitted out in the Ganges by Surville himself and two other gentlemen.[3] After collecting a cargo at Pondicherry, he sailed for the Bashee Islands to the N of the Philippines, and then headed to the SE. He crossed the line during the night of 23 to 24 September but experienced calms and contrary winds which prevented him from making progress until the end of September.[4]

As they made their way southwards the voyagers had noticed many signs of land, and by 6 October, as they continued to head steadily to the SE, these signs became more pronounced. At sunset on 6 October several of the crew believed that they could see land to the SSW, and as day broke on the 7th it was plainly visible from the SE to WSW. At noon the ship's latitude was estimated to be 6° 56' 45'' S and its longitude between 150° 15' E and 152° 28' E (Paris).[5] To the S ¼ SE, at 8 leagues distance, lay an island which Surville named the *île de la Première Vue*, and to the S 5° W lay a high mountain which he named *le Gros Morne*. Fleurieu, in examining the narratives of this voyage, pointed to the existence of an error in the estimated longitude, and suggested that it was a mean error of 3¼° W. In fact, when an attempt is

[1] Bougainville 1771: 10–11.
[2] Fleurieu describes it as 'a particular commercial speculation' (Fleurieu 1791: 107).
[3] Fleurieu 1791: 106.
[4] The source used for this reconstruction of Surville's voyage is the account contained in Fleurieu 1791: 106–63. Fleurieu informs us that he derived his account from four Journals compiled by members of the expedition (Fleurieu 1791: 104–5), and also reproduces charts and views derived from them (see Fleurieu 1791: Plates III, IV, V, VI, VIII). An abstract account of Surville's voyage was attached to the *Instructions* delivered to la Pérouse in 1785 (see Fleurieu 1791: 99–104, where it is reproduced), and an abridged account based on a MS. by Monneron, the author of one of the journals, is to be found appended to the anonymously edited *Nouveau Voyage à la Mer du Sud* of *MM.* Marion and le *Chevalier* Duclesmeur (Marion 1783: 251–90), with a reduced chart of the discoveries (Marion 1783: Plate 7). A reproduction of views of the discoveries made is also to be found in Laborde 1791: 1.
[5] The several estimates of the authors of the four journals (Fleurieu 1791: 109).

made to reconcile Surville's position with the known coastline, it becomes fairly clear that his position was approximately 6° 45′ S, 157° 38′ E (Greenwich). To the S lay the island of Wagina (Ile de la Première Vue) at the southeastern extremity of Choiseul; rather more to the W lay prominent Taura Peak (Gros Morne) rising sharply from Kumboro Cape to 2,050 feet; and beyond it, as the narrative describes, lay a mountainous chain extending westwards, recognizable as the interior of the island of Choiseul.

Concluding that this land could not be Dampier's *Nova Britannia* the members of the expedition decided that, since they knew of no other land having been discovered between *Nova Britannia* and 'the *Tierra Austral* of Quiros', it must be a new discovery. It is not surprising that news of Bougainville's voyage had not reached the French in India, and although Fleurieu remarks that in the journal of Monneron, dated Paris, 4 October 1771, occurs the note, 'We find, however, in the voyage of M. de Bougainville, that he had knowledge of a part of the same land',[1] it is certain that this comment was a post-voyage addition by the author of the journal.

Standing on and off throughout the night of 7 to 8 October, Surville now attempted to beat up towards the Ile de la Première Vue, passing over a bank at 27 fathoms and noting other signs of shoals.[2] As they approached to within two leagues of the island, bottom was sounded in 45 fathoms, by now the peak of Gros Morne seemed to form the 'western point of an immense bay',[3] and four small islets were sighted to the S of the island.[4] A calm enabled Surville to despatch the yawl to explore the Ile de la Première Vue, and the description which its commander brought back of a fertile island with a creek on its northern coast[5] is further evidence for the identification of Wagina Island.

On 9 October a little headway was made to the E, and to the S of the Ile de la Première Vue could be seen what seemed to be 'several isles and islets' and 'some very high mountains', identifiable with the large islands now named Kolombangara, New Georgia and Vangunu to the SW and S of Wagina. From the 9th to the 13th the *St. Jean* was stood on and off, and, although the land was kept in sight, Surville was reluctant to approach it in the prevailing uncertain weather, and in view of its broken appearance and the possibility of reefs and shoals. He himself was uncertain whether he was coasting a continent surrounded by a prodigious number of islands, or an archipelago of islands, and the views sketched during this part of the voyage illustrate his perplexity by providing an accurate representation of the Manning Strait and northern

---

[1] Fleurieu 1791: 110.

[2] The existence of shoals is further evidence of their position, for to the N of Wagina Island there are extensive patches of shoal-water. See Admiralty Chart No. 3416, *New Georgia Group to Choiseul Island*, and the *Pacific Pilot* 1946: I: 408.   [3] As Taura Peak does.

[4] Probably the Arnavon Islands in the Manning Strait. See the view in Fleurieu 1791: Plate V.

[5] Fleurieu 1791: 111–12.

end of Santa Ysabel, an area which, particularly from several miles off-shore, has an extremely broken appearance.

On 13 October Surville decided to examine one of the apparent openings in the hope that it might offer either a passage or an anchorage, and the yawl was sent ahead to reconnoitre. It returned with the report that a good anchorage had been found, and by the 14th the *St. Jean* was safely at anchor in a port to which Surville gave the name *Port Praslin*, and which, from the description,[1] the sketches[2] and chart[3] made by the voyagers, can be identified with the Port Praslin of the modern chart, at the north-western extremity of Santa Ysabel in 7° 26′ S, 158° 17′ E. The position given to the entrance to Port Praslin, 7° 25′ S, 152° 46′ E (Paris),[4] was in error by 3° 11′ W, but there can be little if any doubt as to its identity.

The French remained at Port Praslin for nine days, and during that time acquired sufficient information of the immediate locality to provide an interesting and tolerably informative picture of it,[5] information which was reinforced by questioning a native whom they captured and took away with them. At first their relations with the indigenes were extremely amicable, the French being particularly careful to give no offence, but when the former unprovokedy attempted to lure the ship's boats into an ambush, hostilities developed and prevailed until the *St. Jean* put to sea.

On 21 October the French left Port Praslin, and by the morning of the 22nd were out of sight of land and making some progress eastwards. At noon on the 22nd the *St. Jean* was reckoned to be 40′ E of Port Praslin in 7° 14′ S, and Surville concluded that if the land did continue it must trend to the SE or be interrupted by a wide gulf. In the late afternoon of the 23rd the land became once more visible to the southward 'at a great distance', but by the 24th, when their noon latitude was observed to be 7° 45′ S and longitude 1° 4′ E of Port Praslin, high mountains dominated the horizon from the S to SW ¼S.[6] Thickening weather on the 25th obscured everything except the highest mountains, and a westerly wind which sprang up during the night of the 25th

---

[1] Fleurieu 1791: 114, 126–9. [2] Fleurieu 1791: Plate V.

[3] Fleurieu 1791: Plate IV. Surville admits in his journal that the chart is imperfect, based on rough compass bearings, with distances estimated by eye (Fleurieu 1791: 128). This is quite apparent, as also is the fact that one or two islands have been exaggerated in size, and seen but not recognized twice, and that some of the coastlines are hypothetical.

[4] The mean longitude of the four journals calculated by Fleurieu (Fleurieu 1791: 128). Port Praslin, as has been shown, may have been the passage used by the brigantine during its circumnavigation of Santa Ysabel in 1568.

[5] Fleurieu 1791: 129–44. Of particular interest is the recorded statement of the captured native that his father regularly made voyages of 10 or 12 days duration to 'a nation much less black than his own; that he there changed black men for white, and brought back also fine cloths, covered with designs' (Fleurieu 1791: 143). The reference seems likely to be to voyages to Ontong Java or, less probably, Sikaiana, and to the exchange of prisoners or slaves, with and the acquisition of tapa cloths from, its Polynesian inhabitants. [6] Magnetic bearings, variation 9° 20′ E.

to 26th enabled them to head to the eastwards. On the 26th they were again out of sight of land, and hoped that they had by now reached the most easterly limits of the archipelago. Towards noon on the 26th, however, a small island was sighted to the SE, 5 or 6 leagues distant, to which they gave the name *Inattendue*, and to the S of which could be seen more high land. The distance of the island from the high land to the S was estimated to be 8 or 9 leagues, its extent 2 or 3 leagues from E to W, and it appeared to be in 7° 54′ S or 7° 56′ S, 2° 4′ E of Port Praslin.[1]

It is immediately apparent that after losing sight of the coastline of Santa Ysabel when he left Port Praslin, Surville had fallen to the southwards and seen the mountainous central area of the same island. He had then headed eastwards to sight Ndai Island[2] (in 7° 55′ S and 2° 19′ E of Port Praslin) and the mountains of Malaíta to the southwards. Like his predecessor, Carteret, Surville also concluded that the land to the S of Inattendue was itself an island. Again like Carteret he seems to have failed to appreciate that it might extend to the southwards, for on the morning of the 27th, when he was to the SE of Inattendue, he saw more land between S¼ SE and SW (magnetic) which he concluded to be 'another island'.[3] This was of course the same land which he had seen to the S of Inattendue, the island of Malaíta, off the eastern coast of which he was now sailing. His latitude at noon on the 27th was observed to be 8° 20′ S, and he estimated his longitude to be 3° 2′ E of Port Praslin, remarking of the land that it was the highest which they had yet seen.

Little progress was made during the 27th and 28th, the weather being wet but calm and visibility bad, and at noon on the 28th the ship's position was estimated to be 8° 30′ S, 3° 25′ E of Port Praslin. At 3 in the afternoon the visibility cleared, and high mountains were sighted from the SSW to W at a distance of 10 leagues. At 5 p.m. openings in the land could be seen between W and SW, and on the 29th yet another was sighted. Fleurieu was constrained to note that it was a pity that Surville had not plotted these openings on his chart, but it seems fairly clear that the openings were in fact deceptions caused by the appearance of the higher land of South Malaíta and Maramasike from some distance off-shore, and that Surville himself, as he approached the land more closely, became aware of this.[4]

In the morning of 30 October an island was sighted 8 leagues to the S of SE, and the ship's noon latitude of 9° 20′ S and Surville's chart[5] are sufficient evidence for its identification with Ulawa, the island discovered by Mendaña's expedition, and named by them La Treguada. Surville was virtually becalmed in the vicinity of this island for three days, and in consequence named it the

---

[1] Fleurieu 1791: 146.   [2] Carteret's Gower's Island.   [3] Fleurieu 1791: 146.
[4] See the views of the coastline in Fleurieu 1791: Plate VI. He may have seen the opening between Malaíta and Maramasike which narrows into the Maramasike Passage.
[5] Fleurieu 1791: Plate III.

île des Contrariétés, estimating its latitude to be 9° 46′ S and its longitude to be 4° 20′ E of Port Praslin.[1] As the *St. Jean* lay off the island canoes came out and surrounded her. With presents and signs of friendship the French succeeded in inducing several of the indigenes aboard, including the chief or leader who, with signs of considerable amity towards Surville, endeavoured to persuade the French to go ashore. 'These demonstrations . . . did not inspire Surville with much confidence; the scene at Port Praslin was too recent in his memory',[2] but, in view of the need for refreshments for the scurvy-ridden crew, he sent the yawl towards the shore, well manned and armed. Scarcely had it left the ship before it was surrounded by canoes, the occupants of which began to fit arrows to their bows. Without more ado the French fired their muskets, dispersed the native fleet and retreated to the vessel. Undeterred, the indigenes returned to the attack, but Surville, anxious to 'lessen . . . the danger to which these brave islanders exposed themselves',[3] fired his guns as early as possible, minimizing their damage but causing his attackers to flee in terror.

At sunset on 2 November, as Surville sailed slowly to the S, more land 'having the appearance of an island' became visible to the S¼SE (magnetic). On the following morning two more were sighted which, with the former, made three small islands in line to which the name *les trois Soeurs* was given. Beyond, at what seemed to be a great distance, more land could be seen, and it is quite apparent from the description and Surville's chart that he had sighted the three islands[4] to which Mendaña's expedition had given the name La Tres Marías against the background of the northern coast of the island of Santiago or San Cristóval. During the afternoon of the 4th another island was sighted to the SSW of the most southerly of Les Trois Soeurs, which was named *île du Golfe* identifiable with Ugi, the Ysla de San Juan of Mendaña's discoveries. Anxious lest he be engulfed amongst the lands which lay to the westwards by the prevailing easterly winds, Surville stood close into the wind, and with considerable difficulty, cleared the coast of San Cristóval. At eight in the morning of the 5th some islets were seen dead ahead but at some distance, and at noon the latitude was determined by observation to be 10° 20′S. At sunset the *St. Jean* was 8 or 10 leagues from the islets, to which were given the name *îles de la Délivrance*, and which subsequently revealed themselves as two in number. They seemed to form the end of the archipelago, whilst the cape of the larger land to their W, to which was given the name *Cap Oriental*, seemed to terminate the mainland. As the vessel cleared the two islands, certainly identifiable with the islands of Santa Ana and Santa Catalina at the eastern extremity of San Cristóval, this supposition proved correct, and open sea lay ahead.

[1] Ulawa is in 9° 46′ S, 3° 40′ E of Port Praslin but, in view of the weather and ship's movement, it is hardly surprising that Surville's longitude had developed an error of 1° 10′ in the short distance sailed from Port Praslin.   [2] Fleurieu 1791: 155.   [3] Fleurieu 1761: 156.   [4] Olu Malau.

As Fleurieu remarks, the four authors of the journals were agreed that the 'vast extent of coast' along which they had sailed was in fact an archipelago of large and small islands,[1] a conclusion which the native captured at Port Praslin later confirmed. Since his crew were urgently in need of refreshment, Surville now determined to head for New Zealand, which he believed to be 'the nearest land to that which he was quitting',[2] and this he eventually made on 16 December. In the time between leaving the *Terres des Arsacides* (Lands of the Assassins), as he named the archipelago which he thought he had discovered, and leaving New Zealand on 1 January 1770, thirty-nine of the crew died of scurvy. Abandoning any further attempts at discovery, and presumably the commercial endeavour planned, Surville now headed for South America in an attempt to reach a European settlement before what were left of his complement were dead. Arriving off Callao on 8 April 1770, he himself was drowned when his yawl capsized crossing the Callao Bar, and after a delay of three years, during which nineteen of the crew died and twenty-five deserted, Surville's Lieutenant, M. Labé, raised a Spanish crew and eventually made Port l'Orient in August 1773.

Surville's contribution to the discovery and rediscovery of the Islands of Solomon, though he was totally unaware of it, was perhaps the most important of the three eighteenth-century contributions so far examined, for it provided, particularly in relation to the islands at the south-eastern extremity of the archipelago, knowledge of islands which could be identified with the discoveries recorded by the Spaniards. His longitudinal errors were to cause some slight confusion in the precise reconstruction of the archipelago, but this was a minor factor compared with the overall contribution which he had made. He had discovered part of the north coast of Bougainville's Choiseul or Mendaña's San Márcos; had coasted much of Santa Ysabel's northern shores, perhaps even anchoring in the very place through which the brigantine had passed during its circumnavigation of that island in 1568; had sighted the island previously discovered and named Gower's Island by Carteret; had coasted the eastern side of Malaíta or Ramos[3]; and had rediscovered Ulawa (La Treguada), Olu Malau (Las Tres Marías), Ugi (San Juan), San Cristóval or Santiago, Santa Ana and Santa Catalina. He had, in particular, provided approximate northern and eastern limits for the archipelago within which historians and hydrographers, with additional information at their disposal, were able to postulate the existence of the Islands of Solomon.

[1] Fleurieu 1791: 161.   [2] Fleurieu 1791: 162.
[3] As the Spaniards in 1568 had not done, though they had guessed at its general shape and overestimated its size.

Callander

The postulation of this assumption was not, however, to be made for several years, and in the meantime other ideas were presented and other activities absorbed the attention of those in Europe who were interested in the Pacific. Between 1766 and 1768 John Callander had produced his three-volume *Terra Australis Cognita or Voyages to the Terra Australis, or Southern Hemisphere, during the 16th 17th and 18th Centuries*, an edited version of de Brosses' *Histoire des Navigations*, in which he advocated for the English what de Brosses had advocated for the French: the discovery and colonization of *Terra Australis* and the settlement of Dampier's *Nova Britannia*. He acknowledged a slight indebtedness to de Brosses for the substance and purport of his work, but argued that 'from the nature of our government, the genius of our people, the skill and acknowledged bravery of our navigators' the treatise might 'meet with superior attention from a nation who, by the success of their maritime commerce, have raised themselves to the present distinguished rank they hold among the powers of Europe'.[1]

He reproduced de Brosses' accounts of the voyages of Mendaña, Quirós, le Maire and Tasman, in which the account of Mendaña's first voyage, with its errors, was based on 'Herera's Indian Geography *c.* 27, and the Portuguese History of Lopez Vaz'. Of Mendaña's first voyage he remarks that:

It was on this occasion that the isles called Solomon's . . . were first discovered, lying 800 leagues from the coast of Peru . . . They are situated betwixt the 7th and 12th parallels and towards the 210th meridian.[2] According to the Spanish charts, near 1500 leagues from Lima . . . The inhabitants are black, for the most part, but some of them are red, others white, and others fair; which made some imagine, that they bordered on New Guinea; but without any foundation, seeing the people of that country are black with curled hair.[3]

Remarking on Mendaña's discovery, Callander states that:

It is greatly to be lamented that the latitudes in which they lie are so carelessly laid down. This has produced abundance of confusion . . . Some geographers place them in 255° longitude: and thus there is a difference of a 1,000 leagues in their position. See De l'Isles charts. We must observe too that Mindana, during his second voyage with Quiros in 1595, found some islands under the 250 parallel, which he named after the Marquis of Mendoca . . . his crew took them to be the islands of Solomon. But Mindana told them they were wrong. . . . We are hence led to think, that the true isles called Salomons are those of Isabella, Santa Cruz, etc. lying about the 10° latitude, and 200–210° longitude. This too was the opinion of Gallego.[4]

---

[1] Callander: I: ii.

[2] 210° E of Ferro. He reproduces de Brosses' general chart (Callander 1768: II: front).

[3] Callander 1768: I: 277. He reproduced the two conflicting figures, 800 leagues and 1,500 leagues, recorded by sixteenth-century chroniclers.

[4] Callander 1768: I: 280–1. The longitudes are all E of Ferro.

In fact Callander himself, like de Brosses, reflects the confusion of his age in his acceptance of the current positioning of the Solomons in mid-Pacific. Notwithstanding his attribution of the discovery of the Solomons to Mendaña he remarks in relation to the voyage of Byron that:

The Islands of Solomon are said to have been discovered by Ferdinand de Quiros ... but though the Spaniards have at different times sent several persons in search of these islands, it was always without success: which must probably proceed either from the uncertainty of the latitude in which they are said to be found; or the whole being a fiction.[1]

Again, notwithstanding these remarks, he adds that:

The discoveries begun by Quiros and Mindana, have been little attended to, much less prosecuted, as their importance requires; none that we know of, having visited these latitudes on such a design during two centuries, excepting the Dutchman Roggewein: Schoulen, le Maire, Anson, and others, who have visited these seas, had quite other objects in view. They generally held one course across the Pacific Ocean, and nearly under the same parallels, though, as that intelligent mariner, Captain Rogers, justly observes, there remains a tract of 2,000 leagues of sea, extending from the line to the south pole, which has been little examined, and where, in all probability, there must be some large continent.

Alexander Dalrymple

The year 1769 saw the publication of Alexander Dalrymple's *An Account of the Discoveries made in the South Pacifick Ocean Previous to 1764*, the work of a man whose true contribution to the science of hydrography and to the thought of his day has yet to be fairly and properly assessed. His ... *Account of the Discoveries made in the South Pacifick* ... was in effect a statement of the evidence which Dalrymple believed justified his quite implicit faith in the existence of an austral and antipodean continent.[2] Largely compiled during the siege of Madras, between 1758 and 1759, it was printed in 1767 and eventually published in 1769. It consists of three sections, a 'Geographical Description of Places' an 'Examination of the conduct of the Discoverers in the Tracks they pursued', and 'Investigations of what may further be expected'. Accepting the classical arguments of terrestrial balance as a basic reason for believing in the existence of an austral continent, Dalrymple seems to have accepted, with what must at times be admitted to have been rash enthusiasm, all the evidence which could be mustered for his belief, from the supposed continental discovery of Juan Fernández to the reputed discovery of Theodore Gerrards in 1599:

One of the first Dutch who attempted to voyage into the South Sea, who, after passing the Streights of Magellan, being carried by tempests into 64° South, in that height the country was mountainous and covered with snow, looking like Norway, and seemed to extend towards the Islands of Solomon, that is to the North-western.[3]

[1] Callander 1768: III: 711.
[2] For his belief in the existence of the austral continent see Dalrymple 1773.
[3] Dalrymple 1767: 101–2.

It is all too easy to treat Dalrymple's convictions lightly, for, although the tenacity with which he clung to them in the face of mounting contrary evidence may have been indicative of something less than a scholarly search for truth, at the time when his first major work went to the press there did seem to be considerable if at times doubtful evidence for those convictions.

The voyage of Wallis seemed to add support to the earlier report of continental land in the South Pacific, and Robertson, the Master of the *Dolphin*, never lost faith in his impression that land lay to the S of Tahiti, an impression which he had first obtained on 17 June 1767, shortly before Tahiti was sighted. Even after the Tahitians had informed the English that Tahiti was an island, and not the northern promontory which Robertson thought it to be, he criticized Wallis for failing to head S,[1] and it is certain that Dalrymple had seen the note, probably written by Lord Egmont between 20 May 1768, and 26 February 1769, in Robert Molyneux's[2] journal,[3] which referred to Wallis sighting land 20 leagues S of George's Island (Tahiti).

In his *Account of the Discoveries made . . . Previous to 1764* Dalrymple sidestepped the question of the Islands of Solomon and their identity and position, a question which he was to examine in more detail in a later publication, by limiting the scope of his discourse; but on a *Chart of the South Pacifick Ocean Pointing out the Discoveries made therein Previous to 1764*, which accompanies this work, he firmly identifies them with Dampier's *Nova Britannia* and the south-eastern extremity of New Guinea. Initially his source material for the Spanish voyages was necessarily limited to the account of Herrera for Mendaña's first voyage; to a mutilated version of Figueroa published by Thevenot for Mendaña's second voyage[4]; to the accounts of Torquemada and some of Quirós' *memoriales* for Quirós' voyage of 1605–6[5]; and to the *memorial* of Arias. On the evidence of these sources alone he not only postulated the identification of the Islands of Solomon with New Guinea and *Nova Britannia*, but also deduced Torres' track between New Guinea and New Holland and the certain insularity of the former. His identification of the Islands of Solomon with this locality may have been independently achieved, but it seems more than likely that it owed much, in its initial inception at least, to those charts which identified the 'Southern' Solomons (Guadalcanal, etc.) with the Hooch Landt (New Ireland's north-east coast) of le Maire,[6] and de l'Isle's *L'Hémisphère Méridional* of post 1740, which delineated Dampier's Passage between New Britain and New Guinea as the '*Passage de Dampiere ou Guadalcanal*'. The identification may have been espoused by Dampier,[7] and it

---

[1] Carrington 1948: xxvii–xxix.   [2] Master's Mate on the *Dolphin*.
[3] BM: Egmont MSS. (No. 157).
[4] He later acquired a copy of Figueroa and of Quirós' report to de Morga.
[5] He later acquired a copy of Torres' letter.
[6] See, for example, du Val's *La Mer de Sud* of 1679.   [7] Woodford 1890: 417.

certainly had some support in the assertion of Arias that Torres had sighted land near New Guinea which he took to be *New Guadalcanal*.[1]

The identification of Guadalcanal with the charted coastline at the south-eastern extremity of New Guinea reputedly discovered by the *Geelvink*, and of the remainder of the Solomons with Dampier's *Nova Britannia*, was slightly modified by Dalrymple in the detailed argument and charts contained in his *An Historical Collection of the Several Voyages and Discoveries in the South Pacific Ocean*, published in London in 1770. In a section headed 'Of the Salomon Islands'[2] he remarks that:

Not only our writers, but the Spaniards themselves have committed great errors in re-capitulating the discoveries of these islands: it is, therefore, requisite to treat the subject with the utmost attention, in order to avoid the confusion and perplexity which has been introduced from the want of a cautious examination of authorities.[3]

He then proceeds to explain how, many years before, he had been struck by the similarity between de Bry's Pacific map of 1596 and Dampier's chart of *Nova Britannia*, a similarity which he concluded could only derive from their delineation of the same lands. He describes in some detail how he reconstructed the chart of the Solomons, but his two charts are largely self-explanatory.[4] To Dampier's chart of *Nova Britannia* and New Guinea he added, in the manner of some contemporary cartographers, the supposed discoveries of the *Geelvink* at the south-eastern extremity, and produced in effect the New Guinea coast-line laid down by de Bry. Using Herrera's description of the archipelago, Dalrymple then proceeded to fill in the detail of the Islands of Solomon within the bounds of Dampier's *Nova Britannia*, arguing that the latter had only circumnavigated the area without exploring it, and adducing evidence of straits and an archipelago from references in Dampier's narrative. The details of his reconstruction are not immediately relevant, for they were incorrect, but Dalrymple had made a very near guess, on what at times were perfectly proper basic assumptions. He argued that:

Not only DE BRY's, but all the old maps, call the Assemblage of Islands adjoining to this part of New Guinea, the SALOMON islands, and it is the modern maps only which appropriate this name to islands in the middle of the ocean. ORTELIUS'S maps, 1587, and 1589, lay them down at the termination of NEW-GUINEA, from 1 deg. to 11 deg. S. Lat. The extent eastward is protracted beyond all measure, comprehending 20 deg. of longitude. The two draughts do not agree, and both seem to be laid down at random: of all the ancient charts, DE BRY's seems to be the best and most explanatory.[5]

In relying on those sixteenth-century charts which laid the Solomons down in close proximity to New Guinea Dalrymple was correct, even though they had laid them down as a result of a misconception and underestimate of the

---

[1] Markham 1904: II: 526.   [2] Dalrymple 1770: I: 16–21.   [3] Dalrymple 1770: I: 16.
[4] See Dalrymple 1770: I: facing 16.   [5] Dalrymple 1770: I: 19–20.

relative distance of New Guinea from Perú. Herrera's own map he dismissed as the 'work of some bungling geographer',[1] and he pointed out quite rightly that 'though it will be no difficult matter to trace Herrera in the plan,[2] the size he gives of all the islands is vastly greater than what DAMPIER's observations confine us to'.

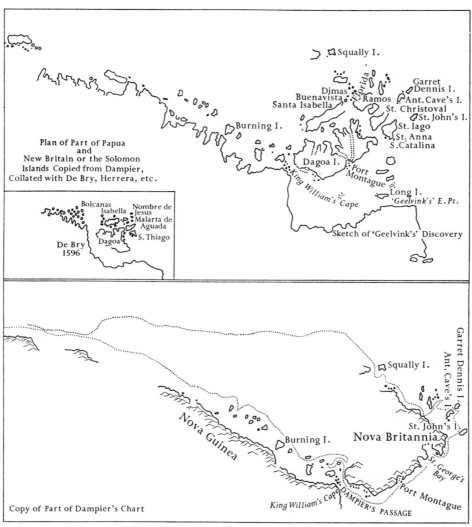

Map XXXVII Two charts from Dalrymple's *An Historical Collection of Voyages* of 1770, redrawn

Dalrymple's identification depended on the assumption that the latitude ascribed to the Islands of Solomon on early charts and in early references were incorrect, although in fact the latitudes were the only really reliable information

[1] Dalrymple 1770: I: 19. One must at times admire the forthrightness of Dalrymple's phrases.
[2] i.e. to follow Herrera's description of the Islands of Solomon on Dampier's chart.

relating to the Islands of Solomon recorded by the discoverers and reproduced by later cartographers and chroniclers. As he wrote:

HERRERA's latitudes, as well as DE BRY's, exceed the truth by many degrees, ISABELLA being placed by them between 8 and 9 deg. S. instead of 4 deg. to 5 deg. S. This error in the latitude has been the great source of the confusion we meet with, and has prevented it from being observed, that the SALOMON islands, discovered in 1567, are in fact NEW-BRITAIN, as a due comparison of DE BRY's map, and HERRERA's description with DAMPIER will plainly evince. The situation of these islands at the extremity of NEW-GUINEA, one would have imagined, pointed this fact too clearly to have been overlooked by geographers, but DANVILLE has not comprehended this part in his map of ASIA, and there is no other modern who deserves the name.[1]

His deductions on the identity of the Islands of Solomon received, as in their time they deserved to receive, support and acceptance. Forrest, in his *Voyage to New Guinea... 1774, 1775 and 1776*, reproduced Dalrymple's comparative charts[2] and, paying tribute to his research, remarked that his identification of Solomon's islands with *Nova Britannia*:

has so far been verified by Captain Carteret's discovering a strait through the middle of New Britain. But a map published by Linschoten in 1695, puts the matter beyond all doubt, as in that map the islands at the east extremity of New Guinea are absolutely named Solomon's islands.[3]

Dalrymple's contribution to the rediscovery and recognition of the Islands of Solomon was to draw attention to the information of the earliest charts that they lay in close proximity to New Guinea, with the possible consequent deduction that the longitudes estimated by the Spaniards in 1567–8 had been in error. It could have been validly argued in reply that the Spaniards had no reason for charting the Solomons close to New Guinea, other than the suspicions of Gallego and Quirós that they were close, and the fact that sixteenth-century charts underestimated the width of the Pacific and placed New Guinea (and only the western and known half of New Guinea at that) to the E of its true position. It could, however, have been argued in reply again, and with even more validity, that the underestimate of the width of the Pacific and the easterly error in the location of New Guinea were themselves partly the result of, and were not immediately appreciated because of, the very same factors which had caused the distance of the Solomons from Perú to be underestimated. Indeed, as the position of New Guinea relative to Perú had been corrected, so the position of the Islands of Solomon should have been corrected with it.

Dalrymple's identification of the Islands of Solomon with Dampier's *Nova Britannia* brought into the open the choice which had to be made, between the evidence which indicated that the Islands of Solomon were in close proximity to New Guinea, and the evidence of the longitudinal estimate of the Spaniards which indicated that the Solomons were well to the east of New Guinea. The

[1] Dalrymple 1770: I: 19.   [2] Forrest 1779: Plate XIV.   [3] Forrest 1779: iv–viii.

two were in conflict, and whilst most eighteenth-century cartographers had so far relied on the latter, in one of its several recorded forms or one of the several ways in which it could be regarded,[1] Dalrymple relied on the former, and he at least had land to show in the position in which he claimed the Solomons lay. It was land, moreover, which bore a striking resemblance to the general outline of the Solomons as they were delineated on one sixteenth-century chart, and which, with some ingenuity, could be reconciled with Herrera's description of the archipelago. On the evidence available, and until the voyages of Carteret, Bougainville and Surville revealed the presence of land to the SE of *Nova Britannia* and the possibility that the latitudes of the Spaniards might have been correct, Dalrymple's deductions were scholarly and reasonable, and were in fact a very near approximation to the truth.

Cook and Latouche-Tréville

When Cook set sail from England in 1768 on the first of his three great voyages of discovery in the Pacific, a voyage for which Dalrymple's writings were in part responsible, five questions loomed large in the minds of those interested in that sea. These were the existence and extent of the supposed antarctic antipodean continent; the easterly extent of New Holland; the eastern limits of New Zealand; the possibility of a passage from the Atlantic to the Pacific N of Canada; and the existence and position of the Islands of Solomon. Tasman had shown that New Holland was not a part of a southern and antarctic continent, but he had given no indication of its easterly limits, and although Bougainville had disproved the likelihood of Quirós' Espíritu Santo being joined to New Guinea, and had penetrated as far W as the Great Barrier Reef, it was Cook who, in 1770, discovered and charted the eastern limits of New Holland and who, with the help of Dalrymple's Pacific chart on which the deduced route of Torres had been laid down, passed through the Torres Straits and showed conclusively that New Guinea was separated from New Holland. Moreover, by his circumnavigation of New Zealand he disproved the suggestion that it might be the western coastline of an antipodean and antarctic continent, and dealt a considerable blow to Dalrymple's theory of such a continent.[2] It was a blow which was considerably strengthened by the

[1] They could, for instance, rely on the 1,500 leagues recorded in Herrera, the 800 leagues recorded in Acosta and also in Herrera, or the 1,610 leagues recorded in Figueroa. They could, alternatively, rely on the 1,850 leagues recorded in Figueroa as the distance of Santa Cruz from Perú, calculating the position of the Solomons relative to it. They could vary these figures in accordance with particular deductions, arguing, for instance, that the 1,610 leagues from Perú to the Baxos de la Candelaria of Figueroa should be reduced to 1,550 or 1,500 leagues to give the position of the eastern extremities of the Solomons; they could attempt to calculate a mean figure; or finally, they could interpret Iberian leagues as degrees in one of several ways.

[2] For Cook's first voyage of 1768–71 see Beaglehole 1955.

additional fact that he had sailed SW from Cape Horn to 60° S, and S of Tahiti to 40° S, without sighting land. Although Cook did not attempt to search for the Islands of Solomon, the Spanish authorities seem to have thought that he did, and in a despatch of 9 October 1771, to the Viceroy of Perú, the Secretary of State for the Indies reported with some vagueness that:

From the said island [Otaheite] they passed on to the Isle of Dogs, whence they went unsuccessfully in search of those called on the maps the Isles of Solomon, and being satisfied that they do not exist, they proceeded southwards to examine New Zealand.[1]

By his second voyage of 1772–5 Cook provided a complete negation of the idea of an antarctic continent, as it had been postulated by Dalrymple, by sailing so extensively throughout the South Pacific as to indicate the impossibility of anything other perhaps than large islands existing north of the 65th parallel, and the inaccessibility or unattractiveness of any continental land which might exist in higher latitudes. Moreover, he did this, not only in the South Pacific, but, equally importantly, in the South Atlantic and South Indian Oceans as well. His second voyage was an astonishing accomplishment, in its achievements far exceeding his instructions, and revealing an interest and ability on Cook's part which has not been exceeded in the annals of maritime discovery.[2] It was unfortunate that his voyage had the effect of discrediting Dalrymple to posterity, though much of this was Dalrymple's own fault and due to his dogmatic acceptance of the available evidence for an antipodean continent, and it was hardly Cook's fault that he became, as Beaglehole has put it, 'a sort of executioner—the executioner of misbegotten hypotheses'.[3]

It may, in view of the sum total of Cook's achievements, be unreasonable to lament the fact that when he visited the New Hebrides, although he had ample time and adequate supplies, he did not proceed to the NW to explore the little known area of ocean which concealed the Islands of Solomon. Nevertheless, his exploration and charting of the New Hebrides was one of the triumphs of the voyage, and his identification of Quirós' Espíritu Santo with a greater accuracy than his predecessor Bougainville was a considerable contribution to the reconstruction and reappraisal of the Spanish discoveries of the late sixteenth and early seventeenth centuries.

Whilst Cook was on his second voyage, a young French naval officer, Louis René Madeleine le Vassor de Latouche-Tréville, made a proposal to the French government for a voyage of exploration and annexation to the South coast of New Holland.[4] His proposal was rejected, but when at the end of July

---

[1] Corney 1908: 66–68.   [2] For Cook's second voyage see Beaglehole 1961.
[3] Beaglehole 1961: ci.
[4] Forsyth 1959: 115–29; and Beaglehole 1961: 695–6, 700–3, provide the necessary information relating to Latouche-Tréville. Forsyth examined the proposal in detail and illustrated its defects (Forsyth 1959: 119).

1775, Cook returned to England, Latouche-Tréville wrote to him congratulating him on his success. Cook replied and invited him to continue the correspondence. With Cook's letter to support his case, Latouche-Tréville sought the Minister of Marine's permission to answer it and to bring the matter of a Pacific voyage of exploration once more to the attention of the King. He again wrote to Cook who, on 10 February 1776, replied from London, informing him that he was about to set out on a third voyage to the Pacific and assuring him that there was plenty there to occupy them both. Referring to those areas which he felt might usefully be explored, he suggested that the area between 10° S and 10° N, particularly the lands discovered by Bougainville and Surville to the SE of New Guinea, deserved attention.

Je crois qu'il serait à propos d'examiner avec plus d'exactitude la terre qui a été découverte par Ms. Surville et Bougainville. Je parle des terres qui touchent la Nouvelle Guinée. Il est à presumer qu'elles peuvent produire des épices ou quelque article précieux pour le commerce . . . Les géographes aussi bien que les navigateurs diffèrent d'opinions sur la situation des isles nommées de Salomon. La route que j'ai marquée éclaircira ce point.[1]

Cook did not suggest that the Islands of Solomon might be the lands discovered by Bougainville and Surville, but he was correct in his suggestion that the exploration of the Pacific W from the Marquesas to the discoveries of Surville and Bougainville, on an equatorial belt from 10° N to 10° S, would clarify the question of their existence or position. In fact Latouche-Tréville never made his proposed voyage, and when the French government did decide to initiate a voyage of Pacific exploration it was under another commander.

Pingré

In 1767 European attention had been directed towards the South Pacific by the need to select a suitable site for the observation of the transit of Venus in 1769, and it was with this particular object that Cook had been instructed to remain for some time at Tahiti. In France the question was taken up by Alexandre Guy Pingré, *Chanoine Régulier et Bibliothécaire de Sainte Geneviève*, and in preparation for it he had, in 1766, translated Figueroa's account of the Spanish discoveries. In 1767 he produced his *Mémoire sur le choix et l'état des lieux ou le passage de Venus du 3 Juin 1769 pourra être observé* . . . , and his views, and a map[2] which he drew to illustrate them, were subsequently incorporated in his *Mémoire sur les découvertes faite dans la Mer du Sud avant les derniers voyages des Anglois et des François autour du monde* of 1778. He threw little light on the question of the Islands of Solomon, for he accepted their position as being between 7°–11° S and 205°–215° E of Ferro (85°–95° W of Lima) in the manner of many contemporary charts, and argued accordingly that:

[1] Beaglehole 1961: 700-1.   [2] Pingré 1778: map at end.

L'Archipel des isles de Salomon forme une espece de chaîne très advantageusement placée, pour arrêter les Astronomes qui jusque-là n'auroient pu trouver de lieu propre à l'observation de Vénus. La Martiniere dit que cet Archipel s'étend depuis le septieme dégré de latitude méridionale jusqu'au Tropique du Capricorne, et je pense qu'il a raison.[1]

He rejected the idea that Santa Cruz was one of the islands in the archipelago, as some eighteenth-century cartographers had delineated it, arguing that the reported distance of Santa Cruz from Perú was 1,850 Spanish leagues (*'donc vers 193 dégrés de longitude'*, i.e. 193° E of Ferro),[2] and that:

il n'est pas possible de donner plus de longitude[3] a l'isle de Ste Croix. Les isles de Guadalcanar & de S. Christophe, que nous avons vu ci-dessus être à peu-près sous le même parallele que l'isle de Ste. Croix, ne sont qu'à 1500 ou 1550 lieues de Lima. Pour confondre une de ces isles avec celle de Ste. Croix, il faudroit dire que Hernan Gallego se seroit trompé de 300 lieues Espagnoles sur la distance de Lima aux isles de Salomon, c'est- à-dire, d'une cinquieme partie de toute sa route. Il n'est pas facile de soupçonner d'une erreur si grossiere un Pilot célébre, qui navigeoit depuis 45 ans.[4]

He had taken the 1,450 leagues from Lima to the Ysla de Jesús and the 160 leagues from Ysla de Jesús to the Baxos de la Candelaria recorded in Figueroa's *Hechos de Don García . . . de Mendoza . . .* to make a total of 1,610 leagues, and had deduced from the description of the archipelago given in the same source that the eastern extremities of the archipelago lay approximately 1,500–1,550 leagues from Perú,[5] or 215° E of Ferro (85° of Lima) as he interpreted it.[6] His deductions, the result of some thought and comparative study of the available source material, were the reverse of those of Dalrymple, for Pingré is perhaps the best example of those cartographers who placed their reliance on the re-corded distance of the Solomons from Perú estimated by their discoverers, and who, as he himself put it, found it difficult to imagine that Gallego might have made a gross error in his estimate.

The Recognition of the Islands of Solomon

The next significant contribution to the recognition of the identity and position of the Islands of Solomon came from Buâche, a French scholar who, on 9 January 1781, presented a memoir to the French Royal Academy of Science on the existence and situation of the Islands of Solomon.[7] His memoir opened with the statement that whilst recent voyages had furnished much knowledge concerning the South Sea, they had at the same time given rise to

---

[1] Pingré 1778.   [2] As it is laid down in his chart.
[3] i.e. longitude E of Ferro.   [4] Pingré 1778: 39.
[5] He noted the contradictory figures of 1,500 leagues and 800 leagues recorded by Herrera.

[6] Pingré 1778: 22, 39. 1,500 Iberian leagues would be approximately 85° of longitude if it was as-sumed that 17½ Iberian leagues did in fact constitute an equatorial degree. Pingré lays the Solomons down extending over 10° of longitude so that they are bisected by the meridian of 210° E of Ferro (90° W of Lima or 170° W of Paris).

[7] Reproduced in Fleurieu 1791: 309–23.

doubts respecting the existence of the Islands of Solomon, and had induced several geographers either to expunge them from their charts or to recommend their removal.

It was for some time rather usual to deny the existence of every country, which was not found at the place assigned to it by the charts; while on the other hand, all those lands which were found in tracts of sea where there were not any marked in the charts, were considered as new discoveries. The more enlightened navigators of the present time, when their researches prove unsuccessful, draw no other conclusion, than that the lands they are unable to find have been ill placed upon their geographical charts; and, before they give a new name to any island that does not appear there, consider attentively all those that appear in the same tracts and at the same latitudes. In the present case, to be qualified to deny the existence of Solomon Islands with any reason, it would be necessary to have sought them in all the situations which different authors have assigned, which has not yet been done. I have examined this point of geography with attention; and it has appeared to me, that to any one who has not made a vow of scepticism, the existence of these islands is sufficiently demonstrated by the accounts of Mendana's voyages. I have also thought that, with the knowledge we now have of the South Sea, we may be able to ascertain their position more precisely, and make them easier to be found by other navigators.[1]

Referring to the accounts of Figueroa, to the fact that Mendaña did depart on a second expedition to his discoveries, and to Quirós' conviction of their existence, as evidence for the certain existence of the Islands of Solomon, Buâche argued that Byron and Carteret had failed to find them because they had only looked for them in places assigned to them on the charts.

Byron observes that having advanced to ten degrees west of the position assigned to them by the French charts of the South Sea, he thought it necessary to abandon the search ... Carteret, in like manner observes, that he had advanced far beyond the situation attributed to them; and that, having arrived at the island of Santa Cruz, which he re-discovered, he gave up the attempt.[2]

He pointed out that two pieces of evidence existed for the determination of the position of the Islands of Solomon; their latitudes recorded by the Spaniards and the distance at which the Spaniards had estimated them to lie from Perú. The former, he argued, would not have been subject to more than inconsiderable errors, and the latter could be used to determine the longitude of the islands within a few degrees, by relating it to the time taken.

Buâche then turned to the evidence of those charts on which the Solomons had been laid down, in an attempt to explain their discrepancies and contradictions. He stressed, as Dalrymple had done, that the earliest charts laid the Islands of Solomon down 'to the east of New Guinea, and at no great distance from it', and cited as examples the charts of de Bry (1596), Witfliet (1597), Herrera, Ortelius (1589) and 'an ancient Portuguese chart of the East Indies, inserted in Thevenot's curious collection of voyages'.[3] This delineation had

---

[1] Fleurieu 1791: 309–10.   [2] Fleurieu 1791: 313.
[3] The chart by João Teixeira (1649) in Thevenot's *Relations des Divers Voyages Curieux*.

persisted until 1646, when Robert Dudley, in his *Arcano del Mare*, had transposed the position of the islands to that of the Marquesas on the grounds that they had been discovered 800 'Spanish' leagues W of Lima and that though they were commonly delineated at 1,800 leagues this was false.

He referred to Delisle's (de l'Isle) initial acceptance of Dudley's delineation, his adoption in 1714 of the estimated distance of the Solomons from Perú of 1,635 'Spanish' leagues and consequent delineation of the islands in 205° E of Ferro, and his final delineation of the Islands of Solomon in 190° E of Ferro[1] on his world-map of 1720, 'determined . . . by the journals of the discoverers, and by tracing their voyages'.[2] He then turned to Bellin, and showed how in 1741 he had begun by placing the Solomons 195° E of Ferro and had justified his delineation in his *Observations on the Construction of the Latter Chart*[3] but how in 1756 he had moved them to 205° E of Ferro,[4] a position also adopted by Green. Danville had adopted what Buâche termed a 'mean position' 200° E of Ferro,[5] but had then omitted the Islands of Solomon from his charts altogether. Finally, he referred to Pingré, who plotted the Solomons on the meridian of 210° E of Ferro,[6] and to Dalrymple's identification of the Solomons with *Nova Britannia*, noting the major flaw in the latter's willingness to accept that the latitudes determined by the discoverers of the archipelago might have been in error by as much as 5 or 6 degrees.

Turning to the chronicles of Acosta, Herrera, López Vaz, Ovalle, Figueroa and Witfliet, a *memorial* by Quirós and the writings of Sir Richard Hawkins, Buâche summarized the often conflicting information which they contained relating to the position of the Islands of Solomon, and dismissed as a gross error the 800 leagues stated by Acosta, Herrera and López Vaz as their distance from Perú. Taking the 1,500 leagues of Quirós' *memorial* and the 1,610 leagues of Figueroa, he suggested that both these figures were underestimates resulting from a failure to allow for current, that:

Mendana, in his first voyage, being as yet unacquainted with this effect of currents and winds, which bore him away perpetually to the west, must have estimated his way at much less than the truth; and his distance, computed at 1,610 leagues, must be much less than it really was.[7]

---

[1] i.e. 110° W of Lima, 170° E of Paris. This delineation seems probably to have been based on Quirós' estimate of 1,850 leagues from Lima to Santa Cruz, and the deduction that the Solomons lay to the W of the latter, the value of the league being taken at 17½ to the degree (110° = 1,925 leagues).

[2] Fleurieu 1791: 315. Buâche did not note that de l'Isle had moved the Solomons yet again to 180° E of Ferro, 160° E of Paris.

[3] 195° E of Ferro, 175° E of Paris, 105° W of Lima. I have not seen Bellin's *Observations* but it seems likely that his estimate of 105° W of Lima was based on Quirós' estimate of 1,850 leagues to Santa Cruz.   [4] Probably following de l'Isle's second stage.

[5] It may have been a mean of contemporary delineations, but it could also have been based on the 1,500 leagues recorded in Herrera, etc. (200° E of Ferro = 100° W of Lima or 180° E of Paris), on the assumption that 15 'Spanish' leagues constituted a degree.

[6] 90° W of Lima, 170° W of Paris.   [7] Fleurieu 1791: 321.

and pointed to Bougainville's observation that:

...all the navigators who have crossed the South Sea have fallen in with New Guinea, much sooner than they ought by their reckoning; and that, consequently, they have given this sea a much smaller extent from east to west than in truth it has: this error he attributes to the effect of favourable winds and currents in that ocean, not taken into their account.[1]

He expressed his preference for the 1,850 leagues from Perú to Santa Cruz recorded by Figueroa after Quirós, indicating that this agreed with the 2,500 English leagues which Hawkins had seen recorded as the distance of the Solomons from Perú 'in a manuscript belonging to the Viceroy of Peru'.[2] In fact Buâche was wrong in this belief, for Hawkins recorded that the distance which he had learnt in Perú was 750 leagues,[3] and even if Hawkins had recorded the distance as 2,500 leagues, it would still not have been correct, as Buâche asserted that:

These 1,850 leagues [i.e. recorded by Figueroa after Quiros from Lima to Santa Cruz], reckoned at the proportion of 15 to a degree, as we find them in the memoirs of the early Spanish navigators, answer exactly to 2,500 English leagues of 20 to a degree.[4]

He then argued that Carteret's voyage had indicated that Santa Cruz lay in 162° 20' E of Paris (164° 40' E of Greenwich),[5] and that Bougainville's voyage had revealed that the eastern extremity of New Guinea lay in 149° 52' E of Paris.[6] From this he concluded that $12\frac{1}{2}°$ of longitude or 247 leagues[7] remained between Santa Cruz and New Guinea, and that the middle of this space would be 156° E of Paris (158° 20' E of Greenwich). This position would be 'just 2,400 French marine leagues from the coast of Peru, the exact distance assigned by Richard Hawkins and Figueroa',[8] and in this position Bougainville, Surville and Carteret had all sighted islands 'which appear to have all the character of those of Solomon'.

M. de Bougainville saw the western part of them, in seven degrees south latitude; and what he reports of the inhabitants of Choiseul Bay, agrees with the description given by Mendana of the natives of the Archipelago discovered by him. M. de Surville was in sight of these lands for the space of 130 leagues, and from the 7th to the 11th degree of latitude ... and what he relates (of the people) is equally conformable to the recital of Mendana. In the same

---

[1] Fleurieu 1791: 320–1. This was rather a bland over-simplification, and something of an overstatement, but basically it was correct.

[2] Fleurieu 1791: 318.   [3] A point which has already been examined.

[4] Fleurieu 1791: 321. Buâche's calculation is quite obvious. If the Spanish league had been 1/15th of an equatorial degree, then 1,850 leagues would have represented 123°, nearly the same distance as 2,500 English leagues reckoned at 20 leagues to the equatorial degree, 125°.

[5] This was almost correct. Carteret had calculated at Santa Cruz that Cape Byron lay 164° 49' E of London.

[6] Bougainville had calculated the longitude of the Cap de la Delivrance, i.e. the eastern extremity of the Louisiade Archipelago as 151° 30' E of Paris, and this was taken as the eastern extremity of New Guinea.   [7] i.e. leagues at 20 to the degree.   [8] Fleurieu 1791: 322.

sea, Carteret, in 1767, had discovered two small islands, which he named Gower's and Simpson's Islands, but was far from imagining that they belonged to the Islands of Solomon, which he had sought so long.[1]

Buâche concluded by remarking that:

Till our navigators shall complete their discoveries in this interesting and little known portion of the globe, I think I can with confidence assert, that The Lands of the Arsacides and Choiseul Bay, are parts of the Archipelago discovered by Mendana; and, consequently that the Islands of Solomon are actually about 1850 Spanish leagues distant from the coast of Peru, and in the vicinity of New Guinea, as the early charts had indicated.[2]

He could indeed make this assertion with confidence, for it was tolerably correct, but it was not entirely correct for the reasons which Buâche imagined. He had based his deduction on two assumptions, the first of which may have been inadequately considered, the second of which was false. In the first place he relied on the evidence of sixteenth-century charts which laid the Solomons down in close proximity to New Guinea, evidence which, though correct, depended on nothing more than the conclusions of Gallego and Quirós that this was so. However, his reference to Bougainville's remark that navigators had failed to appreciate the westerly setting current, and had consequently underestimated the width of the Pacific, may indicate that he realized that, whilst the Pacific's width had originally been underestimated and New Guinea charted to the E of its true position because of an underestimate of the terrestrial circumference, the westerly current and limitations of navigation concealed these errors even after several westerly trans-Pacific voyages. Since these same factors had probably caused Gallego to underestimate the distance of the Solomons from Perú, it could be assumed that the approximate distance of the Solomons from Perú could be determined from the proportion of that estimated distance to the distance at which New Guinea was laid down from Perú on late sixteenth-century charts, bearing in mind that those charts had only laid down the western half of New Guinea. That he was thinking in these terms is perhaps evidenced by his statement that the distance estimated by the discoverers could be related to the time taken over the voyage, to arrive at an approximate longitude, for the time would only have had value in proportion to the time taken by other navigators to sail from the Americas to, say, the Moluccas or Philippines.

Nevertheless, his major argument, that the lands discovered by Bougainville lay 2,500 English leagues, 2,400 French leagues or 1,850 'Spanish' leagues from Perú, was based on the false assumptions that Hawkins had reported the Solomons to lie 2,500 English leagues from Perú; that 1,850 'Spanish' leagues, the distance in fact estimated from Perú to Santa Cruz, corresponded with the latter distance; and that a position at that distance would be on the meridian of

---

[1] Fleurieu 1791: 322-3.   [2] Fleurieu 1791: 323.

156° E of Paris (158° 20′ E of Greenwich). In fact a position 1,850 Iberian leagues W of Lima, in 10° S, would have been very slightly to the W of 100° W of Lima, i.e. in 180° E of Paris (200° E of Ferro, 182° 20′ E of Greenwich),[1] but as a result of his false assumption Buâche did postulate the perfectly correct statement that the Islands of Solomon were bisected by 156° E of Paris (158° 20′ E of Greenwich), for 158° 20′ E of Greenwich is the meridian of the north-western extremity of the island of Santa Ysabel. He had in fact done little more than de l'Isle had implied on his charts, when the latter laid the Solomons down 180° E of Ferro (160° E of Paris) and named Dampier's Passage the *Passage de Dampiere ou Guadalcanal*, but he had justified his delineation in detail and had provided reasons which, in his day, were convincing.[2] He had in fact identified the Islands of Solomon.

The Voyage of Franzisco Antonio Mourelle (Maurelle)[3]

That the Spaniards, the discoverers of the Islands of Solomon, should have made one last sortie to the archipelago at this juncture, when the truth of their discoveries had been almost completely proved, is perhaps in the proper order of things. That this last sortie was accidental, and that it made only one minor contribution to the rediscovery and recognition of the group— albeit a contribution which inaccurate navigation rendered confusing rather than enlightening—is also perhaps appropriate to the mass of confusion which is the epic of the discovery, rediscovery and recognition of the Islands of Solomon.

In 1780 *Don* Franzisco Antonio Mourelle was appointed to Manila as a major of marines, charged with the defence and survey of the port of Cavite. On his arrival, however, he was appointed to the command of the *fragata La Princesa* or *Nuestra Señora de la Rosario*, and was ordered to put to sea bearing sealed instructions which he was not to open until 12 leagues out. These orders, which he opened on 25 August 1780, instructed him to repair to Siciran, a port on the east coast of Luzon, and there to await the further pleasure of Government. Arriving at Siciran on 3 September, he received into his care a box which he was instructed to bear with all haste to the Viceroy of México, sailing immediately for San Blaz or Acapulco.[4]

[1] 1,850 Iberian leagues = 7,400 Roman miles = 5,920 Nautical miles ÷ 59 (at 59 nautical miles to the degree in 10° S) = 100° (approximately).

[2] A chart demonstrating Buâche's identification of the Islands of Solomon and the delineations of other geographers was included in Fleurieu's *Découvertes des François . . .* of 1790 (Fleurieu 1791: Plate XII).   [3] Rendered as Maurelle by French writers.

[4] The primary source of information relating to this voyage is a MS. in the Archivo General de Indias, Sevilla (AGI; Guadalajara 520). It consists of a copy of Mourelle's narrative journal of the voyage lodged in the Viceroy of México's secretariat and entitled *Navegacion hecha por el Alferez del Navio dela Real Armada y Command^{te} dela del Rey nombrada la Princessa, Don Franz^{co} Antonio Mourelle*

That he should have received such orders is strange, for repeated failures had established the impossibility of making the passage from the Philippines to México other than during the season of westerly winds after the month of June, and Mourelle was faced with the prospect of attempting a route S of the equator. Whilst his own statement that:

I . . . considered myself as going to undertake a voyage absolutely new, over tracks of the ocean unknown till that time . . . (and) . . . I may therefore conclude that the track I pursued had never been traced by any navigator,[1]

was an overstatement, his trepidation at making such a voyage, for which he was himself ill-prepared, and for which his vessel was ill-furnished and ill-equipped, is understandable, even though the reader may be excused for tiring of his perpetual references to his own diligence, prudence and zeal to deliver the box to México.

Putting to sea on 21 November, Mourelle passed through the Carolines and crossed the line on 29 December. Passing to the N of the Admiralty Islands and New Ireland,[2] he came on 18 January to 3° 48' S, 27° 9' E of San Bernardino[3]; and on that day a high coast was sighted to the SW which he at first took to be Nueva Bretaña (i.e. Dampier's *Nova Britannia* or New Ireland) but which he subsequently identified as San Juan (St. John).[4] The longitudes of the log-book and the relevant chart in the Museo Naval do not agree, though it may be concluded that the latter, the result of reflection and correction, is probably the more reliable. It is, however, apparent from a reconstruction of his route, and the chart, that Mourelle was indeed off the island of St. John (4° S, 153° 40' E). As the voyage is of marginal significance it would be inappropriate to reproduce here the detailed reconciliation of the available

. . . 1781 (57 ff), a glossary of native words (1 f), a table of positions (2 ff), a table of daily positions (1 f), and the log-book of the pilot, Vásquez, entitled *Diario de la Navegacion Executada por Don Jose Antonio Vasquez primer Piloto de los del numero de la Real Armada desde el Puerto de Manilla . . . a las costas de Neuva Espana . . . con la Fragata de S.M.C. nombrada Nuesta Señora del Rosario (alias la Princesa) mandada por el Alferez de Fragata Don Francisco Antonio Mourelle. Ano de 1780* (Microfilm in the ANL). The part of his route relevant to this study is laid down on two charts in the Museo Naval, Madrid, from the Archivo General de Indias (Microfilm in the ANL). La Pérouse, the French navigator, obtained an extract from Mourelle's journal which was reproduced in translation by Pingré, with a reconstructed route-chart by Buâche, in his posthumous *Voyage round the World* (La Pérouse 1798: I: 340–418, see also 131, 418–39). Fleurieu also reproduced an extract from Mourelle's journal (Fleurieu 1791: 179–83).

[1] La Pérouse 1798: I: 346.

[2] Which he regarded, after Dampier and the chart he was using, as *Nueva Bretaña*.

[3] Vásquez' log-book f75 (AGI: Guadalajara 520). The longitudes in Vásquez' log-book are from San Bernardino which he took to be 121° 40' E of Paris (124° E of Greenwich), and this would seem to have been a reasonably correct prime meridian. The two relevant route charts in the Museo Naval, Madrid, have the meridians laid down from San Bernardino, and in addition the chart of his route around *Nueva Bretaña* lays down the meridians W of San Lucas in California (109° 54' W of Greenwich, 112° 14' W of Paris), and the chart of his route to the E of the Solomons also lays down the meridians from Paris.   [4] Vásquez' log-book ff75–76.

navigational information, for there can be no doubt as to Mourelle's position at this stage.

Heading SE, two low islands were sighted at sunrise on the 19th which Mourelle named *Los Caimáns* but which are identifiable with the Green Islands (de Groene Eylanden).[1] At sunset on the same day two islands were sighted to the S, the most northerly of which was quite small and was named *Santa Ana* (*Anna*), the other, some 7 leagues in extent, being named *Santa Bárbara*.[2] At daybreak on the 29th the middle of a large island, to which Mourelle gave the name *Don Manuel Flores*, and which was dominated by a high mountain, bore to the W of due S and seemed to extend for 6 leagues ESE to WNW. It is quite apparent that Mourelle had sighted the island of Buka on the 19th, confusing the northern cape for a separate island, and that, on the following day, he had sighted the northern coastline of the island of Bougainville.

At eight in the morning of the 19th nine islets came into view to the E which Mourelle immediately concluded to be the 'Ohong Jaba of the French Charts',[3] but which were certainly the atoll islands of Kilinailau. It is interesting, in relation to Carteret's discovery of these islets, that both he and Mourelle should have thought that there were nine islands when there are in fact only six, particularly since they both viewed the archipelago from different quarters. If the sketch-map of the group in Vásquez' log-book is orientated to allow for magnetic variation, the identity of the nine islands becomes fairly clear, and they may be named from the west, and in a clockwise direction, as Jangain, Yecola, Irinalan, Yovo (delineated as three islands situated close together), Yeharnu, Piuli and, at the south-eastern extremity of the atoll, the sand cay which in fact lies to the southward of the southern extremity of the atoll reef.

Natives came out to the frigate, but Mourelle, with an amazing lack of interest, if a commendable zeal to deliver his box post-haste, did not linger to converse with them, remarking that:

... they returned to their islets, upon which it appeared to me impossible that human creatures could subsist. We saw ... palm trees, which, without doubt, produced them fruit, and this with the supply from fishing enabled these creatures to drag on a miserable life.[4]

Continuing to the SE, Mourelle had no sight of land until the night of 22 January when, at ten o'clock, a 'frightful roaring' was heard to the NE and the watch saw, 'broad on the ship's quarter, and at no great distance, the sea quite white with foam'.[5] Mourelle at once stood to the SW and remained on that course until the sound could no longer be heard, when he resumed his original course. Presuming that he had narrowly missed a shoal, Mourelle named it *El Roncador*, and Vásquez estimated its position to be 6° 12′ S, 32° 28′ E of San Bernardino.[6] According to Vásquez' log the difference in longitude

---

[1] Vásquez' log-book f76. [2] Vásquez' log-book f77.
[3] i.e. the Onthong Java of Tasman. [4] La Pérouse 1798: I: 363.
[5] La Pérouse 1798: I: 363. [6] Vásquez' log-book f80.

between *Ohong Jaba* (Kilinailau) and El Roncador was 2° 35', but on the route-chart in the Museo Naval, Madrid, they are separated by 3° 57', El Roncador being laid down 33° 50' E of San Bernardino. If reliance is placed on the latter evidence then the position of El Roncador would be 6° 12' S, 159° 21' E of Greenwich, the position occupied by the large shoal which Mendaña probably sighted and named Los Baxos de la Candelaria. There seems to be very little doubt that El Roncador was the Roncador Reef of the modern chart, for there is no other reef in this latitude in the locality, and Vásquez' underestimate of longitude and previous and subsequent navigation rule out the shoals in 6° 50' S, 160° 50' E which now bear the name Bradley's Shoals.

Assuming that El Roncador can be identified with Mendaña's Los Baxos de la Candelaria, then this was the only contribution which Mourelle had made to the discovery and rediscovery of the Islands of Solomon, for his earlier landfalls had all been previously discovered and charted. Continuing generally eastwards, he found himself almost completely unable to make a satisfactory easting without also being borne further to the S, and by this time his navigational difficulties had become aggravated by a shortage of water and provisions.

Taking all these occurrences into my most serious consideration, I judged it was not possible for me to continue my course towards the north of the line, without putting into some port to replace the water I had lost. I could not flatter myself with gaining the Marian Islands in time; the result of my reflection, therefore, was that I ought to make for Solomon's Islands; I reckoned them to bear west, at a hundred and seven leagues distance; I hoped that the winds, which blew from the northward, would allow me to put in there, and that I might thence with more expediency and certainty gain the Presidency of Monterey.[1]

Mourelle was, of course, already well to the E of the Solomon Islands and, at the time of these deliberations, estimated his position to be 174° 8' E of Paris. If he imagined that the Solomons lay 107 leagues to the E, then he must have believed that their western extremities lay in approximately 180° E of Paris, and his further remark that, on 20 February, he found himself to be 17 leagues to the 'westward of Cape Santa Cruz, or Guadalcanar', indicates that he was in fact using a French chart on which the Solomons were laid down between 175° W and 180° W of Paris, and on which that archipelago was delineated as the one large island of *Saint Elizabet*, with *Saint Croix* and *Guadalcanar* (Guadalcanal) identified as one island to the immediate SW. The route chart in the Museo Naval, Madrid, lays the *Tierras de Salomon* down in exactly this position and form, and illustrates clearly how Mourelle's deliberations were induced.

Contrary winds prevented him from maintaining his easterly course and, imagining that he had narrowly missed Santa Cruz, he headed southwards in the hope of picking up westerly winds which might carry him across the Pacific. He passed through the Tongan Archipelago and then, having got as

---

[1] La Pérouse 1798: I: 367.

far S as 25° 52′, decided to head back to the N, eventually reaching Guam on 31 May. By now the winds favourable for an easterly passage to México N of the line were beginning, and on 20 June he again weighed anchor and eventually reached San Blas on 27 September, having, in terms of fulfilling his mission and through no fault of his own, wasted some six months wandering around the South-West Pacific.

Alexander Dalrymple, 1782-1790

In the face of Buâche's deduction that the Terres des Arsacides of Surville, the Iles de la Louisiade of Bougainville and Gower's and Carteret's Islands were all part of the archipelago of the Islands of Solomon, Dalrymple seems to have revised his identification of these islands with New Britain, New Ireland and New Guinea. In June 1782, he completed his *Memoir concerning the Passages to and from China*, a work which was not published until March 1785, being in the meantime issued by the Secret Committee of the East India Company to the Masters of the Company's China ships. Its purpose, as its title implies, was to provide the information necessary to masters on the run to and from the China coast, at particular times of the year and under particular conditions. Most of the memoir's contents are irrelevant to this study, but Dalrymple refers to the question of the identity of the Solomons in his description of the passage to China via the S of New Holland, and northwards through the Western Pacific.

The Passage between NEW-HOLLAND and NEW-ZEALAND is branched out into several by the Clusters of Islands from the Tropick to NEW-GUINEA. 1st. between NEW-HOLLAND and NEW-CALEDONIA passed by Surville 1769; this again branching into two; Bougainville's Strait between NEW-GUINEA on the West and GUADAL-CANAL on the East; and Surville's Passage to the Eastward of GUADALCANAL. 2nd. The Channel to the Eastward of NEW-CALEDONIA navigated by Cook. 3rd. The Unexplored Channel between NEW-HEBRIDES and the FRIENDLY ISLANDS, and to the Eastward of the STA CRUZ ISLANDS. 4th. The Channel through the FRIENDLY ISLANDS, navigated by Tasman 1643. 5th. The Channel to the Eastward of the FRIENDLY ISLANDS, navigated by the French 1772.[1]

Exactly what Dalrymple meant by 'GUADALCANAL' is clearly demonstrated on the chart accompanying the memoir, on which he identifies the lands discovered by Surville, those discoveries by Bougainville to the S and E of Bougainville's Strait,[2] and presumably Carteret's Malaítan discoveries, as a supposed large island, *Guadalcanal*. The eastern coastline of the island of Bougainville is delineated as a possible north-eastern extremity of New Guinea, adjoining the coastline which Dalrymple believed to have been discovered by the *Geelvink* and Bougainville's Terres de la Louisiade. The name Islands of

---

[1] Dalrymple 1782: 6. [2] i.e. Vella Lavella and Choiseul.

Solomon does not appear on the chart at all, and whilst New Ireland and New Britain are shown as separate islands, after Carteret, they jointly bear Dampier's name *New Britain*.[1]

Dalrymple remarks in this memoir that:

It may be sometimes expedient for Ships from CHINA to come round CAPE HORNE instead of coming by the CAPE of GOOD HOPE; The only Example I know of this Voyage was St. John Baptist 1769 commanded by the Chevalier Surville: They left the BASHEES 24th August, saw no Land 'till 7th October, when they fell in with the East Coast of GUADALCANAL in about 7° So. Lat. They Coasted THIS LAND 'till 7th November when they left it about the Latitude of 12° So.[2]

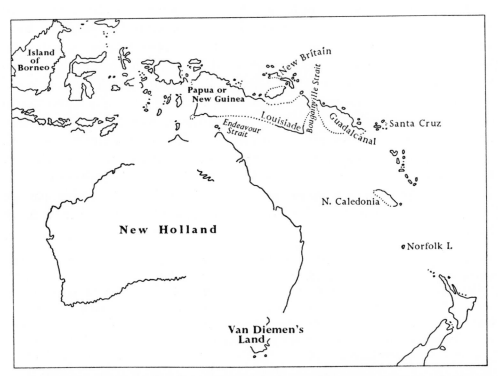

Map XXXVIII   Relevant detail on Dalrymple's chart in his *Memoir concerning the Passages to and from China* of 1782, redrawn

Fleurieu, commenting on his change of opinion, and his apparently ready acceptance of the identification of the discoveries of Bougainville, Surville and Carteret with the Islands of Solomon, was later to remark in praise of Dalrymple: 'A real man of letters earnestly seizes the truth as soon as it is

[1] The British Museum copy of Dalrymple's memoir has the MS. note in the margin of page 6, opposite the words Bougainville's Strait: 'Guadalcanal is divided into several islands so that there are several Passages between that of Bougainville and that of Surville. This Channel has been passed by several Ships recently.' This comment is a later addition, and refers to the several voyages which revealed the inner coastlines of the archipelago and which are the subject of the next chapter.

[2] Dalrymple 1782: 27.

offered to him.'[1] His praise was perhaps a little precipitate for, in 1790, Dalrymple restated his opinion that the Solomon Islands and Dampier's *Nova Britannia* were one and the same, and argued that the discoveries of Surville and Bougainville bore no resemblance to the Islands of Solomon as they were delineated on sixteenth-century charts.[2]

The Voyage of the 'Alliance'

It is generally supposed that the first European voyage along the southern and western limits of the archipelago of the Solomons was made by Lieutenant Shortland of the Royal Navy in the *Alexander* in 1788. This is incorrect, and whilst Shortland is entitled to the credit for part of the discovery of those limits, and indeed to all the credit for providing additional knowledge of the archipelago which could be and was incorporated on contemporary European charts, he was preceded in these western waters by at least one other navigator.

In June 1787 the *Alliance*, an ex-U.S. naval frigate,[3] left Philadelphia bound for Canton, to obtain a cargo of tea and, presumably, to trade furs and guising. She was commanded by Thomas Read, an ex-Commodore in the revolutionary navy, and carried as Mate, Richard Dale, a sailor who had served under both the English and revolutionary ensigns during the war, and had ended it as Captain of a privateer.[4] It seems likely that the voyage of the *Alliance* was one of the early voyages in the race to establish trade with China, and that the particular route followed was an experimental one, planned in the hope of a speedy passage.

Leaving the American coast on 19 June, the *Alliance* called at the Cape Verde Islands and then headed down into the South Atlantic. She passed the Cape of Good Hope, sighted Amsterdam Island (St. Paul) on 24 September, and made Van Diemen's Land on 15 October. Heading northwards, she sailed up the coast of New South Wales, keeping about 200 miles to seaward, and narrowly avoided disaster on the reefs of northern New Caledonia and the coast of Queensland.

[1] Fleurieu 1791: 205.

[2] See Dalrymple 1790. In this memoir on Buâche's deductions Dalrymple restated his belief in some detail and reproduced the relevant charts.

[3] Sold out of the service in 1785 she was owned by R. G. Morris, a merchant and financier concerned with the development of the American China trade.

[4] Dale's log-book is the only source material used for the reconstruction of the route and the details of the voyage. It is, or was, in the possession of Mr. E. C. Read of Bryn Mawr, Pennsylvania, U.S.A. and a photostat of it is lodged in the records of the U.S. Navy Department, Naval Records Collection of the Office of Naval Records and Library (RG.45). I am indebted to the late Mr. J. Forsyth of Sydney for the loan of his microfilm of the log-book, and for drawing my attention to its existence. The log-book is complete and detailed, permitting a fairly precise reconstruction of the route followed. It appears to be a fair copy of the original, but was probably written up by Dale concurrently with his rough log-book.

At 5 a.m. on Friday, 9 November 1787, land was sighted dead ahead extending from NE to NW, at a distance of 9 or 10 leagues. At noon, when Dale recorded a DR position in 8° 53′ S, 157° 19′ E, what appeared to be 'six islands in file' bore from E by N to NW by N, and the nearest land bore N by W at a distance of 3 or 4 leagues. Hardly surprisingly Dale's estimated longitudes are inaccurate, although to no alarming extent; more surprisingly, however, his latitudes are not as accurate as might be expected. Nevertheless, it is possible, if the *Alliance's* recorded course over the several days with which this study is concerned is taken as a whole, if the day's workings in the log-book are plotted independently of the chart, if Dale's descriptions and bearings of the land sighted are related to the known appearance of the land in this locality, and if these are then reconciled, for a fairly precise reconstruction of the course in relation to that land to be made.[1]

At 5 a.m. on the 9th Dale was apparently to the S of Tetipari and Vangunu and some 9 to 10 leagues off-shore. At noon the 'six islands in file' would have been the six high points of Rendova, Tetipari, Gatukai and Vangunu, as seen from a position 15 leagues from Gatukai, 5 leagues from the western extremity of Rendova and 3 leagues to the SE of the nearest point on the Rendova coast. At 5 p.m., after heading NW and then NNW, the western extremity of Rendova had been passed and the northernmost land in sight, identifiable as Kolombangara, bore NNW. At 6 p.m. other islands were sighted which are identifiable with the islands of Vella Lavella and Ranongga (Ganongga). At 3 a.m. on the 10th, after sailing NNW, N and then N by W, a small low island was sighted, which could have been Simbo but seems more probably to have been Gizo. At 5 a.m. the *Alliance* made sail and headed for an opening between two islands bearing NNW, 6 or 7 leagues distant, but on drawing closer found it to be full of small islands and rocks, an almost certain reference to the passage between Gizo and Wana Wana. At noon Dale recorded a position by DR in 156° 53′ E, 8° 11′ S which can be reconciled with a position to the SE of Gizo and to the W of Wana Wana.

---

[1] The most useful basic procedure to follow seems to be to plot the day's work on a scaled transparency; to plot positions relating to, and bearings from, provisionally identified landmarks mentioned in the log on the modern chart; to marry the chart and transparency together as far as possible; and then to complete and correct the picture by reference to the further description of the lands sighted, and in relation to a personal knowledge of the locality or to such information concerning its appearance as may be gleaned from the available hydrographic publications. There are several errors in the log-book which emerge quite clearly when the route reconstruction is attempted. For example: the day's work and remarks for 12 November are written up under 11 November, and *vice-versa*, an error probably resulting from copying from the rough log-book; and the day's work for 19 November contains a Long. In. of 153° 21′ which should be 153° 29′ if the Departure is correct. A Distance of 11 miles and Course of S 31° W gives a D. Lat. of 9·4 and a Departure of 5·7, but Dale gives the D. Lat. as 4, the Departure as 6. If the day's work is related to the day's workings preceding and following, it appears that the Course should be W 12° N, the Distance 15, the Departure 14·5 and the D. Lat. 4. The Observed Latitude is then correct at 4° 40′ S and the Long. In. correct at 153° 20′ 30″ E.

At 1 p.m. on the 10th the vessel was stood for a passage between two islands to leeward, and at 6 p.m. passed through it. This seems to have been the passage between Simbo and Ranongga, and at this time the *Alliance* was visited by some 250 natives in canoes, who came off shore and 'appeared to be friendly'. The approach of darkness and squally weather prevented the Americans, perhaps fortunately, from having any intercourse with them, or from obtaining supplies, and the *Alliance* stood out to sea. At 3 a.m. on the 11th land was sighted to the NW at a distance of 9 or 10 leagues, probably identifiable with Mono, the larger of the Treasury Islands of the modern charts, and Dale remarks with some justification that 'the sea here seamed to abound in Islands'. Little progress seems to have been made during the daylight hours of the 11th, and at midnight (11th to 12th) the land bore NE by E 3 or 4 leagues distant. By this time the *Alliance* was to the SW of Mono, and at 6 a.m. on the 12th what can only have been the peaks of Bougainville were sighted, appearing as 'a number of islands on file'. At 11 a.m. breakers were sighted 'at least 5 leagues from land' identifiable with the position in which off-shore breakers are marked on the modern chart, some 10 miles off the south-western coast of Bougainville.

From noon on the 12th until noon on the 13th the *Alliance* made slow progress in cloudy and drizzly weather, and Dale noted in his log-book that: 'it is unsartin when we shall get Clear of thease chane of Islands among them all we have not seen the least appearance of a harbour, the wind light and Baflin the men taken sick . . .' Nevertheless the vessel was slowly making her way up the west coast of Bougainville, the crew weakened by scurvy and exhausted by the need to work the sails continually in failing and varying breezes, and by late evening on the 13th was abreast of what is now Augusta Bay. By noon on the 15th they were off what Dale describes as 'the northernmost land in sight', which he hoped would 'be the last we shall see untill we Cross the Line and get into a settled wind', and which was certainly the island of Buka. At 5.30 a.m. another island was sighted to the NW which, it was concluded, must be New Ireland, 'which makes St. Georges Channel', and which they intended to keep to the W of. With variable northerly winds the *Alliance* was tacked on and off the coast of New Ireland in an attempt to avoid having to enter St. George's Channel, 'a place not the most Agreeable this time of year', and made slow progress northwards. At 6 a.m. on the 18th another island was sighted to the N which may be identified with St. John's Island and, rounding it, the *Alliance* came very close to Babase, the lesser island immediately to the NE of St. John's (Ambitle); so close indeed that the natives who came down to the beach to observe them could be seen clearly. By the early evening of the 19th the Americans had cleared this last obstacle, no more land could be seen ahead, and they continued their course northwards, eventually reaching Canton on 22 December.

Read had in fact made the entirely new discovery of the west coast of Bougainville, disproving Dalrymple's hypothesis that it was a north-eastern promontory of New Guinea; had further explored the land which Bougainville had sighted to the S of Choiseul; and had opened up a route to China around New Holland other than the known ones through Bougainville's Strait, between Santa Cruz and Surville's Cap Oriental (San Cristóval), or to the E of Santa Cruz. His discoveries in fact made no apparent contribution to contemporary knowledge of the archipelago, other perhaps than amongst Read's merchant acquaintances, and they were not reflected in the work of European cartographers. He may, of course, in the interests of his backers and their future enterprises have kept his newly discovered route secret, but it seems more likely, in view of the slow progress which he had made in the South-West Pacific and the obvious dangers of these waters that, having once used this route, he regarded its unsuitability as proven.

What exactly Read intended or expected when he chose this particular route to Canton is not certain, nor is the extent of his prior information relating to the area. He certainly knew of New Ireland and St. George's Channel, but Dale makes no attempt in his log-book to name or identify any of the lands sighted, even loosely, nor do these Americans, apparently disinterested merchantmen to the soles of their sea-boots, seem to have named their discoveries themselves. It may have been that Read intended to pass through Bougainville's Strait or to the E of Cap Oriental, but the absence of any reference to these routes in Dale's log, and of any explanation for or expression of disappointment or chagrin at their failure to do so, renders this unlikely, even though Dale may have been concealing what he thought was their bad navigation.

The log-book itself conveys the impression that the coastlines sighted between 9° S and New Ireland were unexpected if not surprising landfalls, and that Read and Dale had no knowledge of the discoveries of Surville and Bougainville. If they were not attempting to follow one of the known routes, then the choice of this course seems to have been rash to say the least, particularly since theirs was a commercial enterprise. They may have been using Dalrymple's memoir on the passages to China, and his chart could certainly account for their landfall quite close to the entrance to Bougainville's Strait, but the absence of any reference to the lands to the E, named by Dalrymple *Guadalcanal*, tends to discredit this supposition.

Even Dalrymple himself was later to comment, apropos of his memoir, that, whilst the route to China via New Holland offered advantages in time of war, or for vessels engaged in piratical excursions on the China coast, the suggestion that this was a more expeditious and secure passage than those normally used was the 'offspring of Ignorance'. He argued that to suppose that where no lands were charted it could be assumed lay open sea was foolish, and that these were waters where 'the danger of passing Straits is not removed but increased; the Passage being through unknown, or unfrequented, Straits, instead of through such as are well known'.[1] Whatever their purpose or intent the Americans on the *Alliance* did make a significant if unrealized contribution to knowledge of the archipelago. That it was unrealized, and that the voyage is therefore almost out of context in this study, was the result, if anything, of the partial isolation of America which her independence had brought; of the tendency, then and later, for private merchants to conceal the details of their voyages; and of that lack of co-ordination in amassing and disseminating hydrographic information which was to dog cartography for many years to come.

The Voyage of la Pérouse

The further rediscovery and exploration of the Islands of Solomon was primarily the result of two factors. The first of these was the establishment of the English penal settlement in New South Wales, leading as it did to an immediate concentration and subsequent continuous movement of vessels of the Royal Navy and East India Company in the South-West Pacific, and to some of them heading for Canton or Batavia by way of the waters to the SE of New Guinea. The second of these was the interest of the French in the Pacific, and their continuation of that series of officially sponsored voyages of exploration which they had begun shortly after the English, and which, in the case of the latter, had ended with Cook's third voyage.

The secession of the American colonies presented the British Government with the problem of resettling those Loyalist planters who had had their lands expropriated, and of finding alternative accommodation for those unquiet spirits whom the law regularly sentenced to transportation. That penal settlements were beneficial both to the commonwealth and to their unwilling residents was an accepted dogma of English justice, applauded from pulpit, bench, pamphlet and correspondence column, and one to which Parliament was wedded. Cook's discovery of the east coast of Australia was quickly followed by speeches and pamphlets extolling its virtues as a penal colony,[2] and though it attracted initial official attention as a possible site for the resettlement of the American Loyalists, the proposals that it should become a penal colony culminated in an Order in Council of December 1786, and an Act of 1787, to that effect.[3]

---

[1] Mackaness 1943(b); 21–23, 23–24.

[2] See, however, Dalrymple's pamphlet *A Serious Admonition to the Public on the Intended Thief Colony at Botany Bay* (Mackaness 1943(b)).

[3] On the background to the selection of Botany Bay see Rutter 1937.

In March 1787, a fleet was prepared to transport the first consignment of staff, marines and transportees. It consisted of six transports, the *Alexander, Scarborough, Friendship, Charlotte, Prince of Wales* and *Lady Penrhyn;* three store-ships, the *Golden Grove, Fishburn* and *Borrowdale;* and two armed tenders, the *Supply* and the *Sirius.* Captain Arthur Phillip was appointed to the command of the fleet, and his staff included Lieutenant John Shortland, the Agent for the transports; Post-Captain John Hunter, Phillip's Second-Captain on the *Sirius;* and Lieutenant Philip Gidley King, Phillip's Lieutenant. The *Supply* was under the command of Lieutenant Henry Lidgbird Ball.[1]

The convoy weighed anchor off Portsmouth on 13 May 1787, and eventually reached Botany Bay on 18 January 1788. The disadvantages of this site being immediately apparent, the colony site was moved to Port Jackson on 26 January. On the 24th two vessels bearing French colours were sighted, and these anchored in Botany Bay on the 26th, revealing themselves as the *Boussole* and the *Astrolabe* under the command of the *Comte* de la Pérouse.[2] Cordial greetings were exchanged, mail for the French Ambassador in London was handed to the English, and they learnt from la Pérouse something of the voyage which he had already made.

La Pérouse is the tragic figure in the history of the rediscovery of the Solomons. Despatched from France in 1786, he had, by the time he reached Botany Bay, completed much of a voyage which might well have ranked with those of Cook. He left Botany Bay on 10 March 1788, intending to pursue a course which would almost certainly have added considerably to contemporary knowledge of the Solomons, and have proved beyond reasonable doubt the truth of Buâche's assertion that the Terres des Arsacides of Surville were in fact the Islands of Solomon. He never accomplished his task, for when he sailed from Botany Bay he sailed into oblivion, an oblivion only relieved after the elapse of some twenty-five years by the discovery that his vessels had foundered on the reef of Vanikoro and that such survivors as had escaped the wrath of the indigenes had died there of old age and sickness or had perished in an attempt to sail a small boat towards Batavia.

Louis XVI of France was a monarch greatly interested in geographical discovery, inspired by Cook, and influenced by Charles Claret, *Comte* de Fleurieu, the leading geographer of France, then Director of Ports and Arsenals and later Minister of Marine. In consultation with Fleurieu he conceived a voyage which at once seemed likely to add considerably to contemporary scientific knowledge, and to complement and cap, if not to rival, the achievements of Cook. On the recommendation of the *Marquis* de Castries he appointed la Pérouse to the command of the expedition, and in the instructions which the

---

[1] See Stockdale 1790; Hunter 1793.

[2] Hunter 1793: 43–45; Stockdale 1790: 47–48, 73–74; Phillip's report to Lord Sydney dated 15 May 1788 (Rutter 1937: 135); *Historical Records of N.S.W.* 1893: I: 121; II: 543–7, 391.

latter was given may be seen the outcome of Cook's correspondence with Latouche-Tréville, and the implementation of his suggestion for the exploration of the lands to the SE of New Guinea 'discovered' by Bougainville, Surville and Carteret.

La Pérouse was to sail from Brest by way of Funchal, Trinidad, Georgia and Cape Horn to Easter Island. Here the two frigates were to separate, one going to Otaheite, the other to Pitcairn Island and thereafter in search of the Encarnación, San Juan Bautista, Santelmo, Cuatro Coronadas, San Miguel and Conversión de San Pablo discovered by Quirós in 1606. They were then to rendezvous at Otaheite, to visit the Society Islands and search for Quirós' San Bernardo, to pass N of the Friendly Islands looking for Quirós' Bella Nación (Gente Hermosa), visit the Navigator Islands, the Friendly Islands, the Isle of Pines and New Caledonia, Queen Charlotte's Islands (Santa Cruz), the Terres des Arsacides of Surville, the Louisiade coast of Bougainville, Endeavour Strait, the Gulf of Carpentaria, the Straits of Sunda, the west coast of New Holland, Van Diemen's Land, Cook's Strait, New Zealand, the Marquesas, the Sandwich Islands, the north-west coast of America, Behring's Bay, the Aleutians, Kamtschatka, the Kuriles, Japan, Macao and Canton or Manila, the Tartary coast, the Ladrones, the Carolines, Mindanao, the Moluccas, Ile de France, and to return to France via the Cape of Good Hope.[1] The route instructions proposed a formidable enterprise, and revealed a prodigious study of the known geography of the Pacific by Fleurieu and a very real appreciation of the major gaps in it. The instructions were themselves detailed to a degree, providing la Pérouse with as much information as was available or likely to be of value and, prudently, giving him full authority to alter them in the light of the circumstances as he found them, their purpose being only 'to make known to the Sieur De La Pérouse the discoveries which remain to be made'.[2] Relative to his proposed visit to Queen Charlotte's Islands and the Terres des Arsacides, the *Notes of the King, to serve as a particular instruction to the Sieur De La Pérouse*[3] advised him that:

If, after having run down the south-west coast of New Caledonia, he can make Queen Charlotte's Islands, he will try to reconnoitre the island of Santa Cruz of Mendaña, and determine its extent to the south.

But if the wind should not allow of this course, he will make for the Deliverance Islands, at the east point of the Terre des Arsacides, discovered, in 1769, by Surville; he will run along the south coast, which neither this navigator, nor any other, has examined, and he will satisfy himself whether, as is probable, these lands do not form a group of islands, which he will try to particularize. It is to be presumed, that they are peopled on the coasts to the south, as we know those of the north are; perhaps he may procure there some refreshments.

---

[1] La Pérouse 1798: I: 64–81.   [2] La Pérouse 1798: I: 80–81.   [3] La Pérouse 1798: I: 62–117.

He will endeavour, in like manner, to examine an island to the northwest of the Terre des Arsacides, the eastern coast of which was seen by Bougainville in 1768,[1] but he will pursue this research no farther than to be able without difficulty afterwards, to make Cape Deliverance on the south-east point of Louisiade.[2]

They continued that he:

will carefully examine the productions of these countries, which, being situate under the torrid zone ... may open a new field of speculation in commerce; and, without giving way to the reports, undoubtedly exaggerated, which the ancient Spanish navigators have made of the fertility, and the riches of some of the islands, which they discovered in this part of the world, he will only observe, that the reconcilliation of various accounts, founded upon geographical combinations, and upon the knowledge and information which modern voyages have procured, give room to think, that the lands discovered, in the one part, in 1768, by Bougainville, and in the other in 1769, by Surville, may be the islands discovered in 1567, by Mendaña and known since by the name of Solomon's Islands; which name was given in after-times, by the idea whether true or false that was entertained of their riches.[3]

In a collection of *Notes, Geographical and Historical. To be added to the King's Memoir* ... la Pérouse was referred to the accounts of previous voyages to the South-west Pacific and provided with a synopsis of each, and Mendaña's discoveries of 1568 were listed and described as they were in Figueroa, with the comment that:

Besides these islands, cited in the relation of Christopher Suarez de Figueroa, many others are to be found, named in the descriptions of Herrera, and De Bry, and which may be seen upon ancient charts; such as Saint Nicolas, Arrecifes, Saint Mark, Saint Jerome etc.[4]

He was also referred to Mendaña's discovery, and Carteret's rediscovery in 11° S, 161° 35' E, of the island of Santa Cruz, to the discoveries of Quirós in 1606, and to the voyages of le Maire, Tasman, and Roggewein.

Instructed to consult the accounts of Bougainville and Figueroa, in the test of a synopsis of Surville's voyage, la Pérouse was informed that he would find in the collection of MS. charts committed to his care one which related to the more recent discoveries made in the Terres des Arsacides or Islands of Solomon:

upon which the discoveries of Mendaña have been endeavoured to be represented, as well as they could be laid down, after the description given by Figueroa, Herrera, and other Spanish historians, who do not agree upon the particular extent of the different islands, or on their relative positions, but it was sufficient to show the presumed identity of the discoveries of Mendaña and those of Surville, and it is certain, that the researches which M. de la Pérouse is expected to make will establish that which is here only presented as probability'.[5]

In addition to this chart of the discoveries of Bougainville, Surville and Carteret on which the Solomons were provisionally delineated, la Pérouse was provided with a chart of the South Sea, a fragment of which Fleurieu was

---

[1] i.e. Bougainville Island.   [2] La Pérouse 1798: I: 70.   [3] La Pérouse 1798: I: 85–86.
[4] La Pérouse 1798: I: 156–8.   [5] La Pérouse 1798: I: 180.

later to publish.[1] This latter chart laid down the coastlines of the South-West Pacific as they had been recently charted,[2] and Fleurieu was later to comment that, when it was being prepared:

the latitude and longitude of Choiseul Bay were laid down from the Charts which accompany M. de Bougainville's Journal. To place Surville's Port Praslin the position of it given by that navigator was corrected; and it was fixed, by approximation, from the time and way that he had taken from that place to New Zealand, the longitude of which had been determined by Captain Cook's observations. His île Inattendue was then placed from the difference of its parallel and meridian with respect to Port Praslin; and when it was required to insert the Gower's Island of Carteret, from the determinations given by him, its position turned out to be the very same as that of Inattendue. . . .'[3]

The chart was in fact a very reasonable representation of the discoveries recently made, and illustrates clearly the significant stage which had now been reached in charting the archipelago.[4]

Fleurieu's position within the planning of the expedition was of particular significance for, accepting Buâche's thesis that the discoveries of Surville and Bougainville were identical with the Islands of Solomon, a thesis which he was to develop with additional evidence,[5] the instructions clearly reveal that he saw the expedition as an opportunity to prove or disprove his deductions. Buâche himself provided la Pérouse with certain observations, and in a *Memoir drawn up by the Academy of Science for the . . . learned and scientific persons embarked under the orders of M. De La Pérouse* he remarked that:

The . . . space which deserves to be examined more particularly, is that which is comprised between the New Hebrides and New Guinea. M. De Bougainville and M. De Surville are the only navigators who have passed through it, and from the situation of such parts of the land as they saw, there is every reason to believe, that the land is the same as the ancient islands discovered by Mendaña in 1567, and known afterwards by the name of Solomon's Islands. . . .

As a great part of the ancient discoveries of Mendaña and Quiros have been found again, there is every reason to believe the rest will be found, and with this view their memoirs deserve to be consulted. The island Taumago of Quiros will probably be found again, with those of Chicayana, Guaytopo, Pilen, Naupau, and others near it.[6]

When la Pérouse reached Botany Bay in 1788 he had visited Easter Island, the Sandwich Islands, Behring's Bay, Monterey, Macao, the Philippines, Japan, Kamtschatka, the Navigator and Friendly Islands, and had passed

[1] See Fleurieu 1791: Chart I.

[2] New Guinea's coastlines, however, followed the older charts, there being no recent voyages to improve knowledge of them, and included the coastline reputedly discovered by the *Geelvink*.

[3] Fleurieu 1791: 211.

[4] For some reason the northern extremity of Choiseul was delineated as a separate island, perhaps on the supposition that the open water of the New Georgia Sound, which Bougainville suspected to be a strait or a large bay, was a strait leading to the seas to the N of the Solomons.

[5] In his '*Découvertes des françois en 1768 et 1769, dans le sud-est de la Nouvelle Guinée*' of 1790 (published in English in 1791). [6] La Pérouse 1798: I: 242.

Norfolk Island and Lord Howe. By that time the vagaries of wind and weather had dictated several changes in his proposed itinerary, and it was his intention when he left Botany Bay to explore New Caledonia, Santa Cruz and the Terres des Arsacides, to pass between New Guinea and New Holland, and to explore the Gulf of Carpentaria and the west coast of New Holland. From Macao, in January 1787, he had written of his intention to circumnavigate New Holland, or, if the season prevented this, of heading directly for Cook's Passage in New Zealand, 'the south side of New Caledonia, and the Arsacides and Caroline Islands: then passing through the Moluccas with the north-west monsoon, I shall explore the coast of New Holland, and afterwards proceed to the île de France'.[1] From Avatscha he had written in September of his intention of directing his course to the Kuriles, of running down the parallel of 37°N to Guam, and of then following a course through the Carolines and, should there be any likelihood of success, of passing southwards through Bougainville's Strait, 'by Cape Choiseul in the Terre des Arsacides', and thereafter of bearing away for Queen Charlotte's Sound in New Zealand.

If on the contrary, my own observations and researches should prove the inexpediency of my taking that route ... I shall steer directly from Guam to New Zealand.... From Queen Charlotte's Sound I shall make a run to the Friendly Islands, and shall do everything that I am enjoined by my instructions, in regard to the southern part of New Caledonia; the island of Santa Cruz of Mendaña, or the south coast of Terre des Arsacides; and to Bougainville's Louisiade, by determining whether it be part of New Guinea or separated from it.[2]

The evidence for the disastrous end of la Pérouse's expedition on the reef of Vanikoro will be referred to later in its chronological sequence. Suffice it to say here that the evidence to date points to the loss of both vessels off the one island, to the decimation of many of the crew at the hands of the indigenes, to the subsequent departure of most of the survivors in a boat built from salvaged timber, and to its loss, perhaps in the vicinity of Simbo, the death of its occupants at sea or at the hands of the natives, and to the death from old age or disease of those who remained at Vanikoro.

The Voyage of Lieutenant Shortland

The establishment of the penal settlement at Port Jackson proceeded according to plan, with the result that by 24 March the transports *Charlotte*, *Scarborough* and *Lady Penryhn* had been unloaded, and had left for China to collect

---

[1] La Pérouse 1798: I: 338.

[2] La Pérouse 1798: I: 361. The determination of whether or not Bougainville's Louisiade was part of New Guinea would have been an important achievement, and might have disproved the New Guinea coastline to the S of New Britain laid down on so many charts and reputedly discovered by the *Geelvink*.

a speculative cargo of tea as vessels of the East India Company.[1] By July the *Alexander*, *Friendship*, *Prince of Wales* and *Borrowdale* had been unloaded and prepared for the return journey to England. They were commanded by Lieutenant John Shortland, previously Agent for the transports, who travelled on board the *Alexander*. Making a hasty departure on 14 July, without any arrangements for a rendezvous, the *Prince of Wales* and *Borrowdale* soon forged ahead of the *Alexander* and *Friendship* and pursued an independent voyage to Batavia. It had been agreed, despite the difficulties and uncertainties of this route, that it was advisable in view of the season for the vessels to attempt to make their return passage to England by way of Endeavour Strait or the north coast of New Guinea, rather than by way of Van Diemen's Land and Southern New Holland[2] or Cape Horn.

At noon on Thursday, 31 July, land was sighted from the *Alexander* bearing from N$\frac{1}{2}$W to ENE at a distance of 5 or 6 leagues and, as the ship was now in 10° 52′ S, Shortland at first inclined to the opinion that this must be Carteret's Egmont's Island (Santa Cruz). That this was a different landfall soon became apparent, and as Shortland sailed parallel with the land in a north-westerly direction for some 6 or 7 leagues, he decided that it had the appearance of an island,[3] the two apparent extremities of which he named *Capes Sydney* and *Phillip*. His recorded position at noon of 10° 52′ S, 161° 41′ E[4] reveals quite conclusively when related to the charts and his subsequent voyage that Shortland was off the south coast of the island of San Cristóval, Cape Sydney[5] being the most southerly point of the island sighted and Cape Phillip[6] the extreme westerly point.

He passed Cape Phillip, and continued to head in a north-westerly direction until 7 that evening, when the crew, who were reefing the top-sails, sighted land dead ahead. The two vessels were accordingly brought to and lay throughout the succeeding night with their bows held off the land. The next morning the

[1] Rutter 1937: 98. At this stage, and later, privately owned vessels under the colours of the East India Company transported convicts and supplies to New South Wales under charter to the Admiralty, and were then released from their charter and permitted to make a speculative return voyage via China.

[2] The source material for the details of Shortland's voyage in the *Alexander* consists of the edited narrative in *Governor Phillip's Voyage to Botany Bay* (Stockdale 1798: 185–216). Shortland's *Table of Positions* (Stockdale 1798: Appx. i–vii), two charts prepared under his direction by his son, T. G. Shortland, who accompanied him (Stockdale 1789: 200, 218); the chart *Track of the Alexander . . . from Port Jackson . . . to Batavia* (MLS: M2 801; 1789/1); and the *Chart of New Georgia, Solomon Islands . . . 1790* (BM: Add. MS. 38076 D93), from the collection of Admiral Richard, Earl Howe (d. 1799). See also Fleurieu 1791: 184–208.

[3] Although Shortland refers to it as an island, he seems subsequently to have entertained the possibility that it was part of a mainland.

[4] In the *Table of Positions*, however, the noon longitude is given as 161° 14′ E, and on the chart as 161° 25′ E. These do not contradict the identification of the coastline.

[5] Spelt *Sidney* on Shortland's charts, but named after Lord Sydney.

[6] Spelt *Philip* on Shortland's charts, but named after Governor Arthur Phillip of New South Wales.

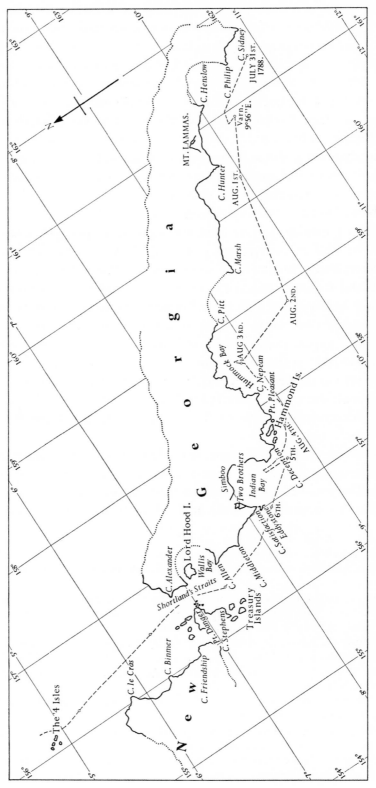

Map XXXIX Thomas Shortland's chart of the coastlines sighted from the *Alexander*, redrawn

English were surprised to find themselves some 5 to 6 leagues off a mountainous coastline extending from NE by E to WNW. This indicated conclusively that the land sighted on the day previously had not been Egmont's Island, and Shortland, assuming that this present land was separated from Cape Phillip by a bay, supposed it to be part of one large island. The vessels were in fact off the south coast of Guadalcanal, a coastline which rises sharply from the sea to heights of as much as 8,000 feet and to the dominant peaks of Marau, Lion's Head and Popomanasiu.

Following this coastline in a generally west-north-westerly direction for 5 or 6 leagues, Shortland named the dominant capes *Henslow* and *Hunter*, and noted one particularly elevated summit to which he gave the name *Mount Lammas* and which seems likely to have been the Lion's Head. Throughout 1 August the two vessels followed the coast westwards, and by 6 in the evening the furthest land in sight, to which was given the name *Cape Marsh*, lay 13 or 14 leagues to the NW by N. From Shortland's chart and the bearings given it seems likely that Cape Marsh was in fact the Russell Islands to the NW of Guadalcanal, but that Shortland assumed them to be the cape of a more distant mainland.

Hazy weather on 2 August prevented Shortland from seeing that Cape Marsh was quite separate from the mainland of Cape Hunter and that it did not extend westwards, and throughout the whole of the day no land was seen, the *Alexander* maintaining a course W by N. At 3 a.m. on 3 August land was again sighted bearing from NNE to NW, and at 6 a.m. it had the appearance of several islands between which an attempt was made to pass. When approached closer, however, the islands resolved themselves into apparently unbroken land, and the supposed passage for which they were heading was seen to be blocked by low-lying tree-covered land. The land as a whole rose in nine roundish points or hummocks,[1] from which the place was named *Hummock Bay*, the extremity of land visible to the E being named *Cape Pitt* and the extremity to the W being named *Cape Nepean*. It is quite clear from Shortland's chart and a reconstruction of the route and the bearings given that Cape Pitt was the island of Gatukai, Cape Nepean the southern extremity of Tetipari; that the passage attempted was the one between Gatukai and Vangunu; and that the nine hummocks were the nine highest points of Gatukai, Vangunu, New Georgia Island, Rendova and Tetipari. By 4 p.m., as Shortland bore out of Hummock Bay and to the westward, Cape Nepean bore NW $\frac{1}{2}$ W at a distance of 5 or 6 leagues, and at 6 p.m. the *Alexander* shortened sail and stood off for the night.

Shortland seems to have imagined that Cape Nepean was probably the western extremity of the land, but on the morning of the 4th found himself

---

[1] In this locality, but from a slightly different position, Dale on the *Alliance* had distinguished only six dominant peaks.

21

to the W of it and 5 or 6 leagues to the SSE of a bluff point to which he gave the name *Point Pleasant*.[1] Point Pleasant seem to have been the south-eastern point of the island of Rendova, but though Shortland appears from his narrative to have recognized that this was an island, on his chart it is joined to Cape Nepean by a firmly outlined coast, perhaps the result of a later deduction that had he been closer he might have seen a continuous coastline. By 4 p.m. the most westerly land in sight bore NW by N at 4 or 5 leagues and, thinking it to be the extremity of the land and realizing subsequently that he had been mistaken, Shortland named it *Cape Deception*. From the chart prepared by Shortland's son it would appear that Cape Deception was not the most westerly point of Rendova, but the point immediately to its SE. The narrative bears this out initially, but the bearings and later references combine to convey the impression that it was the extreme westerly point. Some islands lying close to Cape Deception and seeming to form a good harbour were named *Hammond's Isles*, and though they cannot be identified with certainty it seems likely that Shortland's chart is slightly in error and that, whilst Cape Deception should be identified with the western extremity of Rendova, Hammond's Islands were in fact the islands which form Rendova Harbour on the north-western side of Rendova and are the only islands in this locality.

On the morning of the 5th, having stood on and off during the night in order to be able to determine at dawn whether or not he had reached the extremity of land and could head N, Shortland found himself in what appeared to be a great bay, surrounded from the ENE to W by N $\frac{1}{2}$ N by land rising in six hummocks. In all probability his position was to the W of Raniata Point on Rendova, and in sight of the islands of Simbo, Ranongga (Ganongga), Vella Lavella and Kolombangara, Mount Vina Roni (on the island now known as New Georgia) and Rendova, the six hummocks being the peaks of the five latter points including the two peaks of Rendova. Heading southwards and out of the bay, Shortland resumed a north-westerly course and, between 11 a.m. and noon on the 5th, two hills, to which he gave the name the *Two Brothers*, seemed to form the western extremity of the visible land, and bore NW $\frac{1}{2}$ N at a distance of 10 leagues. This was the island of Simbo, consisting of two volcanic peaks connected by a low narrow neck of land and, as the *Alexander* approached close to it on 6 August, what appeared to be a vessel could be seen some 2 leagues to the SSW of it. So marked was the similarity that the crew thought they could distinguish top-gallants and a signal was made, it being assumed to be either the *Boussole* or *Astrolabe* of la Pérouse or one of the two transports which had left Port Jackson ahead of the *Alexander*. Only when they came to within 4 miles of it did it reveal itself as a rock, to which Shortland gave the

[1] The modern chart names two points on the Rendova coast, Bluff Point and Point Pleasant. It seems clear, however, from Shortland's narrative that they were one and the same place.

name *Eddystone*. This particular formation, which is quite unmistakable and unique, provides very definite evidence for the identification of the island of Simbo with the Two Brothers.[1]

Between 10 and 11 a.m. on the 6th four canoe-loads of islanders came alongside the *Alexander* and allowed themselves to be towed on ropes thrown to them. They exchanged personal ornaments for nails and beads, but could not be induced to go aboard, endeavouring instead to entice the English towards the shore by showing them the rinds of fruit and the feathers of poultry, pointing continuously to the land and uttering the word *Simbo*. Shortland assumed that this was the name of their country, and subsequently applied it to all the land which he had sighted in this locality,[2] though it seems certain that the natives were from and were referring to the island of Simbo. He failed to see that Simbo, the Two Brothers, was a relatively small island and, assuming it to be a southern cape of a large land mass, named it *Cape Satisfaction*. Of the natives Shortland remarks that they were remarkably stout and well-built, and strikingly superior to the aborigines of New South Wales; their canoes, which could hold from six to fourteen men, were well constructed with lofty bows, were carved, stained and similar to those at Otaheite.

Heading slightly to the W of due N from Cape Satisfaction, Shortland sighted more land to the westward at dawn on the 7th; six or more small islands to which he gave the name *Treasury Islands* and which are identifiable with the Treasury and Shortland Islands of the modern chart, Fauro and its neighbours.[3] The lands which Shortland could see to the N and E from this position present something of a problem in terms of reconciling his nomenclature with the known coastlines. It is possible, from a reconstruction of his route and his recorded bearings and narrative, to conclude that Shortland gave the name *Cape Allen* to the northern extremity of Ranonnga, that to its immediate N he sighted the island of Baga, which he named *Lord Hood's Island*, and that the apparent bay formed by Vella Lavella and Ranongga was named *Wallis Bay* without it being realized that these were separate islands. From his chart, however, it appears that the entrance to the New Georgia Sound between Choiseul and Vella Lavella was what Shortland named Wallis Bay. There is no island between Vella Lavella and Choiseul, and it is possible that some confusion arose in Shortland's mind, perhaps as a result of preparing the chart at a later date, and that what he saw and intended to delineate was the northern point of Vella Lavella (Cape Allen), the stretch of water between Vella Lavella and

---

[1] In the past the name *Eddystone* has been incorrectly applied to Simbo. Eddystone Rock consists of two very conspicuous rocks, the highest of 30 feet, about half a mile to the SW of Simbo.

[2] He writes, for instance, of the 'passage between Simbo and Egmont Island' (Santa Cruz), i.e. the passage to the E of San Cristóval.

[3] On his chart Shortland applies the name *Treasury Islands* to all the islands off the southern extremity of Bougainville, but the islands which he sighted initially and called *Treasury Islands* were the Treasury and Shortland Islands of the modern chart.

Choiseul (Wallis Bay) and the island of Baga off Vella Lavella (Lord Hood's Island), but that he erroneously charted the latter to the N of the position in which it was sighted. Alternatively, of course, Lord Hood's Island could have been the particular appearance of part of Choiseul, which seemed to Shortland to be separate from the main body of the land.

At 6 p.m. on the 7th, as the *Alexander* sailed slowly northwards, a passage seemed to be visible 5 or 6 leagues to the N by E.

The Alexander and the Friendship had now run from the latitude of 10° 44′ south, and longitude 161° 30′ east, to the latitude of 7° 10′ south, and longitude 156° 30′ east, the whole way nearly in sight of land. As, therefore, proceeding westward, to the south of the next land, might have entangled them with New Guinea, Lieutenant Shortland determined to try the passage which was now before him, and being very well convinced, before it was dark, that the way was clear, kept under a commanding sail all night.[1]

This was Bougainville's Strait between the island of Choiseul to the E and the islands of Fauro and Bougainville to the W, but Shortland, apparently unaware of the exploits of his predecessor, seems to have regarded it as a new discovery. Had he, instead of risking the strait, withdrawn to the S and attempted to round the land to the westwards, he would have followed the route discovered by the *Alliance* and coasted the west side of the island of Bougainville. He supposed that the lands which he had coasted formed one large tract of land, entertaining doubts only in respect of the areas between Capes Phillip and Henslow, and between Capes Marsh and Pitt, where he suspected that passages might exist which had escaped his observations.

The editor of Shortland's narrative in *Governor Phillip's Voyage to Botany Bay* was rash enough to suggest, in reference to the narrative of Bougainville, the probability of Shortland's Strait being one with Bougainville's Strait, and the probability that 'the island supposed to be called Simboo . . . is the same which was then named Choiseul',[2] probabilities based on the evidence of the similarity of the descriptions of the natives and their canoes, that:

A place called by one of the French navigators, Port Surville, is probably a part of it, as well as Choiseul Bay, but the points seen and described by the French discoverers are very few; and for the knowledge of the form and bearings of the rest of the Coast, throughout the whole extent of near three degrees of latitude and full five of longitude, we are indebted entirely to the researches of our own countryman.[3]

It was a remark which betrayed either arrant nationalism or a crass ignorance of what had been published both in France and England concerning the French discoveries, and brought forth the justifiable scorn of the French,[4] as did the ignorance of Shortland, 'a seaman . . . employed in great navigations, and . . .

---

[1] Stockdale 1789: 198–9.

[2] This was only correct to the extent that all the land sighted to the E of the strait was regarded as one land mass, and that *Simboo* was regarded by Shortland as the native name for the whole area.

[3] Stockdale 1789: 200–1.   [4] See Fleurieu 1791: 201–5.

called to the command of an important convoy', of the routes and discoveries of his predecessors in the waters in which he had to navigate.

Between 10 in the evening of 7 August 1788 and 5 in the morning of 8 August the *Alexander* passed through the strait, and Shortland named the most north-westerly point of land to the E *Cape Alexander*. To the W could be seen remarkably high land which stretched away to the NW, and the names *Cape Friendship* and *Cape Le Cras* were given to the nearest and furthest points of it. Continuing northwards and leaving this the northern coast of Bougainville Island astern, two islands were sighted at 6 p.m. on Saturday, 9 August, lying in 4° 50′ S, 156° 11′ E. From Shortland's chart and from a reconciliation of this estimated position with the known error in his longitude, it is quite clear that the two islands were the most south-easterly of the islands of Kilinailau Atoll. On the morning of the 10th two more came in sight to the SW of the *Alexander's* position, and Shortland, thinking at first that they might be the Nine Islands seen by Carteret, concluded, incorrectly, that their number and longitude did not support this identification.[1] He accordingly determined that, rather than attempt St. George's Channel, he would sail round New Ireland to the N, and this he did.

Unaware or uncertain of the exploits of his French predecessors, Shortland named his discoveries, *New Georgia*, applying the name to the whole area of land which he had sighted both to the NW and SE of the passage which he named the Shortland Straits. He apparently had no ideas or information on the possible identification of this mainland or archipelago with the Islands of Solomon, but such discoveries as he made provided knowledge of the southern limits of the group, and permitted its firm identification with them. The answering of the question of whether or not this was an archipelago or a large island, and of what, if it was the former, lay in the middle, is the final phase in the story of the rediscovery of the Islands of Solomon.

The assertion of the editor of the published account of Shortland's voyage that the discoveries made to the SE of New Guinea were more certain and valuable than those made by the French, and the parallel but unintentional claim implied by Shortland's chart that these were entirely new discoveries, brought forth the fury of Gaul. In his *Mémoire sur la Prétendue Découverte faite en 1788 par des Anglois d'un continent qui n'est autre chose que la Terre des Arsacides découverte en 1768 par . . . Bougainville. . . . et en 1769 par . . . Surville* of 1788 Laborde accused the English of either lacking good faith or of being singularly

[1] Recalling that both Carteret and Mourelle had identified nine islands on this atoll where there are a total of six, Shortland's identification of the four at the eastern perimeter of the atoll, identifiable with Irinalan, Yovo, Yeharnu and Piuli, would seem to indicate (a) that the appearance of nine islands was the result of the bearing from which they were seen, and the conditions under which they were seen, (b) that it was not the result of the existence of more islands on the atoll at that time than exist now, and (c) that at a certain distance, from the NE and under certain conditions of visibility, only the four islands to the E of the atoll are visible.

uninstructed in the discoveries of their predecessors. He recapitulated the discoveries made by Surville and Bougainville, asserting that: '*La gloire de la découverte d'une île aussi considérable que celle des Arsacides appartient donc à ces deux derniers, malgré les injustes efforts de leur rivaux pour la leur enlever*'[1] and ended his *mémoire* with a plea for subscriptions to permit a search for la Pérouse, whom he deduced to have been wrecked off either New Zealand, New Ireland, New Britain or the *Isle des Arsacides*.

Le Comte Claret de Fleurieu

The actual construction of a chart of the discoveries made to the SE of New Guinea from the details of the narratives of Carteret, Surville, Bougainville and Shortland, and the presentation of the closely argued case for the identification of their discoveries with the Islands of Solomon, was the work of Fleurieu. In his *Découvertes des François en 1768 et 1769, dans le Sud-Est de la Nouvelle Guinée* of 1790[2] he defended Buâche's original hypothesis, stated in detail the conclusions which had been manifest in the instructions delivered to La Pérouse, and attempted to reconstruct the actual discoveries of the Spaniards on the new chart. To analyse Fleurieu's work in detail would be a task beyond the bounds of this present study, and it will suffice to summarize his arguments and to reproduce the charts which he prepared and which are largely self-explanatory.[3]

On the basis of Buâche's *mémoire*, which he reproduced as an appendix, Fleurieu began with a recapitulation of the Spanish voyages, based on those secondary sources available to him, the chronicles of Figueroa, Herrera, and Torquemada, Quirós' letter to de Morga and one of his *memoriales*, and then proceeded to narrate the discoveries of Carteret, Bougainville, Surville, Cook, Maurelle (Mourelle) and Shortland. Having poured scorn on the latter for his failure to recognize some of his discoveries as those of Bougainville and the possibility that all his discoveries were in the same locality as those of Surville, particularly since Dalrymple had written on the subject of the French discoveries, he demonstrated which of Shortland's discoveries were already known. He identified Carteret's Gower's Island with the Inattendue of Surville, and Carteret's Island and Simpson's Island with the coastline S of Inattendue which Surville had also sighted. He then turned to Dalrymple's previous identification of the Solomons with *New Britain*, 'as seen by Dampier', and, whilst praising its virtues, pointed out that Dalrymple had to rely on inadmissible

---

[1] Laborde 1788: II. He accepted the discovery as being of one large island.

[2] Published in English in 1791.

[3] His chart of the Solomons and New Guinea shows the coast reputedly discovered by the *Geelvink* in 1705, but in a postscript Fleurieu noted that the appearance of a Dutch map, published by Dalrymple in 1781, which traced the route of the *Geelvink*, revealed that the *Geelvink* coast was erroneously placed at the south-eastern extremity of New Guinea, and its exclusion gave grounds for the belief that Bougainville's Louisiade coast was probably only a chain of islands. This was a correct deduction.

latitudes. He recapitulated on the several reports made of the position of the Islands of Solomon by Figueroa, Quirós, López Vaz, Ovalle, Acosta and Herrera, all of whom agreed that the Solomons lay between 7° S and 12° S. Arguing, on the evidence of Mendaña's voyage of 1595, Quirós' voyage of 1606 and Carteret's rediscovery of Santa Cruz, that the Solomons could not lie any more than 12° E of New Guinea, he accepted the view expressed by Buâche, remarking that from the moment that the latter presented his *mémoire* in 1781, 'the identity of the Islands of Solomon and those of the Arsacides, appeared demonstrated in the eyes of all impartial men. . . .'[1]

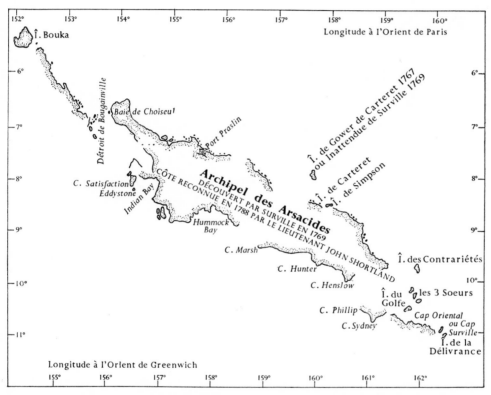

Map XL   Fleurieu's co-ordinated chart containing the coastlines sighted and charted by
Carteret, Bougainville, Surville and Shortland, redrawn

In reconciling the rediscoveries of the eighteenth century with the Spanish discoveries recorded in Figueroa, Fleurieu went into considerable detail irrelevant in this context. In the Northern Solomons he differentiated between the first group of islands sighted by Schouten and le Maire (Ontong Java) and the Onthong Java of Tasman, and identified the latter as being the same as the Marquen of Schouten and le Maire. Tasman's Ontong (Onthong) Java he further identified with the nine islands of Mourelle (Kilinailau); the Baxos de

[1] Fleurieu 1791: 224.

la Candelaria of Mendaña he identified, probably correctly, with Mourelle's El Roncador (Roncador Reef); and he also differentiated between the Nine Islands of Carteret and the Four Islands of Shortland, both in fact Kilinailau[1]. His reconciliation of the coastlines of the archipelago was remarkably near-accurate and a considerable piece of reconstruction. His attempt to identify the Spanish discoveries with the relatively limited coastlines then charted was clearly influenced by the fact that earlier charts of the archipelago had, to

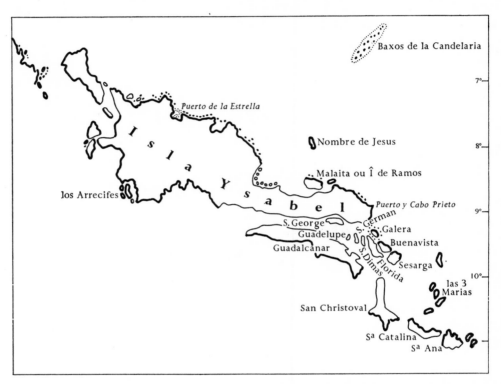

Map XLI   Fleurieu's attempted reconstruction of the Spanish discoveries of 1568 on the basis of his co-ordinated chart, redrawn

varying extents, shown Santa Ysabel as a comparatively large island, and he consequently assumed that the *Isla Ysabel* occupied the greater part of the area of the archipelago or mainland as a whole. He identified Shortland's discoveries between Capes Henslow and Marsh, partly correctly, with *Guadalcanar* 'Guadal-canal), and the Three Sisters of Surville (*les 3 Soeurs*) he identified correctly with Las Tres Marías of the Spaniards. However, whilst he identified Shortland's discovery between Capes Sydney (*Sidney*) and Phillip with *San Christoval* (Cristóval), his longitudinal reconciliation was here distorted. Failing to identify Surville's coastline W of Cap Oriental as the northern coast of this same land, sighted by Shortland, he identified it with Santa Catalina and Santa Ana, when

[1] He also plotted Carteret's Sir Charles Hardy's Island as a small island to the N of Buka (Bouka) which in turn he correctly identified with Carteret's Lord Anson's island.

these were in fact the Iles de la Delivrance of Surville. He correctly identified Carteret's Island with Malaíta, presumably on the basis that it was the only land which had been rediscovered in the relative position assigned by Figueroa to that island, but he identified the Malaítan coastline sighted by Surville with the southern extremity of *Santa Ysabel* terminating in *Cabo Prieto*. *S. George* (San Jorge) he laid down as a hypothetical outline relative to his Malaítan identification of Southern *Ysabel*, and the most southerly part of Malaíta's east coast which Surville had charted Fleurieu broke into three sections[1] which he identified with *la Galera, Buenavista* and *Sesarga*, plotting hypothetical neighbouring islands of *Guadelupe, San German, San Dimas* and *Florida*. The coastlines sighted and charted by Shortland, of the islands which we can recognize as including and between Gatukai and Vella Lavella, Fleurieu identified as part of the western coast of *Ysabel*. He deduced that the strait or bay sighted by Bougainville, and by Shortland, which we know to be the New Georgia Sound between Vella Lavella and Choiseul, was the passage to the sea to the north of Santa Ysabel followed by the brigantine in 1568, and that what Bougainville had named Choiseul was the islands at the north-western extremity of Santa Ysabel, to the S of which the brigantine passed.[2]

What is particularly striking about Fleurieu's reconstruction is not its faults, but its several accurate or near-accurate identifications, and its revelation of an ingenuity and deductive ability which are all the more praiseworthy when the limitations and confusions of Figueroa's description are appreciated.[3] Fleurieu had in fact closed the question of the identity of the Islands of Solomon by presenting a case for their identification with the discoveries of Bougainville, Surville, Carteret, and Shortland which was basically unanswerable. Dalrymple might still protest the invalidity of Fleurieu's assertions,[4] but the identification had been defended in detail, and it was correct. The amendment of Fleurieu's provisional individual identifications could only come with the more detailed exploration of the archipelago, and, indeed, could only come with certainty after considerably more reliable Spanish sources than those of Herrera and Figueroa had been unearthed, and this was not to be for some considerable time thereafter. With Fleurieu, if not with Buâche, the period of rediscovery ended, and the period of exploration began.

[1] He had Surville's references to breaks in the coastline in this locality to justify his action.

[2] Fleurieu identified Ndai Island (Gower's Island or Inattendue) with *Nombre de Dios*, naming it *Nombre de Jesus* on his chart (though the editor of the English edition of his *Découvertes* differentiated between *Nombre de Dios* and *Nombre de Jesus*). On the evidence of sixteenth-century charts, which showed Nombre de Jesús far too close to the Solomons as a whole, his identification was an obvious if an incorrect one.

[3] See Fleurieu 1791: 227–43, for his detailed comments on the application of Figueroa's description to the coastlines charted in the eighteenth century.

[4] See Dalrymple 1790, where he reverts to his identification of New Britain, New Ireland and New Guinea as the Solomons.

The Exploration of the Solomons, 1790-1838

THE effect, in terms of geographical knowledge of the Solomons, of the several voyages of the eighteenth century which have so far been examined, may be seen on the published charts of the period. On Sayer's chart, *The Indian and Pacific Oceans between the Cape of Good Hope, New Holland and Japan*, of 1788,[1] the discoveries of Carteret, Bougainville and Surville are delineated as they were charted by their discoverers; but with the island of Choiseul shown quite decidedly as an island,[2] with the erroneous *Geelvink's Coast* and the Terre de la Louisiade of Bougainville shown as two sides of a triangular land mass separate from New Guinea, and with New Britain divided into two islands.[3] On d'Anville's *Hémisphère Oriental (c. 1775)* we see only the discoveries of Carteret and Bougainville, with Bougainville's Strait laid down as a passage between the extended *Geelvink's* coastline of New Guinea, of which the east coast of Bougainville is itself a north-eastern limit, and the island of Choiseul. On Faden's *Western Hemisphere* of 1775 and Dunn's *Scientia Terrarum et Coelorum* of 1772 the discoveries of Bougainville and Carteret alone are delineated, and in both cases the islands of Bougainville and Choiseul are shown as quite large islands with hypothetical coastlines other than those sighted by Bougainville and, in the case of the latter map, with Choiseul identified as *S Christoval* (San Cristóval).

The same outlines occur on a *Chart of the Southern Hemisphere* in Forster's *Voyage Round the World* of 1771, and on Djurberg and Roberts' *Karte von der Inselwelt Polynesien oder den Funften Welttheile* of 1795, where the eastern coast of Choiseul has been firmly defined, presumably on the basis of Surville's voyage, and to the S of which is a short eastern coastline named *Surville's Island or St. Christoval*. These last four charts are rather debased or rough representations of the discoveries made, though of interest. On Djurberg and Roberts' chart the acknowledgement of the discoveries of Shortland consists of nothing more than the application of the name *Neu Georgien Oder Guadalcanal* to the islands which were originally Bougainville Island and Choiseul, and

---

[1] Sayer 1788: Plate I.

[2] Presumably on the assumption, which Fleurieu also made, that the strait which Bougainville saw (the northern entrance to the New Georgia Sound) led through to the sea to the N, and the further assumption, clearly demonstrated by Sayer, that the gap in the coastline which Surville observed between Gros Morne and Port Praslin indicated the southern extremity of Choiseul. The former assumption was incorrect, the latter correct.   [3] Apparently for no good reason.

although the name *Salomons Inseln* extends from *Neu Brittanien* across the area of the Solomons, the *Salomon Inseln* are also laid down some 40° E of New Guinea in the manner of the French charts of the early eighteenth century. As late as 1783 Sayer and Bennett, in their *Chart of the Greater Part of the South Sea*, had followed Green and laid down *Imaginary Isles of Solomon* 174° W of Greenwich, even though Byron's track was plotted through the middle of them, and plotted Santa Cruz twice in order to accommodate Carteret's rediscovery of it in 196° W of Greenwich and its earlier deduced delineation at the south-western extremity of the large *Isabella* of charts of the early eighteenth century.

An interesting attempt to reconcile the coastlines charted by Carteret, Bougainville, Surville and Shortland was made by Laborde in his *Histoire Abregée de la Mer du Sud*[1] of 1791, repeated on his *Carte pour servir au Voyage de M de Surville*[2] of 1791, where the name *Guad-al-canal* is applied to New Guinea,[3] and where Bougainville Island is also delineated as a north-eastern extension of New Guinea and the Louisiade of Bougainville.[4] Of particular interest is Laurie and Whittle's *New Chart of the Indian and Pacific Oceans* of 1797, which is in fact Sayer's chart of 1788 with the coastlines charted by Shortland added. It adheres closely to the records of the discoverers and presents a not unreasonable delineation of the outer coastlines of the archipelago of the Solomons, but shows *Shortland's Passage* to the E of Choiseul and quite distinct and separate from the *Strait of Bougainville*. To what extent this was the result of an attempt to prove an English discovery, or genuinely derived from the belief that the differences in the longitudes recorded by Bougainville and Shortland justified such a deduction, is by no means clear, but it would be unjust, in view of the latter,[5] to accuse the English cartographers of chauvinism.

Henry Lidgbird Ball of the 'Supply'

It would appear that the next visit to the Solomons after Shortland's was made by Lieutenant Ball in the *Supply*. He left Port Jackson on 17 April 1790, bound for Batavia, carrying Lieutenant King with despatches for the Admiralty. His orders were to attempt to charter a relief vessel for the near-starving settlement at Port Jackson, and King was to make his own way to England from

---

[1] Laborde 1791(a): III: opp. 294.

[2] In his *Cartes de la Mer Pacifique* (Laborde 1791(b): Plate 3). See also Laborde 1791(b): Plate 6.

[3] Laborde admits his indebtedness to Dalrymple (d'Alrimple) for this idea.

[4] This frequent delineation of Bougainville as a north-eastern extension of Bougainville's Louisiade (the Louisiade Archipelago), of the supposed *Geelvink* coastline and of New Guinea, may derive from Bougainville's application of the name Louisiade not only to the Louisiade Archipelago but also to Choiseul and Bougainville, and the inference that they were all allied or connected, together with the fact that his chart indicated the possibility of high land well inland from Bougainville's eastern coast.

[5] Bougainville had charted his strait in 153° E of Paris (155° 20′ E of Greenwich), Shortland had charted it in 156° 30′ E of Greenwich (its actual position is 156° 20′ E), so that there were grounds for the suspicion, if not the firm belief, that they were different straits.

Batavia.[1] Proceeding via Norfolk Island, Ball seems to have intended either to follow Shortland's route, of which he knew, or to sail between Santa Cruz and the Îles de la Délivrance (Santa Ana and Santa Catalina) or, as Shortland referred to the latter route, between 'Simboo and Egmont Island'.

At noon on 3 May the estimated position of the *Supply*, according to King's journal, was 12° 13′ S, 161° 33′ E, and the number of birds and floating logs reinforced their belief that they 'were now drawing near the situation in which Lieutenant Shortland had discovered land'.[2] On the morning of the 5th high land was visible bearing NNW to WNW, and at noon, when the position of the vessel was believed to be 11° 7′ S, 162° 34′ E, the land bore N by W at a distance of 5 leagues. This was the south-eastern extremity of San Cristóval, with Santa Ana and Santa Catalina in the foreground; King subsequently refers to the northernmost land visible as having the appearance of a small island and, later, to the northernmost land being two small islands which appeared to trend NNE to SSW, 'the mainland lying a little to the westward of them'. To the southernmost island (Santa Catalina) Ball gave the name *Massey's Island*, and to the northernmost (Santa Ana) the name *Sirius Island*.

Moving slowly northwards in hot sultry weather, an island was sighted to the NW which Ball named *Smith's Island* and which is identifiable with Ulawa, the La Treguada of the Spaniards or Île des Contrariétés of Surville. Land beyond, which Ball coasted until 9 May and which can be easily identified with the east coast of Maramasike and Malaíta, he supposed to be part of Shortland's *New Georgia*. King concluded that they had rounded the east part of 'that island' which Lieutenant Shortland coasted on its south side and, taking Shortland's positions and those recorded on the *Supply*, calculated that the land mass of *New Georgia* must be 62 miles wide and 436 miles long, extending along a line S 57° E and N 57° W, and concluded correctly that there could not be a great deal of distance between Sirius Island and Queen Charlotte's Islands (Santa Cruz). To the 'north-east coast of this island', by which King seems to have meant the north coast of San Cristóval and the east coast of Malaíta, Ball gave the name *Ball's Maiden Land*, and he named the passage between Sirius Island and Queen Charlotte's Islands *Supply's Passage*. Leaving the Malaítan coast on 9 May, the *Supply* headed NE, and by noon on the 10th was in 7° 16′ S, 162° 23′ E. No more landfalls were made in the vicinity of the Solomons, and the *Supply* eventually reached Batavia on 6 July.

Ball's contribution to knowledge of the archipelago was slight, for, though he provided accurate information relating to the position of the south-eastern extremity of the Solomons, and confirmed Surville's discovery of a navigable

[1] The account of Ball's voyage is contained in Lieutenant King's journal, reproduced in Hunter 1793: 419–33. See also the chart *Track of the Supply* (MLS: M2 800 1790/1) and the *Chart of New Georgia, showing the routes of Lieutenants Shortland and Ball, 1788 and 1790*, from the collection of Admiral Richard Earl Howe (d. 1799) (BM: Add. 38076 D93).   [2] Hunter 1973: 417.

passage between the Îles de la Délivrance and Santa Cruz, he had made no discoveries or rediscoveries. His voyage was significant, however, in that it provided recent and reliable information for English shipping from Port Jackson of the existence of a passage other than that used by Shortland.

Captain Hunter of the 'Waaksamhey'd'

On 27 March 1791, the supply-ship *Waaksamhey'd* left Port Jackson under the command of Captain Hunter bound for Norfolk Island and Batavia. Compelled to abandon his attempt to reach Norfolk Island, Hunter determined to head N and to pass between New Caledonia and the New Hebrides.[1] He mistook the Isle of Pines for the south-west point of New Caledonia, and subsequently found himself in some peril. Avoiding disaster on the coast of New Caledonia, he headed NW to 19° S and then hauled to the NE:

so as to pass between Queen Charlotte's Islands and that large track of land which had been seen by Monsieurs Bougainville and Surville formerly, lately by Lieutenant Shortland, in the Alexander Transport, and more recently still by Lieutenant Ball, in his Majesty's armed tender Supply. The part seen by Lieutenant Ball is, I believe, more to the southward, than that seen by the French, and is no doubt the same as that seen by Lieutenant Shortland; but the one sailed along the east, the other along the west side of it. It is highly probable that there is a continuation of the same track, and it is farther probable, by the breaks which have been observed in it, that it is a chain of islands extending in a south-east and north-west direction, and very nearly connected with New Guinea.[2]

Hunter passed the latitudes of 12° to 10° S in longitudes between 163° E and 163° 33′ E, and in consequence sighted neither the south-eastern extremities of the Solomons nor Santa Cruz, though he expressed some surprise that he had not sighted the latter and concluded that it must lie further E than was generally supposed.[3] From the record of Hunter's account it is possible to trace the route of the *Waaksamhey'd*[4] in a generally northerly direction to the latitude of 8° 30′ S. In that approximate latitude, on the morning of 10 May, land was sighted to the WNW which closer investigation revealed to be five small islands, well wooded and apparently with coconuts, which Hunter at first took to be Carteret's Island. The appearance of the islands and their position, which he calculated to be 163° 18′ E, 8° 26′ S, persuaded Hunter of the error of this

---

[1] The account of the voyage of the *Waaksamhey'd* is contained in Hunter 1793: 214–66. See also the *Chart Shewing the Track of the Waaksamhey'd Transport* in Hunter 1793: 264–5.

[2] Hunter 1793: 219.

[3] Carteret had estimated the position of Cape Byron, the eastern end of Santa Cruz, to be 164° 49′ E (according to his log-book) or 164° 32′ E (according to the chart in Hawkesworth's edited account of his voyage), but his officers had estimated its length to be some 50 miles, so that its western extremity could have been charted in 163° 42′ E, only 12 miles to the E of the longitude in which Hunter claimed to have crossed its latitude.

[4] Hunter reproduces the major navigational contents of his log-book (Hunter 1793: 267–73).

identification, and enable us to identify his landfall and discovery with the Polynesian inhabited atoll of Sikaiana, consisting of the five islands of Sikaiana, Faore, Manduiloto, Barena and Matuavi, in 162° 45′ E, 8° 20′ S.[1] Concluding, correctly, that these islands had not been sighted by a European before, Hunter named them *Stewart's Islands*, 'as a mark of . . . respect for the honourable Keith Stewart', but was not able to determine whether or not they were inhabited. These were, of course, the islands of *Chicayana* of which Quirós had heard, and from an indigene of which, Pedro, he had obtained much of his information of the area.

As they headed NW, breakers were sighted on the starboard bow at 9 in the morning of the 12th, no more than 6 miles distant. Several more patches appeared and Hunter passed between them with considerable caution, naming them *Bradley's Shoals* and recording their position as 6° 52′ S, 161° 06′ E. This is a position only 15 miles to the E of that ascribed to the Bradley's Shoals of the modern chart and, since no other shoals are known to lie in this immediate locality, and as their position is still not fixed with certainty, there seems little doubt that they were the same.

At daybreak on the 14th, having headed generally northwards from a noon position on the 13th in 6° 01′ S, 159° 44′ E, Hunter sighted land which resolved itself into a number of islands, 'some of considerable extent, and many of a smaller size'.

Thirty-two were distinctly counted from the mast-head, bearing from north-west half north to north-east half east; many of them were considerably distant, so far as to make it probable that we did not see the whole of this extensive group.[2]
The Islands appeared very thickly covered with wood, among which the cocoa-nut was very distinguishable. . . . They lie in an east and west direction along that side on which we sailed[3] and their latitude on that side is 5° 30′ south, the longitude from 159° 14′ east to 159° 37′ east.

There can be no doubt that Hunter was off the southern limits of the atoll of Ontong Java in 159° 30′ E, 5° 25′ S, probably discovered previously by Le Maire and Schouten and rediscovered and named by Tasman, and to these islands, which he does not appear to have suspected to have been an earlier discovery, Hunter gave the name *Lord Howe's Groupe*. Some contact was had with the inhabitants, who came off in a 'badly made' outrigger canoe wearing what Hunter described as false beards fringed with teeth, and who are identifiable from his further description with the indigenes of Ontong Java.

Continuing westwards until 8 in the morning of the 18th, he then sighted high land to the SW, and seven islands and a sand bank were sighted to the NW. The position of the most southerly of the islands Hunter observed to be

---

[1] Hunter's position was determined by DR from his previous noon position, and it is unlikely that he allowed sufficiently for the prevalent SW setting current.
[2] Hunter 1793: 221.   [3] The south side.

4° 53' S, 155° 20' E, and he deduced, correctly though with some uncertainty, that these were the Nine Islands of Carteret. The high land to the SW seemed to be broken, and Hunter supposed this break to be Shortland's Strait, particularly since Shortland had recorded that shortly after leaving the strait he had fallen in with four islands 'which he took to be part of Carteret's nine islands'. The strait Hunter observed to be in 5° 25' S, 154° 30' E, and it seems highly probably that what he in fact saw was the two islands of Bougainville and Buka, the appearance of a strait being created by the passage between them[1] and by the low-lying nature of the northern extremity of Bougainville. At daylight on the morning of the 19th he sighted and recognized Sir Charles Hardy's Island (The Green Islands) and 'Winchelsea or Lord Anson's Island' (Buka), presumably without realizing that the latter identification contradicted his suppositious identification of Shortland's Strait. From Kilinailau he headed westwards, passed through St. George's Channel between New Britain and New Ireland, and eventually reached Batavia on 27 September.

Captain Edwards of the 'Pandora'

Quite another event which was to have repercussions leading to discoveries in the Solomon Islands was the celebrated mutiny on the *Bounty*. The publication of Bligh's account of it, and of his incredible voyage over 3,168 miles to Timor, excited considerable sympathy, and the Admiralty fitted out an expedition to apprehend the mutineers and return them to England. A frigate, the *Pandora*, was commissioned for the purpose and placed under the command of Captain Edward Edwards.[2] As Basil Thomson has remarked of Edwards, he:

belonged to that useful class of public servant that lives upon instructions. With a roving commission in an ocean studded with undiscovered islands the possibilities of scientific discovery were immense, but he faced them like a blinkered horse that has his eyes fixed on the narrow track before him. . . . Edwards, in the eye of posterity was almost the worst man that could have been chosen.[3]

Leaving England in November 1790, the *Pandora* sailed for the Pacific by way of Cape Horn and made directly for Otaheite, which she reached on 23 March. Edwards narrowly missed sighting Pitcairn, the abode of Christian

---

[1] Buka Passage. On the chart of the track of the *Waaksamhey'd* in Hunter's *Travels* (Hunter 1793 : 264–5) Shortland's Passage is shown correctly, and as distinct from what is clearly Buka Passage, bearing the inscription *Appearance of a Strait*. As the chart was probably the result of later reflection, we may conclude that Hunter afterwards revised his opinion and realized that the 'appearance of a strait' was to the NW of the true position of Shortland's Strait. The same chart also applies the name *Duke of York's Island* to Kilinailau, though in fact the Duke of York's Island was the large island between New Britain and New Ireland, so named by Carteret, and so recognized and referred to by Hunter in his narrative.

[2] For the details of the voyage see Edwards and Hamilton 1915, which contains the accounts of Captain Edwards and his Surgeon, George Hamilton.   [3] Edwards and Hamilton 1915: 4.

and his fellow mutineers, but at Tahiti he arrested fourteen who had remained there. From Tahiti he went as far to the NW as Nukunono in the Union Group and then ran southwards to Samoa, searching between Nomuka, Tofoa, Samoa, Vavua, Pylstaart, Tongatabu and Ewa, and returning to Nomuka at the close of his search.

Edwards now shaped a course for Wallis Island (Uvea), which he sighted on 5 August and where he made contact with the indigenes. He then bore away to the westward, intending to run between Espíritu Santo and Santa Cruz, and on the 8th sighted Rotuma. On the morning of August 12 a small island, 'which met in two high hummocks and a steeple rock which lies high on the West side of the hummocks',[1] was sighted in 11° 49′ S, 190° 04′ 30″ W (169° 55′ 30″ E) and named *Mitre Island*.[2] Shortly afterwards another island, of considerable height but small girth, was sighted in 11° 37′ S, 190° 19′ 30″ W (169° 40′ 30″ E), which appeared to be inhabited and cultivated and which Edwards named *Cherry's Island*.[3] These were the two most easterly islands within the present political boundary of the Solomon Islands, and Edwards appears to have been the first European to sight them.

On the 13th August a little before noon we saw an island bearing about NW by N. In general it is high, but . . . the mountains tapered down to a round point of moderate height. It abounds with wood, even the summits of the mountain are covered with trees. In the SE there was the appearance of a harbour, and from that place the reefs run along the South side to the Westernmost extremity. In some places its distance is not much more than a mile from the shore, in other places it is considerably more. . . . The haziness of the weather prevented us from seeing objects distinctly, yet we saw smoke very plain, from which it may be presumed that the island is inhabited. It is six or seven leagues long and of considerable breadth. I called it Pitt's Island. Its latitude is 11° 50′ 30″ S . . . and longitude 193° 14′ 15″ W.[4]

His last landfall was, of course, the island of Vanikoro, named Ourry's Island or New Alderney by Carteret, and at the time of Edwards' visit there were survivors of la Pérouse's expedition alive on the island. Had Edwards been of a rather more curious and inquisitive disposition, he might well have solved the mystery of la Pérouse's disappearance.

At midnight between the 16th and 17th, after pursuing a westerly course from *Pitt's Island* and whilst laid to for the night, Edwards sighted breakers a mile ahead, and the ship was worn and stood away from them. More breakers which appeared on the beam were avoided by dint of putting on more sail, and at daylight the *Pandora* was put about with the intention of examining them. Edwards estimated the position of these shoals, which consisted of a

---

[1] Edwards and Hamilton 1915: 66.

[2] The Mitre Island of the modern chart, in 11° 55′ S, 170° 12′ E. It is described in the *Pacific Island Pilot* as 'steep, covered with trees, and consisting of two hills and a rock which give it the appearance of a mitre'.

[3] In honour of the Commissioner of the Victualling Office. This was the Cherry Island of the modern chart in 11° 35′ S, 169° 51′ E.   [4] Edwards and Hamilton 1915: 67–68.

double reef below water, 7 miles in extent and enclosing a partial lagoon, to be 12° 20′ S, 200° 2′ W (159° 58′ E), and it is certain that they are identifiable with the Indispensable Reef[1] of the modern chart, though the certainty of their discovery by Edwards suggests that they would properly be referred to by the name which he gave them, *Willis's Shoals*. Continuing westwards Edwards sighted New Guinea on 23 August, discovered the Murray Islands on 25 August, and on the 28th, whilst attempting to make Endeavour Strait, the *Pandora* grounded on a reef and sank after eleven hours. The four ship's boats sailed for Timor, which they reached after eleven days and a voyage for which Edwards, despite his failings, is justly remembered in maritime history.

The First Expedition of Dentrecasteaux

That vessels out from Port Jackson were now beginning to use Bougain-ville's Strait as a matter of course is illustrated in an extract from the *Minutes of the Justice of the Peace of Morlaix* in France. These recorded that George Bowen, captain of the ship *Albemarle*, who had been carried into Morlaix whilst *en route* from Bombay to Lonon, had reported how, whilst sailing from Port Jackson to Bombay in December 1791, he had been on the coast of *New Georgia*.[2] There he had seen pieces of the wreckage of a ship floating upon the water and, having been ashore, gathered from the natives that a vessel had touched on their coasts and that they now knew the use of iron. He added that to his knowledge the only ships which had been on these coasts were those of Bougainville, Shortland, la Pérouse[3] and himself.[4] The authorities of Morlaix were interested in his report as possible evidence of the fate or whereabouts of la Pérouse, and it is by no means impossible that Bowen had sighted wreckage from the boat constructed by the survivors of la Pérouse's expedition at Vani-koro, in which they had attempted to reach Batavia. It is also possible, either that he was mistaken in his identification of debris as wreckage, or that it was

---

[1] So named apparently in the mistaken impression that they were discovered by Captain Wilkinson in the *Indispensable*, an error which will be referred to later. Indispensable Reef, lying 30 miles S of Rennel Island, consists of three separate reefs extending 57 miles NW–SE. North Reef is 12 miles long and 4 miles wide and encloses a deep-water lagoon. Middle Reef is 2 miles to the S of North Reef, 22 Miles SE–NW and 10 miles N–S. South Reef is 2 miles further S again, is 13 miles long and 5 miles wide, and encloses a deep-water lagoon.

[2] His position could have been anywhere along the coastlines chartered by Shortland. From his reference to *New Georgia* it seems likely that he was off the southern limits of the Solomons, and that he was heading for Bougainville's Strait (Shortland's Strait).

[3] The belief that la Pérouse had been on these coasts could only have been deduced from the fact that he intended to visit them. Bowen could not have had any evidence that la Pérouse ever reached them.

[4] There was, of course, also the *Alliance*, and there may have been other American ships in the early days of the race to establish the tea trade.

22

the wreckage of a vessel, perhaps an American vessel engaged like the *Alliance* in opening up new routes to China, of which we know nothing.[1]

In 1791, three years after the disappearance of la Pérouse, the Parisian Society of Natural History made representations to the Constituent Assembly and induced it to petition the King to finance an expedition to search for La Pérouse and to continue the geographical, scientific, commercial and navigational research of previous official expeditions, of which la Pérouse's own had been the most notable. Two vessels, the *Recherche* and the *Espérance*, were commissioned and placed under the command of *Contre-Amiral* Bruny-Dentrecasteaux. He was accompanied by Major and Post-Captain Huon Kermadec, and an *entourage* which included the naturalist Labillardière, Lieutenant Rossel and the hydrographer Beautemps-Beaupré.[2]

The instructions given to Dentrecasteaux[3] are an interesting study in themselves, laying down the route which he was to follow in fairly minute detail and advising him, in respect of his search in the area of Santa Cruz and the Islands of Solomon, to acquaint himself with the work of Fleurieu with its reproduction of the accounts of those who had previously visited these islands. They added that:

Il importe que le sieur Dentrecasteaux puise verifer le récit du voyageur Espagnol, qui avoit abordé a plusieurs; et qu'il s'occupe a detailler cet archipel, dont il est d'autant plus interessant d'acquerir une connoissance parfaite, qu'on peut avec raison le regarder comme une découverte des François, puis qu'il était resté ignoré et inconnu pendant les deux siècles qui s'étoient écoulés depuis que les Espagnols en avoient fait la première découverte.[4]

The fact that his instructions implicitly required him to obtain '*une connoissance parfaite*' of the Solomons, and that he was equipped with such information of them as was available in 1791, offered him a unique opportunity to explore the archipelago and to add considerably to contemporary knowledge of it.

Dentrecasteaux's expedition left Brest on 28 September 1791, and made for Cape Town. Here he received two depositions from Frenchmen in Batavia to the effect that Captain Hunter and several officers of the *Sirius*[5] had reported seeing natives off the Admiralty Islands wearing uniforms of the French navy, and had expressed the belief that la Pérouse had been wrecked there. Hunter, however, who left Cape Town for England two days after Dentrecasteaux

---

[1] For Bowen's statement see La Pérouse 1798: 51. He arrived in Port Jackson on 13 October 1791, and departed later in the year. See *Historical Records of New South Wales* 1893: I (Part 2): 422, 487, 532, 558–9; and Collins 1798: I: 181–2, 190.

[2] For Dentrecasteaux's voyage see the account of Dentrecasteaux himself, edited by Rossel (Rossel 1808); the account of Labillardière (Labillardière 1800); and the *Atlas du Voyage de Bruny d'Entrecasteaux* of Beautemps-Beaupré (1807). The charts in the latter publication, though laying down the route of Dentrecasteaux's expedition and demonstrating the cartographical developments and achievements made by it, are also indebted to the voyage of Captain Manning in 1792.

[3] Rossel 1808: I: xix–xlv.   [4] Rossel 1808: I: xxxiii–xxxiv.

[5] They were on board the *Waaksamhey'd* following the wreck of the *Sirius*.

arrived without contacting him, had denied the truth of these reports to several people in Cape Town.[1] From the Cape Dentrecasteaux made for the S of New Holland and Van Diemen's Land, and then headed N to New Caledonia and the Terres des Arsacides.

At 10 in the morning of 9 July 1792, land was sighted which Dentrecasteaux identified as the Arsacides in the vicinity of Cape Nepean. At 4.30 p.m. Eddystone Rock was sighted and recognized and, like Shortland, Dentrecasteaux at first mistook it for a vessel under sail.[2] As they headed NW, without apparently sighting anything more than Eddystone, Simbo,[3] and part of the south-western coast of Ranongga, the Treasury Islands were sighted on the following day. Beautemps-Beaupré's chart[4] reveals that by these were meant the island of Mono and the small islet on its southern coast,[5] but the *Recherche* also sailed in close towards the south coast of the largest of the islands which now bear the name Shortland's Islands, and recognized that it was separated from the coast of Bougainville. Dentrecasteaux now followed and charted the west coast of Bougainville Island northwards, following, although he did not realize it, in the wake of the *Alliance*.

At noon on the 14th the channel between Bouka (Buka) and Bougainville was sighted, and once the expedition had made the north cape of the former they congratulated themselves on having explored their eastern coasts. On the 16th, as the two vessels were headed towards New Ireland, Sir Charles Hardy's Island (the Green Islands) was sighted to the N, and recognized. Dentrecasteaux made a short stay at Carteret Harbour, and then sailed through St. George's Channel for Amboyna. From Amboyna he sailed S along the west coast of New Holland, eastwards and around Van Diemen's Land, and then headed for the northern extremity of New Zealand, the Friendly Islands and New Caledonia. He left the latter on 10 May 1793, bound once again for the Solomon Islands.

Captain Manning of the 'Pitt'

In the meantime, however, between his departure in July 1792, and his return in May 1793, the archipelago was visited by at least three other navigators. At some time during the year 1792, Captain Edward Manning took the

[1] This is perplexing, for there seems no good reason why Hunter should have concocted the story or denied it if true, or, for that matter, why the French in Batavia should have concocted the story of Hunter's report.

[2] The two narratives, and the *Tables of Positions* and maps contained in them, together with the charts in Beautemps-Beaupré's *Atlas*, leave no doubt as to the approximate route followed and the landfalls made. The *Table of Positions* for the *Recherche* is included in Rossel 1808, and for the *Espérance* in Labillardière 1800. See Beautemps-Beaupré 1808: No. 24.

[3] Which Beautemps-Beaupré's chart shows they suspected to be a promontory, as Shortland had done, and for which the name Cape Satisfaction was retained.

[4] Beautemps-Beaupré 1807: No. 24.   [5] Charted as four small islets.

East India Company vessel *Pitt* N from Port Jackson between the Russell Islands and Buraku, and NW through the straits between Santa Ysabel and Choiseul which now bear the name Manning Straits. The exact date of Manning's voyage is uncertain, though he was certainly at Port Jackson in February, 1792, having arrived there on the 14th of that month from England.[1] No account of the voyage appears to be readily available,[2] but a copy of Manning's chart is,[3] and his route is laid down on several charts of the period.[4]

How Manning came to discover this particular route is not clear, though it seems likely that he intended to use Shortland's Passage/Bougainville's Strait, but was either misled by the discovery of open water where mainland had been charted by Shortland into thinking that he had reached Shortland's Passage or, more probably, decided to explore to the N in the hope of finding a better passage than that for which he was sailing.

It appears from his chart that he sighted the south coast of San Cristóval, identifying Cape Phillip; passed to the S of Guadalcanal on a north-westerly course, identifying Cape Henslow; and that he came upon the Russell Islands of the modern chart, to which he gave the name *MacCaulay's Archipelago*. Although he realized that this was an archipelago, he still seems to have imagined that it was off Shortland's Cape Marsh, itself contiguous with the mainland behind Cape Henslow. The main island of the Russells, Pavuvu, which forms the western side of the group, he also suspected of being a cape, perhaps contiguous with Cape Marsh (with which it should probably have been identified), and named it *Cape Raban*. To the W he came upon Buraku (Baruku) which he named *Murray's Island*, and just short of it he headed N into what probably appeared to be open water.

He now seems to have come within sight of the west coast of Santa Ysabel, naming the high land *Keate's Mountains*, and the most southerly visible point *Cape Robertson*. For three days he followed a varied course between Santa Ysabel to the NE and the northern coastline of the New Georgia Group to the SW, naming the island of Gatukai *Cape Traverse* and apparently assuming that this coastline was a continuous one. He then sailed to the NW, apparently searching for a passage to the W of Keate's Mountains and naming a prominent point on the coast of Ysabel *Cape Foxhall*, and came to the shoal patches to the

[1] See *Historical Records of New South Wales* 1893: I (Part 2): 496, 526; Collins 1798: I: 201. The *Pitt* seems to have been owned by George Mackenzie Macaulay Esquire, and to have been employed by the Royal Navy for the voyage out to Port Jackson and by the East India Company for the commercial return voyage. See *Historical Records of New South Wales* 1893: II: 39.

[2] Two log-books from the *Pitt* for voyages between 1788–90 and 1794–5 do exist but do not relate to this voyage.

[3] ... *Chart describing the Track and Discoveries of the Ship Pitt, Captn Edward Manning in the Service of the Honble East India Company, On the Western coast of the Solomon Islands, made in a Voyage from Port Jackson to Batavia in the Year 1792.* MLS: Admiralty Hydrographic Collection, e15 shelf Pc.

[4] See, for example, A. Arrowsmith's *Chart of the Pacific Ocean*, 1798, Sheet 3, and Krusenstern's *Carte Systematique de l'Archipel des Isles de Salomon* of 1824 in Krusenstern 1827: Chart No. 9.

S of Manning Strait. From his chart it appears that he sailed through Pasco Passage, the most easterly of the three navigable channels through them, and came to the passage between Ysabel and Choiseul. To the W he sighted Taura Peak,[1] which he named *Mount Elphinstone*, and assumed that it formed the north-eastern limit of a coastline of which Cape Traverse was also a part. Gagi Island[2] he charted but did not name, and Nidero Island,[3] off the coast of Ysabel, he named *Nairne's Island*.

On the modern charts the name Manning Strait is applied to the stretch of water between the Arnavon Islands[4] and Santa Ysabel, but it is quite clear from his chart that Manning actually used the Kologilo Passage between Molakobi[5] and Gagi Island, two of the group of islands at the north-western extremity of Santa Ysabel. His choice of this apparently less suitable route than one to the NW, may have been dictated by the sight of the sea breaking off Kerihikapa Island[6] and the shoal patches which extend well out to westward as far as 157° 51' E, 7° 14' S. Manning's *Remarks* on his chart are further evidence that the passage used was Kologilo Passage, that what he named *Half-Drowned Bay* was the bay between the Perigo Shoal[7] and Remark Islet[8] of the modern chart, and that what he named *Cape Comfort* was the extreme northern point of Bates Island.[9]

Captain Bond of the 'Royal Admiral'

In December 1792, Captain Henry Essex Bond in the *Royal Admiral* left Port Jackson bound for Canton and sailed through the passage between Santa Cruz and San Cristóval without sighting land. His log-book[10] clearly disproves the fiction of several contemporary charts,[11] which laid down his route to the immediate E of Santa Cruz and S of the Swallow or Reef Islands, and the statement by Purdy that:

The Great Eastern Passage to China: Bond's Passage: This Passage, by an East India ship, was first attempted in 1792 and 1793, by Captain Bond of the Royal Admiral. From Port Jackson . . . he passed about 40 leagues westwards of Lord Howe's Island . . . doubled the reef off the north-west end of New Caledonia, came to the easternmost point of Santa

---

[1] Surville's Gros Morne.   [2] 7° 25' S, 158° 14' E.   [3] 7° 40' S, 158° 28' E.
[4] 7° 26' S, 158° 01' E.   [5] 7° 22' S, 158° 07' E.   [6] 7° 25' S, 158° 01' E.
[7] 7° 21' S, 158° 11' E.
[8] 7° 22' S, 158° 11' E: Manning refers in his *Remarks* to a tall tree on Remark Islet which still survives.   [9] 7° 21' S, 158° 13' E.
[10] CRO (Military Records Section, Old India Office): 338F.
[11] See, for example, Laurie and Whittle's *New Chart of the Indian and Pacific Oceans* of 1797, and Butler's chart in their *East India Pilot* (Laurie and Whittle 1799: Chart 87 Laurie and Whittle 1803: II: 125). See also Laurie and Whittle 1799: Chart 1, and Laurie and Whittle 1803: II: Chart 1, where his route is laid down correctly between Santa Cruz and San Cristoval.

Cruz or Egmont Island, and having sailed between that point and Swallow Island, crossed the Line in 166° 10′ of East longitude.[1]

The error is understandable when it is realized that Santa Cruz was currently charted to the W of its true position,[2] and when it is noted that Bond in his log-book entry for 4 December 1792 remarks, apropos a position at 8 p.m. on the 3rd between 164° 19′ E and 164° 47′ E and slightly N of 11° S, that:

Being near the Situation of the Island of Santa Cruz or Queen Charlotte's Island as laid down in the Chart. No land in sight hove too and sounded as per log—it is laid down erroneously or we must have seen it our longitude being correct and to be relied on.

It would appear that Bond did not in fact pass to the E of Santa Cruz, but that in the light of his recorded positions and the current error in the charting of Santa Cruz it was assumed by contemporary cartographers that he must have done so.[3]

Captain Boyd of the 'Bellona'

In March 1793, the Solomons were visited again by an East Indiaman, this time the *Bellona* under the command of Captain Matthew Boyd.[4] Leaving Port Jackson on 19 February, Boyd had reached a position in 12° S, 160° E by the morning of 3 March. At 5 a.m. he sighted part of Indispensable Reef, previously discovered by Edwards and named by him Willis's Shoals, and at 8.30 a.m. saw land to the NE which he took to be 'the Island of Arsacides'. By noon, as he approached more closely, he realized that it was a much smaller island in 11° 36′ S, 160° 10′ E, and it is identifiable with the island of Rennell.[5] At 1 a.m. on the 4th another island, some 8 miles long, was sighted to the NNW of the first island, and 7 leagues distant from it. This second island is identifiable with the island of Bellona, and after coasting it to the W Boyd headed northwards. At 8.30 a.m. land was sighted to the NE by N, which would seem to have been the south coast of Guadalcanal, and at noon Boyd recorded a position in 10° 06′ S, 159° 00′ E.

Heading generally WNW, he sighted the Russell Islands (MacCaulay's Archipelago) and Buraku (Murray's Island), and between 5 and 11 March generally followed Shortland's route to the S of Vangunu, Tetipari, Rendova

---

[1] Purdy 1816: 685. The passage between Santa Cruz and the Solomons had of course already been sailed by Surville, Ball and Hunter, but Bond was probably the first East-Indiaman to use it.

[2] See Laurie and Whittle's *New Chart of the Indian and Pacific Oceans* of 1797. On Butler's chart of 1799 (Laurie and Whittle 1803: II: 125), Santa Cruz is correctly positioned.

[3] On the *Royal Admiral* see *Historical Records of New South Wales* 1893: I (Part 2): 620, 665; II: 33, 470, 789, 793; and Collins 1798: I: 236.

[4] See his log-book, CRO (Military Records Section, Old India Office): 353A. See also *Historical Records of New South Wales* 1893: II: 13, and Collins, 1798: I: 261–3, 268.

[5] The position of the island of Rennell has recently been corrected on Admiralty Charts and moved slightly to the N of its original position. Boyd's observed position was correct and conforms with the recently recharted one.

and Simbo, to the W of Ranongga and Vella Lavella, through the strait between Choiseul and Bougainville, and then northwards. He makes no reference
in his log-book to the possible identification of the lands sighted, other than
to refer to them generally as the *Island of Arsacides* and to refer specifically to
Shortland's Strait, of which he obviously knew and which he intended to use.
Nor does he seem to have accorded any names to his two discoveries, the islands
of Rennell and Bellona, and although the latter name seems likely to have been
accorded in honour of his vessel, perhaps by a hydrographer, the origin of the
name Rennell is uncertain.[1]

The Second Expedition of Dentrecasteaux

Dentrecasteaux, whom we left *en route* from New Caledonia for the Solomons in May 1793, sighted Santa Cruz during the morning of 20 May, 22
miles to the NW. He coasted the southern,[2] western and northern sides of the
island, charting it with commendable accuracy and fixing the position of Cape
Byron within 10 miles of its true position. After sailing NNE from Cape
Byron for a short distance without sighting Swallow Island (the Reef Islands),
and being prevented by contrary winds from entering Graciosa Bay, he then
made sail to the W 'for the Islands of the Arsacides'.

At 10 a.m. on 26 May the Îles de la Délivrance were sighted to the W,[3]
with the land of the Arsacides beyond them. Throughout the 27th and 28th
Dentrecasteaux's two vessels coasted to the S of the land, which appeared to be
quite mountainous, rounded Cape Phillip, and discovered the passage between
what were correctly identified as San Cristóval and Guadalcanal.[4] Naming the
north-western cape of the former *Cap de la Recherche*, Dentrecasteaux sailed as
far as E as the Île des Contrariétés of Surville,[5] sighting Les Trois Soeurs, the
Île du Golfe[6] and rediscovering Bio island to the NW of the latter. The

---

[1] Arrowsmith's *Chart of the Pacific Ocean* of 1798 lays down Indispensable or Willis's Reef, with the
inscription 'Shoal discovered by the Bellona 1790'; and the two islands of Rennell and Bellona, though
only the latter is named. The erroneous date and the attribution of the discovery of the shoal to the
Bellona instead of to the *Pandora* are unfortunately typical of the confusion and inconsistencies relating
to these islands and Indispensable Reef in the work of several contemporary hydrographers.

[2] Beautemps-Beaupré's chart of the Santa Cruz Group is perplexing for it lays down Carteret's
Edgecombe's and Ourry's Islands (Utupua and Vanikoro), but also lays down an *Ile de la Recherche*
to their SE in 11° 40' S. As the latter can only have been Vanikoro, it seems highly likely that Utupua,
viewed from the SW and into the deep bay which it surrounds on three sides, appeared to be two
islands. Assuming that Carteret's chart, which laid down Edgecombe's and Ourry's Islands too
close together, supported this, Dentrecasteaux further assumed that the islands of Vanikoro was a new
discovery, and charted and named it without visiting it. See Beautemps-Beaupré 1807: Charts Nos.
19 and 20.

[3] See Beautemps-Beaupré 1807: Chart No. 22, where the Îles de la Délivrance are correctly identified as Santa *Anna* (Ana) and Santa Catalina, and Rossel 1808: I: 381–2.

[4] Beautemps-Beaupré 1807: Chart No. 22; Rossel 1808: I: 387.

[5] La Treguada of the Spaniards, or Ulawa.   [6] The San Juan of the Spaniards.

south-west coast of Malaíta was sighted and charted, though its identity was not hazarded, and the expedition then headed westwards along the south coast of Guadalcanal. He came to its western extremity, to which the name *Cap de l'Espérance* was given,[1] and to the Russell Islands or MacCaulay's Archipelago, which he recognized as Shortland's Cape Marsh but which he charted as separate from Guadalcanal.

He passed to the S of Buraku, which Beautemps-Beaupré later identified as Manning's Murray's Island,[2] and coasted Shortland's Cape Pitt, Hummock Bay, Cape Nepean and Cape Pleasant, and charted them with recognizable accuracy. At the south-western extremity of Rendova Dentrecasteaux bore away to the S as far as 11° 30′ S, and then headed W towards the Louisiade of Bougainville, convinced that the survey made left no room to doubt that these Islands of Arsacides were indeed the Islands of Solomon. Coasting Bougainville's Louisiade to the N, he confirmed the suspicion that this was only a chain of islands extending south-eastwards from New Guinea, and dispelled once and for all the idea that the coastline which earlier cartographers had believed the *Geelvink* to have discovered did exist. He passed through Dampier's Strait, coasted the west side of New Britain and New Ireland, and made the Admiralty Islands in July 1793, where he died. The remainder of the expedition reached the Dutch East Indies in October 1793, hearing there for the first time of the creation of the French Republic and the execution of the King in the previous January. It was here, with the impounding of the vessels by the Dutch and the division of the *expeditionaires* into Royalist and Republican factions, that the expedition ended.

Although the achievements of the expedition were not inconsiderable, they were considerably less than might, in the circumstances, have been expected. Dentrecasteaux brought no light to bear on the fate of la Pérouse, and provided only limited new information concerning the islands of Solomon. Such charting as was done was of a high order, but it hardly fulfilled the instruction to obtain *une connoissance parfaite* and left the great body of the archipelago still either unknown or but vaguely charted. Apart from its accurate surveying, its charting of the western coast of Bougainville, its identification of Santa Ana, Santa Catalina, San Cristóval and Guadalcanal, its recognition that Cape Marsh was separate from Guadalcanal, and its charting of Savo, the expedition had achieved nothing. It had certainly clarified much that was already vaguely known and delineated but, apart from one brief foray between San Cristóval, Guadalcanal and Malaíta, it had made no attempt to penetrate the archipelago and clarify the all-important question of the delineation of the interior coastlines, contenting itself in fact with a re-examination of coastlines which, with the exception of the western coast of Bougainville, were already known.

[1] From Cap de l'Espérance the island of Savo (the Sesarga of the Spaniards) was sighted and charted, but not recognized or identified (Rossel 1808: I: 396).   [2] Beautemps-Beaupré 1807: No. 23.

Captains Wilkinson (Indispensable) and Page (Halcyon)

A significant contribution to knowledge of the eastern parts of the archipelago was made in 1794 by Captain Wilkinson in the *Indispensable* and Captain Benjamin Page in the American merchantman *Halcyon*, who sailed in company through the strait between San Cristóval and Guadalcanal, and between the Nggela Group and Malaíta, now known as Indispensable Strait. In the contemporary charts and pilots some confusion occurs as to the date of Wilkinson's voyage, but there can be no doubt that the year 1794 is the correct one. His route is laid down on Butler's *Chart of the Western Part of the Pacific Ocean* of 1800,[1] attributed to the year 1790; on Norie's chart of the Western Pacific of 1833,[2] attributed to the year 1796; in part on Norie's *Chart of the Islands and Passages in the vicinity of Papua or New Guinea* of 1841 and on Krusenstern's *Carte Systematique de l'Archipel des Isles de Salomon* of 1824,[3] attributed, correctly, to the year 1794.

From the charts it appears that Wilkinson came N from Port Jackson, bound for Bengal, sighted Willis's Shoals,[4] which were subsequently named *Indispensable Reef*[5]; passed between the islands of Rennel and Bellona, previously discovered by Boyd in the *Bellona;* and made for the passage between San Cristóval and Guadalcanal. It is unlikely that he had any other information to go on than Shortland's belief that there might be a passage between Cape Phillip and Cape Henslow, for he could hardly have known of Dentrecasteaux's partial exploration of this area. That 1794 was the year in which Wilkinson made the discovery of this passage is supported by the apparent absence of any evidence to the effect that he was in these waters at an earlier date,[6] and by the fact that he was accompanied in his voyage through the passage by the American *Halcyon*. The latter vessel had left Providence, Rhode Island, with a speculative

---

[1] Laurie and Whittle 1803: II: 125.   [2] Norie 1833: Chart No. 26A.

[3] Krusenstern 1827: Chart No. 9. See also Krusenstern 1824: 165.

[4] On some charts of the period Willis's Shoals are laid down as separate from Indispensable Reef with the name *Wells Reef*.

[5] Purdy 1816: 100, cites Wilkinson 'in 1790' as his authority for positioning Indispensable Reef between 12° 46′ S, 160° 40′ E and 11° 44′ S, 159° 58′ E and *Rennell's Isles* in 11° 13′ S, 159° 58′ E (i.e. the 'Eastern Island' or Rennel, the name *Rennell's Isles* including both Rennel and Bellona). Rienzi mistakenly attributes the discovery of Rennel and Bellona to Butler in the *Walpole* in 1794, but adds: '*et revue dans la même année par l'Indispensable*' (Rienzi 1855: II: 383). He also remarks, correctly, that '*le récif de la Pandora découvert par le capitaine Edwards en 1791 sans doute le même qui fut revu en 1794 par l'Indispensable*'. Findlay incorrectly attributes Wilkinson with the discovery in 1790 of Rennel's Island and Indispensable Reef (Findlay 1851: xxiii).

[6] *The Historical Records of New South Wales* 1893: II: 82–84, 237, record that the *Indispensable* arrived in Sydney for the first time on 24 May 1794, and returned again in 1796. See also Collins 1798: I: 254 *et seq*, 261, 374, 370, 378–9; II: 317, which provides further details of the arrival and departure of the *Halcyon* and *Indispensable*. Wilkinson did in fact sail through Indispensable Strait again in 1796 (see Krusenstern 1824: 165, and Laurie's *Chart of the Islands and Passages in the vicinity of Papua or New Guinea* of 1841).

cargo for Sydney, arriving there on 14 June 1794. She left on 8 July, bound for Canton, and accompanied the *Indispensable* through the passage[1] which, though it was to become known to English seamen as *Indispensable Strait*, was also to become known 'as Page's Straits to a generation of American Ship-masters'.[2] Sailing northwards between Guadalcanal and Malaíta, Nggela and Malaíta, and Santa Ysabel and Malaíta, the *Indispensable* passed to the E of the small island in 8° 15′ 30″ S, 160° 11′ E which now bears the erroneous name of *Ramos* and came to the clear water to the N, having in fact discovered an infinitely more suitable passage than those of either Bougainville and Shortland or Manning. Wilkinson now appears to have headed NW, for he is credited in several contemporary hydrographic sources with the sighting of a group of islands in 4° 36′ S, 156° 30′ E to which he gave the name *Cocos Islands*. It[3] seems likely that these were the islands of Tau'u Atoll, previously discovered by Schouten and le Maire, and named by them Marquen, but it also seems likely that, *en route* to them, Wilkinson passed to the S and in sight of Ontong Java, the Lord Howe's Groupe of Hunter.[4] He again passed through the strait two years later, in 1796, this time sailing to the W of the small island between the northern extremity of Malaíta and Santa Ysabel.[5]

[1] In a statement relating to two convicts who had escaped from Port Jackson on board the *Indispensable* in July 1794, and who had been the subject of a letter from the Navy Board in London to Under-Secretary King dated 13 May 1795, Wilkinson explained that: 'After being from the land some considerable distance Mr. Pitt brought a strange man out of his cabin. "Good God" said I "we must return back", but the wind being strong off the land was impossible. The man's name was Richard Haynes. A short time after Captn Page of the Halcyon in company, hailed me and said: "I have got one of the convicts on board; what whall we do?" ' (*Historical Records of New South Wales* 1893: II: 295–6). The statement was probably made when Wilkinson returned to Port Jackson in 1796, but since the *Indispensable* was a well-armed but short-handed ship, and since Wilkinson carried a letter of marque, it was probably made with tongue in cheek.

[2] Kenny 1958. See also the log-books of Benjamin Page Jnr. and Christopher Bently (John Carter Brown Library) and the journal of Dr. Benjamin Bowen Carter (Library of the Rhode Island Historical Society) which relate to a voyage by Benjamin Page in the *Ann and Hope* in November 1798, through Indispensable Strait. The Strait is described with the names given to its landmarks by Page in 1794. I am most grateful to Professor Kenny of Brown University for valuable information on the two voyages of Captain Page.

[3] See Findlay 1851: 1015–16, who gives the date as 1790 and identifies the islands with the Marqueen (Marquen) of le Maire and Schouten, and Krusenstern 1824: 174, who gives the date as 1794. On Laurie's *Chart of the Islands and Passages in the vicinity of Papua or New Guinea* of 1841 they are laid down in 4° 30′ S, 156° 30′ E, identified with Marquen, and described as rediscovered by Wilkinson in 1794. On Krusenstern's *Carte Systematique . . . des Isles de Salomon* of 1824 they are similarly laid down (Krusenstern 1827: Chart No. 9), and also on Arrowsmith's *Chart of the Pacific Ocean* of 1832.

[4] According to Purdy, Wilkinson was his authority for positioning *Howe's Group* (*Barrington or SW Isle*), i.e. Ontong Java, in 5° 35′ S, 159° 15′ E. The several islands charted by Hunter from the *Waaksamhey'd* in the Ontong Java Groupe, and named by him Lord Howe's Group, seem to have subsequently acquired a variety of individual names including *Barrington*, *Curtis*, *Parker*, *Hotham* and *Hammond*, (see Norrie 1833: Chart No. 26A). It is possible that either Wilkinson or Hunter was responsible for these names. See Purdy 1816: 100. The Cocos Islands (Tau'u) may also be the *New Spice Island* described as having recently been discovered by Captain Page of the *Halcyon* in the *Boston Independent Chronicle*, 9 July 1795, and the *Connecticut Gazette*, 16 July 1795. [5] Krusenstern 1824: 165.

Captains Butler and Mortlock

Another East Indiaman who has been erroneously credited with the discovery of the islands of Rennell and Bellona in 1794[1] is Captain Thomas Butler of the *Walpole*. In fact, his own chart and log-book[2] reveal that he was barely near the Solomons at all. He was off Van Diemen's Land on 1 November 1794, headed for China from England and Table Bay, and reached Norfolk Island on 15 November. His object was to follow the channel between New Caledonia and the New Hebrides, and to the 'westward of Santa Cruz, or the isles called Queen Charlotte's Isles',[3] but in fact he passed between Tanna and Erronan in the Southern New Hebrides, and then ran northwards, passing to the E of Cherry Island and Mitre Island and crossing the line in 166° 15′ E.

In 1795 another East Indiaman, the *Young William*, commanded by Captain James Mortlock, seems to have passed through the Solomons, and to have sighted Tau'u.[4] His voyage is of little interest in this study, other than for the fact that it added yet another name, *Hunter's Islands*,[5] to the islands along the northern perimeter of the Solomons, but Mortlock did position the atoll with accuracy in 4° 48′ S, 157° 0′ E. His route through the Solomons has not been plotted but, since the three main passages S to N through the archipelago had now been opened up, it is doubtful if it brought any new light to bear on the interior configuration of the Solomons as a whole.[6] If anything Mortlock's sighting of Tau'u Atoll probably added to the increasing confusion of contemporary charts, which were beginning to become cluttered with repetitions of the same islands due to slight differences in the estimated positions accorded to them by successive navigators.

[1] See, for example, *The Colonial Magazine and Commercial Maritime Journal*, Vol. VI, September-December 1841, p. 84; Rienzi 1855: III: 383; and Krusenstern 1824: 172.

[2] Butler's *Chart of the Western Part of the Pacific Ocean* of 1800 in Laurie and Whittle 1803: II: 125, on which his route in 1794 is plotted. CRO (Military Records Section: Old India Office): 293R, *Log-book of the Walpole (Captain Thos. Butler) to China 1794–5*.   [3] Purdy 1816: 691.

[4] The Marquen of le Maire, and Cocos Islands of Wilkinson.

[5] Mortlock may have named them *Hunter's Islands* in the belief that these were the seven islands sighted by Hunter from the *Waaksamheyd* (Kilinailau).

[6] His log-book is extant, CRO (Military Records Section: Old India Office). The *Young William* arrived in Sydney on 4 October 1795, and departed for Whampoa on 29 October (Collins 1798: I: 429, 431). See also *Historical Records of New South Wales* 1893: II: 284, 296. According to Findlay, 'MORTLOCK ISLES—a group to which Admiral Krusenstern applied this name, was discovered by Capt. Mortlock, in the Young William, in 1795, in lat. 4° 45′ S., and lon. 157° 0′ E. He called them Hunters Islands; but as this name is given to several others in the Pacific, that of this discoverer was preferred. They do not appear to have been since seen, but are evidently a distinct group from the other, described above' (i.e. Lord Howe's Islands) (Findlay 1851: 1015). Purdy describes *Ontong Java-Southern Isle* as being in 4° 48′ E, 157° 00′ E, on the authority of 'Mortlock in the ship Young William, 1795' (Purdy 1816: 100), Krusenstern states that Mortlock discovered *Hunter islands* in 4° 45′ S, 157° 00′ E in 1795 (Krusenstern 1824: 174, see also Krusenstern 1827: Chart No. 9), and Rienzi states that Mortlock discovered islands which he named Hunter's Islands, which he (Rienzi) identified with Marquen (Rienzi 1855: III: 384). See also Horsburgh 1809: 478.

Captain Hogan of the 'Cornwallis'

By this stage in the history of European navigation through the Solomons it is very likely that more vessels were passing through the archipelago than are known about. The fact that navigators had knowledge of the existence of three passages through the group, and the quite considerable amount of English and American shipping which was now sailing N from Sydney, render this supposition very probable. Nevertheless, provided this probability is borne in mind, it can be argued that the voyages which contributed to cartographical knowledge were in fact those of which we know, from references to them in contemporary hydrographic material,[1] and that it is with these that such a study as this must be primarily concerned.

One such voyage which, though making no new discoveries or significant rediscoveries, did provide further information for the correction of charts and the compilation of hydrographic data, was that of the *Marquis Cornwallis* under the command of Captain Hogan. Arriving at Sydney on 11 February 1796,[2] with convicts from Ireland,[3] she left in May,[4] bound for India. An extract from Hogan's log-book was reproduced by Purdy,[5] and his route is laid down on Butler's *Chart of the Western Part of the Pacific Ocean*[6] and on Norie's Pacific chart of 1833.[7]

He sailed northwards between Tanna and Erronan in the New Hebrides, and by 26 June was off the island of Aurora. On the following day he made Santa Cruz and:

Having run along that island from East to West, and sought in vain for the two islands Edgecumbe and Ourry, as laid down by Captain Carteret . . . close in with the south-east part of this shore, on a small scale, I am now very much inclined to believe that he must have meant two isles seen by us in the morning, and to which I will give no name, although (with due submission to that able navigator) he has entirely mistaken their size and situation, as well as the position of this Isle of Egmont.[8]

Hogan was quite correct in this deduction, but he was himself slightly in error in locating Ourry (Vanikoro) in 11° 37′ S, 167° 11′ E, Edgecumbe (Utupua) in 11° 19′ S, 166° 55′ E, the south-west cape of Santa Cruz in 10° 55′ S, 166° 10′ E, and Volcano Island (Tinakula) in 10° 38′ S, 166° 12′ E.[9]

---

[1] It seems quite likely that a particularly American body of hydrographic information concerning the Pacific was developing at this time, largely independent of European hydrography. I have not had the opportunity to pursue this aspect, contenting myself primarily with the development of European knowledge of the archipelago of the Solomons, but it might well provide an interesting avenue for research. The voyages of, for example, the *Alliance* and the *Halcyon*, may have contributed to the emergence of a peculiarly American chart of the Western Pacific with a particularly American nomenclature.

[2] Collins 1798: I: 45.   [3] *Historical Records of New South Wales* 1893: II: 299–300, 315, 335, 356.

[4] Collins 1798: I: 478.   [5] Purdy 1816: 675–8.   [6] Laurie and Whittle 1803: II: 125.

[7] Norie 1833: Chart 26A. See also Rienzi 1855: III: 382.   [8] Purdy 1816: 676.

[9] Hogan prided himself on his use of Earnshaw's chronometer and the results obtained. Purdy was later to abandon Edward's position for Pitt's Island (Ourry or Vanikoro) of 11° 50′ 30″ S, 166° 45′ 45″ E, in favour of Hogan's less accurate longitudinal but more accurate latitudinal position (Purdy 1816: 98).

From Cape Boscawen Hogan headed NW and sighted one of 'the small isles, which Captain Hunter named Stewart's Islands' which he located in 8° 31′ S, 162° 57′ E.[1] Passing to the S, he made Gower's Island[2] on the 2nd of July and shortly afterwards sighted the *Arsacides Land* to the W. He followed the northern coastlines of the Solomons, identifying Manning's Strait and Shortland's Strait, remarking of the coastline of Bougainville that it was the highest he had ever seen, 'and some of it remarkably picturesque', and eventually making New Ireland and St. George's Channel.

Captain Wilson of the 'Duff'

Increasing European activity in the Pacific, and the emergence of the evangelical movement in England, combined to produce the appearance of Protestant missions. Whilst the extension of their activities to the Solomons was not to occur for some time, the establishment of one mission in the Eastern Pacific was to result in a quite accidental contribution to the rediscovery and exploration of them. In 1796 the London Missionary Society decided to establish missions on the islands of Otaheite, Samoa, the Marquesas and Pelew, and a vessel was prepared to implement this project. The *Duff* was placed under the command of Captain James Wilson, who was granted considerable discretionary powers in the delivery of the missionaries to their respective islands, and who, having completed his task, was to proceed to Canton to obtain a cargo of tea from the East India Company factory. Quite where the crew, whom one of the missionaries described as ever 'wishing to be instrumental in so blessed a service', were recruited from, is a matter for interesting conjecture.

The *Duff* left Spithead on 10 August 1796, cleared from Portsmouth on the 24th, and sailed S of the Cape of Good Hope, New Holland and New Zealand, to arrive at Otaheite on 4 March 1797. She then proceeded to Tongatabu and the Marquesas, and returned to Otaheite after completing the delivery of the missionaries. She left Otaheite on 4 August, called again at Tongatabu, which she left on 7 September, and then headed NW and W. She passed N of the Fiji Group,[3] sighted Rotumah on 16 September, and was then headed 'NW by W to W and W by S for 8 days'.[4]

At 8 a.m. on 25 September land was sighted to the NW by N, and the ship was immediately headed towards it. It soon resolved itself into 'ten or

---

[1] Sikaiana. Purdy 1816: 19, 677.
[2] Which he placed in 7° 54′ S, 160° 48′ S.   [3] See Henderson 1933: 195–214.
[4] The account of the voyage is derived from two principal sources, the published account of the voyage (Wilson 1799) and the log-book of the Second Officer, Thomas Godsell, CRO (Military Records Section, Old India Office): HO7A. See also the *Naval Chronicle* January-July, 1800, pp. 54–55; Wilson 1841; and the *Universal Navigator and Modern Tourist* of 1805. Wilson's route is laid down on Arrowsmith's *Chart of the Pacific Ocean* of 1798.

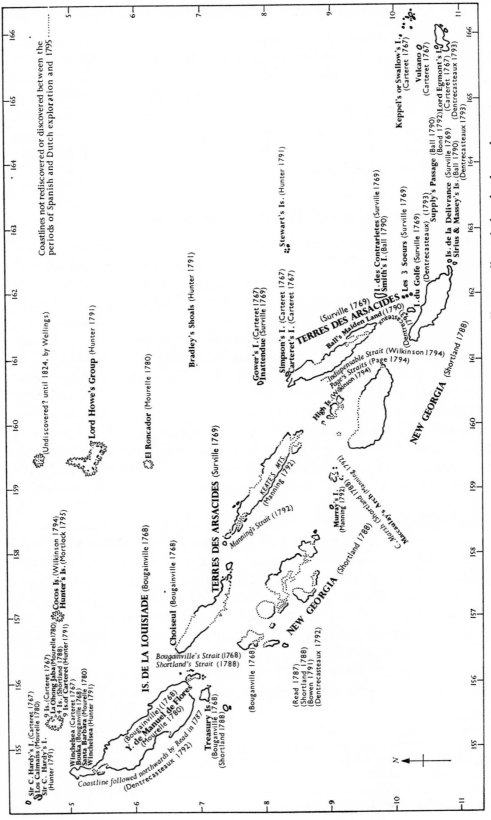

Map XLIIa   Chart showing the coastlines sighted by Carteret, Bougainville, Surville and Shortland, etc. by 1795

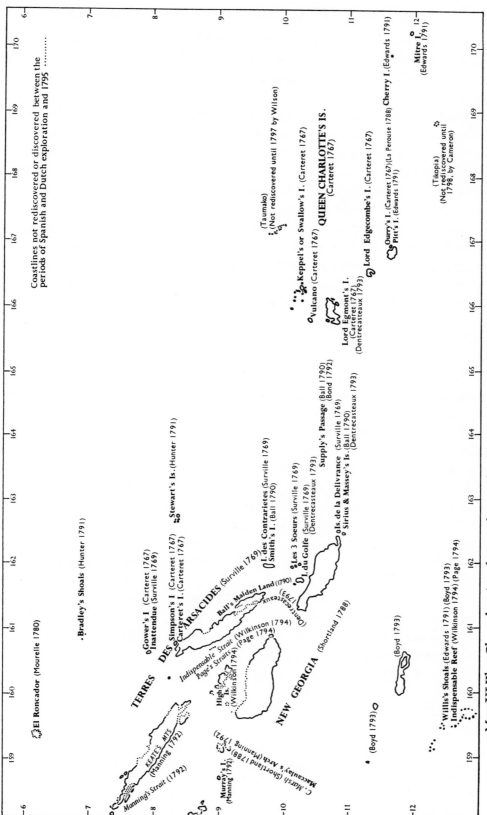

Coastlines not rediscovered or discovered between the
periods of Spanish and Dutch exploration and 1795 ....

Map XLIIb   Chart showing the coastlines sighted by Carteret, Bougainville, Surville and Shortland, etc. by 1795

eleven' separate islands, two or three of which were of 'considerable size'. Wilson attempted to approach the largest of the islands on the following day, but being unable to approach close enough to cover the jolly-boat, which he proposed to send ashore, he bore away. The description of the islands and their inhabitants in the published narrative, the details of Godsell's log-book and Wilson's chart,[1] and the position which he calculated for the main island, 9° 57' S, 167° E, leave no doubt that Wilson had in fact rediscovered the *Taumaco* of Quirós, the island of Taumako in 9° 57' S, 167° 12' 30" E.[2] To this island was given the name *Disappointment Island* and the group as a whole was given the name *Duff's Group* which it bears today.

From Taumako Wilson headed W by S and sighted, identified and passed to the N of Swallow Island (the Reef Islands). To the southwards he sighted and recognized Egmont's Island (Santa Cruz) and Volcano Island (Tinakula), and passed to the S of Nukapu, Nalogo and Nupani.[3] As he headed WNW, Stewart's Islands (Sikaiana) were sighted at a distance of 9 miles to the NE on 30 September, and were recognized; and at 1 p.m. on 1 October, 'high land . . . which we take to be part of New Georgia', and which was almost certainly North-Eastern Malaíta, was sighted about 12½ leagues to the SW ½ S. On 10 October the *Duff* crossed the line in 152° E without having sighted any more land, passed through the Ladrones, and headed W through the Pelew Islands and then NW to Canton.

Wilson's rediscovery of Taumako and its immediate neighbours was shortly followed by the rediscovery of Quirós' other discovery of 1606 in these waters, the island of Tikopia. On 17 September 1798, the *Barwell* left Sydney, under the command of Captain John Cameron, bound for China.[4] The log-book of the Master[5] indicates that he generally followed the track of Butler in the *Walpole*, by what was to become known as the *Outer Passage*,[6] and that on Sunday, 14 October, an island was sighted in 12° 14' S, 168° 59' E to which was given the name *Barwell Island*. There can be little doubt that this was the island of Tikopia in 12° 18' S, 168° 49' E.[7] On the following day at 10.30 a.m. two more islands were sighted and, although the navigational record of Cameron's log-book for the two days following the sighting of Barwell Island is limited and precludes any certain identification of these islands, it seems very likely that they were part of the Duff Islands.

[1] See the *Chart of the Duff's Track in the Pacific Ocean* (Wilson 1799: 1).

[2] Wilson was not aware of his rediscovery.

[3] These three islands were almost certainly new discoveries.

[4] See Collins 1798: II: 111–12, 125–6.

[5] CRO (Military Records Section, Old India Office): 4209.   [6] Horsburgh 1809: 476–7.

[7] See Horsburgh 1809: 476–7, where Barwell Island is described as being 18 or 20 leagues WSW of Mitre Island. Dillon was later to assert that when the *Hunter* visited Tikopia in 1813, she was, according to the natives, the second vessel to visit them. A vessel had earlier attempted to land a long-boat but it had been driven off by the indigenes, and Dillon believed that this must have been the *Barwell* in 1798 (Rienzi 1855: II: 260).

Nineteenth-Century Cartography

It could be argued that by the end of the eighteenth century all the Spanish discoveries in the Islands of Solomon had been rediscovered, if not identified, examined and charted, and this would certainly be true of the Spanish discoveries in the Santa Cruz Group and its outlyers. Such a statement in relation to the Solomons would assume that the Nggela Group (La Galera, Florida, Buena Vista, San German, San Dimas, Guadalupe) was what Wilkinson from the *Indispensable* had charted as *High Islands* [1] and whilst it is probably true that all the land which the Spaniards had sighted had been resighted, it was still necessary for later navigators to add to the rediscoveries of Manning, Dentrecasteaux and Wilkinson within the group, by coasting and charting the Nggela Group and the northern coast of Guadalcanal, and by examining more closely the southern extremities of Santa Ysabel and Malaíta, before the same knowledge which Mendaña's expedition of 1568 had acquired had been reacquired, and before the discoveries of the Spaniards could be identified completely.

Spanish exploration and knowledge of the group had been limited, and by the late eighteenth century other areas of the archipelago were known, and well known, which they had not discovered or explored. Nevertheless, in simple terms of the acquisition of geographical and hydrographic knowledge, and quite apart from the academic question of rediscovery, certain areas of the archipelago needed to be coasted, or explored more closely, before hydrographers had the basic material at their disposal, conflicting, imprecise, confusing and limited though some of it might be, from which they could prepare a tolerably representative chart of the archipelago as a whole. The coastlines of Northern Guadalcanal, Southern Choiseul and the Nggela Group,[2] and most of what is now known as the New Georgia Group, had to be coasted before such information was available. In addition, the atoll of Nukumanu to the north of Ontong Java still had to be discovered before all the outlying island groups could be described as known.[3]

It would require a detailed study in itself to trace the history of the accurate charting of the archipelago, to examine the several varied attempts of nineteenth-century cartographers and hydrographers to produce charts from the information available to them, or to trace the several attempts to identify the discoveries made by the Spaniards in 1568. Some brief allusion will be made to them, but the period with which this study is concerned ends with the

---

[1] See, for example, Butler's chart of 1800, Laurie and Whittle 1803: II: 125.

[2] Malaíta and Santa Ysabel were approximately and almost completely delineated, but their southwestern extremities needed to be coasted for more accurate knowledge.

[3] The suggestion that this atoll may have been discovered by le Maire or Tasman has been dismissed.

approximate delineation of the several islands of the archipelago, for thereafter the problem was one of survey rather than of discovery or exploration.

The nineteenth century was well in its stride before the blank spaces in the chart of the Solomons were almost completely filled in, despite the fact that this was a period of not inconsiderable European activity within and around the group. That this was so can perhaps be attributed to three reasons. In the first place, by the end of the eighteenth century the three known channels through[1] and the three channels around[2] the group provided vessels bound for India and China with safe and alternative routes, to the use of which their insurance may often have bound them, and precluded the necessity for such vessels to explore for new routes. Secondly, those navigators who were particularly active in the Solomons were primarily concerned with the pursuit of whales or trade, and tended to keep their movements secret; and, thirdly, voyages which were specifically for exploration were limited.

Of the several charts and publications which may be described as representative of the various attempts to reconstruct the detailed outline of the Solomons at the end of the eighteenth and beginning of the nineteenth centuries, some deserve particular mention. Laurie and Whittle's *New Chart of the Indian and Pacific Oceans* of 1797 delineates the archipelago as it was known before the voyages of Manning and Wilkinson, as a single land mass.[3] It provides an interesting comparison with Arrowsmith's *Chart of the Pacific Ocean* of 1798, where the results of these two later voyages are shown, and where it is assumed that a coastline linked the lands seen to the westward of Indispensable Strait, that is Santa Ysabel, the Nggela Group and Guadalcanal.[4]

Of particular importance is Thomas Butler's *Chart of the Western Part of the Pacific Ocean*,[5] which lays down the routes of the later rediscoverers and explorers, and clearly reflects the ignorance which existed in respect of the areas between Choiseul and the New Georgia Group and between Guadalcanal and Santa Ysabel, the confusion surrounding the outlying islands and atolls to the

---

[1] Bougainville or Shortland's Strait.
   Manning's Strait.
   Indispensable Strait.
[2] *The Outer Passage*—to the E of Mitre and Cherry Islands.
   The Great Eastern, Bond's or Supply's Passage—between Santa Cruz and San Cristóval.
   The Inner Passage between Bougainville Island and New Britain, then through St. George's Channel or to the E of New Ireland.
[3] For a similar delineation see Walch's *Australien auch Polynesian oder Inselwelt* of 1802 and Buchanan's *Southern Hemisphere* of 1816.
[4] This chart also delineates Malaíta (unnamed) as one island, and shows a very reasonable attempt to delineate the area now known as the New Georgia Group (Gatukai-Vella Lavella) from the information provided by Shortland and Manning.
[5] See Laurie and Whittle 1799: Chart 87: Laurie and Whittle 1803: II: 125. Although the chart bears the inscription: 'Published May 20th, 1800 by Laurie and Whittle' it is also to be found in their one volume *Complete East India Pilot* dated 1799.

N of the archipelago,[1] and an inevitable imprecision of positioning and delineation.[2] Horsburgh's *Directions for Sailing to and from the East Indies, New Holland* ..., published between 1809 and 1811, provide a clear indication of contemporary knowledge of the area,[3] and Purdy's *The Oriental Navigator or Directions for Sailing* ... published by Laurie and Whittle in 1816,[4] is in reality a more detailed partner to it.

Captains Page, Simpson, Coutance and Nicolls

That the passages through the Solomons were being used by an increasing number of merchant vessels is evidenced by the details of the voyage of the American vessel *Ann and Hope*, under the command of Benjamin Page, through Indispensable Strait or Page's Straits in company with the *Jenny* of Boston.[5] That maritime activity around the Solomons generally was increasing is also perhaps indicated by the report of Captain Simpson of the *Nautilus* of his 'discovery' of *Kenedy's Island* or *Mattooetee* in a position which was reported variously as 8° 36' S, 167° 50' E,[6] 11° 17' S, 167° 58' E,[7] and 8° 40' S, 167° 45' E.[8] There is no land in any of these positions, and the name *Mattooetee*, probably a corruption of the Polynesian expression *motu-iti* (small island), offers as little evidence for purposes of identification as Simpson's brief description of its beautiful appearance, populousness, 'Savage, artful and treacherous' inhabitants, and abundance of hogs. That it was not Taumako is evidenced by Simpson's other references to the 'Island Disappointment' of 'Dexter's Group'[9] or Duff's Group',[10] but exactly what it was it seems impossible for the moment to determine.

In 1803 the French privateer the *Adèle*, under the command of Roualt Coutance, passed within sight of Willis's Shoals or Indispensable Reef,[11] but apparently did not sight the Solomons. In April 1811, the *Union* of Calcutta, *en*

---

[1] Butler admits that 'The Longitudinal situation of these Islands is very uncertain'.

[2] For a similar delineation of the Solomons see L. S. de la Rochette's *A Chart of the Indian Ocean* of 1803 (based on a chart by Mannevillette) and, in a less complicated form, Faden's *Southern Hemisphere* of 1802.   [3] Horsburgh 1809: 470–8.   [4] Purdy 1816: 93–106, 675–92.

[5] See Kenny 1958; JCB: *Log-book of Benjamin Page Jnr 1798–9*; *Log-book of Christopher Bently 1798–9*; LRIHS: *Journal of Dr. B. Bowen Carter*.

[6] Woodford 1895: 333. Woodford suggested that it might be one of the islands of Sikaiana.

[7] *Naval Chronicle*, 1806: XVII: 195; *The Salem Register*, 9 June 1803.

[8] Norie 1833: Chart 26A. There are many other references to Kenedy's Island.

[9] Apparently another name applied to the Duff Islands, and also perhaps indicative of another mariner who had visited them.

[10] *The Salem Register*, 9 June 1803. Simpson also recorded finding at Taumako the wreckage (the remains of 'a very large lower mast' and 'the keel') of what he thought might have been 'some large Spanish ship' which 'had been wrecked upon it, but it must have been long since, as the timber was greatly decayed'. The only Spanish vessel which we know to have disappeared in these waters was the *Almiranta* of Mendaña's expedition of 1595, which disappeared off Santa Cruz.

[11] Rienzi 1855: III: 383; Krusenstern 1824: 172.

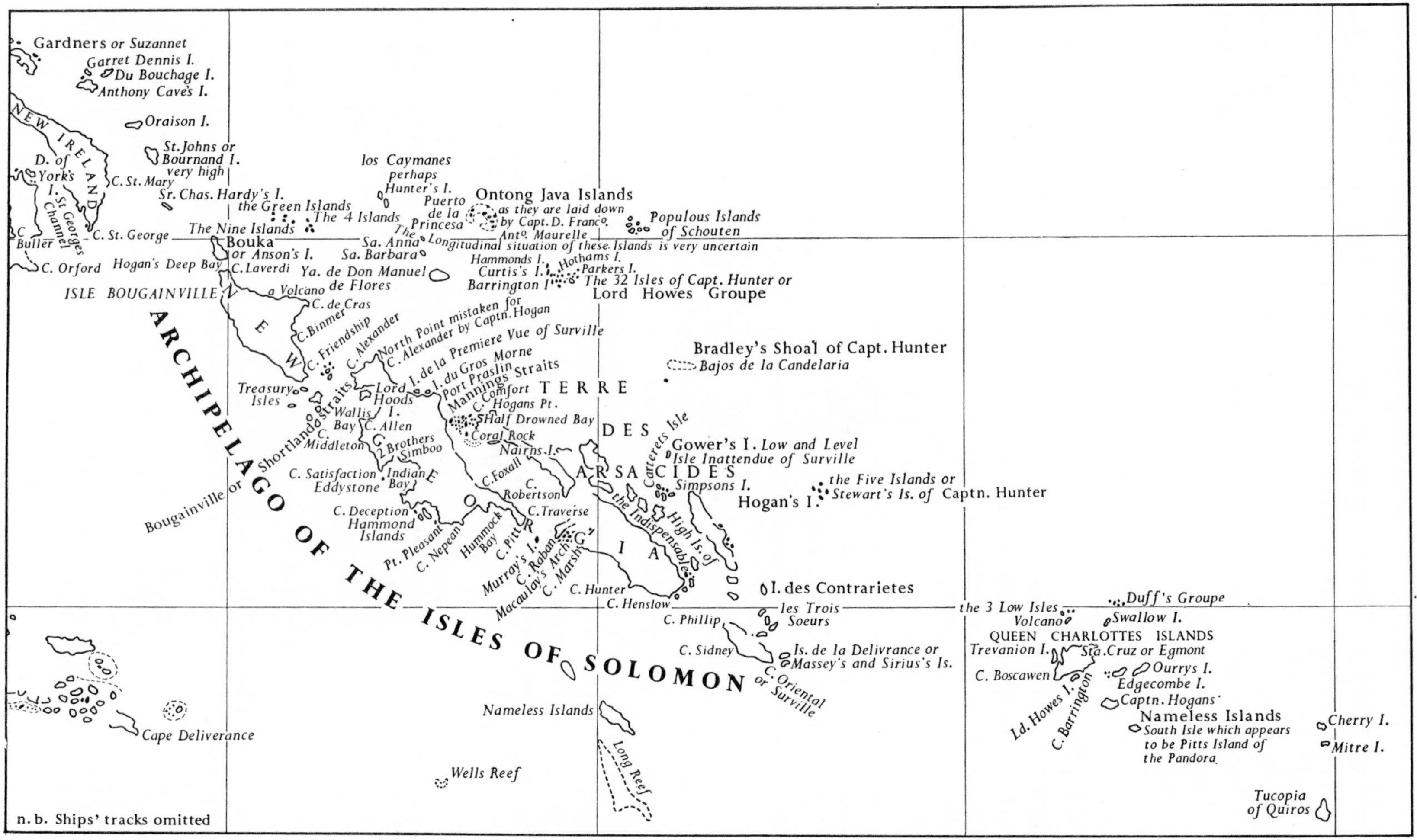

Map XLIII Section from Butler's Chart of the Western Part of the Pacific Ocean of 1800, redrawn

n. b. Ships' tracks omitted

ARCHIPELAGO OF THE ISLES OF SOLOMON

NEW IRELAND

ISLE BOUGAINVILLE

TERRE DES ARSACIDES

Gardners or Suzannet
Garret Dennis I.
Du Bouchage I.
Anthony Cavès I.
Oraison I.
St. Johns or
Bourand I.
very high
St. Chas. Hardy's I.
the Green Islands
The Nine Islands
Bouka
or Anson's I.
C. Laverdi
C. de Cras
C. Bimmet

los Caymanes
perhaps
Hunter's I.
The 4 Islands
Sa. Anna
Sa. Barbara
Ya. de Don Manuel
Ya. de Flores
a Volcano

Ontong Java Islands
as they are laid down
by Capt. D. Franc.o
Longitudinal situation of these islands is very uncertain
Hammonds I.
Curtis's I.
Barrington I.
Parkers I.
The 32 Isles of Capt. Hunter or
Lord Howes Groupe

Puerto
de la
Princesa
Ante. Maurelle

Populous Islands
of Schouten

Bradley's Shoal of Capt. Hunter
Bajos de la Candelaria

Gower's I. Low and Level
Isle Inattendue of Surville
the Five Islands or
Stewart's Is. of Captn. Hunter
Simpsons I.
Hogan's I. of Captn. Hunter

I. des Contrarietes
les Trois
Soeurs
Is. de la Delivrance or
Massey's and Sirius's Is.
C. Oriental
or Surville
C. Sidney
C. Phillip
C. Henslow
C. Hunter

High Is. of
the Indispensable

Nameless Islands

Long Reef

Wells Reef

Cape Deliverance

C. Bimmet
C. Alexander Premiere Vue of Surville
Second Point mistaken for
C. Alexander by Captn. Hogan
Third Point
la Gros Straits
N.C. Hogans Pt.
Port Comfort Bay
Drowned Bay
Coral Rock
Nairns Is.
Lord. de la Prasln Straits
Hoods
Wallis
C. Allen
Brothers
Simboo
C. Traverse
C. Robertson
Macaulay's Arch.
C. Robm
Murrays
Pt. Marsh
C. Nepean
Pt. Pleasant
Hummock
Bay
Hammond
Islands
C. Deception
Indian
Bay
C. Satisfaction
Eddystone
C. Middleton

Treasury
Isles
Friendly
Isles

Bougainville or Short-land

D. of
Yorks
St. Georges
Channel
C. St. George
C. Orford
Hogan's Deep Bay
C. Buller
St. Georges

Duff's Groupe
Swallow I.
Volcano
QUEEN CHARLOTTES ISLANDS
Trevanion I.
Sta. Cruz or Egmont
C. Boscawen
C. Barrington
L'd Howes I.
Edgecombe I.
Ourrys I.
Captn. Hogans
Nameless Islands
South Isle which appears
to be Pitts Island of
the Pandora

Cherry I.
Mitre I.

Tucopia
of Quiros

route from Australia to Penang under the command of John Nichols, put a boat ashore at an island in 8° 18′ S, 156° 30′ E which is identifiable with Simbo. The First Officer, James Hobbs, sighted what appeared to be wreckage in the channel on the east side of the island, wreckage which it was later suggested might have come from one of La Pérouse's vessels.[1] In 1812 Captain Abraham Bristow of the *Thames* seems to have cruised quite extensively in the vicinity of the Green Islands, Buka and Bougainville, and to have visited Simbo and Murray's Island.[2]

Burney

A significant contribution to the historiography of the Solomons was made with the publication between 1803 and 1817 of Burney's *A Chronological History of the Discoveries in the South Sea or Pacific Ocean*, in which the author, apart from recounting the voyages made in the past, endeavoured to summarize contemporary knowledge of the Solomons[3] and to identify the individual Spanish discoveries.[4] He was no more successful in this latter attempt than Fleurieu had been, and in fact failed to take full advantage of all the hydrographic information available in 1803, although, as he rightly pointed out:

The discoveries of the last forty years have verified the discoveries of Mendaña, though the knowledge obtained of the geography of the Salomon Islands is not more than sufficient to explain their general position. Very few of the points marked in the original account have been recognized and identified.[5]

He realized that the size attributed to Santa Ysabel in Figueroa's account of the discoveries of 1568 must have been erroneous,[6] but assumed that the Spaniards had circumnavigated several islands under the illusion that they were circumnavigating one island.

Peter Dillon

The first of the series of events which were to culminate in the discovery that la Pérouse's expedition had foundered off Vanikoro occurred in 1813 when Peter Dillon[7] sailed as Third Officer in the Calcutta ship *Hunter* from New

---

[1] Rienzi 1855: III: 400. It could well have been the wreckage of the vessel built by the survivors at Vanikoro, for their obvious route would have been to the S of the Solomons in the direction of St. George's Channel.

[2] Purdy 1816: 100, 103–4, 106; Findlay 1851: 1016.   [3] Burney 1803: I: 287–91.

[4] Burney 1803: I: 276–7. *A Sketch of the Salomon Islands designed to assist in comparing the Modern Discoveries with the Early Spanish Accounts*.   [5] Burney 1803: I: 288.

[6] Burney 1803: I: 291. Burney included a chart of the discoveries made previous to 1579 (Burney 1803: I: Frontispiece), on which he delineated the Solomons with their known outline immediately after Shortland's voyage of 1788.

[7] For a concise and scholarly study of Dillon see Davidson 1956.

South Wales to Fiji, under the command of Captain Robson, to collect sandal-wood. Engaged at Norfolk Island, Dillon had already spent several years in Fiji and Tahiti and when, after little success in the collection of sandal wood and after participating in the internecine battles of the Fijians, Robson turned on the Fijians and was soundly beaten by them, Dillon acquitted himself gallantly and assumed command of the *Hunter's* tender, the *Elizabeth*. In the *Elizabeth* Dillon carried a German, Martin Bushart, and a lascar named Joe, both of whom had been living in Fiji, together with three Fijian women. Bushart, his Fijian wife and Joe, were landed at their request at Tikopia, the first island sighted after leaving the Fiji Group and the name of which Dillon understood to be *Tucopia*. To the W of Tikopia, and in sight of a large high island which can be identified as Vanikoro, the *Hunter* and *Elizabeth* separated, Robson sailing for India, Dillon for New South Wales, but this simple act of landing these three persons at Tikopia was 'a chance action whose conse-quences were to bring Dillon, many years later, the greatest triumph of his career'.[1]

Mitre and Cherry Islands were visited in 1822 by the Russian Kroutcheff,[2] and in 1823 Duperrey, in command of the *Coquille*, passed by Vanikoro and Utupua during the night of 1 and 2 August, and visited Santa Cruz, Bougainville, Buka and the Green Islands without making any further contri-bution to contemporary knowledge of the area.[3] In 1824 the first certain dis-covery of the atoll of Nukumanu[4] seems to have been made by a Captain Wellings,[5] and with him it can be said that the discovery of the outlying islands of the archipelago had been completed.

Krusenstern

The publication in 1824 of Krusenstern's *Carte Systematique de l'Archipel des Isles de Salomon* and *Mémoire pour servir d'analyse et d'explication à la Carte Systematique ...*,[6] based on the charts of Dentrecasteaux and Arrowsmith,[7]

[1] Davidson 1956: 311. See Dillon 1830 and Dillon 1829: I.   [2] Findlay 1851: 963.
[3] Duperry 1826; Rienzi 1855: III: 381, 384, 397, 408; Findlay 1851: 956. Duperrey, who had accompanied Freycinet on the *Uranie* during the latter's Pacific voyage of exploration between 1817 and 1820, was accompanied by Dumont d'Urville. The prime object of the voyage seems to have been research into the question of magnetic variation.   [4] 4° 30′ S, 159° 30′ E.
[5] Findlay 1851: 1015; Cheyne 1855: 68. Findlay referred to them as *Le Maire and Tasman's Isles* with the statement that 'After Tasman had made the island ... of Ontong Java ... he saw to the N.N.W. of them, another group'. Cheyne suggested that these 'low islands' seen by Wellings in 4° 29′ S, 159° 28′ E might be the same as the coral islands reputedly seen by Captain Simpson of Sydney in 4° 52′ S, 160° 12′ E, which Findlay referred to as *Simpson's Coral Islands*. See also the *Nautical Magazine*, of 1848: 574. Simpson's Coral Islands could have been part of Ontong Java. For Welling's discovery see also Laurie's *Chart of the Islands and Passages in the vicinity of New Guinea* of 1841, and Krusenstern 1827: Chart No. 9.
[6] Krusenstern 1827: Chart No. 9; Krusenstern 1824: 157–83.
[7] His *Chart of the Islands and Passages to the East of New Guinea*.

and on Fleurieu's publication, was the next major step in the cartographical reconstruction of the Solomons and the identification of the Spanish discoveries. From the outline reproduction of his chart it can be seen that in terms of creating a chart of the archipelago from contemporary or recent information, Krusenstern was remarkably successful. He postulated a southern coastline for

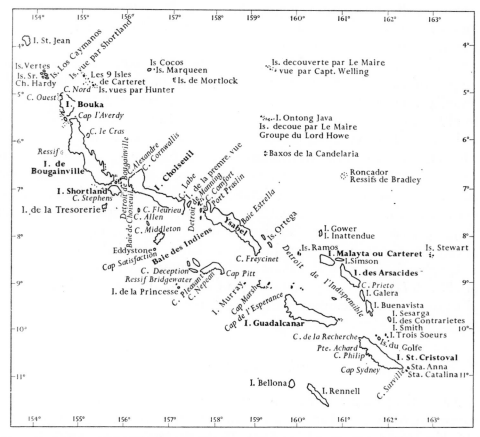

Map XLIV   Krusenstern's *Carte Systematique de l'Archipel des Isles de Salomon* of 1824, redrawn

Choiseul and a northern coastline for *Guadalcanar* (Guadalcanal) which, though far from accurate, were relatively representative. He might have placed more reliance on Shortland's description and charting of the coastline between Cape Pitt and Cape Allen to produce a rather more embodied delineation of that area,[1] but in attempting to utilize the descriptions of the Islands of Solomon derived from the narratives of the Spaniards as a source of cartographic information additional to that provided more recently, he was misled to delineate

[1] To the SW of Cape Deception Krusenstern lays down *Bridgewater Reef* and *Princessa Island*, and cites Arrowsmith as his authority. There is at present neither a reef nor an island in this position and the origin of this delineation by Arrowsmith has not been traced.

Malaíta as a group of islands and to produce a deteriorated representation. The Nggela Group is conspicuous by its absence from his chart, except perhaps as the few small islands (excluding Savo which had been charted by Dentrecasteaux) off the north coast of *Guadalcanar*, presumably derived from information of the two voyages of Wilkinson; but Krustensern did make a very reasonable attempt to reconcile the reports of the four atolls and two reefs which lie off the Northern Solomons and which had been severally, variously and confusingly reported, only duplicating Tau'u as the *Is de Mortlock* in one position and as the *Is Marqueen* or *Is Cocos* in a nearby position.

In endeavouring to identify the Spanish discoveries Krusenstern succeeded in respect of Santa Ysabel, in locating the approximate position of the Bahía de la Estrella and in locating the Baxos de la Candelaria in what is in fact the position of Roncador Reef, even though he identified El Roncador with Bradley's Shoals. Thereafter, however, he became involved in confusion.

It seems to have been Krusenstern who was first guilty of the erroneous application to the small island between the northern extremity of Malaíta and Santa Ysabel, and which from a distance appears to be two islands,[1] of the name *Ramos* which it bears today. He correctly identified Carteret's Island with *Malayta* (Malaíta), but applied this identification only to the part seen by Carteret. Moreover, he postulated the belief that the remainder of what other cartographers had charted as Malaíta was in fact three islands,[2] which he named from N to S *I des Arsacides* (terminating in *Cabo Prieto*),[3] *Galera* and *Buenavista*, and in consequence identified the Île des Contrariétés of Surville (Ulawa) as *Sesarga*.

Dillon and Vanikoro

During the period following his visit to Tikopia in 1813 Peter Dillon had been employed in the Indian 'country trade'; in three voyages in his own vessel, the *Calder*, from Calcutta to New South Wales; and in a series of voyages in the Pacific and between Valparaiso, New South Wales and Calcutta.[4] On 13 May 1826, whilst taking his second ship, the *St. Patrick*, from New Zealand to Bengal with a cargo of *kauri* spars, he came in sight of the island of Tikopia.[5]

---

[1] See Krusenstern's *Carte Systematique*. . . . Wilkinson in the *Indispensable* apparently took it to be two islands (Krusenstern 1824: 165).   [2] Krusenstern 1824: 167.

[3] He rejected the idea that Cabo Prieto was the south-eastern extremity of Santa Ysabel (Krusenstern 1824–165, 167), and identified San Jorge (not named on his chart) with an island in Indispensable Strait: 'Ortega découvrit une isle qu'il nomma St. George, gisant OSO a 5 ou 7 lieues d'Espagne du Cap Prieto; cette isle correspond exactement avec celle qui avoit été vue par l'Indispensable, si on place le Cap à la longitude et latitude que je lui ai designées' (Krusenstern 1824: 168). Quite what the island was which Wilkinson saw from the *Indispensable* is, in the absence of his log-book or original chart, impossible to determine, but it seems highly likely that it was the Nggela Group.

[4] Davidson 1956: 311–13.   [5] Which Dillon refers to as *Tucopia*.

Canoes came off, in one of which he sighted Bushart and the lascar, Joe. From the former he learnt that during the first eleven years of his residence on the island no vessels had been sighted but that 'twenty months back' a whaler had worked off the island for a month, and that ten months previously another one had passed. One of Dillon's officers now informed him that the lascar Joe had sold the armourer a silver sword guard and, on enquiry, Dillon learnt that this and many other European relics had been obtained at a 'distant island, which they called Malicolo'.[1] Bushart had been informed by the Tikopians that two ships had been wrecked on that island when the old men of Tikopia were boys, and Joe confirmed that six years previously, whilst on a visit to *Malicolo*, he had conversed with two old men who were survivors from the ships. A Tikopian further confirmed the information, and Dillon at once concluded that the two vessels wrecked there must have been those of La Pérouse. On further enquiry the Tikopians asserted that although several ships had passed the island of *Malicolo*, none had actually been there since the two in question. Dillon now determined to visit the island, primarily to rescue the two survivors, and Bushart agreed to accompany him provided Dillon would return him to Tikopia. On the second day out from Tikopia, heading westwards with light breezes and occasional calms, Dillon sighted Vanikoro, but here, eight leagues off shore with his ship leaking and his provisions running low, he lay becalmed for seven days. He was compelled to abandon the attempt for the moment and ran before a light breeze 'for the island of Indenny, commonly called Santa Cruz',[2] passed Tinakula, and then headed for New Ireland, the Moluccas and Bengal.[3]

In Calcutta, which he reached at the end of August 1826, Dillon approached the government with the request that they support his return to Vanikoro, and eventually secured command of the Honourable East India Company vessel the *Research* and the support of both the British government in India and the French administration at Chandernagore. He left India on 23 January 1827, proceeded to Van Diemen's Land and anchored at Hobart. After a delay

---

[1] Dillon 1829: II: 33. Dillon adds in a footnote: 'Since ascertained to be more correctly called Mannicolo or Vannicolo', i.e. Vanikoro.   [2] Dillon 1829: II: 35.

[3] The *Asiatic Journal* for October 1825, reprinted from the *Constitutional* the statement that 'Admiral Manby, of the English Royal Navy has recently arrived in Paris with the news, which is strongly supported by presumptive evidence, that the place where the intrepid Peyrouse with his brave crew perished 40 years back is now known. An English whale ship has discovered a long and low island surrounded with innumerable rocks between New Caledonia and New Guinea, at nearly equal distance from those islands. When the inhabitants came on board, they perceived that one of the chiefs had, as an ornament, a Cross of St. Louis hanging from his ear. Other natives had swords upon which was marked the word Paris, and some medals of Louis XVI were seen in other hands. When they were asked how they became possessed of these articles, one of their chiefs, of about 50 years of age, answered that when he was a boy, a large vessel was wrecked in a violent tempest upon a coral reef, and that all the men that were in her perished.' On the evidence available it would be rash to hazard any conclusions from this report. See Langdon 1961 and Jack-Hinton 1961(a).

there caused by his mutinous Surgeon, Dr. Tytler, Dillon sailed for New Zealand and Tongatapu, passed Mitre Island on 4 September,[1] and arrived at Tikopia on 5 September.[2] On 7 September he sighted Vanikoro and landed the following day. Here the story which he had learnt from the Tikopians was confirmed; he discovered that of the two last survivors one had died and the other had left; and he also discovered that those who had earlier survived the wreck and the onslaught of the indigenes had constructed a two-masted vessel and had set sail in it. He obtained more relics of la Pérouse's expedition and convincing proof that this was the place where the expedition had ended,[3] making a twofold contribution to the story of Solomons' discovery in charting Vanikoro[4] and in determining the fate of la Pérouse's expedition.

Dumont d'Urville

In 1825 Dumont d'Urville, who had served as the First Officer of Duperrey during the latter's Pacific voyage in the *Coquille*, had been appointed to the command of that vessel, renamed the *Astrolabe*. He had been instructed to proceed to the Pacific and continue the work of Duperrey, to explore the principal archipelagos N and S of the line, particularly New Zealand and New Guinea, and to search for information concerning la Pérouse. His voyage was yet another of those which successive French governments, with singularly enlightened and enquiring outlooks, and no doubt with some commercial motivation, had despatched into the Pacific.[5]

D'Urville sailed from Toulon on 25 April 1826, and proceeded by way of Trinidad, Brazil and the South Atlantic to South-Western Australia, Bass Strait and Port Jackson. From Port Jackson he sailed for New Zealand, where he spent three months, Tonga and the Fiji Group, and then passed to the S of

[1] The native name of which he learnt from Bushart as *Fatacca* (Fataka), and the position of which he determined correctly to be 11° 56′ S, 170° 17′ E. He also discovered that the native name for Cherry Island was *Anuta*.

[2] Here he collected five Europeans who had arrived in a long boat and claimed to have been on a Liverpool whaler. Dillon concluded that they were escaped convicts from New South Wales on the grounds, which throw some light on the increased European activity in the South Sea, that 'the only ports in Great Britain from which Southseamen are fitted out are London and Milford Haven'.

[3] The evidence points to the fact that both of la Pérouse's vessels were wrecked on Vanikoro. An expedition in 1960 discovered relics of what appears to have been the *Astrolabe*, and a native diver recently located (at the end of 1961) what may be the wreckage of the *Boussole*. See *Pacific Islands Monthly*, April 1958; Filewood 1958; James 1958; Discombe and Anthonioz 1960; Langdon 1961; Jack-Hinton 1961(a). (Since going to print a French expedition has recovered material from the *Boussole* site.)

[4] See the reproduction of his chart *Island of Mannicolo* in Dillon 1829: II: 172.

[5] Dumont d'Urville 1827; 1828; 1829; 1830; 1833: 398–426; 1834; Dixon 1936: Hapdé 1829; Rienzi 1855: 400–7; Wright 1950: 1–20.

the Solomons through Dampier's Strait, along the north coast of New Guinea to the Moluccas and Java, and then around Australia to Hobart. His intention was to return to New Zealand, but here at Hobart he heard for the first time of Dillon's discovery at Tikopia and of his return to Vanikoro in the *Research* by way of Hobart earlier in the year. He also heard from Hobbs of his discovery of wreckage on Simbo whilst serving in the *Union* in 1811 and, recalling the deposition made by Bowen of the *Albemarle*, realized that these two stories could not be discounted. Whilst his first task was survey, d'Urville's secondary orders to search for information relating to the fate of la Pérouse clearly took precedence in the light of the information which he had obtained at Hobart, and he determined to follow Dillon. He left Hobart on 5 January 1828, and, sailing via Norfolk Island, Mitre[1] and to the S of Cherry Island,[2] reached Tikopia on 10 February.[3]

At Tikopia he met Bushart, who had only recently been returned there in the *Governor Macquarrie, en route* to Tonga, and learnt from him the details of Dillon's discoveries. From the lascar Joe he received a letter written by Dillon whilst at Tikopia, stating that he was proceeding to Pitt Island, but d'Urville does not seem to have appreciated that this was the name given to Vanikoro by Edwards of the *Pandora*. D'Urville now sailed for Vanikoro, as he himself understood the name of this island which he identified with the *Mallicolo* mentioned by Quirós, and which he reached on 15 February. Here he confirmed Dillon's discoveries,[4] obtained some relics, erected a cairn, and did some surveying. In view of the stories of Hobbs and Bowen he felt obliged to make some search for the wreckage of the boat built by the survivors of la Pérouse's expedition, concluding that their obvious route would have been for New Ireland and the Moluccas or Philippines, and even expressing the opinion that 'in the future, some indications will probably be found in the west coast of the Solomon Islands'.[5] From Vanikoro he headed N in a search for the Kennedy (Kenedy) island of the *Nautilus* and Quirós' Taumako, which he concluded might be one and the same island,[6] apparently failing to realize that Taumako had been rediscovered, though not recognized, by Wilson in the *Duff*. The deteriorated health of his crew prevented d'Urville from continuing his search for signs of the survivors of la Pérouse's expedition in the main body of the Solomon Islands and he accordingly made for Guam, Batavia and Europe.[7]

[1] The name of which he learnt to be *Fataka*.
[2] The name of which he learnt to be *Anouda*.
[3] See d'Urville's route chart in Dumont d'Urville 1830: Atlas: Plate 32. It will be recalled that d'Urville had previously passed Tikopia and Vanikoro in 1823 on board the *Coquille*.
[4] Rienzi 1855: 405–6.   [5] Rienzi 1855: 406.
[6] Dumont d'Urville 1833: 407–8, 427.
[7] See d'Urville's *Carte Generale de l'Ocean Pacifique* (Dumont D'Urville 1830(b): Plate 1) which is clearly based on Krusenstern's *Carte Systematique* ... of 1824 for its delineation of the Solomons.

Although several voyages were made through the Solomons in the inter-vening years,[1] it was not until d'Urville returned there in November, 1838, that the next, and indeed the last, major individual contribution to the carto-graphy and geographical knowledge of the archipelago was made. In the period following his return to France in 1829 d'Urville had been required to occupy himself in petty naval duties at Toulon, and had incurred disfavour for his outspoken views. During this time, however, he revealed himself to be a true scholar, publishing the account of his voyage and his *Voyage Pittoresque Autour du Monde* and studying the linguistics and ethnography of Oceania. By the end of 1836 he required additional material for his private research, particularly in linguistics, and endeavoured to interest the authorities in a further voyage of Pacific exploration. Hardly surprisingly the authorities saw little value in his proposals, but at this time Louis-Philippe had developed a desire to see France to the fore in the exploration of Antarctica, and d'Urville was conveniently appointed to command an expedition to the Antarctic and the Pacific.[2]

On 7 September 1837, he set sail from Toulon with the *Astrolabe* and the *Zélée*, and sailed for the Brazilian coast, Tierra del Fuego and the Antarctic. Between January and March 1838, he explored in the area of the South Ork-neys, South Shetlands and what is now known as Graham Land, and then headed for Valparaiso. From Valparaiso he headed westwards to Gambier's Islands,[3] the Marquesas, Tahiti and Fiji. Leaving Fiji on 20 October 1838, the two corvettes were headed for the Solomon Islands[4]; the New Hebrides were

---

[1] In 1828 de Tromelin in the *Baionaisse* visited Tikopia, Vanikoro, Santa Cruz and the Reef Islands (of which he learnt the native names of nine, perhaps the nine names applied to the central islands today, i.e. Ngailo (the three islands named Lomlom on the modern chart), Pokoli (Nimbanga Tema), Pangani (Nimbanga Nendi), Fenualoa, Nifiloli, Pileni, Makalobu, Tekaueha and Matema). On Krusenstern's *Carte de l'Archipel de Santa Cruz* (dated 1824, but obviously corrected after 1828—see Krusenstern 1827: Plate 7, and Krusenstern 1835: 50–52) the island of Nukapu is named the *Isle Tromelin*. See also Cheyne 1855: 66. For Tromelin's voyage see Rienzi 1855: 407; Journal des Voyages 1829: XLII: 39–56. In 1830 the American Morrell in the *Atlantic* visited Kilinailau and Buka in search of *bêche-de-mer* (see Morrell 1832; Rienzi 1855: 366–381; *Colombian Centinel*, 3 September 1831; Findlay 1851: 1016). He returned again in 1834 in the *Margaret Oakley*, and sailed along the west coast of Bougainville, through Bougainville Strait, coasted the north-eastern side of Choiseul and Santa Ysabel, the north side of the Nggela Group and Savo and the north-western coast of Guadal-canal, visited Rennell, Bellona, San Cristóval and Santa Cruz, and then headed SSE for the New Hebrides (see Jacobs 1844). The voyage could have contributed quite considerably to contemporary knowledge, but Morrell seems to have been a tourist at heart and to have had little interest or compe-tence as a hydrographer. Whalers were particularly active at this time, and by 1841 there were even Europeans, deserters and escaped convicts, living in the Solomons. See *The Colonial Magazine and Commercial Maritime Journal*, May–August 1841, September–December 1841; an extract from the *Singapore Chronicle* of 1834 in the *Pacific Islands Monthly*, August 1958–51; the reference to the whalers *Alfred* and *John Bull* in the *Asiatic Journal*, December 1828: 757–8, the *Sydney Herald*, 12 December 1832, and the *Asiatic Journal*, June 1832: 103–4, to the brig *Hammond* in the *Nautical Magazine*, 1840: 467–8, to the brig *William* in *The Australian*, 2 March 1839: 3, 21 March 1839: 2, and to the *Marshall Bennet*, in the *Nautical Magazine*, 1840: 467. See also Cheyne 1855: 68, 71, 75, 78.

[2] Dumont d'Urville 1841: I: lxiv.   [3] Timoe and Mangareva.

[4] Dumond d'Urville 1841(b): V: 1.

sighted on 1 November, and Vanikoro was reached on 6 November.[1] After a brief visit ashore, d'Urville continued by way of Utupua to Santa Cruz where he lay becalmed off Tinakula until the 9th. It was not until noon on 12 November that San Cristóval became visible and, as the two vessels approached more closely, that he sighted Santa Ana and Santa Catalina.[2] Passing to the N of the latter, d'Urville coasted the north side of San Cristóval and then headed N towards Malaíta, which he identified. Following its western coast northwards, he gave the south-western extremity of Maramasike or Small Malaíta the name Cape Zélée, noted the Maramasike Passage which divides Small Malaíta from Malaíta, and passed between Malaíta and Alite Reef, to which he gave the name *Recif Bejean*. Continuing northwards, the two vessels passed Fauabu Bay, which d'Urville suspected to be a passage dividing the island and, in the evening of 16 November, sighted the north-western cape of Malaíta, which he named *Cap Astrolabe*, and the island erroneously named *Ramos* which, like his predecessors, he mistook for two small islands.

Anxious to clarify the question of the locality and identity of the islands of 'Galera, Florida, Sesarga and Buena Vista', reported by Ortega and apparently situated immediately to the SE of Cape Prieto, which d'Urville identified as the south-eastern cape of Santa Ysabel, he now headed to the SW towards the high mountains of Guadalcanal. He soon sighted the chain of islands of the Nggela Group, and identified them collectively as those discovered by Ortega and Gallego under the names 'Sesarga, Florida, Buena Vista and Galera'. Unfortunately, he approached their western extremity from the NE, and in consequence was only able to identify La Galera and Buena Vista with certainty, applying the names Florida and Sesarga to the coastline visible to the SE. Heading NW towards Santa Ysabel, he recognized Thousand Ships Bay and San Jorge and rediscovered the channel between San Jorge and Santa Ysabel used by the brigantine in 1568, to which he gave the name *Canal Ortega*. He followed the southern coast of Santa Ysabel north-westwards, passed through the Manning Strait, and coasted to the N of Choiseul, Bougainville Strait, Bougainville and Buka. He now headed northwards to the Mariannas, then to the Philippines, Java, Tasmania, due S to the Antarctic coast, back to Tasmania, and thence to New Zealand, the Torres Straits, Timor and the direct route to France.

By the time the results of d'Urville's explorations and rediscoveries of 1838 had been published the only areas within the Solomons which were still relatively unknown were the area of and between the south coast of

---

[1] Dumont d'Urville 1841(b): V: 7–13.

[2] For d'Urville's passage through the Solomons see Dumont d'Urville 1841(b): V: 16–115. See also Dumont d'Urville 1841(b): *Hydrographie*, Vol. II: 76–89, and the *Carte des Iles Salomon . . . par M. Vincendon Dumoulin* in Dumont d'Urville 1841(b): Atlas, Vol. II: *Carte 5eme*.

Choiseul and the north coast of the New Georgia group[1] and the north coast of Guadalcanal.[2] His contribution to the cartography of the Solomons emerges very clearly from a comparison of Dumoulin's *Carte des Iles Salomon*,[3] prepared during d'Urville's voyage, with Krusenstern's *Carte Systematique* of 1824 or with Chart 26A in *The Country Trade or Free Mariner's Journal* of 1833.[4] Even by 1846, however, Norie was still publishing his *A New and Correct Outline Chart* of 1833, avowedly corrected to the year 1846, without those corrections which d'Urville's exploration necessitated, and there was quite considerable discrepancy between the publications of contemporary cartographers.[5]

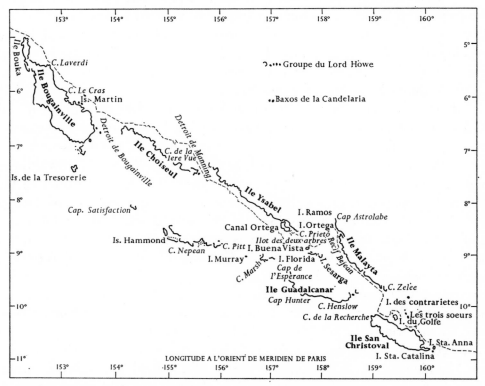

Map XLV   The *Carte des Iles Salomon* by Dumoulin, d'Urville's hydrographer in 1838

[1] The limited application of the name *New Georgia* to the group of islands between Gatukai and Vella Lavella seems first to have been made by Krusenstern (as *Georgia*), see Findlay 1851: 1010. Cheyne 1855: 74, refers to it (after Shortland's name for those coastlines of the archipelago which he saw as a whole) as *New Georgia*, and applies the name *Georgia* to what seemed to be the main island in the group but was in fact Kolombangara, New Georgia, Vangunu and Gatukai.

[2] Manning, Wilkinson and d'Urville had seen enough of the north coast of Guadalcanal to permit an approximate delineation of it.   [3] Dumont d'Urville 1841(b): Atlas Vol. II: *Carte* 5.

[4] Norie 1833. This chart, like Norie's *A New and Correct Outline Chart Intended for the Use of the Officers in the Royal Navy and Merchants' Service* of 1833, is substantially Thomas Butler's *Chart of the Western Part of the Pacific*.

[5] Basically, however, the Solomons were delineated according to either Krusenstern and d'Urville or Butler.

The variations of individual cartographers apart, by 1841 sufficient information did exist for the preparation of a reasonably accurate chart of the Solomon Islands, the area between New Georgia and Choiseul excepted, and such a chart was achieved to a considerable degree with the publication in 1841 of Laurie's *Chart of the Islands and Passages in the vicinity of Papua or New Guinea between the Sea of Banda and the Eastern Extremity of the Solomon Islands*. Laurie laid down dotted coastline between the eastern and western extremities of Choiseul and New Georgia, but Krusenstern had postulated a southern coastline for Choiseul, and d'Urville, with the additional evidence of the impressions he had received of the area from the entrance to Manning Strait, seems to have agreed with him[1]. Laurie, unlike Krusenstern, delineated a much fuller southern coastline for the New Georgia Group, on the evidence of Shortland's chart, and if the charts of Krusenstern, d'Urville and Laurie are taken together, and if Manning's delineation of the north-eastern coastline of the New Georgia Group is added to them, all that is required for completion is the exact delineation of the islands of the New Georgia Group and of part of the south coast of Choiseul.

The completion of this gap in the chart of the Solomons was a slow process to which many navigators contributed. As late as 1877 Findlay was still obliged to remark that knowledge of the south coast of Choiseul was imperfect, and that 'no recent navigators have given an account of it',[2] and also stated that New Georgia, previously thought to be one island, was then better known and recognized to be a group of islands.[3]

In the period after 1841 whalers and traders were apparently active in the New Georgia area and contributed to an increased knowledge of it, though the improvement of the chart of the Solomons in respect of this particular area was the result of surveys, by Commander Balfour in the *Penguin* in 1893–5 in the New Georgia area, by Commander Pasco in the *Dart* around Santa Ysabel in 1902, and by F. I. Bayldon in the SS. *Moresby* around Vella Lavella and Ranongga.[4] *Admiralty Chart No.* 214, with corrections to 1925, still delineated the south coast of Choiseul as a dotted line and part of the New Georgia group with uncertainty, and was still based on the charts of Dentrecasteaux, Krusenstern and d'Urville, with amendments made as a result of naval surveys and the observations of missionaries of the Melanesian Mission and of C. R. Woodford and W. T. Wawn. It is with the year 1841, however, and the publication of Laurie's chart and the commencement of the publication of the results of d'Urville's exploration, that this study properly ends. By that time the Solomon Islands were known and reasonably charted, and the

---

[1] See Dumont d'Urville 1841: Atlas Vol. II: *Carte 5*.
[2] Findlay 1877: 777. See pp. 758–95 for the Solomons generally.
[3] Findlay 1877: 772–4. On Choiseul and New Georgia see also Findlay 1851: 1010–12 and Cheyne 1855: 74.   [4] Letter from The Hydrographer, dated 11 May 1961.

identification of the Spanish discoveries of 1568 could have been generally achieved.

The Islands of Solomon were the first major group in the South Pacific to be discovered by Europeans, and from the time of their discovery they were variously a source of interest, attraction, perplexity, doubt and confusion. For over 200 years their delineation on charts of the Pacific was a question of considerable cartographical importance, and the detailed story of their discovery, rediscovery and exploration, which in this brief study it has only been possible to summarize, is perhaps the most fascinating in the history of the South Pacific. It is a microcosm of the epic of European maritime expansion set against a background of the development of the art and science of navigation and the development of cartography and hydrography. It is a story of courage and endurance, of men pitting themselves, often with disastrous consequences, against the largest and most inappropriately named ocean in the world, but nonetheless the most attractively islanded and peopled ocean in the world. It embraces the greatest period of European endeavour, when the sailors of five nations, with various motivations but always with the same spirit, took their vessels to the four corners of the earth and, for better or worse, discovered and charted the way for their colonial and commercial successors. The discovery of the Solomons was the result of a romantic quest, the quest for *Ophir*, and it is perhaps appropriate that these islands should still bear the historically inaccurate but romantically apposite name—Islands of Solomon.

BIBLIOGRAPHY

(i) A bibliographical note on Spanish archival sources relating to the expeditions of 1567–1606.

(ii) A bibliography of archival material cited and consulted.

(iii) A bibliography of published works and modern MS. sources cited and consulted.

(iv) A bibliography of newspapers and magazines cited.

(v) A bibliography of maps, charts and globes cited and consulted.

(i) A BIBLIOGRAPHICAL NOTE ON SPANISH ARCHIVAL SOURCES

The following notes provide a brief synopsis of the several main sources relating immediately and solely to the three Spanish voyages to the South-West Pacific, 1567–1606.

MENDAÑA'S FIRST VOYAGE, 1567–9

A. The *Relación* of Hernán Gallego.

The most important single document describing the first voyage of Mendaña is the *relación* or log-book of the Chief Pilot, Hernán Gallego. This exists in two forms which can conveniently be named *The Long Version* and *The Short Version*.

The Long Version

Four MS. editions of this version are known to exist, none of which has any claim to being the original prepared by Gallego. They all contain detectable errors, generally consistent, which were unlikely to have existed in the original, and which can be attributed to dictation to an amanuensis. The MSS. are

(i) The MS. in the Museo Naval, Madrid (MNM), (MS. 921).

(ii) The MS. in the Archivo General de Indias (AGI), Seville (*Patronato, legajo* 18 (1–1–1/18), *No.* 10, *Ramo* 4).

(iii) The MS. in the British Museum (BM), London (Add. MS. 17.623). This MS. was partially translated by Guppy.[1]

(iv) The MS. in the Alexander Turnbull Library (ATL), Wellington, New Zealand. This MS. was originally owned by Lord Amherst of Hackney and was translated by him.[2]

Amherst refers to a MS. in the Royal Library (Biblioteca de Palacio), Madrid,[3] but I am informed by Father Celsus Kelly, who has made a detailed search and study of the Spanish archival sources, that he has been unable to locate this MS. It seems likely that Amherst was referring in fact to the MS. in the Museo Naval, Madrid.

---

[1] Guppy 1887: 192–245.   [2] Amherst 1901: I: 5–80.   [3] Amherst 1901: I: vii.

The Short Version

This version may have been written by Gallego for the *Licenciado* Lope García de Castro,[1] although it is quite possible that it is an abbreviated version of the long *relación*, perhaps with corrections. A MS. copy of it was recently located by Father Celsus Kelly in the Archives of Santa Casa de Loyola, Guipúzcoa (MS. *De Marina* 10–5–14, ff104v–121). The MS. contains, in addition to the copy of Gallego's short *relación*, several papers written by Quirós. It is certainly a copy of Gallego's *relación*, and not the original, and may well be a copy of the copy made by Quirós, which he consulted, along with the *Long Version*, whilst participating in Mendaña's second voyage in 1595.

In making the present study I have relied primarily on the Museo Naval MS. and the Santa Casa MS. The other MSS. have been examined, primarily for comparative purposes, and although most of the source references are to the MNM MS. a few, where necessary, relate to the other MSS.

B. The *Relación* of the Chief Purser Gomez Hernández Catoira (Dated La Plata, 4: vi: 1573).

Addressed to the *Licenciado* de Castro, and to be found in the British Museum (Add. MS. No. 9944, ff225–306), this is an important account, second only to Gallego's *relación*, and secondary only by virtue of its dearth of navigational detail. It is by far the most picturesque, detailed and literary account of the voyage, and, though often reporting at second-hand, provides the most complete picture of the internal politics of the expedition, the personalities of the *expedicionarios*, the islands, their inhabitants' customs and appearance, and the nature of Ibero-Melanesian contact. A translation of this MS. was made by Amherst[2] which, although containing some bowdlerization, is generally reliable.[3]

C. An Anonymous MS. in the Bibliothèque Nationale, Paris. (MS. No. N325).

This MS. is useful as an additional source.[4]

D. The Report of Álvaro de Mendaña to the *Licenciado* de Castro, Governor of Perú.

This incomplete MS. is of considerable value within the framework of source material. Two copies to be found:

(i) In the Archivo General de Indias (AGI), Sevilla, (*Patronato, legajo* 18, *No.* 10, *Ramo* 5, 'Relación de lo acaecido . . .'), and
(ii) In the Real Academia de la Historia (RAH), (*Colección Muñoz*, Vol. XXXVII, ff230–64).[5]

E. The Report of Álvaro de Mendaña to the King (11 September 1569).

A copy of this MS. is to be found in the Real Academia de la Historia (RAH) Madrid (*Colección de Velázquez*, Vol. XXXVI, *No.* 8, ff185–194v).[6]

---

[1] See Zaragoza 1876: I: 187, where Quirós quotes from the *Short Version* and describes his source as Gallego's *relación* for the *Licenciado* de Castro, and Mendaña's letter to de Castro in which he remarks that 'as the Chief Pilot, Hernan Gallego, will give your Lordship a particular account of the courses and latitudes of our navigation, and of all things touching the navigation . . . I will not state them here' (Amherst 1901: I: 97).   [2] Amherst 1901: II: 217 *et seq.*

[3] I have utilized a microfilm of a transcript of the MS. made by Father Celsus Kelly and deposited in the National Library, Canberra.

[4] See Amherst 1901: II: 195 *et seq.* for a translation, and also Charton 1854: IV: 187.

[5] It is transcribed in Pacheco 1864: V: 221–85, and translated in Amherst 1901: I: 97–158.

[6] It is transcribed in Zaragoza 1876: II: 15 *et seq*, and translated in Amherst 1901: I: 161 *et seq.*

F. The Report of Dr. Barros.

This is the report of a Commission of Enquiry set up under Dr. Barros in 1573 to examine members of the expedition and, by means of leading questions, to prove the importance of the part played by Sarmiento de Gamboa in the expedition, Mendaña's indebtedness to him, and Mendaña's incompetence and failure to carry out his instructions. The statements made to Dr. Barros are valuable as revealing the impressions of the 'rank and file' and 'lower deck' of the expedition. It is to be found in the Real Academia de la Historia (RAH), (*Colección Muñoz*, Vol. X, ff197–212).[1]

G. An Anonymous Account of the expedition, which Amherst translated and attributed to Sarmiento,[2] and which Forsyth identified as the concluding part of the *Barros Report*,[3] would appear in fact to be the work of Sarmiento. It appears to be an extract from a longer narrative by Sarmiento to be found in RAH: *Collección Muñoz*, Vol. XXXVII, ff266–83 and AGI: *Patronato, legajo 18, No. 10, Ramo 8*, However, since the extract was made at La Plata, the site of the Barros Enquiry, and since the Barros Enquiry was clearly instituted in Sarmiento's interest, a close association between the extract and the Enquiry seems fairly certain.

MENDAÑA'S SECOND VOYAGE, 1595

A. The Quirós-Bermúdez *Relación*.

This account is generally attributable to Pedro Fernández de Quirós, Chief Pilot of the expedition, but owes much to another, almost certainly identifiable with his secretary of later years, Luis de Belmonte Bermúdez.[4] The *relación* consists of three sections, the first providing an account of Mendaña's voyage of 1567–9, which seems to be based on the *Short Version* of Gallego's *relación*,[5] the second describing the second voyage of Mendaña in 1595, and the third describing Quirós' voyage of 1606.

Two MS. copies of the Quirós-Bermúdez *relación* are known to exist,

(i) in the Biblioteca de Palacio (BPM), Madrid (MS. 1686), with the loose title '*Varios Diarios de los Viajes a la Mar del Sur y descubrimientos de las Yslas de Salomon, las Marquesas, las de Santa Cruz, Tierras del Espiritu Santo, y otras de la parte Austral incognitas, Executados por Albaro de Mendaña y Fernando de Quiros desde el año de 1567, hasta el de 606; y escritos por Hernan Gallego, Piloto de Mendaña*',

(ii) in the Museo Naval (MNM), Madrid (MS. 951), with the equally loose and incorrect title '*Dos relaciónes del viaje del illustre Alvaro de Mendaña en el descrubimiento de las islas de Poniente ó Salomon—Año de 1567*'.

A transcription of the *relación* is to be found in Zaragoza 1876: I: 1–402, and a translation of all but the account of the voyage of 1567–9 in Markham 1904: I: 3–146.[6] Zaragoza

---

[1] Translated in Conway 1946: 139–51.

[2] RAH: *Collección Muñoz*, Vol. XXXVII, ff3–7; Amherst 1901: I: 82 *et seq*.

[3] Forsyth 1955: 37. See also Pacheco 1864: V: 210; and Duro 1896: II: 260.

[4] Zaragoza 1876: I: LIX; Markham 1904: I: xi–xii; Kelly 1960.

[5] Zaragoza 1876: I: 1–22. Though Quirós certainly used the *Short Version* of Gallego's *relación* several of his comments would seem to indicate that he also used the *Long Version* as well.

[6] Markham's scholarly abilities, prodigious editing and enthusiasm were not, unfortunately, equalled by his knowledge of Spanish. Whilst his translation provides a useful basis it must be used with considerable care and reference to either the Spanish MSS. or Zaragoza. See Diffie and Bernstein 1937. There is also an abbreviated version of the *relación* in Figueroa. See Figueroa 1631: Book VI: 324 *et seq*; and Figueroa 1861: 126 *et seq*.

used the Museo Naval MS., but, as Kelly has pointed out, his footnotes seem to indicate that he used the Biblioteca de Palacio MS.[1]

B. A Report by Quirós to Dr. Antonio de Morga, Lieutenant General of the Philippines. This is contained in Antonio de Morga's *Sucesos de las Islas Philipinas*, México, 1609.[2]

C. There is also a brief account of the expedition entitled *Vreve Relacion de el biaje que albaro de mendaña aquien su mag^d dio la conquista poblacon y pacificacion de las yslas occidentales de la mar del sur*... in the Archivo General de Indias (AGI), Seville (*México* 116).

QUIRÓS' VOYAGE OF 1606

A. The Quirós-Bermúdez *Relación*.

MNM: MS. 951.
BPM: MS. 1686.
Zaragoza 1876: I: 192 *et seq.*
Markham 1904: I: 261 *et seq.*

B. The log-book of the Chief Pilot, Gaspar González de Leza.

The original MS. of his log-book is in the Biblioteca Nacional (BNM), Madrid (MS. 3212), and a transcription of it is to be found in the British Museum (BM), London (Michelena Collection Add. 17625).[3]

C. The *Relación* of *Don* Diego de Prado y Tovar (*c.* 1615).

This is probably a copy of an original written *c.* 1608, the MS. of which was discovered in the second decade of this century in a collection of books and papers auctioned at Sotheby's. A translation by Barwick and a transcript of it is to be found in Stevens 1929: 86–205. MLS: Safe 1/73a.

D. The Account of Fray Martín de Munilla O.F.M.

This MS. account is in the Archivum Generale Ordinis Fratrum Minorum (MS. XI–33 *México, Relationes et Descriptiones*, S XV–VII).

E. An Account by Juan de Iturbe, Accountant to the Expedition.

This account, which is unsigned, but which is to be found in one archival source (AGS) attached to the correspondence of Juan de Iturbe to the King and the Constable of Castille and to a ministerial summary of the contents of those letters, is entitled *Sumario brebe de la Relacion y Derrotero del Viaje que hizo el Capitàn... de Quiros... en el descubrimiento de las tierras incognitas de la parte Austral de la Mar del Sur*. AGS. *Estado, legajo* 219. BNM: MS. 3099, ff109–128v; RAH: *Colección de Jesuitas*, CXVIII, 87: MNM: MS 196, ff16–27v. This account also provides a summary of previous voyages to the South-West Pacific and their achievements.

---

[1] Kelly 1959: 189.
[2] Transcribed in Zaragoza 1876: II: 51–61, and translated in Stanley 1868: 65–74 and Markham 1904: I: 149–57.   [3] See also Zaragoza 1876: III: 76, and Markham 1904: II: 323.

F. The Letters of Luis Váez de Torres.

(i) Letter to the King, Manila, 12 July 1607.

AGS: *Estado, legajo* 209.

BNM: MS. 3099, ff30–42, translated in Stanley 1868: 402 *et seq*, and Stevens 1929: 214–37.

A copy was obtained by Alexander Dalrymple and translated by him. See Burney 1803: III: 467–78; Major 1859: 31, and Markham 1904: II: 455, which are all reproductions of Dalrymple's translation.

(ii) Letter to Quirós, 15 June 1607.

A part of this letter only is included in a *memorial* from Quirós to the King of 1610.[1]

G. Secondary Documents.

The account of *Fray* Juan de Torquemada.[2] This account, included in Torquemada's *Monarchia Indiana* of 1614, is only of interest in relation to the primary sources by virtue of Torquemada's position as Provincial of the Franciscans in México at the time of Quirós' return, and the strong possibility that his account was derived directly from Quirós. Two other Franciscan accounts, by *Fray* Antonio Daza and *Fray* Diego de Córdova, seem to have been derived from Torquemada.

In addition to these main sources relating to the actual voyage, there is a wealth of reference to and description of the expedition in the *memoriales* of Quirós, the correspondence of the other members of the expedition, and the recorded deliberations of the several councils. Such sources I have referred to in the main body of this study as they arise, but have not included in this brief synopsis of the principal sources.

(Since the MS. of this book went to the printers Father Celsus Kelly has published a *Calendar of Documents* relating to Spanish voyages in the Pacific, Franciscan-Historical Studies, Australia, and Archivo Ibero-Americano, Madrid, MCMLXV, to which the interested reader is referred.)

(ii) BIBLIOGRAPHY OF ARCHIVAL MATERIAL[3] CITED AND CONSULTED

Alexander Turnbull Library, Wellington (ATL)

Gallego, Hernán. Relacion cierta y verdadera de la navegacion de las Islas del Poniente.

Archivo de Universidad, Salamanca (AUS)

Three memoriales of P. F. de Quirós to the King (1597), MS. CCCXXXVII, ff121–125v.

Archivo General de Indias, Sevilla (AGI)

Patronato, legajo 18, *No.* 10, *Ramo* 4 (Gallego—*relación*).
Patronato, legajo 18, *No.* 10, *Ramo* 5.
Patronato, legajo 18, *No.* 10, *Ramo* 6.
Patronato, legajo 18, *No.* 10, *Ramo* 8.
Patronato, legajo 51, *No.* 3, *Ramo* 8.

---

[1] Zaragoza 1876: II: 296–9.   [2] Torquemada 1723: I: 738–56; Markham 1904: II: 407 *et seq*.
[3] With the exception of material in the Mitchell Library and Dixson Collection, Sydney, this material, or relevant parts of it, has all been examined in either microfilm or photocopies.

Indiferente General, legajo 750.
Indiferente General, legajo 1085.
Indiferente General, legajos 1383B, 1384–5.
Lima 125.
Lima 570, *Lib.* 14, ff333–343v.
Lima 570, *Lib.* 15, ff224v–228v.
Filipinas 19, 20.
Filipinas 82 (*Fray Ignacio Muñoz*, 15: IV: 1674).
Guadalajara 51, *doc.* 145.
México 116.

Archivo General de Simancas (AGS)

Estado, legajo K, 1631, *docs.* 33, 34, 34bis, 243, 244, 245.
Mapas y Planos.
Estado, legajo 196, 206, 209, 213, 219, 228, 249, 252, 2640, 2641, 2642, 2644, 2746, 2747, 2773, 2637, 2638, 196.

Arthur A. Houghton Jnr. Collection, New York

Derrotero General—Pedro Baena.
Descripción y Derotero de las Costas Pueros—Nicholás de Espinoza.

Australian National Library, Canberra (ANL)

Uncatalogued maps and charts.

Biblioteca de Palacio, Madrid (BPM)

MS. 1686 (*Quirós-Bermúdez relación*).
MS. 2227, ff254–257.

Biblioteca Nacional, Madrid (BNM)

Catalogo de Manuscritos de America.
MS. 3099 (*Papeles de Quirós*).
MS. 3212.
MS. 3048, ff53–58v.
Memoriales por Fray Juan de Silva, 1613, 2/51255.

Bibliothèque Nationale, Paris (BNP)

Duchess of Berry Atlas (Ge. F. F. 14409).

Bibliothèque Royale, Brussels (BRB)

Erédia: Declaracam de Malaca, MS. 7264.

British Museum, London (BM)

J. Dee—The Great Volume of Famous and Rich Discoveries—1577 (Vitellius, C, VII, Cotton MSS.).
Hernán Gallego—Relación (Add. MS. 17.623).
Relación de Gómez Hernández Catoira (Add. MS. 9.944, ff225–306).
Eighth Memorial of P. F. de Quirós (Add. MS. 13.974).
Memorial de Juan Arias, c. 1615 (*Papeles Tocantes à la Iglesia Española*, 4745).

A petition by Andrés de Medina-Dávila of 1661 (Gayangos FU/65 Medina).

W. Hack(e)—Description of the Sea Coasts of Monomapata, etc. (Maritime VI–V Vol. 9/Tab. 37).

W Hack—Transcript and translation of the Spanish derrotero captured by Captain Sharp in 1681 (Harl. 4034).

W. Hack—Drawing of the Wagoner of the Great South Sea (7 Tab. K Mar. VIII: 15).

W. Hack—Charts of the Pacific Coasts of America (Harl. 4034).

W. Hack—A Description of all the Navigable Parts of the World (Add. 1 5414 art. 6).

A Discovery of Lands beyond the Equinoctiall, 1573 (Landsdowne MS. 100, ff142–146).

John Welbe's scheme for the discovery of Terra Australis, 1715 (Sloane MS. 4044, ff214v–217).

Royal MS. 20 E IX ff29v–30.

Sloane MS. No. 5222 Art. 12 Verkleind.

Maps and Charts

Egmont MSS. (No. 157).

J. Carter Brown Library, Rhode Island (JCB)

Juan López de Velasco—Demarcacion y Diuision de las Indias, c. 1575.

MS. log-book of the Ann and Hope (1798–9) by the Mate, Christopher Bentley.

MS. log-book of the Ann and Hope (1798–9) by the son of the Master, B. Page Jnr.

Commonwealth Relations Office (CRO)—Old India Office—Military Records Section

MS. log-book of the Royal Admiral to Port Jackson and Whampoa 8/4/1792–25/9/1793 by the Master, Captain E. H. Bond (338F).

MS. log-book of the Bellona to Port Jackson and Whampoa 24/7/1792–29/9/1794 by the Master, Captain Mathew Boyd (353A).

MS. log-book of the Duff to Rio de Janeiro, Otaheite and Whampoa 1/7/1796–31/7/1798 by the Mate, Thomas Godsell (H07A).

MS. log-book of the Barwell 1797–1799 by the Master, Captain Cameron (420G).

Huntingdon Library, San Merino (HL)

A Spanish roteiro dated Panama 1669 (HM 918).

Atlas of 18 folios (HM 39).

Koninklijke Bibliotheek, The Hague (KB)

MS. Atlas (129 A 25).

Library of Congress, Washington (LC)

Atlas of João Teixeira, c. 1630.

Mitchell Library, Sydney (MLS)

Maps and charts.

Tasman's Journal (The Huydecoper MS.) with a MS. translation by P. K. Roest.

Memoriales of Quirós (Safe 1/5).

Admiralty Hydrographic Collection.

MSS. C401, C402, C403, C404, B1436, B690.

Relación of de Prado (Safe 1/73a).

Dixson Collection, Sydney (MLS (Dixson))

    Captain Philip Carteret's log-book of the Swallow, 1767.
    Memoriales of Quirós.
    Maps and charts.

Museo Naval, Madrid (MNM)

    MS. 921, *Gallego—relación.*
    MS. 951, *Quirós-Bermúdez relación.*
    MS. 196, ff1–6, 41–44, 155–63.
    MS. 142, *Doc. No. 5* and *Doc. No. 8.*
    MS. 328, ff123–123v.

National Archives, The Hague (NAH)

    Collection of Leupe 493.

National Archives, Washington (NAW)

    MS. log-book of the Alliance from Philadelphia to Canton, 1787, by the Mate, Richard Dale.

New York Public Library (NYPL)

    Fray Miguel de Balboa's Miscelena Antarctica of 1566.

Public Records Office, London (PRO)

    Admiralty 2/1332, pp. 99–100, *Instructions to Captain Byron.*
                 pp. 145–22, *Secret Instructions to Captain Wallis.*
                 pp. 160 *et seq, Secret Instructions to Captain Cook.*

Real Academia de la Historia, Madrid (RAH)

    Salazar F23, ff59v–139v and 140–153.
    Papeles Varios de Indias D90.
    Colección de Velázquez, Vol. XXXVI, *No. 8,* ff185–194v.
    Colección Muñoz, Vol. XXXVII, ff3–7, 230–64, 266–83.
    Colección Muñoz, Vol. XXXVIII, ff42–48; 49–54.
    Pinelo—Epítome de la Bibliotheca. . . .
    Colección de Jesuitas, Vol. CXVIII, 87.
    Colección Muñoz, Vol. X, ff197–212.

Rhode Island Historical Society, Library (LRIHS)

    Journal of Dr. B. Bowen Carter.

Santa Casa de Loyala, Guipúzcoa (Santa Casa)

    MS. *De Marina, Estante 10, Pluteo 5, No. 14.*

Vatican Archives (VSdS), Rome.

    Segreteria (dei Brevi) di Stato, Vol. CCCXIX, ff73–77v.

Archivum Generale Ordinis Fratrum Minorum (VAGOFM), Rome.

> *Relación de Fray Martín Munilla*, MS. XI-33 México, *Relationes et Descriptiones*, S, XVI–VII.

> *Missiones Apostólicas... de la Santa Provincia de los Doce Apostoles de Lima... por el R. P. F. Fernando Rodríguez de Tena...* MS. XI-41.

Archivio de Propaganda Fide (VAPF), Rome.

> *Two memorials of Dr. Sebastian Clemente to Pope Gregory XV* (*Scritture originali riferite nelle Congregazioni Generali Memoriali del an 1662*. CCCLXXXII, ff156–157v, 164–167v).

(iii) BIBLIOGRAPHY OF PUBLISHED WORKS AND MODERN MS. SOURCES CITED AND CONSULTED

ACOSTA, J. de, 1880. *The Natural and Moral History of the Indies*, 2 vols., ed. C. R. Markham London. (The English translation of Edward Grimston, 1604).

ACTON, Lord 1960. 'The New World.' *Lectures on Modern History*. London, pp. 61–77.

ALGUNS DOCUMENTOS *do Archivo Nacional da Tôrre do tombo ácerca das Navegações e Conquistas Portuguezas* (ed. by J. Ramos Coelho), 1892. Lisbon.

ALMAGIÀ, R. 1948. 'Carte geographiche a stampa di particolare pregio o rarita.' *Monumenta Cartographica Vaticana*, Vol. II. Rome.

AMHERST, Lord and THOMSON, B. 1901. *The Discovery of the Solomon Islands by Alvaro de Mendaña in 1568*, 2 vols. London.

ANON, 1767. *A Voyage round the World, in HM ship the Dolphin... by an officer on board the said ship*. London.

ANON, 1841. *The Missionary Voyages to the South Sea Islands performed in the years 1796, 1797, and 1798 in the ship Duff commanded by Captain James Wilson*. London.

ANTHIAUME, A. 1916. *Cartes Marines, Constructions Navales; Voyages de Découverte chez les Normands 1500–1650*, 2 vols. Paris.

ARDEN-CLOSE, C. 1947. *Geographical By-Ways*. London.

ARISTOTLE, 1947. *De Caelo* (translation by J. L. Stocks in *The Works of Aristotle* edited by W. D. Ross, Vol. II). Oxford.

BACON, R. 1928. *Opus Majus* (c. 1267) (translation by R. B. Burke). Philadelphia.

BAGROW, L. 1945. 'The origin of Ptolemy's Geographia.' *Geografiska Annaler*, pp. 318–87.

—— 1947. 'Supplementary notices to "The origin of Ptolemy's Geographia".' *Imago Mundi*, Vol. IV, pp. 71–2.

—— 1951. *Geschichte der Kartographie*. Berlin.

BAIÃO, A. *et al.* 1939. *História da Expansão Portuguesa no Mundo*, Vol. II. Lisbon.

BAKHUIZEN VAN DEN BRINK, R. C. 1865. 'Isaac Le Maire—Eene Voorlezing.' *De Gids*, Vol. IV. The Hague.

BARLOW, R. 1932. *A Brief Summe of Geographie* (ed. E. G. R. Taylor). London.

BARROS, J. de 1615. *Década Quarta da Asia*. Madrid.

BAYLY, G. 1885. *Sea Life Sixty Years Ago*. London.

BAYLDON, F. J. 1927. 'Alexander Dalrymple.' *Journal of the Royal Australian Historical Society*, Vol. 13, p. 41.

—— 1932. 'Remarks on navigators of the Pacific, from Magellan to Cook.' *Journal of the Royal Australian Historical Society*, Vol. 18, p. 134.

BAYLDON, F. J. 1933. 'Remarks on criticisms of explorers in the Pacific Ocean.' *Journal of the Royal Australian Historical Society*, Vol. 19, p. 141.

BEAGLEHOLE, J. C. 1934. *The Exploration of the Pacific*. London.

—— (Ed.) 1955. *The Journals of Captain James Cook*, Vol. I. Cambridge.

—— (Ed.) 1961. *The Journals of Captain James Cook*, Vol. II. Cambridge.

BEALE, T. 1839. *The Natural History of the Sperm Whale . . . to which is added a Sketch of a South-Sea Whaling Voyage*. London.

BEAUTEMPS-BEAUPRÉ. 1807. *Atlas du Voyage de Bruny-Dentrecasteaux . . . fait par ordre du gouvernement en 1791, 1792 et 1793*. Paris.

BENEDETTO, L. F. 1928. *Marco Polo—Il Milione*. Firenze.

BENSAUDE, J. 1912. *L'Astronomie Nautique au Portugal*. Geneva.

—— 1917. *Historie de la Science Nautique Portugaise*. Geneva.

—— 1917–20. *Les Légendes Allemandes sur l'Histoire des Découvertes Maritimes Portugaises*. Geneva.

BENSON, E. F. 1929. *Ferdinand Magellan*. London.

BETTEN, F. S. 1923. 'The knowledge of the sphericity of the earth in the early Middle Ages.' *Catholic Historical Review*, New Series, Vol. III, No. 1, pp. 74–90.

BEYNEN, K. (Ed.) 1876. *Gerrit de Veer: The Three Voyages of William Barents to the North-East*. London.

BIRDWOOD, G. 1891. *Report on the Old Records of the India Office with Supplementary Note and Appendices*. London (2nd reprint).

BLAEU, J. 1648. *Atlas*. Amsterdam.

—— 1663. *Le Grand Atlas ou Cosmographie Blaviane en laquelle est exactement descrite la Terre, la Mer et le Ciel*, 12 vols. Amsterdam.

BLAIR, E. M. and ROBERTSON, J. A. 1903. *The Philippine Islands*, Vols. I, XXVIII, XXXVI, XXXVII. Cleveland.

BOUGAINVILLE, M. M. de 1771. *Le Voyage de Bougainville autour du Monde, par la frégate du roi la Boudeuse et la flûte l'Étoile, en 1766, 1767, 1768 et 1769*. Paris.

BOURNE, E. G. 1891. 'History and determination of the line of demarcation of Pope Alexander VI between the Spanish and Portuguese fields of discovery.' *Annual Report of the American Historical Association*, pp. 103–30.

BOURNE, W. 1578. *Treasure for Travailers*.

—— 1581. *A Regiment of the Sea*.

BOWEN, E. 1752. *A Complete Atlas*. London.

BOXER, C. R. 1934. 'Portuguese roteiros 1500–1700.' *Mariner's Mirror*, Vol. XX: pp. 171–86.

BRUCE, J. 1810. *Annals of the Honorable East India Company*, Vol. I. London.

BUCK, P. H. 1938. *Ethnology of Mangareva. B. P. Bishop Museum Bulletin No. 157*. Honolulu.

BUFFET, H-Fr. 1950. 'Voyage à la découverte du port-Louisien Surville.' Extrait des Mémoires de la Société d'Histoire et d'Archéologie de Bretagne, Tome XXX.

BUNBURY, E. H. 1959. *A History of Ancient Geography among the Greeks and Romans from the Earliest Age till the Fall of the Roman Empire*. 2 vols. New York.

BURNEY, J. 1803. *A Chronological History of the Discoveries in the South Sea or Pacific Ocean*, 5 vols. London.

BURON, E. 1930. *Ymago Mundi de Pierre d'Ailly . . . (1350–1420). Texte latin et traduction française . . . et des notes marginales de Christophe Colomb*, 3 vols. Paris.

BURPEE, C. J. 1935. *The Search for the Western Sea*, 2 vols.

CALLANDER, J. 1766. *Terra Australis Cognita: or Voyages to the Terra Australis, or Southern Hemisphere, during the 16th, 17th and 18th centuries*, 3 vols. Edinburgh.

BIBLIOGRAPHY

CALVERT, A. F. 1893. *A Collection of Maps to illustrate the Discovery of Australia.* Sydney.

CAMPBELL, W. S. 1918. 'The East India Company and Australian trade.' *Journal of the Royal Australian Historical Society*, Vol. IV, Part V.

CARACI, G. 1926. *Tabulae Geographicae Vestutiores in Italia Adservatae*, 3 vols. Florence.

CARRINGTON, H. (Ed.) 1948. *The Discovery of Tahiti—A Journal of the Second Voyage of H.M.S. Dolphin round the World, under the command of Captain Wallis R.N. written by her master George Robertson.* London.

CAWSTON, G. and KEANE, A. H. 1896. *The Early Chartered Companies.* London.

CHARTON, E. 1854. *Voyageurs Anciens et Modernes*, 2 vols. Paris.

CHEYNE, A. 1852. *A Description of Islands in the Western Pacific Ocean.* London.

—— 1855. *Sailing Directions from New South Wales to China including the whole islands and dangers in the Western Pacific Ocean, the coasts of New Guinea and safest route through Torres Strait.* London.

CHICOTEAU, M. 1959. 'Early Cartography.' *Cartography*, Journal of the Australian Institute of Cartographers, Vol. 3, No. 2, September, pp. 76–77.

CHRISTIAN, F. W. 1924. *Early Maori Migration as evidenced by Physical Geography and Language. Report to the 16th Meeting of the Australasian Association for the Advancement of Science.* Wellington.

CHURCHILL, J. and A. 1704. *A Collection of Voyages in Four Volumes.* London.

CLEOMEDES. 1932. *On the Orbits of the Heavenly Bodies*, Book I (translation by T. L. Heath). London.

CLISSOLD, P. 1959. 'Early ocean-going craft in the Eastern Pacific.' *Mariner's Mirror*, Vol. 45, No. 3, pp. 234–42.

CLISSOLD, S. 1954. *Conquistador: the Life of Don Pedro Sarmiento de Gamboa.* Verschoyle.

COELLO, F. 1885. 'Conflicto Hispano.' *Boletín de la Real Sociedad Geográfica*, Tomo 19. Madrid.

COHEN, M. R. and DRABKIN, I. E. 1948. *A Source Book of Greek Science.*

COLLINDER, P. 1954. *A History of Marine Navigation.* London.

COLLINGRIDGE, G. 1891–2. 'Early Australian discovery.' *Journal of the Royal Geographical Society of Australia* (N.S.W.), Vol. 5.

—— 1895. *The Discovery of Australia.* Sydney.

—— 1906. *The First Discovery of Australia and New Guinea.* Sydney.

COLLINS, D. 1798. *An Account of the English Colony in New South Wales.* London.

COLONIAL CALENDAR, East Indies, 1617–21, Nos. 143, 159, 325. London.

COMMONWEALTH RELATIONS OFFICE, *Printed List of Marine Records—List of East India Company Ships' Logs in the Military Records Section, Old India Office.* London.

CONWAY, G. R. G. 1946. Translation of the Report of Dr. Barros to Toledo, Governor of Perú, on his examination of members of Mendaña's expedition of 1567 in June 1573 *American Neptune*, Vol. 6. April, pp. 139–51.

COOTE, C. H. 1894. *The Voyage from Lisbon to India.* London.

CORNEY, B. G. (Ed.) 1908. *The Voyage of Captain Don Felipe González . . . to Easter Island in 1770–1: Preceded by an Extract from . . . Roggeveen's . . . Log . . . in 1722.* Cambridge.

—— 1915. *The Quest and Occupation of Tahiti by Emissaries of Spain 1772–1776*, 3 vols. London.

CORTESÃO, A. 1915. 'Noticia de un atlas del siglo XVI manuscrito y desconocida.' *Boletín de la Real Sociedad Geográfica.* Madrid.

—— 1935. *Cartografia e Cartógrafos Portugueses dos Séculos XV e XVI*, 2 vols. Lisbon.

—— 1960. *Portugaliae Monumenta Cartographica*, 4 vols. Lisbon.

CORTÉS, M. 1589. *The Arte of Navigation* (translation by R. Cortés). London.

COSMAS, 1897. *The Christian Topography* (translation by J. W. McCrindle). London.

COUTO, D. do 1612. *Década Quinta da Asia*. Lisbon.

CROZET, M. 1783. *Nouveau Voyage a la Mer du Sud. . . . On a joint a ce Voyage un extrait de celui de Surville dans les mêmes parages*. Paris.

CUNNINGHAM, W. 1559. *A Cosmographical Glasse*. London.

CUTLER, 1728. *Atlas Maritimus et Commercialis*. (The first volume by Daniel Defoe?)

DAGH-REGISTER, *gehonden int Casteel Batavia van't passerende daer ter plaetse als over geheel Nederlandts-India 1643-44*, 1896. The Hague.

DAHLGREN, E. W. 1916. *Were the Hawaiian Islands visited by the Spaniards before Captain Cook?* Stockholm.

D'AILLY, P. 1930. See Buron 1930.

DALRYMPLE, A. 1767. *An Account of the Discoveries made in the South Pacifick Ocean previous to 1764*. London (published 1769).

—— 1770. *An Historical Collection of the Several Voyages and Discoveries in the South Pacific Ocean*. London.

—— 1773. *A Letter from Mr. Dalrymple to Dr. Hawkesworth, occasioned by some groundless and illiberal imputations in His Account of the late Voyages to the South*. London.

—— 1785. *Memoir concerning the Passages to and from China*. London (printed 1782).

—— 1790. *Considerations on M. Buache's Memoir concerning New-Britain and the North Coast of New Guinea*. London.

DALY, C. P. 1879. 'On the early history of cartography.' *Journal of the American Geographical Society*, Vol. XI, No. 1, pp. 1-37.

DAMPIER, W. 1906. *Voyages*, 2 vols. London (Ed. by J. Masefield).

DAVENPORT, F. G. 1917. *European Treaties bearing on the History of the United States and its Dependencies to 1648*. Washington.

DAVIDSON, J. W. 1956. 'Peter Dillon and the South Seas.' *History Today*, Vol. 6, pp. 307-17.

DAVIS, J. 1607. *The Seaman's Secrets*. London (see Markham 1880: 229-337).

DAWSON, S. E. 1899. 'The line of demarcation of Pope Alexander VI . . . with an inquiry concerning the metrology of Ancient and Medieval Times.' *Proceedings and Transactions of the Royal Society of Canada*, Series II, Vol. V, pp. 467-546.

DE BROSSES, C. 1756. *Histoire des Navigations aux Terres Australes*, 2 vols. Paris.

DENUCÉ, J. 1907. 'Les Îles Lequios et Ophir.' *Bulletin de la Société Royale Belgique de Géographie*, Vol. XXXI.

—— 1911. 'Magellan, la question des Molucques et la première circumnavigation du globe.' *Mémoires de l'Académie Royale de Belgique*, Ser. II, Vol. IV.

DIFFIE, B. W. and BERNSTEIN, H. 1937. 'Sir Clements Markham as a translator.' *The Hispanic American Historical Review*, Vol. XVII, November.

DILLON, P. 1829. *Narrative and Successful Result of a Voyage in the South Seas . . . to ascertain the fate of La Pérouse's expedition, interspersed with accounts of the religion, manners . . . of the South-Sea Islanders*. 2 vols. London.

—— 1830. *Voyage aux Îles de la Mer du Sud en 1827 et 1829, et relation de la découverte du sort de la Pérouse*, 2 vols. Paris.

DISCOMBE, R. and ANTHONIOZ, P. 1960. 'Voyage to Vanikoro.' *Pacific Discovery*, Vol. XIII, No. 1, January-February, pp. 4-15.

DIXON, W. 1936. 'Dumont d'Urville and Laperouse.' *Journal of the Royal Australian Historical Society*, Vol. XXI.

—— 1931. 'Notes and Comments on "New Light on the Discovery of Australia" by H. N. Stevens etc.' *Journal of the Royal Australian Historical Society*, Vol. XVII.

DONCKER, H. 1660. *De Zee-Atlas ofte Water-Waereld vertoonende alle de Zee-Kusten.* Amsterdam.

DOURADO, F. V. 1948. *Atlas of 1571.* Porto (Biblioteca História De Portugal, Ebrasil).

DUDLEY, D. R. 1647. *Arcano del Mare.*

—— 1661. *Arcano del Mare.*

DUMONT D'URVILLE, J. S. C. 1825. 'Note sur les collections et les observations recueillies . . . durant la campagne de la Coquille autour du monde en 1822, 1823, 1824 et 1825 . . . .' Reprinted from *Annales des Sciences Naturelles,* mai. Paris.

—— 1827. A report dated Amboina, 7 October 1827, published in the *Annales Maritimes et Commerciales (Bulletin de la Société de Géographie,* 73ᵉ numero). Paris.

—— 1828. 'Extrait du rapport addressé a S. Ex. le Ministre de la Marine sur les operations de la corvette l'Astrolabe, depuis son départ d'Hobart-Town, jusqu'a son arrivée a Batavia. . . . Janvier 1828. (In Hapdé 1829: 46.)

—— 1829. 'Rapport sur le voyage de l'Astrolabe lu a l'Académie Royale des Sciences, 1829, par M. Dumont D'Urville.' (In *Journal des Voyages,* Vol. XLII: pp. 150–215. Paris.)

—— 1830. *Voyage de la corvette l'Astrolabe, executé par ordre du roi, pendant les années 1826–29, sous le commandement de J. Dumont D'Urville,* 13 vols. and 4 *Atlases.* Paris.

—— 1833. *Voyage de Découvertes de l'Astrolabe executée dans les années 1826–29 sous le commandement de M. J. Dumont D'Urville . . . Observations nautiques, metreologiques, hydrographiques et de physique.* Paris.

—— 1834. *Voyage Pittoresque autour du Monde, resumé general des voyages des découvertes publié sous le direction de M. Dumont D'Urville.* Paris.

—— 1841(a). *Expédition au Pôle Austral et dans l'Océanie des corvettes de Sa Majesté l'Astrolabe et la Zélée sous le commandement de . . . M. Dumont D'Urville.* Paris.

—— 1841(b). *Voyage au Pôle Sud et dans l'Océanie sur les corvettes l'Astrolabe et la Zélée, executé par ordre du roi pendant les années 1837–1840 . . .,* 13 vols. and 7 Atlases. Paris.

DUPERREY, L. I. 1826. *Voyage autour du Monde executé par ordre du roi, sur la corvette de Sa Majesté, la Coquille, pendant les années 1822–25* (incl. Atlas). Paris.

—— 1827. *Mémoire sur les Operations Géographiques faites dans la campagne de la corvette de S. M. la Coquille pendant les années 1822–25.* Paris.

DURO, F. 1903. 'Discovery of the Solomon Islands.' *Boletín de la Real Sociedad de Geográfia,* Vol. XLV. Madrid.

DURO, G. F. 1896. *Armada Española,* Vol. II. Madrid.

D'URVILLE—see Dumont d'Urville.

EASTWOOD, E. 1927. *Memoir on Jodocus Hondius' World-map of 1608, accompanying a facsimile, by the Royal Geographical Society,* London.

EDWARDS, E. and HAMILTON, G. 1915. *Voyage of H.M.S. Pandora . . . 1790–91.* London.

EMORY, K. P. 1939. *Archaeology of Mangareva and Neighbouring Atolls.* B.P. Bishop Museum Bulletin No. *163.* Honolulu.

ENCISCO, M. F. de 1519. *Suma de Geographia.*

ENGELBRECHT, W. A., and HERWERDEN P. J. van 1945. *De Ontdekkingsreis van Jacob Le Maire en Willem Cornelisz Schouten in de jaren 1615-1617. Journalen, documenten en andere bescheiden.* . . . The Hague.

ERÉDIA, M. G. de 1882. *Declaracam de Malacca* (1613) (translation by L. Janssen in *Malaca l'Inde Méridionale*). Brussels. (See also Mills, 1930.)

ESPADA, M. J. de la 1879. *Tres Relaciones de Antiquedades Peruanas. Publicalas el Ministerio de Fomento, con motivo del Congreso Internacional de Americanistas que ha de celebrarse en Bruselas el presente año.* Madrid.

ESPADA, M. J. 1891. 'Las Islas de los Galápagos y otras más á poniente.' *Boletín de la Sociedad Geográfica de Madrid*, Vol XXI.

FARO, M. 1955. *Manuel Godinho de Erédia Cosmógrafo*. Lisbon (reproduced in *Panorama*, Series II, Nos. 13–14).

FERNÁNDEZ, V. 1922. *O Livro de Marco Polo* (Lisbon, 1502) (edited by F. M. E. Pereira). Lisbon.

FERRAND, G. 1918. 'Malaka, le Malayu et Malayur.' *Journal Asiatique*, Onzième Serie, Tome XI, No. 3, mai-juin, pp. 391–484. Paris.

FIGUEROA, C. S. de 1613. *Hechos de Don García Hurtado de Mendoza cuarto Marqués de Cañete*. Madrid. (See also *Colección de Historiadores de Chile*, Tom 5, Santiago, 1851, where it is reproduced with an introduction by Don Barros Araña.)

FILEWOOD, L. W. 1958. 'Markings on lead ballast may help to confirm La Pérouse relics.' *Pacific Islands Monthly*, May.

FINDLAY, A. G. 1851. *A Directory for the Navigation of the South Pacific Ocean; with descriptions of its coasts, islands, etc . . . its winds, currents and passages*. London.

FISCHER, J. and WIESER, F. von 1903. *The Oldest Map with the name America of the year 1507 and the Carta Marina of the year 1516 by M. Waldseemüller*. Innsbruck.

FLEURIEU, M. L. C. de 1790. *Découvertes des François, en 1768 et 1769, dans le Sud-Est de la Nouvelle Guinée*. Paris.

—— 1791. *Discoveries of the French in 1768 and 1769 to the South-East of New Guinea*. London.

FONTENEAU (or ALPHONSE) de SAINTONGEOIS, JEAN 1904. *La Cosmographie avec l'Espère et Régime du Soleil et du Nord* (1544), ed. by G. Musset. Paris.

FORNANDER, A. 1880. *An Account of the Polynesian Race*. London.

FORREST, T. 1779. *A Voyage to New Guinea and the Moluccas from Balambangan . . . in the Tartar Galley belonging to The Honourable East India Company . . . 1774, 1775 and 1776*. London.

FORSYTH, J. 1955. 'Australia in French geographical documents of the Renaissance by M. R. Herve' (ed. and trans.). *Journal of the Royal Australian Historical Society*, Vol. 41, Part 1.

—— 1959. 'Latouche-Tréville and his proposal to explore the south coast of New Holland.' *Mariner's Mirror*, Vol. 45, pp. 115–29.

FOSTER, W. 1911. 'An early chart of Tasmania.' *Geographical Journal*, Vol. 37, May, pp. 550–1.

FOSTER, W. 1933. *England's Quest of Eastern Trade*. London.

FREISLEBEN, H. C. 1960. 'Limitations of the dead reckoning reference at sea.' *Journal of the Institute of Navigation*, Vol. XIII, No. 1, January, pp. 13–19.

FREYCINET, L. de 1825. *Voyage Autour du Monde, enterpris par ordre du roi, executé sur les corvettes de S.M. l'Uranie et la Physicienne, pendant les années 1817–1820*, 2 vols. Paris.

GALLOIS, L. 1890. *Les géographes allemands de la Renaissance*. Lyon.

GALVANO, A. 1862. *Tratado* (1563). *The original Portuguese document together with The Discoveries of the World, the English edition of Richard Hakluyt* (1601). (Ed. C. A. Bethune.) London.

GERINI, G. E. 1909. *Researches on Ptolemy's Geography of Eastern Asia*. Asiatic Society Monographs, No. 1. London.

GIFFORD, E. W. 1929. *Tongan Society*. B.P. Bishop Museum, *Bulletin No. 61*, Honolulu.

GOOS, P. 1676. *De Zee-Atlas ofte Water-Wereld*. Amsterdam.

GOTTSCHALK, P. 1927. *The Earliest Diplomatic Documents on America. The Papal Bulls of 1493 and the Treaty of Tordesillas reproduced and translated*. Berlin.

GREENLEE, W. B. 1938. *The Voyage of Pedro Alvarez Cabral to Brazil and India*. London.

GREGORY, J. W. 1917. 'The evolution of the map of the world.' *Scottish Geographical Magazine*, Vol. XXXIII, pp. 49–65.

GSCHAEDLER, A. 1954. *Mexico and the Pacific 1546–1565: the Voyages of Villalobos and Legazpi and the Preparations made for them.* (Ph.D. thesis, University of Columbia.)

—— 1948. 'Religious aspects of the Spanish voyages in the Pacific during the 16th century and the early part of the 17th century.' *The Americas*, Vol. IV, No. 3, January, p. 302.

—— 1950. 'Seventeenth Century documents on Spanish navigation in the Mitchell Library of Sydney, Australia.' *The Hispanic American Historical Review*, August, pp. 397–9.

GUILLEMARD, F. H. H. 1890. *The Life of Ferdinand Magellan, 1480–1521.*

GUPPY, H. B. 1887. *The Solomon Islands and their Natives.* London.

HACHETTE, 1954. *La Tragique Expedition de Lapérouse et Langle.* Paris.

HAKLUYT, R. 1903. *The Principal Navigations Voyages Traffiques and Discoveries of the English Nation* (the 1598–1600 edition). Glasgow.

HAMBIS, L. 1955. *Marco Polo—La Description du Monde.* Paris.

HAMY, E. T. 1877. 'Commentaires sur quelques cartes anciennes de la Nouvelle-Guinée pour servir à l'histoire de la découverte de ce pays par les navigateurs espagnols, (1528–1606).' *Bulletin de la Société de Géographie*, nov. pp. 449–89. Paris (and also in *Études Historiques*, 1896, p. 187).

—— 1878. 'Le descobridor, Godinho de Eredia.' *Bulletin de la Société de Géographie*, Juin, pp. 511–41 (and also in *Études historiques et géographiques*, 1896, p. 281). See Dr. Hamy 1878: 41–71.

—— 1879. 'Cook et Dalrymple: (discours prononcé devant la Société de Géographie à l'occasion du centenaire de la mort de Cook).' *Bulletin de la Société de Géographie*, mai.

—— 1894(a). 'Declaration de Bartolomieu Viell.' *Bulletin de Géographie, historique et descriptif.*

—— 1894(b). 'Francisque et Andre d'Allaigne.' *Bulletin de Géographie, historique et descriptif,* pp. 405 *et seq.*

—— 1899. 'Nouveaux documents sur les frères d'Allaigne.' *Bulletin de Géographie, historique et descriptif.*

—— 1903. 'Documents relatifs a un projet . . . en 1570.' *Bulletin de Géographie, historique et descriptif.*

—— 1907. 'Luis Vaës de Torres et Diego de Prado y Tovar, explorateurs de la Nouvelle-Guinée 1606–1607: étude géographique et ethnographique.' *Bulletin de Géographie, historique et descriptif.*

HAPDÉ, A. 1829. *Expedition et Naufrage de La Pérouse, recueil historique de faits événements, découvertes, etc. appuyés de documents officiels avec un état general nominatif des officiers, etc. embarqués sur la Boussole et l'Astrolabe, et l'enumeration authentique de tous les débris du naufrage.* Paris.

HARING, C. H. 1918. *Trade and Navigation between Spain and the Indies.*

HARRIS, J. 1744. *Navigantum atque Itinerantium Bibliotheca; or a Complete Collection of Voyages and Travels,* 2 vols. London.

HARRISSE, H. 1892. *The Discovery of North America.* London.

HAWKESWORTH, J. 1773. *An Account of the Voyage undertaken by the Order of His Present Majesty for making Discoveries in the Southern Hemisphere, and successively performed by Commodore Byron, Captain Wallis, Captain Carteret and Captain Cook,* 3 vols. London.

HEAWOOD, E. 1921. 'The world map before and after Magellan's voyage.' *Geographical Journal*, Vol. LVII, No. 6, pp. 431–46.

HEERES, J. E. 1898. *Abel Janszoon Tasman's Journal . . . with documents relating to his exploration of Australia in 1644 . . . being photolithographic facsimiles of the original manuscripts in the colonial archives at the Hague with an English translation and facsimiles of original maps to which are added: Life and Labours of Abel Janszoon Tasman by J. E. Heeres.* Amsterdam.

HEERES, J. E. 1899. *The Part Borne by the Dutch in the Discovery of Australia, 1606–1765.* London.

HENDERSON, G. C. 1933. *The Discoverers of the Fiji Islands.* London.

HENNIG, R. 1948. 'The representation of the Magalhães Straits before their discovery.' *Imago Mundi*, Vol. V, p. 36.

HERRERA y TORDESILLAS, A. de 1601(a). *Descripcion de las Yndias Occidentales.* Madrid.

—— 1601(b) *Historia General de los Hechos de los Castellanos.* Madrid.

—— 1622. *Novus Orbis sive Descriptio Indiae Occidentalis. Auctore Antonio de Herrera— Accesserunt et Aliorum Indiae Occidentalis Descriptiones. . . .* Amsterdam.

HEWSON, J. B. 1951. *A History of the Practice of Navigation.* Glasgow.

HEYERDAHL, T. 1952. *American Indians of the Pacific.* London.

HILDEBRAND, A. S. 1924(a) 'Magellan.' *Harper's Magazine*, Vol. CXLIX, pp. 466–79.

—— 1924(b) 'Magellan crosses the Pacific.' *Harper's Magazine*, Vol. CXLIX, pp. 781–94.

HISTORICAL RECORDS OF NEW SOUTH WALES, 1893–. Vols, I, II and III. Sydney.

HONDIUS, J. 1907. *Hondius' Map of the World—1611* (ed. by Stevenson and Fischer for the Hispanic Society). New York.

HORNELL, J. 1946. 'How did the sweet potato reach Oceania?' *Journal of the Linnean Society*, Vol. LIII, No. 348. London.

HORSBURGH, J. 1809–. *Directions for Sailing to and from the East Indies, China, New Holland, Cape of Good Hope. . . . Compiled from Original Journals at the East India House.* London.

HOURANI, G. F. 1951. *Arab Seafaring in the Indian Ocean in Ancient and Early Medieval Times.* Princeton.

HUES, R. 1889. *Tractatus de Globis et Eorum Usu (1592)* (ed. by C. R. Markham). London.

HULOT, Baron 1894. 'D'Entrecasteaux 1737–1793.' *Bulletin de la Société de Géographie*, Serie 7, Tome XV, 3ᵉ Trimestre, pp. 263–402.

HUME, M. A. S. 1940. *Spain 1479–1788.* Cambridge.

HUMPHREYS, A. L. 1926. *Old Decorative Maps and Charts.* London.

HUNTER, J. 1793. *An Historical Journal of the Transactions at Port Jackson and Norfolk Island.* London.

HYMA, A. 1953. *A History of the Dutch in the Far East.* Michigan.

IVENS, W. G. 1926. 'Notes on the Spanish account of the Solomon Islands.' *Journal of the Royal Geographical Society*, April.

JACK-HINTON, C. 1961(a) 'The fate of the La Pérouse survivors.' *Pacific Islands Monthly*, April.

—— 1961(b). 'The importance of personal acquaintance in the identification of island discoveries.' *Journal of the Polynesian Society*, Vol. 70, No. 2, June, pp. 233–9.

—— 1962. 'Personal acquaintance in the identification of island discoveries.' *Journal of the Polynesian Society*, Vol. 71, No. 1, March, pp. 124–6.

—— 1964(a) 'Marco Polo in South East Asia.' *The Journal Southeast Asian History*, Vol. 5, No. 2, September, pp. 43–103, Singapore.

—— 1964(b) 'The political and cosmographical background to the Spanish incursion into the Pacific in the Sixteenth Century.' *Journal of the Malaysian Branch, Royal Asiatic Society*, Vol. XXXVII, Part 2, pp. 125–61. Kuala Lumpur.

JACK, R. L. 1921. *Northmost Australia. Three centuries of exploration, discovery and adventure in and around the Cape York Peninsula, Queensland.* London.

JACOBS, T. J. 1844. *Scenes, Incidents and Adventures in the Pacific Ocean or the Islands of the Australasian Sea, during the cruise of the clipper Margaret Oakley under Captain Benjamin Morrell.* New York.

JAMES, P. L. 1958. 'The key to the fate of a La Pérouse ship.' *Pacific Islands Monthly*, August.

JAMESON, J. F. 1926. 'Despatches of Castlenau.' *American Historical Review*, Vol. 31, pp. 285–96.

JANE, C. 1930. *Select Documents Illustrating the Four Voyages of Columbus*, 2 vols. London.

JENKINS, J. S. 1853. *Recent Exploring Expeditions to the Pacific and South Seas*. London.

JODE, C. DE 1578. *Speculum Orbis Terrarum*. Antwerp.

—— 1593. *Speculum Orbis Terrarum*. Antwerp.

JOMARD, E. F. 1862. *Les Monuments de la Géographie*. Paris.

JONES, J. W. 1850. *Divers Voyages touching the Discovery of America*. London.

JOSEPHUS, 1950. *Jewish Antiquities* (edited with an English translation by H. St. J. Thackeray), Vol. V. London.

JOURNAL DES VOYAGES, 1829. 'Voyage autour du Monde, executé par M. Legourant de Tromelin, Capitaine de Frégate, commandant la corvette du roi la Baionnaise', Vol. XLII, pp. 39–56. Paris.

KAMAL, S. A. Y. 1926. *Monumenta Cartographica Africae et Aegypti*, Vol. II. Le Claire.

KELLY, C. 1946. 'Catholic missionaries in the Pacific.' *Catholic Review*, Vol. II, Nos. 5 and 6, August and September, pp. 257–74.

—— 1948. 'Terra Australis, a Franciscan quest.' *The Americas*, Vol. IV, pp. 429–48, Vol. V, pp. 68–94.

—— 1959. 'Geographical knowledge and speculation in regard to Spanish Pacific voyages.' *Historical Studies*, Vol. 9, No. 33.

—— 1960. 'The narrative of Pedro Fernandez de Quirós.' *Historical Studies*, Vol. 9, No. 34.

—— 1961(a) 'Some early maps relating to Queirós-Torres discoveries of 1606.' *ACTAS. Congresso Internacional de História dos Descobrimentos*, Vol. II, pp. 203–54. Lisbon.

—— 1961(b). 'Pedro Fernandez de Queirós the last Portuguese navigator.' *ACTAS*. Vol. III, pp. 289–313. Lisbon.

KENNY, C. E. 1947. *The Quadrant and the Quill*. London.

KENNY, R. W. 1958. 'The maiden voyage of the Ann and Hope of Providence to Botany Bay and Canton 1798–1799.' *American Neptune*, Vol. XVIII, No. 2, April 1958.

KERR, R. 1824. *A General History and Collection of Voyages and Travels*. Edinburgh.

KEUNING, J. 1947. 'The history of an atlas.' *Imago Mundi*, Vol. IV, pp. 37–62. Stockholm.

—— 1951. 'The Novus Atlas of Johannes Janssonius.' *Imago Mundi*, Vol. VIII, pp. 71–98. Stockholm.

KIMBLE, G. H. T. 1938. *Geography in the Middle Ages*. London. (See also Pereira 1937.)

KIRKPATRICK, F. A. 1946. *The Spanish Conquistadores*. London.

KLERCK, E. S. de 1938. *History of the Netherlands East Indies*. Rotterdam.

KOHL, J. G. 1860. *Die Beiden Aeltesten General-Karten von Amerika*. Berlin.

KRETSCHMER, 1889. *Die Physiche Erdkunde im Christlichen Mittelalter*. Berlin.

—— 1891. *Zietschrift fur Erdkunde*. Berlin.

—— 1892. *Die Entdeckung Amerikas in Ihrer Bedetung fur die Geschichte fur des Weltbildes*. Munich.

KRUSENSTERN, A. I. 1824. 'Mémoire pour servire d'analyse et d'explication a la Carte Systematique de l'Archipel des Isles de Salomon.' In his *Recueil de Mémoires Hydrographiques pour servir d'analyse et d'explication à l'Atlas de l'Ocean Pacifique*. Saint-Petersbourg.

—— 1827. *Atlas de l'Ocean Pacifique dressé par M de Krusenstern Contre-Amiral et Directeur du Corps des Cadets de la Marine*. Saint-Petersbourg.

—— 1835. *Supplemens au Recueil de Mémoires Hydrographiques*. Saint-Petersbourg.

LABILLARDIÈRE, J. J. H. de 1800(a). *Voyage in Search of La Pérouse ... during the years 1791, 1792 and 1794*, 2 vols. (translated from the French). London.

LABILLARDIÈRE, J. J. H. de 1800(b). *Relation du Voyage à la Recherche de La Pérouse*, 2 vols. and Atlas. Paris.

LABORDE, J. B. 1788. *Mémoire sur la Prétendue Découverte faite en 1788 par des Anglois d'un continent qui n'est autre chose que la Terre des Arsacides, découverte . . . par M de Bougainville . . . et . . . M de Surville.* Paris.

―― 1791(a). *Histoire Abrégée de la Mer du Sud; ornée de plusieurs cartes . . . ,* 4 vols. (Vol. III). Paris.

―― 1791(b). *Cartes de la Mer Pacifique.* Paris.

LANGDON, R. A. 1961. 'The mystery of the Cross of St. Louis.' *Pacific Islands Monthly*, Vol. XXXI, No. 7, February.

LANGENES, 1609. *Hand-boeck of Cort Begrijp der Caerten ende Beschryvinghen van alle Landen des Werelds van niews oversien ende vermeerdert door Jacobius Viverius.* Amsterdam.

LA PÉROUSE, J. F. G. de 1797. *Voyage autour du Monde*, 3 vols. Paris.

―― 1798. *A Voyage Round the World . . . ,* 3 vols. London.

LATCHAM, R. E. 1928. *Prehistoria Chilena.* Santiago.

LAURIE, R. and WHITTLE, J. 1799. *The Country Trade East-India Pilot . . . chiefly composed from Actual Surveys and Draughts communicated by experienced Officers of the East-India Company and from the Neptune Oriental of M. D'Apres de Mannevillette.* London.

―― 1803. *The Complete East India Pilot, or Oriental Navigator*, 2 vols. London.

LEA, H. C. 1908. *The Inquisition in the Spanish Dependencies.* New York.

LE GUILLOU, É. 1843. *Voyage autour du Monde de l'Astrolabe et de la Zélée . . . pendant les années 1837, 1838, 1839 et 1840*, 2 vols. Paris.

LEE, I. 1920. *Captain Bligh's Second Voyage to the South Sea.* London.

LELEWEL. 1852. *Géographie du Moyen Age.*

LEVILLIER, R. 1921–. *Gobernantes del Perú, cartas y papeles, siglo XVI: documentos del Archivo de Indias*, 14 vols. Madrid.

LEWEL, J. 1850. *Atlas.* Brussels.

LINSCHOTEN, J. H. van 1596. *Itinerario.*

―― 1885. *The Voyage of John Huyghen van Linschoten to the East Indies (the Old English translation of 1598—The First Book containing his Description of the East)*, 2 vols. (ed. by A. C. Burnell and P. A. Thiele). London.

LIVERMORE, H. 1958. *A History of Spain.* London.

LOTHROP, S. K. 1932. *Aboriginal Navigation off the West Coast of South America.* Publications of the Royal Anthropological Institute, Vol. LXII. London.

MACKANESS, G. 1942. 'Some proposals for establishing colonies in the South Seas.' *Australian Historical Monographs*, No. 6. Sydney.

―― 1943(a). 'Some proposals for establishing colonies in the South Seas.' *Journal of the Royal Australian Historical Society*, Vol. XXIX, Part V.

―― 1943(b). 'Alexander Dalrymple's "A Serious Admonition to the Public on the Intended Thief Colony at Botany Bay".' *Australian Historical Monographs*, No. 7 Sydney.

MACKENNA, V. 1883. *History of the Island of Juan Fernandez.* Santiago.

MADARIAGA, S. de 1942. *Hernán Cortes.* London 1947. *The Rise of the Spanish Empire.* London.

―― 1949. *Christopher Columbus.* London.

MAGGS BROS LTD. 1921. *The Voyages and Discoveries of Early Travellers and Missionaries—Part 2—Australasia*, Catalogue No. 413. London.

―― 1927. *Australia and the South Seas*, Catalogue No. 491. London.

MAHAN, A. J. 1892. *The Influence of Sea Power upon History, 1660–1783.* London.

MAJOR, R. H. 1859. *Early Voyages to Terra Australis now called Australia.* London.

MAJOR, R. H. 1861. 'The discovery of Australia.' *Archaeologia*, Vol. 44.

MANGIN, A. 1880. *Voyages et Découvertes Outre-Mer au XIXᵉ siècle.*

MARCEL, G. 1886. *Recueil de Portulans.* Paris.

—— 1889. *Un Globe Manuscrit de l'École de Schoener.* Compte rendu du 4ᵐᵉ Congress international de Géographie, Vol. I, pp. 518–24. Paris.

—— 1898. *Mendaña et la Découverte des Îles Marquises.* Paris.

MARION, et CHEVALIER du CLESSNEUR. 1783. *Nouveau Voyage au Mer du Sud.* Paris.

MARKHAM, A. H. 1880. *The Voyages and Works of John Davies.* London.

MARKHAM, C. R. 1865. *The Travels of Pedro de Cieza de Leon—The First Part of his Chronicle of Peru, 1532–1550.* London.

—— 1870. *Garcilasso—Royal Commentaries of the Incas.* London.

—— 1872. *Garcilasso—Royal Commentaries of the Incas.* London.

—— 1873. *Narratives of the Rites and Laws of the Incas.* London.

—— 1878(a). *The Hawkins Voyages during the reigns of Henry VIII, Queen Elizabeth and James I.* London.

—— 1878(b). *The Voyages of Sir James Lancaster to the East Indies.* London.

—— 1884. *The Second Part of the Chronicle of Peru, 1532–1550.* London.

—— 1895. *Narratives of the Voyages of Pedro Sarmiento de Gamboa to the Straits of Magellan.* London.

—— 1904. *The Voyages of Pedro Fernandez de Quiros 1595–1606*, 2 vols. London.

—— 1907. *Sarmiento de Gamboa—History of the Incas.* London.

—— 1911. *Early Spanish Voyages to the Straits of Magellan.* London.

MARTYR, P. 1555. *The Decades of the New World of West India* (translation by Rychard Eden). London.

MAUDE, H. E. 1959. 'Spanish discoveries in the Central Pacific.' *Journal of the Polynesian Society*, Vol. 68, No. 4, December, pp. 285–326.

—— 'Post Spanish discoveries in the Central Pacific.' *Journal of the Polynesian Society*, Vol. 70, No. 1, March, pp. 67–111.

MEANS, P. A. 1942. 'Pre-Spanish navigation off the Andean coast.' *American Neptune*, Vol. II, No. 2.

MEDINA, J. T. 1888. *Colección de Documentos Inéditos para la Historia de Chile*, 3 vols. Santiago.

MENDOZA, J. G. de 1854 *A Historie of the Kingdome of China—Second Part, 2 Vols.* (ed. by Sir G. T. Staunton, introduction by R. H. Major). London.

MEYJES, R. P. 1919. *De Reizen van Abel . . . Tasman en Franchoys . . . Visscher . . . en 1642/3 en 1644.* The Hague.

MILLS, J. V. 1930. 'Malacca, Meridional India and Cathay.' *Journal of the Royal Asiatic Society, Malayan Branch*, Vol. 8.

MINISTERIO DE FOMENTO 1877. *Cartas de Indias.* Madrid.

MOLL, H. 1723. *The Compleat Geographer or the Chorography and Topography of all the Known Parts of the Earth.* London.

MOLLEMA, J. C. 1935. *De Eerste Schipvaart der Hollanders naar Oost-Indie 1595–7*, Vol. II. s'Gravenhage.

MONTÉMONT, A. 1853. *Histoire des Voyages*, Vol. II. Paris.

MOORE, J. H. 1780. *A New and Complete Collection of Voyages and Travels*, Vol. I. London.

MORGAN, E. D. 1891. 'Early discovery of Australia.' *Transactions and Proceedings of the Royal Geographical Society of Australia, N.S.W. Branch*, Vol. V, pp. 90–96.

MORISON, S. E. 1942(a). *Admiral of the Ocean Sea.* Boston.

—— 1942(b). *Admiral of the Ocean Sea.* 2 vols, Boston.

MORRELL, A. J. 1833. *Narrative of a Voyage to the Ethiopic and South Atlantic Ocean, Indian Ocean, Chinese Sea, North and South Pacific Oceans in the years 1829, 1830, 1831.* New York.

MORRELL, B. 1832. *A Narrative of Four Voyages to the South Sea, North and South Pacific Oceans, Chinese Sea, Ethipopic and Southern Atlantic Ocean, Indian and Antarctic Ocean for the years 1822–1831.* New York.

MOSES, B. 1894. 'The Casa de Contractación of Seville.' *Annual Report of the American Historical Association*, pp. 92–123.

MOULE, A. C. and PELIOT, P. 1938 *Marco-Polo—The Description of the World*, 2 vols. London.

MULLER, F. and CO. 1843. *Catalogue of Maps and Atlases.* Amsterdam.

——1894–. *Remarkable Maps of the XVIth and XVIIth Centuries reproduced in their original size.* Amsterdam.

MURDIN, 1759. *Collection of State Papers.* London.

MUTCH, T. D. 1942. 'The first discovery of Australia.' *Journal of the Royal Australian Historical Society*, Vol. 28, pp. 303–52.

McCRINDLE, J. W. 1897. *The Topographia Christiana of Cosmos Indicopleustes, an Egyptian Monk.* London.

McELROY, J. W. 1941. 'The ocean navigation of Columbus on his first voyage.' *American Neptune*, Vol. I, July, pp. 200–41.

McNUTT, F. A. 1912. *De Orbo Novo. The Eight Decades of Peter Martyr d'Anghera.* New York.

NAVAL RECORDS SOCIETY, 1928. *Naval Miscellanies*, Vol. III, pp. 343–50.

NAVARRETE, F. de 1825. *Colección de los Viages y Descubrimientos que hicieron por mar los Españoles desde fines del siglo XV con varios documentos inéditos concernientes a la Historia de la Marina Castellana y de los Establecimientos Españoles en las Indias, coordinada e illustrada por don Martín F. de Navarette*, 5 vols. Madrid.

—— 1842. *Colección de Documentos Inéditos para la Historia de España.* Madrid.

—— 1851. *Biblioteca Maritima Española, obra póstuma*, 2 vols. Madrid.

NICHOLSON, J. 1717. *Atlas Geographus*, Vol. V.

NORDENSKIÖLD, A. E. 1889. *Facsimile Atlas to the Early History of Cartography with reproductions of the most important maps printed in the XVth and XVIth Centuries.* Stockholm.

—— 1897. *Periplus—An Essay on the Early History of Charts and Sailing Directions.* Stockholm.

NORIE, J. W. 1833. *The Country Trade and Free Mariner's Pilot.* London.

NOWELL, C. E. 1945. 'The Treaty of Tordesillas and the diplomatic background of American history.' In *Greater America—Essays in Honor of Herbert Eugene Bolton*, pp. 1–18. Berkeley and Los Angeles.

NUNN, G. E. 1932. 'The Columbus and Magellan concepts of South American geography.' *The Geographical Review*, pp. 26–27.

—— 1936. 'Magellan's route in the Pacific.' *The Geographical Review*.

NUTTALL, Z. 1914. *New Light on Drake: A Collection of Documents relating to his Voyage of Circumnavigation, 1577–1580.* London.

OLSCHKI, L. 1960. *Marco Polo's Asia, an Introduction to his Description of the World called Il Milione.* Berkeley.

ORNSTEIN, M. 1913. *The Role of Scientific Societies in the Seventeenth Century.* Chicago.

ORTELIUS, A. 1570 *et al.* Successive editions of his *Theatrum Orbis Terrarum.*

OVALLE, A. d' 1703. *An Historical Relation of the Kingdom of Chile (1646)* ... : *Translated from the Spanish.* (See also Churchill 1704: III.)

OVIDEO Y VALDES, G. F. de 1853. *Historia General y Natural de las Indias, Islas y Tierra Firme del Mar Océano, por el Capitán Gonzalo Fernandez de Ovideo y Valdés, Primer Cronista del Nuevo Mundo*, 4 vols. Madrid.

PACHECO, J. F., CÁRDENAS, F. de, y MENDOZA, L. T. De 1864–. *Colección de Documentos Inéditos relativos al Descubrimiento, Conquista y Colonización de las Posesiones Españolas en América y Oceanía sacados . . . del Real Archivo de Indias*, Vols. V and XXIII. Madrid.

—— 1885–. *Colección de Documentos Inéditos . . . de ultramar*, Vols. II and III.

PACIFIC ISLANDS PILOT, 1946. 3 vols. with supplements. London. (Published by the Admiralty Hydrographic Department.)

PARKINSON, S. 1784. *A Journal of a Voyage to the South Seas, In His Majesty's Ships the Endeavour. . . . from the Papers of the late Sydney Parkinson . . . and an Appendix Containing an Account of the Voyages of . . . Captain Carteret . . . and Monsieur Bougainville.* London.

PARKS, R. B. 1928. *Richard Hakluyt and the English Voyages.* New York.

PATERSON, G. 1811. *History of New South Wales.* Newcastle on Tyne.

PELHAM, C. 1806. *The World; or the present state of the universe: being a general and complete collection of modern voyages and travels . . .* 2 vols. London.

PELLIOT, P. 1904. 'Deux itinéraires de Chine en Inde' à la fin du XIIIᵉ siècle. *Bulletin de l'École Française d'Extrême-Orient*, Vol. IV.

PENZER, N. M. 1929. *The Most Noble and Famous Travels of Marco Polo together with the Travels of Nicolo de Conti. Edited from the Elizabethan translation of John Frampton.* London.

PEREIRA, D. P. 1937. *Esmeraldo de Situ Orbis* (1505–8) (ed. by G. H. T. Kimble). London.

PEREIRA, J. de S. 1609. *Disputationem de Indiarum Jure.* Madrid.

PÉROUSE—see La Pérouse.

PHILLIP, W. 1619. *The Relation of a Wonderful Voiage by William Cornelison Schouten of Horne.* London.

PINGRÉ, M. 1767. *Mémoire sur le Choix et l'État des Lieux où le Passage de Venus du 3 juin 1796 pourra être observé.* Paris.

—— 1778. *Mémoire sur les Découvertes faites dans la Mer du Sud avant les Derniers Voyages des Anglois et des François Autour du Monde.* Paris.

PINKERTON, J. 1808. *Voyages and Travels*, Vols. XIV and XI. London.

PLINY, 1938. *Natural History—Book II* (edited with an English translation by H. Rackham), Vol. I. London.

—— 1942. *Natural History—Book IV* (edited with an English translation by H. Rackham), Vol. II, London.

POLO, M. 1949. *Marco Polo's Travels. Facsimile reproduction of the original 1485 Antwerp edition.* Tokyo.

PRESTAGE, E. 1933. *The Portuguese Pioneers.* London.

PTOLEMY, C. 1932. *Geographia* (English translation by E. L. Stevenson of the 1507 Rome edition). New York.

PURCHAS, S. 1905. *Hakluytus Posthumus or Purchas His Pilgrimes*, 20 vols. Glasgow.

PURDY, J. 1816. *Tables of the Positions, or of the Latitudes and Longitudes, of Places, composed to accompany the Oriental Navigator, or Sailing Directions for the East Indies, China, Australia, etc. with notes.* London.

RAINAUD, A. 1893. *Le Continent Austral, Hypothèses et Découvertes.* Paris.

READ, B. M. 1914. *Chronological Digest of Documentos Inéditos de las Indias.* Albuquerque.

RICCI, A. 1950. *The Travels of Marco Polo* (English translation of Benedetto's transcript of the *Italian Geographic Text*. See Benedetto 1928). London.

RIENZI, M. G. D. de 1855. 'Histoire et Description de tous les Peuples.' Vol. III of his *Océanie, ou Cinquième Partie du Monde.* Paris.

RIVET, P. 1928. *Relations Commerciales préColombiennes entre l'Océanie et l'Amérique.* Vienna.

ROSENBLAT, A. 1950. *Pedro Sarmiento de Gamboa.* Buenos Aires.

Rossel, M. de 1808. *Voyage de Dentrecasteaux*, 2 vols. Paris.

Rowe, J. H. 1944. 'An introduction to the archaeology of Cuzco.' *Papers of the Peabody Museum*, Cambridge, Mass., Vol. XXVII, No. 2, pp. 55–59.

—— 1946. 'Inca culture at the time of the Spanish Conquest.' (In Steward 1946.)

Rozpides, R. B. Y. 1844. *La Polinesia*. Madrid.

—— 1891. *Descubrimiento de la Oceanía por los Españoles*. Madrid.

Rundall, T. 1849. *Narratives of Voyages towards the North-West, in search of a passage to Cathay and India*. London.

Rutter, O. 1937. *The First Fleet. The Record of the Foundation of Australia . . . compiled from the original documents in the Public Records Office*. London.

Sainsbury, W. N. 1862. *Calendar of State Papers, Colonial Series, East Indies . . . 1513–1616*, Public Records Office. London.

—— 1870. *Calendar of State Papers, Colonial Series, East Indies . . . 1617–1621*. Public Records Office. London.

San Vitores, D. L. de 1669. *Memorial que el P. Diego Luys de San Vitores . . . pidiendo le ayuden, y oscorran para la fundacion de la Mission de dichas Islas*. México.

—— 1670. *Noticia de los progressos de nuestra Santa Fe, en las Islas Marianas . . . .* México.

Santa Cruz, A. de 1918. 'Isolario general de todas las islas del mundo.' *Boletín de la Real Sociedad de Geográfia*, Madrid, Vol. 60, pp. 46–49.

Sayer, R. 1788. *A New Pilot for the Country Trade in the East Indies and Oriental Seas within the limits of the East India Company*. London.

Schoff, W. H. 1912. *The Periplus of the Erythrean Sea*.

Schuster, M. 1669. *Dissertatio Geographica de Terra Australi. . . .*

Sharp, A. 1960. *The Discovery of the Pacific Islands*. Oxford.

Shattum, O. 1908. *Ofir-studien*. Kristiana.

Silva, J. de 1621. *Advertencias importantes acerca del buen Govierno y Administración de las Indias assi en lo espiritual como en lo temporal*. Madrid.

Skelton, R. A. 1952. *Decorative Printed Maps of the 15th to 18th Centuries*. London.

—— 1958. *Explorers' Maps*. London.

—— 1960. 'The cartography of Columbus' first voyage.' (In Vigneras 1960: 217–27.)

Sölver, C. V., and Marcus, G. J. 1958. 'Dead reckoning and the ocean voyages of the past.' *Mariner's Mirror*, Vol. 44.

Spate, O. H. K. 1957(a). 'Godinho de Eredia.' *Meanjin*, pp. 109–22.

—— 1957(b). 'Terra Australis-Cognita?' *Historical Studies—Australia and New Zealand*, Vol. 8, No. 29, November.

Stanley, H. E. J. 1868. *Antonio de Morga: The Philippine Islands . . . at the close of the Sixteenth Century*. London.

Stanley, Lord 1874. *The First Voyage round the World, by Magellan*. London.

Stapel, F. W. 1943. *De Oostindische Compagnie en Australie*. Amsterdam.

Starbuck, A. 1885. *A History of the American Whale-Fishery* (in *Appendix to the Report of the Commissioner for Fish and Fisheries for 1875*).Washington.

Stephens, H. M. and Bolton, H. E. 1917. *The Pacific Ocean in History*.

Stevens, H. 1886. *Court Minutes of the East India Company*, Vol. I.

Stevens, H. N. 1929. *New Light on the Discovery of Australia as revealed by the journal of Captain Don Diego Prado y Tovar*. London.

Stevens, J. 1816. *The Oriental Navigator or Directions for Sailing. . . . being a requisite Companion to the Charts and Plans which constitute the East-India Pilot*. London.

Stevens, ?. 1888. *Johann Schöner. A reproduction of his Globe of 1523 long lost and the 'De Moluccis' of Maximilianus Transylvanus*. London.

STEVENSON, E. L. 1921. *Terrestrial and Celestial Globes*. Hispanic Society of America, 2 vols. New Haven.

—— 1932. *Geography of Claudius Ptolemy*. New York.

STEWARD, J. H. 1946. *The Andean Civilizations*, Vol. II. Bulletin 143 of the Smithsonian Institute. Washington.

STOCKDALE, J. (Publisher), 1790. *The Voyage of Governor Philip to Botany Bay . . . to which are added the Journals of Lieutenants Shortland, Watts, Ball, and Captain Marshall with an account of their New Discoveries*. London.

STRABO 1942. *Geography* (Translation by H. L. Jones), Vol. I.

SZCZESNIAK, B. 1943. 'Notes on the penetration of the Copernican theory into China.' *Journal of the Royal Asiatic Society (Great Britain)*. London.

TATE, V. D. 1941. 'The "Instrucion Nautica" of 1587.' *American Neptune*, Vol. I, April, pp. 191–5.

TAYLOR, E. G. R. 1929(a). 'Master John Dee: Drake and the Straits of Anian.' *Mariner's Mirror*, April.

—— 1929(b). 'Jean Rotz: His neglected treatise on nautical science.' *Geographical Journal*, May.

—— 1930(a). 'French cosmographical navigators in England and Scotland. 1542–1547.' *Scottish Geographical Magazine*, January.

—— 1930(b). 'The missing draft project of Drake's voyage of 1577–80.' *Geographical Journal*, January.

—— 1930(c). *Tudor Geography*. London.

—— 1931. 'A sixteenth century navigating manual.' *Geographical Journal*, October.

—— 1932. Introduction to Barlow 1932.

—— 1933. Supplementary Introduction to Jane 1933 : II.

—— 1934(a). 'Early empire building projects in the Pacific Ocean, 1565–85.' *Hispanic American Historical Review*, Vol. XIV, No. 3, pp. 296–304.

—— 1934(b). *Late Tudor and Early Stuart Geography*. London.

—— 1935(a). 'Some Notes on Early Ideas on the Form and Size of the Earth.' *Geographical Journal*, Vol. LXXXV, pp. 65–68.

—— 1935(b). *The Original Writings and Correspondence of the Two Richard Hakluyts*. London.

—— 1956. *The Haven Finding Art*. London.

TENCH, W. 1789. *Narrative of an Expedition to Botany Bay*. London.

TEXEIRA, JOÃO. 1630. *Atlas* (in the Library of Congress, Washington).

THEALL, G. McC. 1898–. *Records of South-Eastern Africa*. Cape Colony.

THEVENOT, M. 1681. *Recueil des Voyages*. Paris.

—— 1696. *Relations des Divers Voyages*. Paris. (Also published in 1664.)

THEVET, A. 1575. *La Cosmographie Universelle . . .*, Vol. I. Paris.

—— 1558. *Les Singularitez de la France Antarctique*. Paris.

TIELE, P. A. 1960. *Mémoire Bibliographique sur les Journaux des Navigateurs Nederlandais*. Amsterdam.

TORQUEMADA, J. de 1723. *Monarchia Indiana con el Origen y Guerras de las Indias Occidentales, de las Poblaciones, Descubrimiento, Conquista, Conversion y otras cosas maravillosas de la mesma tierra distribuidos en tres tomos*, 3 vols. Madrid.

TORRES LANZAS, DON P. 1925. *Catálogo de los Documentos relativos a las Islas Filipinas existentes en el Archivo de las Indias de Sevilla*. Barcelona.

TREVOR DAVIES, R. 1954. *The Golden Century of Spain*. London.

—— 1957. *Spain in Decline*. London.

UNITED STATES: Department of Agriculture, 1938. *Atlas of Climatic Charts of the Oceans*. Washington.

UNITED STATES: Hydrographic Office, 1955. *Atlas of Pilot Charts—South Pacific and Indian Oceans*. Washington.

—— 1944. *Atlas of Surface Currents—South-western Pacific Ocean*. Washington.

UNITED STATES: Works Progress Administration of Massachussets, Central Pacific Islands Project, 1940. *Research in Records of American Activities in the Central Pacific 1790–1870*. Boston. (Typescript.)

VALENTIJN F. 1726. *Oud en Niew Oost-Indien*. Doordrecht and Amsterdam.

VANDER LINDEN, H. 1916. 'Alexander VI and the demarcation of the maritime and colonial domains of Spain and Portugal, 1493–1494.' *American Historical Review*, Vol. XXII.

VAZ DOURADO, L. 1948. *Atlas* (1571). Reproduced by the Biblioteca Histórica de Portugal, Ebrasil.

VIDAL, P. J. 1674. *Carta escrita en el Ciudad de México a Don Gerónimo Sanvitores del Consejo de su Magesdad*. Mexico.

VIGNERAS, L. A. 1960. *The Journal of Christopher Columbus*. London.

VILLIERS, J. A. J. de 1906. *The East and West Indian Mirror*. London.

VISSCHER, N. (undated). *Atlas Minor sive Geographia Compendiosa qua Orbis Terrarum*. Amsterdam.

VON HAGEN, V. W. 1957. *Realm of the Incas*. New York.

—— 1959. *The Incas of Pedro Cieza de Leon* (translation by H. de Onis). University of Oklahoma.

WAFER, L. 1934. *A New Voyage*. London.

WAGNER, H. R. 1926. *Sir Francis Drake's Voyage around the World*. San Francisco.

—— 1929. *Spanish Voyages to the North West Coast of America in the 16th Century*. Special Publication No. 4 of the Californian Historical Society, San Francisco.

—— 1937. *The Cartography of the North-West Coast of America to the Year 1800*. San Francisco.

WALKER, J. 1896. *A Collection of Papers relating to Abel Janszoon Tasman and his Voyages*. National Library, Canberra.

WALLIS, H. M. 1951. 'The first English globe.' *Geographical Journal*, Vol. CXVII, Part 3, September.

—— 1952. 'The Molyneux globes.' *British Museum Quarterly*, Vol. XVI, No. 4, pp. 89–90.

—— 1953. 'A contemporary handbook of the Molyneux globes.' *British Museum Quarterly*, Vol. XVIII, No. 3, pp. 68 *et seq.*

—— 1954. *The Exploration of the South Sea, 1519–1644. A Study of the Influence of the Physical factors with a Reconstruction of the Routes of the Explorers*. Unpublished D.Phil. dissertation, University of Oxford.

—— 1955. 'Further light on the Molyneux globes.' *Geographical Journal*, Vol. CXXI, September.

WARD, J. M. 1947. 'British policy in the exploration of the Pacific 1699–1793.' *Journal of the Royal Australian Historical Society*, Vol. 33, pp. 25 *et seq.*

WATERS, D. W. 1958. *The Art of Navigation in England in Elizabethan and Early Stuart Times*. London.

WATTER, R. 1748. *Voyage*. London.

WIEDER, F. C. 1914. 'El premier portolano holandes de la Mar del Sur.' *Actas y Memori, Congreso de Historia y Geografía Hispano-Americana celebrado en Sevilla*, pp. 517–22. Madrid.

—— 1925-. *Monumenta Cartographica*, 5 vols. The Hague.

—— 1942. *Tasman's Kaart van zijn Australische Ontdekkingen 1644; de Bonaparte-kaart*. s'Gravenhage.

WIESER, F. 1881. *Magalhaes-Strasse und Austral-Continent auf den Globen den Johann Schöner.* Innsbruck.

WILGUS, A. C. 1941. *The Development of Hispanic America.* New York.

WILLIAMSON, J. C. 1929. *The Voyages of the Cabots and the English Discovery of North America under Henry VII and Henry VIII.* London.

—— 1933. *The Observations of Sir Richard Hawkins—edited from the Text of 1622.* London.

—— 1946. *The Age of Drake.* London.

WILSON, J. 1799. *A Missionary Voyage to the Southern Pacific Ocean performed in the years 1796, 1797, 1798 in the ship Duff, commanded by Captain James Wilson, compiled from the Journals of the Officers and Missionaries. . . .* London.

WINSTEDT, E. O. 1909. *The Christian Topography of Cosmas Indicopleustes.* Cambridge.

WINWOOD, R. 1725. *State Papers,* Vol. I. London.

WOODFORD, C. M. 1888. 'Exploration of the Solomon Islands.' *Proceedings of the Royal Geographical Society,* Vol. 10, pp. 351–76.

—— 1890. 'Further exploration of the Solomon Islands.' *Proceedings of the Royal Geographical Society,* Vol. 12, pp. 393–418.

—— 1895. 'The Gilbert Islands.' *Geographical Journal,* Vol. 6, October, pp. 325–50.

—— 1909. 'Note on the atoll of Ontong Java.' *Geographical Journal,* Vol. 34, November, pp. 544–9.

—— 1916. 'On some little-known Polynesian settlements in the neighbourhood of the Solomon Islands.' *Geographical Journal,* Vol. 48, July, pp. 26–54.

—— 1926. 'Notes on the Solomon Islands.' *Geographical Journal,* Vol. 68, December, pp. 481–7.

WRIGHT, H. 1932. 'A manuscript journal of Tasman's voyage 1642–3.' *Journal of the Royal Australian Historical Society,* Vol. 18, p. 155.

WRIGHT, I. S. 1945. 'Early Spanish voyages from America to the Far East, 1527–1565.' In *Greater America—Essays in Honor of Herbert Eugene Bolton,* pp. 59–78. Berkeley and Los Angeles.

WRIGHT, O. 1950. *New Zealand 1826–1827 from the French of Dumont D'Urville.* Wellington.

—— 1955. *The Voyage of the Astrolabe 1840.* Wellington.

WROTH, L. C. 1944. *The Early Cartography of the Pacific.* Papers of the Bibliographical Society of America, Vol. 38, No. 2. Portland.

WYRTKI, K. 1960. *The Surface Circulation in the Coral and Tasman Seas.* Commonwealth Scientific and Industrial Research Organization, Australia, Division of Fisheries and Oceanography, Technical Paper No. 8.

WYTFLIET, C. 1605. *Histoire Universelle des Indes Orientales et Occidentales divisée en deux livres, le premier par Cornille Wytfliet. . . . Douay.* (The French edition of his *Descriptionis Ptolemaicae Augmentum* of 1597.)

YULE, H. 1866. *Cathay and the Way Thither,* 2 vols. London.

—— 1903. *The Book of Ser Marco Polo,* 3 vols. London.

ZARAGOZA, DON J. 1876–. *Historia del Descubrimiento de las Regiones Austriales hecho por el General Pedro Fernandez de Quirós.* 3 vols. Madrid.

—— 1878. 'Descubrimientos de los Españoles en el Mar del Sur y en las costas de la Nueva-Guinea (con la tradución de Mr. Hamy, por Don Martín Ferreiro, . . .), por Don Justo Zaragoza.' *Boletín de la Sociedad Geográfica de Madrid,* pp. 7–67.

—— 1894. *Geografía y Descripción Universal de las Indias recopilada por el Cosmógrafo-Cronista Juan López de Velasco desde el Año de 1574, publicada en el Boletín de la Sociedad Geográfica de Madrid.* Madrid.

(iv) BIBLIOGRAPHY OF NEWSPAPERS AND MAGAZINES CITED

Asiatic Journal: October 1825; December 1828, Vol XXVI, pp. 757–8; June 1832, Vol. VII, pp. 103–4.

Australian: 21 May 1828; 2 March 1839; 21 March 1839.

Baltimore Patriot: November 1831.

Boston Daily Advertiser: 7 September 1831; 20 June 1857.

Boston Independent Chronicle: 9 July 1795.

The Colonial Magazine and Commercial Maritime Journal: May-August 1841, pp. 459–69; September-December 1841, pp. 74–85.

Columbian Centinel, Boston: 3 September 1831.

Connecticut Gazette: 16 July 1795.

The European Magazine and London Review: November 1802.

London Chronicle: 16–19 March 1771.

Mercantile Advertiser: November 1831.

The Nautical Magazine and Naval Chronicle: 1834, 1840, 1847, 1848.

Naval Chronicle: January-July 1800, pp. 54–55; Vol. XVII, 1806, p. 195.

New England Palladium, Boston: 2 September 1831.

Oriental Herald and Advertiser: October 1828.

Pacific Islands Monthly: August 1958, pp. 51.

The Salem Register: 9 June 1803.

Sydney Herald: 12 December 1832.

(v) BIBLIOGRAPHY OF MAPS, CHARTS AND GLOBES[1] CITED AND CONSULTED

BEATUS 13th century. *World-map* (Wroth 1944: Plate II).

PTOLEMY, C. 1460. *World-map* (in the Ebner MS. of his *Geographia*) (Stevenson 1922: Plate 1).

—— 1482. *World-map* (Wroth 1944: Plate 1).

MELA, P. ? *World-map* (Bunbury 1959: II: Map 4).

—— 1482. *World-map* (in the 1482 edition of his *Cosmographia*) (Maggs 1927: Plate I).

MACROBIUS. 1483. *World-map* (in the 1483 Breschia edition of his *In Somnium Scipionis*) (Wroth 1944: Plate III).

ESCHVIDIUS, J. 1489. *World-map* (in his *Summa . . . Anglicana*). (Nordenskiöld 1889: Plate XXXI).

MELA, P. 1498. *World-map* (in the 1498 Salamanca edition of his *Cosmographia*) (Maggs 1927: Plate II).

REISCH, G. 1503. *World-map* (in his *Margarita Philosophica*). (Nordenskiöld 1889: Plate XXXI).

WALDSEEMULLER, M. 1507. *World-map* (Fischer 1903).

STOBNICZA, J. de 1512. *World-map* (Wroth 1944: Plate IV).

VINCI, L. da 1513–15. *World-map* (Nordenskiöld 1889: figure 45).

---

[1] References (bracketed) are to the site of the original, with abbreviations as in the Bibliography of Archival Material; or to publications in which the map or chart is reproduced, relating to the Bibliography of Published Works.

SCHÖNER, J. 1515. *Globe* (Nordenskiöld 1889: Figure 47).

—— 1520. *Globe* (Kretschmer 1891: Plate XIII).

—— 1523–4. *Globe* (Wieder 1925: I: Plates I–III).

LA SALLE 1521. *World-map* (Nordenskiöld 1889: Figure 18).

FRANCISCUS 1526. *World-map* (Lewel 1850: 127).

THORNE, R. 1527. *World-map* (Nordenskiöld 1889: Plate XLI).

RIBEIRO, D. 1529. *World-map* (Two states: (*a*) Grand Ducal Library, Weimar, (*b*) College of the Propaganda, Rome).

FINAEUS, O. 1531. *Nova et Integra Universi Orbis Descriptio* (Nordenskiöld 1889: Plate XLI).

MAILLARD, J. 1536–40. *World-map* (Chicoteau 1959: 79).

MERCATOR, G. 1538. *World-map* (Nordenskiöld 1889: Plate XLIII).

DESLIENS, N. 1541. *World-map* (Forsyth 1955: Figure I).

ROTZ, J. 1542. *World-map* (BM: Royal MS. 20E IX ff29v–30).

CARTE DU DAUPHIN, *c.* 1542. *World-map* (Chicoteau 1959: 77).

DESCELIERS, P. 1550. *World-map* (Chicoteau 1959: 80).

GASTALDI, J. *c.* 1555. *World-map* (Bibliothèque Nationale, Paris).

LE TESTU, G. 1555–6. *MS Atlas* (Bibliothèque du Ministre de la Geurre, Paris, MS. Atlas No. 607).

DESLIENS, N. 1566. *World-map* (Bibliothèque Nationale, Paris).

—— 1567. *World-map* (National Maritime Museum).

MERCATOR, G. 1569. *World-map* (Jomard 1862: Plate XXI).

MERCATOR, M. post 1569. *Americae sive India Nova* (Copy in the Australian National Library).

ORTELIUS, A. 1570. *Typus Orbis Terrarum* (Nordenskiöld 1889: Plate XLVI).

VELASCO, J. L. de *c.* 1575. Two charts of the Indies (JCB: Velasto).

JODE, C. de 1578. *Universi Orbis seu Terreno Globi in plano effigies* (Jode) 1578.

POSTEL 1581. *Pola Captata Nova Charta Universii.*

POPPELINIER 1582. *World-map.*

ORTELIUS, A. 1587. *Typus Orbis Terrarum* (Ortelius 1590; Wroth 1944: Plate XIV).

——1587. *Americae sive Novi Orbis Nova Descriptio* (Ortelius 1601; Wagner 1937: II: No. 147).

MERCATOR, R. 1587. *Orbis Terrae Compendiosa Descriptio* (Nordenskiold 1889: Plate XLVII).

ORTELIUS, A. 1589. *Maris Pacifici* (Ortelius 1601: Skelton 1958: Figure 128).

MAZZA, G. 1589–93. *Americae et Proximar Regionum Orae Descriptio* (Müller 1894: Plate 12).

LASSO, B. 1590. Map from his *Este Libro de Cosmographia* (Mollema 1925: II: Plate LXVI).

PLANCIUS, P. 1590. *Orbis Terrarum Typus de Integro Multis in Locis Emendatus* (BM: PS 0/8955. 920(279)).

—— 1592. *Nova et Exacta Terrarum Orbis Tabula Geographica ac Hydrographica* (Wieder 1925: II: Plates 26 and 31).

MOLYNEUX, E. 1592. *Globe.* Petworth Hall, England (Later edition of 1603 in the Middle Temple, London).

JODE, C. de 1593. *Novae Guineae. Forma et Situs* (Jode 1593: 39).

—— 1593. *Hemispheriŭ ab Aeqvinoctiali Linea, ad Circulŭ Poli Ătarctici* (Nordenskiöld 1889: Plate XLVIII).

PLANCIUS, P. 1594. *World-map* (Hakluyt 1903: IX).

——1595? One sheet from a planisphere. (Wieder 1925: II: Plate 40 ter).

BRY, T. de 1596. *Western Hemisphere* (Fleurieu 1790: Chart X).

LINSCHOTEN, J. H. VAN 1596. *Insulae Indiae Orientalis* (Nordenskiöld 1897: Plate LX; Wroth 1944: Plate XV).

RUGHESI, F. 1597. *Carta dell Americana* (Almagia 1948: Tav XXIII).

—— *Mappa Mondo* (Almagia 1948: Tav XXV).

WYTFLIET, C. 1597. *Chica sive Patagonica et Australis Terra* (Wytfliet 1605: 70–71).

WOLFE, J. 1598. *Map of the Moluccas.*

WRIGHT/MOLYNEUX 1598–1600. *The Shakespeare New/Hakluyt World-map* (Hakluyt 1903: I; Nordenskiöld 1889: Plate L).

TATTON, S. late 16th century. *Map of the Pacific Ocean* (Caraci 1926: I: Plates XV–XVII).

HERRERA, A. de 1601. Two charts of the Indies (Herrera 1601(a); 1622).

ANON. post 1606. Chart of the discoveries of the *Duyfken* (NAH: Collection of Leupe 493).

HONDIUS, J. 1608. *World-map* (reproduced by the Royal Geographical Society, London, 1927).

—— 1609. *Typus Orbis Terrarum* (Langenes 1609: I).

QUADUS, M. 1608. *Fasciculus Geographicus* (Nordenskiöld 1889: Plate XLIX).

LANGENES 1609. *Nieu Guinea* (Langenes 1609: 755).

—— *Beschryvinghe van Nieu Guinea* (Langenes 1609: 756).

WRIGHT, E. 1610. *World-map* (British Museum).

HONDIUS, J. 1611. *World-map* (Hondius 1907).

ERÉDIA, M. G. de 1613. *Typus Orbis Terrarum* (in his *Declaracam de Malaca*) (Bibliothèque Royale, Brussels, MS. 7264).

GASTALDI, J. 1613–40. *Nova Totius Orbis Descriptio.*

TORQUEMADA, J. de 1615. Map of America and the Pacific (Torquemada 1723: I).

VISSCHER, N. 1617. *Insulae Moluccae* (Hakluyt 1903: XI).

ANON. 1618. *Kaart vande Zuydzee vertonende wat wech Willem Schoutzen.* (Engelbrecht 1945: 172.)

—— *Caarte van Nova Guinea* (Engelbrecht 1945: 200–1).

—— 1619. *Nova Totius Orbis Terrarum Descriptio* (Villiers 1906: II).

—— *Chart of the Itinerary of Jacob Le Maire* (Villiers 1906: 186).

—— 1622. *Caerte van de zeylage van Iacob le Maire* (Engelbrecht 90–91).

—— *Caerte vande Landen vande Papouas* (Engelbrecht 100–1).

GERRITSZ, H. 1622. Map of the Pacific (MLS: M2 910/1622(i)—copy).

ANON, 1615–23. *The Duchess of Berry Atlas* (BNP: Ge FF 14409).

SANCHES, A. 1623. *World-map* (BM: Add. I MS. 22874).

LECONSFIELD. *World-map,* c. 1625. (See Francis Edwards' Catalogue No. 603.)

TEIXEIRA, J. 1630. *Mapa de Archipelago de la India Oriental* (LC: Atlas of João Teixeira, Map No. 7).

VAN LANGREN, A. F. 1630? *Globe* (BNP: Globe Room).

HONDIUS, H. 1630. *Nova Totius Terrarum Orbis Geographica ac Hydrographica Tabula* (In Hexham's edition of Mercator's *Atlas,* 1636—BM: Maps 34d8, and in Jansson's *Atlas*—BM: Maps 88 e 1).

BLAEU, G. J. 1630? *America Nova Tabula* (MLS (Dixson): Cb63/1).

GUERARD, J. 1634. *Carte Universelle Hydrographique* (BNP: E122; MLS: M2–100/1634(i)).

BLAEU, G. J. 1635? *Nova Totius Terrarum Orbis Geographica ac Hydrographica Tabula* (MLS (Dixson) Cb 63/4).

PISANI, O. 1637. *Globus Terrestris Planisphericus* (MLS: MB2–100/1637(i)).

DANIELL, J. 1639. (*Portolano* No. 23 in a collection of charts in the Bibliotheca Nazionale, Florence).

VISSCHER, J. 1639. *Orbis Terrarum Typus de Integro Multis in Locis Emendatus* (Calvert 1893: 105).

SANCHES, A. 1641. Chart of the Pacific (KB: 129 A 25 Chart No. 10).

COLOM, J. A. 1642. *Oost-Indische PasCaart Nieulycks Beschreven door Jacob Aertz Colom* (Maggs 1927: Plate XI).

VISSCHER, F. J. 1643. Chart of Amsterdam Eylandt, Heemsckercks Droochton and Prins Wyllem's Eylanden (MLS: Huydecoper MS.; Henderson 1933: 46, 84).

GERRITZ, H. 1628–43. Chart of the East Indies and Southland (MLS: Huydecoper MS.).

TASMAN, A. 1643. Chart of Amsterdam Eylandt etc. and Prins Wyllem's Eylanden (Heeres 1898; Henderson 1933: 50, 82).

TASMAN, A. J. 1643–4. *Kaart* of his voyage of 1642–3 (*The Bonaparte Map*) (MLS).

JANSSONIUS, J. and KAERIUS, P. 1645. *Nova Totius Terrarum Orbis Geographica*. . . . (MLS (Dixson Cb 64/3)).

DUDLEY, D. R. 1647. *Mar del Sur* (Dudley 1661: Map XXIII).

TURQUET, L. de M. 1648. *Petit pourtrait du Globe Terrestre* (BM: P10649/Maps 920(53)).

BLAEU, J. 1648. *Weltkarte* (Bagrow 1951: Plate 99).

—— *Nova Totius Terrarum Orbis Tabula* (Wieder 1925: III).

TEIXEIRA, J. 1649. (Thevenot 1696: tome I.)

JANSSONIUS, J. 1650. *Mar del Zur Hispanis—Mare Pacificum* (Nordenskiöld 1897: Plate LVII).

VISSCHER, N. 1652. *Nova Totius Terrarum Orbis Geographica ac Hydrographica Tabula* (Doncke 1660).

——1658? *Novissima et Accuratissima Totius Americae Descriptio* (MLS (Dixson) Cb 65/22).

DE WIT, c. 1660. *Nova Totius Terrarum Orbis Tabula* (Weider 1925: III).

BLAEU, J. 1662. *Nova et Accuratissima Totius Terrarum Orbis Tabula* (BM: Maps 64 e 1).

GOOS, P. 1665. *Pascaerte vande Zuyd-Zee* (Goos 1676: Plate 40).

THEVENOT, M. 1666. Chart of the Dutch discoveries (Thevenot 1681: 10–11; Nordenskiöld 1897: 197).

VISSCHER, F. J. post 1666. Chart of Tasman's voyage (The *Algemeene* or *Eugene Map*) (Weider 1925: IV: Plate 96; see also BM: Sloane MS. No. 5222 Art 12 Verkleind for an English copy of c. 1697).

GOOS, P. 1666. *Pascaerte vande Zuyd-Zee* (MLS: M2 910/1666(1)).

ANON, 1669. Chart of some of the discoveries of the Spaniards in the South-West Pacific (see the several states of this chart in the *derroteros*—BM: Harl. 4034; HL: HM918; Zaragoza 1876: III: End Map).

ANSALDO, M. c. 1669. *Carta de Australia* (Ministerio de Fomento 1877: Mapa 1).

SANSON (d'Abbeville). 1670? *Mappe-monde*. . . . (ANL).

LHUILIER, G. 1674. *Mappa Mondo* (BM: Maps 39 f7).

SELLER, J. 1675. *A Chart of the South Sea* (ANL).

GOOS, P. 1676. *Paskaerte beschreyen door Arent Roggeveen met octroy van de HM Staten General* (ANL).

DU VAL, P. 1677. *Carte Universelle du Commerce* (ANL).

SANSON (d'Abbeville), N. 1678. *Mappe-monde . . . en deux plan-hémisphères* (ANL).

DU VAL, P. 1679. *La Mer de Sud, dite autrement Mer Pacifique*.

BERRY, W. 1680. *A Map of all the World in two hemispheres* (ANL).

ALLARD, C. 168? *Planisphaerium Terrestre* (MLS (Dixson): Cb 68/2).

WIT, F. de 168? *Nova Totius Terrarum Orbis Tabula, ex officiana* . . . (MLS (Dixson): Cb 68/8).

—— 168? *Novissima et Accuratissima Totius Americae Descriptio* (MLS (Dixson): Cb 68/7).

GREENE, R. 1686. *A New Mapp of the World* (ANL).

HACK, W. 1687. *Chart of the South Sea* (in his *Charts of the Pacific Coasts of America*) (BM: Harl. 4034).

CORONELLI, P. M. 1690. *Mar del Sud detto altrimenti Mare Pacifico* (ANL).

JAILLOT, A. H. 1694. *Mappe-monde* (MLS (Dixson): Cb 69/i).

VAN KEULEN, J. 1695. *Pascaerte vande Zuyd Zee en een gedeelte van Brasil* (ANL).

DANCKERTS, I. 169? *Recentissima Novi Orbis sive Americae Septentrionalis et Meridionalis Tabula* (MLS (Dixson): Cb 69/7).

ALLARD, C. 1696. *Recentissima Novi Orbis sive Americae Septentrionalis et Meridionalis Tabula* (MLS (Dixson): Cb 69/7).

DANCKERTS, I. 169? *Nova Totius Terrarum Orbis Tabula* (MLS (Dixson): Cb 69/9).

HACK, W. 1700. *World-Map* (in his *Description of the Sea Coasts of Monomapata*—BM: Maritime VI–V, Vol. 9, Tab. 37, No. 97).

DELISLE (de l'Isle), G. 1700. *Mappe-monde* (BM: Maps 37f. 13).

—— *c.* 1700. *Mappa Totius Mundi* (ANL).

—— *c.* 1700. *Hémisphère pour voir les terres* (ANL).

SANSON (d' Abbeville), N. 1700. *Mappe-monde* (ANL).

SCHENK, P. *Americae Septentrionalis Novissima* (MLS (Dixson) 70/8).

SANSON (d'Abbeville), N. 1706. *Mappe-monde Geo-hydrographique* (MLS (Dixson) Cb 70/3).

DE WITT 1707. *Novissima et Accuratissima Septentrionalis ac Meridionalis Americae Descriptio* (MLS (Dixson): Cb 70/9).

SCHENK, P. 1706. *Diversa Orbis Terrae* (MLS (Dixson): Cb 70/6).

DELISLE (de l'Isle), G. 1708. *L'Amerique Méridionale* . . . (MLS (Dixson) Cb 70/2).

ZUERNER, A. F. 1709. *Americae tam Septentrionalis quam Meridionalis* (MLS (Dixson) Cb 70/7).

MOLL, H. 1709. *A New and Correct Map of the World* (MLS: M4 100 a/1709/1).

—— 1717. *New Guinea, New Britain and New Holland* (Nicholson 1717: 5).

—— 1717. *A Map of South America* (Nicholson 1717: 77).

DELISLE (de l'Isle), G. 1720. *Mappemonde* (BM: Maps 37f. 15(2)).

—— 1720. *Hémisphère Occidental* (ANL).

—— 1720? *Mappe-monde* (MLS (Dixson): Cb 72/3).

VALENTIJN, F. 1726. *Kaart der Reyse van Abel Tasman volgens syn eygen opstel* (Valentijn 1726: 46–7; Stapel 1943: 88–9).

SEUTTER, M. 1730. *Diversi Globi Terr-Aquei.* . . . (in Seutter's *Atlas Novus* of 1730—BM: Maps 40f. 2 Vol. 1).

HOMANN, J. B. 173? *Planiglobi Terrestris cum utroq Hemisphaerio Caelesti generalis exhibitio* . . . (MLS) (Dixson): Cb 73/4).

OTTENS, R. and I. (Publishers), 173? *Magnum Mare del Zur* . . . (MLS (Dixson): Cb 73/5).

DELISLE (de l'Isle), G. 1740? *Hémisphère Méridional pour voir plus distinctement les Terres Australes* (Corney 1908: Map V). (Solomons laid down twice—255° E of Ferro and 205° E of Ferro).

—— post 1740? *Hémisphère Méridional pour voir plus distinctement les Terres Australes* (MLS (Dixson): Cb 74/7) Solomons laid down 180° E of Ferro).

LETH, H. de 174? *Mappe Monde* (MLS (Dixson): Cb 74/15).

—— *c.* 1740. *Carte Nouvelle de la Mer du Sud* (ANL).

BUÂCHE, P. 1744. *Carte Physique de la Grande Mer* (ANL).

BOWEN, E. 1744. *A New and Accurate Map of the World* (Harris 1744: I: 6–7).

TIRION, I. 1744. *Wereld-kaart* (MLS (Dixson): Cb 74/11).

LOWITZ, C. M. 1746. *Planiglobi Terrestris* (MLS (Dixson): Cb 74/10).

BOWEN, E. 1750–2. *A New and Accurate Chart of the World* (ANL).

—— 1752. *A New and Accurate Map of all the Known World* (BM: Maps 89, d, Z).

VAUGONDY, R. de 1752. *Orbis Vetus in Utraque Continente* (ANL).

TIRION, I. 1754. *Niewe Kaart van het Westelykste Deel der Weereld* (MLS (Dixson): Cb 75/5).

CRUZ, T. L. y J. de la 1756. *Mapa Nautico* (MLS: F 18/94—photograph of the original in the John Carter Brown Library).

VAUGONDY, R. de 1756. *Carte Generale* (De Brosses 1756: II: Plate I).

—— 1756. *Carte Réduite de la Mer du Sud* (De Brosses 1756: II: Plate II).

BENNETT 1761. *A New and Correct Map of the World* (NLC).

PINGRÉ, M. 1767. *Carte Nouvelle de la Partie Meridionale de la Mer du Sud* (Pingré 1778).

DALRYMPLE, A. 1767. *Chart of the South Pacifick Ocean* (Dalrymple 1767).

CARTERET, P. 1767. *Chart of Queen Charlotte's Islands* (Hawkesworth 1773: I: 348-9).

BOUGAINVILLE, L. A. de 1768. Charts of his route and landfalls off the Louisiade Archipelago and the Solomons (Fleurieu 1790: Plate II).

SURVILLE, J. F. M. de 1769. Chart of the Terres des Arsacides (Fleurieu 1791: Plate III; Marion 1783: Plate 7).

CLOVET, A. 1769. *Mappe-monde* (ANL).

WHITCHURCH, W. 1770. *Chart of a Part of the South Sea* (ANL).

DALRYMPLE, A. 1770. *Plan of Part of Papua and New Britain or Solomon Islands* (Dalrymple 1770: I: 16).

—— 1770. *Copy of Part of Dampier's chart* (Dalrymple 1770: I: 16).

KITCHIN, T. 1771. *Map of the World* (ANL).

ANON, 1771. *Chart of the Southern Hemisphere* (Forster 1771).

DUNN, S. 1772. *Scientia Terrarum et Coelorum* (MLS: m4 600/1772/1).

D'ANVILLE, J. B. *c.* 1775. *Hémisphère Oriental* (MLS (Dixson): Cb 78/3). (dated 1761 but with additions to the plate post 1761).

FADEN, W. 1775. *Two Hemispheres* (MLS: M2 100a/1775).

SCHREIBERS, E. 1780. *Karte von Australien oder Polynesien* (MLS: M1-910/1780(i)).

ANON, *c.* 1781. *Carta que comprendes varias yslas adyacentes a las de Nuevas Bretaña y Guinea en el año de 1781 con la fragata Princesa mandada por el Alferes Maurelle* (AGI).

SAYER, R. and BENNETT, J. 1783. *Chart containing the Greater Part of the South Sea* (MLS: M2-916/1783(i)).

ANON, 1785. Fragment of a chart prepared for la Pérouse (Fleurieu 1790: Plate I).

SAYER 1788. *The Indian and Pacific Oceans between the Cape of Good Hope, New Holland and Japan* (Sayer 1788: Plate I).

SHORTLAND, T. G. 1789. *Chart of the Track of the Alexander Transport* (MLS: M2 801/1789).

—— 1789. Two charts of the route and landfalls of Shortland in the Alexander, 1788, by T. G. Shortland (Stockdale 1789: 200, 218).

DJURBERG, D. 1789. *Polynesian* (ANL).

FLEURIEU, C. M. F. de 1790. *Carte Réduite des Terres des Arsacides* (Fleurieu 1790: Plate III).

—— 1790. *Nouvelle Carte . . . de l'Archipel Des Arsacides* (Fleurieu 1790: Plate VIII).

—— 1790. *Carte Réduite des Découvertes des François* Fleurieu 1790: Plate IX).

—— 1790. *Carte Systématique des Îles de Salomon* (Fleurieu 1790: Plate XI).

FADEN, W. 1790. *Southern Hemisphere* (ANL).

KING, P. G. 1790. *The Track of the Supply—Lt. H. L. Ball* (MLS: M2 800/1790/1).

LABORDE, M. de 1791. *Carte pour servir au Voyage de M de Surville* (Laborde 1791 (b): Plate 3).

—— 1791. *Carte d'une Partie de la Nouvelle Hollande* (Laborde 1791(b): Plate 6).

——1791. *Carte de l'Îsle des Arsacides* (Laborde 1791(a): III: 294).

MANNING, E. 1792. *Track of the Pitt . . . under Captain Manning* (MLS: Admiralty Hydrographic Collection e 15 shelf Pc—photograph).

DJURBERG and ROBERTS, 1795. *Karte von der Inselwelt Polynesien oder dem funften welttheile* (ANL).

LAURIE and WHITTLE, 1797. *New Chart of the Indian and Pacific Oceans* (MLS: M4–800/1797 (1)).

WILSON, J. 1797. *Sketch of the Duff's Groupe* (Wilson 1799).

—— 1797. *Chart of the Duff's Track in the Pacific* (Wilson 1799).

ANON. 1799. *New Georgia, Solomon Islands, showing the Routes of Lts. Shortland and Ball, 1788 and 1790, from the collection of Admiral Richard Earl Howe* (d. 1799) (BM: Add. 38076, D93).

BUTLER, T. 1800. *Chart of the Western Part of the Pacific Ocean* (Laurie and Whittle 1803: II: 125).

FADEN, W. 1802. *Southern Hemisphere* (MLS: M2 140/1802 (1)).

BURNEY, J. 1803. *A Sketch of the Solomon Islands designed to assist in comparing the Modern Discoveries with the Early Spanish Accounts* (Burney 1803: I: 276–7).

ROCHETTE, L. S. de la. *A Chart of the Indian Ocean and Part of the Pacific Ocean* (MLS: M4 110/1803(1)).

BEAUTEMPS-BEAUPRÉ, C. F. 1806. *Carte des Archipels des Îles Salomon* (MLS: M3–922/1806. (1)); Beautemps-Beaupré 1807: Chart No. 22 etc.).

—— 1806. *Carte de l'Archipel de Santa Cruz* (Beautemps-Beaupré 1807: Chart No. 20).

KRUSENSTERN, M. de 1824. *Carte Systématique de l'Archipel des Îsles de Salomon* (Krusenstern 1827: Chart No. 9).

—— 1824. *Carte de l'Archipel de Santa Cruz* (Krusenstern 1827: Chart No. 7).

GRESSIEN 1828. *Routes de la corvette l'Astrolabe près des Îles Vanikoro* (Dumont d'Urville 1830: Hydrographie: Plate 32).

DILLON, P. 1829. *Island of Mannicolo* (Dillon 1829: II: 172).

D'URVILLE, D. 1830. *Carte Generale de l'Ocean Pacifique* (Dumont d'Urville 1830(b): Plate 1).

ARROWSMITH, J. 1832. *Pacific Ocean* (MLS: M2–910/1832(1)).

NORIE, J. W. 1833. Chart No. 26A in his *The Country Trade or Free Mariners Pilot*.

DUMOULIN, V. 1838. *Carte des Îles Salomon ... dressée ... a bord de la corvette l'Astrolabe* (Dumont d'Urville 1841(b): Hydrographie, Vol. II: Carte 5eme).

LAURIE, R. H. 1841. *Chart of the Islands and Passages in the vicinity of Papua or New Guinea* (MLS: uncatalogued).

NORIE, J. W. 1846. *New and Correct Outline Chart of 1833 corrected to 1846* (MLS: M3–100/1846(1)).

INDEX